OUR CONRAD

OUR CONRAD

Constituting American Modernity

PETER LANCELOT MALLIOS

Stanford University Press
Stanford, California

Stanford University Press
Stanford, California

A portion of Chapter 3 was originally published in *Modern Fiction Studies* 47.2 (2001). Reprinted with permission.

Printed in the United States of America on acid-free, archival-quality paper

Library of Congress Cataloging-in-Publication Data

Mallios, Peter Lancelot.
  Our Conrad : constituting American modernity / Peter Lancelot Mallios.
    p. cm.
  Includes bibliographical references and index.
  ISBN 978-0-8047-5791-1 (cloth : alk. paper)
  1. Conrad, Joseph, 1857–1924—Appreciation—United States. 2. Conrad, Joseph, 1857–1924—Criticism and interpretation. 3. Conrad, Joseph, 1857–1924—Influence. 4. Modernism (Literature)—United States. I. Title.
  PR6005.O4Z7667 2010
  823'.912—dc22

                        2010006863

Designed by Bruce Lundquist
Typeset at Stanford University Press in 10/15 Minion

For Elizabeth

[We need more] to interpret interpretations than to interpret things; and more books upon books than any other subject; we do nothing but comment upon one another. Every place swarms with commentaries; of authors there is great scarcity. . . . Our opinions are grafted on one another; the first serves as a stock to the second, the second to the third, and so forth; thus step by step we climb the ladder: whence it comes to pass that he who has mounted highest, has often more honor than merit, for his is got up but an inch upon the shoulders of the last one.

—Michel Montaigne, 1575

But there it is, the newest and in some ways the best of those amazing documents which are . . . utterly national and of today. And when our Conrad . . . comes, such books as this will have cleared the way. Out of these enormous and often muddy lakes of sincere and sophisticated observation will flow the clear stream—if there is to be a clear stream at all.   —F. Scott Fitzgerald, 1923

CONTENTS

PREFACE

This book is a literary and cultural history of the modern American invention of Joseph Conrad as a "master" literary figure between 1914 and 1939. It is primarily a book about reading: reading war and peace; reading crises of U.S. and world history; reading conflicts of culture, democracy, coloniality, nation; asking why we read, and how, and whom; reading U.S. Americans who once read Joseph Conrad, and asking what this stands to contribute to contemporary comparativist and international developments in the fields of Americanist, modernist, and Conrad studies. This is also a book about dialogue: the cultural dialogue that produced Conrad as a "master" literary figure in the United States during and after the First World War, and the potential for dialogue between American studies and Conrad studies, Americanist endeavor and transnational modernist literary inquiry more generally, in ways that have been more foreclosed than one might think. Finally, this book concerns methodology. Although the empirical recovery of Conrad's "heterotopic" cultural and political resonance in the modern United States is this book's scholarly priority, it is also an occasion to advance and argue for an extended practice of what I call "capillary comparativism," a critical approach predicated on the minute investigation of the constitution and contestation of "domestic" spaces by "foreign" signs. Throughout and *through* Conrad, *Our Conrad* seeks to emphasize the revisionist power of and need for this approach in contributing to other recent efforts to transnationalize the terms of global literary and cultural studies in a (still) formidably and often frighteningly nationalized world.

I hope it will be clear that the Americanist emphases of this book are professional (i.e., it is my field—and that field, I argue, includes Conrad) and strategic, not appropriative or territorializing. Though the original American meaning of "our Conrad," as we shall see, was quite possessive, the last thing I would wish is that whatever energy and intensity one might find in this book should be construed as a gesture of "claiming" Conrad for Americans (or Americanists)—especially when what inspired this book in the first place was the example of so many different world scholars of Conrad who have pioneered different strategies of world contact, conversation, and contemplation through the genuinely plural and planetary frame of Conrad's writings. It is an Americanist desire to participate in this global conversation, and to extend back to U.S. literary and cultural studies some of its own defamiliarizing implications and complications, that centrally motivates this study.

. . .

This book, my first, has been a while in the making and would not have made it at all were it not for the limitless generosity and insight of many friends and colleagues. My first thanks are to my teachers. I am indebted to Albert Gelpi, George Dekker, Thomas Moser Sr., and Bill Solomon—for wisdom and generosity far beyond the confines of this book. I especially thank Al Gelpi for opening American literature to me, and for one of the great guiding friendships of my life. Barbara Gelpi, David Riggs, Jay Fliegelman, and Marjorie Perloff also provided crucial support from the beginning; Ian Watt and Albert Guerard were foundational to this book's conception; and D. A. Miller and Cass Sunstein were the first to raise enduring questions of how to write and what to write for.

The heart of this book was written during sixteen months spent at the National Humanities Center on fellowship support provided by the National Endowment for the Humanities and the General Research Board of the University of Maryland. I sincerely thank Geoffrey Harpham, intrepid director and infectious thinker, and Kent Mullikin for their perfect hospitality and invigorating friendship; Theresa Braunschneider, Paul Saint-Amour, Phil Rupprecht, and Scott Casper for a remarkable community of collaborative criticism and convivial fun; Alice Donohue, Sheryl Kroen, Ann Firor Scott, Kyeong-Hee Choi, Mark Fiege, Catherine Gallagher, Martin Jay, Mary Kinzie, Gary Macy, and Mark Maslan for suggestive conversations relating to this book and many other things; and Bernice Patterson, Lois Whittington, Sarah Payne, Corbett Capps, James Getkin, Phillip Barron, Josh Bond, Sue Boyd, Marie Brubaker, Karen Carroll, Betsy Dain, Joel Elliott, Jean Houston, Martha Johnson, Caren Koplik, Barbara Mormile, Lynwood Parish, Eliza Robertson, Richard Schramm, Pat Schreiber, Don Solomon, Stephanie Tucker, Marianne Wason, Michelle Walton-Snow, and Felisha Wilson for making me (and everyone else) feel perfectly at home.

At the University of Maryland, I've been fortunate in the support I've received from my own department and college. Bob Levine, in one of many acts of unstinting friendship, read completely and commented incisively on the most important draft of the manuscript. Sangeeta Ray made an especially valuable critique of the Introduction. Michael Israel, Brian Richardson, Elizabeth Arnold, Ralph Bauer, Richard Cross, Matt Kirschenbaum, Ted Leinwand, Susan Leonardi, Beth Loizeaux, Isabella Moulton, Howard Norman, Zita Nuñes, Randy Ontiveros, Carla Peterson, Martha Nell Smith, Josh Weiner, and David Wyatt all did and said things that directly mattered to this book—perhaps more than they know. John Auchard, most generously of all, knew exactly what to say and when to say it throughout the most important period of this book's composition.

Among Conrad scholars, my debts are truly too extensive to enumerate—but I must at least try to thank Keith Carabine and Allan Simmons, remarkable friends who have from the beginning generously supported and crucially advised this book; Zdzisław Najder, who graciously spent many pages and hours vitally informing its contents; Laurence Davies, who thoughtfully gave me advance access to Conrad's later letters; Gene Moore, Don Rude, Grażyna Branny, and Jack Peters, who all provided me with valuable materials on Conrad in the United States that I was not aware of; Carola Kaplan and Andrea White, comrades-in-arms in a project that ran parallel to this book; Edward W. Said, whom I met only once during the writing of this book but who impacted it significantly through that experience; Robert Hampson, whose insights on Conrad's "late" work I've found indispensable; Terry Collitts, whose remarkable *Postcolonial Conrad* and Conradian correspondence I have never properly thanked him for or acknowledged the pleasure they brought me; Robert Caserio, whose kind and sagacious words never fail to come at exactly the right time; Debra Romanick-Baldwin, whose thoughts on narrative solidarity are an inspiration; and Anthony Fothergill, who gave a talk years ago in London on Conrad in Weimar Germany that first made me think that *perhaps* a book on Conrad in the United States could be written: his incomparable *Secret Sharers: Joseph Conrad's Cultural Reception in Germany* (2006), which I first encountered in the final stages of writing this book, is the true origin of what lies here. Finally, Norris Pope, Emily-Jane Cohen, Sarah Crane Newman, Carolyn Brown, and Cynthia Lindlof at Stanford University Press have been the most meticulous, professional, expeditious, supportive editors I could possibly imagine working with.

There are six to whom I owe the greatest thanks of all. Bill and Ronna Mallios were there every step of the way with great patience and cheering support—as they always have been. Seth Mallios is quite right to empathize with Moby-Dick, not only on the grounds he once explained to me but also because I do not know a figure whose company I would chase (harpoons aside) with more compulsive interest and excitement than his. And finally, most fortunately for me, Sam and Annabelle are the bright lights, and Elizabeth Dahl the central star, whose love and support made it possible for me to complete this book—and realize that the best parts of life lie outside Conrad.

PM

ABBREVIATIONS

Citations to Conrad's writings are to the *Collected Edition of the Works of Joseph Conrad* (London: Dent, 1946–55), reprinted in the Oxford World Classics series. Where the introduction or annotation of a Conrad novel in a different edition is cited, that text is cited separately.

AF	*Almayer's Folly*	TU	*Tales of Unrest*
AG	*The Arrow of Gold*	UWE	*Under Western Eyes*
C	*Chance*	V	*Victory*
In	*The Inheritors*	WT	*Within the Tides*
LE	*Last Essays*	YOS	*Youth, a Narrative; and Two Other Stories*
LJ	*Lord Jim*		
MS	*The Mirror of the Sea*	CL	*The Collected Letters of Joseph Conrad,* ed. Frederick R. Karl and Laurence Davies (Cambridge: Cambridge University Press, 1983–).
N	*Nostromo*		
NLL	*Notes on Life and Letters*		
NN	*The Nigger of the "Narcissus"*		
OI	*An Outcast of the Islands*		
PR	*A Personal Record*		
Re	*The Rescue*		
Ro	*The Rover*		
SA	*The Secret Agent*		
SL	*The Shadow-Line*		
SS	*A Set of Six*		
Su	*Suspense*		
TH	*Tales of Hearsay*		
TLS	*'Twixt Land and Sea*		
TOT	*Typhoon and Other Tales*		

OUR CONRAD

INTRODUCTION

The American Invention of Joseph Conrad

The position which Conrad's name holds in America is really a remarkable one and touched with the quality of romance. His is not only the fame of a writer, but the fame of a personality, and it is not alone fame, it is glamour, as though his genius and career had really stirred a responsive chord in the generous heart of the great Republic. His individuality has, I believe, impressed itself more firmly upon the imagination of America than that of any other contemporary author, and though tastes differ and fashions change, Conrad's reputation does seem immune from the chances of time.   —Richard Curle, *The Last Twelve Years of Joseph Conrad* (1928)

We, too, have our place in the world. We have our obligations, our aggressions, our social chasms, our internal diseases. We are unready to deal with them. We are committed to responsibilities we do not understand. We are the victims of interests and deceptive ideas. We, too, can blunder into horror.

—"The End of American Isolation," *New Republic* (November 7, 1914)

"American studies was conceived on the banks of the Congo," writes Amy Kaplan in her introduction to *Cultures of United States Imperialism* (1994), an essay and a volume that have justly become as influential as any in Americanist criticism in recent years.[1] The reference is to the famous "Congo epiphany" Perry Miller describes in the preface to *Errand into the Wilderness* (1956). There Miller recounts how "three decades" before "at Matadi on the banks of the Congo," he first discovered a "determination" to articulate "the innermost propulsion of the United States": to commence a body of work and an academic field devoted to exploring and expressing "the massive narrative of the movement of European culture into the vacant wilderness of America."[2] Kaplan's purpose is to brush Miller against the grain. She demonstrates how the "America" Miller believes he's "left alone with" in the Congo is intimately dependent on the elided conception of "Africa" that serves him as a narrative frame; how this "Africa" functions as an imperial unconscious through which many American historical materialities (slavery, removal, imperialism) are disavowed; and how Miller reduces a triangle of historical relations among Europe, Africa, and the United States to a dyadic narrative of a European "errand" into an American "vacant wilderness," itself a vacated and monadic construction of an exceptionalized "America."[3]

Kaplan also brings up Joseph Conrad twice. First, she describes Miller's "own journey into the fabled 'Heart of Darkness'" as leading "not to Marlow's 'beginning of the world,' but to the origins of American culture, not to Kurtz's breakdown of the European subject, but to the vocation of American historian"; and at the end, in an inspired discussion of Francis Ford Coppola's *Apocalypse Now* (1979), Kaplan argues that Coppola's film, "a recent revision of Conrad's classic text of European imperialism," significantly duplicates as a matter of the material circumstances of its filming the very imperialist practices it seeks to critique.[4] But throughout her nine-page close reading of Miller's four-page preface, Kaplan considers Conrad only as an *externality* of the younger Miller's experience and the older Miller's text: as a suggestive analogue to but not an informing or constituent element of either. Kaplan's Conrad is outside both the historical fields and the intertextual mediations at issue in Miller's text and life.

Miller, however, went to the Congo in 1926: the same year that Conrad's *Congo Diary*, the raw autobiographical record of Conrad's own experiences in the Congo, was first published in the United States with great fanfare. This was also a time, as the epigraph above from Conrad's English friend Richard Curle suggests, of exceptional currency and popularity for Conrad in the United States: two years after Conrad's widely mourned death; three years after his celebrated U.S. visit and appearance on the cover of *Time* magazine; a general period in which "our Conrad,"[5] in F. Scott Fitzgerald's phrase, had become embraced and exalted in the United States as a "master" literary figure; and five years after the first performance of Eugene O'Neill's *The Emperor Jones* (inspired by *Heart of Darkness*, just as *Congo Diary* provides the raw material for *Heart of Darkness*)—shortly before Perry Miller became an intimate of the Provincetown Players.[6] The conspicuously Conradian details of Miller's preface may be considered in this historical light. Much like *Heart of Darkness*, Miller's tale concerns a smart, alienated, "atypical" white man employed on a ship for an imperialist operation in the Congo (Miller was "unloading drums of case oil" for a U.S. company).[7] Sitting "disconsolate on the edge of a jungle in central Africa," the young Miller, also like Conrad's Marlow, experiences a series of radical temporal, spatial, and ideological reversals, all generally involving vague and primitivizing constructions of Africans, all specifically marshaled in a queerly interior and impressionistic defense of the social power of "ideas," and finally resulting in a dramatic and shocking epiphany concerning both Western imperialism and his home country.[8] These echoes are by no means the pure products of retrospective narrative imposition: the older Miller's, Kaplan's, or mine. They are a product of the social history that sent Miller to the Congo in the first place. In the United States in the earlier 1920s, especially among young white males of "literary" inclination, one of the few gestures less original and more socially prescribed than having a burning desire to live out one of Conrad's stories was to have a "national" epiphany while doing so.

What would it mean to say that American studies was conceived *via Conrad* on the banks of the Congo? What are the historical and aesthetic circumstances of Conrad's production in the United States during and after the Great War that illuminate this question? What happens to American literary and cultural studies when Kaplan's Miller, who immaculately "conceives" his exceptionalist lifework in the self-declared void of the Congo, becomes replaced by a more subtly historical Miller whose very presence and thinking in the Congo were the complex consequence of *both* the most influential European text ever written in relation to Africa *and* the American sociohistorical field that created that text and its author as figures of "mastery"? I ask these questions to advance a series of broader ones through Conrad concerning the very transnational, post-national, and internationalist dimensions of American studies that the work of Kaplan and others has recently opened up. What global vistas does Conrad, arguably the twentieth century's most internationally rewritten novelist, offer American studies? More polemically, how might a systematic blindspot with respect to Conrad in even the most innovative postnationalist and post-Americanist interventions in the field draw attention to unwittingly circular and inherited assumptions of field imaginary and procedure that presently limit it? How might the example of Conrad in the United States—a special but by no means exclusive example—open the door to a new transnational comparativist emphasis in American studies: one whose emphasis is the capillary constitution and interpenetration of the United States by "foreign" signs; one that does not assume that the primary U.S. literary mechanism of political self-assertion, negotiation, and contestation is to be found in native authored texts; one that does not assume that practices and discourses of international aesthetics and authorship, no matter how "high" or aestheticized the terms of their reception, are somehow outside the intrinsic province of either engaged politics or American studies; one, in short, whose focus is not the reception, proliferation, or likeness of U.S. texts outside the United States but rather the circulation, engagement, and recognition of non-U.S. texts within and as part of a worldly situated (and saturated) American scene? Finally, what happens to the study of *Conrad*—just as effectively insulated, one should point out, from U.S. contextualization by the critical discourses that principally route it (British, European modernist, postcolonial) as any efforts by Americanists—when considered under Americanist eyes? What happens when we take seriously the fact that in the irreducibly plural and global field of Conrad's original reception—and well over three decades before F. R. Leavis formally acknowledged Conrad's place in British letters in *The Great Tradition* (1948)—the first mass-scale public project of reverencing and institutionalizing Conrad was well under way in the United States, a place Conrad never once visited until the year before his death and generally disdained and suspected among nations perhaps more than any other throughout his life?

These are the questions that frame and preoccupy this book, itself a study of what I will be calling the modern American invention of Conrad as a "master" literary figure. This development happened in the United States in the decade following the onset of the Great War (1914–24), with significant aesthetic and cultural-political implications for the following fifteen years as well. Simultaneously a literary and a cultural history, historicist in emphasis, of Conrad's production and contemplation in the United States during this time, this book advances the general argument that "our Conrad" emerged in the United States as a figure of aesthetic mastery as a complex and cascading social function of competing *ideological* attempts to master and contest in Conrad's image the domestic terms and worldly relations of "our America" (in Waldo Frank's contemporary phrase). Through a process of escalating intensity and rhizomatically self-extending breadth, Conrad's fiction and persona, I argue, came to mediate and cross-correlate an enormous range of U.S. domestic and international cultural-political concerns. With ever-expanding radius, Conrad became produced and reproduced as a collective object of U.S. literary veneration through the widening range of "American" cultural-political debates conducted in his provocatively and plurally foreign, surreptitiously domestic, irreducibly ambiguous, and remarkably appropriable image. "Our Conrad" became a space in which "America" itself was generated, queried, troubled, challenged: sometimes, as with Perry Miller or Edith or Theodore Roosevelt, in neatly (though not unreflectively) exceptionalist terms; at other times, as with H. L. Mencken, Willa Cather, William Faulkner, or Richard Wright, in highly varying degrees and terms of locality and opposition; but always, apropos of the metaphors of Columbus repeatedly used when Conrad "first sailed" to the United States, in terms that combined aesthetic and political "discovery."[9] The American invention of Conrad is an instance of an international aesthetic figure becoming transformed into a domestic political and cultural currency of great consequence; and it is the purpose of this book to begin to recover both the vast range of contrapuntal voices who participated in this signifying economy and the complex network of domestic and international issues whose fault lines animated the conversation.

Our Conrad, hence, is not directly a study of Conrad's fiction per se but rather a study of the interpretations of that fiction through which a diverse intersection of U.S. individuals and institutions, often anticipating the inter-pretive frontiers of our own moment in both Conrad studies and American studies, turned to the works of an ostensibly perfect stranger to negotiate the relationship between Americanness and larger global developments of modern-ism and modernity. More generally, my twin critical priorities in what follows are to offer the inherently internationalist domain of Conrad (and modernist) studies the first sustained and historicist consideration of Conrad in a large U.S. context,[10] and to complicate American studies by broadly rewriting and reconsidering modern U.S. literary and cultural history through the foreigniz-ing, globalizing figure of Conrad—each field estranging the other through a restoration of the contact that both have worked rigorously and ahistorically to preclude.[11] Neither an "influence" nor a "reception" study in any conven-tional sense, though I do draw on both domains of inquiry when useful, *Our Conrad* is fundamentally an investigation and semiotic archaeology of a for-eign signifying presence within U.S. cultural discourse: a presence, indeed, both so foreign and so ubiquitously particular to the United States that such solid conceptual oppositions as self and other, native and alien, foreign and domestic, "Eastern" and "Western" hemispheres and cultural spheres, aesthet-ics and politics, find themselves decomposing irrecoverably into one another. Not unlike the titular figure of his own *Nostromo*, the central and foreign na-tional hero of the imaginary Latin American country of Costaguana whom all the competing factions (mis)take as "our man" through his remarkable and contradictory capacity to appear to each as "just the man they take me for" (*N* 151), the "Conrad" of this book is a fundamentally *specular* figure: a complex, exotic, polymorphic, endlessly resonant reflector through whose multiple mirror relations and interferences the United States becomes written, rewritten, unwritten, from a variety of local and global vantages. Not unlike the figure of Razumov in *Under Western Eyes*, "our Conrad" is also a story of mistaken interpretation, misidentification, and multiple alliances and allegiances, often self-contradictory. Though my ultimate purpose in writing this book is to present a general model for future Americanist inquiry into the "foreign" and "literary" that well exceeds the specific instance of Conrad, I will also be arguing that there is a special singularity to the kind of elaborate and effusive "secret sharing" that Conrad was able to effect with modern U.S. Americans—the product of both the distinct *heterotopic* nature of his fiction and the specific historical circumstances and moment, never really escaped throughout the entirety of the twentieth century, in which "our Conrad" was originally generated. I began this introduction with reference to Amy Kaplan's work and to questions of modern American imperialism that Kaplan instrumentally formulates and that Conrad, as this book emphasizes from beginning to end, complexly historically mediates. But perhaps an even clearer critical intertext to glimpse the large Americanist disorientation foregrounded in this book is one, actually indispensable to its original conception, that I have meant to invoke implicitly both in my title and historical cross-references to "our America": Walter Benn Michaels's *Our America: Nativism, Modernism, Pluralism* (1995). Like Kaplan, Michaels has written insightfully and politically about *Heart of Darkness* in the context of *Apocalypse Now*;[12] yet also like Kaplan, Michaels in *Our America*, a text that emphasizes precisely the "modern" historical period and a good number of the literary figures that this book does, tells a U.S. American story that externalizes and precludes from consideration Conrad or any other "foreign" author as a constitutive and complicating aspect of the American scene. *Our Conrad* asks what happens—methodologically, epistemologically, aesthetically, cultural-politically, transnationally, literary-historically, pedagogically—when Michaels's *Our America* is forced to account for Conrad as an interpretive context and problem, as an element and distortion of the *tabula* of the modern American vocabulary; more generally, this project directs attention to the degree to which, even in the present "transnational" moment, the disciplinary premises of the field of American literary and cultural studies continue *ex ante* to determine (and delimit) what is "foreign" to the materiality of the United States and the means by which its global imbrications may be perceived.

To these ends, *Our Conrad* empirically blends a broad examination of Conrad's modern U.S. cultural production—in newspapers, magazines, the book publishing industry, academia, film, theater, literary criticism, social and political criticism, linguistic tracts, and elsewhere—with detailed investigations of the simultaneously aesthetic and political terms that made Conradian forms, themes, and tropes especially useful (and/or objectionable, but always inescapable) for a number of U.S. writers: among them, H. L. Mencken, Van Wyck Brooks, Randolph Bourne, Theodore Roosevelt, Edith Roosevelt, Willa Cather, Mary Austin, Elia Peattie, Langston Hughes, Countee Cullen, W. E. B. Du Bois, Richard Wright, Eugene O'Neill, F. Scott Fitzgerald, Ernest Hemingway, T. S. Eliot, Frances Newman, Robert Penn Warren, W. J. Cash, and William Faulkner. All of these voices, media, and social institutions seize upon the mediating occasion and catalyst of Conrad to conduct dissensual dialogue over various American projects of—and an ever-expanding field of terms concerning—U.S. boundaries, internal spatialization and cultural relations, and global implications and proximity. This book is divided into three parts, in which I trace in roughly chronological order the three major spatial economies of Conrad's modern U.S. production: (1) an initial "national" economy centered in the Northeast and arising through U.S. experiences of the First World War; (2) an "international" expatriate economy arising in the war's aftermath; and (3) a Southern "regional" economy emerging in the 1920s but with implications extending through the civil rights movement—all subject to the "foreign" dislocations endemic to Conrad's contemplation with respect to them. Part 1 charts Conrad's rise in the modern U.S. public imagination through the context of the Great War and the volcanic catalyst, inciting much of the reaction and extension formations to come, of Baltimore newspaperman, magazine editor, literary critic, and sociopolitical iconoclast H. L. Mencken. Chapter 1 examines how Mencken, by provocationally converting the ambiguities of Conrad's relation to "Englishness" into a triply mapped assault on American "Anglo-Saxon" ideologies of international policy, domestic racial and immigration norms, and political democracy, introduced "our Conrad" as an American object and agency of dissensus, disruption, and controversy. Chapter 2 elaborates the converse rise, both during and after the war, of a number of different individual and institutional efforts—in publishing, mass media, academia, popular culture, and various cultures of literary expression—to tame, contain, reverse, and remarkably extend the range and nuance of Conrad's domestic and international cultural-political mediations; at issue here are not only Conrad's mediations of complex questions of "Anglo-Saxonness," Russian Bolshevism, and imperialism and self-determination on a world scale in the aftermath of the Treaty of Versailles, all in a manner folded back on the United States, but also the beginning of this book's broader recovery of the significance and ideological polyphony and diversity of Conrad's interest as a "Jewish" writer, and among African American and U.S. women readers and rewriters. Part 2 shifts to an expatriate postwar context and reconsiders several major figures and narratives of the "Lost Generation"—principally, those of Eliot, Hemingway, and Fitzgerald—in light of their imprint as products of a "Conrad Generation." Challenging conventional associations and hierarchizations of these three U.S. expatriate authors, I argue that the very different terms of intense interest that each took in Conrad constitute part of a political conversation that runs between them in their writings, each author using intelligent readings and rewritings of Conrad to articulate questions and formulations of nationhood and national imagining enabled by their own expatriate displacement. Part 3 consists of two chapters concerning Conrad's postwar reception in the modern South. Chapter 4 historicizes Conrad's remarkable (and hotly contested) boom in the South in the 1920s as an expression of radically diverse sectional interests and conflicts emerging from three internal poles of production: (1) "modern" little magazines centered in Richmond, Virginia; New Orleans; and Fayetteville, Arkansas; (2) the more conservative writings of the Vanderbilt Fugitives and Agrarians; and (3) an idiosyncratic nexus that included Thomas Wolfe, W. J. Cash (the author of *The Mind of the South*), and William Faulkner. Chapter 5 considers Faulkner's lifelong aesthetic interest in and symbiosis with Conrad in relation to the Southern social and race relations that Conrad both helps and haunts Faulkner into scripting; I close with a brief glimpse at how remarkable continuities of political and social history between Conrad's native Poland and Faulkner's postbellum U.S. South might be used to ground an account of the uncanny aesthetic convergences that run between Conrad and Faulkner as well as the interest and resonance of the experimental forms of both authors in Latin America—the furthest "postnational" horizon this book has to offer.

Throughout, *Our Conrad* turns on a paradox of inverse reciprocity. This paradox is that the remarkably "global" Conrad—the Polish-born, Russian-exiled, temporarily French, ultimately English novelist of and sailor/traveler throughout so much of the world's European, Slavic, East Asian, South Asian, Oceanic, African, Arab, and Latin American places and cultures—should experience his first large explosion of popular celebrity and wide public reverence in the United States: one of the few places of the earth that Conrad not only failed to make direct contact with and rarely felt charitably toward until the very end of his life, but also never once set his fiction in and seldom derived his characters from, invariably unflatteringly when so. The modern American embrace of an ostensibly perfect alien is a paradox I explain, as the fundamental historical argument of this book, as the doubly mapped product of *both* the manifestly superabundant international interest *and* the latently extensive domestic resonances of Conrad's fiction and image in the United States in the historical moment of World War I and its aftermath. In the tortuous international and domestic era that arose under Woodrow Wilson's presidency (1914–20, especially); in a decade of both extreme tensions within and unprecedented internationalist crisis and awakening for the United States (1914–24); in an epochal moment beset by the "horror," as the editors of the *New Republic* put it in their inaugural issue of November 1914, that "We, too, have our place in the world"—Conrad quite naturally became an American obsession. Conrad's fiction and image, I argue, offered a United States already disrupted in its traditional isolationist and exceptionalist complacencies a *heterotopic* site in which a vast field of densely consolidated global relations (British, European, Russian, Zionist, Latin American, African, Arab, Asian) could be imagined and contested not only as an *external* constituent of vital bearing on the United States but also as an uncanny and estranging mirror image of race relations, radical class politics, political democracy, immigration debates, gender conflict, imperialism, and much more *within* the United States. The production and containment of Conrad as an American heterotopic site—a space absolutely outside the United States yet somehow comprehensively deconstructive and reconstructive of its sense of external and internal boundary; a site of perpetual interference and recovery with respect to U.S. macronarratives of isolationism and exceptionalism; a genetic source constantly expanding in its terms of application yet also ultimately unfixable and irresolvable in its ideological determinations—is the mechanism of Conrad's invention in the United States as a figure of *literary* mastery. And if this invention was particular to a very specific U.S. historical moment and set of circumstances, without which Conrad almost certainly would not have emerged as the seminal "American" literary and cultural figure he became, Conrad's heterotopic fictions and functions are ultimately part of a global trajectory of interest in Conrad that, from the perspective of Conrad studies, I seek to reconnect with its forgotten U.S. coparticipants. I develop these heterotopic and historical arguments more fully in the second half of this introduction and as the overarching conceptual premises of the chapters that follow, but before turning to them, I want first to address some of the larger questions presented earlier concerning the implications of this book *beyond* the specific example of Conrad (and the U.S. estrangements particular to his recovery) and *for* internationalist practices of U.S. literary and cultural studies generally. Although I do not intend what follows to be exclusive of readers coming to *Our Conrad* from the vantage of Conrad studies and the British, European modernist, and postcolonial discourses that principally route it— indeed, as I've suggested above, the abrasive and productive contact of these discourses with American studies is an important priority of this book—it is possible for non-Americanist readers to skip to the next section of this introduction without worry that the remainder of the book is written with a dual audience, never quite reconcilable in its terms, focally and consistently in mind.

CAPILLARY COMPARATIVISM:
"OUR AMERICA" AND SIGNS OF THE FOREIGN

In *Through Other Continents: American Literature Across Deep Time* (2006), Wai Chee Dimock proposes a model of contemplating U.S. literature that stretches its horizons of context and implication to the very limits of planetary space and human history. Pulling back radically from a scale of vision coordinated by the temporal and territorial boundaries of the U.S. nation, Dimock proposes a "scale enlargement" in which "durable diachronic axes" of understanding are sought across massive stretches of world space and history.[13] We are asked to assume a distanced perspective from which the *totality* of world history may be visualized as a unit, from which the hermeneutics of its understanding may be derived from the *longue durée* of planetary history itself.[14] From this vantage, Thoreau and the *Bhagavad Gita* become reconnected as joint theorists of global civil society; Henry James, Dante, and *Gilgamesh* collectively anticipate world systems analysis through the genre of epic; black vernacular English in the United States becomes rethreaded through an astonishing array of world-historical "Creole" tongues (including Old and "standard" modern English); and all in all, the nation recedes as any kind of fundamental unit of analysis or organizing and delimiting boundary. The U.S. nation, however, is not transcended entirely: the book, after all, does highlight the category of *"American* literature" in its title, and most of the chapters are organized, in a manner that speaks to the fundamental stakes and structure of the project, in terms of the radical worldly estrangement of a primary U.S. author—often very canonical, nationally hyperinscribed and overdetermined, and surely chosen in part for these reasons. The power of Dimock's project thus turns on a *double* movement: the simultaneous articulation of multiple global possibilities *and* an implicit but no less pointed critique and corrosion of the primary nationalizing frames through which canonical figures of U.S. literature have been captured, canonical conceptions of U.S. literature have been advanced. The nation is not avoided or eclipsed by the articulation of global possibilities; it is engaged, corrosively and dialectically, through the opportunity of their articulation.

This book shares Dimock's double priorities, but its methods of execution are essentially the extreme reverse, or perhaps obverse, of the "deep time" model. Whereas Dimock conducts her double critique through an optic that pulls back so far from a national frame of vision that what once were its coordinating figures now become constellated by a much larger transtemporal and transspatial planetary frame, this book proposes a model of pulling so closely *within* the territory claimed by a national frame of vision that what once were its coordinating figures are now seen as part of a terrain which, examined at the microscopic level, is found to be pervasively and indissociably constituted and coinhabited by "foreign" signs and mediations. (Conrad's fiction and persona are an instance—a very special and revealing instance—of the kind of "foreign" signs one finds *everywhere inside* U.S. territory—literary, cultural, and otherwise—when that territory is examined at the level of the pixel and high grain, rather than through a nationalizing frame and focus that harmonizes, backgrounds, and otherwise resolves such "alien interference.") Whereas Dimock looks to a *longue durée* to engulf and to challenge with macroscopic immensity the limiting space and temporality of the U.S. nation-state, this book urges, through the example of Conrad, that we look with molecular intensity at the capillary "foreign" elements and filaments through which the U.S. nation-space has been composed, and through whose vexed and plural negotiation a cosmos of planetary concerns, transnationally mapping the global and the local, is already embedded. Whereas Dimock eloquently champions the pursuit of a "deep time" which, in "inter-threading . . . the long durations of [non-U.S.] cultures into the short chronology of the United States," "thickens time, lengthens it, shadowing in its midst the abiding traces of the planet's multitudinous life," "binding continents and millennia into many loops of relations, a densely interactive fabric"—this book champions what might be called *thin* time and the play of *surfaces*: it resists the "empty and homogeneous" temporality of the nation not through recourse to a thicker, deeper frame, but rather by immersing in the unregulated play of signs in a series of *contemporary* moments, moments not yet claimed by taming or temporalizing narrative, not yet divested of the danger of their immanent futurity.[15] Finally, whereas Dimock does ultimately to some degree reinscribe, or so it seems to me, a distinction between "American literature" and the literary or cultural expression of "*other* continents"—that is, we never really forget or find challenged who or what counts as "American literature," even as the significance of this category is placed in endlessly suggestive global eclipse—this book argues that the category of U.S. American literature and its study must be revised and reunderstood to include the foreign-authored textuality that manifestly and materially make up the field of "writing *in* the US,"[16] the literature *of* the United States. In 1922—a year sometimes described as the most significant year of literary production in the twentieth century, for reasons this book may lead us to revise—the writings of the multiforeign Conrad were as published and printed in, celebrated and contested by, conceptually present to, and materially and historically a part of U.S. culture as those of any American-born (much less foreign-born) author; not to understand Conrad's works as American and "American literature" (among many other things, of course) is the kind of historical, empirical, disciplinary, and institutional mistake against which this book is most strongly positioned. Indeed, though I am aware of the complex history of the term "comparative" in the discipline of comparative literature,[17] and though I also intend this book as a complement and contribution to contemporary comparativist developments in American studies, one of the implicit claims that runs throughout this book is that no logic of "comparison" (at least to the extent this term implies the cross-consideration of *separate* domains of inquiry) is actually required to justify Americanist consideration of the "foreign" literary figures broadly implicated by this project.

Our Conrad, hence, offers a particular critical mode, predicated on attention to signs produced and negotiated in the United States as "literary" and "foreign," of participating in the recent globalist and "post-Americanist" turn in American literary and cultural studies: a turn marked by a general desire, as the nine essayists who take their stand at the outset of *Post-nationalist American Studies* (2000) express it, "to contribute to a version of American studies that is less insular and parochial, and more internationalist and comparative."[18] The term "post-Americanist,"[19] which usefully places the field itself centrally in question, encompasses at least two strategies of direct relevance to this book: one, the "postnational," which at the very least involves counter-hegemonic rejections of celebratory nationalism and uncritical recuperations (i.e., mythic, ahistorical, monocultural, exceptionalist) of what Lauren Berlant calls the "National Symbolic," while also potentially challenging "the nation" as a valid social category or meaningful political form/reality altogether; the other, by no means categorically distinct, the "transnational"—the emphasis here falls on both comparativist defamiliarizations of national and nationalist assumptions and the articulation of international and extranational textual, cultural, conceptual, and sociopolitical economies.[20] As I have suggested of Dimock's work, this book is defined by the intersection of both of these vectors of analysis. On the one hand, although many voices have usefully and provocatively asserted the obsolescence—analytically, ethically, sociopolitically, global-economically—of the nation-form and critical vocabularies responsive to it,[21] I should clarify here that I am among those postnationalists who understand the term dialectically and who are at least provisionally content to embrace the irony Ulf Hannerz discerns in "the tendency of the term 'transnational' to draw attention to what it negates—that is, to the continued significance of the national."[22] Though it remains to be seen whether, as Julia Kristeva wrote in 1990, "within and through the nation . . . the economic, political, and cultural future of the coming century will be played out,"[23] I understand that the very idea, frame, and historical-empirical problem of "our Conrad" *makes* a nation-based assumption, one derived from and faithful to the complexities of the historical moment and problem I am studying; and, as in certain moments of the work of Amy Kaplan and John Carlos Rowe, I am principally interested in critically exposing the internationalist vectors and signifiers that have worked historically to constitute (and destabilize) that assumption and the domestic ideological work transacted through and in relation to it.[24]

It is, however, among the work of the transnational comparativists—work that, in Paul Gilroy's phrase, emphasizes "transnational structures of circulation and exchange," "mutuality and reciprocity"[25]—that *Our Conrad* finds perhaps its closest home. For even as this book concentrates on a national domain of engagement, it does so with the fundamental aspiration of using a world-authorial figure like Conrad to collapse and connect U.S. and global spheres of political, cultural, and literary activity; to demonstrate the thoroughgoing *saturation* of self-declaredly nationalized domains by "foreign" world-political and transnational literary traces; to illustrate the historical dependency through which, as Laura Doyle observes,

Transnationalism and nationalism have since the seventeenth century arisen together and unfolded dialectically. Their frictions have catalyzed their further instantiations. Some transnational scholarship assumes a sequence in which nations come first and then transnational migrations, economies, and impulses move against these national boundaries.... [Yet] the nation's "imaginary" centripetality and insistence on commonality ... arises, at least in part, under centrifugal, transnational pressures—economic, political, psychological, [literary].[26]

Doyle writes specifically of Atlantic modernity; and in part, this book seeks specifically to contribute to the "British-American" subfield within modern Atlantic studies, some of whose important recent voices include Doyle, Amanda Claybaugh, Lawrence Buell, and Paul Giles (whose work I will return to shortly).[27] More so than most British authors, however, the Polish-born, multiforeign, hypertraveled Conrad was much more than, and much more to modern U.S. Americans than, singularly, normatively, or even dependably "British." The expansive stakes of recovering Conrad within a British-American "Anglo-Saxon" transatlantic framework mark the crucial beginnings of this book's inquiries, but this frame does not define either the book's ultimate historical scope (which includes Black Atlantic, hemispheric, world systems, and other pointed planetary dimensions as well) or the ultimate stakes for transnational American studies of its methodology.

Closer to this book's central intention is the specific *strategy* Giles demonstrates in an ambitious trilogy of recent books in which he broadly rewrites the field of British and American transatlantic relations (literary, cultural, political) during the past three centuries.[28] Arguing trenchantly for the necessity of assuming positions of estrangement and externality in contemplating self-declaredly "national" traditions, Giles's work turns on an innovative vocabulary of "bi-focal" and "virtual" operations through which various forms of national literatures and cultures may be used to estrange one another, especially with respect to the nationalizing, harmonizing, and self-distinguishing tendencies of nationalist ideology. To participate in one national literary discursive stream while "bi-focally" eyeing and inscribing the techniques and conventions of another, or to approach one's own national space "virtually" through the outside perspective of a similar but distinct national other, is to introduce a "structural alienation," a new and estranged center of gravity, into one's "national" vision.[29] "National histories," Giles argues, "cannot be written simply from the inside. The scope and significance of their narrative involve not just the incorporation of multiple or discordant voices in a pre-established framework of unity, but also an acknowledgment of external points of reference that serve to relativize the whole conceptual field, pulling the circumference of national identity itself into strange, 'elliptical' shapes."[30]

This elliptical function, in which the charmed circle of the nation becomes estranged through the introduction of an alien focus, is very much a central function performed by "our Conrad" in the modern United States, and it is one I will be formulating through Foucault's notion of "heterotopia," itself expressly articulated through the trope of the "virtual,"[31] to emphasize both the distinctive nature of Conrad's fiction and the peculiar fullness of exposed spatial relations that can emerge from it. Giles, moreover, argues in several recent essays that a "virtual" approach to literary studies can help reveal how U.S. literary history has been systematically conceptualized, periodized, "territorialized" to privilege a self-sufficiently nationalist orientation: the nineteenth century, for instance, traditionally overshadowing the explicitly and expansively transnational earlier centuries; more recently, the Civil War emerging in criticism as the nation's generative struggle par excellence.[32] This book takes a similar tack with respect to the era of World War I: an expansive period of military, socioeconomic, and diplomatic upheaval too often reduced (in traditional, but also more recent, Americanist literary scholarship) to a purely foreign Event, itself further reduced to the little more than a year's worth of active U.S. military participation in that event, and finally sealed off (rather than explored) in the image of the kind of abstract "scar," unnamable "wound," and symbolic displacement featured in Faulkner's first, Hemingway's second, and Fitzgerald's third novels. Hence the profoundly internationalized decade of "our Conrad"—

which is one way to conceive both "the war" and the years 1914–24[33]—becomes perversely reduced to a vague traumatic threshold and wholly self-referential seam *within* U.S. modernity; and so too, at least the first half of this decade, and many of the rich imbrications of the national and transnational extending from it that underwrite the second half, become lost on considerations of "American modernism" of the 1920s and 1930s, which, divorced from its earlier animating contexts, become artificially and excessively divided between nativist and internationalist poles. To "virtually" reconsider U.S. literary and cultural history through "our Conrad"—or, and this is to say significantly the same thing, to imagine such a thing as "Wilsonian modernism"—is to transgress, disrupt, and ultimately begin counter- and globally renarrativizing one of the most important periodizing boundaries and strategies through which hermetic conceptions of U.S. literary history have historically articulated themselves.

Here, however, is a list of names that do not receive significant discussion in Giles—or anywhere else in contemporary Americanist criticism to my knowledge. It will be clear from the national-ethnic composition of my list that my point is not to criticize Giles,[34] but rather to suggest a major and systematic lacuna in the field of American studies generally. The list: Conrad, Shaw, Wells, Hardy, Bennett, Kipling, Walpole, Galsworthy, Strachey, Norman Douglas, George Moore, Stevenson, Huxley, Mansfield, Masefield, May Sinclair, Dorothy Richardson, Tolstoy, Dostoevsky, Pushkin, Ibsen, Dumas, Proust, Anatole France, Mann, Knut Hamsun, Huysmans, Rabindranath Tagore, Benavente, D'Annunzio, Sigrid Unset, Ricardo Léon, Gjellerve, Gunnerson, Spittel, and Heidensturm. Absent from contemporary American studies, these "foreign" literary signifiers *do* appear and receive significant discussion in the 1921 and 1922 issues of the *Reviewer* (Richmond, Virginia), perhaps the most influential U.S. Southern literary and cultural magazine of the postwar period. Such "foreign" literary figures thus constitute not only terms of American historical engagement but the very field of U.S. literary and cultural textuality; it is only belatedly, and through a process of repressing their complex constitutive and disruptive role in U.S. ideological self-production, that they become neatly generated as nationally "other." Hence, though Conrad's specific ideological production in venues like the *Reviewer* is the focus of this book, the larger aim of *Our Conrad* is to help break open the "foreign" and "literary" responsibilities of American studies more generally: to initiate a broader spectrum of inquiry into how foreign authorship and textuality become produced in the

United States as "literary" and "aesthetic," and through a process by which they are converted and exchanged as a *domestic* cultural currency of transacting and negotiating, consolidating and contesting, estranging and elaborating the spatial dimensions and worldly relations of U.S. territoriality. I see this domain of inquiry as significantly specific to the work of criticism in the age of digitality: much in this book turns on large quantities of primary historical materials not readily available without the tools and institutions of a digital age; in such a culture of hyperaccessible information lie the possibilities of a "new empiricism" among whose Americanist purposes is the radical recovery and reconceptualization of the United States as a global literary contact-space, connected with the world precisely and even in the most extreme attempts to disavow it. The immediate comparativist emphasis here lies less on eclipsing U.S. boundaries—though this does and must happen, to take the resistance afforded by "foreign" signs seriously—than on a strategically robust critical pursuit of the infinitely complicated ways (and the myriad globally and locally resonant vectors) through which the "foreign" and "literary" have saturated "American" territory, constituting its boundaries and occasioning their contestation. In sympathy with but different from the many comparativist projects that have helped to inspire this book—new extranational ontologies of the novel (economic, ethnosocial, geopolitical, etc.); new comparativist estrangements of national ideology through the novel; new international engagements with the extranational dissemination of U.S. novels—*Our Conrad* attempts to open up inquiry into the status of foreign literature as *domestic cultural-political signs*: as both a material part of the U.S. domestic sphere of signification and part of what constitutes and globally complicates it *as* domestic.

One might object that the "liberating" tenor of these claims is curiously at odds with the white, male, European writers emphasized in the above list from the *Reviewer*: hardly the terrain, in John Muthyala's difficult but useful formulation, where we might expect to "develop critical vocabularies that would foreground and address the multivalent complexity of transcontinental patterns of social and cultural interaction and the transborder geopolitical determinations that engender global disjunctions and local sedimentations in the flow of power, capital, commodities, ideas, peoples, and symbols within, between, and across the Americas"; hardly the sort of "recovery" that might be expected to help us most "effectively contest the nationalist, linguistic, religious, geopolitical, and ethnocentric biases that have, historically, informed the construction of Eurocentric America."[35] Yet one might be surprised by the multivalent complexity of transcontinental and transborder management strategies inscribed in the American vogue of writers like Kipling (whose U.S. popularity, incidentally, is what prompted Doubleday to take the risk on Conrad), W. H. Hudson, Shaw, France, or Mann; or the internationalist interest that important African American magazines like the *Crisis* and the *Half-Century Magazine* took in Galsworthy, Wells, Stevenson, Pushkin, and Dostoevsky; or the vast array of non-Western and women writers featured in political magazines like the *New Republic* and published by major publishing houses including Knopf and Boni & Liveright; or the thoroughgoing deconstructions, reconstructions, and pluralizing contextualizations of "Eurocentric America"—to the point where that polemically productive phrase begins to lose its probative value—made possible through a writer like Conrad. A number of the authors named above, moreover, are seminal figures in global literary formations—genealogical streams of writers who write like or in some form of response to them—that are themselves "transcontinental patterns of social and cultural interactions" with their own "global disjunctions" and "local sedimentations," irreducibly postnational and unpredictable in political formation. Furthermore, one of the strong claims of this book is that it is really impossible to predict and deduce in advance the diversity of voices or array of interchanges and dialogue made available by the recovery of an author from the identity (national, political, racial, etc.) of that author. Frances Newman, a brilliant maverick feminist Southern author who very richly and perceptively abominated Conrad, probably becomes more recovered in this book on Conrad than most of what American and Southern studies have managed during the past fifty years; the very network of modern Southern voices who become connected, interconversant, and globally re-placed through Conrad is also a significant estrangement and enhancement of current understandings. The complex story of modern African-American responses to Conrad, and the cultural routes through which they come to (and against) Conrad, is an important story with global implications that remains almost completely untold. Even a figure like H. L. Mencken becomes recoverable through Conrad as a figure of much greater complexity and alterity than "American" studies alone have been able to account for. In sum, I do not at all mean the previous list from the *Reviewer* to be exclusive or even in a certain sense representative of the kind of "foreign" and "literary" investigation licensed by this book; but at the same time I would insist that the kind of archaeology advocated by this book at its largest level of Americanist generality must include those authors mentioned in the *Reviewer*, lest we arbitrarily and partially refortify the very hermetic procedures of U.S. literary and cultural history we seek to overcome.

This book, then, advances through the example of Conrad a mode of post-Americanist inquiry predicated on the investigation of signs of the "literary" and "foreign" and challenging five general assumptions that frequently determine practices in the field: first, that foreign-authored textuality constitutes a category external to or separable from U.S. culture and the field of American studies; second, that U.S. nativist, nationalist, and exceptionalist politics, nested in a field of local and global counterflows, "naturally" find their most forceful literary expression, instrumentation, and contestation through native-authored texts; third, that transnational American studies can succeed in de-fetishizing "the nation" while refetishizing (by refusing to reexamine) crucial domains and figures of national/transnational intersection; and fourth and fifth, that "aesthetics" and "the author" are suspicious categories for conducting cultural-political analysis, rather than a primary instrumentation and a powerful mechanism of social constellation and coordination of diverse political issues, respectively.[36] These assumptions have prevented "Conrad" and his various configurations of likeness from emerging in Americanist discourse, and they are flanked by a series of assumptions in Conrad and modernist studies, as I have already begun to suggest,[37] that have similarly hindered the otherwise worldwide study of Conrad from genuine historical contact with the United States. It is to the specific problem of "our Conrad"—which I mean, among its many historical usages, as a term not of possession but rather the possibility of reintegration between U.S. and global spheres through Conrad's mediation—to which we turn now.

THE HEART OF THE MATTER: CONRAD'S HETEROTOPIC FICTIONS[38]

I emphasized at the outset of this introduction that *Our Conrad*, as a matter of its specific and fundamental historical argument, rests on a paradox of inverse reciprocity. This paradox is aptly illustrated by the "map" of Conrad's works that originally appeared as the front endpapers of the first U.S. edition of *Victory* (1915) (see Figure 1). There beneath bold red lines and circles lies the world: thoroughly circumnavigated and plotted, circumscribed and dotted, by all the

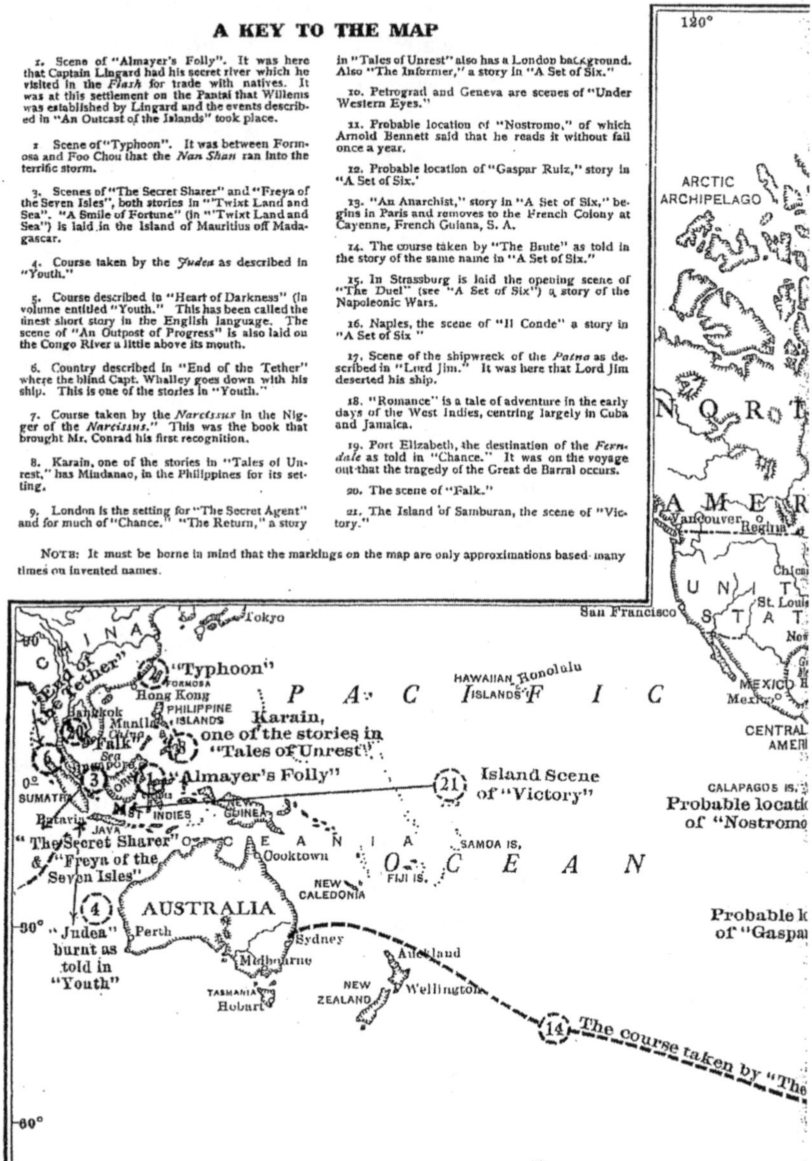

A KEY TO THE MAP

FIGURE 1. Front endpapers of the first U.S. edition of *Victory*. All superimposed type originally appeared in red.

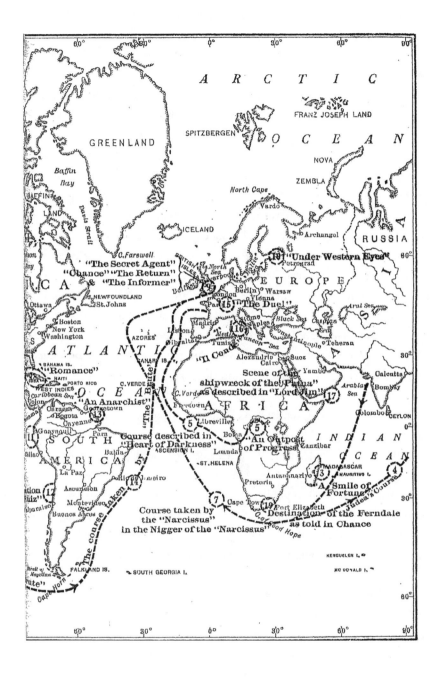

various European, Slavic, African, Latin American, East Asian, Australasian, Arab, and maritime traces and passages of Conrad's life and works. And here at the center of the world—which is to say, the map itself, the reader's presumed perspective, Doubleday's marketing strategy, and the public "boom" in Conrad underwriting it all—is the United States: the one place (along with Canada and Greenland) with which Conrad's works share no common ground; the one space that Conrad's works do not touch and say I shall go there.

This is not to say, as critics have sometimes suggested, that the United States is not a pervasive and crucial coordinating element across Conrad's life and fiction. As I have argued elsewhere,[39] Conrad's life was in fact filled with contact with U.S. American cultural forces and people (including several of his most intimate male and female friends, and some of the writers, critics, and publishers he most highly esteemed); Conrad's correspondence, even (and sometimes precisely) at its most anti-American, demonstrates extensive awareness of U.S. literature, culture, and politics (domestic and international). The very *idea* of America, I have suggested, is an indispensable negative counterpoint of Conrad's own distinct sense of "European" politics and agonized modernity; and perhaps most important for our purposes here, no one understood better than Conrad the basic proposition on which both this book and much about Conrad's own fiction (including the relative absence of the United States) is premised. As Conrad put it to his agent J. B. Pinker as early as August 5, 1907: "If the money *or the public* ever comes to us it will be from there [the United States]. We must treat them well" (*CL* 3.463, emphasis in original). Very little that Conrad wrote—from his first two novels in 1895 and 1896, both delayed in publication due to U.S. production and copyright problems, to his "later" fiction, whose oft-remarked formal sea change owes much to the American audience it self-consciously (if commercially) prioritizes and negotiates—fails to presuppose the United States in some significant, if not always flattering, way.

Nevertheless, we are still left with that paradox that Conrad would call—in direct reference to the United States—"the effusiveness of the Other Side": that the United States, a national space in so many ways most strange and estranging to Conrad should play such a primary role in producing him as a popular, celebrated, and revered writer—indeed generating, for the first time in the world and through a strange romance of the hyperforeign, what an astonished Conrad himself would describe (again referring specifically to the United States) as "this 'intensive culture' of Conrad success."[40] We have already begun to see some of the basic ideological dynamics involved in this process, but specifically how and why Conrad's fiction and image were able to enter the crosscurrents of U.S. public and artistic cultures so broadly and so resonantly—and at the particular historical moment that they did, not precisely coincident with the original publication dates of most of the fiction usually considered Conrad's "greatest"—is a mystery whose terms we've barely begun to articulate, much less account for. Why Conrad's *Chance*, originally written for and serialized in the *New York Herald* in 1912, and with an interview advertising Conrad as a "woman's writer," became the first Conrad text to attract "large" "general public" attention (*C* viii); why F. N. Doubleday and Alfred Knopf could begin to launch what would become a massive U.S. campaign to promote and distribute cheap and expensive editions of Conrad's works in 1913 and 1914; why, by 1915, the Yale English Department had made Conrad the subject of its annual essay competition, and H. L. Mencken began sensing an American "boom in Conrad's works";[41] why in the same year the *New York Times* could advertise *Victory* as "The Island Love Tale That Will Win America for Conrad," *Current Opinion* (New York) described Conrad as "The Most Remarkable Phenomenon in Modern Literature," and the Catholic magazine *America* confessed to "a severe attack of the Conrad fever, now so widely raging";[42] why in 1917 the city of Cincinnati hosted two "living-picture" shows of Conrad's works, and the first Conrad society in the world (American) reached two thousand members and proposed a "Conrad trophy" for the most notable annual work of *American* fiction;[43] why in 1918 the Los Angeles–based Kauser agency began approaching Conrad for extensive film rights to his work; why in 1919 *The Arrow of Gold* became the second best-selling novel in the United States;[44] why *every* new novel Conrad published during the remainder of his life, precisely as his "high" artistic vogue was peaking, also became an American best seller;[45] why in April 1923 Conrad appeared on the covers of both *Time* and *Outlook* magazines; why in May 1923 Conrad's U.S. visit was hailed "the most notable literary event of the year" and "an important part of the intellectual history of our time";[46] why in July 1923 Conrad's manuscripts were auctioned off in New York for a staggering 1,000 percent ($110,998) of what (American) John Quinn originally paid for them, an absolutely unprecedented amount for a living author and one Christopher Morley estimated as larger than the gate intake of a recent World Series game;[47] and why, in the several years leading up to Conrad's death in August 1924, such "American" remarks as these appeared:

[Mr. Conrad is a man] of natural American sympathies. . . . He is not only our first novelist, a creator of fiction ranking in the great succession—he is one of the first minds of his time. (*New York Tribune*, 1920)

He is a very great man—possibly the greatest man now living. (Wilson Follett, *New York Times Book Review*, 1923)

What strikes me the most is that my name seems to be worth something to the American public. . . . I am made to feel a considerable person. . . . All this is very curious, very attractive . . . something unprecedented. . . . I simply have become a *personality*. (Conrad, Letters of March, May, and November 1923)

[Though] in 1910 Doubleday Page sold only 585 copies of all Conrad's works . . . up to the present half a million of his books have been distributed in America, and he was among the few authors who could be counted on to sell over 100,000 copies annually. Millions of Americans will feel his death as a personal loss. (*Literary Digest*, September 1924)

It was his fortune to die in the plenitude of his fame. To obscurity, gradually enlightened by the approval of the few, had succeeded a wide popularity and unchallenged creative pre-eminence as the first active creative artist of his time. (*New York Times*, August 1924)

—all of these partake of the paradox of the U.S. embrace of the perfect alien, the absolute outsider whose fictions of utterly foreign people and places succeeded in capturing and perplexing the modern American imagination, both in the decade of the Great War and beyond.[48] Why?

In his celebrated 1967 lecture "Of Other Spaces," Foucault uses the term "heterotopia" to describe those spaces "outside of all places" and "absolutely different from all the sites they reflect and speak about," which nevertheless "have the curious property of being in relation with all the other sites, but in such a way as to suspect, neutralize, or invert the set of relationships they happen to designate, mirror, or reflect."[49] Heterotopias comprise, as Cesare Casarino explains in a masterful recent book exploring the heterotopic premises of Conrad's earlier sea fiction, "a special kind of space from which one can make new and different sense of all the other spaces"; they are also, as Natalie Melas argues in a book combining separate but suggestive discussions of heterotopia and Conrad's earlier colonial fiction, "an 'elsewhere' that

produces the effect of dislocating one's fundamental sense of fully inhabit-
ing a single space," an "other space" that "at once brings the totality of the
world into apprehension and destabilizes and contests" prior delimitations
of "relationality."[50] In Foucault's articulation of 1967, heterotopias are principally defined by an unusually *comprehensive* collapsing into a single site of
surrounding spaces and logics of partition and boundary, each of which, as
a result of the collective conflation, becomes *negated* in its claims of authority, naturalization, delimited relation, self-limited implication, and totalizing
coherence. As such, heterotopias are also generally built on several complementary principles: most notably, they are *compositionally hybrid*, "capable
of juxtaposing in a single real space . . . several sites that are in themselves
incompatible"; they are *heterochronous*, "most often linked to slices of time"
when traditional patterns of temporality and history are disrupted; they
are *semiautonomous*, set in a situation of pronounced and distinctive self-
enclosed remove, yet also "always presuppos[ing] a system of opening and
closing that both isolates them and makes them penetrable"; and—especially
suggestively for our purposes—they lend themselves to a *double purposiveness*, "unfold[ing] between two extreme poles": "Either their role is to create
a space of illusion that exposes every real space, all the sites inside of which
human life is partitioned, as still more illusory. . . . Or else, on the contrary,
their role is to create a space that is other, another real space, as perfect, as
meticulous, as well arranged as ours is messy, ill-constructed, and jumbled."[51]
Finally, we should add that Foucault's physical-spatial account of heterotopias
in "Of Other Spaces" (1967) is preceded by a linguistic-textual account in *The
Order of Things* (1966), where heterotopias are defined less in terms of inhabit-
able physical places than of textual spaces; such heterotopias, like Foucault's
famous example of Borges's "Chinese encyclopedia," exist in the "non-place
of language," presenting radically "heteroclite" linguistic properties whose
incommensurate and uncontainable multiple registers defy and expose the
tabula of underlying rules and boundaries upon which any given system of
language or articulation invisibly depends.[52] Though some emphasize the distinction between these two accounts, for us the fundamental point is the con-
gruence between these two heterotopic models, the physical-spatial and the
linguistic-textual, the ideological dissolution and reassertion of geopolitical
domain and dimension and the kind of textuality that makes such things
happen at the level of (political) epistemology and (nationalized) language.

Such a conception of heterotopia—an irreducibly "outside" (foreign) space compositionally possessed of the power intricately, extensively, and controversially to summon, interfere with, and even incite urgent reassertion of the boundaries and relations through which "home" spaces are constructed, their worldviews transacted—is how this book defines the complex status, role, and phenomena of "Conrad"—or rather, "the world of Conradia," in the *New York Herald*'s phrase of 1922—in the modern United States. Joseph Conrad's fiction, nonfiction, and persona composed a single textual site of broad and ineluctable foreignness, expansive shadowy ("uncanny") U.S. proximity and implication, immensely condensed intersection and hybridity, peculiarly heteroclite and untotalizable pieces, and radically negative and ambiguous properties so extreme that they simultaneously generated and authorized, through the very multiple vocabularies of their disruption, an array of oppositional countermandates *for* order (and *against* the "double" property suggested previously)[53]—all situated so as to summon, cancel, haunt, reinforce, and ultimately dialogize much of the greater grid of the ideological, cultural, and geopolitical American *tabula*. Modern U.S. Americans in effect invented Conrad as a "master" literary figure through a dialogic cascade of oppositional engagements with Conrad's heterotopic writings and persona, exploited both for their capacity to subvert and reinscribe (U.S.) "American" boundaries, and for their specific application across a remarkably wide array of domestic and global domains of U.S. concern. At some ultimate level, the modern U.S. invention of Conrad as a master literary figure is foundationally a matter of this heterotopic "Conrad" interfacing both with and against the grain of the two great ideological spatializers of the U.S. American imagination, isolationism and exceptionalism—a drama one can see borne out in the Janus faces of the Doubleday map itself. Does it confirm the isolated and exceptional relation of the United States to all those places in the world to which Conrad's works do travel, or rather the central and circumscribing implication of the United States in and by all the rest of the world? Yet lest we misunderstand that the heterotopic properties of Conrad's fiction are peculiar to the United States, rather than a globally applicable quality significantly endemic to Conrad's fiction that flourished first in the United States for particular contextual reasons, we must briefly inquire into the heterotopic nature of Conrad's fiction itself generally before plunging further into the specific historical details of Conrad's U.S. emergence, whose framing is the culminating point of this introduction and whose execution is the province of the book proper. "Conrad's heterotopic fictions," a phrase I have borrowed from a provocative recent essay by Robert Hampson,[54] is an idea that has come into increasing, though only partial, currency during the past six years; at issue in a clear and comprehensive framing of Conrad's fiction in this manner is not only a template that the rest of this book can work from but the pointing up of a global range of access points conceivable, connectable, and interconversant through Conrad—including but not restricted to the U.S. concerns and voices this book emphasizes.

Nearly all of Conrad's fiction lends itself to a general hermeneutics of heterotopia, in part because a basic gamble of Conrad's fiction is precisely that of occupying "other spaces." Whereas the Doubleday map of 1915 makes it seem that Conrad's work has a uniquely "foreign" relation with the United States, Conrad's fiction is in fact presumptively set in hyperexotic, unusually distant, or at least distinctively liminal ("queer," in one of Conrad's repeated locutions) places: spaces quite "other" as a matter of location and familiarity to *any* of the primary audiences Conrad originally assumed. Such "other spaces" have themselves, of course, generated some of Conrad's most incisive global readers, rewriters, and critics over the course of the past century, and at least part of the reason why derives from the heterotopic richness—the catholicity of estranging questions, relations, and negations, amid vexing limitations as well—built into Conrad's fiction at its most foundational levels, which is what makes it worthwhile responding to Conrad even when one is objecting to him. As Hampson notes, it is difficult to read Conrad and "Of Other Spaces" together without noticing remarkable continuity;[55] and this heterotopic continuity begins, I would argue, at the fundamental level of the archetypal Conradian *scene.* One thinks of the Sulaco of *Nostromo* (1904): a presumptively distant, semiautonomous space on the western South American seaboard, defined both by formidable geographic self-enclosure from the operations of history, and, as that "slice of time" that is historical global capitalism begins to penetrate Sulaco, by a negative superabundance of imperialist and nationalizing forces—British, U.S. American, Italian, French, Creole, indigenous, etc.—each rendered, through the experience of contact, as fictive, fraught, and denaturalized in its claims to space and authority as the curiously fictive and empty (and homogeneous) character who gives title to the novel, Nostromo. One thinks also of Conrad's next two major "political" novels, *The Secret Agent* (1907) and *Under Western Eyes* (1911). The former is set in the seedy reaches of liminal London, in the weirdly self-perpetuating vortex of a Soho neighborhood that has the peculiar effect of negatively collapsing and revealing all the different ostensibly oppositional parts through which domestic British space is physically and conceptually segregated—police/anarchist, public/private, familial/political, native/foreign, metropole/colony, mass media/personal expression—as systemic *components* of one another. The latter is set in two overlapping heterotopic places, the heart of Russia, St. Petersburg, and "la Petite Russie" neighborhood of Geneva. The first, as Christopher GoGwilt keenly observes, is posited by the impercipient, cliché-ridden British narrator in absolutely "Other" and oppositional relation to the West precisely so that the novel may demonstrate the dependency of "Russia" and "the West" as complementary elements of the same spatial-ideological imaginary.[56] The second is a concretely hybrid and composite space—simultaneously a "respectable and passionless abode of democratic liberty," "the heart of democracy," *and* the exilic gathering space of Russian nihilism, anarchism, and proto-Bolshevism (*UWE* 205, 357)—gathered together under the ironic sign and statue of Rousseau, precisely to underscore an ancestral commonality of radical Russian and Western democratic thought and folly that will not brook artificial boundary.[57] *Under Western Eyes* is fundamentally a story about the *production* of boundaries: about how Razumov, a character defined by an a priori lack of differentiation and affiliation within the sphere of "Russia,"[58] becomes suddenly transformed, through shocking and repulsive contact with the revolutionist Haldin, into a figure of oppositional identity and fierce autocratic allegiance—yet one whose new boundaries and even fervent commitment can never relieve Razumov of a sense of underlying relation to and alliance with the archetypal "other," Haldin. Predicated on the recovery of the multiple relations and intersectional implications that boundaries repress, *Under Western Eyes* offers up the perfect anti-image of its own heterotopic project in the Genevan island where Razumov, beneath the false-iconic statue of Rousseau, fancies his ability to begin writing. This "hexagonal islet with a soil of gravel and its shores faced with dressed stone" is cut off from all worldly relations as much as possible, its "perfection of puerile neatness" accessible by only one "narrow" and complexly angled bridge: "If solitude could ever be secured in the open air in the middle of a town, he would have it there on this absurd island, together with the faculty of watching the only approach" (*UWE* 290).

No less than such European spaces, the sea is also a prominent heterotopic space in Conrad, as Cesare Casarino, building on Foucault's suggestion that "the ship is the heterotopia *par excellence*," demonstrates in acutely sensitive readings of *The Nigger of the "Narcissus"* (1897) and "The Secret Sharer" (1910), both instances of what Casarino argues is the larger heterotopic genre of the "modernist sea narrative."[59] For Casarino, the modernist sea narrative as practiced by writers like Conrad and Melville is primarily a later nineteenth-century genre whose conceptual dislocations have their historical moorings in the liminal vantage and heterotopic "alternative laboratory" and space afforded by the nineteenth-century merchant marine.[60] However, in the general analytic spirit of Casarino's account, though from a very different historical and ideological vantage, I introduce here as a microcosm of heterotopic scene and effect a passage from a later Conrad sea novel that Casarino does not consider—for the very good reason that the historical conditions of the nineteenth-century merchant marine are not its primary animating factor—but one whose quoted words below did appear in a review of the novel in the *Boston Evening Herald* in May 1917, about a month after the United States entered World War I. This passage comes from *The Shadow-Line* (1917) at the moment when Conrad's young captain (and narrator in first-person retrospect) has just assumed his first command of a ship somewhere in the Far East:

Nothing could equal the fullness of that moment, the ideal completeness of that emotional experience which had come to me without the preliminary toil and disenchantments of an obscure career. My rapid glance ran over her [the ship], enveloped, appropriated the form concreting the abstract sentiment of my command. A lot of details perceptible to a seaman struck my eye at that instant. For the rest, I saw her disengaged from the material conditions of her being. The shore to which she was moored was as if it did not exist. What were to me all the countries of the globe? In all the parts of the world washed by navigable waters our relations to each other would be the same— and more intimate than there are words to explain in the language. Apart from that, every scene and episode would be passing show. The very gang of yellow coolies busy about the main hatch were less substantial than the stuff dreams are made of. (*SL* 50)

Here, from the freshly "appropriated" heterotopic space and vantage of the ship at sea, a curious drama of comprehensive cancellation and unboundaried negative recovery unfolds. On the one hand, the detached, semiautonomous, "outside" space of the ship (with respect to "land") seems to occasion a solipsistic reverie for the young captain in which all the boundaries and relations structuring all the "material conditions" and "countries of the globe" become "disengaged," suspended, neutralized, dissolved—"as if [they] did not exist." But in fact, this disengagement happens in a fashion that does not, like Razumov's island, simply essay to do away with the world, but rather one that folds, builds back, and conflates all aspects of the world's negation—that is, in the "toil and disenchantments" the young captain mentions but that *are not* a part of his career; in the "lot of details" he observes but does *not* narrate; in "all the other parts of the world" and the "gang of yellow coolies" that are necessary to the ship but *not* "substantial" enough for the captain's reverie; in the very logic of "concreting the abstract" by canceling the concrete that runs throughout this passage—into the fundamental articulative condition and undifferentiated conceptual space of the ship itself. The ship is a heterotopic space where there are no worldly boundaries precisely because it is defined by—literally composed of—their comprehensive desiccation, where there are no worldly relations precisely to the degree that all old formulas delimiting the possibility of conceiving relations are placed under a kind of asymptotic erasure, opening up fresh possibilities for perceiving intersection and contact. "What were to me *all* the countries of the globe?": this is not simply a rhetorical question expressing nationalist and/or postnationalist indifference but a precise formulation of *all* the vast, unboundaried global space and field of relations that are simultaneously divested of prior provincializing cartography and folded back into the collective negative experimental imaginary of the ship. "In all the parts of the world washed by navigable waters *our relations to each other would be the same*": the defining ambiguity of referent here (is it the ship or "all the parts of the world" that constitutes the other half of "our"?) renders *coterminous* a permanent relation to the ship with a radically leveling and deterritorialized relation to all that lies outside it. Here, in this tale of paralyzing calm at sea whose immediate animating historical anxiety is the grueling stasis of the endless international violence of World War I; here, in a young captain's mind that is directly and repeatedly articulated through the image of Hamlet ("passeth show," etc.) to highlight irruptive uncertainties that lie beneath his newfound posture of command; here, in a passage that appeals to the *Boston Evening Herald* because, one month after the United States entered the Great War, it offered the United States a vision of grand international transcendence in a moment (and text) immured in and haunted by nationalized and imperialistic world politics—the very tenuous coherence of Conrad's ship itself has its meaning in the heterotopic comprehensivity with which it inversely implicates and is implicated by all the world outside it.

Of course "the colony" is a final seminal heterotopic site that runs through-out Conrad. In *Heart of Darkness* (1899), the Congo is that "outside" space, simultaneously isolate and distantly penetrable, wherein "all Europe" that "contributed to the making of Mr. Kurtz" (*YOS* 117) finds itself negated and col-lapsed in absolute identification with everything it posits as "other." In *Victory*, Heyst's island, former site of the Tropical Belt Coal Company and still a space of distinctive hybridities, is a zone of willful remove nevertheless defined by the comprehensivity with which, in the allegorical form of Mr. Jones, Martin Ricardo, and Pedro, "*the world itself* come[s] to pay you a visit" (*V* 379, emphasis added); and each of the novels that make up Conrad's Malay trilogy—*Almayer's Folly* (1895), *An Outcast of the Islands* (1896), and *The Rescue* (1920)—are predi-cated on "secret" heterotopic loci wherein hierarchies of imperialism, and the conceptual segregations endemic to them, are folded into a single social space in which cultures and races are multiple, power is plurally distributed, and all methods, boundaries, alliances, and attachments are provisional, subject to no naturalizing or exceptionalizing claims. There may be no clearer expression of heterotopic effect, at least in its dissolving and disruptive counterspatial as-pects, in all of Conrad than the long lyric passage that introduces *The Rescue*'s principal setting, "The Shore of Refuge": a small coastline of "blurred outline" and "dissolving shore"; a "land without form," with "no distinctive features," with "not a single landmark to point the way through the intricate channels"; a fundamentally unmapped and unmappable space with "no specific names on the charts, and [such that] geography manuals don't mention it at all" (*Re* 63). Finally, we must include the ever-illuminating example of *Lord Jim* (1900): for here one finds not only the symbiotic conjunction of *two* major heterotopic sites, the "ship" from which Jim jumps (the *Patna*) and the "colony" (Patusan) that serves as a site of consolation, resolution, and containment for that crisis; one also finds a distinct bipartite narrative form that makes the point about *oppositionality*—combining and lending itself to extremes of both dissolution *and* containment, radical disorder *and* overdetermined reassertions of order—that I have been arguing is fundamental to the double nature of heterotopias in themselves and the polemical terms that often define their engagement.[61]

Heterotopia, then, is a *general* property of Conrad's fiction: manifest across it as a matter of site and scene; global in its dimensions and disruptive range; deeply implicating the fiction's thematics, formal experimentalism, and complications of interpretation and reception; further intensified in its "heteroclite" status by the inclusion of Conrad's *non*fiction and discourse about his persona[62]—and all in all, emphatically *not* dependent on any exclusive relation with the United States. Nor are Conrad's writings' heterotopic properties exclusively or fundamentally rooted in any particular historical field of experience. Though the rich and elastic interpretive yield of Casarino's model, for instance, allows us to see how all Conrad's fiction could be considered "sea" fiction—which is what it would mean to think the whole fiction through the heterotopic *analogy* of Conrad's sea tales, to make it "sea," in Geoffrey Harpham's clever and suggestive pun[63]—neither a later sea tale like *The Shadow-Line* (which, I've suggested, is coordinated by significantly different national and international concerns than the earlier sea fiction) nor the large majority of Conrad's fiction as a whole, which does not centrally concern the sea, is easily or genuinely reducible to any absolute or all-encompassing determinations of the nineteenth-century merchant marine. Rather, across its many genres and wide fields of historical experience, Conrad's fiction demonstrates a hypernegative and itinerant heterotopic impulse that is curiously transgenerated and transapplicable in character: one that Harpham, who without using the term "heterotopia" may be the origins of its power in contemporary Conrad studies, formulates in terms of the hypernegated and hypernegating national space of nineteenth-century Poland; one that Edward Said, from the beginning of his work to the end, traces to Conrad's conditions and qualities of exile;[64] one that many commentators including Said and Melas have connected to the formative contradictions of Conrad's colonial experiences;[65] one that I will formulate in terms of historical crises of the World War I era; one, indeed, that nearly all of Conrad's most discerning critics from the beginning have anticipated from a bewildering variety of vantages, through an implicit heterotopic tropology of semiautonomous external spaces, inverted boundaries and exposed relations, and murmurs of revolutionary revelation and contestation, a radical conflation of inside and outside that effectively turns any "home" space inside out.[66]

Why, then, amid this wide geotemporal field of implication and application, did Conrad's heterotopic invention as a master literary figure and iconic public celebrity happen so early and with such force in the modern United States? What specific U.S. circumstances led the young American critic Van Wyck Brooks, author of what I will argue is the first major heterotopic formulation of Conrad in November 1914, to posit a new "epoch of alien turmoil" in which "speculation gathers about Conrad" through whom "the spirit of revolt, of 'unrest' is prefigured"? What U.S. angle of vision leads a critic like Brooks, who was hard at work on his seminal manifesto *America's Coming-of-Age* (1915) at the time, to turn to and herald Conrad as "not a novelist of ideas" himself but rather "supremely the cause of ideas in others"; "a figure not more remarkable in himself than in his relations"; an artist whose work "is of the greatest importance and should receive the greatest attention" both because of the "several hitherto impossible things" it combines and the amazingly plural effect this "most fugue-like of writers" has in generating conversation?[67] What U.S. particularities, domestic and global, inform the equally heterotopic assessment of Wilson Follett, the American professor who in 1916 wrote what Conrad described as "the first intelligent attempt to understand fundamental ideas of my work" (*CL* 5.576), that "the final significance of Conrad" lies in the "relation to reality . . . that [Conrad] creates . . . and that he constantly re-creates": that "nearer he comes to us, the farther away he is seen to be"?[68]

This book answers these questions by arguing that the particularity of Conrad's heterotopic rise in the modern United States, and the reason "our Conrad" was invented then and there as a master literary figure, is a function of, first, Conrad's fiction's powerful exclusion of the United States, and even more important, the relationship between the unique intensity with which the United States excludes itself from the rest of the world through narratives of isolationism and exceptionalism and the capacious degree to which, as a matter of both international relations and domestic composition, Conrad's writings directly evoke and uncannily summon wide fields of U.S. concern and territory, consequently disrupting, dialogizing, and placing into controversy vast domains of U.S. knowledge hitherto administered by a grounding tabula of isolationist and exceptionalist logic. "Our Conrad," simply put, is a matter of the most ideologically hyperboundaried, aggressively self-distinguishing of nations meeting the most comprehensive site of heterotopic evocation and interference with it: at just the right historical moment—the rise of the Great War, the dawn of U.S. emergence as both an international power and a modern nation entwined in global crisis. The catholicity of the "foreign" world and its modalities of human interaction that Conrad could bring "home" to the United States, combined with the resistance of U.S. national and regional assertions of difference and distance in a moment of profound world-interpenetrative apprehension and shock, is what mobilized Conrad as such a singular site of heterotopic contestation and containment in the modern United States. If, as we have already begun to see, the commencement of mass and ever-expanding hostilities in Europe in August 1914 dramatically activated in the U.S. imagination a crisis of what we might call the United States' "*relation* to all the space that remains [in] the general organization of terrestrial space,"[69] the role of Conrad was one, to quote the inaugural editorial in the *New Republic* in November 1914, of mediating and elaborating the new "horror" that "We, too, have our place in the world": a double horror of both being placed within the world's sphere of power relations (contra isolationism) and being placed as more fundamentally *related* to the rest of the world (contra exceptionalism).[70]

Three important assumptions underlying this argument remain to be elaborated. The first is that Conrad became of special U.S. interest in the historical circumstances outlined above, not simply because of the general pressure his writings place on questions of "boundary" but also because of the specific interface between his writings and some of the major narrative semes and strategies through which modern U.S. exclusivity and self-distinction have been most powerfully asserted. Conrad's fiction continually turns, this is to say, on privileged sites and nodes of haunting Americanist propensity: most notably, (1) a slippery discourse of *Englishness*, capable of both suturing and subverting U.S. "Anglo-Saxon" articulations of world relation and domestic boundary and hierarchy; (2) the idea of *revolutionary/Bolshevik Russia*, both the absolute Other of the United States and a dark mirror of its class tensions and "democratic" (state-terroristic) excesses; (3) global practices of *imperialism* and the race ideologies subtending them, both a plural flashpoint of self-recognition and probably the most emphatic consistent focus of U.S. self-disavowal; (4) the idea of *the nation* itself, both emphatically valorized by Conrad and equally evacuated by his writings of ontological authority; and (5) an inconsistent but significant *hypermasculine asymmetry of vision*, paradoxically engendering both conservative and alternative responses to gender-essentialist and heteronormative constructions of U.S. national and social cultures. This shared proximity of seam between hegemonic formulations of the United States and "the world of Conradia"—this deeply resonant obverse reciprocity between the macro-vocabularies upon which the two worlds are constructed, pulling one another apart and back together—in further combination with the significantly heteroclite domains and registers placed in uncertain, multiformulable contiguity *across* the seams, is an important engine of Conrad's heterotopic expansion in the United States.

The second assumption, perhaps even more fundamental, is a profound sense of material historical overlap, in a certain sense "fueling" the kind of engagement that happens at the metalevel of "boundary"—supplying it with fresh repositories of material; sustaining and perpetuating it across diverse fields of U.S. experience and implication—between the superabundant world of Conrad's fiction and the most acute, often doubly mappable regions of U.S. international interest and domestic territory. From the international side alone, the omni-"foreign" Conrad quite naturally became a U.S. fascination at the crossroads of war. Not only did the vast international panorama of his fiction offer a kind of portal to and virtual education in all the pressing world events and places that *now* seemed of national consequence. (The Bolshevik Revolution, for instance, could be considered in light of the Russia of *Under Western Eyes*; Pancho Villa and the Mexican Revolution in relation to *Nostromo*; the rebirth of Poland in light of *Lord Jim* and Conrad's own Polishness; worldwide crises of imperialism [both giving rise to and as extended by the war] with respect to Conrad's [anti-]imperialist fiction, especially *The Rescue*; and the Great War itself and its complex European aftermath in light of complex contemporary negotiations in *The Shadow-Line*, *The Rover*, and *Suspense*.) In addition, Conrad's fiction, despite a general refusal to "place" the United States, does also directly target and powerfully resonate with many aspects of U.S. wartime and postwar involvement in the international sphere. (*Nostromo*, for instance, which aggressively asserts the anti-exceptional place of the United States among the world's Western imperialist powers, was republished with a new introduction in the United States in 1917, the year the United States joined the *other* imperial powers in the Great War—and continued much imperialist activity in the Caribbean and Latin America. Similarly, *Victory* [1915], the key text in Conrad's U.S. popularization and first published earlier in the war when the official U.S. policy was "Neutrality in thought and deed," is essentially the tale of an *isolationist* enterprise gone awry at the hands of sinister European forces, especially German and English. As a final example, *Lord Jim*'s towering appeal in the postwar, post–League of Nations, "disillusioned" United States must be understood in the context of a general cultural sense that the United States had "jumped" into the war unprepared, and that the fate met by the idealistic, romantic, and utterly unprepared President Woodrow Wilson was not all that different from what befell "Lord" Jim—or Tom Lingard in *The Rescue*.)

But the fundamental power of Conrad's heterotopic captivation of the modern U.S. imagination, and the vast processes of dialogue and debate that produced him as a "master" literary figure, ultimately derive, not simply from his explicit implications in the international sphere, but from the double mappability of *both* Conrad's superabundant "foreign" interest *and* his equally extensive if surreptitious *domestic* "American" resonances. I mean this latter "Americanizing" claim neither in metaphysical nor proprietary terms, though my point here may help to account for the long line of U.S. readers and writers who, as Robert Secor and Debra Moddelmog document, have since the beginning of the twentieth century been eager to claim Conrad as "American" on spiritual, temperamental, and aesthetic grounds.[71] My point is rather that Conrad's writings, "beneath" and within their apparently wholly exotic surfaces, and in mappable relation to their ostensibly foreign and metanational fields of concern, are broadly and intimately predicated on a wide range of personal experiences (Conrad's) and objective cultural-political concerns and issues that either mirror or directly implicate key cultural-political fault lines and governing circumstances of the modern United States. This sociocultural overlap between "Conrad" and the modern United States—effecting a vast field of "uncanny" recovery and estrangement, dislocation and recognition, between the two—includes shared focal problematics and conditions of: immigration and emigration, expatriation and exile, nationalist ambivalence and national in-betweenness, extreme linguistic and ethnic multiplicity (and their apprehensions), black/white racialized conflict and segregation and their relation to radical class politics, democracy and its liabilities, modern media culture and "public opinion," coloniality and national independence, domestic imperialism and its disavowal, Anglophilia and Germanophobia, Jewishness (and Catholicity) and their detectability, gender difference and feminist assertion—as well as a striking array of convergences between the political and cultural histories of Conrad's native Poland and the modern U.S. American South. This list, of course, names many elements that are not in themselves particular either to the United States or the relation of the modern United States to Conrad; but taken together, and placed in relation to the field of international and metanational concerns Conrad's fiction also articulates—for example, larger arcs of imperialism and its disavowal; Anglo-Saxonism and its subversion; Bolshevism and its elaboration; Pan-Africanism and postnational alliances/analogies of race and class generally; "American" hemispheric relations; isolationism as a means of deliberate and effective political action—this list does name the *network* of concerns that link "our Conrad" and "our America." The creation of the former emerged from the dialectics of the latter; the U.S. availability and proximity of the former gave rise to the dialogue concerning the latter. And indeed, it is precisely because Conrad's heterotopic fiction, its categorically "alien" appearances notwithstanding, was so richly and plurally amenable to interpenetrating so many different historical aspects of modern U.S. experience—was both more and less "American," in this sense, than any specific native place or person or text could be—that "our Conrad" could become specially invented in the United States as a literary master.

The third and final assumption is the general *absence* of the United States from direct placement by Conrad's fiction: the key lacuna, curious and fundamental in origin, that makes the heterotopic multiplicity of "our Conrad" possible. In this light, we might imagine the relation between Conrad and the modern United States in conjunction with Foucault's famous discussion of the Velázquez painting *Las Meninas* at the outset of *The Order of Things*, immediately after his discussion of heterotopias in the preface. The painting presents Velázquez himself, in the company of various observers, painting the king and queen of Spain, but the two sovereign figures themselves are located outside the visible field of the painting, only faintly registered in a small mirror at the back of the painting, rather omnipresent in their importance as the structuring *occasion* of everything represented and enacted in the painting. It is a good metaphor for Foucault to begin his investigations of the sovereign structures and figures that invisibly guarantee our sense of the order of things. Now imagine for a moment that instead of a true sovereign coordinating the painting, there were instead in the sovereign space—which is also the space where the *audience* of the painting must stand—something like a lord of misrule: a heterotopic figure capable of replicating but grotesquely distorting, negating but also offering up for urgent resolution, all the lines and boundaries and gestures and gazes that Velázquez paints so cleanly. That painting would be something like the structure of this book; that *idea* is the governing idea of the empirical history it documents; and the imaginary picture you have formed is something like the picture of Conrad with which the first chapter begins.

PART I

The Nation in the World, the World in the Nation

1 IN THE CRUCIBLE OF WAR
Immigration, Foreign Relations,
Democracy, and H. L. Mencken

Joseph Conrad, rover of the seven seas, has never set foot in the United States. Now he is coming. At about the end of this month the man who holds probably the most exalted position in contemporary English letters is to arrive here for a visit. . . . He looks forward to it in a spirit of adventure. —*Time*, April 7, 1923

I am going away with a strong impression of American large-heartedness and generosity. I have not for a moment felt like a stranger in this great country. . . . I am proud to have had from it an unexpected warmth of public recognition and the gift of precious private friendships. —Conrad to Elbridge Adams, May 31, 1923

Yes; he was a castaway. A poor emigrant from central Europe . . . washed up here in a storm. And for him, who knew nothing of the earth, this was an undiscovered country. . . . He could talk to no one and had no hope of understanding anybody. Upon my word, I wonder he did not go mad. He didn't know where he was. Somewhere very far from his mountains—somewhere over the sea. Was this America, he wondered? —Conrad, "Amy Foster" (1901)

ONE OF US?

On April 7, 1923, Joseph Conrad appeared on the cover of America's *Time* magazine. The occasion was Conrad's first and only visit to the United States, which began in May and was anticipated throughout the preceding month. The mood was one of high romance, as Conrad, "rover of the seven seas" and "probably the most exalted [figure] in contemporary English letters," was finally embarking on the most exotic adventure of them all:

Despite all the countries and seas of the world which he has made his own and presented to his readers, Mr. Conrad has never come closer to this coast than on the first voyage of his sea-life in 1875, which took him through the Florida Channel to the West Indies. It will be our especial opportunity to greet him here at last.[1]

As these words suggest, there is a curious element of destiny and circular homecoming that underwrites this narrative of ultimate distance, a paradox registered in the two mythic figures most widely in circulation to gloss Conrad's latest journey: Ulysses, the archetypal alien wanderer, and Columbus, the "discoverer" and a narrative foundation of "America."[2] This paradox is also registered in the picture on the cover of *Time*, unique in its artistry among contemporary numbers of the magazine (see Figures 2 and 3 on pages 44 and 45). There is a portrait of Conrad looking very much the familiar venerable writer: stately, solemn, neatly anchor bearded, grandfatherly wise. Yet this image of Conrad is embedded in a rush of dark, heavy streaks, not the background for but the occlusive and estranging medium in and through which this Conrad exists. This flattened surface creates an extraordinary—and defining—optical illusion, especially evident in the original glossy format of the *Time* cover. It presents Conrad simultaneously as a spectral apparition who has come from afar and as a face one might see if one looked in the mirror.

This is the image of the "distant mirror" through which I would have us understand Conrad's heterotopic construction in and captivation of the American imagination from 1914 to 1939, and it is one quite explicitly and self-consciously used in several U.S. appreciations of Conrad during this period.[3] Yale professor William Lyon Phelps, for instance, observes in *The Advance of the English Novel* (1916) that whereas "Dickens is a refracting telescope, Conrad is a reflector," and goes on to identify a mirror *of* the mirror of Conrad's fiction in the same dualized and shrouded image of Conrad's face that the *Time* cover presents visually:

His face to some extent is a map of his soul. He looks like a competent, fearless, and highly intelligent clipper captain. His eyes have looked on the brutality of nature and the brutality of men and are unafraid. . . . It is a face that knows the very worst of the ocean and the very worst of the heart of man, and, while taking no risks, realizing all dangers, is calmly, pessimistically resolute. This is not a man to lead a forlorn hope, but unquestionably the man to leave in charge; grave, steady, reliable.[4]

This double Conrad—his "eyes" reflecting both reassuring safety and vast penumbral stretches of distance and darkness—is also presented by Christopher Morley in *The Mentor* in 1925. Morley, too, begins by introducing Conrad's fiction in terms of its "mirror" function and then elaborates that function through an even more intensely dualized reading of a recent bust of Conrad by U.S. sculptor Jacob Epstein:

[Conrad] had, as highly as any man of our time perhaps, the genuinely poetic mind which dreams about its experiences in life and, by its magic faculty of seeing secret resemblances and analogies, builds a fable which mirrors ourselves. . . . The great sculptor Epstein has done a bust of Conrad which has startled some of those who loved him because they do not find it "like the Conrad they knew." It isn't: it is great sculpture because it is like the Conrad they didn't know, that probably no one knew: the secret and fierce and imagination-wracked soul of the great poet—with an enemy in his breast.[5]

The Epstein bust is, in fact, quite representative of the many curiously and variously distorted images of Conrad in circulation in the United States at the time; but perhaps the most precise contemporary formulation of the "distant mirror" of Conrad's fiction, struggling through and against difference to arrive at and to erode an image of identity, may be found in the work of idiosyncratic Brown professor, public essayist, and future editor and novelist Wilson Follett (perhaps most famously known for his *Modern American Usage*). In an important essay in the *Atlantic Monthly* in February 1917, Follett presents the whole of Conrad's fiction through the exemplar of "The Secret Sharer"; in particular, Follett emphasizes the captain-narrator's "secret," specular fascination with the mutinous Leggatt—who is "the *negation* of tranquility in a solid and respectable ship's company," "a negation of [all] the serene immensity of the cosmos that mocks him"—to theorize Conrad's fiction in terms of mirror operations that negate and "disentangle" all the artificial boundaries preventing identification.[6] Taking his cue from the claim in the Preface to *The Nigger of the "Narcissus"* that the artist's "task" is to "awaken" a "feeling of unavoidable solidarity" among "all humanity" (*NN* ix), Follett argues that Conrad's characters, always "outside" of and "outcast" from our normative spheres of reference, are nevertheless "so near to being ordinary characters that we see ourselves *reflected* in them." The crucial element of this "perception," however, is not the "nearness to common life" but rather "the strangeness that underlies the familiarity; the strangeness that comes from the something inexplicable and nameless at the center of every soul, which makes it eternally foreign to every other." Whether with respect to "the mystery of race," "a world in which East is East and West is West," or the local psychology through which "everyman [becomes] a foreigner to his neighbor," "the secret and invisible thing

FIFTEEN CENTS

TIME

The Weekly News-Magazine

VOL. I, NO. 6

JOSEPH CONRAD
"Toward New Adventure"—See page 15

APRIL 7, 1923

FIGURE 2. Cover of *Time*, April 7, 1923.

FIGURE 3. Contemporary covers of *Time*, March and April 1923. Pictured clockwise beginning from upper left: Joseph Cannon, Warren G. Harding, Foad I, Winston Churchill.

that renders us alien to each other is the thing Mr. Conrad is always trying to disentangle." Conrad's fiction, by effecting identification through the negative prism of alienation, comprises a "mirror" through which the "outward wrappings" in which are lives are "suffused" become momentarily collapsed into the space of the alien.[7]

All of the previous formulations speak to a sense of Conrad's fiction—as well as his persona, invariably invoked to explain the fiction's anomalous character and to contain its unstable and contradictory applications—as a matrix of spatio-conceptual difficulty: a shadow-line of foreign and familiar space; an interference in the constitution of boundaried identity; an *excess* of narrativity that becomes blurred together in a common undifferentiated contact zone; an external virtual vantage through which—as happens when one looks in the mirror—presumptive self-integration itself becomes displaced by an expanded, estranged, reversed, derealized image of one's self in a *world*. Such modern U.S. reactions to Conrad, hence, are much like the "sort of counteraction on the position" of the observer that Foucault theorizes of *heterotopias* through the instance and analogy of the mirror:

From the standpoint of the mirror I discover my absence from the place where I am since I see my self over there. Starting from the gaze that is, as it were, directed toward me, from the ground of this virtual space that is on the other side of the glass, I come back toward myself; I begin again to direct my eyes toward myself and to reconstitute myself there where I am. The mirror functions as a heterotopia in this respect: it makes this place I occupy at the moment when I look at myself in the glass at once absolutely real, connected with all the space that surrounds it, and absolutely unreal, since in order to be perceived it has to pass through this virtual point which is over there.[8]

Conrad performs this kind of desanctification of space in the modern United States, as I begin to tell the story in this chapter. Offering up an entire "external" world in mirror relation to the United States, the United States becomes not only absolutely realized in all its worldly connectedness and implication but also absolutely derealized (and variously rerealized) with respect to all the narrative and ideological machinery through which the United States has traditionally constructed itself as an emphatically separate, exceptional, self-reliant, self-determined, fundamentally self-contained space. Making the conception of "America" pass through the vantage of the foreign, Conrad becomes an American *problem* whose contestation and proliferation emerge from the degree to which he turns the United States into a contested space—*not* by taking a "position" with respect to it but by rendering problematic, susceptible to controversy, as a species of *trouble*, the very vocabularies through which the United States constitutes itself as a fundamentally distinct and distinctly self-regulated national domain.

Richard Curle, hence, is only partially right in his attempt in 1928 to explain Conrad's "tremendous" stature in the United States—why "to numbers of Americans, he is the author of all authors, the one writer to whom they pay a single-minded homage"—in terms of "sheer" difference:

At first sight this was astonishing, because the kind of admiration which amounts to worship is usually bound up with deep spiritual affinity, but I have come to the conclusion that it is the *sheer exoticism* of much of Conrad's atmosphere which appeals so particularly to the Americans. It is, in brief, *the romance of contrast*. . . . [I]t is in romance that one may discover the final secret of Conrad's hold upon America. . . . Conrad awakens the American sense of adventure.[9]

Rather, it is the very *question* of difference, the very clusters of "American" relations that are unsettled, reasserted, fiercely contested, and finally unfixable in Conrad's image, that makes for the romance of and with Conrad in the modern United States. "I dare say there were multitudinous Conrads," Christopher Morley observed in late 1924;[10] and from these many Conrads, generating and mediating equally multitudinous fissures and suturings of the U.S. spatial and ideological imaginary, arise many of the signature aspects of Conrad's discursive production—especially his remarkable ability to be processed on *any* side of many binaries (cosmopolitan/national; metropolitan/provincial; democratic/aristocratic; elitist/popular; reactionary/radical; aesthetic/political; imperialist/anti-imperialist; masculinist/womanist), and his simultaneous overdetermination *and* underdetermination by the idea of "debate" itself.[11] Conrad, in short, allows modern Americans to ask and engage with unusual depth and extension the "unhomely" question that Conrad's aptly named *Yanko* Goorall poses to himself in "Amy Foster": "Was this America, he wondered?" (*TOT* 129).[12]

History, I have suggested, emerging at just the right "slice of time," is the key to Conrad's U.S. cultural emergence, and in this chapter we begin to consider the relation between the rise of Conrad as a modern U.S. fascination and the historical threshold and U.S. cultural-political implications and circumstances of the Great War. The focus of this chapter is H. L. Mencken, one of the major oppositional figures in U.S. history and a primary cultural generator of Conrad as a figure of trouble, interference, and neutralizing subversion and inversion in the modern United States. The first section begins by discussing the general terms, affectual and perceptual, of Mencken's attraction to Conrad, and the exilic positionality that enables Mencken to become a powerful disseminating force of Conrad—well beyond his own writings and this chapter. The following sections trace Mencken's specific inscription and construction of Conrad in terms of a triply mapped assault on the idea of the "Anglo-Saxon"—a nexus of foreign relations, racialized response to immigration, and "Puritanical" ethos of democratic government and culture—all made visible and actionable through the crucible of war. The "distant mirror" of Conrad for many modern Americans begins with Mencken—and as we shall see throughout this book, it never entirely escapes him.

AS HLM SAW IT

Mencken's vigor is astonishing. It is like an electric current. In all he writes there is a crackle of blue sparks like those one sees in a dynamo house amongst the revolting masses of metal that give you a sense of enormous hidden power. . . . When he takes up a man he snatches him away and fashions him into something that (in my case) he is pleased with—luckily for me, for had I not pleased him he would have torn me limb from limb. Whereas as it is he exalts me above the stars. It makes me giddy. Who could quarrel with such generosity, such vibrating sympathy and with a mind so intensely alive?   —Conrad to George T. Keating, December 14, 1922

The blue sparks of Conrad in the modern U.S. imagination begin with Baltimore iconoclast H. L. Mencken. Though by no means the first American to discover or become passionately attached to Conrad, Mencken was the primary force that first galvanized Conrad as a figure of broad public recognition, and his are the surging volcanic tones—richly and fiercely heterotopic in character—that not only provoked but established many of the terms of the larger American counterpoint of Conrad to follow. This Menckenian awakening of "our Conrad" must be understood in the more general context of the literary, cultural, and political impact that Mencken had on the generations that came of age during World War I, an impact that one ignores at the risk of evading a primary cultural interface of "our America." Described by Walter Lippmann in 1926 as "the most powerful influence on this whole generation of educated people" and by the *New York*

Times in 1927 as "the most powerful private citizen in America," by his friend Huntington Cairns in retrospect as "the closest embodiment of the Johnsonian dictatorship that the U.S. has ever known," and by Vincent O'Sullivan in 1919 as simply "the first American critic, since Poe," Mencken may be considered as something of the Ralph Waldo Emerson of modern U.S. letters.[13] In recovering the terms of Mencken's claims to twentieth-century Emersonian centrality—a proposition I advance heuristically and historically, not didactically—we begin to recover not only the large field and mechanism of affectual and cultural-political controversy that propelled Conrad's invention as a master literary figure but also, through Conrad, a good deal of the peculiar genius and complexity of Mencken.

Mencken is sufficiently important to the genealogy of Conrad that runs throughout this book to elaborate the Emersonian analogy in more detail. Like his heretical nineteenth-century precursor, Mencken captured the imagination of the younger generation in corpse-cold modern America by combining an infectious irreverence of spirit with a bold, invigorating, temple-smashing prose style. Also like Emerson, Mencken expressed his signature voice and attitude across a massively diverse and positively unruly body of work, one of whose key effects was to facilitate *contact* and *correspondences* among widely divergent spheres of cultural activity. Though Mencken was neither truly nor only a poet, a philosopher, a literary or cultural critic, a political theorist, a linguist, an ideological polemicist, or even a straight newspaperman, his work ran its rough, electric fingers through them all. Mencken created a cosmos of discursive interrelation and intersection in the various columns, ultimately nationally syndicated, he wrote regularly for the Baltimore *Herald* and then *Sunpapers* from 1906 through World War II; in the 182 essays reviewing some two thousand books that he wrote in various editorial capacities at the *Smart Set* from 1908 to 1923; in his contributions as cofounder and chief editor from 1924 to 1933 of the politically fearless *American Mercury*, whose pugnacious spirit made the magazine "rank first among those sold in the Harvard University Bookstore, at Columbia University, and other campuses across the country";[14] and in the *forty* books, several of them pioneering, that Mencken wrote on such subjects as Nietzsche, Shaw, Ibsen, socialism, U.S. politics and culture, feminism, religion, democracy, and literary criticism, and including the first major modern treatise on the "American" language. As with Emerson, the special and seminal aspect of this body of work lies less in the consistent originality or incisiveness of the individual parts than in the pulsating expanses of relays and homologies—the literary, linguistic, cultural, and political planes of expression and activity that are made to interpenetrate one another—effected by the textual whole. Simply put, for Mencken to promote Conrad was for Conrad to become vitally inserted into probably the most culturally extensive, publicly accessible, vociferously aggressive "personal" discursive fabric the United States had to offer at the time.

It was for Conrad also to be inserted within a matrix of *controversy*: for Mencken was nothing if not an agent provocateur with respect to many of the major national fault lines and ideological cruxes not only of his own moment but also of the remainder of the century. Fred Hobson's remarkable study of Mencken's impact on the South in the 1920s, for instance, is keenly premised on the silent intuition of Mencken as a type of the civil rights movement of the 1960s.[15] So, too, Mencken's foundational battles on behalf of freedom of expression in a moment when the First Amendment afforded few protections, and various forms of what he called "fundamental human rights"[16] and what we now call the "right to privacy," including sexual and marital autonomy, reproductive rights, and anti-Prohibition liberties, would come to inspire both anti-McCarthyite and liberal activists during the cold war period and more conservative opponents of "political correctness" in recent years.[17] Moving matters further to the right, Terry Teachout, the author of one of the three full-length Mencken biographies that have appeared over the last two decades, is certainly correct to emphasize that Mencken's "libertarian" politics include not only unlimited freedom of expression but also unlimited suspicion of large Progressive government; meantime, back on the left, the publication of Mencken's diary in the late 1980s occasioned a fresh series of debates concerning the place of race, gender, and anti-Semitism in his thinking, the many sides of which—even when most forcefully denouncing Mencken—all implicitly confirm the twentieth-century cultural centrality of his writings.[18]

Conrad, hence, becomes injected by Mencken both horizontally and vertically into several of the most major and politically volatile arteries of twentieth-century U.S. culture—and via a mediator, again recalling Emerson, whose ideological centrality walks hand in hand with his signature gift for not only contradictory *reception* but also, fundamentally, *self*-contradiction. Invoking the Emersonian disciple who at times seems to incarnate this principle, Hobson makes the point nicely: "As Whitman embraced multitudes, so Mencken vilified multitudes";[19] and in both cases, the ability of Emerson/Whitman and Mencken to get away with speaking to and for "multitudes" whose constituent terms are ultimately *not* commensurate lies in the fact that the rhetorical power of all three authors was never really traceable to the systematicity or clarity of their thought in the first place. Rather, theirs is the prophet's rhetorical mode of (controversial) provocation and (polysemous) intimation, with Mencken in particular given to provoking thought and interchange—to inciting and instantiating the very principle of free speech for which he most vitally and violently stands—by mirroring his own characteristic denunciations of others as absurd with an artifice of self-contradiction that maximizes its own chances for denunciation and ultimately commands its own renunciation as absurd. This point, elaborated throughout this chapter, is fundamental to any historical and/or textual understanding of Mencken, and its specific application to the case of Conrad is this: well before Conrad's famous "ambiguities" concretely become the occasion of U.S. controversy, Mencken's cries from the wilderness hailing Conrad's coming have positioned him as such—in part because Mencken understood himself to be mirroring Conrad.

All of this leads to a final corollary between Emerson and Mencken, who, of course, as a matter of good cheer, national enthusiasm and allegiance, isolationist propensity, nativist complacency, and exceptionalist license could not be further apart. The America that the Anglo-American Emerson champions in the highest universal terms is very much the United States that the German-American Mencken endlessly deplores through strategies of estranged vantage and foreignization. Similarly, Emerson's perennial recovery among Americanists—even when the project is no longer one of secular hagiography, even when the priorities are postnational or multicultural[20]—is categorically the opposite of the speechless blanks, frequently against the grain of the field's own ostensible priorities, invariably induced by the unsanitary, undomesticatable, irreducibly disconcerting (and not college-educated: horrors!) figure of Mencken. The very project, indeed, of thinking U.S. literary history through Mencken involves a self-consciously alienated relationship to its object that is the inverse of the Ishmael-identification "consensus" project that Sacvan Berkovitch has identified at the traditional core of American studies, and that the lacuna of Mencken *across* critical generations presents as a continuing question. Yet in the end, we may bring Emerson and Mencken forcefully back together, for with both much of their significance to U.S. history lies in the "simmering, simmering, simmering" fields of *literary* creative activity they were able to cultivate, coordinate, clear space for, and otherwise help to "bring to a boil." Alongside the familiar genealogy of influence, dialogue, and discourse descending from Emerson, we may observe that the careers of U.S. writers, including Theodore Dreiser, Sinclair Lewis, and F. Scott Fitzgerald, are unthinkable as we know them in the absence of Mencken; that Willa Cather, Eugene O'Neill, Sherwood Anderson, Abraham Cahan, Edgar Lee Masters, James Branch Cabell, James Weldon Johnson, and even William Faulkner were all boldly published and/or promoted by Mencken at breakthrough early moments; that Richard Wright dated his emergence as a writer to the discovery of Mencken's *A Book of Prefaces* (1917), and that W. E. B. Du Bois, Countee Cullen, and Langston Hughes were all printed by Mencken, as were important lesser-known figures, including Julia Peterkin, Ruth Suckow, Frances Newman, Luiz Muñoz Marin, and Avrahm Yarmolinsky. Even Pound (discussed frequently and favorably by Mencken throughout the 1910s, despite his general distrust of poetry) and Frost, Tolstoy and Joyce, Djuna Barnes and Ibsen, appeared in the *Smart Set* (a literary magazine, as we shall see, that it is unwise to underestimate) on account of Mencken. Perhaps most important of all, moreover, was the distinctive kind of literary atmosphere that Mencken strove to create: on the one hand, championing with great force and in impassioned detail a number of European writers, critics, and philosophers; and on the other hand, always targeting and prioritizing the development of young American writers and the effect they (and he) might have on various baseline aspects of U.S. culture and its institutions. Much as Emerson calls for a new American poetry at the opening of "The American Scholar" (1837), Mencken, who cites this moment in the opening of "The National Letters" (1920), devotes much of his writing from 1908 to 1923 to clearing space and cultivating an atmosphere for a new kind of U.S. literature—one situated in the United States but not narrowly *of* it—to arise. Much as Emerson calls at the outset of *Nature* (1836), "Our age is retrospective. It builds the sepulchers of the fathers. . . . Why should not we also enjoy an original relation to the universe?" Mencken, in deliberate echo, near the end of the first of four long essays concerning the future of the American novel and its cultures that make up *A Book of Prefaces*, writes: "We are not dead yet; we are here, and it is now. Therefore, let us venture, opine, guess."[21] The title of the essay from which these words come is "Joseph Conrad." The next sentences read: "My own conviction, sweeping all those living reaches of fiction that I know, is that Conrad's figure stands out from the field like the Alps from the Piedmont plain. He not only has no masters in the novel; he has scarcely a colorable peer." And finally, in the very last sentence of *A Book of Prefaces*, at the close of the tour de force essay "Puritanism as a Literary Force," one finds for the very first time a U.S. American looking to the future and expressing his hopes of literary salvation in terms of the coming of, in Mencken's exact phrase, "our Conrad."[22]

Though much has been said about Mencken's enthusiasms for and influential canon-shaping campaigns on behalf of *American* writers—especially Poe, Twain, Dreiser, and Lewis—there is no serious question that by far the most consistent, ecstatic, unqualified, and thoroughgoing literary enthusiasm of Mencken's life was Joseph Conrad. Nor are the two matters unrelated. When Mencken bookends *A Book of Prefaces*—which, as Marion Rodgers observes, Mencken came to understand as the "most important book in its effect on his professional career," and about which Mencken wrote in the *Smart Set* in January 1918, "If I die, bury me beneath it"[23]—with an opening essay on and a closing appeal to "our Conrad," he reveals the degree to which his campaign on behalf of the "new" American novel and its assault on U.S. culture and its institutions is coordinated in Conrad's image. Indeed, though Theodore Dreiser is usually understood—and quite correctly—as the answer to Mencken's search in the 1910s for "an author who would serve me as a sort of tank in my war upon the frauds and dolts who still reign in American letters," the choice of Dreiser as an American assault vehicle is clearly informed by the practical need of doing battle with a native "tank"; and the force that through the fuse drives this tank—as Mencken's many essays on Dreiser, the subject of the second essay in *A Book of Prefaces*, routinely reveal—is repeatedly Conrad.[24]

Mencken's fascination with Conrad begins with his second *Smart Set* essay in December 1908 and runs through the diary pages and several autobiographies he wrote much later in life;[25] Teachout tells the story that even after his stroke and in his seventies, Mencken would have William Manchester come to his home four mornings a week to read aloud to him from Conrad and Twain.[26] Not coincidentally, Mencken's affection for Conrad discovers its distinctive terms and takes on extremes of force, volume, and urgency during the Great War (1914–18)—which is also the very time that the German-American firebrand, increasingly precluded from direct political expression elsewhere, became chief editor of the *Smart Set* and published, within months of returning from a behind-the-scenes visit to Germany and the formal U.S. entry into the war in April 1917, *A Book of Prefaces*. Through the crucible of war, but as a means of conceptualizing and contesting more generally U.S. culture and its worldly relations, Mencken, that most ferociously unforgiving and unsentimental of commentators, developed a reverence for Conrad that would express itself in terms such as this:

I put in a blue afternoon last week re-reading Joseph Conrad's *Youth*. A *blue* afternoon? What nonsense! The touch of the man is like the touch of Schubert. One approaches him in various and unhappy moods: depressed, dubious, despairing; one leaves him in the clear, yellow sunshine that Nietzsche found in Bizet's music. But here again the phrase is inept. Sunshine suggests the imbecile, barnyard joy kohlrabi—the official optimism of a steadily delighted and increasingly insane Republic. What the enigmatical Pole has to offer is something quite different. If its parallel is to be found in music, it is not in Schubert, but in Beethoven—perhaps even more accurately in Johann Sebastian Bach. It is the joy, not of mere satisfaction, but of understanding—the profound but surely not merry delight which goes with the comprehension of a fundamental fact— above all, of a fact that has been coy and elusive.[27]

These words come from the opening of "Conrad Revisited," an important essay that first appeared in the *Smart Set* in December 1922 and that Mencken revised and reprinted on at least two other occasions. Though we will come to understand the significance of Mencken's conspicuous investment in *German* high-cultural figures, his denigration of the "official optimism" of a *democratic* republic like the United States as "imbecile," and his emphasis on Conrad "the enigmatical Pole" as an unmelted British *immigrant*, the most striking aspect of the passage is simply its unguarded emotionalism, Mencken's describing as an experience of very personal grace his being released through Conrad from "blue" depression into the "yellow sunshine." To this point, Mencken's discussion of Conrad's *Youth*—the collection that includes the three stories "Youth," *Heart of Darkness*, and *The End of the Tether*, all in all "probably the best book of imaginative writing that the English literature of the twentieth century can yet show"[28]—principally concerns the story "Youth." But the musical metaphors ("Whenever I think of anything properly describable as a beautiful ideas, it is always in the form of music," Mencken writes elsewhere)[29] and rhetorical superlatives only become stronger as Mencken turns to *Heart of Darkness*: "There is in *Heart of Darkness* a perfection of design which one encounters only rarely and miraculously in prose fiction. . . . I can't imagine taking a single sentence out of that stupendous tale without leaving a visible gap; it is as thoroughly *durch componiert* as a fugue. And I can't imagine adding anything to it, even so little as a word, without doing it damage. As it stands it is austerely and beautifully perfect, just as the slow movement of the Unfinished Symphony."[30] And he concludes "Conrad Revisited" in this way:

A very great man, this Mr. Conrad. As yet, I believe, decidedly underestimated, even by many of his advocates. . . . When one reflects that the Nobel Prize has been given to such third-raters as Knut Hamsun and Rabindranath Tagore, with Conrad disdainfully passed over, one begins to grasp the depth and density of the ignorance prevailing in the world, even among the relatively enlightened. One *Lord Jim*, as human document and as work of art, is worth all the works produced by all the Hamsuns and Tagores since the time of Ramses II. It is, indeed, an indecency of criticism to speak of such unlike things in the same breath: as well talk of Mendelssohn in terms of Brahms. Nor is *Lord Jim* a chance masterpiece, an isolated peak. On the contrary, it is but one unit in a long series of extraordinary and almost incomparable works— a series sprung suddenly and overwhelmingly into full dignity with *Almayer's Folly*. I challenge the nobility and gentry of Christendom to point to another Opus 1 as magnificently planned and turned out as *Almayer's Folly*. The more one studies it the more it seems miraculous. If it is not a work of absolute genius, then no other work of absolute genius exists on this earth.[31]

How are we to understand these words: zealous to the point of rapture, partisan beyond discrimination, singular even in the context of Mencken's other great literary enthusiasms? Are they empty hyperbole, or rather as freighted with resonance and suggestive meaning as they are deeply felt? How indeed might we understand these words as densely affectively and culturally-politically charged: so that what Stephen Greenblatt would call the "social energy" galvanized in Conrad through the dynamo of Mencken could become available as a field of national heterotopic contention?[32] One way to answer these questions lies in the unlikely parallel of Edward Said, who, in the interview at the close of *Conrad in the Twenty-first Century*, especially in his discussions of *Heart of Darkness* and *Nostromo*, speaks in a language of lyric reverence, soaring and unqualified superlatives, musical analogies, simple personal passion, and even comparisons with Nietzsche, Beethoven, and Bach that is surprisingly indistinguishable from the passages presented above.[33] There are of course distinct differences, both of subtlety and of insight, between the first great American Conradian and perhaps the most recent. Yet the striking fact remains that the two fundamental elements that structure Said's attraction to Conrad—(1) the *affect of exile*, and (2) the *commitment to unreconciled and uncompromised counter-hegemonic thinking*, always against the imperial State and especially against Anglo-Saxon structures of imperialist and Statist power—are precisely the elements that structure Mencken's attraction to Conrad, and in elaboration of which, at lesser degrees of abstraction, Mencken inscribes and introduces Conrad as an object of interference, controversy, and dialogue for the U.S. public. The subsequent sections of this chapter detail the multiply mapped particularities of Mencken's use of Conrad to assault "Anglo-Saxon" assertions and consolidations of international and domestic power. Here, however, it is important to attend to the more general structures of feeling and cognition Mencken apprehends in Conrad first, for these constitute, beyond the local particularities and specific political battles Mencken inscribes in Conrad, something of the macro-vocabulary and articulative conditions of possibility, simultaneously affectual-subjective and objectively historical, through which many modern U.S. Americans will discover their own specific relations to Conrad.

We can trace the double nature of Conrad's status as a structure of feeling and thinking for Mencken by exploring two commensurate but nonidentical strands of Mencken's commentary with respect to the two Conrad texts that were central for him: "Youth" and *Heart of Darkness*. Since 1911, "Youth" was a story Mencken had been "yowling over" as "the best short story in English"; it was a text Mencken truly loved and claimed to reread every year—"I shall not miss it, believe me!" he wrote in the *Smart Set* in April 1916—along with *Huckleberry Finn* as an annual rite of spring.[34] Indeed, tellingly as a matter of both interpretation and canon construction, Mencken understood "Youth" and *Huckleberry Finn* as fundamentally the same story: "Has anyone ever noticed that the two stories are as alike as two peas, that the fundamental idea of the one is the fundamental idea of the other, that their very management is identical?"[35] What Mencken means by this becomes clearer in his 1917 review of Conrad's *The Shadow-Line*. There he describes "Youth" as "a study of the reaction of young blood to the terrifying,"[36] a simultaneously narrative and thematic observation that implicitly connects Huck's peculiar youthful resilience as he encounters trauma after trauma, "horror" after "horror," along the Mississippi River, to the redemptive postadolescent romanticism of young Marlow, for whom all is glory and adventure even though (or rather precisely because) his ship is doomed to every imaginable disaster, while the voyage of the *Judea* itself "seem[s] ordered" for a distinctly futilitarian "illustration of life": "You fight, work, sweat, nearly kill yourself, sometimes do kill yourself, trying to accomplish something—and you can't. Not from any fault of yours. You simply can do nothing, neither great nor little—not a thing in the world" (*YOS* 3–4). For young Marlow, the more apocalyptic the disaster, the greater the glamour; yet for Mencken, the precarious balance between a fatalistic and menacing universe and the resilient strength and energizing misrecognitions afforded by the "illusions" of "youth" is not in the end what most appeals about "Youth." Rather, the appeal lies in the pathos of the *older* Marlow who, precisely as he is narrating this tale about his youth, repeatedly and troublingly ("Pass the bottle") finds himself cast irrecoverably beyond the "shadow-line" *of* "youth." "To me," Mencken emphasizes, aptly conjoining two titles and metaphors with the affect of exile and expulsion for which they must ultimately stand, "'Youth''s significance, like that of *The Shadow-Line*, is *all subjective*; it is *an aging man's elegy upon the hope and high resolution that the years have blown away*, a sentimental reminiscence of what the enigmatical gods have had their jest with, leaving only its gallant memory behind."[37]

This point is so fundamental—so universally applicable throughout and archetypally personal to Mencken's sense of the order of things—that he makes it again[38] in the key episode of *Newspaper Days, 1899–1906*, the second of Mencken's autobiographical volumes recounting his earliest days as a reporter. Here Mencken describes the "valiant" efforts of his younger Marlow-aged self and other reporters at the Baltimore *Herald* to cover the great Baltimore fire, which ultimately claimed the *Herald* building itself, of February 1904. As Hobson and Rodgers have noted, Mencken's tale of how the "hot gas of youth kept me going," turning a "brain-fagging" and "back-breaking" experience into an "adventure" "grand beyond compare," is self-consciously scripted through "Youth"; yet once again, apropos of the narrative complexities of Conrad's story and Conrad generally, the defining note that the older narrating Mencken strikes at the outset of his tale, relating how he first discovered "Youth" a few weeks after the fire when he was on a banana boat headed for Jamaica, is not one of returning to but rather everlasting dislocation from youth:

The uproar over, and the *Herald* on an even keel again, I picked up one day a volume of stories by a new writer named Joseph Conrad, and therein found a tale of a young sailor that struck home to me as this history of Judas must strike home to many a bloated bishop, though the sailor naturally made his odyssey in a ship, not on a newspaper and the scene was not a provincial town in America. *Today, so long afterward. I too "remember my youth and the feeling that will never come back any more—that feeling that I could last forever, outlast the sea, the earth, and all men. . . . Youth! All [sic] youth! The silly, charming, beautiful youth!"*[39]

Newspaper Days, 1899–1906 is more than strict autobiography. Like "Youth" and *Huckleberry Finn*, it is a "study of the reaction of young blood to the terrifying" conditions of modernity: specifically, the crowded tenements, grossly unsanitary conditions and food, hazardous roads and buildings, miserable school system, and mismanaged government for which Baltimore was notorious at the time and that the young Marlow-aged Mencken was "discovering" as a reporter. *Newspaper Days*, moreover, may be compared with *Happy Days, 1880–1892*, the first of Mencken's autobiographical volumes devoted to his childhood years, in which the "shadow-line" of modernity itself is precisely in ontological question. That is, the signature ambiguity (and charm) of *Happy Days* lies in the ultimate narrative inability to discern to what degree the text genuinely is claiming 1880s Baltimore as an objective, essentially Edenic, premodern sociohistoric space, and to what degree that space and those "happy days" are the residual product of a child's insulated viewpoint. Certainly many of the major objective fault lines that would come to define U.S. modernity—"new" immigration, urbanization, industrialization, organized struggles between capital and labor, racial segregation and racial-ethnic conflict, rising direct democracy—are unsettlingly, self-consciously, ironically anticipated in *Happy Days*; and as a consequence, the text flickers between objective historical and psychofamilial accounts of the premodern space it relates. What does not flicker, however, is the subjective reality of that space, nor, across Mencken's writings, a profound and irremediable sense of expulsion from any space that could meaningfully be called "home." This is not to make a wistful, melancholy romantic of Mencken but to appreciate the pronounced sense of alienation and existential homelessness that lies at the very core of the jocular but unmistakably bitter blast of all Mencken's writings; it is, indeed, to understand Mencken as presciently, pointedly, expansively in touch with two objective *historical* structures of feeling—the affect of *exile* and the compensatory compulsions of *nostalgia*—that would come to predominate in the modern United States, especially after the conceptual catalyst of the war. Put another way, the Mencken who lived all but five years of his life in his childhood home in never-quite-recoverable Baltimore, and the Mencken whose large orbits of national and international celebrity, activity, and interest never removed his center of gravity from that not-quite-Baltimore, is the same Mencken who understood in tropes of exile and nostalgia the perfect narrative means of expressing the historical experiences of not only the jarring (and disempowering) macrosocial dislocations of U.S. modernity but also his own subject position as a "hyphenated" German-American within it. The "alien," indeed, is an obsessive trope that runs lifelong throughout Mencken's writings; and echoing earlier descriptions of himself as "essentially foreign" and a "homesick foreigner," Mencken makes clear in the later pages of his diary that his immigrant heritage has always been a significant element of his sense of "alienation": "My grandfather, I believe, made a mistake when he came to this country. He was an unhappy man himself and his descendants have had many troubles. . . . I believe my chances in Germany would have been at least as good as they have been in America, and maybe a great deal better. . . . I was born here and so were my father and mother, and I have spent all of my 62 years here, but I find it impossible to fit myself into accepted patterns of American life and thought. *After all these years I remain a foreigner.*"[40]

This is the Mencken—caught in an affectual nexus of exile and nostalgia—who loved "Youth" to the "blue" limits of rhetorical expression, if perhaps also sometimes beyond his patience or gifts for hypernuanced literary-critical elaboration. This Mencken is also a very good reader of "Youth": a tale whose historical underpinnings in the advent of modernity (many Conrad tales, especially those of the sea, turn on the subjective reaction to objective "modern" historical shifts) and whose ethnoexistential underpinnings in emigration (the ship's motto, "*Judea,* London. Do or Die," suggests something of the dualized identity and cultural ambitions inscribed in the "voyage") are central to its meaning. But perhaps most important, Mencken demonstrates himself here to be among the very first to identify in Conrad the complex historical structure of feeling—open to many concrete articulations and specific terms and contexts of elaboration—that would come vitally to define the American appeal of "shadow-line" texts like "Youth," *Lord Jim,* and *The Shadow-Line* after the great psychic fault line of the war. When T. S. Eliot generates "fear in a handful of dust" from "Youth"'s "heat of life in a handful of dust" (*YOS* 37) to express *The Waste Land*'s forlorn sense of spiritual regeneration; when F. Scott Fitzgerald, after describing the closing pages of "Youth" as among "the most remarkable passages in English prose written these thirty years," demonstrates seminal sensitivity to those pages in the wistful conclusion of *The Great Gatsby*;

and when Willa Cather, as we shall see, powerfully evokes and interprets *Lord Jim* to articulate the epic vision of *My Ántonia*, they all are participating in a modern U.S. culture of Conrad that recognizes his engagements with affects of exile and nostalgia in terms of (U.S.) *American* socioeconomic dislocations of modernity and/or (U.S.) *American* immigrant or migrant experience: sometimes, as in the case of Cather and Mencken, in the very question of the relation between the two.[41] This kind of "translation" of Conrad to U.S. terms and historical grounding is fundamental to U.S. cultures of "our Conrad."

Heart of Darkness is the critical obverse of—the analytic antidote to and aggressively externalized redirection of—the exilic/nostalgic structure of feeling we have thus far been tracing. For if part of what it means to be an exile is to have at least the fantasy of a lost home and to be subject to its nostalgic narrative temptations, exile also implies an estrangement of circumstances that works to relativize and deflate such sentimentality—to cross it out precisely as it is being felt and uttered—as well as an estranged sensibility that finds itself at cross-purposes with the naturalizing, harmonizing, exceptionalizing, and sentimentalizing operations of its "new" environment. The exile, this is to say, is well positioned to think critically with respect to the situated character and arbitrary power operations of culture, and for Mencken *Heart of Darkness* is "the archetype of [Conrad's] whole work and the keystone of his metaphysical system" because of the extremity and variety with which it does just that.[42] As a matter of first blush, *Heart of Darkness* is the exemplary Conrad text for Mencken because of the radical unsentimentality, to the point of ruthlessly sardonic laughter, with which it exposes the vast farce and folly of all human affairs: "Here we have all imaginable hopes and aspirations reduced to one common denominator of folly and failure, and here we have a play of humor that is infinitely mordant and searching."[43] We should note that in Mencken's moments of fullest contemplation, it is precisely the *comprehensivity* with which Conrad *both* empathetically captures *and* absolutely preserves critical distance from human experience that marks Conrad's singularity as an author. This is the point of the second and third essays in the original *Prejudices* (1919), in which each half of the dyad of H. G. Wells and Arnold Bennett fails to match the simultaneously empathetic and caustic standard of Conrad; it is also the point of Mencken's remarkable claim: "I have said that [Conrad] does not criticize God. One might even imagine him pitying God."[44] But with respect to *Heart of Darkness*, the terms of Mencken's appreciation are entirely corrosive, negative, critical. For Mencken, *Heart of Darkness* is Mr. Kurtz's story, and "the exact point of the story of Kurtz . . . is that it is pointless, that Kurtz's death is as meaningless as his life, that the moral of such a tragedy is the wholesale negation of all morals."[45]

These words may in part be understood as an expression of the futilitarian spirit described previously, with Kurtz providing yet another example of "the blind groping we call aspiration," the "conviction that human life is a seeking without a finding," the "cosmic implacability" that renders "all sweating and striving thus useless"—a line of analysis whose general politics, at least heading into the war, hover evenhandedly between a general swipe at the Progressive reformist/activist spirit and the more subtle suggestion, not at all incompatible with Walter Lippmann's *A Preface to Politics* (1915) (which Mencken reviewed sympathetically), that Progressives might be more effective if they were better readers of humanity and of more discerning books *about* humanity.[46] (After the war, Mencken's deterministic and Conradian politics seemed to many simply diagnostic, prophetic, correct.) As with "Youth," however, the most crucial conceptual stakes for Mencken lie elsewhere. For Mencken, the point of the pointlessness of Kurtz's story, of Kurtz's death being "as meaningless as his life," of the tale's only moral being "the wholesale negation of all morals," lies in the radical cancellations and collapsing of distinctions effected by Conrad's text: in the radical *openness* with which the text declares and provokes its questions beyond the sealed symmetries of established and authoritative hierarchies, categories, and laws, especially those of a moral nature. "Kurtz," Mencken emphasizes, "is at once the most abominable of all rogues and the most fantastic of all dreamers. It is impossible to differentiate between his visions and his crimes, though all we look upon as order in the universe stands between them." In Kurtz, Mencken extends the argument elsewhere, "one glimpses a depravity so vast it takes on an aspect of the heroic"; he epitomizes the proclivity in Conrad "to show the bare side of every virtue, the hidden heroism of every vice and crime."[47] Geoffrey Harpham, in a phrase Mencken would have enjoyed, observes in Conrad's fiction a "*truly* comprehensive" quality that "confuses the moralizing mind and is, indeed, genuinely confusing"—and for both Harpham and Mencken, this "quality of excess" (or in Mencken's phrase, "capacity" for "the whole point of view") derives from the endless "negations" (Harpham) and "anarchy of valuations" (Mencken) through which Conrad the alien par excellence refuses to be confined within

any moral or ideological point of view. Rather, Mencken puts the point incisively, there is in Conrad "a difference revolutionary and abysmal": a negative
superfecundity borne of an infinitely agnostic "absolute detachment" and a
corrosively hypergenerative "disdainful skepticism" and "universal irony"—
both of which, in addition to replicating the heterotopic model I articulated
through the image of the ship in *The Shadow-Line* in this book's Introduction,[48] presuppose the strong sense of the arbitrariness of human linguistic and
conceptual systems that one associates with Nietzsche, and a nearly anarchic
commitment to *declaring* this premise.[49]

When Mencken claims Conrad as a "great artistic revolutionist" for
predicating his fiction on the insight that "life is meaningless, that it has no
purpose, that its so-called lessons are balderdash"—indeed, when Mencken
claims this insight as "the capital discovery of our day, the one supreme truth
that must revise and condition every other truth"[50]—he does not mean that
life is unimportant or absolutely bootless; he means, apropos of his pioneering book on and "discovery" of the point in Nietzsche, that "meaning" and
"purpose" and "lessons" are *arbitrary* and contingent qualities imposed by
human beings on otherwise inert, unfathomable, resistant, and certainly not
moral primary processes and elements of "life." Moreover, like Nietzsche,
Mencken is principally interested not merely in the contingency of epistemological systems but in how they come to function ("genealogically") as
systems of power/knowledge: in particular, how moral systems—the "revived
and reinforced *Sklavenmoral* that besets all of us of English speech"—generate "taboos" that "penalize courage and curiosity with inescapable dudgeon,"
interpellating and intimidating subjects "so that they become partisans of
the existing order and, per corollary, of the existing ethic." With Conrad,
"his absolute detachment from that heresy that would make [his art] no
more than a servant to some bald and depressing theory of conduct," and
his commitment to understanding life *extramorally* in terms of "inexorable
and uncompassionate struggle" and *dialogically and dialectically* against the
grain of authorized vocabularies, makes for a fiction of radical resistance.[51]
It makes for a fiction, indeed, that incarnates much of Mencken's own fundamental commitment to principles of *counter-hegemonic free expression*. This
happens in part through the emphasis on speaking, many voices, and vitality
of discussion in Conrad, always unsettling and refusing confinement within
any authorized, legalized, moralized, or ideological plane of discourse, and

continually raising questions of context, power, and contingency. This commitment to a multiplicity of voices—Conrad's fiction itself constituting what Justice Oliver Wendell Holmes Jr. would call a "marketplace of ideas"[52]—is complemented by a further emphasis on destabilization and uncertainty of meaning in Conrad, whose fiction "faces squarely the massive and intolerable fact" that there can be no authoritative voice of meaning in an ultimately illegible universe. Premised on this metathematic "confession of unintelligibility," there can be no monopoly of speaking privileges: Conrad's fiction perpetually "pauses to explain, speculate, look about" because it rejects at the very level of *form* the kind of "omniscience" that could articulate itself with hegemonic finality.[53] Finally, Mencken emphasizes a Conradian tactic that brings us back to his fascination with the figure of Kurtz and that may be described, in one of Mencken's own favorite phrases, as a poetics of *reductio ad absurdum*. This is a tactic in which poles of opposition—the two faces of Kurtz or London and Africa in *Heart of Darkness*, Jim and Gentleman Brown in *Lord Jim*, the Professor and Inspector Heat in *The Secret Agent*, Haldin and Razumov in *Under Western Eyes* (etc.)—taken to their logical conclusion find a "secret sharer" in one another; *this is the very self-negating poetic structure, as we have already begun to see, of Mencken's own discourse of provocation and self-contradiction*; and the content of this form in Mencken's eyes—its "one supreme truth that must revise and condition every other truth"—is a commitment to the process, principle, and stimulation of counter-hegemonic free speech itself. For Mencken, Conrad stands not only for the recovery of oppositional voices but also for the assertion and protection of those practices of critical voicing that would turn the various procedures, technologies, and *figures* of monologic hegemony—which is exactly what Kurtz is when he goes to the Congo—into their own opposition. For this reason, Conrad's "doctrine can only fill the Anglo-Saxon mind with wonder and fury"; like James Gibbons Huneker, the critic whom Mencken credited as Conrad's American discoverer, Conrad speaks in a "not only un-national, but anti-national" voice, one that "under cover of charm . . . has diligently poisoned the American mind with heretical ideas."[54] And it is precisely in Mencken's assault on perhaps the most multiply mapped and ideologically cathected narrative seam in the modern U.S. imaginary—the trope of the "Anglo-Saxon"—that this theory of Conrad's counter-hegemonic oppositionality assumes its first concrete heterotopic form.

THE WAR ON ANGLO-SAXONDOM

The Anglo-Saxon of the great herd is, in many important respects, the least civilized of white men and the least capable of true civilization. His political ideas are crude and shallow. He is almost wholly devoid of esthetic feeling. The most elementary facts about the visible universe alarm him, and incite him to put them down. Educate him, make a professor of him, teach him how to express his soul, and he still remains palpably third-rate. He fears ideas almost more cravenly than he fears men. . . . No other known man, indeed, is so violently the blowhard, save it be his English kinsman.

—Mencken, "The Anglo-Saxon" (1923)

A war would do us good.

—Mencken, "Free Lance," *Baltimore Evening Sun*, August 4, 1914

The key text through which to enter Mencken's construction of Conrad as a triply mapped assault on the idea of the "Anglo-Saxon" is *A Book of Prefaces*, and what it is essential to appreciate about the work, written by Mencken at a time of increasingly repressive and punitive political censorship in the United States, is that it is a coded war text. When war was originally declared in Europe in August 1914, Mencken was by no means either a pacifist or neutral. Rather, as he expressed his outspoken opinion repeatedly in his "Free Lance" columns in the *Baltimore Evening Sun*, Mencken believed "a war would do us good"—and that in "the inevitable struggle to the death between the German *Weltanschauung* and the Anglo-Saxon *Weltanschauung*" "the Germans were wholly right": a victory for England "would be a victory for all the ideas and ideals I most ardently detest." "I am for the hellish deutsche until hell freezes over," Mencken advised his German-American friend Dreiser, who felt the same way.[55] Mencken would go on to defend the sinking of the *Lusitania*, to conduct a behind-the-scenes visit to Germany in early 1917 (between drafts of *A Book of Prefaces*), and in his private conscience to support the German cause even after the United States entered the war. Yet from very early on, as the nation's various "preparedness" campaigns and other Anglocentric national realities began to make it clear that the United States was hardly genuinely "neutral," Mencken devoted his principal energies less to championing the kaiser than to challenging "the ignorant and vicious libels of English propagandists and their dupes."[56] Even so, the rising constraints of censorship, first as a matter of *Sun* policy and eventually as a matter of U.S. law, soon squelched even this form of direct political expression; as a consequence, Mencken turned to the *Smart Set* and *A Book of Prefaces*, both of which, with more than a hint of *occupatio,* offer solemn assurances that they "avoid any discussion of war,"[57] as strategic venues to convey the politics that dare not speak its name. Much in *A Book of Prefaces* derives from less-censored wartime essays Mencken wrote for the *Smart Set. A Book of Prefaces* itself—which consists of four long interrelated essays on, respectively, Conrad, the *German*-American Dreiser, the "purely *Irish* in blood"[58] and "not only un-national, but anti-national" Huneker, and "Puritanism as a Literary Force"—combines an explicit and principally literary assault on "Puritanical" Anglo-American culture with an implicit and fiercely political assault on "Anglo-Saxon" hegemony within and upon the United States, as made especially visible by the war.

Mencken's first target is England, specifically its efforts to lure the United States into the war and the more general "colonial" (Mencken's word) and ideological project exemplified by its success. With respect to Conrad, Mencken's first and fundamental move is to emphasize that "Conrad's place" within "the culture of Anglo-Saxondom" is one of distance and irreducible estrangement: "That place is isolated and remote; he is neither of it nor quite in it."[59] In this reading, Conrad occupies an aleatory, liminal, and residually alien space from which to think against Britain's moral, ideological, and macrodiscursive grain, and through which an American, following Conrad's heterotopic lead, might question the ostensibly "natural" or "historic" or "moral" Anglophile and pro-British structurations of her own culture. For not only did Conrad come to England "almost by accident" and essentially as "a chance passerby." Not only was his artistic decision to "write [in] English instead of French" essentially "far afield" and incidental, and a choice that "once made . . . concerned him no further." As well Conrad persists in his "alien" relation "to his place and time," if anything increasing the ways he is "not actually an Englishman," indeed "obviously no Englishman": "In his first book he was plainly a stranger, and all himself; in his last he is a stranger still—strange in his manner of speech, strange in his view of life, strange, above all, in his glowing and gorgeous artistry, . . . his absolute detachment from all infra- and ultra-artistic purpose."[60] Mencken's valorization of "absolute . . . artistic purpose" here should not be mistaken as an anticipation of (U.S.) New Critical ahistoricism. Indeed, few could be more aware, as Mencken's very first *Prejudices* essay, originally published in the *Smart Set* the same month that *A Book of Prefaces* came out, readily demonstrates, that "beauty as we know it in this world" "has its social, its political, even its moral implications"; that "the springs of beauty are not within itself alone, nor even genius alone, but often in things without"; that what is "colossal in beauty" is also "colossal in revolt: it says something against something."[61] Rather, Mencken's point is that Conrad sees more—indeed, "makes you *see*"[62] more of the world and *against* the grain of normative ideological-narrative routings—through his absolute "repudiation of the role of propagandist." In this, Conrad is especially the opposite of his contemporary British literary compatriots: "In the midst of the hysterical splutterings and battle-cries of the Kiplings and Chestertons, the booming pedagogics of the Wellses and Shaws, and the smirking at keyholes of the Bennetts and de Morgans, [Conrad] stands apart and almost alone, observing the sardonic comedy of man with an eye that sees every point and significance of it, but vouchsafing none of that sophomoric indignation, that Hyde Park wisdom, that flabby moralizing which freight and swamp the modern English novel."[63]

The focus on British literary figures and their "moralizing" here—a specific instance of a larger wartime and "Anglo-Saxon" phenomenon—must be understood in the context of the secret literary department (secret as a matter of organization, not output) of the British War Propaganda Bureau organized by C. F. G. Masterman at Wellington House beginning in September 1914. At that time, Masterman invited to his office twenty-five of England's most influential men of letters to coordinate what would become a powerful British literary propaganda effort, in no small part intended to complement the "most important special branch"[64] of the Bureau that Masterman also created (soon to be headed by Sir Gilbert Parker) to coordinate British propaganda in the United States. (Getting the United States into the war, or at least preventing the U.S. from allying with the Central Powers, was one of the primary goals of British propaganda throughout the war.) All of the names Mencken mentions above except Shaw were on the list and played significant roles in the Masterman project. Bennett, whose "book on the war" (*Over There: War Scenes of the Western Front* [1915]) and "book on the United States" (*Your United States: Impressions of a First Visit* [1912]) Mencken criticized as Bennett at his "worst," briefly became head of the British Ministry of Information in March 1918.[65] Wells wrote five books concerning the war. One, *The War That Will End War* (1914), ends with "An Appeal to the American People" in which Wells emphasizes that by joining England, "you may play a part such as no nation has ever played since the world began. . . . It is not for ourselves we make this appeal to you; it is for the whole future of mankind." Another, Wells's best-selling novel *Mr. Britling*

Sees It Through (1916), Mencken shrewdly and by no means dismissively attacks for "present[ing] a fifth-rate Englishman in a heroic aspect. Because it sentimentalized the whole reaction of the English proletariat to the War, it offered a subtle sort of flattery to other fifth-rate Englishmen, and per corollary, to Americans of corresponding degree, to wit, the second."[66] Rudyard Kipling, whose "whooping a pothouse patriotism" and "hurling hysterical objurgations at the foe" make for a constant refrain throughout the Conrad essay in *A Book of Prefaces*, to the point that Kipling becomes the arch-counterpoint of that essay, was simply the most powerful prowar British literary voice in the United States: his poems regularly appearing in the *New York Times* and himself a childhood hero of Mencken.[67] It should be emphasized that Bennett, Wells, and Kipling are British writers that Mencken attacks precisely because, in various respects, he sees great value and power in them, power that has become compromised by the hysteria of the war. This is not always the case with other British writers like Arthur Conan Doyle, J. M. Barrie, Arthur Quiller-Couch, and Anthony Hope Hawkins, all of whom Mencken also attacks in the Conrad essay, and all of whom were also involved, Conan Doyle ferociously, in the Masterman project.

Though Mencken could not know about the Masterman project itself, he did not need to know to be perfectly aware of its output, outlook, and flush, even exemplary, relation to the more general and massive British war propaganda campaign in the United States, as well as the cultural, institutional, financial, and political forces within the United States that were also increasingly pressing for war, invariably disguising much of their true animations, in pro-British terms. Similarly, though *A Book of Prefaces*, published after American entry into the war, never explicitly mentions the Great War or insists that pro-British and Allied war propaganda is the kind of "Anglo-Saxon" moralizing it is assaulting, it consistently and strategically invites this reading—indeed, as we shall see in a moment, it cannot truly be "read" without it—precisely as it also consistently invites the (American) reader to consider Conrad as an antithesis and antidote. Indeed, Mencken makes this point expressly—explicitly positioning Conrad as the opposite and undoing of the ideological corruption of wartime British literature, directly positing Conrad as a hostile and almost "German" figure of resistance to pro-British wartime propaganda—in an earlier and fuller version of lines quoted previously that was printed in the *Smart Set* in January 1916, a moment less constrained by anti-German war hysteria, the Espionage and Sedition Acts of 1917–1918, and the Supreme Court jurisprudence that dependably facilitated and licensed them all. The passage is sufficiently important to be quoted in full:

More than any other allied country [since the war began], England shows signs of surgical shock, of concussion of the heart and brain, of a spiritual collapse, and more than any other class of Englishmen, not even accepting bishops and the politicians, the authors of the tight little isle are its victims. H. G. Wells, for example, has frankly gone to pot; the stuff he has done during the past year calls for charity rather than criticism. And such fellows as Arnold Bennett, G. K. Chesterton and Rudyard Kipling have suffered even worse. Kipling, indeed, has apparently passed into a state of mind which can only be described as pathological. The literary artist of yesteryear has departed, one fears, forever; what remains is only a frightened householder in a flapping nightshirt, bawling for the police down an alley. . . . And what of Conrad? Has he been damaged as badly as the others? Despite the curious banality of his account of his Polish experiences [i.e., *A Personal Record*], I presume to doubt it. *While others rant and blubber, he has next to nothing to say. . . . One detects in that silence something characteristically and magnificently ironical: the immigrant's but half-concealed sneer at the native. For Conrad, after all is not an Englishman but a Pole.* He comes from a race that is proud and *undemocratic*, a race that *Nietzsche*, with his fine sense of the heroic, regarded with almost superstitious veneration, a race that knows how to endure without complaint. One wonders just what, in his inmost heart, he thinks of the bellowing of Kipling, the feeble paralogy of Chesterton, the middle-class fustian of Wells and Bennett. What, indeed, must he think of (in [John] Palmer's phrase) "insolence as fine art"? Of the cad as artist?[68]

The connection with Nietzsche is revealing. In the important essay "The Mailed Fist and Its Prophet," which appeared in the *Atlantic Monthly* in November 1914, Mencken goes out of his way to gloss Nietzsche in "Polish" and "Slavic" terms that make for a crossing between Nietzsche—considered by many the intellectual author of the war from the German side—and Conrad;[69] and indeed, once we understand Mencken's Conrad as a Nietzschean figure "sneering at the [Anglo-Saxon] native," offering a "half-concealed" and "magnificently ironical" challenge to both pious British wartime propaganda and its "colonial" American echoes and elaborations, Mencken's essay in *A Book of Prefaces* begins to crackle with energy and subtlety that otherwise remain invisible. Mencken concludes his discussion of *Heart of Darkness*, for instance, with a prescient but nevertheless seemingly straightforward appreciation of the irony of the closing scene between Marlow and Kurtz's "Intended" fiancée: "In *Heart of Darkness* we get [Conrad's] typical view of it. Over all the frenzy and horror of the tale itself floats the irony of a trusting heart back in Brussels. Here we have his measure of the master sentimentality of them all."[70] The edge on this remark, however, which everyone in 1917 would have understood, lies in its implicit equation between "Belgian" sentimentality in Conrad's novella—radically, criminally detached from the actualities of the colonial Belgian Congo—and the greatest and "master sentimentality" of British propaganda in America during the Great War: the "barbarous" German invasion of and "atrocities" committed against "innocent" Belgium. An apex of British misinformation and sensationalist manipulation (most notoriously, in the report of Viscount Bryce's Committee on Alleged German atrocities in May 1915) and the demonizing moral template through which the idea of the "savage Hun" entered the U.S. imagination, "the case of Belgium," as the *New York Times* was able to recognize as early as November 1914, "seems in many instances to have been the chief factor in determining the American viewpoint"; "the violation of Belgian neutrality by the Germans," George Bernard Shaw would put it later, "was the mainstay of [British] righteousness, and we played it off in America for much more than it was worth. I guessed that when the German account of our dealings with Belgium reached the United States, backed with an array of facsimiles of secret diplomatic documents discovered by them in Brussels, it would be found that our own treatment of Belgium was as little compatible with neutrality as the German invasion."[71] Simple and obvious misrepresentation aside, moreover, sentimentalized Belgium epitomized for Mencken precisely the kind of "moralistic" hermeneutic—the misreading of human affairs in terms of first principles of "good" and "evil," of British "liberty" and "democracy" and "freedom" as opposed to German "militarism" and "autocracy" and "tyranny"—that Mencken rails against throughout *A Book of Prefaces*, and whose application to the war makes Mencken so often turn to the figure of Kurtz. To understand of Kurtz, as the Belgian Intended does not, and as Conrad, who situates the telling of Marlow's tale of absolute "darkness" in a boat *in England*, clearly does, that "*it is impossible to differentiate between his visions and his crimes, though all we look upon as order in the world stands between them,*" is to be able to understand that the same England that fights the war genuinely championing ideals of liberty and democracy is also an England that certainly did *not* enter the War to "save" Belgium, that imposed a naval blockade one of whose express purposes was the arguable "atrocity" (as many did argue) of starving the German civilian population, that had warily eyed rising industrial Germany for decades and relished the opportunity to defeat its naval ambitions, that never had any intentions of summarily relinquishing its own empire and indeed saw the war as a means of extending it, that unsparingly suppressed the Irish Rising of Easter 1916 and executed Roger Casement (whom at least one American at the time understood as a figure of Kurtz)[72] after viciously smearing him as a homosexual and pedophile in, among other places, the U.S. press—etc. To understand Kurtz, this is to say, is to be able to perform the heterotopic operation of holding a distant and destabilizing mirror up to British moralizing rhetoric, annihilating its boundaries by conflating it with its self-declared opposites (material self-interest, the "savage" German "other")—and consequently exposing its situatedness within a fuller set of world relations. Or, to express the matter in a manner that picks up further on Mencken's fascination with Kurtz's Germanic naming and Nietzschean affinities, to appreciate Kurtz is to seek out the wills-to-power that lurk behind and beyond perversely idealized events like the Great War; it is to suspect the *Lusitania*, as the commander in Conrad's "The Tale" certainly would have, of carrying the enemy arms it very plausibly was; and it is indeed, to switch the focus from the British and Germans to Americans, to see the absurdity of American fulminations like those of Theodore Roosevelt who would seize the occasion of Belgium to *moralize* U.S. entry into the war: "What this doctrine demands that one believe is this: that the man [Roosevelt] who, for mere commercial advantage and (in Frederick the Great's phrase) 'to make himself talked of in the world' tore up the treaty of 1846 between the United States and New Granada, whereby the U.S. forever granted the 'sovereignty of ownership' of the Colombians in the isthmus of Panama—that this same man, thirteen years afterward, was shocked and horrified beyond expression when Germany, facing powerful foes on two fronts, tore up the treaty of 1832, guaranteeing not sovereignty but the mere neutrality of Belgium."[73]

"Conrad," Mencken emphasizes in *A Book of Prefaces* with great literal force, "makes war on nothing"—and this precisely because "he is pre-eminently *not* a moralist," "he swings, indeed, as far from revolt and moralizing as possible," instead effecting in tales like *Heart of Darkness* a kind of antiwar on the ethical, ideological, and patriotic modes of narrativity that war in a modern democratic age, one of mass media and "public opinion," presumes.[74] The discrepancy between war and idealized accounts of its animation and resolution deeply informs Mencken's appreciation of "The Duel." Originally published in 1908 and first and fittingly republished in the United States in 1915, Conrad's tale concerns two officers in Napoleon's army whose endless and irreconcilable antagonism, whose personal war that has no end but further war, defies any narrative of rational foundation or ultimate purposiveness. For Mencken, "The Duel" serves as an acid rejoinder to President Wilson's idea of a war that would end all wars, and also a prescient anatomy of the forgettable foundations of the war and the stylized conventions that sustain it: "The original cause of their quarrel soon fades into the background; in the course of time, indeed, they actually forget it. But with sword, cutlass, pistol, on horseback and afoot, they pursue their incomprehensible feud with grim and laborious ferocity, until, in the end, they are so old they can scarcely lift their arms. No more penetrating *reductio ad absurdum* of the punctilio could be imagined."[75] With respect to *The Secret Agent*, Mencken connects "all the classical doings of anarchists" presented in it to the political manipulation of images "copiously credited of late to German spies" to make a point about not simply the aims but the tactics and topography of pro-British war propaganda in the United States.[76] I have written elsewhere at length of *The Secret Agent*'s perceptive attention to the power of mass media in organizing and policing public opinion,[77] a point whose application to the wartime British and American press Mencken (the newspaperman) understands perfectly. But *The Secret Agent* also places much emphasis on *propaganda par fait*, the need for propaganda in the form of "facts" (*SA* 31)—"a distinct, significant fact," "an alarming fact" (18)—as opposed to polemical rhetoric, "cock-and-bull stories" (31); and as several commentators have observed, this emphasis on persuasion through "bare fact," calculated to convince and alarm through the very appearance of objectivity, was a mainstay of British propaganda efforts both in the press and among person-to-person networks, and nowhere more effective than in the British counterespionage efforts that disclosed a number of high-ranking German and Austrian officials in the United States as linked to anti-American sabotage rings in 1915 and 1916.[78]

Perhaps most devastating of all, however, is the attack Mencken launches through Conrad's wildly popular *Victory* (1915), Mencken's "American" answer to *Mr. Britling Sees It Through*. Here Mencken, emphasizing Conrad's title and reading the essential spirit of the novel quite correctly, converts the very Master Sign of Allied success, righteous vindication, and patriotic blackmail—ubiquitous in newspapers, speeches, slogans, as the title of various war bonds—into a deadly ironic corrosive: "*The whole Conradean system sums itself up in the title of 'Victory,'* an incomparable piece of irony. Imagine a better label for that tragic record of heroic and yet bootless effort, that matchless picture, in microcosm, of the relentlessly cruel revolutions in the macrocosm! . . . *Victory* ends with a massacre of all the chief personages, a veritable catastrophe of blood."[79] Hence Mencken's assessment of the general efficacy, outcome, and moral value of U.S. participation in the Great War; and hence also Mencken's critique of the tenets of Wilsonian idealism (self-determination, League of Nations, etc.), significantly enabled by an ignorance of European geopolitical history and an arrogance of American moral exceptionalism, that narrativized the greater American "purpose" in the war. For Mencken, there could be no more Conradian character than the "Archangel Woodrow"; the vainly "romantic" Lord Jim, Nostromo, the would-be isolationist (as Wilson was well into 1917) Heyst, and Woodrow Wilson "one and all . . . destroyed and made a mockery of by the blind and incomprehensible forces that beset them." This, too, was Conrad's assessment of Wilson, as he expressed the matter to Hugh Walpole on, of all days, Armistice Day:

I cannot confess to an easy mind. *Great and very blind forces are set free catastrophically all over the world.* This only I know that if we are called upon to restore order in Europe (as it may well be) then we shall be safe at home too. To me the call is already manifest— *but it may be declined on idealistic or political grounds.* It is a question of courage in the leaders who are never as good as the people. (*CL* 6.302, emphasis added)[80]

. . .

British war propaganda and U.S. political rhetoric commensurate with it, hence, immediately occasion and offer the most urgent political subtext of Mencken's initial thunderings on behalf of Conrad. As Mencken knew perfectly well, the Anglophilic bias of U.S. policy from the beginning, actually quite resisted by Woodrow Wilson, was driven much less by moral than pragmatic factors: advantages of common language and culture; a virtual British news monopoly with respect to Europe once communication cables between the United States and Germany had been cut; an Atlantic blockade that first favored British-American trade and eventually generated an unprecedented American financial investment in British victory; and Anglophiles across key U.S. institutions of political, economic, journalistic, religious, and academic power. And in Conrad, Mencken inscribed and offered the American public an anti-Kipling through which to question, in Christopher Hitchens's phrase, "that an Anglo-American partnership [was] in the natural order of things."[81] But the war was also symptomatic for Mencken of a much larger Anglo-American "colonial" deference syndrome, and one that frames Conrad's construction across the more general course of Mencken's writings. As Mencken himself makes the "colonial" point in "On Being an American" (1922), an important essay first published two months before "Conrad Revisited": "When [one] recalls the amazing feats of the English war propagandists between 1914 and 1917 . . . [one] is apt to ask himself quite gravely if he belongs to a free nation *or to a crown colony*."[82] If during the war "the office of the American Secretary of State [Lansing] was little more than an antechamber of the British Foreign Office"; if "Dr. Wilson himself, in the conduct of his policy, differed only legally from such colonial premiers as Hughes and Smuts"; if "such anatomists as Bryce" and such statesman as "the Balfours and Lloyd Georges" were able to manipulate the United States as yet another of Britain's "far flung and exhausting colonial enterprises"; and if "even after the United States got into the war it was more swagger for a Young American to wear a British uniform than an American uniform," then these were hardly wartime anomalies.[83] Such a relationship of Anglo-American political coloniality—what Carroll Quigley, with conspiratorial undertones, would come to call the "Anglo-American establishment"—was far older than the Kipling poem ("The White Man's Burden") written expressly to prod Theodore Roosevelt on in the Spanish-American War; as current as the yielding of "everything to English interests" at Paris and Versailles in 1919, the "obvious surrender to English hegemony" in the Disarmament Treaty of 1921–22, or American susceptibility to the British proposal for a U.S. mandate in Armenia; and as prospectively ominous as the "special relationship" by which Britain, increasingly confronted with the fragility of its own empire, would surely continue to attempt compensation through various schemes of collusion and coordination involving and often steering the colonially complicit United States.[84]

The same is true, moreover, *culturally* of "the American colonist."[85] The wartime contingencies that resulted in British control of international news, and the larger British guidance of American policy and viewpoint throughout the war, were only emblematic of a larger process by which "the gaping colonists of Yankeedom" broadly rendered themselves systematically and "spontaneously servile" to every form of British dependency: through general infrastructural reliance on British journalistic resources and foreign expertise; through "wholesale borrowing" of every scholarly, aesthetic, and social standard or taste; through "intellectual servitude" to such obvious colonial apparatuses as "a cargo of national prejudices" like the *Encyclopaedia Britannica*, as explicitly opposed to Mencken's aggressively entitled and anticolonial study *The American Language* (1919); and perhaps most important, through abdication of all contact with "the aims and interests of all other nations" except insofar as they arrive through "the clearing house and transformer station" of imperial Britain.[86] All in all, Mencken argues in "The National Letters," against the grain of both U.S. isolationist and exceptionalist fantasy, despite "the current highfalutin about melting pots and national destinies the United States remains almost as much an English colonial possession, intellectually and spiritually, as it was on July 3, 1776"; the relationship is fundamentally "a business of subalterns."[87]

The stakes here, as we shall see in a moment, are as domestic as they are international, although to ascribe the previously stated views, even in all their historical exaggeration, simply to a resurgent American "nationalism" is to miss the point of both the extreme cultural internationalism Mencken genuinely champions and the irreducibly negative and counter-hegemonic attitude Mencken brings to bear on any articulation of the "boobus Americanus" or the naïve fantasy that one can simply "declare" independence from Britain. Rather, one needs continually to redeclare and be aware of the terms of one's embattled imbrication within structures of coloniality;[88] and in this, Mencken argues in the *Smart Set* in March 1917, the month before the United States formally entered the war, there can be few better models than the new school of *Irish* writing that includes Joyce, Yeats, George William Russell, Lady Gregory, Dunsay, McDonough, and Synge, building generally on the precedent of Wilde, Symons, and Moore. These anticolonial writers declare war on the very language of the English colonizer they ultimately inhabit, and through the experience of oppositionality itself develop, not simply an "original" relation to the universe but also an intelligent, fiercely dynamic and dialectical, simultaneously aesthetic and political one:

They tell us that no great literature is ever written in a tongue foreign to its makers; [yet] the Irish invade the language of the conqueror with Gaelic idioms and Gaelic modes of thought, and make a new English that is as sonorous and savory as Marlowe's. They tell us that letters cannot prosper in the turmoil of politics; the Irish turn from the land laws to rhapsody without batting an eye, and stop a peasant comedy to shoot a red-coat, and face a firing squad with sheaves under their arms. . . . In Ireland there has been no forgetting. The fathers of the new literature, indeed, were political agitators almost more than they were literary pioneers. They essay to dethrone England, English, the English, and all Englishdom. They turned to ancient demi-gods as to inspiring heroes of nationality; they called upon the Gael to be a Gael once more. One and all, they learned Gaelic, thought in Gaelic, made Gaelic their weapon. But the forces they faced were too sturdy for them. The English language engulfed them in its gigantic and irresistible tide; they were forced willy-nilly to yield to it; they ended by making it their own. No stranger surrender has ever been seen, and no stranger conquest by the conquered. The neo-Celts, pumping not only their materials, but even their forms out of Gaelic, have emptied into English the most lavish stream of new idioms and rhythms it has received since the days of Elizabeth.[89]

Substitute "Polish" or "Slav" for "Gaelic" here—as much a "weapon" of difference used *against* "English" as a new mother lode "pumped" into it—and one arrives at Mencken's anti-British, anticolonial construction of Conrad: a "long hymn" to whom, retracing Mencken's fascination with Conrad from its "opening anthem" in 1908 to its status as "a cantata still going," immediately follows and manifestly, homologously grids Mencken's discussion of the new Irish writers.[90] Mencken, in fact, makes this substitution himself in "Conrad Revisited," contextualizing and grounding the over-the-top rhetorical effusiveness of that essay, and explaining why that frequently reprinted text could be originally written in the same anticolonial, anti-British rhetorical breath as "On Being an American." You have just heard these words—twice—in another transcultural key:

I observe of late a tendency to examine the English of Conrad rather biliously. This folly is cultivated chiefly in England, where, I suppose, chauvinistic motives enter into the matter. It is just the boast of great empires that they draw in talents from near and far, exhausting the little nations to augment their own puissance; it is their misfortune that these talents often remain defectively assimilated. Conrad remained the Slav to the end. The people of his tales, whatever he calls them, are always as much Slavs as he is, the language in which he describes them retains a sharp, exotic flavor. But to say that this flavor constitutes a blemish is to say something so preposterous that only schoolmasters and their dupes may be thought of as giving it credit. The truly first-rate writer is not one who uses language as such dolts demand that it be used; he is one who re-works it in spite of their prohibitions. It is his distinction that he thinks in a manner different from the thinking of ordinary men; that he is free from that slavery to embalmed ideas which makes them so respectable and so dull. . . . What Conrad brought into English literature was a new concept of the relations between fact and fact, idea and idea, and what he contributed to the complex and difficult art of writing in English was a new way of putting words together. His style now amazes and irritates pedants because it does not roll along in the old ruts. . . . It was precisely that avoidance that made him what he is. No Oxford mincing is in him. . . . If he cannot find a phrase above the salt, he seeks it below. His English, in a word, is innocent. And if, at times, there gets into it a color that is strange and even bizarre, then the fact is something to rejoice over, for a living language is like a man suffering incessantly from small internal hemorrhages, and what it needs above all else is constant transfusions of new blood from other tongues. The day the gates go up, that day it begins to die.[91]

Conrad, hence, is not a "gaping colonial." Like the new Irish writers, Conrad refuses to the play the part of the colonial raw materials that "great empires" extract and exhaust from "the little nations" they dominate so as "to augment their puissance" and finish and process those materials in their own image. Just like the Irish who "call upon the Gael to be a Gael once more," Conrad remains in every fundamental aspect "the Slav to the end"; he retains the "sharp exotic flavor" that is the mark not of the colonial subject matter of or phantasmatic colonial annexations performed by his novels,[92] but rather his own personal anticolonial resistance within them. His relationship to England and the English culture and language is anything but one of "slavery" and subservience to British imperial authority, anything but a ratification of the colonizing techniques of the schoolmaster or Oxford manner. Indeed, the "small internal hemorrhages" that fiction like Conrad's causes in the English-speaking imagination are the insurgent kin of the "lavish stream of new idioms and rhythms" that the Irish "pump" and "empty"—like the newly invented machine gun—into the English language. And all in all, of course, the ultimate referent of Mencken's construction of both Conrad and the new Irish writers is "the business of the subaltern" *in the United States.* In an exceptional passage in "The National Letters," Mencken describes how the "extraordinary [American] colonist, moved to give utterance to the ideas bubbling within him," finds himself "vastly handicapped, for he must submit them to the test of a culture that, in the last analysis, is never quite his own culture, despite its dominance."[93] Neither of it nor quite in it, as Mencken's earlier phrase ran of Conrad, the American "looking within himself . . . finds that he is different, that he diverges from the English standard, that he is authentically American—and to be authentically American is to be officially inferior. He thus faces dismay at the very start: support is lacking when he needs it most."[94] Mencken points to Poe and Whitman as rare anticolonial examples of Americans who through their "obscure, inner necessity" refuse to make "the slightest concession to what was predominant in English tastes, the prevailing English authority." The phrase "obscure, inner necessity"—which Mencken uses more than once in this essay, which often refers to Conrad—is a slight misquotation of Conrad's *A Personal Record*; hence, through Conrad Mencken is attempting to imagine and fashion a new past and present U.S. literary culture, one simultaneously opened to the vast field of world colonial analogies at issue in Conrad's writings and also defiant of, resistant to, the British coloniality that Mencken understands as a national (yet transnational) syndrome.[95] For all those young U.S. writers and cultural observers who read "The National Letters" with keen interest, Conrad becomes mobilized as an external space through which, from an internationalized perspective, the United States becomes both opened to colonial vocabularies and authorized in its disruptions—and further self-interrogations, and self-evasions—of colonial paradigms.

. . .

But for Mencken to end the "Conrad Revisited" passage on the note of "the gates going up"—indeed, for Mencken to organize the entire analysis between extremes of "defective assimilation" (by which Mencken means *too* assimilated) and the joy of "constant transfusions of new blood from other tongues"—is to introduce the domestic element of *immigration* into a "colonial" equation that to this point we have been discussing principally in international "Anglo-Saxon" terms. Taking advantage of Conrad's status as *both* an anticolonial writer and an immigrant writer, Mencken effects through Conrad a double mapping of two different spheres of Anglo-Saxon sociocultural and political relations. Mencken connects and doubly maps through Conrad the resistance to two kinds of Anglo-Saxon *international* imperialist assertion—the kind by which Britain dominates "colonies" like the United States, and the kind by which the United States attempts to assert itself (on both the non-Western world and Europe) on Britain's self-righteous, moralizing model—onto the resistance to *domestic* Anglo-Saxon discourses of race and "Americanization" that do their work, among other targets and means, to the imperialized and exclusionary disadvantage of (recent) immigrants. The bankrupt imperialism of the international sphere is rendered akin to domestic practices and discourses of domination in the United States that systematically disavow the label "imperialism"; those very domestic discourses, in turn, find their naturalizing appeals to biology and nation upset by the transparent power-based facticity of such appeals to Anglo-Saxon genealogy, loyalty, and morality in the international sphere; the absurd idea of America saving Europe from barbarism is shown to complement the absurd illusion that the United States is not an agent of barbarism toward those Europeans who would become U.S. citizens; and all of this—a *speaking through* the discursive blockades of U.S. isolationism and exceptionalism—becomes possible through Conrad ultimately because of the heterotopic distance that makes him both like and unlike, categorically outside of yet intimately connected to, the inverse of and a comprehensive interference with, the American scene.

On the domestic side, the crucible of war is once again crucial. As we have been noticing all along, Mencken's essays in and around the war period figure Conrad obsessively, even talismanically, as, if not always a "sneering immigrant," then certainly an intransigent and indelibly alien one. For Mencken, Conrad remains at core an "enigmatical Pole" or "Slav" and "obviously no Englishman" despite his "place" within a "culture"—like that of the United States, of course—of hegemonic "Anglo-Saxondom." So often, indeed, did Mencken emphasize Conrad's "Slavic" difference and distance that Conrad himself protests this construction in his 1919 Author's Note to his autobiographical *A Personal Record*—as he does again in a December 1922 letter to (American) George T. Keating, in which, although generally expressing sincere appreciation and respect for the author of "Conrad Revisited," Conrad nevertheless wonders why "a personality so genuine in its sensations, so independent in judgment, should now and then condescend to mere parrot talk; for his *harping on my Slavonism* is only that. I wonder what meaning he attaches to the word?"[96] The answer to Conrad's question—much closer to Conrad's soul than the self-declared "*homo duplex* in more ways than one," especially eager here not to be associated with Bolshevik Russia, is giving Mencken credit for—lies in *A Book of Prefaces*. There "Slav" is explicitly defined not "in the direction . . . of nationality" but in terms of a contextually oppositional temperament that "carries the study of man and fate to a point that seems morbid to westerners."[97] There also Conrad "the extraordinary Pole" is repeatedly championed for preserving his "marks of origin" and the "foreign smack" in his "multi-lingual thinking" and "mongrel" style.[98] He is likened in "a hundred ways" to the German-American Dreiser, the subject of the second essay in *A Book of Prefaces* and another "alien to his place and time" whom, if he is increasingly cast by "bawling" "patrioteer[s]" "into a German frame" and "as an agent of Prussian frightfulness in letters," is actually "obviously Germanic [in] name and ancestry," thoroughly "the Teuton" in "racial patience and pertinacity and all the racial lack of humor," and generally "of mongrel blood, with the German . . . predominating."[99] Finally, Conrad is the template for the "un-national," "anti-national," and "true cosmopolitan" Huneker, the focus of the third essay in *A Book of Prefaces.* In a truly remarkable portrait and flight of fancy that frequently mentions and never strays far from Conrad, Mencken introduces Huneker as the "purely Irish"-American grandson of a distinguished Fenian poet and then proceeds to contemplate Huneker as a temperamentally German-American, self-declaredly "Celto-Magyar," culturally "Celto-Czech," occasionally gastronomically Celto-Viennese, and ultimately spiritually "Czech-Irish" ("or is it Magyar-Irish [or] Czech-Irish?") "marriage of unearthly elements."[100]

Among the many agendas embedded in this sea of hyphens and the palimpsest of portraits that string them together, the most immediately subversive agenda is also the one most easily missed. In a general historical moment in which the number of U.S. immigrants was reaching a peak of roughly 15 million (about 15 percent of the population), and in a specific moment (November 1917) when, as John Higham observes, "about one third of America's foreign-born derived from enemy territory," the overwhelming majority of these immigrants from German-allied territories having not yet acquired U.S. citizenship,[101] Mencken goes out of his way in *A Book of Prefaces* to stitch together through and under the cover of the "Polish" Conrad a veritable cosmos of anti-Allied allegiance: German, Irish, Austrian, various Slovak, Magyar, and Bohemian nationalities within the Austro-Hungarian empire, and even the ultimate "Slavic" wild card of revolutionary Russia. Effected through hyphens, this cultural celebration and integration of the enemy is an intensely domestic as well as international gesture, defining what it means to be Mencken's *anti-Statist* kind of (counter-) American, and also drawing attention to the very sources of domestic opposition and instability—concentrated German and Irish populations in the Midwest and Northeast (respectively), predominant Magyar and Slavic labor in the eastern coal fields and in the iron and steel industries, the more general threat of labor revolt epitomized by radical Russia—that contemporary discourses and programs of "Americanism" (Wilson's 1916 campaign theme), "Americanization" (at least in the more virulent varieties of this assimilationist program), and "100% Americanism" (the toxic wartime apotheosis of coercive immigrant loyalty and assimilationist regimes) were designed to neutralize.[102] Put another way, at the very (wartime) moment when domestic ideologies of "Americanism" and "Americanization" are being most aggressively deployed to coerce complete loyalty to the State and (as a function thereof) an Anglo-Saxon political alliance with the British, Mencken demands attention to and alliance with everything that is the enemy of the Anglo-Saxon aligned State— including a hyphenated relation to it.

The hyphens in *A Book of Prefaces*, hence, significantly denote *political* opposition to the American State. The hyphenated categories clearly derive from peoples with which the State is at war; the relationship of hyphenation signifies the kind of estrangement and divided allegiance that makes Conrad a "public enemy" and "rebel against current assurances" in England;[103] the significance of Conrad as hyphenated immigrant in *A Book of Prefaces* lies less in how he *is* (ethnoracially) "Polish" or "Slavic" than in how in being those things he is *not* and a negation of Anglo-Saxon Statist authority; and all in all, "hyphenation" is a term—like *A Book of Prefaces* itself—that has its principal meaning in and is expressly meant to target and bring these matters home to the United States. This political assault on the American State is extended through Conrad in two important "cultural" ways. First, in using Conrad as a template and trigger to celebrate the "high civilization" of the enemy over the "tragic aesthetic wilderness" of the Anglo-Saxon-allied nations,[104] Mencken reverses the rampant U.S. war propaganda championing high Anglo-Saxon achievement to the absolute exclusion of the "savage Hun": for example, the widespread assertions that no significant intellectual or cultural achievements had ever come from Germany, or the ubiquitous State-engineered War Issues Courses whose notorious purpose was to deduce Germany's guilt for the war from its "barbaric" history and to cast Britain and its colonies as transhistorical agencies of sweetness and light.[105] Though there are manifestly high ideological stakes here, the even more devastating attack lies in Mencken's turning the charges of "barbarism" against the Anglo-Saxons. Beginning in the essay on Conrad and drawing on strategies of cancellation and civilization/savagery reversal derived from *Heart of Darkness*, Mencken casts the *German*-identified powers as truly "civilized" and the Anglo-Saxon *Americans* in particular in terms of an "alert and bellicose Puritanism," an "unmatchable intolerance of opposition," "savage cruelty of attack," and a "lust for relentless and barbarous persecution."[106] The unmistakable target—this being a moment before most of the American troops had even landed in Europe—is the repressive American war State itself at home, most especially in the context of the savage barbarity and hypocrisy of the wartime persecution of German-Americans. For to obsessively emphasize the "high civilization" of German-Americans (Mencken, Dreiser, temperamentally Huneker) and their suspicious like is to implicitly draw attention to the barbarism of the American State and its infinite apparatuses that persecute them: e.g., the mob that lynched Robert Prager, and the jury that acquitted that mob; the endless state and local boards of education that banned the teaching of German in public schools as "a language that disseminates the ideas of autocracy, brutality, and hatred"; the institutional persecution at all educational levels of individuals associated with German; the myriad spy networks, loyalty leagues, and bilingual watchdog groups whose purpose was the surveillance, protection, and punishment of anything less than "100% American" behavior among German-Americans; the various measures resulting in the disappearance of German clubs and the punishment of German cultural habits; the federal demonization of all German history through George Creel's Committee on Public Information; the instrumentalization and abetting of all this by a president who long had urged that the "poison of disloyalty" "must be crushed out"; and even the Congress that officially renamed the hamburger and sauerkraut as the "liberty sandwich" and "liberty cabbage."[107] These attempts to exterminate the German brute within constitute the silenced context and true "horrors" of *A Book of Prefaces*. They lie at the heart precisely and politically of not only what Mencken cannot say in 1917 but why and how he cannot say them. And when Mencken turns to Conrad as an exemplar of the "implacable comprehension" of how "right and wrong, savagery and civilization, are equal and indifferent,"[108] he articulates through Conrad a critique of the American State that, for the first but not the last time in Mencken's career, effectively turns the United States into Conrad's Congo.

But there is another layer to the "hyphenate" in Conrad that lies beyond the strictly political. In an unusually balanced and measured essay Mencken wrote on the occasion of Theodore Roosevelt's death in March 1920, Mencken returns to the issue of hyphenates. Conceding the legitimacy of the ex-president's wartime concerns with national unity, Mencken nevertheless deplores the extremity of Roosevelt's "furious denunciations of Americans of divided allegiance":

The hyphenate of 1915 is still a hyphenate in his heart—with genuine and unforgettable grievances to justify him. Roosevelt, very characteristically, went too far. In opposing German hyphenism he contrived to give impetus to English hyphenism—and this new banshee will be even harder to lay than the old one. Instead of a national solidarity following the war, we have only a revival of Know Nothingism, which failed colossally a century ago. One party of hyphenates tries to exterminate the other party.[109]

The hyphenate here, however, is actually quite different from what it was for Mencken in 1915. Whereas for Mencken being a German-American hyphenate in 1915 meant being affiliated with one of the oldest, most established, most assimilable and reputable of U.S. immigrant groups, but one that had come recently into a sense of *political* division with respect to the internationally Anglo-Saxon-aligned State, by March 1920 "German hyphenism" for Mencken is clearly not only a political but also an ethnic term. The opposite of "German hyphenism" is now not simply patriotism but "English hyphenism" (Mencken's subversive *ethnicizing* of the Anglo-American); and by "the revival of Know Nothingism" Mencken means not the rise of a new political party but the soaring Anglo-Saxon ethnoracial chauvinism and nativism of the 1920s. "Exterminat[ing]" the German brute is now both a political and a cultural and racialized project. As in the international sphere of "Anglo-Saxon" British-American relations, in the domestic sphere Mencken discovers through the crucible of war both a specific application and a more general paradigm of Anglo-Saxon power; and for the Mencken who discovered himself during the war "a member of a race lately in worse odor among 100% Americans than either Jews or Negroes,"[110] the more general paradigm lay in the appreciation of Anglo-Saxonism as not simply a political occasion but also a much larger racial and cultural machinery of U.S. hegemonic assertion. As I have suggested, the overall brilliance of Conrad for Mencken owes much to the fact that as both an anticolonial and an immigrant writer, Conrad enabled mappings between Anglo-Saxon imperialist dynamics in the international sphere and Anglo-Saxon racialized, cultural, and political critiques of domination in the domestic sphere, doubly undoing from a "virtual," composite, and externalized vantage what would have remained segregated spheres of inquiry without that disruptive vantage. The anti-imperialist domestic critique of cultural and racialized ideologies of the Anglo-Saxon that Mencken inscribes in Conrad works in two ways.

The first is the use of Conrad to assault extremist programs of Americanization—those associated with Henry Ford's "melting pot" pageants, Royal Dixon's *Americanization* (1916), and Peter Roberts's *The Problem of Americanization* (1920), all premised on the "100%" assimilation of immigrants beyond civic and cultural identification with any country but the United States[111]—and also immigrant exclusion programs sharing the same nativist logic and agenda of Anglo-Saxon racial and cultural supremacy. Mencken constructs Conrad as the opposite of these programs, his mastery betokening their bankruptcy. Thus, when Mencken obsessively emphasizes Conrad's unmeltable, non-Anglo-Saxon alterity; when he "harp[s] on [Conrad's] Slavonism"; when he insists on Conrad's preserved "origins" and "foreign smack"; when he deduces a veritable cosmos of multicultural hyphenism in Conrad's image in *A Book of Prefaces*—he is championing through Conrad a foreignized, transnational, xenophilic vision of immigration and the United States, one very much like Randolph Bourne's and Horace Kallen's vision of a "transnational America," though in certain respects, as we shall see, both more and less far-sighted. Mencken's Conrad, hence, is the repudiation of both assimilationist "Americanization" ideology and immigrant restriction policies crafted in Anglo-Saxon terms. Conrad stands for the rejection of the "defective assimilation" that would make "English hyphenism" (and "English only"[112]) the monolithic U.S. cultural norm, and also "the gate[s] going up"—as they would with the Immigration Restriction Acts of 1921 and 1924—in terms carefully designed to preserve, monitor, and engineer Anglo-Saxon racial dominance. The foreignizing impulse that leads Mencken to champion "constant transfusions of new blood" and "small internal hemorrhages" of culture and language in Conrad's image in "Conrad Revisited" (1923) is the same impulse that leads Mencken seven months later in "The Anglo-Saxon" to extol the "mongrel" and "mixed population[s]" and the "areas of recent immigration" in the United States over the blowhard strongholds of the self-proclaimed "'purest Anglo-Saxon blood in the world.'"[113] The same Mencken who champions Conrad as the writer par excellence is also the Mencken who singularly championed among U.S. politicians Senator James Reed of Missouri, the one senator who voted against the Dillingham Immigrant Restriction Act of 1921, and who further wrote in the run-up to the Johnson-(David A.) Reed Immigration Act of 1924: "In the fine arts, in the sciences and even in the more complex sorts of businesses the children of the later immigrants are running away from the descendants of the early settlers. To call the roll of Americans eminent in almost any field of human endeavor above the elemental is to call a list of strange and often outlandish names. . . . *The fact that they increase is the best hope for civilization in America.*"[114] Indeed, the very paradigm of the hybrid and transnational immigrant writer that leads Mencken to celebrate Conrad and Henry James in 1915 as the only writers worth considering in England—"the one a Pole and the other an American!"—becomes a template for promoting other foreignizing American immigrant and immigrant-related texts including:

- Sholom Asch's *America* (1918), which "avoid[s] all the customary gabble about melting-pots" and appreciates that "the immigrant does not come to Ellis Island to be melted into a pot" but rather "to make it with the least possible yielding of his native customs and habits of mind";

- Abraham Cahan's *The Rise of David Lewinsky* (1918), a "miracle" and "really quite astonishing" book whose sensitive evocation of Russian Jewish experience is expressed in an "absolutely perfect English" that is "not merely correct English" but the kind of "musical" and "highly felicitous" expansiveness that rarely comes from "native novelists";

- Edward Bok's *The Americanization of Edward Bok* (1921), which one would expect Mencken to dislike, but which Mencken ingeniously frames as the story of how "this plu-normal Mr. Bok *failed* in his supreme enterprise: he never quite became 100% American," hence producing the "inconvenient moral" that "[Bok's] chief human value lay in his failure to become wholly Americanized, that he was a man of mark in direct proportion as he was not 100% American";

- Ezra Pound's Chinese translations, which are to be celebrated for "creating a Chinese spirit and getting it into English forms," a matter alarming to "English Comstocks" in part because of the absolute gulf posited between China and the United States by the (foundationally anti-immigrant) Chinese Exclusion Acts of the 1880s; and

- Mencken's own *American Language*, whose attention to the fluid English *of* and "Non-English Dialects *in* America" derive from an ideologically charged "central objective" of "convinc[ing] 100% Americans that language is really interesting, and not only interesting but important [i.e., to who they are]."[115]

Conrad, hence, both figures within and is a coordinating figure of an expansive antinativist project: he is, indeed, a coordinating interference and relay between the unspeakable U.S. determination by the international sphere and the erased coloniality of the domestic sphere. Mencken's primary domestic rationale for casting Conrad in this light, moreover, consists less in a commitment to cultural pluralism per se—though this is part of what it means to valorize Conrad as an "enigmatical Pole" simply because he is and remains an ethnic Pole—than in a commitment to the dynamic processes through which cultural pluralism engenders what we have already described, by way of Oliver Wendell Holmes Jr., as a "marketplace of ideas": a forum of open competition and exchange among maximally free and diverse voices toward goals of perpetually agnosticized truth and tolerant standards of civil and civilized society. "The battle of ideas in the United States," Mencken writes in "The National Letters," "is largely carried on under strange flags, and even the stray natives on the side of free inquiry have to sacrifice something of their nationality when they enlist." "Without this rebellion of immigrant iconoclasts," Mencken continues, "the whole body of the national literature would sink to the 100% American level of such patriotic literary business men as the president of the Author's League"; "whenever one encounters a novel that rises [to] superior [levels] the thing takes on an unmistakable foreignness"; "the native author of any genuine force and originality is almost invariably found to be under strong foreign influences"; "in other words, we must put up with aesthetic Bolshevism of the Europeans and Asiatics who rage in the land, for without them we might not have any literature at all."[116] Such an ideal of a multiplicity of voices, intersecting with and chafing against one another, undermining any omniscient or normative authority that might be imposed by one on another, is, as we have already seen, a fundamental "content" of Conrad's novels for Mencken; and hence we may add here that Conrad's fiction incarnates for Mencken not simply a certain kind of immigrant voice, but a kind of immigrant microcosm and vision in whose image one might stylize a dynamic and foreignized United States.

But in "harping on [Conrad's] *Slav*onism," Mencken also insists on an aggressively racialized category that, notwithstanding Mencken's occasional hedging with respect to the term "Slav," adds to the dynamic cultural pluralist critique in which he inserts Conrad an additional attack on the "Anglo-Saxon" as a racialized discourse of power/knowledge. In the essay "The Anglo-Saxon" (1923), Mencken delights in taking the prominent American race theorists of his day—

the likes of Lothrop Stoddard, Madison Grant, Thomas Dixon—at their white supremacist word in affirming that the Anglo-Saxon "designates a genuinely distinct and differentiated race," "separated definitely, in character and habits of thought, from the men of all other recognizable strains," and "represent[ing], among all the people of the earth, almost a special species [to which] he runs true to type." Mencken does so to trash the truly singular "Anglo-Saxon" as a "race" whose "real" and "overwhelming" "inferiority" "must be obvious to any impartial observer." "Civilization is at its lowest in the United States precisely in those areas where the Anglo-Saxon presumes to rule," Mencken argues; indeed, the only hope for "civilization" in the United States lies in the "mongrel" admixture and "stimulus of other and less exhausted strains."[117] Conrad the Slav meshes with this critique as a racialized member, in Matthew Jacobson's phrase, of one of the "white Others of Anglo-Saxondom."[118] For Conrad to be a Slav, and not only a Slav but superior to anything Anglo-Saxon precisely insofar as he is and "remains" so, is to repudiate the ideology of Anglo-Saxon supremacy in its own terms. Moreover, not only is Conrad the Slav the supreme literary example of the superiority of racial Otherness *to* the Anglo-Saxon; in the process, Conrad becomes part of a scorched-earth project, very much like that of *Heart of Darkness*, wherein the premise of a certain kind of white racial superiority and difference taken to its logical and considered conclusion leads to a breakdown and sabotage of the discourse of "race" altogether. For although Chinua Achebe is not wrong—in his famous argument, less famously born of U.S. circumstances[119]—to suspect the racist and racialized politics and deployment of *Heart of Darkness*, one primary effect of that novella is to compromise the polarizing assertion of racial difference by significantly neutralizing the vocabulary of its assertion; and so, too, in "The Anglo-Saxon" are white supremacists left with a discourse of Anglo-Saxon singularity that is significantly useless to them.

Finally, just as Mencken emphasizes in "Conrad Revisited" "bilious" British attempts to use Anglo-Saxonism as a means of "prohibition," "slavery, "and punishment for Conrad, so he is also keenly attuned throughout this period to what he would later call "crackers hugging fortuitously their idiotic whiteness"[120] as a means of punishing and denying civic protections and social empowerment to non-Anglo-Saxons in the United States. Without ever being completely outside conceptual investments in race, this is to say, Mencken understands very well the principle of the mutable and situated constructability of "race" that

Theodore Allen identifies with the phrase "the relativity of race"; and Mencken also, as something of the John the Baptist of whiteness studies, understands perfectly the political deployment of "race" to assert shifting terms of power and control over historically changing internal minorities, as Higham identifies this practice as central to the history of American "nativism."[121] The latter is what Mencken means by excoriating the American Anglo-Saxon for historically "penaliz[ing]" the "foreigner" "he admits . . . to his country . . . absurdly for his mere foreignness": "The Anglo-Saxon American is always trying to do it; his history is a history of recurrent outbreaks of blind rage against people who have begun to worst him." The former is implicit in Mencken's discussion of the "false label[s]" of "race" through which "grotesque and extravagant forms" of punishment are asserted over people whose only crime is varying terms of newness and difference: "Laws are passed to hobble and cage the citizen of newer stocks in a hundred fantastic ways. It is made difficult and socially dangerous for him to teach his children the speech of his fathers, or to maintain the cultural attitudes he has inherited from them. Every divergence from the norm of the low-cast Anglo-Saxon is treated as an *attentat* against the commonwealth, and punished with eager ferocity."[122] Though written in 1923, these comments seminally derive from Mencken's experiences as an ethnic German during the war; they are connected to Mencken's outspoken defense of Howard University professor Kelly Miller's eloquent call for African-American political equality in 1917; they are also connected to Mencken's fierce denunciations of the Klan, as well as bold and early defenses of Emma Goldman, Alexander Berkman, Carlo Tresca, and Sacco and Vanzetti in the 1920s, each treated unfairly in Mencken's view by virtue of his or her immigrant status; and what connects them all is the same objection to the racial Anglo-Saxonization of full citizenship that Mencken also inscribes within Conrad.[123]

THE THIRD ANGLO-SAXON MAPPING:
ARISTOCRACY, DEMOCRACY, "PURITANISM"
Mencken, Brooks, Bourne, Lippmann

Does all of the above mean that through "Conrad" we arrive at a Mencken significantly different from the one presently known, one outside not only present competing views of Mencken in American studies but also, at least incipiently, the agonistic limitations of his own time? In part, yes. Much of the empirical information presented above is new, not only to the general areas of Americanist and modernist studies but even to the more specialized domains of Conrad and Mencken scholarship. The gesture of considering this information, especially as it concerns and becomes intermediable through Conrad, in light of contemporary Americanist discourses of race, imperialism, coloniality, Anglophilia, transnational political relations, and jurisprudence is also significantly new. But alongside confirming what I take to be the cardinal truth of the matter with respect to Mencken in the years emphasized above—that he was an enormously disruptive force, one whom no informed person on the left or the right should dismiss—the occasion of "Conrad," whose capillary investigation exposes both the aesthetic sophistication and the tremendous cultural and political range of Mencken's work, finds its fundamental effect in undermining what has truly impeded Mencken's emergence in Americanist scholarship of the past two generations: the assumption of Mencken's "thinness." To the contrary, through the sign of Conrad, pursued as a material constituent and global integrant of the American scene, one recovers a Mencken of enormous extension, implication, strategy, and dimension, a Mencken whom one can genuinely understand as the momentous Emersonian cultural force he simply really was, both within his own moment and toward the remainder of the century.

But none of this is to suggest, of course, that Mencken *escapes* his historical moment through the agency or recovery of Conrad. Indeed, that very fantasy of transcendence—which nearly always involves retrospectively conceiving one's object of inquiry as an anticipation of one's idealized self—is precisely what the irreducibly messy and situated example of Mencken helps to avoid. Mencken's ensnarement within his own moment is especially clear in his discussions of race, which, as we have just seen, indict and even negate the abuse and facticity of "race" while nonetheless reinscribing race in crucial ways, ultimately never failing to relinquish fundamental investments in either the explanatory power or the incendiary occasion of "blood." Actually quite facilitated by Conrad, whose writings, as we explore further throughout the course of this book, invariably assume stereotypes that are critically interrogated but never truly eclipsed or replaced, the contradiction that runs throughout Mencken's work between neutralizing and embracing racialized explanation, between deconstructing and deriding racist assertion and, sometimes in the very same essay, engaging in the crudest racial slurs, is the product of a number of factors: among them, laziness, callousness, and genuine incoherence; a comprehensive preference for the posture of agent provocateur;[124] changing viewpoints over time (Mencken's challenges to "race" are most extreme in the years during and shortly after the Great War); an iconoclastic mode that, amid its flurry of pugnacious blows, implicitly shields, conceals, and prevents the interrogation of reactionary premises; and finally and especially, the assumption of the United States as a historical refuge of failures and the lowest caliber of humanity generally, making it possible to belittle *any* self-aggrandizing assertion of identity among U.S. Americans—including but not limited to racialized assertions—without compromising the fundamental logic (say, of race) underlying the assertion itself.

But perhaps most fundamental to Mencken's capacity for racial self-contradiction is the fact that (de)racializing the terms of America, though always a crucial context and inseparable field of engagement and implication, is ultimately not the central political project or anxiety through which Mencken's writings self-consciously articulate themselves. Indeed, though Walter Benn Michaels has suggestively demonstrated how the rhetoric of class and cultural pluralism in the modern United States is frequently predicated on a concealed racist premise and project,[125] this has the matter significantly backward with respect to Mencken, who does not emerge in Michaels's *Our America* perhaps for this reason. Mencken's appeals to and indictments of race from 1915 to 1925 are *never* concealed and frequently not reducible to a logic of identity;[126] his foremost impulse and effect during this time is to *resist* resolution and consolidation, much less celebration, of the terms and boundaries of "America"; and throughout his writings, Mencken's inconsistencies with respect to race must be understood as interwoven with and subtended by two complementary political and metanarrative fixations: one, the idea of "aristocracy," itself by no means a race-neutral term in the modern United States, though also not univocally determined or materially grounded in its racialized or class significance;[127] and two, the use of this ideal, not to denote or authorize any living class or race of "superior" people in the United States, but rather as a figure of American impossibility: as a *strategic negative and counterfactual means* of illuminating the kind of civic and expressive protections from government and majority rule that the United States radically denies, and the historical reasons why this has come to be the case. Against the grain of U.S. self-celebration in terms of "liberty," this is to say, Mencken uses a negative (mutually exclusive) figure of "aristocracy" to raise and theorize counter-hegemonic challenge to contemporary excesses of U.S. *democracy*, the effectively unchecked power it consolidates and facilitates in the U.S. State, and a supporting U.S. culture of moralistic and majoritarian domination tactics—labeled by Mencken and others of this time as "Puritan." For Mencken, "aristocracy" lies at the constant core of what is and has always been most vitally *missing* in U.S. culture and politics. And though Mencken expresses this idea with reference to historically bygone and socially distant class formations of people, themselves often articulated through narratives of "stock" and "blood," though generally in a fashion that valorizes race mixing and never reduces to simple race exclusion, Mencken's coordinating purpose is to use "aristocracy" as a converse and oppositional vantage from which to challenge coercive excesses fundamental to earlier twentieth-century U.S. democracy and its "Puritan" instrumentations and extensions—both of which Mencken styles as fundamentally "Anglo-Saxon." It is here we thus arrive at the third and final Anglo-Saxon mapping of Mencken's Conrad: contra-democratic and anti-Puritan in character.

Throughout his writings, Mencken's emphasis on Conrad as a "Slav" is flanked by an equal emphasis on the image of Conrad as an aristocrat: on Conrad's "essential *superiority* as a *civilized* man." For Mencken, Conrad is "a Pole of noble lineage," "by birth and training an aristocrat," "the son of a Polish aristocrat, bred to carry on the family [tradition]," "a country gentleman from the Ukraine"—what Joseph Hergesheimer, following Mencken, would call "ideally the aristocratic genius"—and insofar as he is these "aristocratic" things, Conrad "has the gift of emotional detachment. The lures of facile doctrine do not move him. In his irony there is a disdain which plays about even the ironist himself."[128] "Aristocracy," a complex because inversely elastic (with respect to the United States) term in the Menckenian lexicon, means here more than anything else a kind of "interior security" born of a class "secure in its position," "beyond responsibility to the general masses" and their "decrees," and "delighting in the battle of ideas for its own sake." The "extraordinary detachment" of Conrad's fiction thus befits its aristocratic maker, positioned above and insulated from pressures of ideological conformity; and, as we have already seen, the "interior security" that Conrad has in himself makes for a "destructive criticism" and exteriorized perspective—a sort of "lofty severity" advanced as if "from a high window, looking down"—that is the bane and ironic undoing of the moralizing and propagandizing engines of the Great War.[129] But for Mencken, as he emphasizes in the essay on Conrad in *A Book of Prefaces*, the "Anglo-Saxon"—English or American, warmonger or progressive reformer, imperialist, fundamentalist, socialist, or even pacifist—is always eager to declare a crusade or Holy War on behalf of something: "Mountebanks almost innumerable tell us what we should believe and practice, in politics, religion, philosophy and the arts. England and the United States, between them, house more creeds than all the rest of the world together, and they are more absurd. They rise, they flame, they fall and go out, but always there are new ones, always the latest is worse than the last. . . . Let a new messiah leap up with a new message in any part of the world, and at once there is a response from the two great free nations."[130] Crusading moralism is a cultural pathology with Anglo-Saxons, especially in the United States; hence, combining elements of Nietzsche's notion of will-to-power and George Santayana's critique of American "Genteel" culture, Mencken complements his "colonial" and transatlantic critique of Anglo-Saxondom, itself the inverse of what Amanda Claybaugh has recently described as a late nineteenth-century Anglo-American transatlantic economy of "purpose,"[131] with a more fundamental critique of U.S. culture as predicated on an Anglo-Saxon ethos of "Puritanism": abstractly, an extreme separation between the spiritual and ("sinful") material, inherited from the original Puritans, that has given rise, through a series of systematic social disjunctions, to a ferociously punitive culture of moral obsession, imposition, inquisition.[132] It is in opposition to this American "Puritanism" that Mencken presents the antimoral Conrad in the first essay of *A Book of Prefaces*, and "our Conrad" at the end of the final essay in the volume, "Puritanism as a Literary Force."

Neither Puritanism nor aristocracy, however, is simply a matter of abstract definition for Mencken. In "Puritanism as a Literary Force," he emphasizes that the American Puritanical ethos cannot be understood outside the "complex of social and economic conditions which have worked in countless irresistible ways" to facilitate a "campaign of repression and punishment perhaps unequalled in the rest of the world, . . . an art of militant morality as complex in technique and as rich in professors as the elder art of iniquity."[133] In part, Mencken has in mind here the large number of federal, state, and local laws curtailing personal liberty and enabling extraordinary abuses of police power in the name of social improvement and moral danger that came into operation during the fifty years following the U.S. Civil War. Mencken names the Comstock Act of 1873 (regulating obscenity), the Mann Act of 1910 (sexual conduct), the Webb Act of 1913 (alcohol), and various vice statutes in *A Book of Prefaces*; he goes on to challenge the Espionage and Sedition Acts (targeting political expression, civil liberties), the Palmer Raids (privacy, civil liberties), "the grotesque anti-syndicalist laws of California," antievolution laws in Tennessee and Mississippi, and antimiscegenation and anticontraception statutes shortly thereafter.[134] But even beyond such statutory and other formal legal measures, Mencken's political critique extends to the large web of social institutions and inculcating mechanisms—what Althusser would call State "apparatuses": churches, newspapers, universities, chambers of commerce, the infinite leagues and organizations on the model of the Rotary or YMCA or Anti-Saloon League—through which a culture of majoritarian morality becomes engineered and enforced: "The whole drift of our law is toward the absolute prohibition of all ideas that diverge in the slightest from accepted platitudes, and behind that drift of law there is a far more potent force of growing custom, and under that custom there is a natural philosophy [and social machinery] which erects conformity into the noblest virtues and the free functioning of personality into a capital crime against society."[135] Mencken's fundamental problem, as he articulates the matter most fully in *Notes on Democracy* (1926), is with the entire framework (the "hegemony" in Gramsci's sense) of American *democratic* culture itself: i.e., not simply as a matter of the majoritarian laws it passes, but the majoritarian *culture* the content of whose newspapers, the wisdom of whose churches, the belletristic and obscure pieties of whose professors, the circus of whose fraternal organizations, the vulgarity and machine-corruption of whose politicians, and the manipulation of whose plutocrats are but reflections and instrumentations of the rule of America's tyrannically mediocre *demos*—ever subject to alarmist manipulation by the U.S. State and its consolidating "material interests," ever engineering the terms and expectations to which that State is ultimately answerable. In the absence of an actively functioning Bill of Rights—many of whose crucial qualities and protections were only beginning to be judicially imagined at this time—contemporary U.S. "democracy," in "its perfect correspondence with the imbecility of mob thinking," its circularity of popular and State hysteria, its authoritarian susceptibility to "the Puritan fear of ideas that is the master of them all," becomes the engine of that majority-mobilized, ethically rationalized will-to-power that is Puritanism.[136] Absent a robust core of "common rights"[137] protecting various domains of personal and political liberty and privacy from the infringements of a "rigidly partitioned ethical field," democracy and Puritanism, Mencken argues in *Notes on Democracy*, become coterminous: "If democracy had not lain implicit in Puritanism, Puritanism would have had to invent it. Each is necessary to the other. Democracy provides the machinery that Puritanism needs for the quick and ruthless execution of its preposterous inventions."[138] And consequently, Mencken arrives in *A Book of Prefaces* at a formulation he will repeat and develop many times after. The problem with America is it lacks a *sensibility* and social(izing) center of gravity that would check coercive excesses of tyrannical democracy: that its "commonwealth of peasants and small traders," its "paradise of the third-rate," is "almost wholly unchecked by the more sophisticated and civilized ideas of an aristocracy": "The difference between the United States and any other nation [does] not lie in any essential difference between American peasants and other peasants, but simply in the fact that here, alone, the voice of the peasant [is] the single voice of the nation"; "it is the lack of a civilized aristocracy, secure in its position, animated by an intelligent curiosity, skeptical of all facile generalizations, superior to the sentimentality of the mob, and delighting in the battle of ideas for its own sake" that prevents the United States from becoming both a civil and a civilized country.[139] Note here that "aristocracy" is not being put forth as a viable U.S. sociopolitical model or covert endorsement of certain social or ethnic groups or historical aspects of the United States; rather, it is an idea whose very American *preclusion*—whose absolute counterfactuality—enables a complexly consolidated articulation (and historical archaeology) of the need for changes within the American democratic system and also the practice of assuming a critical relationship to it.

Conrad fits into this critique—much more shrewd and subtle than Mencken's critics at the level of political philosophy have yet to acknowledge—in two fundamental ways. First, in the Conrad essay that opens *A Book of Prefaces*, Mencken devotes a long section—the essay's longest—to the specific debunking of "the vast repertoire of delusions which go along with democracy . . . particularly the master delusion that human problems, in the last analysis, are soluble, and that all that is required for their solution is to take counsel freely, to listen to wizards, to count votes, to agree upon legislation."[140] Conrad the aristocrat is the opposite of such democratic "delusions." His fiction suggests that many human problems are not "soluble"; that they are dialectical in origin—the product of "inexorable and uncompassionate struggle"[141]—rather than the product of spiritual or pragmatic confusion; that human perspectives and attempts at collective activity are frequently fatally underinformed, disrupted by cognitive dissonance, and otherwise not amenable to popular coordination; and finally, that the will of the majority and the agents and agencies of its fascination and expression are not the best means of deciding the course of a ship, be it of State or at sea. Conrad's "aristocracy" is for Mencken a *figure* of the "interior security" and "absolute detachment" with which Conrad's fiction divests itself from the animating fictions of (Anglo-)American democracy, deactivating and interfering with its self-authorizing social and political premises.

Yet as important as this point is, the even more important point—and one that gets to the heart of Conrad's effectiveness for Mencken as a political weapon—is that the aristocratic Conrad is also an aesthetic and affectual *agency* through which Mencken attempts—performatively—not simply to argue for but to cultivate and effect a sensibility of counter-hegemonic relation to the American democratic State and the Puritan-democratic culture that both authorizes and reproduces its effects. That is, when Mencken attacks through Conrad in the Conrad essay "the prime and immovable doctrine of the *mobile vulgus* set free"—"this notion that there is some mysterious infallibility in the sense of the majority," "this theory that the consensus of opinion is inspired"[142]—his point is not simply to use Conrad to debunk a belief that is, in the end, fairly obviously erroneous. It is also to use Conrad as a functional means, combining ideas with aesthetic spectacle and affectual experience, of cultivating and galvanizing a set of tastes and sensibility—what Mencken himself, apropos of the title of his most famous book series, would call "prejudices"—against majoritarian-Puritan democratic culture and its State, and the uncritical identification of the American democratic subject with either. Just as Mencken knows that the United States never had or will have a European-style aristocracy, and just as his strategic appeals to aristocracy are negatively designed to identify weaknesses and prompt a search for correctives within the American democratic system, Mencken also knows that the evolution of the American democratic framework, along lines whose priorities he aestheticizes and itemizes as "aristocratic," ultimately depends on a sea change in the American cultural infrastructure grounding it. For "the fundamental causes of all the grotesque . . . phenomena flowing out of [American democracy] are to be sought," Mencken argues, not in economics or formal politics but rather "in the habits of mind of the American people"; for meaningful democratic evolution to happen, "it must wait until a sense of reason and justice shows itself in the American people."[143] Given this need for a sea change in the "mind" and "sense"—really, the *sensibility and culture*—of the American people so as to support and ground changes in the nature of American democratic civil society, Mencken uses Conrad *both* as an exponent of critically democratic and anti-Statist ideas *and* as a kind of "dynamo" (to bring back Conrad's own metaphor for Mencken) to galvanize those ideas with the seductive spark of all those aesthetic and affectually engaging aspects of Conrad's fiction and persona. Conrad's aristocracy thus enfolds not only Conrad's critical distance but also his chivalric glamour, exoticism, romanticism, worldly wisdom, lyric eloquence, aura of mystery, bold experimentalism, dash of scorn, uncompromised vision, unmistakable individuality, exilic wanderings—all means by which Mencken seeks to create a *taste*, "prejudice," sensibility *through* Conrad for contra-democratic, counter-hegemonic, anti-Puritan values and questions. If there could be no true aristocracy—nor really would one want one—to check the operations of raw U.S. democracy at this historical nadir in U.S. judicial and constitutional history, there could be a new quasi-aristocracy of *critically* democratic tastes and values; or rather, there could be the *equivalent* of the effect of aristocracy in the cultivation of a counter-hegemonic and critically democratic sense and sensibility, not simply among a new cultural elite attuned to priorities of expression, liberty, privacy, and equal protection, but also in the larger democratic U.S. mainstream in whose idioms and for whom as an audience Mencken, to the frustration of academic professionals ever since, significantly and very effectively wrote.

I emphasize this point because at issue in it is the power of "our Conrad" as mobilized by Mencken and the power of Mencken as it stands to be recovered by the proximity of "our Conrad." For as Walter Lippmann understood in 1926, and as Americanist inquiry since Perry Miller has had trouble integrating ever since, what's special about the general arc of Mencken's work as a whole, and what accounts for his peculiar power in the United States in the years following the Great War, is his flanking of critical analysis with aesthetic and affectual focus: his understanding that at the most fundamental levels "the established [democratic] scheme is *not supported by reason but by prejudice, prestige, and reverence*, and that a good joke is more devastating than a sound argument."[144] Like Rousseau's *Social Contract* and Thomas Paine's *Rights of Man*, Lippmann argues, each "far inferior as works of the mind to the best [political] thought of the eighteenth century," Mencken's works exert "incalculably great influence because they *alter men's prejudices*": they find their singular power not at the level of ideas but in being "addressed to those vital preferences which lie deeper than coherent thinking."[145] Profoundly in tune with the structures of feeling in his own moment, Mencken seizes in particular on ideals of popular sovereignty and majority rule that no longer carry the explanatory force they did in 1776 or 1789 or 1848—and Mencken attacks these ideals at the level of affect and aesthetics:

> The effect of his polemic is to destroy, by rendering ridiculous and unfashionable, the democratic tradition of the American pioneers. This attack on the divine right of demos is an almost exact equivalent of their earlier attacks on the kings, the nobles and the priests. *He strikes at the sovereign power,* which in America to-day consists of the evangelical churches in the small communities, the proletarian masses in the cities, and the organized smaller business men everywhere. . . . Mr. Mencken does not argue with them. He lays violent hands upon them. . . . Mr. Mencken is so effective just because his appeal is not from mind to mind but from viscera to viscera. . . . He presents an experience, and if he gets you . . . if he succeeds with you, he implants in you a sense of sin, and then he revives you with grace, and disposes you to a new and somewhat fierce pride in a nongregarious excellence.[146]

In *A Book of Prefaces* and other works of this period, Mr. Mencken is trying to "get you" with Conrad: not through the same violently jocular affect of his own work but nevertheless through a complementary aesthetic "experience" of Conrad that, if it succeeds with you, will cultivate within you that secular sensibility of sin that is a counter-hegemonic, antipatriotic relationship to U.S. democratic culture and government. In a moment in which there is effectively no Bill of Rights protective of nonmajoritarian individual liberties, Mencken devotes pages after pages of adoration to Conrad not simply to argue on behalf of a skeptical relation to the State and its apparatuses but also to implant a felt sense of self defined by such subversive and nonnormative possibilities. "Aristocracy" is the term, exemplified by the master figure of Conrad, that defines this style of self-sufficient, experimentally expressive, *prospectively* counter-hegemonic (which is why the term must remain to some degree undefined) relationship to majoritarian rule. Moreover, the very archetypal tale Conrad has to tell—about the sea and "men who are conquered and undone" by such "elemental forces"—bespeaks the never-ending heroic struggle that one must wage against the State: "He sees it as the Eternal Enemy, deceitful in its caresses, sudden in its rages, relentless in its enmities."[147] If Mencken's primary U.S. historical significance, then, is that of helping to cultivate the cultural background and sensibility that made much of what we now understand by the Bill of Rights possible, what I am arguing, and what we will continue to see throughout this book, is that Conrad also played a crucial role in this modern "constitution" of the United States.

. . .

At this point, the structure of this book becomes explicitly contrapuntal: the following chapter presenting a number of voices repudiating each of the anti-Anglo-Saxon elements of Mencken's "Conrad," that chapter and the ones that follow also further expanding and exploring the range of "American" issues heterotopically articulable and contestable through Conrad. As a prelude to such dialogue, I close this chapter by juxtaposing with Mencken two equally early, important, anti-Puritan, antiestablishment, and significantly anti-"Anglo-Saxon" constructions of Conrad that illustrate how complexly and significantly counterpointed even ostensibly "parallel" constructions of Conrad can be. The two new voices are those of Van Wyck Brooks and Randolph S. Bourne, both prominent New York "Young Intellectuals" of the 1910s: the former a major early figure in the U.S. invention of Conrad as a master literary figure, precisely at the time he was working on his seminal critical treatise, *America's Coming-of-Age* (1915); the latter less so, though revealing in his striking construction of Conrad in part for this reason. Together, these voices offer a conversation with Mencken that rounds out the substantial complexities of the anti-"Anglo-Saxon" pole of constructing Conrad traced in this chapter, and against, beyond, and in recuperation of which the following chapters unfold.

As I suggested in the Introduction, in an important review essay that appeared in the *New Republic* in December 1914 Brooks offers the world its first major heterotopic articulation of Conrad: one that understands Conrad's fiction through the broad interference it effects with respect to normative American, among other, templates of self- and world understanding, which Conrad's fiction achieves by collapsing a wide field of presumptive oppositions into the same space, and extensively probing, not the boundaries, but rather the "relations," that exist between them.[148] It is this quality, Brooks argues, that makes it so "the natural history of [Conrad]'s art, baffling as it is, is of the greatest importance and should receive the greatest attention"; it is also why, in Brooks's memorable phrase, "although Conrad is himself not a novelist of ideas he is supremely the cause of ideas in others."[149] Like Mencken, however, Brooks does not let Conrad's broad heterotopic properties of interference and disarticulation preclude him from *locating* "his" Conrad. Indeed, in reciprocally self-conscious correspondence with Mencken, who himself admired Brooks and was beginning to develop his own wider anti-"Anglo-Saxon" conception of Conrad at this time, Brooks situates his understanding of Conrad in a Santayanan (dualized, anti-Genteel, anti-Puritan) line of critique—only whereas, for Mencken, the crux concern lies with a U.S. culture of punitive moral obsession that has emerged as a consequence of the historical Puritans' harsh subjection of the material to the spiritual, for Brooks, the underlying cultural concern, circumscribing the history of the United States as a nation, lies in the unbridgeable division between the spiritual and the material in itself. Brooks's Conrad, ultimately a kind of negative objective correlative for the United States, must be sought in this context.

Nearly all the works of Brooks's remarkable "earlier" period—from *The Wine of the Puritans* (1908) to *The Pilgrimage of Henry James* (1925), a body of work highly underestimated in its internationalist literary dimensions—turn on a fundamental problem and vocabulary of "division" and "dissociation": "the peculiar dualism that lies at the root of our national point of view."[150] This predicament, Brooks argues, arises from the extreme qualities and tendencies of American ("historical") Puritan, pioneer, and industrial experiences and manifests itself in terms of a sharp separation between American cultural practices of the spirit, intellect, and humanities and the mainstream of its practical, economic, and political "enterprises." These two extremes, Brooks continues, are never united in "a middle tradition . . . which effectively combines theory and action"; never placed in any relation of integrated interface or "vital connection" or "contact" with one another; never ultimately allow for the development of a "platform of collective experience," a "foundation" of "connected" and "cumulative culture," a "resisting background" of "organic" cultural experience through which American society could check and guide its (capitalistic) operations in the interests of human self- and social fulfillment.[151] America's lack of this kind of collective and cumulative culture means a lack of control over both its larger sociopolitical capitalistic and democratic-individualistic excesses and its ability to generate a field of experience in which human meaning and expression can become cultivated, developed, distributed, shared among individuals.

Conrad enters this field of argument with special prominence in Brooks's *The World of H. G. Wells* (1915), a book written in the same breath as both the *New Republic* essay described earlier and *America's Coming-of-Age*, Brooks's most famous expression of the above position. *Wells* turns on two basic propositions: first, H. G. Wells as a model of the kind of *socialism* Brooks champions, predicated not on economic orthodoxy or fixed doctrine but rather the imaginative call for an anterior, revisionary, and integrative culture that will support the "*designing* [of] the world in a positive and rewarding fashion," the evolution of a State capable of intelligent and beneficent response to the haphazard, atomistic, and destructive excesses of competitive capitalism and "democratic individualism"; and second, Wells as a type of the "spirit of America"—someone whose "mind, like the American mind, is a disinherited mind, not connected with tradition"; someone whose "instincts," like the qualities of extreme abstraction and dissociation that mark American "ideas" (Puritan, Transcendental, Genteel), "are all . . . instincts of the intelligence." Wells, indeed, is an ideal type of the American spirit precisely because he combines with this rest-position of abstract, fantastic, materially divested, intellectual disinheritance a "visionary burden" and "synthetic motive" of completely reengaging and reimagining the concrete world, such that a "new order of things, a "new *world* of instinct," can become possible.[152]

Conrad, the only literary figure Brooks discusses at any length besides Wells, emerges as Wells's opposite in the book's climactic final chapter where the "American" claim is advanced. Whereas Wells "naturally grasps and interprets life in light of *ideas*," Brooks argues, Conrad, "the greatest and most typical figure of the opposite camp," does so "in light of *experience*," as a matter of "life approached through experience."[153] Interestingly, Conrad's anti-intellectual world of "experience" is presented in terms that uncannily recall Brooks's more general—and generally highly unfavorable—narratives of *American* Puritan and pioneer experience. Conrad's rugged, self-reliant, nature-determined world of "ships . . . set off against the impersonal, appalling sea"; his characters embattled in strenuous elemental struggles against "hunger, icy winds, storm and shipwreck, and the abysmal forces of nature"; their becoming bonded in a windswept crucible of community "forged through immemorial suffering and effort"; their existence where "the relations of things are in a peculiar sense abiding and . . . only one [intellectual] problem exists, the problem of character"; Conrad's consequent assumption of a "moral" rather than "social" "point of view," his interest in "elemental" struggles "between man and his Maker," his "bitterly profound wisdom" that emerges in relation to "an equally profound contempt for the [intellectualist's] play of ideas, so irresponsible in comparison" with the "deep, obscure conviction of the 'plain man'"—all these have the distinct ring of the American frontier and its religious and pioneer cultures, not to mention traditional formulations of the American literary "romance."[154]

It is not at all clear, however, that Brooks draws these parallels intentionally; rather, these "American" shades in Conrad's presentation, which many others *would* come to emphasize quite self-consciously, are perhaps best regarded as symptomatic of both the profound Americanist point of view that orchestrates everything Brooks writes and Brooks's keen sense of the intimate American stakes in offering up Conrad, through the idea of "experience," as the *converse* of the U.S. national-cultural historical predicament.

For just as Mencken uses "aristocracy" as a strategic negative figure of oppositional American revelation, "experience" is a term of art throughout Brooks's earlier work for precisely that thickened, resistant, resonant point of view that emerges from the kind of long-standing "organic" and "cumulative" cultures that the United States has not.[155] In offering up Conrad as an "elemental" figure of the sea and its "abiding" maritime traditions, challenges, and "relations," Brooks presents Conrad as an icon and archetype of the very continuous, complex, organically evolving material/spiritual integration that "America" chronically lacks. (To see things through accumulated "experience" rather than abstract "ideas" is to see things this way.) Indeed, in describing Conrad, quite distinctly from Wells, as someone whose richly accumulated "state of instinct, intensive experience, and the immemorial immediacies of duty and [sea]" make it so the full robust province of "humanity" and "all the ideal things, morality, philosophy, art" quite *naturally* belong in Conrad's fiction, Brooks is pointing to qualities that are missing from, and not "natural" to, the terrain of American fiction.[156] And whereas Wells is offered as a utopic figure through which Americans can learn to transform their dissociated "intellect" into "experience" to make a Beloved State, Brooks offers Conrad as a heterotopic figure who reveals all the "experience" that American "ideas" and social structures have hitherto precluded, canceled out from visibility and actualization. This heterotopic figuration helps to explain Brooks's fascination with typing Conrad as a "Russian" literary figure: Russia, prior to the Bolshevik Revolution, often serves Brooks as a kind of reverse mirror image of the United States, its richly evolved cultural fabric lacking in the very modern ideas and material opportunities the United States has at the expense of such a culture.[157] The previous formulation also helps to explain why, much as Mencken ends *A Book of Prefaces* with an appeal to "our Conrad," Brooks closes one of the most culturally significant national documents of his generation, *America's Coming-of-Age*, by quoting (with some liberties) the epigraph from *Lord Jim*: "My belief becomes indefinitely more certain to me as soon as another shares it." This "observation," Brooks argues, "all good Americans ought to ponder," because in its emphasis on "intimate feeling," "intimate intellectual contact," and an "all-dissolving" framework of shared interchange and experience, it names the qualities "we chiefly lack."[158] Channeling *Lord Jim*'s fundamental question of what it means to be "one of us," America "comes of age" here through the Conradian revelation of its own *lack* of constitution as a nation—and the earnest hope of some more worldly articulate and robustly inclusive national model.

This "experiential" reading of Conrad is not so far away from Mencken as it might seem. Both Brooks and Mencken champion Conrad in relation to radical antiestablishment political programs (socialism, libertarianism); both conceive Conrad in the image of envisioned "checks" to macro sociopolitical excesses of democracy and plutocracy; both understand Conrad as a figure of tremendous affect and feeling, constituting much of his potential for social power; both explicitly formulate Conrad through their anti-Puritan discourses, and to varying degrees (though Mencken much more venomously so than Brooks) challenge wider Anglo-Saxon premises through Conrad; both understand "national" questions as intimately bound up in the transnational mediation of "foreign" and "literary" figures like Conrad; both are fundamentally invested in heterotopic formulations of Conrad with respect to the United States. But whereas Mencken's heterotopic Conrad is almost exclusively *negative* and *negating* in the purely counter-hegemonic relation it encourages Americans to assume with respect to U.S. democratic institutions and culture, Brooks's heterotopic Conrad is principally the negative ideal image of a *positive* quotient he would like Americans to create, construct, establish, integrate, in the place of boundaries now revealed to be void. One cannot imagine Mencken describing Conrad in Brooks's "moral," "elemental," communal, "plain man" terms for precisely this reason—not because Mencken would not appreciate Brooks's argument, and not because Brooks is any less "aristocratic" (Brooks's word) in his sense of who must guide the "organic" culture of the "plain man,"[159] but rather because Mencken sees in Conrad an exhaustive means of attack on precisely the comprehensivity of qualities that Brooks, from the distant, disintegrated, and "impossible" vantage of the United States, marvels at Conrad's ability to connect and collapse together.[160] There are larger political implications here, too. Whereas the radically negative Mencken is eminently specific and concrete, not only in the Anglo-Saxon political State he attacks through Conrad but also, as I have shown, in the thoroughly oppositional attitude he uses Conrad to bring to bear upon that State, the democratic processes and cultures that both authorize and are manipulated by it, the various ethnic and internationalist measures advanced through and in relation to it, and the field of basic civil rights ultimately denied by it, the visionary Brooks is much more vague and diffuse. Beyond an overarching, prophetic sense of instructive and constructive purposiveness, Brooks's Conrad remains in many respects as nebulous in his specific U.S. applications and implications as Brooks's socialist politics—which he was often "suspiciously inclined to define by metaphor," as Raymond Nelson notes—are in themselves.[161] For though Brooks is clear that the "Great State" and "sense of the State" he imagines will come (no less than for Mencken) from a cultivated cultural space outside governmental institutions—"through an enlightened individualism, outside the recognized governmental institutions, [by which] the ostensible States will be superseded virtually by informal centres of gravity quite independent of them"—Brooks's socialism is lacking in any sense of *dialectical*, genuinely necessary, and fundamental counter-hegemonic relation to the political State. It avoids, in part by way of a distantly posited Conrad, the very irreconcilable tensions between individual liberty and cultural prosperity, on the one hand, and the political State, contemporary democracy, their "moral" apparatuses, ethnic nationalism, and colonial/imperialist internationalism, on the other, that ground and proliferate throughout Mencken's sense of Conrad.[162] In short, whereas Mencken and his Conrad assume a thoroughly oppositional, purely *counter-hegemonic nationalist* frame, Brooks and his Conrad—to advance a charged historical claim that could be elaborated elsewhere—may usefully be understood in terms of *pragmatist nationalism*:[163] what matters is a useful and organic relation between instrument and cultural-national field rather than any values embedded in the instrument of inquiry. Brooks's earlier writings, often quite emphatic in their call for a singular "national point of view," are unclear in their relation to the diverse immigrant populations of the United States and its counter-discourses of ethnic Anglo-Saxonism;[164] Brooks also, though he for a long time opposed U.S. entrance into the Great War, famously came around to the view, as the key bridge figure in the editorial inner circle of the *Seven Arts*, that he couldn't "see why a magazine of art should destroy itself by opposing the war."[165] Brooks's Conrad is structured by similar pragmatist, and pragmatic, ambiguity: what matters are not the qualities of the nation that he stands for but that he stands for and instrumentalizes—in negative, experiential relief—the organic quality of the nation as such.

Brooks's friend Randolph Bourne, who coined the term "transnational" in unequivocal *support* of a hybrid and diverse conception of U.S. culture, and who steadfastly opposed U.S. military involvement in the Great War until the day he died, offers a final early contra-Anglo-Saxon construction of Conrad to the conversation. Bourne, though not a major figure in the U.S. invention of Conrad, reveals precisely the extension and striking mutability Conrad would come to have even among those not self-consciously committed to, or unconflicted about, his propagation. Though Bourne had been exposed to Conrad from the beginning of his undergraduate years at Columbia (1910–12), which he attended with future U.S. Conrad editor Alfred Knopf, Bourne's touchstone contact with Conrad comes in the signature essay of his earlier writings, "Youth" (1912). Bourne wrote this essay, which became the eponymous lead piece of Bourne's first book, *Youth and Life* (1913), at the suggestion of *Atlantic Monthly* editor Ellery Sedgwick, who offered Bourne the timely advice that he write "an essay along the lines of Conrad's story 'Youth.'"[166] Despite this conceptual seed and the precedent of Conrad's "Youth" and *Youth and Other Stories* on which Bourne opportunistically capitalizes, Bourne's "Youth" writings fundamentally evade and quietly negate Conrad's writings rather than palpably engage or elaborate them. Unlike the early writings of Mencken and Brooks, Bourne's earnest, lyrical first-person paeans to the dynamic and "radical" vitality of the youthful spirit, effected through a quietly erudite network of allusions to Wells, Kipling, and Emerson, abjure the critical and heterotopic edge of Conrad. If anything, they embrace the spirit of the younger Marlow's ebullient "illusions" of "youth" rather than the more complex and seasoned skepticism of Conrad's story "Youth" as a whole. Overall, the twenty-five-year-old Bourne's writings simply cannot place the robust register of Conrad they are both conspicuously generated and authorized by—and struggle even to come to negative terms with.

This sense of an *awkward* Conrad, both provoking and resisting articulation, increases in dimension and resonance as Bourne's own relation to world literature and politics, the U.S. State and its cultures, rapidly matures and undergoes sharp oppositional transformation as the United States moves toward and finally enters the Great War in April 1917. Highly revealing is the most expansive passage Bourne ever wrote about Conrad—in a review of Mencken's *Book of Prefaces* that appeared in the *New Republic* in November 1917. Despite some sympathies with the counter-hegemonic aspects of Mencken's general enterprise, Bourne's fundamental critique of Mencken, here and elsewhere,

is that through the very zeal of his crusade against "Puritans" and "Demos,"
Mencken reproduces the culture of pathological "moralism" he seeks to decry.[167]
Yet of all the essays in *A Book of Prefaces*, Bourne argues,

Mr. Mencken's moralism infects the essay on Conrad perhaps the least. With considerable effort the critic shakes himself loose from the clutches of his Puritan enemies and
sets Conrad very justly in relation to his time. "What he sees and describes in his books,"
Mr. Mencken says, "is not merely this man's aspirations or that woman's destiny, but the
overwhelming sweep and devastation of universal forces, the great central drama that is
at the heart of all other dramas, the tragic struggles of the soul of man under the gross
stupidity and obscene joking of the gods."[168]

A curious doubleness defines this passage: which, on the one hand, despite
its grudging praise of the Conrad essay relative to the rest of the volume, and
despite the genuinely striking claim that Mencken "sets Conrad very justly
in relation to his time," is governed by a reticence that discloses remarkably
little about Conrad himself. Bourne's discussion of each of the other essays
and major figures in *A Book of Prefaces* is significantly more substantial and
transparent; the arresting—because both significant and sincere—claim about
"set[ting] Conrad very justly in relation to his time" is crucially undermined
by Bourne's failure to elaborate, not only why this is so, but exactly when, and
in what relation to the present, Conrad's "time" is; and even the long closing
quotation from Mencken, which consumes more space than the entirety of
Bourne's original prose in the passage, through Bourne's refusal to interpret
and ground it ends up locking Conrad in an abstract register that shields the
concrete details and implications of Conrad's "universal" and fundamental
importance. It is as if, far from offering a "construction" of Conrad, Bourne is
going out of his way not to do so.

Yet on the other hand, to read Bourne's "Mencken" essay and its Conrad
passage in the context of Bourne's other writings of this period is to reveal, in
tandem with the discursive reticence we have been tracing thus far, a quite contrary precision and intensity with which Bourne constructs Conrad: altogether
making for a kind of awkward intimacy that refuses, at least too loudly, to declare
its name. All of Bourne's political essays of this time—from "The War and the
Intellectuals" (June 1917) to "The State" (1919)—do in fact adhere to a master
narrative of "this man's aspiration and that woman's destiny" being caught up
in an "overwhelming sweep and devastation of universal forces," "the great cen-

tral drama that is at the heart of all the other dramas" of Bourne's prose being precisely "the tragic struggles of the soul of man under the gross stupidity and obscene joking of the gods"—if we only understand "gods" here as a metaphor for the secular power of the sovereign State to sweep all human and social forces to its obscene, ill-considered, and all-consuming ends in times of war. Bourne's political essays of this period, this is to say, center on the "inexorable,"[169] fatally and fatalistically determinative, all-consuming power of the U.S. State and its "war technique" to marshal every potentially resistant aspect of U.S. foreign policy, U.S. domestic socioeconomic organization, and U.S. culture and individual subjectivity to its relentlessly self-determining and destructive ends. Bourne has constructed—or rather, adjusted—from Mencken a "Conrad" who is "very justly" in line with Bourne's critique of his own "time"; and the nature of this critique, apropos of, though not precisely coincident with, Mencken's loaded claim that "Conrad makes war on nothing,"[170] produces a conception of Conrad that is aggressively *antipragmatist/progressive-liberal* and ultimately *pacifist* in its terms. That is: Bourne's fatalistic Conrad, in which the "overwhelming sweep and devastation of universal forces" and victimized human "soul[s]" become organized by a "stupid," "obscene," absurd, all-totalizing sovereign power, is perfectly flush with the kind of "inexorable" force Bourne is at central and great pains to help Americans see in the U.S. war State, one in which *"there are literally no forces moving in another direction.* War determines its own end,—victory, and government crushes out automatically all forces that deflect, or threaten to deflect, energy from the path of organization to that end."[171] To place Conrad in this context is to offer an antipragmatist and anti-progressive-liberal construction of Conrad—one whose subtlety Conradians will appreciate in light of Conrad's famous metaphor of the "knitting machine," which indomitably knits the world in a certain way despite idealizing attempts to "embroider" it otherwise (*CL* 1.425)—because Bourne's principal target at this time is precisely those pragmatist social philosophers, like John Dewey, and progressive-liberals, like those in the Oval Office and at the *New Republic*, who arrogantly presume, with knowing swagger and "with liberal naivete," a "pragmatic" and technocratic ability to manage and steer to beneficent ends the conduct and consequences of a war whose entry in itself was beyond their powers to resist.[172] Sorely in need of reading Conrad—or at least so Mencken would make the point in juxtaposing a review of Conrad's *Victory* with one of Walter Lippmann's *Drift and Mastery* (1914)[173]—such individuals "are hostile to [all] impossibilism, to apathy, to any attitude that is not a cheerful and brisk setting to work to use the emergency to consolidate the gains of democracy"; "to talk as if war were anything other than an [all-consuming] poison is to show your philosophy has never been confronted with the pathless and inexorable, and that, only dimly feeling the change, it goes ahead acting out of its depth."[174] Bourne's is a pacifist construction of Conrad, moreover, because Bourne's sober pessimism, against the grain of his general pragmatist enthusiasm and sincere commitment to egalitarian and internationalist social justice, is confined to circumstances of the State at war. Whereas for Mencken, all progressive efforts are subject to a "great central drama" of "gross stupidity" and "obscene" manipulation, for Bourne, the "inexorable" Conrad is placed by Mencken "very justly in relation to his time" precisely because that time is a time of war—where the only meaningful alternative is the aloof, critically neutral Conradian posture of "declar[ing] war on nothing," refusing the partisan terms and tactics of bellicosity altogether.

But to return to the dialectic of reticence and consequence: one may speculate that the phenomenon of Conrad's "awkward" expressivity in Bourne, that is, the *tension* between the instances and opportunities of Conrad's evocation and their manifest resistance,[175] results from any of several ambivalences Bourne may have felt toward Conrad: on generational grounds; as too amenable to Mencken's antiprogressivist constructions; as too amenable to *pro*-"Anglo-Saxon" and "English" constructions of a kind we will observe throughout the next chapter. One ground of silencing, however, does not require our speculation. At the close of the review of Mencken's *Book of Prefaces*, Bourne reiterates that the fundamental problem with Mencken is his excessive and self-circumscribing concern with the "majority of Americans," the very Puritans and democratic masses whom he insists are beneath contempt:

Mr. Mencken's mode of critical attack thus plays into the hands of the philistines, demoralizes the artist, and demoralizes his own critical power. Why cannot Demos be left alone for a while to its commercial magazines and its mawkish novels? All good writing is produced in serene unconsciousness of what Demos desires or demands. It cannot be created at all if the artist worries about what Demos will think of him or do to him.[176]

Bourne advocates here not engagement with but a shield between "true art" and the prohibitively coercive forum of mass culture, people, politics. It is the same shield, or rather "shelter," the same divorced and nondialectical conception of art, that Bourne advocates in "A War Diary" in response to the inexorable war State: "One keeps healthy in wartime not by a series of religious and political consolations that something good is coming out of it all, but by a vigorous assertion of values in which war has no part. Our skepticism can be made a shelter behind which is built up a wider consciousness of the personal and social and artistic ideals which American civilization needs to lead the good life." "The war—or American promise," Bourne continues: "one must choose. One cannot be interested in both. For the effect of the war will be to impoverish American promise. . . . Americans who desire to cultivate the promises of American life need not lift a finger to obstruct the war, but they cannot conscientiously accept it."[177] This Brooksian conception of art as a regenerative cultural force of national promise—not rooted in any situated anterior or counter-hegemonic relation to political and social power, and indeed often best avoiding such mass political fields of contestation and capture so as to incubate and actualize its national "potential"—is allied with a genuinely *posthegemonic nationalist* vision of "American nationalism" beyond the terms of "the nationalisms of twentieth century Europe" that Bourne articulates in the essay "Trans-national America" (1916).[178] One obvious liability of Bourne's formulation, however, is that it makes impossible and deflects the production and articulation of "art" insofar as its primary stakes and implications, as well as its primary practitioners and audience, lie in the widest and most contentious domains of the "democratic" public and political sphere. The politically ultrademocratic Bourne, hence, is inclined to bracket, underarticulate, silence those aspects of Conrad and all other artists that most directly engage the public sphere and its cultures—because for Bourne, the most urgent possibilities of art lie elsewhere. Conversely, Mencken, the self-declared champion of "aristocracy," becomes revealed in Bourne's own terms as the greatest democratic artistic agent of them all: for it is Mencken whose fundamental purpose is to engage, not only elite artists and intellectuals but "the majority of Americans," and to do so in a fashion that makes "art" like that of Conrad a vital counter-hegemonic aspect and agency, conceptual and affectual, of U.S. politics and culture broadly construed. For this reason, Bourne, though arguably the true U.S. intellectual giant of the Great War years, was not nearly the social force Mencken would become in the decade that followed.

2 APPOSITIONS
Jews, Anglo-Saxons, Women, African-Americans

I was down at Colonel and Mrs. Roosevelt's house in the autumn. The Colonel is a great admirer of yours, but in particular Mrs. Roosevelt is. I gave her Curle's book on you and that set her to re-reading *Nostromo* at once.

—John Quinn to Conrad, January 28, 1916

Thank you warmly for remembering to send me Conrad's *Typhoon*. I shall look forward with greatest pleasure to reading it, and I thank you for your kindness.

—Woodrow Wilson to Secretary of War Newton D. Baker, August 29, 1917

Since the war most of us have been conscious of living in a world of trouble—a disordered, disgruntled earth, where nations, peoples, men and women, are at odds. Conrad from the first realized that struggle in his stories. . . . The reason why Conrad has meant so much to us, and more since the last bloody assize of war, is no doubt because he has used his pen as to make his tale the fable of ourselves.

—Ernest Rhys, "An Interview with Conrad," in *Bookman* (NY), December 1922

Joseph Conrad, the great novelist, is dead. Young colored folk who want to write should read his life and his novels.   —W. E. B. Du Bois, *Crisis*, October 1924

I am afraid it would be some vanity on my part to think I could add anything to Mr. Conrad's memory by way of literature. However as an avid reader of everything he has written and as one under obligation for many hours of great pleasure, I would be glad to support any memorial to his memory.

—Herbert Hoover, Seamans' Church Memorial Statement, 1925

MR. CONRAD IS NOT A JEW
In August 1918, shortly before the second printing of H. L. Mencken's *Book of Prefaces*, a letter appeared in the *New Republic*, the nation's foremost progressive political magazine and a staunch advocate of the Wilson administration at the

time, under the heading "Mr. Conrad is Not a Jew" (Figure 4). This letter affords a glimpse at the basic trajectory of this chapter, whose double purpose is to trace a broad cultural reaction formation to every aspect of Mencken's anti-"Anglo-Saxon" construction of Conrad and to demonstrate how this central axis of contestation is nested in and gives rise to a widening field of other specific aspects of Conrad's domestic and international heterotopic contemplation in the United States—like the question of Conrad's Jewishness. The structure of this chapter combines a linear reversal of each of the Anglo-Saxon elements considered in the previous chapter with a centrifugal expansion of the specific sites of Conrad's U.S. implications and applications, international and domestic. Because of its (anti-Menckenian) emphasis on *containment* and *assertions* of order rather than their presumptive subversion, this chapter also highlights the proposition advanced in the Introduction about the order(s) that heterotopic sites presuppose and demand.

The letter in the *New Republic*, actually an excerpt of a longer letter written privately to and independently forwarded by an unnamed "friend of Mr. Conrad's," presents Conrad himself responding to a recent prominent identification (also unnamed) of him as Jewish. Though the excerpt begins with Conrad insisting that he does not "feel annoyed in the least" by the identification, and that were he Jewish he "would never [deny] being a member of a race occupying such a unique place in the history of mankind," the rest of the letter does its best anxiously to extinguish this possibility. Conrad itemizes at least six different Polish historical documentations of his racial and religious identity as Polish and Catholic, not Jewish. He adds in a post-Polish historical record of exemplary conduct—"V.G. as to 'character' and V.G. as to abilities"—in the British merchant marine and as a British author and citizen, both also apparently incommensurate with a concealed Jewish identity. Finally, he responds to the charge of Jewishness less as a religious or ethnic matter than as an almost criminal violation of his word and the public trust: as something akin to being declared "a forger, a burglar, a pickpocket, or a cardsharp," "an anarchist, a forger of bank notes, or anything like that."[1]

One may take three points about this excerpt from Conrad, itself only less striking than its appearance in so high profile a political venue as the *New Republic* a mere handful of months before the close of the war in November 1918. The first point is that this fragment is both more and less progressive than it might seem—in ways the *New Republic* actively constructs through processes

They had not been good enough for Peter. That seemed grievance enough.

He did not imagine yet that they could murder the likes of Peter by the thousand, without a tremor.

He loved the fine lines of the boy's profile, he marked his delicate and healthy complexion. Peter was like some wonderful new instrument in perfect condition. And all these other youngsters too had something of the same clean fire. . . .

Was it all to be spent upon love-making and pleasure-seeking and play? Was this exquisite hope and desire presently to be thrown aside, rusted by base uses, bent or broken? " The generations running to waste—like rapids. . . ."

He still thought in that phrase. The Niagara of death so near to them all now to which these rapids were head-

ing; still did not hear, did not suspect its nearness. . . .

And Joan—. From Peter his thoughts drifted to Joan. Joan apparently could find nothing better to do in life than dance. . . .

Suddenly Peter took a deep breath, sat back, and began to clap. The whole house broke out into a pelting storm of approval.

" Ripping! " said Peter. " Oh! ripping."

He turned his bright face to Oswald. " They do it so well," he said smiling. " I had forgotten it was in Russian. I seemed to understand every word."

Oswald turned his eye again to Hamlet in Gordon Craig's fantastic setting—which Moscow in her artistic profusion could produce when London was too poor to do so.   H. G. WELLS.

CORRESPONDENCE

Mr. Conrad is Not a Jew

A FRIEND of Mr. Conrad's has kindly communicated to us the following letter denying some assertions that appeared in this country not long ago:

. . . I imagine that —— called me a Jew in his publication as a manner of insult and in the hope of causing me extreme annoyance.

But I don't feel annoyed in the least. Had I been an Israelite I would never have denied being a member of a race occupying such a unique place in the religious history of mankind. I send you this disclaimer simply in the interest of truth.

I imagine there is no scruple which would prevent —— from calling me Mohammedan or a worshipper of Baal, for some reason of his own, or from the mere love of lying. Neither is there anything in him to prevent him calling me a forger, a burglar, a pickpocket or a cardsharp. This is a statement of fact which can be disproved as follows:

I am in possession of the following documents:

(1.) A passport in the name of Alexander II, Emperor of all the Russias, and signed by Prince Galitzin, Governor of the Province, granted in 1868 to my father, " the Nobleman Appolinary N. Korzeniowski, and his son, Conrad, aged ten years, to travel abroad for the benefit of his health for three years, etc., etc."

(2.) Copy of my parents' marriage certificate from the register of the Roman Catholic Consistorium of the government of Volhynia.

(3.) My baptismal certificate delivered in the usual way by the officiating priest and registered in the parish church.

(4.) The Act of Decease of my father (28 May, 1869, Cracow), delivered by the parish priest of that quarter of the town, minor canon of the cathedral, stating distinctly that the deceased died in the Roman Catholic religion and duly shriven according to the rites of the church.

(5.) An official advice from the Burgomaster certifying that I had been elected Burgess of the city of Cracow with the remission of the usual fees, " to honor the memory of his father as a Patriot and Man of Letters," and addressed to the Highborn Lady Teofila Bobrowska as the (maternal) grandmother and the natural guardian of the minor (1869) Conrad Korzeniowski.

(This last document established my descent on my mother's side.)

In sending these and other documents in 1864, when I became a British subject, my maternal uncle advised me that if I wanted to know something more about my descent I would find it in the archives of the Province of Podolia, relating mainly to the eighteenth century, but (he wrote to me at the same time) that he had had researches made already, which showed that during that century my paternal ancestors were men of substance and what may be called " prominent citizens " frequently elected to provincial offices of trust, and forming alliances in their own modest sphere after the usual several years' service in the armies of the republic. My paternal grandfather served in the Polish army from 1817 to 1820, when he sold his land in Podolia and came to live on his wife's estate in Volhynia. Their fortune, which descended to my father, his brother and his sister, was confiscated by the Russian government in consequence of the rebellion of 1863. Those are the origins and this is my history before my arrival in England. After that it is carried on documentarily by a series of my discharges (V. G. as to " character " and V. G. as to abilities) as seaman and officer in the British Merchant Service up to the year '94. From that time to the present day it is carried on by my written and published pages, eighteen volumes in all, which have obtained a certain amount of recognition. The police of the County of Kent have nothing against me—in fact, if anything, I am rather honorably known to them; even to the extent that one day when our car broke down on the road the son of our local superintendent of police came out to the rescue—five miles—in his own car, and was perfectly charming. But that may have been on account of my wife, who is a very popular person, and—I may also add—*not* a Jewess.

So if it pleases —— to declare me an anarchist, a forger of bank notes or anything like that, I trust you will be good enough to affirm to everybody that it can be disproved on documentary evidence.

JOSEPH CONRAD.

London.

Because I Am a Jugoslav

SIR: May I not congratulate the New Republic for having recognized and so splendidly expounded the necessity of the complete liberation of all the Slavic races as the only means of securing a lasting peace and of checking permanently the German aggression? But we, the Slavs, have more reason to be satisfied when we see that the

FIGURE 4. "Mr. Conrad is Not a Jew," *New Republic*, August 24, 1918.

of excision, excerption, and, as we shall see later, mistranscription. The "friend" to whom Conrad wrote the letter was Hebrew Union College (Cincinnati) seminary student and future rabbi Lewis Browne, a remarkable figure soon to become a vigorous socialist activist but not a political radical or oppositional figure with respect to the Wilson administration at this point. Browne, who did not know Conrad personally, originally wrote Conrad concerning his Jewish beliefs and heritage in response to an article that Frank Harris, the Irish-American firebrand and editor of *Pearson's Magazine* (New York), wrote in February 1918 identifying Conrad as Jewish. In this article, Harris, whose relationship to anti-Semitism is notoriously complicated, and whose magazine in fact sometimes valorizes Jews in line with Harris's increasingly leftist and sympathetically Bolshevist politics,[2] writes:

It is a good thing, I am glad to say, to be a Jew today, for various reasons. If you take up any art or wish merely to write books you can easily find a publisher, for you are sure of a public and most kindly sympathetic critics. I cannot otherwise explain the immediate extravagant success of [Israel] Zangwill or Conrad: true, Conrad has an excellent prose style and a special seaman's knowledge of eastern seas and scenes. . . . But . . . to puff [a book a thin book like *The Shadow-Line*] extravagantly and beyond all measure simply annoys both the critic and the reader.[3]

The wartime context of *The Shadow-Line*, a nautical tale resonant with patriotic structures of feeling and expressly dedicated to Conrad's eldest son, Borys, and others of his generation who were fighting in the war, is revealing. For of Harris's many notorieties, the most prominent of this moment was his fiercely outspoken critique of Wilson as the United States moved toward war on the British side; indeed, Harris's coy continuation of this critique, even under the muted terms mandated by the Espionage and Sedition Acts, earned *Pearson's* a formal "warning" from federal authorities in the very month of February 1918. The war is a crucial context for Browne, too: for although Browne and his fellow students at Hebrew Union College seem genuinely to have wondered and cared whether Conrad was Jewish, Browne's fundamental purpose in writing to Conrad, as his one surviving letter to Conrad makes clear, was less to clarify Conrad's Jewishness in itself than to use such clarification as a means of discrediting Harris's general veracity with respect to his overarching "radical" and "heterodox" antiwar, anti-Wilsonian, sympathetically Bolshevist views.[4] Likewise, Conrad's fundamental anxiety in writing to Browne, as the full text of his central letter emphasizes, derives not from any "criminal" assessment of Jewishness per se (which Conrad surely would not have expressed to a future rabbi, even if he felt this way) but rather from Conrad's sense of the criminal intentions and effects involved in Harris's misidentification of him (as a kind of duplicitous "secret agent") as such.[5] Browne sent the full text of Conrad's letter to the *New Republic* as the logical Progressive place to embarrass Harris, but the *New Republic*, excising several situating paragraphs and all references to Harris and Browne, refuses to take the bait and produces a "Conrad" for its own purposes. This "Mr. Conrad" is emphatically "not" a Jew, neither for privately Jewish nor certainly for any anti-Semitic reasons (two of the five central editors of the magazine at the time, Walter Weyl and Walter Lippmann, were Jewish), but rather directly in line with the *New Republic*'s strong and ongoing commitment to challenging and exposing false attributions and representations of all kinds concerning Jews, generally punitive and hysterical in character.[6] The *New Republic*, this is to say, enlists the instance of Conrad to challenge a broad U.S. culture of false "Jewish" attribution and stigma; the magazine actively constructs Conrad's Jewishness as *the* central, focalized social issue to a degree much more so than the original letter or its contexts; and ironically enough, the very degree to which the *New Republic* highlights Conrad anxiously disclaiming any implication by Jewishness only underscores a vulnerability to anti-Semitic stereotype that recovers Conrad's common ground with Jews after all.

This leads to the second point: pace Conrad and the *New Republic*, it was entirely historically plausible for U.S. Americans to construct Conrad as Jewish in this moment. As *A Personal Record* (1912) had made plain, Conrad was born in 1857 in the Russian-controlled Polish Ukraine: specifically in the town of Berdichev, an exceptionally diverse (and, as Keith Carabine points out, highly antagonized)[7] domain within the Pale of Settlement, roughly three-quarters of whose population of nearly fifty thousand was Jewish, making Berdichev the second-largest Jewish community in the Russian empire. Though there is no real evidence, at least to my knowledge, of Jewish ancestry on either side of Conrad's family, Conrad's emigration from the coercive circumstances of the Russian periphery—and perhaps *toward* the United States, if one follows the hint in "Amy Foster"[8]—for many contemporary U.S. Americans easily fit the general pattern and timing of the nearly 2 million Russian and Polish Jews who emigrated to the United States between 1880 and 1914. Moreover, though Conrad's fiction generally refrains from representing Jews and even occasionally engages in anti-Semitic portraits (as in "Amy Foster") and premises (as in the Shylock/Rothschild archetype that seems invisibly to underwrite the presentation of de Barral in *Chance*), there is much about Conrad's fiction that recalls Jewish, and especially Jewish émigré, expression and experiences. For example, Mary Antin's *The Promised Land* (1912), the widely celebrated Jewish-American autobiography published on the eve of the U.S. boom in Conrad, is anything but distinct from *Lord Jim* in its sharply bipartite "from . . . to" structure, its conspicuous narrative transition from harrowing realism to patriotic romance, and even the coy attention it draws to the cultural erasures and translations endemic to the project of emigratory prose—perhaps, indeed, because the two texts are ultimately practices of a similar mode of immigrant narrative.[9] So, too, Conrad's greater thematics of diaspora, marginalized and embattled community, and deferred and thwarted search for a homeland, as well as his conflicted and decentered relation to hegemonic nationalistic assertion, his internationalized perspective on questions of human politics, and his critical disinterest in Christian morality and metaphysics, all open themselves up to Jewish corollaries—as Conrad's interest has blossomed for a wide variety of Jewish writers throughout the twentieth and into the twenty-first centuries.[10] Finally, as I have argued elsewhere, even Conrad's presentation of Señor Hirsch in *Nostromo* is radically open to interpretation as *either* an anti-Semitic stereotype *or* a figure (in every sense of the word) whose arbitrary and blameless torturing mirrors the torture (physical, conceptual, narrative) through which Jews have been historically scapegoated for autonomous Western advances in capitalism—a *critical* reading that, as we shall see, may have been how Willa Cather, after much revisitation of her own anti-Semitism, came to understand this crux in Conrad.[11]

For these and other reasons, far beyond the local interplay of Frank Harris and the *New Republic*, Conrad was continually linked with (and severed from) the idea of Jewishness throughout the wartime and postwar United States. Ford Madox Hueffer (later Ford) inadvertently opens the door in 1911 with an important article in the *English Review* (London) introducing Conrad's fiction through the story of an encounter with a passionate Jewish appreciator of literature.[12] In *Current Opinion* (New York) in May 1915, a long article whose opening section details how "during the next decade New York is destined to become the Athens of Jewish literature," and how "during the last six months the Yiddish Ghetto has been kept busy arranging receptions for its literary guests—writers driven out of Europe, out of Russia especially, by the repelling forces of the war and the Jewish prosecutions [*sic*] abroad"—including Abraham Raisin, Sholom Asch, Perez Hirschbeim, and Sholom Alecheim, is followed by a long full-portrait discussion of Conrad as "the most remarkable phenomenon in modern English literature."[13] H. L. Mencken, as we have seen, was already drawing such "Jewish" parallels in the *Smart Set*; and in a subsequent article in *Current Opinion* in March 1918, the "Russian spirit" and fictional methods that Abraham Cahan brings to American writing are placed through Mencken's discussion of Conrad in *A Book of Prefaces*.[14] Similarly, a diverse range of Jewish-Americans, including anthropologist/linguist Edward Sapir, writer and society figure Dorothy Parker (née Rothschild), and writer Anzia Yezierska, variously link themselves to Conrad during this time.[15] Obversely and on a more phobic note, by the time Conrad visited the United States and gave a high-society reading of his work at the Curtiss James home on May 10, 1923, a commentator in the audience could describe how "the ladies in blue" in their "gilt ease chairs" "were uneasily wondering if he were not a Jew (so many came out of Galicia and surely Galicia was in Poland)"; Perriton Maxwell in the *New York Herald and New York Tribune Magazine* in 1924 relates that the first time he met Conrad he was confronted with "the quaintest figure I had seen since David Warfield's Yiddish characterization in 'The Auctioneer,'" a figure "identical with that of a conventional stage Hebrew"; and even as late as 1928, an article in the *New York Times* insists that Jules Verne was "not a Polish Jew by birth" but conspicuously leaves the case open with respect to Conrad.[16]

Other voices, of course, take the *New Republic*'s line in distancing Conrad from articulations of Jewishness, albeit with varying complexities of referent and motivation. R. L. Mégroz, in an influential piece on Conrad reprinted in the United States in 1926, opines: "[Conrad] was the immortal Marlow in manner and the Anglicized Polish genius in aspect. (How absurd was that statement of Mr. Frank Harris that Conrad was a Jew!)."[17] From a very different point of view, Mencken, in a tellingly tepid review of Conrad's *Notes on Life and Letters* in 1921, distances Conrad from Jews by *criticizing* Conrad's patriotic Polish essays for their blind disregard of "the aimless, senseless massacre of Jews" during the dark pogroms that accompanied the rebirth of the Polish republic from 1919 to 1921.[18] There were also a variety of attempts to place Conrad directly and enthusiastically in an anti-Semitic continuum. Several U.S. articles parse Conrad's fiction through imposed anti-Semitic frames like those of "the accursed wandering Jew";[19] John Quinn, the American purchaser of all Conrad's handwritten manuscripts, fills his letters to Conrad with a torrent of presumed (and unreciprocated) anti-Semitism; and one (highly dubious and appalling) article in the Protestant magazine *Outlook* (New York) in 1920—an essay whose politics, domestic and international, are the precise reverse of Mencken's in the *Notes on Life and Letters* review—proudly presents Konstantin Buszczynski, the once consul-general of Poland to the United States, fondly recalling the childhood days in Cracow when he and Conrad had "great fun" tormenting Jews: "'Josef and I used to throw toy torpedoes down on the black caftans of passing Jews, enjoying ourselves hugely when they exploded. . . . A pogrom, I suppose,' he laughed. Poles to-day don't relish that word, or the way it has been misused over here."[20] All in all, hence, whether one's sympathies were pro-Jewish or anti-Semitic; and whether one's purpose was to trivialize Jewish victimization in Poland and Jewish representation in the United States, or rather to accentuate and translate the importance (or threat) of Jewish expression and experience for the United States, Conrad's implication by Jewishness offered a remarkable fertile and pliable occasion for articulation and engagement—a local motor no less significant to Conrad's contrapuntal invention as a "master" literary figure than the parallel question of whether and to what degree Mr. Conrad was a Catholic.[21]

But the *New Republic*—and this is third and overarching point—for all its strategic focus on the question of Conrad's Jewishness, even as it cuts off and backgrounds certain contexts, all the more heavily introduces and invests itself in others. For the magazine, precisely as it concentrates attention on the issue of Conrad's Jewishness, attacking the bankruptcy of anti-Semitic projection while at the same time freeing up space for Jews (ironically, in Conrad's image) outside the space of such projections, does so in a fashion whose very vocabulary of disavowal offers Conrad up as an exemplary image of the magazine's own patriotic Anglo-Saxon wartime priorities, international and domestic. Internationally, the *New Republic*, always an Anglophile publication during the modern era, was especially so during the joint British-American war effort, devoting primary energies from April 1917 through November 1918 to global news and analysis underwritten by a strong sense of British-American allegiance. Conrad, similarly, presents himself beyond anti-Semitic projection precisely through his consistently demonstrated reverence for England. In the Conrad letter, in allowing Conrad to present himself not only as a proud "British subject" but also as a dedicated *external* admirer and figure of convergent sympathy with British traditions—as the product of a family of Polish patriots who were "frequently elected to provincial offices of trust," performed "several years' service in the armies of the republic," even served as officers in the (storied) "Polish Army from 1817 to 1820": all avatars of Conrad's own exemplary conduct as "seaman and officer in the British Merchant Service" and as a dutiful British author, *all pointing naturally toward a reverence of British values and a sense of British solidarity, albeit from without*—the *New Republic* is using Conrad, not simply as a figure of British patriotism, but to model Anglophilia for Americans. Conrad thus serves the *New Republic* as a model of American reverence of, alliance with, and service alongside the British—*not* (simply) because Conrad is nobly British but precisely because his sense of British appreciation and sympathy originally came from somewhere else (i.e., an external but kindred space like the United States). This sense of Anglophile solidarity is reinforced by Conrad's cutting reference to "Russia," which, unlike Conrad and the loyalist values for which he stands, had recently proved an undependable ally to the British in the war. It is further underscored by the idea that "Mr. Conrad is not a Jew," not as a matter of religious or ethnic impossibility but rather as a disavowal of *any* undisclosed aspects that might undermine Conrad's transparent "100% British" profferings. Ultimately, like so many other British literary figures—H. G. Wells most visibly and recurrently among them—whose words appeared in the *New Republic* during this time, Conrad is presented here for Americans as an unqualified ratifying authority of the British-allied war cause, as squarely and centrally behind it as the address from which he writes ("London"), and as steadfastly committed to it as his own project of adopted citizenship since "1864, when I became a British subject."[22]

Both of these last details, however, are errors of transcription: Conrad did not write or sign this letter from London (he wrote from Capel House, in Kent), and his original letter also reports his British naturalization not in 1864 but in 1894, the correct year actually being 1886 (*CL* 6.215, 217). These two "mistakes"—though perhaps a stronger term is warranted—are highly revealing of the complementary *domestic* narrative the *New Republic* seeks to advance through Conrad as well. For it is not difficult to see, of course, that the centralizing (like London) tendencies of the letter with respect to Anglo-American foreign policy are also a recipe for a totalizing conception of Anglo-Saxon-identified American citizenship: the British-American military action and alliance being advocated through Conrad in the international sphere declares

itself through Conrad's model of transparent disclosure and absolute subordination of any dissident or "foreign" alterity to the national, nationalist, and
Statist dictates of the Anglo-normative domestic sphere. Conrad's distinctively
defensive presentation of his own patriotic British citizenship—which is surely
the defining note of his letter—in effect becomes a model for "100% American"
citizenship. Here, though the *New Republic*'s immediate purpose in the letter
is genuinely to challenge an encroaching culture of anti-Semitic hysteria, one
cannot overlook the fact that the letter affords no space to validate Jews—or
anyone else—outside the "100%" cooperation with the war- and nation-state
Conrad seems to epitomize. Here, too, in this wartime context, though the *New
Republic* will soon issue bold defenses of minority and dissident rights, not least
to defuse the related issues of anti-Semitic and anti-Bolshevist/Socialist persecution, both implicit in the title of the letter,[23] the fact remains that the valorized
image of Conrad affords no protection to any kind of political or ethnic relation
to the nation-state that is not ultimately in perfect conformity with that State
and the priority of its dominant assimilating "Anglo-Saxon" culture. Indeed,
by backdating Conrad's British naturalization from 1894 to 1864, the *New Republic*, again probably trying to accentuate the irresponsibility of the "Jewish"
attribution, capitulates to an additional, and by no means unfamiliar at this
time,[24] xenophobic narrative strategy and effect. The gesture effectively dissoci-
ates Conrad from all the "new" immigrants (Russian Jews prominently among
them) who came to the United States beginning in the 1890s and also makes
the example of Conrad's model assimilation apply only to those immigrants
whose naturalization begins when they are very young (Conrad was seven in
1864); others—and most of the "new" immigrants fit this category—remain
undependably outside the true "Anglo-Saxon" American frame.

The *New Republic*, then, in using Conrad (in war circumstances) to shore
up *both* an Anglo-American international alliance and Anglo-Saxon domestic
political and ethnic hegemony, exactly counters the image of Conrad generated by Mencken outlined in the previous chapter. It is a fundamental point
of this chapter, moreover, that the myriad local economies of Conrad's interest (i.e., specific topics like whether and how Conrad was Jewish, Catholic,
Polish, or relevance to the Monroe Doctrine or League of Nations, etc.) both
situate and are situated by, activate and are activated by, the larger heterotopic seams of Conrad's American engagement, which, like the template of
the "Anglo-Saxon," not only grid and propel Conrad's cascading applications

but ensure his dissemination as a species of dialogue and dissension. Hence, amid the many issues, contexts, and audiences enfolded in this chapter, the "Anglo-Saxon" frame whose disruption by Mencken was the focus of the previous chapter is countered by this frame's reverse *containment* and *elaboration* as the linear backbone of this chapter. This contrapuntal cultural counter-formation—which, taken together with the forces its resists, is the true dynamic mechanism of Conrad's dissemination in the U.S.—plays itself out across a wide variety of voices, institutions, and contexts whose generative origins profoundly lie, as we shall now see, with Conrad's exclusive U.S. publisher beginning in 1913: Doubleday, Page, and Company. Something of an institutional anti-Mencken, and largely, intelligently, and with equal force positioned in dialogic relation to Mencken, Doubleday, Page helped galvanize and mass-market a "Conrad" of American self-ratification and self-confirmation in a time of world peril and domestic unrest. Through marketing efforts that shrewdly capitalize on contemporary events and aggressively intercede in the public sphere, mass media, academia, and popular discourses and culture, Doubleday, Page engendered the beginning of a nationally *consolidating* "Conrad," oscillating between extremes of violent and complacent conservatism and the sort of meliorist, progressive, anti-imperialist national idealism typical of the *New Republic* after the war. Against the grain of Mencken's positively anarchic, infinitely counter-hegemonic construction of Conrad, though also a product of the very same sense of heterotopic provocation *in* Conrad, this obverse *orderly* stream of Conradian production, and the contexts, complications, and implications to which it gives rise, compose the "appositions" of this chapter.

A TALE OF TWO PUBLISHERS

To [Alfred] Knopf more than to any one person, Conrad owes his fame and popularity and the reading public a debt of gratitude.

—George Doran, qtd. in Geoffrey Hellman, "A Very Dignified Pavane" (1948)

I've been sitting back with a pipe and reviewing as much as I know of all you've done and made and caused to be and set in motion in your own land, and outside of it. . . . It seemed to me somehow that it wasn't merely the methods and manners of publishing, but the whole spirit and outlook of it, that you have revolutionized by your work first in the US and then over here. I'm putting aside all the money and material part

of it that benefited your employees, because, after all, this is less important than the
spiritual side.   —Rudyard Kipling to F. N. Doubleday, September 7, 1926

In what would become a vital counterpoint to Mencken and each aspect of his
assault on the "Anglo-Saxon" American imaginary through Conrad, the second
foundational engine of Conrad's U.S. invention as a master literary figure came
into being sometime in or around September 1912 through two of the very greatest figures in the history of U.S. publishing crossing paths: Alfred A. Knopf and
Frank Nelson Doubleday. At this time, the twenty-year-old Knopf, fresh from
graduating Columbia and a trip to England where he met John Galsworthy and
discovered, through a Tauschnitz edition of *A Set of Six*, "my idol" in Joseph
Conrad, began working in the accounting department of the new Garden City
facility of Doubleday, Page, and Company.[25] Knopf's quick ascent to editorial
duties at this prominent and ever-expanding publishing house, headed by the
commanding fifty-year-old F. N. Doubleday, coincided with the signature task of
Knopf's eighteen-month tenure at the firm: spearheading an extensive campaign
to acquire and promote Conrad's books, only five of which Doubleday had the
U.S. rights to through Doubleday's takeover of his friend and former partner S. S.
McClure's book company in 1908. Conrad's works had been spread among eight
different U.S. publishers to this point (the product of large advances demanded
by Conrad's agent, J. B. Pinker, that did not pay for themselves and precluded
further investment); and as Doubleday and Knopf worked together to gather
the collective rights to and plan various reissue and collected editions of Conrad's texts, Knopf was given the power to seize on the impending publication of
Chance (1913–14) to coordinate a publicity effort worthy of both his "uncontrol-
lable urge" "as a Conrad disciple" and his already-evident publishing genius.[26]

The first American reader to read the full manuscript of *Chance* when it
came to Doubleday in later 1912, Knopf quickly began a series of supplemen-
tary research efforts: he initiated an important correspondence of trust with
Conrad himself; he contacted the American lawyer John Quinn, who held all
of Conrad's manuscripts and through whose correspondence with Conrad
Knopf discovered much information, including his "hero's [financial] plight";
and he made an appointment with H. L. Mencken at the Baltimore *Sun* offices,
the beginning of what Knopf would come to describe as "my most intimate
friend[ship]" with "[the person who] influenced me more than anyone else."[27]
Following up on these preliminary efforts, Knopf also commissioned two appreciations of Conrad's works, one by John Macy, literary editor of the *Boston*

Herald, that appeared in *Forum*, the other by Alleyne Ireland for *Metropolitan*; he personally contacted numerous booksellers and universities, from Manhattan to Purdue University, to encourage the distribution and adoption of Conrad's texts; he instigated a "Conrad Committee" headed by Booth Tarkington, whose immediate purpose was to facilitate a *Festschrift* of essays by literati (including Edith Wharton) for Conrad, and which quickly became the first formal and multi-thousand member Conrad Society in the world. Perhaps most importantly, moreover, Knopf, on his personal letterhead (to disguise any direct commercial connection with Doubleday), wrote letters of appeal and sent advance copies of *Chance* to several dozen of the most popular and "famous living American writers" of the day—such as Dreiser, Howells, Mary Austin, Jack London, Ellen Glasgow, Harold Bell Wright, Basil King, David Belasco, Rex Beach, Winston Churchill, Meredith Nicholson, Louis Joseph Vance, Robert W. Service, and George Barr McCutcheon—asking for personal testimonials concerning the superlative nature of Conrad's achievements.[28] Knopf mysteriously assured his correspondents, nearly all of whom responded enthusiastically, that if they took the time to write about Conrad, "I would manage somehow to see that his publishers used it"; the result, combined with other solicited and excerpted commentaries, was an inexhaustible fund of critical adulation that has no genuine parallel in Doubleday's advertising efforts before or since that time and that Doubleday liberally and repeatedly drew upon in full-page spreads like the one that appeared in its best-selling magazine, *Country Life in America*, in April 1914 (see Figure 5).[29]

These efforts, as Knopf would later write, set up the publication of *Chance* with such wide exposure and "such a battery of critical praise that its success was ensured and indeed the ground laid for a substantial market for many years for all of Conrad's books"; yet Knopf's true pièce de résistance was his own *Joseph Conrad: The Romance of His Life and of His Books*, a handsome, free twenty-five-page booklet released under Doubleday's imprimatur and Knopf's name in the summer of 1913 in two printings of twenty-five hundred copies each, the second following from the great demand of the first.[30] Attractively combining a central and serious narrative of Conrad's life and books with various photos, icons, testimonials, bibliographic references, manuscript facsimiles, and an excerpted introductory article by James Huneker, Knopf's booklet, itself essentially a compendium of all the work he did on Conrad during his time at Doubleday from fall 1912 through spring 1914, is one of the most important docu-

James Huneker

The famous critic says that Conrad is:

The only man in England today who belongs to the immortal company of Meredith, Hardy and Henry James.

Edwin Björkman

Translator of Strindberg, and well-known critic, says:

I believe that no other writer has surpassed Conrad in the picturing of those two fields of human endeavor — the endlessly variable sea, and the tropics.

J. E. Spingarn

Formerly Professor of Comparative Literature at Columbia University says:

Of course "Chance" is a powerful book, like everything Conrad writes. This, you say, is literature! this is imagination! this, after all, is real English!

H. G. Wells

Famous English Novelist, author of "The Passionate Friends," "Tono-Bungay," etc., says:

One of my chief claims to distinction in the world is that I wrote the first long appreciative review of Joseph Conrad's work.

John Macy

Literary Critic of "The Boston Herald."

Mr. Joseph Conrad's "Chance" is the first important English fiction I have seen this year. It has the imaginative power of "Nostromo" and "Lord Jim" and the infallible excellence of style which has made Mr. Conrad the foremost artist of his time in English prose. He reveals anew his extraordinary perception of the motives and emotions of human beings.

Maria Thompson Daviess

Author of "The Melting of Molly," "Andrew the Glad," etc.

Conrad's "Chance" is a noble piece of work, fine in theme and worked out with great and leisurely scholarliness. I don't think many novels that read as if they were a story within a story, as "Chance" does, could be so wonderfully sustained in incident and interest.

Carl Hovey

Editor of the Metropolitan Magazine says:

Joseph Conrad's "Chance" is a book with an idea. In a manner less grim and tragic, yet scarcely less impressive than that of the Greek drama, Mr. Conrad makes us feel that the biggest events of our lives are frequently controlled by trifling things which almost escape us at the time. *The story is one of those which sink into you, never to be forgotten.*

Rex Beach

Famous novelist, author of "The Iron Trail," "The Net," etc., etc., says.

Joseph Conrad stands for the highest mark in present day English fiction.

I consider him the greatest living author in the English language and have read nearly everything he has written. That his books are not more widely circulated in this country has always been a mystery to me.

Winston Churchill

Author of "The Inside of the Cup," etc.

I have long been an admirer of his work, and it will make me very happy if, through your efforts, his books shall get that attention here which they so richly deserve.

CHANCE

By Joseph Conrad

AT ALL BOOKSELLERS   Net **$1.35**

A reader says of this new story by Conrad:

"Here is a book that so possesses my mind, though I finished it a month ago, that the story of Flora de Barral seems to be in some way a part of my own life. For the first half of the book I kept telling myself that I was not greatly interested, yet I was not content to stop. Unconsciously I was inserting myself into the narrow little lives of the Fynes, into the strange case of the Great de Barral, into the blundering, triumphant love affair of Flora and Anthony.

"In one tremendous chapter where the scattered threads of several lives are caught up, the puzzle of fortuitous human actions pieces itself together into an unforgettable picture, and Chance, that unseen dealer of the cards of life, lays his hand face down upon the table before you. . . . ."

John Galsworthy

The English novelist, author of "The Dark Flower," etc., wrote of Conrad's books in 1908.

The writings of these ten books is probably the only writing of the last twelve years that will enrich the English language to any great extent.

. . . . The essential virtue of such writing consists in its intensely individual point of view, in the manner and method of presentation not in the thing presented. This kind of "living" full-charged, dramatic, all-embracing, could alone be revealed by this one man.
The London Times.

There is great work in the book — great not only as art, for literature does not begin and end there. From these magnanimous pages breathes the spirit of a man who has lived and learnt the lessons of life.
Evening Standard and St. James Gazette.

. . . . The whole book is in the absolute proportion of a work of art . . . . he (Conrad) is one of the really great original creators. His people live in the assurance of an everlasting existence. They are not creatures of time at all, for they are not made simply to reflect modern problems, but are essentially the immortal inhabitants of a peopled world — our own world made deathless.
The English Review.

Every critic will delight in this book as a characteristic piece of Mr. Conrad's workmanship. One can scarcely think of a novel whose writer has made us see more precisely just what he intended. All these have the mark of intimate, final, unforced delineation that is Mr. Conrad's supreme gift.
The Pall Mall Gazette.

It is a red-letter day in the life of a reviewer, when a new novel by Mr. Conrad falls to his lot. . . . Sailormen all the world over must thank Mr. Conrad for adding to his wonderful gallery two such splendid portraits of heroic unselfishness and simple loyalty as Captain Anthony and Mr. Charles Powell of the "Ferndale."
The Spectator.

Coming straight from its spell, indeed still in the entrancement which Mr. Conrad's writing produces, one may well declare the latest to be the best of his books. . . . . In this completeness and relevancy, Mr. Conrad has never surpassed "Chance" — that is to say in the sheer art of the thing.
The London Daily Chronicle.

Basil King

Author of "The Inner Shrine," "The Street Called Straight," "Way Home," etc., etc., says of "Chance."

It is a book to be read with the concentration of the tastes with which one savors good wines. The flashes of observation thrown out by those who tell the tale — wise, humorous, or tender, as the case may be — are as remarkable as the tale itself, like the precious stones set in the binding of a missal. But of the book's many striking qualities none is to me more impressive than the degree to which the concluding sentence justifies the quotation from Thomas Browne on the title page, delimiting the signification of the title itself, and rounding out the sphere of the author's thought. Unity of purpose could go no further.

Meredith Nicholson

Author of "Otherwise Phyllis," "The House of a Thousand Candles," etc., etc., says:

I am one of these benighted people who like style for style's sake, and I look on Conrad as a great master. I know of no contemporary writer who can build a scene before the eye as vividly as Conrad, or who can push a character through the door and leave him to speak for himself as Conrad does.

Kate Langley Bosher

Author of "Mary Cary" and other books.

Joseph Conrad has earned and deserves the place he holds among the best English writers of to-day, and his sincerity of purpose, devotion to art, and skill of craftsmanship are admitted by all intelligent readers of his books. . . . May the people indeed praise him — as well as the critics — for this his last book, and may they not only praise but BUY!!

Walter Prichard Eaton

Well-known critic and short-story writer, says:

It is that story which absorbs us, as it absorbed him, and we are tense always for his next discovery. The method gives to Flora a curious lifelikeness, impossible to describe, for it keeps her perpetually but half-revealed to us. It is the method of an artist who knows full well what he is about.

Gouverneur Morris

Well-known writer of short stories says:

More and more I hear people say: "Have you read Conrad's latest?" Those who haven't read him are not well-read. Those who don't intend to read him are of a foolish and slovenly mental habit. As for those who are engaged in reading him — for the first time — oh, my word, how I envy them!

Doubleday, Page & Company   Garden City, New York

FIGURE 5. Advertisement for *Chance* in *Country Life in America*, April 1914.

ments in the history of Conrad's U.S. cultural production because it offered a template of claims and narratives that other U.S. voices and media endlessly reproduced, elaborated, and interpreted. But if this booklet alone epitomizes the plausibility of (fellow publisher) George Doran's claim, "To Knopf more than to any one person, Conrad owes his fame and popularity and the reading public a debt of gratitude,"[31] what we must emphasize—before turning to what is actually the more important figure and cultural institution of Doubleday, but against the grain of traditional Conrad scholarship, which loses its limited interest in Knopf the moment he departs Doubleday—is that Knopf's active facilitation of a modern U.S. culture of Conrad does not cease when, after leaving Doubleday and spending a short interim year at Mitchell Kennerly, he starts his own publishing house in May 1915. Though Alfred A. Knopf did not publish a single book by Conrad, most of what his firm did publish during at least the first decade of its existence was in some way powerfully linked to the expansion and the precedent of Conrad's U.S. cultural interest and authority. Knopf's initial ambition was to publish innovative (U.S.) American fiction, but both the scarcity of that resource and the rapidly internationalizing circumstances of World War I altered his vision to what would become his firm's defining focus and innovating achievement: the task of "introducing major foreign authors to American audiences."[32] The parameters of the "foreign" here were as broad as they were distinctly, catholically Conradian. Like the Polish-English novelist Knopf had championed so successfully at Doubleday, the first novelist the Knopf firm published was Poland's "greatest living writer" Stanisław Przbyszewski.[33] On the model of Conrad's exotic cross-cultural British imperial fiction, and with Conrad's personal endorsement, the first commercially successful Knopf novel was W. H. Hudson's *Green Mansions* (1916). Apropos of the rich "Slavic" subtexts of so much of Conrad's U.S. allure, the Knopf firm's first major publishing innovation was to seize on how "hard put" "the Allies were . . . to explain their Russian partner" as an occasion to acquire and publish in the United States the many translations of Russian fiction then available in England.[34] And overall, very much in the capaciously "foreign" and foreignizing vein of (at least one vision of) Conrad's fiction, a fundamental project of the Knopf firm during the 1910s and 1920s was to secure an unprecedented international range of fiction in translation—by authors who would come to include, among nine Nobel Prize winners, Maupassant, Gide, Mann, Kafka, Hamsun, Gibran, Sigrid Unset, Gogol, Andrejev, Dostoevski, Bunin, Ladislas Reymont, F. E. Sillanpää, and Johannes Jensen —and to provide this fiction to a large American audience. Many of these international Knopf authors were advertised, or rather culturally translated, as having a "foreign air" or "method curiously like that of Joseph Conrad."[35] A number of Knopf's most prominent British and American texts also kept Conrad focally in view: among them, Richard Curle's *The Echo of Voices* (1917) and Thomas Beer's seminal biography *Stephen Crane: A Study in American Letters* (1923), both introduced by Conrad; the twelve-volume complete edition of Crane (1924), introduced by a number of conspicuous Conradians; the novels of Joseph Hergesheimer, one of Knopf's two star American novelists and continually compared to Conrad; Edward Garnett's *Friday Night: Literary Criticism and Appreciations* (1922), which contains several defining essays on Conrad; and finally, much of the work of Henry Louis Mencken, whose *Book of Prefaces, American Mercury, The American Language*, and many other books were all published by Knopf. The Knopf publishing house was, in short, a vital and continuous instrument of Conrad's modern U.S. production, both extending and extended itself through the license of Conrad's U.S. cultural interest, and in terms more or less commensurate with the "foreignizing," aristocratizing ("highbrow" but widely directed) priorities of Knopf's close friend Mencken.

But Doubleday, Page was in fact the far more consequential publishing engine behind "our Conrad"—not by perpetuating the terms of the Menckenian pole of Conrad's U.S. production but by facilitating a rich field of tension and counter-point with it. Doubleday, a large commercial publishing house whose formidable energy and intelligence should be underestimated no less than Mencken's, dur-ing the very years of its U.S. cultivation of Conrad was consolidating its status among the world's most massive and profitable publishing institutions; it did so, as the previous epigraph from Kipling suggests, through an aggressive "spiritual" expansion of the dimensions of the "field of cultural production"[36] that it could successfully mass-capitalize. With specific respect to Conrad, two aspects of Doubleday's efforts must be foregrounded: the first is the sheer enormity of the enterprise. It is important to remember (and easy for us, not the U.S. moderns themselves, to forget) that *every year from 1914 to 1926* with the exception of two saw the release of at least one genuinely new Conrad book: a novel or volume of short fiction or prose that had never been published in any book form before, two in 1925. This steady stream of new releases, each heavily advertised, Doubleday flanked with enormous collateral distributive efforts during this general period. These efforts include individual reissues of most previously published Conrad texts; no less than five complete collected editions of Conrad's works, ranging from mass-market soft-cover editions to limited autograph sets; at least four selected volumes of Conrad's tales; one volume of Conrad's prefaces and no less than five anthologies containing significant autobiographical expression by Conrad; four volumes of personal testimonial concerning Conrad, including the many notable voices gathered in George T. Keating's *A Conrad Memorial Library* (1929); two editions of Conrad's letters, including the definitive edition for many decades to come (G. Jean-Aubry's *Joseph Conrad: Life and Letters* [1927]); and several volumes of literary criticism of Conrad, including the two earliest and most important book-length studies of their time, Richard Curle's *Joseph Conrad: A Study* (1914) and Wilson Follett's *Joseph Conrad: A Short Study* (1915).[37] These were incredible efforts for a living author (during most of this time), and they were further complemented by Doubleday's relentless and often quite inspired advertising opportunism. Far beyond Knopf's original campaign of 1913, most Doubleday reissues of Conrad include some "new" element of individuation requiring fresh purchase for the full or "authentic" experience of Conrad;[38] all new Conrad titles come with clever slogans affirming their Conradian essentiality and singularity;[39] autographs, limited editions, collector's items, and special author's notes are a constant lure; a flood of pictures, maps, and biographical sketches of Conrad *personalize* Conrad's allure much more so than in Britain;[40] various contests are organized involving Conrad's works, generally given out as prizes for literary and literary-critical competitions, but once the subject of a contest to complete (Conrad's unfinished) *Suspense* in the *Saturday Review of Literature* in 1925;[41] and all the while, perhaps Doubleday's shrewdest stroke is the repeated circulation of the disclaimer "The art of self-advertising, which is pretty generally practiced by writers on both sides of the Atlantic, is altogether unknown to [Joseph Conrad]."[42]

Finally, in addition to its own direct efforts, perhaps Doubleday's greatest contribution to the U.S. proliferation of Conrad lay in its strategic insinuation of Conrad into, or simply making Conrad available for, other (and quite diverse) advertising and media outlets. Whether placing Conrad's new "Author's Notes" in bourgeois venues like *Bookman* (NY) or in the (newly) avant-garde *Dial*;[43] whether advancing its critical studies of Conrad in *Bookman* or having them extended in the genteel *Atlantic Monthly* (Boston);[44] whether lavishly advertising Conrad in or leaking suggestive information about Conrad to the major mass New York newspapers or to the trendy *Saturday Review of Literature* (one of whose central editors, Christopher Morley, once worked for Doubleday); whether materially facilitating an academic culture of Conrad at Yale or helping to give rise to a middle-class book-club craze for Conrad in the "Monday Study Club of Sabetha, Kansas" and other "multitudinous, select and earnest Browning Societies dotted about the Middle West States of America [that] have enthusiastically turned themselves into Conrad circles,"[45] Doubleday disseminated, transposed, and infused Conrad with remarkable latitude. It eschewed no opportunity to transfuse Conrad into the capillary networks of U.S. discourse and culture, into the sinews of various sectors of social "apparatus" commensurate with Doubleday's purposes; and where it did not directly extend or cross-wire Conrad, it helped materially give rise to a much larger cultural and institutional network of parallel and commensurate interest and investment in Conrad. Hence, far beyond its own immediate agency, Doubleday, with force not only simultaneous with but also as formidable as Mencken's, engendered the material foundation, opportunity, and momentum through which a much wider arc of "our Conrad" became possible.

But Doubleday, of course, as a large commercial publisher sought not the differentiation, polarization, or strategic antagonization of Conrad's U.S. audiences on the model of Mencken, but rather a harmonizing image and register of Conrad through which to appeal to them all, on which to sell Conrad to them all. That this does not simply, exclusively, mean the dilution or "popularization" of Conrad for mass appeal—indeed, that Doubleday's Conrad is no less complex in its heterotopic premises or keen and catholic in its sense of cultural-political engagement than Mencken's Conrad—is suggested by an article that appeared in *Bookman* (NY) in July 1919, its information clearly prompted by Doubleday, its closing quotation deriving from an important letter Conrad wrote Doubleday that the latter circulated widely during this period. What's especially important to note about the excerpt below is the *difference* between the "popular" remarks with which it begins and the "democrat[ic]" claims of the Conrad quotation with which it closes; the context here is the surging success of the new Conrad novel that, as noted in the Introduction, became the second best-selling novel in the United States in 1919:

The Arrow of Gold, published late in the fall and now in its fifth large printing, has already exceeded by over one-third the sale of *Chance*, Conrad's next best seller, which appeared five years ago, and by more than half again that of any of his other novels. Just before the appearance of his novel Conrad had remarked in a letter to his publishers:

"I am sufficiently a democrat to detest the idea of being a writer of any 'coterie' of some small self-appointed aristocracy in the vast domain of art and letters. As a matter of feeling—not as a matter of business—I want to be read by many eyes and all kinds of them like that." [46]

Doubleday generally marketed *The Arrow of Gold*, the best-selling (to this point) and also probably most uneven of Conrad's underappreciated later fiction, as "A Great Love Story by Joseph Conrad":[47] a "popular" frame very much in line with *Bookman*'s opening emphasis on high sales, this information itself clearly provided by Doubleday. As Gene Moore has shown, moreover, this kind of "popular" framing was also crucial to another important development of this moment, a strong wave of U.S. *cinematic* adaptations of Conrad: a phenomenon that, if it was encouraged by Conrad's own arrival in the United States in May 1923 with a lecture entitled "Author and Cinematograph," which Conrad first delivered at Doubleday's plant, was also largely made possible by Doubleday's prior demonstration that Conrad could be a "popular" artist in the first place.[48] But the closing "democrat[ic]" quotation from Conrad, equally orchestrated and disseminated by Doubleday, by no means simply mirrors the terms of *Bookman*'s "popular" opening frame. For even as it presents Conrad as "sufficiently a democrat to detest" exclusive association with an artistic "aristocracy," it implicitly validates Conrad's appeal in the latter circles; far from presenting Conrad as an exclusively "popular" author, Doubleday carefully foregrounds Conrad articulating a plural desire "to be read by *many eyes* and *all kinds of them* like that." Even more important, just as "aristocracy" in the Menckenian lexicon (where the term, of course, is expressly associated *with* Conrad) enfolds a wide range of social concerns and critique, by no means simply reducible to any class of socioeconomic opportunity or aesthetic taste, so, too, the converse term "democracy" is an enormously elastic coinage with no absolute anchoring in either populist demographics and political theory or the standards of the "popular" culture industry. Indeed, as any survey of book titles published in the United States during this period readily reveals, the term "democratic" signifies, less as a strictly anchored term at all, than as a highly charged and widely transposable rhetorical means not only of championing and connecting any of a number of diverse and self-declared "new" or emblematic U.S. policy proposals—in areas of world politics (Wilson), domestic governance (Croly), opinion management (Lippmann), philosophy and public education (Dewey), ethnicity (Kallen/Boune), journalism, literature, art, and much more —*but of championing and connecting these visions as distinctively or triumphally "American."* What "democracy" ultimately means at this moment of U.S. modernity, this is to say—and this, without evacuating the term of all grounding in a certain body of political ideas and their "traveling" application elsewhere; this too, as a means of emphasizing and understanding why *both* conservative and progressive voices lay such strong claims to the term— is the ratification and confirmation of "American" distinctiveness, aspiration, and/or collectivity at the most general levels of hegemonic narrative formation. This highly flexible rhetorical elision of the "American" and the "democratic," opening itself up to a wide diversity of specific applications and locations of Conrad, is the more general harmonizing frame that Doubleday sets in motion for the U.S. public: appealing as capaciously and affirmatively across "American" audiences as Mencken does negatively, acerbically. Whereas Mencken presents Conrad as the negation of any attempt at American self-confirmation, Doubleday, with the same broad elasticity, the same shrewd sense of both Conrad's wide contemporary world-historical resonance and the depth of Conrad's capacity for heterotopic provocation, presents Conrad as a "democratic" confirmation, not simply of any particular vision of American order but of the triumph or at least dignity of American assertions of order generally.

What, then, were some of the specific terms and historical circumstances of Doubleday's wartime construction of Conrad? What were some of the specific political concerns through which Doubleday both proliferated and replicated a larger *anti*-Menckenian pole of Conrad's production, itself a species of cascading dialogic complexity? The answer begins with a point-for-point refutation of each element of the anti-Anglo-Saxon critique presented in the previous chapter. We begin with the vantage of U.S. international relations, centering on the issue of U.S. participation in and conduct of the war. The key terms of Conrad's articulation in this context are suggested by the three central icons with which Doubleday floods its earlier promotion of Conrad: first, the Winged Victory of Samothrace, the famous Hellenic statue of the goddess Nike descending to herald military victory, an icon of militaristic participation and affirmation (Figure 6) and the key image through which Doubleday advertised *Victory* (1915) (Figure 7); second, a circular engraved image of a storm-bound ship at sea (Figure 8), Doubleday's trademark image for Conrad's works, and one inscribing, as we will explore later, within its "adventurous" aura and ambiguous maritime iconography a deep *military-patriotic structure of feeling*; and third, the image of Rudyard Kipling, the ultimate iconic literary linkage between the specific righteousness of the British allied war cause and a larger

FIGURE 6. "Share in the Victory," War Savings Stamps Poster, U.S. Treasury Department, March 1918.

A New Novel
"Victory"
By Joseph Conrad

H. L. MENCKEN
Editor of "Smart Set" says:

THIS is the story of Axel Heyst and the girl from a travelling Ladies' Orchestra with whom Heyst runs away and lives on the almost desert island of Samburan in the Southern Pacific, amid the ruined buildings of the once flourishing Tropical Belt Coal Company.

¶ Thus stated, this new romance of Mr. Conrad's sounds prosaic enough, but in reality nothing about Heyst is prosaic. A man of title in his own country, a dreamer, unfitted for life by an impractical and skeptical parent, Heyst wakes up to a new quality in the world of things when a girl comes into his vision. From that day in Schomberg's hotel when he answers the look of mute appeal in Lena's eyes, a new current of life sweeps Heyst along.

¶ Among those who knew him, Heyst and elopement were unthinkable, and yet it is this "looker-on at life" who plans the details of the escape from Schomberg's, enlists the help of the graven-image wife of the hotel-keeper, and snatches the girl away from under the nose of the infuriated German.

¶ And then begins that strange life of Heyst and Lena amid the ruined splendors of the Tropical Belt Coal Company's headquarters on Samburan. Vague filterings of news come through Davidson, who takes his vessel past Samburan every month in the hope of being signalled for help. But it is only with the visit to Samburan of Mr. Jones and Ricardo, that well-mated pair of scoundrels, that the veil is lifted on the life of Heyst and the girl and the reader understands for the first time the tenderness and the pathos of this strange romance.

¶ "Victory" is specially notable for the directness of the narrative. In this respect it is the complete antithesis of "Chance." And yet it has much in common with "Chance," especially that quality of evoking from the reader a compassionate affection for the two souls that ever strive for, and ever miss, the fulness of understanding. If Flora de Barral, of "Chance," is to be written down first among Conrad's women, Lena, of "Victory," shall be her sister. Seated pale, distracted, at bay before Ricardo, every sense battling beneath a supernatural calm for Heyst's life, she will remain a radiant memory, inexpressibly tender and appealing.

"A narrative that gets under way on the very first page, and proceeds uninterruptedly to a *sforzando* and melodramatic close. The story sets a new style for Conrad, and one obviously likely to increase his audience. Not even 'Falk' or 'Typhoon' has more naked action in it. Conrad applies to the unfolding of it all the resources of his extraordinary art, and particularly all his gift for the dark, the threatening, the sinister. From the moment that Jones and Ricardo reach the crazy island jetty, sun-blistered, purple-faced, half dead of thirst—from this moment to the last scene of all, there is no halting or turning aside. Put upon paper by a lesser man it would become a mere penny-dreadful. But as it is told by Conrad it takes on the Homeric proportions of an epic, a saga. Told in a straightforward, almost bald manner, with no apparent effort to build up effects, it yet leaves upon the mind a picture almost as vivid and as haunting as that left by "Heart of Darkness." It is closer to the conventional novel than anything else he has done, and yet it is full of his characteristic touches."

Copyright Underwood & Underwood

"Deep Sea" Edition of Joseph Conrad
A SET OF SIX
A New Book of Short Stories
Containing five short stories never before published in America, and "The Duel," formerly published as "The Point of Honor"

The New York Times says of the stories:
"In every one there are touches peculiarly Conradian—little searchlights turned on, as it were, that give the reader flashes of insight into the minds of the characters, or down into dark places in the social machine."
Cloth, net, $1.35; "Deep Sea" Leather, net, $1.50

OTHER VOLUMES

Almayer's Folly	An Outcast of the Islands
The Nigger of the Narcissus	Typhoon
Youth	Falk
'Twixt Land and Sea	Chance
Romance	Lord Jim

In "Deep Sea" Leather, net, $1.50

C.L.A.
5-15

GENTLEMEN:

Enclosed find....
for which please send

me .... copies of
"Victory" just published.
(Price $1.35 plus postage).

NAME.......................

ADDRESS...................
....

SEND THIS TO YOUR BOOKSELLER OR TO DOUBLEDAY, PAGE & CO.

One Reader says:
"As I read I marvelled at the vividness of Heyst and Lena, the affection I felt for them in their mutual misunderstanding and their helplessness in the clutches of Ricardo and "plain Mr. Jones."

Those who have never read Conrad will find "Victory" the best introduction to his genius.
Net, $1.35

Garden City Doubleday, Page & Co. New York

FIGURE 7. Advertisement for *Victory* in *Country Life in America*, May 1915.

FIGURE 8. Doubleday's trademark Conrad icon from the cover of Alfred Knopf, *Joseph Conrad: The Romance of His Life and of His Books* (1913).

Anglo-American sense of imperial concord and "Anglo-Saxon" cultural-racial solidarity. Doubleday's prior U.S. marketing of Kipling's works provided the direct precedent and stimulus for its Conrad campaign and is a continual source of cross-reference and ideological linkage within it. Let us explore these three central images and the complex cultural-political fields of their elaboration and dialogic contestation in order.

Nike, with wings and without, like its semantic translation in the English word *victory*, served as a central figure in U.S. patriotic wartime and postwar discourse. Her image abounds in patriotic poems, advertisements, hortatory political tracts, and pictorial representations—very much in the vein of the government-sponsored war poster "Share in the Victory: Buy War Savings

Stamps" (Figure 6), put out by the U.S. Treasury in March 1918.[49] Of all the Nikes, the Winged Victory in particular, its eternal classical lines (derided by contemporary avant-garde figures like Italian futurist F. N. Marinetti) co-existing with the damage and loss of its head and arms over time, epitomized in the United States during this time a spirit of military commitment, sacrifice, participation, moral value, and ultimately glorious celebration. Hence, whereas for Mencken the title of Conrad's *Victory*, the most important text in Conrad's U.S. popularization, signals an ironic blast at precisely this kind of culture of righteous war promotion and patriotic self-galvanization, Doubleday seizes the reverse opportunity. By presenting *Victory* in the image of the Winged Victory, as the later "Share in the Victory" poster makes deadly clear, Doubleday not only thoroughly aligns Conrad *with* U.S. war preparation and promotion efforts; Doubleday also suggests that Conrad's works are somehow fundamentally of and about, framed and inscribed by, the experiences, hardships, and values of war in itself. If Mencken's Conrad emphatically "makes war on nothing," Doubleday positions Conrad to be "prepared" (key word) to comprehend, accommodate, and be thoroughly implicated by war generally.

This strategic construction of Conrad as a (pro-)war writer had actually caught fire in the United States well before the first American release of *Victory* in March 1915. As is typical of Doubleday's self-integrating and adaptive relation to other mainstream public institutions, this construction originally emerged through a series of complementary efforts between Doubleday and the mass-commercial press dating back to the war's beginning. When the war broke out in Europe in August 1914, Conrad and his family, for purely personal and coincidental reasons, had just arrived to visit friends in Poland, where they quickly found themselves behind enemy lines. The *New York Times*, among other major U.S. newspapers, relying to an important extent on "information" leaked by Doubleday, could not make enough of this circumstance. On October 4, 1914, an alarmist piece in the *Times* reports that "no one knows" the whereabouts of and "nothing" has been "heard" from Conrad since he left for Poland in late July; his friends "fear that his being a Pole by birth and also a member of the British Royal Naval Reserve" (Conrad was not in the RNR) "may make his journey dangerous."[50] On October 22, the article "Joseph Conrad Is War Bound" relates new rumors that "the Polish-English author is safe in a little town in the mountains of Galicia."[51] On November 8, the *Times* enfolds the war with a novel Conrad would not pick up for the next four years: "Word has been received from Joseph Conrad, for whose safety his friends entertained much fear, that he is living in a small town in the Polish mountains, where he is hard at work on his new novel, 'The Big Rescue.'"[52] On December 20, the *Times* further mistakenly militarizes the novel Conrad had completed before departing England: "The new novel which Joseph Conrad has been writing in a Polish village where he was *immured by the war* will be published in the Spring by Doubleday, Page & Company. It is called *Victory*, and will reintroduce to his readers a character in one of the author's former books."[53] Later, *Bookman* (NY) reports that "it is possible that in his next novel Joseph Conrad will relate his experiences in those months following the outbreak of war when he was isolated from the rest of the world in Poland"; "it becomes more and more certain that Mr. Conrad's experiences in getting out of Poland were of the sort to make interesting reading."[54] Here, the opportunistic synergy of commercial publisher (Doubleday) and mass commercial press alike combines to produce a "war" writer and at least three "war novels"; this synergy is further extended in its *American* appeal by dramatic reports of the Conrad family's "rescue" by U.S. Ambassador (to Austria-Hungary) Frederic Courtland Penfield;[55] and finally, lest we believe Doubleday's claim that "the art of self-advertising is . . . altogether unknown to Mr. Conrad," Conrad himself, assisted by the staunchly Anglophile *Boston Evening Transcript*, promotes this war frame by swiftly publishing upon returning to England a series of essays concerning his wartime journey to Poland. "Poland Revisited," a consolidation of these essays, has little to do with Poland itself. Rather, as the use of the word *war* in every one of the serial titles that ran in the *Transcript* in March and April 1917 suggests—"The Shock of War: Through Germany to Cracow," "To Poland in War-Time: A Journey into the East," "Poland Revisited: The North Sea on the Eve of War," and "My Return to Cracow: Poland in War-Time"—"Poland Revisited" fundamentally concerns the Conrads' journey *through Germany* amid looming circumstances of war; it concentrates on the discrepancy between Conrad's captivating Polish memories and his inability to recognize the omnipresent wartime menace of contemporary Germany. "Poland Revisited" is the first of several essays in which Conrad declares himself unequivocally and in emphatically *moral* terms *behind* the British war effort and *against* Germany; the essay indeed first appeared in its complete form in Edith Wharton's Allied war charity volume, *The Book of the Homeless* (Scribner 1916); it is the beginning of several Conrad-related Allied war charity efforts that would include the living-picture show "An Evening with Conrad's People" that American Book Company publisher W. T. H. Howe organized in Cincinnati in June or July 1917;[56] and for the first but not last time, it presents Conrad in nonfictional prose form not only endorsing the British war enterprise but flirting with the relation between his own writings and experience and war.

Victory is an interesting text in this context precisely because of the *lack* of simplicity in its reception—notwithstanding Doubleday's strong "military" framing of the novel, Mencken's strong framing of the reverse, and a critical tradition that to this day puzzles over and generally demurs at the novel's "popular" status without ever meaningfully inquiring into to whom and why the novel was popular in the first place.[57] Although many other Conrad texts became popular in the United States during this time because of their ability to be formulated in terms of sharp assertions of American war promotion and/or Order, *Victory*, the most "popular" text of them all, struck a particular chord with the U.S. public in 1915, not principally because of the polemical and partisan positioning to which it was ultimately quite amenable, but rather because of the objective and uncanny accuracy with which its story—i.e., of a would-be isolationist and neutral (Heyst), fatally menaced by an encroaching rivalry of sinister European forces, German (Schomberg) and British (Jones and Ricardo), all subject to a final moral warning (Lena's) to enter the field of world action on the side of right before it is too late—directly mirrored U.S. anxieties of war entry and world relation during its pre-entry and nominally "neutral" years. (*Victory* also rendered this U.S. intimacy, as I have argued elsewhere, in a new accessible "democratic" idiom and form, such that its implications, for arguably the first time in Conrad's career, were widely publicly legible and could be read back, pedagogically, into other Conrad texts.)[58] U.S. responses to the "popular" *Victory*, often directly prompted by its popularizing publisher and related institutions, were consequently by no means generally simplistic or monovocal. For example, in her first of many articles on Conrad, Elia Peattie, the pioneering feminist, journalist, and prolific fictionalist, begins her review of *Victory* in the *Chicago Daily Tribune* on May 1, 1915, by commending Conrad's publishers for the map of Conrad's works that appears at the outset of *Victory*. This map, Peattie argues, allows the reader to readily apprehend the wide range of world spaces, "spots well known and spots little known," that have "their established place in the English imagination" because of this "most geographical of novelists"; in addition, the map draws attention to the general educative use and function of Conrad's fiction: that of reporting back, based on Conrad's broad and genuine world experience, to tell "the folk 'at home' how foreigners of various complexions were doing things." The "foreign" world that *Victory* reports on and compendiously allegorizes, however, is noticeably grim: a site "of monstrous jealousies, of immeasurable meanness, [of] predatory and slimy creatures, having fangs filled with poison," for whom "violence is an instinct" and the only pretense to liberty is "the hideous freedom that man eating beasts have."[59] Indeed, the moral lesson of *Victory*, far from any ultimate affirmation of the redemptive spiritual value of human love and solidarity or the need for timely and active intervention in the greater sphere of world affairs (which is how the conventional reading of *Victory* would come to run),[60] is relentlessly negative and haunting (or rather, haunted). Dark at every turn, just as Edward Said would suggest of the novel six months before he died nearly ninety years later,[61] *Victory* is a story that severely charts "how Heyst, being *betrayed into friendship* by force of circumstances, laid the foundations of his destruction, and how, later, developing pity and love, his overthrow was completed." It is not Heyst's "inhumanity but his humanity [that] brought him to disaster"; there is no redeeming force of human love and solidarity, of moral or social "victory," however venerable these qualities may be, that the "foreign" world of this novel is capable of supporting; and even Lena's final sacrifice of her own life for Heyst at the very end, Conrad's pièce de résistance, is just as haunted by concrete and costly meaninglessness as the "cloak of mystic femininity" through which Conrad narratively dramatizes Lena's (patriarchal) marginalization, psychic victimization, meaning-only-for-others, throughout.[62]

Peattie's *Victory* is, in short, an *isolationist* harbinger of redemptionless and self-immolating entanglement with the foreign world; and it is not difficult to see in this profoundly apprehensive portrait of "Conrad's brutal but fascinating realism," its chilling anxieties with respect not only to the truly sinister elements in the world but also to moralized and idealized fantasies of "friendship" and alliance that stand to leave one no better off than Lena (in an inspired feminist cross-correlation with the larger world-political critique) in such a world, the imprint of Peattie's own isolationist anxieties at this moment, her own tenuously Bryanite antiwar views[63]—not to mention the strong isolationist political views for which Colonel Robert McCormick's *Chicago Tribune* papers would long be well known. But just as Peattie's reading is not simple ideology but rather a genuinely haunted engagement with a textscape whose disconcertingly inexorable clutches she finds it difficult, in a Gothic metaphor she repeatedly uses, to "escape,"[64] so, too, two weeks before in the *New Republic*, Edith Borie had reviewed *Victory* from an equally vexed but very different point of view: one also, not coincidentally, framed by the politics of the magazine for which she was writing. Like Peattie, Borie foregrounds the contemporary value of Conrad in the wide and complex access to the "surrounding world" his works afford; this is a point underscored in its timeliness by large advertisements for *Victory* in the *New Republic* that Doubleday juxtaposes with advertisements of various "foreign" texts explicitly linked to diverse hot spots in the Great War.[65] Also like Peattie, Borie, writing for a magazine whose official policy at the time was no less "our neutrality"[66] than the *Chicago Daily Tribune*'s, offers a narrative aligning *Victory* with world detachment. The argument here, though, extends not from the irredeemably sinister or untrustworthy character of the foreign world but from Conrad's distinctive *narrative* "aloofness as a creator" in *Victory*. Drawing on now-famous language from *A Personal Record* in which Conrad rejects an inherently (i.e., mystically, ontologically) "ethical view" for a "purely spectacular view" of the universe (*PR* 92), Borie presents the narrative distance and artistic self-sufficiency of *Victory* as a signature example of the "detached curiosity" and "steeled heart" with which Conrad insists that we gaze down, or out, at the world of human affairs to neutrally discern rather than morally fabricate its truth. But such "serene detachment," its "high clean wind" of probative but ultimately only passive power, is not an end in itself in Conrad. Indeed, "Look on—make no sound," the deathbed counsel of Heyst's philosopher-father, rejecting alike any "belief in action" and any moral or conceptual foundation on which activist intervention might be based, is precisely the "devil's work" that *Victory* presents so as to challenge. Even in a world of radical uncertainty and complex moral flux and duplicity, Borie argues, ultimate "powerlessness to trust recklessly in the human heart, and to proclaim trust, must seem to Conrad an evil state of soul characteristic of the 'man of the last hour.'" Lena, like all of Conrad's "women supremely," is rife with "actuality" and "tense with life at its best" precisely in the fullness and agency with which she struggles against this "state of soul." In the end, in "the last hour," "doubt, taking refuge in proud silence," is the central "theme" that *Victory* decisively, if not completely unequivocally, rejects.[67]

Here again we find the complex yet visceral impress of politics. The critical reference to "taking refuge in proud silence" is an unmistakable rejoinder to the contemporary (Wilsonian, at this moment) antiwar slogan "Too proud to fight"; it positions *Victory* against that neutral and isolationist position—and yet it takes Borie a good while, with much unresolved tension concerning her opening emphasis on "detachment," to arrive at this ultimate conclusion. More generally, we may say that throughout her article Borie articulates *Victory* with a double consciousness that alternates between values of objective remove and of righteous action and commitment. This ambivalence mirrors the *New Republic*'s own sliding and self-conflicted stance on the war in earlier 1915: on the one hand, officially proclaiming a position of "detached neutrality"; on the other, inclined from the beginning toward intervention alongside Britain in a cause whose morality, public trust, considered pragmatism, and ultimate urgency of military "victory" the magazine would soon actively exclaim. Borie, hence, reproduces the ideological complexities of the *New Republic* in and through her reading of *Victory*—and she does so in a manner that, like Peattie though to very different ends, strategically enfolds gender into her analysis, making women's empowerment, recognition, and agency a yardstick by which Conrad himself measures the "victories" of the world.

A third and final example of the complexity of earlier U.S. engagements with *Victory*, each in some way affiliated with the *assertion* of U.S. boundary or idealized order (whether isolationist or internationalist), each also in some way prompted by the remarkably flexible Doubleday and the general context of war, appears in the work of Wilson Follett, among academics, the most sensitive U.S. literary critic of this era to write on Conrad.[68] Follett, a Harvard-educated literary scholar and pianist who between 1909 and 1918 taught literature at Texas A&M, Dartmouth, and Brown, thereafter leaving the profession to become a longtime editor at Yale University Press, wrote during the 1910s alone several articles and three critical books foregrounding Conrad: the first, the serious 111-page monograph *Joseph Conrad: A Short Study* (1915), was published and distributed by Doubleday as a promotional freebie.[69] All of Follett's Conrad works from this era share a similar theme: "the ironic or tragic unfitness of things," the discrepancy and tension between the meaninglessness, entropy, and anarchic tendencies of "ultimate" realities of self and world, and the "immediate" strategies of human imagination and action through which human meaning and social comity and concord can be effected.[70] Follett's is a *hopeful* if also perennially thwarted Conrad: someone for whom the ultimate indifference of the universe is actually a "blank signed cheque" on which human meaning and solidarity stand to be written, against whatever residual forces of antagonism and irreconciliation invariably remain; someone for whom the "indestructible" and "inexorable" "barriers" separating peoples, plunging them into conflict and forestalling "the secret aspiration of mankind—the dream of brotherhood," is always the primary challenge to be overcome.[71] It is clear from the beginning of *Joseph Conrad: A Short Study*—in a sequence of readings that begins with *Victory* and frequently returns to it as Conrad's purest "symbolic" expression of this problem—that Follett's interest in Conrad is rooted in the parallel circumstances and urgent needs of the comity-challenged, conflict-ridden, war-ravaged contemporary world. Follett would come to make this connection explicitly in the preface to *Some Modern Novelists* (1918), entitled "The War and the Reader"; in that preface he calls for a "new humanism" (invoking but fundamentally critiquing the frame of Harvard influence Irving Babbitt) predicated on "modern" textuality squarely addressing the world's contemporary problems. In that volume's culminating essay on Conrad, Follett writes: "[Conrad] deals not only with a world in which East is East and West is West, but also a world in which everyone is foreign to his neighbor. The secret and invisible thing that makes us alien each to the other is the thing that Mr. Conrad is always trying to disentangle." How, then, in a world as bitterly antagonized and atomized as that of *Victory* or earth from 1914 to 1918, is one to form large human structures of understanding and community? How is it possible to "unite men in a democracy of endeavor" such that "the instinct of comradeship [becomes] made flesh"?[72]

As do Peattie and Borie, Follett answers this question through a double frame of vision. On the one hand, as early as *Joseph Conrad: A Study* though with increasing sharpness as the war progresses, Follett argues that the very radical vulnerability of imagined communities to "ultimate" predatory disruptions puts a premium on *national* structures of solidarity; as Conrad puts it at the end of *The Mirror of the Sea*, "In this ceaseless rush of shadows and shades, that, like the fantastic forms of clouds cast darkly upon the waters on a windy day, fly past us to fall headlong below the hard edge of an implacable horizon, we must turn to the national spirit which, superior in its force and continuity to good and evil fortune, can alone give us the feeling of an enduring existence and of an invincible power against the fates" (194). Sometimes, Follett argues, Conrad hypostatizes such appeals to "nationality" in the form of the "ship"; even more importantly, they are at other times advanced, as in the case of Heyst, through *negative* images like those of the expatriate: "In other words,

Conrad's mode of arguing the supreme worth of human solidarity is to exhibit the whole array of difficulties which tragically interfere with that ideal, sometimes turning the pursuit of it into appalling tragedy. *Writing about the terrible loneliness of expatriates, [Conrad] is really celebrating the indispensable security of home and country.* In fact, his consistent way of affirming anything is to deny its opposite." Follett, indeed, frequently glosses Conrad through key words— "Conscience, Service, Fidelity, Honor," "Loyalty"—which in the United States at *any* time during the Great War would have carried nationalist and military overtones.[73] Yet in "The War and the Reader," Follett also emphasizes, without any reference to or delimitation of "nation" at all, that the primary task of the contemporary novelist is "always . . . to cross or break down the innumerable barriers of race, of creed, of class, to increase the feeling of kinship among all the members and groups of the human guild." This panhuman idiom is, in fact, far more typical of Follett: ever given to emphasize "a world so shrunken we must live at the center of it"; that "art is valuable, in short, because it is a negation of all the prides and prejudices and hates. . . . It is one of many weapons, one of many promises of eventual triumph, in the context of which every other is subordinate and ephemeral—the struggle for [world] union, the war against war." In the essay on Conrad that follows, Follett offers an internationalist vision of Conrad—one predicated on an impulse toward "World Federation"—whose premise is the precedent of the nation, but whose purpose, whose indomitable challenge, is precisely to transcend it:

Briefly, [nationalized] man triumphs over his individual differences so far as to conclude that fellowship must be the supreme logic of creation. Then, having to that extent learned the lesson of brotherhood, man looks outside the immediate world of his own kind, and discovers that fellowship is not the logic of creation at all—that in the chaos of warring species and mute constellations there *is* no decipherable human logic. And again he despairs of the frail human sodality. If the universe is framed for lawlessness, if disaster is as natural in it as triumph, and war as inevitable as peace, why should man take the trouble to invent loyalties and organized brotherhoods? Why should he not assert the separateness of his identity and get what he can for himself out of a precarious existence, let what may happen to others? *These are, of course, the questions raised by such pessimism as that of Heyst in Victory . . . [and Mr. Conrad] answers that, if the universal affair is desperate, it is so much the more necessary for the human affair to be hopeful, and that men's standing together against the universal threat is one way to cheat adverse destiny.*[74]

The "universal affair" here means human existence considered at its largest world horizon of collective and concordant possibility. What Follett is proposing is a nationalist and internationalist vision of Conrad perfectly fused, the former enabling the latter: a perfectly plausible conjunction in this moment, of course, because what Follett is essentially confirming (and to some degree, anticipating as early as 1915) in the image of Conrad is the very combination of U.S. nationalism and U.S.-style liberal internationalism, each idealized in its most effective and most culturally sensitive light,[75] through which the Wilson administration guided the United States into and through the war. Follett's reading of *Victory*, this is to say, takes the unqualified internationalist and interventionist step on which Borie and the earlier *New Republic* equivocate; in doing so, it confirms and renders coincident *two* conceptions of American order, U.S. nationalism and U.S.-style liberal internationalism, which would quickly come apart after the war and the debacle of the Paris Peace Conference—perhaps accounting for the fact that Follett, the very best academic reader of Conrad in the United States in the 1910s, would leave academics by the end of 1918 and would by 1928 write an essay on Conrad recanting much of what he had written during the previous decade.[76]

Victory, of course, had many more starkly polemical formulations than those of Peattie, Borie, and Follett, and what we must now turn to is the general ideological "militarization" of Conrad's works that was, in fact, a conspicuous development of the wartime years. One remarkable example is the treatment *Lord Jim* receives in the article "A Kansas Critic of Conrad" in the *New York Times* on February 2, 1916. This article sets out at great and curiously unprovoked length to ridicule the Monday Study Club of Sabetha, Kansas, for devoting the winter to reading Conrad's books. Apparently beyond Kansans' middlebrow interpretive range, Conrad receives at the crude hands of the club "about as severe judgment and summary execution as Lord Jim at the hands of the old heathen chief whose son has been killed by the former's policy of pacifism."[77] Far from an incidental political reference, this framing of *Lord Jim* as a critique of Jim's "policy of pacifism" (which, in this reading, is responsible for Doramin's son being killed) and by implication as a critique of pacifist "policy" generally, is in fact the true seed of the entire article. For the *Times*'s obnoxious elitism, on display in this article in such plain and puzzlingly gratuitous proportion, is not the origin but the means by which the *Times* expresses and dismisses the true historical source of its hostility: the pacifist movement in the United States itself. Two weeks before, the governor of Kansas, Arthur Capper, had publicly endorsed an antiwar, antipreparedness position that the *Times* harshly denounced as an effort "to spread a spineless pacifism in the Sunflower State and to incite opposition to preparedness"; Capper's efforts were part of a more general antimilitarist movement in the central West, dominated by (Bryanite) populist rather than the pro-British social and business interests predominant in the Northeast, which the *Times* obsessively documented and pilloried. Hence, in "A Kansas Critic of Conrad," the *Times* uses the occasion of Conrad to attack, not simply or ultimately the cultural sophistication of Kansans, but rather through that incendiary and demeaning idiom a variety of war-resistance viewpoints, Kansan and otherwise, whose "pacifism" the *Times* generally telescopes and relentlessly stigmatizes and pathologizes.[78]

In the process, moreover, the *Times* advances a not uninteresting reading of *Lord Jim*. For although the character "Lord" Jim engineers far too many wars within Patusan to be identified with any general "policy of pacifism," the idea that the novel somehow fundamentally is concerned with and offers a critique of pacifism—that it is grounded in experiences *like* war, and what it studies and pathologizes are the conditions that prevent one from fulfilling the standards of duty and service one *should* do—not only directly responds to the explicitly pacifist and neutral formulations of Conrad posited by Bourne and Mencken, respectively; it also has some later authority from Conrad himself. In "His War Book: A Preface to Stephen Crane's *The Red Badge of Courage*," the preface Conrad wrote to the first U.S. reissue of Crane's novel in 1925, Conrad makes much of, among other manifest and self-conscious correlations between Crane's novel and *Lord Jim*, Crane's depiction of a "young" "untried" hero "deprived of the moral support [of] a tried body of men matured in achievement to the consciousness of its worth" who "jumps" up and then panics in a moment of "danger," "running from battle" such that he is "left alone" with a highly symbolic and "unfathomable" but not "morbid" "problem of courage," and ultimately granted an opportunity to redeem his honor and sense of duty (*LE* 121–24). Conrad here clearly codes *The Red Badge* in the image of *Lord Jim*: what, then, is the preface "His War Book" if not an obverse coding of *Lord Jim* as Conrad's own war (and to some important extent, pro-war) book?

Other Conrad texts become militarized as well as the United States inches toward entry into war. A review of *Within the Tides* (1916) in *Nation* (NY) in

February 1916 reads that volume's epigraph, referencing "ante-bellum pages" written "in the last month of peace," as intimating a new explicitly war-directed turn in Conrad's fiction.[79] Shortly thereafter, *Bookman* (NY) reports rumors of a new Conrad novel based on Conrad's Polish "war" experiences, later flanked with testimony of how British sailors "carried to sea" copies of *The Mirror of the Sea* on "voyages during the war."[80] In February 1918, Conrad's "The Tale," expressly concerned with submarine warfare, appears in *Metropolitan Magazine*; and in September 1918, *Current Opinion* uses Conrad's sea fiction like *The Nigger of the "Narcissus"* to situate and authenticate Eugene O'Neill's new maritime war drama *Into the Zone*, which the magazine prints without any evident awareness (certainly not in how it uses Conrad) that O'Neill's play is a significantly antiwar (antihysteria) text.[81] Most important, however, is the one major new Conrad text of this period after *Victory*: one current modernist criticism again tends to underestimate; one Frank Harris and H. L. Mencken in their own moment predictably marginalize; and one Doubleday, ever inspired in matters of timely intervention, insisted on releasing in the United States on April 27, 1917—a mere three weeks after the United States formally entered the war. This text is *The Shadow-Line*. Edith Roosevelt, wife of the ex-president and "a great admirer of Conrad's works," believed *The Shadow-Line* to be "very wonderful, one of Conrad's greatest, I think";[82] this kind of comment must be understood within the specific U.S. circumstances of its reception. Although readers in Britain, where the first edition of the book was exhausted in four days, were well aware of the wartime resonances and grounding of *The Shadow-Line*—its tale of paralyzing calm at sea mirroring the contemporary paralysis of trench warfare, its tale of Conrad's own "first command" offered in some parallel relation to the contemporary experience of young British soldiers, who "have crossed / in early youth the shadow-line / of their generation" (*SL* 1)—the difference in the United States was an additional synergy between the novel's master metaphor ("the shadow-line," a metaphor of *threshold*) and the imminent U.S. experience of crossing the threshold of entry into the war (and toward international maturity). *The Shadow-Line* offered a tale and key figure uncannily resonant with the current experience of U.S. war entry: perfectly poised, indeed, to narrativize, legitimize, socially galvanize, ideologize the traversing of that "shadow-line"—in much the same way that Theodore Roosevelt had earlier narratively justified nationalized causes of war.

Illustrative here is the massive pictorialized review "A Conrad Hero's Quest for Truth" that appeared in the ever-vigilant *New York Times* on April 22, 1917. This review, whose essential purpose is to use *The Shadow-Line* both to sanctify U.S. Anglo-allied war entry as a kind of valiant crusade and to provide a model of conduct for young Americans soon to be called into the "quest" of military service, begins by suggesting that perhaps Conrad's novels have not been "popular" precisely because "they are novels of great quests and absorbing passions, which is to say, they are not, spiritually speaking, of this day and generation"—that is, apathetic, ironic, modern, self-involved.[83] However, with "the cataclysm now whelming the world," horizons have changed; Conrad's fiction—whose "great stakes" include "nothing less than all [we] are and can hope to be in this world and the next," whose greatest "conviction" lies in "the idea of Fidelity" and "Service"—have now struck a new chord of contemporary resonance, value, possibility, urgency. In *The Shadow-Line*, "it is as though the great writer, weary not only with years but with the madness of the world, had by a supreme effort of the will thrown off the burden of personal anxieties and of hopes and fears for his native and adopted countries, and had gone back to that great passion for the sea" in which lies all "the permanent things in nature and the soul of man" that "underlie" and "outlast" and must ultimately be vindicated by war. In *The Shadow-Line*, Conrad begins with a disaffected and alienated young narrator—"Perhaps most young people have this feeling at one time or another"—who, by being "faithful to his task [when] the Call came to him," is able to realize such permanent values, and as such to become "faithful to himself," the true calling of "liberty," and the mature discovery of "his manhood, the place in the world of men and of nature appointed to him from the beginning." Whereas most Conrad novels leave their heroes vanquished in insurmountable "fight[s] with villainy or stupidity or mere inertia," *The Shadow-Line* offers young American men true to a higher cause the reverse model: "[Though] now and then there is struck a note of intense foreboding . . . the gods of disaster are disarmed for once by the youth and courage shining beneath their hand." Personal maturity and disciplined military service, a coming-of-age, a crossing of the shadow-line, both for the redeemed youth of the United States called into service and the United States as a nation itself crossing an epic threshold of world affairs and world stature, are ultimately vindicated by *The Shadow-Line*, as the *Times* article concludes with a remarkable paragraph of prophecy, looping back to the "great passions" and chivalric values with which it began, and making perfectly explicit the values and context of the "sword" framing its, and future, "American" appreciations of Conrad:

At the beginning of this review it was suggested that the novels of Joseph Conrad lack a general popularity—for the same reason, it may be added, as do Malory's tales of King Arthur, because they are records of great passions and of desperate quests. The time is near, we believe, when they shall come into their own. Within the past three years hundreds of thousands of young men have gone in search of "the truth that is to be got out of" life or death. They who have gone, those who have remained behind, must, if they had not already done so, have crossed perforce each his own Shadow Line. The world, to its own astonishment, has learned anew that passion is not a flame to be avoided but a sword to be grasped; it has learned anew the beauty of quest, and the splendor of fidelity. After the war is over we shall read more of Sir Thomas Malory than we have done—and more of Joseph Conrad.[84]

These words suggest the exceptional degree to which Conrad's fiction could be, and was, mobilized to the cause of war in the United States. Even more, in its immense appeals to affect and abstract considerations of spirit, in its almost religious reliance on metaphors of conversion, redemption, and fidelity to soldiering faith as values in themselves, the *Times* article highlights the important degree to which Conrad's works became militarized in the United States, not simply because of the complex fecundity with which they mediated questions of U.S. international-military *policy* (e.g., issues of isolationism, internationalism, pacifism, preparedness, the moral premises and rhetoric of war) but also because of a *military-patriotic structure of feeling* that Conrad's works foundationally inscribe—and offer just as forcefully as the counter-hegemonic *sensibility* we have already seen Mencken locate and mobilize in Conrad. (There is no contradiction, moreover, in this apparent contradiction of multiple purposiveness: the simultaneous emanation of strong and utterly incompatible assertions of order from a field that presupposes, like a Möbius strip, their origin in and ultimate return to one another, is precisely what we have been saying all along defines the field of "Conrad" as heterotopic, boundary neutralizing.) What it means to say that Conrad's works deeply inscribe a military-patriotic structure of feeling is a matter we can clarify with reference to Mark Wollaeger's recent discussion of Conrad's "The Unlighted Coast," a little-known war propaganda essay the British Admiralty commissioned Conrad to write in late 1916. Based on one in a series of nights Conrad spent aboard the disguised brigantine *Ready* off the British coast during a wartime blackout, "The Unlighted Coast" was never published until well after the war: in part, Wollaeger argues, because not much happened to write about during Conrad's time aboard the *Ready*, but also, more importantly, because Conrad, "not a natural propagandist," finds his "modernist" propensities interfering with his propagandizing mission and intentions. In "The Unlighted Coast," "Conrad's failure as a propagandist" is in fact "his success as a modernist," for where that essay goes wrong is in its conspicuous efforts to rewrite that "dark" British evening at sea in terms of the modernist precedent of *Heart of Darkness*, and how it goes wrong, resulting in prose "unlikely to produce recruits or trigger a surge of patriotism," is by undermining its own propagandistic enterprise with the kind of modernist critical self-reflexiveness and self-consciousness with respect to political language and ideology that one finds in *Heart of Darkness*.[85]

This formulation is robust enough to accommodate the reverse conjecture: what if the "modernism" of *Heart of Darkness* is just as invested in "propaganda" as "The Unlighted Coast" is in modernism? As Wollaeger points out, from the beginning of *Heart of Darkness*, Marlow's famous denunciation of "the conquest of the earth" as "the taking it away from those who have a different complexion or slightly flatter noses than ourselves" is immediately undermined by two propagandizing appeals: Marlow's tribute to British colonial "efficiency" that introduces the statement, and the strange rhetoric of idolatry that completes it (affirming the ultimate need for a belief "you can set up and bow down before, and offer a sacrifice to").[86] But more, I think, than Wollaeger lets on; more than his convincing demonstrations of how *Heart of Darkness* both inscribes and critically scrutinizes propagandistic ideology suggest; more, indeed, in ultimate conformity with the very complex understanding of "propaganda" Wollaeger advocates, encompassing tendentious and interested political statements as well as any form of conceptual or emotional appeal whose persuasive force turns on a "progressive adaptation to a certain order of things,"[87] on the larger social integration such appeals are able to effect, *Heart of Darkness* may be read as not simply engaging equivocally with but rather fundamentally *incarnating* at least one very important form of propaganda. This form is its centering ideology of "restraint": a strangely tactile and psychologized political ethos of work, discipline, service, and tradition, produced and championed in circumstances of overwhelming and engulfing chaos and "darkness," which everything in the novella works toward validating (*HD* 105). "Restraint" may be considered a propaganda formation in which the world, including the self, is presented as radically in need of discipline, but wherein what fundamentally authorizes this ontological claim is the affectual and intellectual satisfaction (as well as social power) to which it gives rise, the kind of gratifying integrations and interface the ideology of restraint affords in navigating the modern world. Far from simplistic, this "idea" (in Marlow's sense; *HD* 51) of restraint encourages and often depends on elaborate, if ultimately circular, flights of self-consciousness; it also fundamentally derives from the very extreme environmental challenges of conceptual orientation and integration that make Marlow so convinced of its necessity—and that Conrad produces to make the case for its necessity. Above all, this ideology of restraint is not only an "idea" or an ethos but a regime of aesthetic and affectual engagement: a means, this is to say, evinced in the very "impressionist" form and "will-to-style"[88] of the novella itself, of both grati-fying, to immense sensory and psycho-emotional degrees, wide impulses of dissidence and subversion *and also ultimately preserving and mandating their capture*;[89] of both confirming the authenticity of existential and "horrifying" insight and using this new spectrum of disruptive vision "to make you *hear*, to make you *feel*, . . . to make you *see*" (the entire regimen of sensory and af-fectual appeal is important) the redemptive necessity of discipline, security, spiritually stabilized formations of social order (*NN* x). *Heart of Darkness*, then, may be read as "propaganda" precisely to the extent it *works* (affectively and stylistically, as well as conceptually) as a "modernist" text; it works, this is to say, precisely as it affectively and aesthetically inculcates the reader in the same will-to-discipline, the same Marlovian angle of ontological and politi-cal vision, the same dialectic of desire and repudiation, the same ideology of restraint that defines not only the text's final ethical stance but also Marlow's own curiously idolatrous relation (gratified yet only to a point) to Kurtz. And so, too, might we return to "The Unlighted Coast" as actually quite effective propaganda, not at the level of jingoism or bald defamation, but rather in the very modernist affect of restraint that organizes its power: the seductive allure of "dark" authenticity combined with the heroic prospect of disciplined con-duct and consequence, all situated in a context of attempting to recruit young British men to the cause of *patria* and military service, which makes clear the deep roots of "restraint" in a *military-patriotic structure of feeling*. It is on this affectual ground that "The Unlighted Coast" exerts its recruiting function; it is on this basis that the essay presents itself as "spiritually strengthen[ing]," "very powerful—like a revelation of some deeper truth," unprecedented in "an intense consciousness of itself" [*LE* 48].

These (revisionist) observations are important because "The Unlighted Coast," an essay we have been using to charge into the modernist heart of Conrad to reverse expectations about propagandism, is actually quite atypical of the lyric ease and expanse with which most of Conrad's essays post-1914 lavishly declare and extol both the British war cause and the military-patriotic structure of feeling we have been tracing—and link such things back to Conrad's fiction. "The Dover Patrol," for instance, which follows "The Unlighted Coast" in *Last Essays*, Conrad wrote in 1921 at the request of Lord Northcliffe to accompany the unveiling of a monument commemorating British naval efforts to guard the English Channel during the war. The essay literally begins and ends on the all-important note of feeling—"The worth of a *sentiment*" and "the indomitable *hearts* of the men of the Dover Patrol" (*LE* 58, 65, emphases added)—and in between, we learn all the values and aesthetic-affectual prompts through which such valiant British "hearts" are pulled together in disciplinary formation, creating a "feeling of spiritual exaltation which enabled [the sailors] each in his station, from the Admiral commanding to the youngest member of the smallest drifter's crew, to defy the enmity of nature and the hostility of men":

Unable to put up a fight and without speed to get away, they made a sacrifice of their lives every time they went out for a turn of duty; they concentrated their valour on the calm, seamanlike execution of their work amongst the exploding mines and bursting shells. It was their conception of their honour, and they carried it out of this war unblemished by a single display of weakness, by the slightest notion of hesitation in the long tale of dangerous service. (*LE* 60, 64)

Such values (sacrifice, duty, valor, honor, strength, danger, service) are touchstones of the military-patriotic "sentiment" (*LE* 58) "The Dover Patrol" champions; they are also championed in *all* the essays composing the strong middle of the "Life" section of *Notes on Life and Letters* (1921), most of these originally appearing during the war itself. Of these—"First News" (1918), "Well Done" (1918), "Tradition" (1918), and "Confidence" (1919)—especially revealing is the second, explicitly written to "commend the seamen of Great Britain" for having "done well" during "the last four years" (*NLL* 179), and published twice in the United States in its original stand-alone form, in *Living Age* in October

1918 and *Current Opinion* in November 1918. There are three key points to take
here. First, "Well Done," like many of the essays in *Notes on Life and Letters*
and *Last Essays*, aggressively elides the distinction between the regular British navy and the British merchant marine such that to speak of the animating "spirit" and "sentiment" of the one is also to speak of the other.[90] So far as
Conrad's nonfiction is concerned, then, the military-patriotic structure of feeling explicitly anatomized and celebrated in "The Dover Patrol" (which makes
the same elision) is essentially the same as those traditions and sentiments
elaborated and lionized in the essays more focused on the merchant marine—
a domain of signature personal identification for Conrad himself, of course.
Second, just as "The Unlighted Coast" sets out to rewrite *Heart of Darkness*,
and just as "His War Book" rewrites *Lord Jim*, so too the second part of "Well
Done" directly and elaborately rewrites *The Nigger of the "Narcissus"*—i.e.,
in its general "eulogy of seamen," its meditations on the "devouring enigma"
of the sea, its figurative interests in death and color, its overarching tale of a
"mysterious" seaman whose "deeds of darkness" test "the solidarity of a ship's
company," etc. (*NLL* 184–89)—with all of the strong politics of the staunchly
pro-British, pro-war essays. In "Well Done," Conrad thus glosses not only his
sea prose but his own sea fiction, epitomized by *The Nigger of the "Narcissus,"*
in terms of the pro-British viewpoint and military-patriotic structure of feeling expressly articulated in the wartime essays: a proposition that, without at
all dismissing the national and political complexities of Conrad's sea fiction,
most readers will not have trouble recognizing as a plausible interpretation of
it.[91] Third and finally, "Well Done" ends by focusing on a specific icon—"The
ship, this ship, our ship, the ship we serve, [a]s the moral symbol of our life"—
which it comes to identify with both a distinctively British "spirit of service"
and an equally British "spirit of adventure" (*NLL* 188, 189). Here at last we are
able culturally to decode Doubleday's trademark icon for Conrad, the image
of the storm-bound ship at sea (see Figure 8). This ship, ambiguous in referent, invites and conflates both naval/military and merchant marine projection;
its surrounding "storm" gestures to contemporary historical perils associable
with the sea, including both the war and imperialist extension; its seafaring
pedigree elicits, though not to the exclusion of the United States, British and
Anglophile association; and enfolding them all, its aura is that of a "spirit of
adventure"—not simply a good reason to read Conrad but also, as the *New York
Times*, Doubleday, and Conrad all (variously) understood, crucially energizing

to any modern military-patriotic structure of feeling, not least in the United States. As the *Times* put it on March 21, 1916:

The great majority of [our] boys . . . are shown by the record of their recent activities to be the soundest sort of Americans, uncorrupted by any of the current aspirations for peace at any price, perfectly correct on the preparedness question, and *possessing that instinctive urge toward adventure and that slight regard for personal danger which befit the youth of any land—the absence of which from the youth of any land means the land's decline by a not very remote enslavement by some sturdier race.*[92]

These are the terms in which Conrad becomes available as a British-allied war agency, and it remains to clarify, for the moment from the vantage of U.S. international relations (i.e., to be cross-correlated shortly with a larger field of U.S. domestic considerations), the degree to which Conrad's construction *as English* underwrites this "Anglo-Saxon" war engine. Central here is the figure of Rudyard Kipling, whose immediately prior fantastic marketing success by Doubleday provides the direct stimulus and template for the publisher's turn to Conrad. Nearly all of Doubleday's local strategies in advertising Conrad replicate the Kipling campaign, effectively slotting Conrad for Americans in the image of Kipling: for example, the "blue limp leather" editions of Conrad are modeled on the "green cloth" and "flexible red leather" complete Kiplings; the "Deep Sea" edition of Conrad repeats exotic titles like the "Seven Seas" edition of Kipling; the various edition formats of Conrad—"affordable," "de Luxe," complete, autographed, "limited," boxed, mapped, biographically supplemented, iconically and/or exotically illustrated—all extend the precedent of Kipling. Similarly, between 1914 and 1920, the major magazines Doubleday, Page publishes and controls, including the enormously popular *Country Life in America* and the *World's Work*, relentlessly advertise Conrad and Kipling together: in conjunct and heavily pictorialized terms that include their mutual investments in the sea, the war, struggles at "the frontier of civilization," romance and adventure, foreign exoticism, masculine and multiply gendered appeal, and also their status as simply "The Two Most Distinguished Living Writers in English."[93] Overarching and intertwining all these is the sense of an ultra-British (especially *for Americans*) Kipling: a strident champion, not only of the British and British-allied effort, but of a larger "Anglo-Saxon" conviction of British imperialist legitimacy and shared Anglo-American, Anglo-Saxon (white man's) "burden" generally. This political conception is at the root of Mencken's repeated fulminations against constructing Conrad in the image of Kipling, as the "beyond-Kipling"; and what Doubleday culturally accomplishes by aligning the two is not simply to present Conrad as British, as pro-British, and/or as English as Kipling but also to offer precisely such questions for the U.S. public. During the war period of 1914–18, a strong line of U.S. discourse hence follows (and regenerates) Doubleday's lead by complementing Conrad's general militarization with aggressive constructions of him in Anglophile terms. Conrad's staunchly pro-British wartime essays—affirming that for "right and justice, England will keep on fighting for years if necessary," and that "I have never, never seen any British seaman refuse any risk, any exertion, and effort of spirit or body up to the extremest demands of their calling" (*NLL* 178, 198)—lay the foundations for a U.S. culture of Conrad the Anglophile. The reappearance of Conrad's essay on Henry James in the *North American Review* in April 1916, on the occasion of James's death, helps Americans to ponder how "each [author] found something in the spirit of England and its institutions that won his allegiance and veneration"; the appearance of Conrad's new preface to the *Youth* volume in *Bookman* (NY) in March 1918 presents Conrad affirming that "I have been all my life—all my two lives—the spoiled adopted child of Great Britain"; an essay by the intellectual and once-pacifist J. M. Robertson, MP, in the (Boston-based, venerably Anglophile) *North American Review* in September 1918 emphasizes Conrad's dedication to the English tradition of letters; and Katharine Fullerton Gerould, the conservative New England cultural critic and elegantly unabashed proponent of Kipling, presents Conrad as, though "early *dépaysé*," ultimately grounded in a moral framework compatible with that other "greatest living master of English style," Kipling.[94]

This U.S. *wartime* construction of Conrad—less as an incarnation of Englishness or Britishness than as a reverencer of such things, less as an object of American Anglophilia than as a model for it—changes dramatically after the war, when Conrad becomes, in repeated U.S. articulations, the epitome and essence of the truest possible Briton:

- "Conrad is a Pole by nativity, and an Englishman by sympathy and naturalization" (*Sewanee Review*, January 1922).

- "When he speaks of himself, with pride in the avowal, as 'a man of Kent,' and tells you his sons have grown up with a sure sense of their English birthright, you know how deep that attachment has become" (*Bookman* [NY], December 1922).

• "Welded, as it were, to a British birthright . . . [Conrad is] a more impassioned British patriot than native Britons were" (*New York Times*, May 1923, qtg. Captain Muirhead Bone).

• "Whatever his nationality, he became as thorough a Briton as the world has ever known" (*Christian Science Monitor*, 1924).

• "The chapters here including certain phases of the Great War as he saw them, at sea and on land, moving with perfect comprehension among soldiers and sailors alike, help us to realize how extraordinarily at home Conrad was among the English; how eagerly, how naturally, how inevitably he came to identify himself with those whose literature and language he has so signally enriched by his transcendent genius" (Review of *Last Essays*, *Christian Science Monitor*, April 1926).

• "The result, it would seem, could hardly fail to be a decision that Joseph Conrad was at heart very moral, very British. . . . Conrad was ever interested in morality (in the better sense of the word), he was ever sound, ever sturdy, ever thoroughly British" (*Boston Evening Transcript*, April 1926).

• "*Briefly, Conrad is a Briton by deliberate self-determination*" (H. I. Brock, *New York Times*, May 1923, emphasis added).[95]

There is more at stake in these remarks—domestically—than we can presently account for; suffice it to say, however, that with respect to the international sphere, the difference between the wartime Anglophile and the postwar "essentially English" constructions of Conrad is the ideological difference between the need to propel the United States into the war in alliance with Britain and the postwar desire to administer the world *between* the United States and the best face that Britain could put on (whatever the terms of that face might be, epitomized in "our Conrad" from a variety of U.S. perspectives). This raises a series of postwar international questions concerning the ever-broadening terms and turf of Conrad's U.S. interest and appeal, questions we must at least touch on before returning to the "Anglo-Saxon" politics of Conrad's construction in the domestic sphere. We may take preliminary note, however, of H. I. Brock's inspired formulation, "Conrad is a Briton by deliberate self-determination," which witnesses Conrad's "English" essentialization through his absolute commitment

to that most American of contemporary ideologies, "self-determination." It is to
Conrad's mediation of U.S. ideas and concerns of "self-determination" in the
international sphere in the immediate aftermath of the war that we now briefly
turn, before reintegrating the "world" mediated by Conrad with (other) domestic concerns of immigration, State, and race.

ON SELF-DETERMINATION, ANTI-BOLSHEVISM:
A PROLEPTIC DIGRESSION

Against the grain of Menckenite deployments of Conrad in the postwar period,
some of whose anticolonial and counter-hegemonic elements we have already
seen, and whose further nationalist complications are an important element of
the following chapter, the *order* of war galvanized through Conrad during the
wartime period shifts to two different seams of asserted American order during
the postwar period: self-determination and anti-Bolshevism. Exploring Conrad's articulation through these two seams allows us to continue our recovery
of "late" Conrad as a site of aesthetic and political vitality; to recognize Conrad's
mediation of American "order" as not only a conservative, isolationist, and/or
militarist but also a liberal-internationalist phenomenon; and finally, to understand how the "Anglo-Saxon" engine of Conrad's original production comes to
enfold many different world spaces.

Regarding self-determination, there are few more revealing expressions of
"The Meaning of Conrad" than the one that appeared in an article of that title
in the *New Republic*, a consistent champion of liberal internationalism long
after the United States refused to join the League of Nations and despite its own
break with Wilson over the Treaty of Versailles, on the occasion of Conrad's
death in August 1924. Though the *New Republic* had long served as a forum in
which many voices—both occasional writers like Van Wyck Brooks and Edith
Borie and regular contributors like Frances Hackett, Percy Boynton, and especially lead literary editor Philip Littell—had written individually to champion
Conrad, "The Meaning of Conrad" is different in that it is a general editorial
anonymously authored in the magazine's front editorial section, collectively
speaking for the magazine's values as a whole. Directly engaging Mencken, the
editorial challenges purely "ironic" and politically neutralizing accounts of
Conrad with an appeal to Conrad's ultimate spirit of engaged and indomitable
idealism: "It is true his heroes are not conquerors in the material sphere, but
the significant thing is that they continue to strive. The theme which Conrad

presents most constantly is one of affection, devotion, protection, tested by danger . . . calling out courage, loyalty, endurance, sacrifice."[96] Though this rhetoric of "devotion" recalls the *Times*'s militaristic wartime appeals to *The Shadow-Line*, the order of American self-conception being confirmed here is actually quite different. Far from the dogmatically bellicose and nationalist priorities of the *Times*, the "moral index of the world" at issue here is pacifist and international in its ultimate priorities, and defined by the deference of international military force to the right of all world peoples, regardless of race, power, or colonial status, to ultimately determine the terms of their own destiny. This is how the *New Republic* crucially contextualizes the kind of idealism to which Conrad vindicates "devotion":

Often Conrad's theme is the loyalty between men of a different race, of white men to brown, or brown to white. [In this context,] it is hard to miss the meaning of Lord Jim's sacrifice, as in expiation alike of his long ago faithlessness and the treachery of the men of his own race, he goes to Dorman to die by his hand—*a witness to the imperial truth that the test of a man's fitness to rule by his fellow men is his willingness to die, not only for them and with them, but by them.* If Conrad had not presented this theme so constantly, his own comment, sparse as it is, would give us a definite idea of his moral index of the world.[97]

Whereas the *Times* in 1916 reads the end of *Lord Jim* as a "moral index" of nationalist military preparedness, the *New Republic* in 1924 reads the end of the novel as an affirmation of liberal internationalism: the necessary subjection of any national or international assertion of armed force to Wilsonian principles of native self-determination. This is what it means to celebrate "Lord" Jim, the white figure of superior arms on Patusan, for *submitting* to the ultimate authority of the native chief Doramin. It is also why Jim's "sacrifice" to the will of Doramin and his people—"his willingness to die, not only for them and with them, but *by* them"—may be considered an "expiation" of prior Western imperialist sins of treacherous self-assertion. The *New Republic*'s field of reference (and disavowal) here is clearly colonial in dimension; its formulation, however, is of course complicated because the "imperial truth" the magazine advocates in Conrad's image does not truly reject imperialism so much as delimit and qualify the perceived necessity of its practice with "American" ideals of self-determination. One clear context of this meditation on *Lord Jim*, for example, is the recent spike of U.S. military interventions in the Caribbean and

Central America. Both Haiti and Santo Domingo in particular were subject to notoriously obscene, violent, and racist instances of U.S. military oppression in the early 1920s, prompting the *New Republic* boldly to write, representatively and repeatedly, of Santo Domingo, "Have we so far forgotten our republican principles so as to charter our bureaucrats and soldiers to subjugate whatever weaker peoples they may find convenient?"; and of Haiti: "Our Marines have been murdering Haitians. . . . There is nothing in the worst annals of imperialism to exceed the savage callousness of the behavior of our own forces in Haiti. . . . In Haiti the military are irresponsible, and we want to see them made responsible. This means an American civil occupation that has somebody besides mere officeholders in it, and that dominates the use of force."[98] In "The Meaning of Conrad," the *New Republic* constructs Jim as the reverse ideal of this imperialist abuse: he is a figure of disinterested and deferential service in the international sphere, a figure whose lack of imperialist ambition and militarist arrogation of authority is of the kind that legitimizes narrow, temporary, "necessary" claims of "colony" and "protectorate" and "mandate," the idealized standard by which U.S. delinquency and atrocity in Hispaniola may be measured and held accountable. More generally, the *New Republic* articulates Conrad here through a principle of self-determination—ultimate sovereign authority of native peoples—which, since at least 1919, the magazine had advanced as its own axiomatic "moral index" in every major world boundary and sovereignty dispute, whether the context was the much wider sphere of U.S. intervention in Latin America and the Philippines, renewed European and Japanese imperialist assertions in Africa, the Near East, Ireland, and on the Asian continent, or "punitive" appropriations of territory in continental Europe itself.

But Jim is also a colonial figure, however benevolent, and as the *New Republic*'s recommendation of an "American civil occupation" in Haiti suggests, its principle of self-determination is not at all necessarily preclusive of external intervention in non-Western territories. The magazine's liberal internationalism is also a (racialized) liberal imperialism: for even as the *New Republic* genuinely insists on standards of international disinterest and ultimate popular sovereignty, and even as it often severely indicts and more generally adduces a critical stance of *suspecting* imperialist endeavor, it also inclines to presupposing a need for provisional "guidance" into modernity among some supposedly "backward" non-Western peoples—living in a dangerous world context (or so the argument goes) that cannot tolerate a power vacuum. Conrad, indeed, becomes of such great interest in "liberal" American venues like the *New Republic* in significant part precisely because his fiction straddles the boundary between fierce imperialist critique/disavowal and a disarticulated imperialism's necessary/benevolent recovery[99]—a hallmark of U.S. exceptionalist self-articulation. Conrad's fiction becomes an ideological means through which ideals of self-determination and different concrete practices of world imperialism become adjusted to one another—generally and comparatively vindicating, if not always actual U.S. conduct, at least an idealized (exceptionalist, self-determinationist, fundamentally anti-imperialist) conception of what the terms of American international order *should* be. Similarly, Conrad's "duplex" relation to Britishness plays a central role as well: for even as the *New Republic* seeks aggressively to hold the United States to an exceptionalist standard of distinction from "imperialist" Europe, it often does so in terms that vindicate the comparative imperial benevolence of and the practical necessity of power alliance with Britain, if not "Anglo-Saxon" cultural superiority as well. Overall, whether critiquing or endorsing U.S. world activity, whether indicting or defending international assertions of "protectorate," and whether distinguishing or analogizing the United States and Britain, "The Meaning of Conrad" fundamentally turns on an idealized Wilsonian rhetoricization of the United States in terms of self-determinationist goals: curiously justifying American stewardship of a new world order by being ever prepared to harmonize, differentiate, or project the terms of its own imperialist betrayal.

This context of "self-determination" goes far in explaining the remarkable American popularity of *The Rescue* both with the public and diverse critics.[100] Though set on an obscure coast of Borneo in the mid-nineteenth century, *The Rescue* opens itself up to contemporary Americans in at least three immediate ways. First, Conrad's dedication of the novel "To / Fredric Courtland Penfield / last Ambassador of the United States / of America to the late Austrian Empire / . . . in memory of the rescue of certain / distressed travelers effected by him in / the world's great storm of the year / 1914" (*Re* v) links the novel not only to the U.S. ambassador's wartime "rescue" of the Conrads; it also links the "rescue" at issue in the novel to the greater historical context of the war itself ("the world's greatest storm")—playing into, and inserting the novel interpretively into, a widespread postwar U.S. sense and discourse of "America" as "rescuer" of the civilized world and defender of its oppressed peoples in that war.[101] More plausible than it initially sounds,[102] this "reading" of *The Rescue* as an oblique allegory of U.S. heroism in the war (or is it reckless interventionism predicated on loftily dysfunctional conceptions of "Peace"? [*Re* 435]) is further facilitated by the obvious subtexts of the Great War underwriting the end of the novel (the part Conrad wrote *after* the summer of 1918)—just as this "heroic" interpretation is complicated by the fact that Tom Lingard's rescue efforts are, after all, significantly a failure. Second, though there are many ways of articulating a literary genealogy of the central character Tom Lingard,[103] one is as a close kin of James Fenimore Cooper's Natty Bumppo (a character Conrad mentions on more than one occasion, created by an author Conrad admired). The plain-spoken, democratic and earthy, curiously impulsive, impudent, and even child-ish Lingard, a romantic adventurer and wanderer of the frontier, defined by his mediation between two conflicting races, both privy to and outside the claims of each, a figure simultaneously of social innocence and seasoned experience, an outsider at odds with the very forces of historical transition he helps to ful-fill, is easily legible in the image of Hawkeye; Tom's crucial liminal relation to *England*—he is both historically from it yet largely independent of it—only reinforces this "American" legibility. Third, there is an actual U.S American character in *The Rescue*: a racist gunrunning New Englander connected to the U.S.–Mexican War (1846–48) through his sale of "Mexican war rifles" (*Re* 98) and linked to a wider and more latent critique of U.S. imperialism that Conrad sets in motion by having one of the major European characters, the Spanish D'Alcacer, nephew of the colonial governor-general of the Philippines, enter the novel by way of visiting his uncle in Manila. To raise the Philippines is to introduce an important comparative context under colonial occupation in 1920, not by Spain but by the United States.

Such intimations of U.S. imperialism are precisely what the American em-brace of *The Rescue* is centrally predicated on disavowing, for alongside those who relished the novel for its absolute distance from U.S. implication alto-gether,[104] an even stronger suit of enthusiasts understood the novel in perfectly self-reflexive and ultimately idealizing, if immediately devastating terms. Here we must incorporate into our analysis of the novel's "American" openness a more careful consideration of the novel's plot as legible in different war and postwar contexts. As suggested previously, with respect to the war itself, *The Rescue*'s basic premise, Tom Lingard's heroic rescue of a *very* British yacht and its "civilized" European ally (D'Alcacer) from a desperately mired struggle with a "savage" enemy, naturally lends itself to projective (onto the "American" Tom)

U.S. fantasies of having "rescued" Allied Europe from the "savage" Germans during the war. In the more immediate and disillusioned postwar context of 1920, however, it is rather a more complex understanding of Tom's *failure* that strikes several uncanny notes in the U.S. liberal imagination. This is so because in both the highly problematic claims of racial solidarity and hazy "origin" through which Tom becomes seduced into alliance with and ultimate betrayal by the British-led European allies on the yacht, and even more importantly, in Tom's fundamental failure (this is the central drama of *The Rescue*) *to reconcile this "Western" alliance with much more long-standing and fundamental ethical obligations to the right of native self-rule by and the restoration of native political authority under Wajo royalty Hassim and Immada* (this is what first brings Tom to the "Shore of Refuge"; the Europeans' "savage enemies" are Tom's most honorable and long-standing friends—and he unwittingly destroys them)— liberal Americans could readily conceive an elaborate metaphor for the *tragedy* of U.S. world involvement during the war and its aftermath. The Traverses and D'Alcacer offer a complex vocabulary for imagining the troubled, seductive, ultimately entirely self-interested European imperialist interests that helped "seduce" the United States into a "rescue" effort it perhaps never should have entered (or so the self-insulating "American" story goes); and even more importantly, Tom, already positioned to be read in "American" literary terms, offers a perfect mirror of President Woodrow Wilson's moral failure on a world scale at the Paris Peace Conference: innocently (or ignorantly or recklessly or arrogantly: contemporary American narratives are emphatically plural on this point) traduced and betrayed by scheming imperialist Allies, and traducing and betraying in turn the principles of the Fourteen Points on whose fundamental premise and promise of sovereign self-determination so many of the world's occupied and colonized peoples depended. This, in any event, is the general context and stream of ideological macronarratives that lead the *New Republic* in "The Meaning of Conrad" to highlight *The Rescue* as a central example of Conrad's "constant" "devotion" to the "theme" and "moral index" of ultimate self-determination. As in the magazine's reading of *Lord Jim*, it is only "fidelity to the claims of race" and devotion to the highest standards of disinterested "intentions" and "conscience" that could even possibly and provisionally justify continued Western intervention in the colonized world—terms whose self-determinationist idealism Tom Lingard upholds even in his catastrophic failure to execute them. Similarly, Philip Littell's euphoric embrace of *The Rescue*—its "fittest criticism," he asserts, "would be a song of thanksgiving for the privilege of being alive while Mr. Conrad is alive"—as well as Littell's more sober assessment, as perhaps the most underrated U.S. critic of Conrad in this period, of *The Rescue*'s vindication of Conrad as "in our day the greatest imaginer of human relations," assumes a fundamentally Wilsonian frame of reference. In the context of contemporary numbers of the *New Republic*, Littell's central affirmation in Conrad of a high moral "courage never to submit and yield," combined with an "understanding sympathy" for even the most dedicated idealists "who cannot stand the nerve shattering tests he subjects them to,"[105] must be understood as a pointed intervention in the magazine's wider critique of Wilson (his principles compromised, his nerves shattered by stroke) that nonetheless vindicates Wilsonian ideals. As these and other examples suggest, the liberal response to *The Rescue* does not turn questions of imperialism back on a deexceptionalized United States so much as try to hold it to an idealized American standard and shield, one whose progressive wisdom and colonial equivocation alike find mutable terms of ratification in Conrad.

The same is true of Conrad's last unfinished novel, *Suspense* (1925). Probably the one Conrad novel more than any other whose immense historical and aesthetic interest has become lost to history, *Suspense* is set in Genoa during Napoleon's first exile in early 1815: as the Congress of Vienna deliberates on the terms of a new postwar Europe, rumors are rife of Napoleon's reemergence from nearby Elba. As Conrad's contemporary readers, U.S. and otherwise, readily understood, *Suspense* is articulated through a double historical frame, one whose terms Conrad expresses with special force in "The Dover Patrol." There Conrad begins with an elaborate comparison of "the Great War of the twentieth century" and the "Great War" of "the opening years of the nineteenth century," analogizing not only the "attempt at universal dominion" at fundamental issue in both the Napoleonic Wars and the First World War but also the unsettled "suspense" of the terms and stability of the new international order in the aftermath of each. Conrad comments in this essay of 1921:

When [the war against Napoleon] ended it left the world as weary, indeed, as it is to-day ... unsettled in its thoughts and emotions about the spiritual value of the monstrous experience.... When the hour of peace struck in 1815 ... there must have been the feeling that there never would be such a war again; a feeling of relief, mingled, no doubt, with a half-acknowledged sense of regret for the occupation that was gone. *The great question arising at the end of every prolonged effort made by mankind—And now—what*

next? asked without misgivings in the consciousness of an accomplished duty—was not free
from a certain uneasiness as to the days that would follow in other and unknown condi-
tions. (*LE* 59, emphasis added)

The "suspense" of *Suspense* is thus not simply a historical phenomenon but
a quite self-consciously transhistorical one. Though the novel does pretend to
adopt the conventions of the standard historical novel,[106] foregrounding local
character lives against a backdrop of larger historical and political personages,
forces, and developments, its true suspense lies in its transhistorical conflation
of the political indeterminacy of Napoleon's Elban episode—would he return?
with what response by the powers in Vienna? toward what terms and prospects
of international order?—with anxious implicit meditation on the "suspended,"
indeterminate, deeply precarious state of the world after the Treaty of Versailles.
"Napoleon" as a typically Conradian character site of plural romantic projection
(one thinks of other displaced and multiply fetishized characters like Jim or
Nostromo or James Wait) becomes a nineteenth-century figure in and around
which the historical and ideological potentialities of the earlier twentieth century
are contemplated and negotiated. As William W. Bonney recently suggests in
a game-changing essay on *Suspense*, one way to understand the contemporary
politics of the novel is in relation to the rise and potential spread of Russian Bolshevism. In this reading, the point is not simply that Conrad's presentation of
Napoleon, the historical "great man" who, in Sir Charles Latham's view, connotes
"forces that pushed people to rash or unseemly actions" (*S* 36, 107), inscribes a
contemporary threat and anxieties of mass-galvanizing, transnational, revolutionary Bolshevism. It is that the very project of Conrad's novel—apropos of
the above question "what next?", but through the novel's reverse obsession with
deconstructing and neutralizing, holding in epistemological "suspense," any
possibilities of meaningful action, activist "doing"—is to defuse and negate any
ethically or pragmatically viable answer to the question "What Is to Be Done?":
a "rhetorical formulation," since long before Lenin's 1902 tract of that title and
Conrad's 1925 preoccupation with its tropes, firmly historically "identified with
working class revolt."[107] This anti-Bolshevist intervention of *Suspense*, however,
whose American significance we will be able to gauge shortly, must be considered
alongside an even more immediate contemporary subtext of Napoleon (of whom
the novel licenses so many "contrasted views" [*S* 38]): the threat of resurgent
German militarism. As one U.S. editorial expressed this widespread cultural
analogy on the centenary of Napoleon's death in May 1921: "It seems almost

impossible to resist the obvious reflection that this is not a propitious time for France to remind the world that the most ruthless imperialist of modern times, the one to whom we are so largely indebted for the terrible burden of standing armies, was not of German origin."[108] France's repeated reminder, however, of the continuing military threat posed by Germany is precisely what the historical premise and Napoleonic analogy of *Suspense* is positioned to confirm; for if one titanic military-imperialist menace, its autocratic fanaticism articulated through claims of cultural and scientific superiority, could "return" from Elba, why not another? This is a question begged by the novel that most readers in 1925 likely would have considered self-evident.

To these Bolshevist and proto-fascist subtexts of Conrad's Napoleon, we may add a third horizon of contemporary history contemplated in his image in *Suspense*: one reflective of the complexity with which Conrad, as a Pole, actually regarded Napoleon,[109] including Conrad's tacit validation, to at least some degree, of the "new force" of "new-born ideas" "amongst the imperfectly awakened nations of Europe" that Conrad attributes to Napoleon in "The Dover Patrol" (*LE* 59). This third horizon is that of liberal internationalism, and it is here that U.S. liberal self-affirmation, already implicitly invited by the novel's anti-Bolshevist and antimilitarist premises, finds the occasion to express itself most directly. Highly illuminating in this context, not only of the politics of *Suspense*'s reception but of the eagerness with which U.S. readers greeted the novel generally, is the contest held in the *Saturday Review of Literature* in 1925 (while the magazine serialized Conrad's "unfinished" text) asking readers to "complete" Conrad's novel by submitting articles projecting and defending their accounts of "exactly how the author intended to finish the story."[110] Among the hundreds of contest entries, second place went to Dartmouth English professor David Lambuth, who begins his account, published in the *Saturday Review* in November 1926, with a by now familiar (anti-Menckenite) appeal to Conrad's affirmation of "fidelity" to the "ideal" in a fundamentally "insoluble" and "chaotic" world.[111] In the case of Cosmo, however, the young English protagonist of *Suspense* who wanders innocently into a Genoese labyrinth of Napoleonic intrigue, Lambuth clarifies this "fidelity," ever at odds with "despair," in pointedly *Anglophile* and *liberal* terms. These terms, indeed, are ultimately precisely those of "self-determination":

Despair, for Conrad, is always the last impiety. And it invariably exacts its toll. It is by way of contrast, perhaps, that we get in *Suspense* the adventurousness of Cosmo. "For

Englishmen especially, of all the races of the earth, a task, any task, undertaken in an adventurous spirit acquires the merit of romance." *And the merit of which Conrad speaks is the merit of self-determination.*[112]

By "self-determination," Lambuth means in part here the purely character-ological observation that Cosmo, whose name means "world," exposes himself to various domains of world culture and society without ever relinquishing his fundamental posture of principled and independent decision making—a stance, Lambuth argues, Conrad would have affirmed in completing the novel. But a larger political vision is at stake here, too; for in Lambuth's read-ing, the self-determining Cosmo is attracted to Napoleon precisely because he envisions in the latter the liberal political principles that would become apo-theosized in the earlier twentieth-century ideology of "self-determination." Cosmo, this is to say, assumes a conception of Napoleon as "at heart a liberal, a lover of nationalities, a friend of peace," the "apostle" of a freely formed and fully internally free "United States of Europe"[113]—a military figure only by historical necessity, to make possible the conditions for the realization of the best principles of the French Revolution—all a view that Napoleon himself worked very hard to popularize toward the end of his life: and that Conrad (critically, of course) understands as an important and complicating ideo-logical element of Napoleon's social "meaning" before and since. Against the grain, then, (not of Napoleon himself but) of "Napoleonic Europe, with its welter of conflicting forces, with its hopeless tangle of loyalties, of greeds, of aspirations, wherein individuals sink into insignificance, and through which no man can see clearly either meaning or end," Lambuth reads Napoleon as the liberal "Man of Destiny" who attracts Cosmo's "instinctive admiration" for this "radical" transformative reason. Napoleon is the perfect projection of Cosmo's "young radical" sympathies welcoming deliverance from and "any ending [to] the resuscitated *ancien régime* in France and the sorry spectacle of greed and bad faith being enacted in Vienna." Lambuth even goes so far as to envision Cosmo visiting Napoleon and "hear[ing] the Emperor reiterate emphatically his desire to reinstate French liberties and French honor in the midst of a peaceful Europe"; he imagines Cosmo later "dismayed by the re-ports of the increasing autocracy of Napoleon's conduct and the inevitability of renewed war," which only reinforces the liberal principles at issue for Cosmo all along; and finally, Lambuth emphasizes Cosmo's "conflicting loyalties" be-tween English *patria* and idealized Napoleonic principles throughout—which is to say that vindicated as England is, it is only in an idealized space *outside* it that the "true merit of self-determination" can be imagined.[114]

This is obviously a very "American" reading of *Suspense*, one which takes a novel whose historical premises exclude precisely as its contemporary resonance invites consideration of the United States, and then reads the novel's field of contemporary resonance—that is, bad faith imperialist "peace" conferences; hopeless tangles of self-interested politics; appeals to new principles and historical "destiny" also entangled in questions of power; questions of English and Anglo-allied moral authority—entirely in vindication of U.S. principles of self-determination, entirely in the image of American self-confirmation. The message is the same as in the *New Republic*: even in a hopelessly "chaotic" and "insoluble" world, one imperiled by Bolshevist, proto-fascist, and duplicitous threats from without, and equally haunted by isolationist and imperialist forces from within, one must remain "devoted" to the "ideal" of self-determination—as the "liberal" Cosmo does, and as the liberal-progressive vision of capitalist democracy promoted for the world ("cosmo") through Cosmo's and Conrad's Americanized images is intended to do. Nor is this a wholly empty, though clearly tendentious, reading of *Suspense*, for we learn at least as much from Lambuth about the interest of the novel as we do from most readers in the twentieth century—though at the distinct expense of the reticence toward the United States that Conrad himself builds into the novel. As the late Sylvère Monod keenly observes, Conrad, though sometimes professing himself "a true friend of the United States" (*CL* 6.103), evinced pronounced "distrust" of the United States during the wartime and postwar years; he was especially concerned, in a manner that recalls the recklessly blind interference of Tom Lingard, with U.S. intervention in "problems of peace 'extremely complicated, purely European, involving deep-seated feelings, aspirations and convictions absolutely foreign to American mentality and even to American emotions.'"[115] All of Conrad's fiction from *Victory* forward, that is, fiction written at a time when Conrad self-consciously recognizes the importance of his (booming, profitable) U.S. audiences, expresses this political reticence toward the United States, more urgent in its terms than it ever had been before, by keeping the United States as *backgrounded* in his fiction as it ever was before. *Suspense* is the exemplary manifestation of this phenomenon: for like the novel's presentation of Napoleon, a figure of force and historical inevitability ("Fate") distrusted in his rhetoric and power and emphatically backgrounded by the novel in part in resistance to him, the United States in *Suspense*, by the very force of the novel's setting (an ideological *choice* on Conrad's part), is both historically irrelevant and contemplatively hyperrelevant to the questions of international order the novel presents. Set in 1815 before and beyond the emergence of the United States as a world power but also equally addressed to 1925 where the terms of U.S. involvement as a world power are very much a focal question, *Suspense* seduces U.S. self-projection at the same time it backgrounds and prevents the United States from having any authoritative claims upon it. Such suggestive exclusion, of course, had been the key to Conrad's "heterotopic" U.S. appeal in all his texts—but with a particular note, not only of anxiety, but also of poignancy in his final novel *Suspense*. Whereas a contemporary review in the *Times* (London) praises *Suspense* for a final contribution to "the great collection which this *visitor* to our shores bequeathed to us; an incomparable legacy indeed in return for *our hospitality*,"[116] one almost never finds this firm double-edged rhetoric of "visitor" as opposed to "us," alien "legacy" as opposed to "our hospitality," all so confident in its sense of final boundary, among Conrad's celebrants in the United States—which Conrad, of course, regarded as anything but "home." Instead, the actually quite mixed U.S. reviews of *Suspense* itself—including major articles by Sinclair Lewis and Albert Guerard Sr.[117]—constitute an occasion to champion the nature of Conrad's achievement generally, through a general superlative vocabulary as divested of boundaries as it is ratifying of the American imagination to reconceive them.

The idea of self-determination, so expansive in its American applications throughout Conrad because it incarnates at the level of general problem and principle the concrete questions of territorial and ideological boundary animating U.S. interests in Conrad all along, suggests how more specific world regions could become heterotopically mediated by the different specific "places" foregrounded in Conrad's fiction. Here, the wide international latitude of Conrad's fiction facilitates not only general heterotopic contemplation of the terms of American international order but also specific contestation of the vocabularies of U.S. relation to and conception of particular world domains. *Nostromo*, for instance, was from the beginning centrally received in the United States as confirming the essential and endemic revolutionary instability of Latin America. Beginning in the immediate aftermath of Panamanian independence (facilitated by the United States in 1903; an important subtext of *Nostromo*) and continuing through a wider pattern of actual and threatened U.S. interventions in Latin

America during the next three decades, *Nostromo*'s mainstream discussions and reviews in the United States invariably emphasize the novel's "vividly real" rendering of the "particularly tragical form of revolution and intrigue that is *indigenous* to tropical America."[118] Such formulations essentialize revolution as a fundamental and internal ("indigenous") condition of Latin America while immunizing the United States and other imperial powers from active and ongoing responsibility for conditions of crisis, instability, dependency; they also ultimately authorize, under the Monroe Doctrine and pursuant to principles of "benevolent" intervention and "ultimate" self-determination, U.S. external intervention to rectify this otherwise irremediable "tragical" condition. *Nostromo*, hence, through its vertiginous and iterative presentation of Latin American revolution without indigenous means of resolution, facilitates both U.S. American repudiation of Latin American capacities of self-determination and U.S. harmonization of its own interventions in Latin America with idealized principles of self-determination. However, beginning with the first decade of "our Conrad," a powerful U.S. countertradition of interpreting *Nostromo* also emerges: Mencken, who knew all along that *Nostromo* is the greatest of Conrad's texts, dubs his lineage of Conrad readers "Conradistas" to indicate their parallelism to the Mexican Revolution and hostility in Conrad's Latinized image to the imperial U.S. state; and Wilson Follett, in his key wartime essay of 1917, could not be more clear that *Nostromo*, far from essentializing Latin American revolution, "is complete enough as Mr. Conrad depicts it to revolutionize, among other things, one's idea of South American revolutions."[119] With a sharp eye cast on U.S. activity and ambitions in Latin America and Conrad's expression of them through the U.S. American character Holroyd, Follett contextualizes the rise of U.S.-style and U.S.-financed imperial capitalism in Latin America with the novel's "successive pictures" of imperialist "exploitation" and domination from "different eras." This global historical field, Follett argues, is the ultimate condition and horizon of Latin American "conflict"; its latest imperialist instance, Follett continues, quoting a key passage from Dr. Monygham, in the form of economically secured "material interests" is neither categorically different from nor more ultimately stabilizing in its "continuity," "force," and moral human "rectitude" than prior imperialist forms. Moreover, against the grain of U.S. interventionist apology, *Nostromo* stands for the final proposition that the logic of global economic development and its supporting ideologies of "progress" must remain answerable to the higher "moral principle" of native sovereign self-determination in countries like those of Latin America. Follett closes his reading of *Nostromo* with this remarkable summation: "And reverberating through the book, literally from the first page to the last, haunting every chapter like the wandering echo of some lost truth, is the suggestion that the world's problems are more than economic, *that national identities must not be tampered with from outside in the name of progress.*"[120]

Follett thus enlists *Nostromo* both to critique and champion idealized conceptions of international U.S. American order in a specific (Latin American) global context; and so, too, more than can be fully charted here, do other world domains find complex and reciprocal "American" mediation through other specific Conrad texts. Conrad's Malay novels, for instance, which in the instance of *The Rescue* we have already seen many Americans *identify with* so as to disclaim U.S. imperialism, University of Chicago English professor Robert Morss Lovett aggressively *distinguishes from* a fundamentally "American" literary tradition of South Seas travel and fiction writing—to make much the same U.S. exceptionalist point with grave domestic implications.[121] Similarly, Conrad's "Africa" as presented in *Heart of Darkness*, which we shall explore more shortly from contemporary African-American viewpoints, offers a transnational vantage from which to both authorize and disavow, critically clarify and perversely misrecognize, U.S. situatedness within world continuities of race and imperial power relations.

Poland, moreover, a site of keen world interest in 1919 precisely because every inch of its hotly contested and freshly resurrected boundaries begged questions of self-determination and international security, placed Conrad at issue in the United States in both expected and unexpected ways. As Zdzisław Najder points out, "The Crime of Partition" (1919), by far the most elaborate and impassioned of Conrad's defenses of Polish history and a reborn Polish state, is strategically "addressed . . . mainly to his American readers": Conrad was aware of British public and high political reticence toward Polish territorial aspirations in early 1919, and dating from at least President Wilson's famous "thirteenth point" declaring an independent Poland an American military priority in January 1918, Conrad was attuned to Polish sympathies in the United States.[122] However, neither "The Crime of Partition" (written in December 1918), nor any of Conrad's other and earlier essays concerning Poland eventually published in *Notes on Life and Letters* (1921), nor any of Conrad's novels (which do not explicitly reference Poland at all), substantially address the truly perplexing "Polish" question of the immediate postwar period (1919–21): which was less whether an independent Poland should exist than where its boundaries should be. As might be expected, this lacuna, far from stifling American self-referential expression, instead produced at least two poles of stanching and elaborating its indeterminacy. At one extreme, John Quinn, the prominent New York lawyer and longtime solitary purchaser of Conrad's manuscripts, also an ardent capitalist and vocal anti-Semite, forwarded to the *New York Tribune* on April 2, 1920, an excerpt from a private letter by Conrad, which Quinn prefaces by affirming his and the *Tribune*'s "shar[ed] . . . belief" that "the fate of the new Poland is the real test of the peace settlement," and in which Conrad expresses his "gratification at the thought that the unbroken Polish front keeps Bolshevism off and that apparently the reborn [Polish] state has one heart and soul, one indomitable will, from the poorest peasant to the highest magnate."[123] The immediate context is the Polish-Soviet War of 1920, and in his quoted letter Conrad goes on expressly to advocate, as a bulwark and barrier against the "moral and physical pestilence bred in Russia," as a buffer to the "enormous seething mass of sheer moral corruption" looming from the Bolshevik East, a Polish national boundary extending "on a line from the Baltic provinces to the present frontier of Rumania."[124] This is about where, after a miraculous Polish military turn of events in August, the Treaty of Riga would ultimately place the boundary in March 1921—and about two hundred miles east of what the Paris peacemakers had recommended in 1919, enfolding many non-Polish ethnic minorities.

The *Tribune* not only endorses "Joseph Conrad's eloquent message"; it prints an adjacent editorial demonizing anyone who might disagree as parties of that "pacific cast" "who have been consistently wrong during the past five years" in declaring the war "impossible," fighting "every item of preparedness," "urg[ing] neutrality," "speak[ing] softly of Germany," "regrett[ing] our entrance into the war," and finally "urg[ing] that we fight as gently as possible . . . above all, avoid[ing] a peace with victory." Those "precious intelligences" who have suspected Poland of "wicked and imperialist" intentions do not understand Conrad's message of the menace of the "new czarism"—and foolishly probably hope that "the sooner [Poland and the United States are] overrun by the Bolshevists the better." They do not understand that "those basic instincts of Western civilization which made the great war inevitable" are again on the line, and they manufacture "slanderous pogrom charges" that (it is heavily implied) probably have their corollary in sympathies with ethnic (e.g., Jewish) and worker dissidence in the United States as well. But to the contrary, Conrad, a man of "peculiar authority" attuned to "natural American sympathies," not only *"our* first novelist" but also "one of the first minds of his time," offers a "Polish" question and cause that summon "every truly American instinct—of recollection for valiant Polish heroes who fought under our flag in the American Revolution, of admiration for a superb nationalism that knows not defeat, of fellowship with the spirit of Western liberty."[125] Clearly the *Tribune* instances here old wine offered in new bottles: the rhetorical template and tactics of Conrad's mobilization in a prior (anti-German) war, Conrad's bellicose patriotization to the exclusion of all class and ethnic alternative viewpoints and subtleties, shifted, via the convenient occasion of Poland, to the fresh fields, equally powerfully articulable through Conrad, of a new war against "Russian Bolshevism." Yet foremost among the "precious intelligences" whom the *Tribune* attacks, of course, is the liberal (and crosstown) *New Republic*, whose editors may very well have agreed with Quinn and the *Tribune* that the Polish question held "more interest in it than . . . any other one political and military issue . . . dealt with since the armistice,"[126] but with the reverse sympathies and reverse investments in Conrad. Though by no means hostile to Polish national rebirth and independence generally, the *New Republic* constructs Conrad in "The Meaning of Conrad" in a manner that, beyond its earlier pro-Jewish deployment of Conrad, must be understood in relation to the principles of self-determination by which throughout 1919 and 1920 the magazine centrally and repeatedly (1) supports the significantly more moderate territorial claims of Polish president Józef Piłsudski over the much broader claims advanced at Paris by Roman Dmowski, and (2) questions the anti-Russian and Red Scare hysteria through which U.S. daily newspapers like the *Times* and *Tribune* make it impossible to have any sober discussion of political territoriality in Central and Eastern Europe. Whereas for the *Times* and *Tribune*, "Lord" Jim's duping by Gentleman Brown suggests pacifist inattention to imminent threats like militarist Germany or Bolshevik Russia, for the *New Republic* Jim's ethical submission of his armed might to the sovereign will of the native chief Doramin suggests the principles to which Poland and the United States must adhere, *usque ad finem*, in engaging with "other" peoples and boundaries in Central and Eastern Europe. Though Conrad would have sided with the *Tribune* and had little patience for "American" Wilsonian abstraction as concerns the specific issue of Russia, it is worth noting that Conrad quite decisively preferred Piłsudski over Dmowski in matters of Polish politics[127]—and that "The Crime of Partition" repeatedly sounds themes of moral blamelessness, purely voluntary association, "democratised . . . institutions," and a "sacred tradition of freedom . . . and respect for the rights of individuals and States" that beg the question of the *New Republic*'s interpretation (*NLL* 132, 133).

Russia itself, already so prominently figuring in the discussion above, is a final specific international site that Conrad's writings directly mediate for the modern U.S. imagination. As always, this heterotopic mediation arises from the doubleness of a space posited as absolutely "other" becoming a "secret sharer" of the United States, simultaneously divesting the latter of its vocabularies of order and boundary while also declaring the means and emergency circumstances of their urgent reassertion. On the one hand, although Conrad's "Russian" fiction had always performed an important "educational" function in the United States,[128] the Bolshevik Revolution in October 1917 initiated an anxious turn to Conrad's writings concerning Russia as a pedagogical means of categorically discriminating and differentiating the pathologically self-destructive terms of Russian experience. "Russia is a world apart: that is the sum and substance of the tale," Mencken had written of *Under Western Eyes* as early as 1912[129]—and much of the resurgence, or rather, acute onset of U.S. interest in Conrad's "Russian" writings after the October Revolution are devoted to elaborating this proposition. *Under Western Eyes*, which immediately provoked an offer of dramatization by New York theater impresario H. Neagle in December 1917 (*CL* 6.157), and also an actual dramatization by Russian American writer S. Karrakis in 1921 (*CL* 7.334, 337), offered U.S. Americans attempting to "interpret" the revolution not only a central vocabulary of "Russian" as opposed to "Western" "eyes," experience, character, but also a general project of politically psychologizing Russia in terms of a "senseless" cycle of "tyranny" and "revolution" whose fundamental "moral anarchism" makes the "oppressors and oppressed" involved distinctively and hopelessly "all Russians together" (*UWE* vii, x). So, too, *The Secret Agent*, which went through many plans of American staging in 1920,[130] presents a figure of archetypal Russian "autocracy" in the sinister Mr. Vladimir; "Autocracy and War," reprinted with many American accolades of its "prophetic" qualities in *Notes on Life and Letters*, derides Russia as a vast "*néant*," "simply the negation of everything worth living for" (*NLL* 100); and finally, *The Rover* (1923), the last of Conrad's wildly popular (in the United States) and critically underdiscussed late texts, plainly inscribes within its lurid presentations of the French Revo-lution—its "red-capped mobs," its "ragamuffin patriots" and "revolutionary jargon," its "feebly struggling spirit of terrorism" dispensing bloodthirsty class warfare amid "the clamouring falsehoods of revolution"[131]—the absolutely "othered" contemporary context of the Russian Revolution. Repeated U.S. articulations of Russia and Russian writers "representing the *negation* of the austere virtues that [Conrad] stands for," of Conrad's "hat[ing] to hear [his] name pronounced in the same breath as [that of literary Russians],"[132] reflects this larger political field of U.S. Manichean self-construction with respect to Russia via Conrad's mediation.

Yet the very breadth of Conrad's U.S. cultural/political reception suggests something more than this neatly oppositional and reactionary, if ever nervously interpenetrated with the need for reassertion, "Russian" differentiation. When the *New Republic*, for example, in August 1924 in the important and revealingly entitled article "Nostr' Omo," which has nothing to do with *Nostromo*, advances the truly striking primary claim that "*The Secret Agent* is *the outstanding fact in the fiction of the generation now passing*,"[133] this proposition simply cannot be understood as an affirmation in the image of the "autocratic" Mr. Vladi-mir of all the anti-Russian, antisocialist hysteria that the *New Republic* spent the postwar years of the Red Scare in the United States (1919–21) deploring and contesting. Rather, as the title of the article, recognizing Conrad as "*our man*" through a prism of foreign translation, implies, the singular value and timeliness of *The Secret Agent* lies in the uncanny application of its ostensibly "foreign" story of a Russian-engineered plot to effect a civil rights crackdown, manipulating institutions of the press and mainstream anxieties of immigrants, leftist radicalism, and terroristic praxis, to contemporary U.S. circumstances and tactics during the Red Scare *as mobilized by the U.S. government*. The fact that Vladimir's and Verloc's plan fails is irrelevant: the reason the *New Repub-lic* champions *The Secret Agent* is that the very text that *could* be mobilized to legitimate Russia's absolute "autocratic" (or "radical" revolutionary) otherness turns out to be a pointed diagnosis of the very tactics of civil rights intrusion, elaborate surveillance, manufactured hysteria, press manipulation, xenophobia, terroristic fabrication, and domestic antileftist repression practiced by the U.S. State under the auspices of Attorney General A. Mitchell Palmer in 1919–20. A bomb, in fact, not unlike the one Stevie unsuccessfully attempts to explode near Greenwich Observatory, was quite successfully exploded, and ideologically manipulated by the U.S. State in its explosion, on Palmer's porch in June 1919: that is, what the novel posits as otherworldly conspiracy the United States recognizes as domestic circumstance at the levels of both radical violence *and* State autocracy. Similarly, *The Rover* (recalling the parallel indeterminacy of and multiple contemporary contexts for "Napoleon" in *Suspense*) does not simply posit the French Revolution as a "code" for the radical, violent, illiberal extremes of autocracy transacted by the Russian Bolsheviks in the name of the "people" and absolutely egalitarian ideals; it also *simultaneously* comprehends the French Revolution as a seminal birthplace of modern Western democracy—hence enfolding the two genealogies, the latter pointedly including the United States, into the same suspect "democratic" inheritance and historical pattern of liability and abuse. To appreciate the "genius" of *The Rover*, as Philip Littell observes in 1923, is to feel the sanction of "ultrapatriotic" assertions of difference literally "exile[d]" of the terrain of their articulation;[134] and so, too, as both Jacques Berthoud and Christopher GoGwilt have differently shown of *Under Western Eyes*, are its "Western" and "Russian" confluences as important as its asseverations of difference. As GoGwilt beautifully explains, the novel's central image of Rousseau's statue in Geneva, metonymizing both that "respectable and passionless abode of democratic liberty" and its Russophile "international conspirators of every shade" (*UWE* 357), "situates the institutions of European democracy and the rhetoric of Russian revolutionary and autocratic thinking under the same mistaken [Rousseauian] legacy."[135] *Under Western Eyes* thus announces the perpetual challenge by which liberal democracy must continue to confront its shadow in the autocracy of the general will and mass-manipulated State, which, with respect to the United States, was Mencken's "antidemocratic" point in invoking Conrad all along.

DOMESTIC FRONTS: IMMIGRATION, RACE RELATIONS, AFRICAN-AMERICAN VOICES

I have been arguing that an "Anglo-Saxon" axis of mediation and contention, one predicated on British alliance and British-allied war galvanization during the Great War, and one also generating further major seams (e.g., self-determination, anti-Bolshevism) and sites of international heterotopic contemplation, foundationally propels Conrad's rise in the modern U.S. imagination. Unfolding contrapuntally along and outward from this Anglo-Saxon axis, the various terms of American international order (Anglophile, moral/idealist, anti-imperialist, nationalist and internationalist, democratic) affirmed in this chapter directly reverse the emphases of the previous chapter. I have argued that such a perpetual dialogic of contention and containment, subversion and capture—never fully resolved, never sufficiently reasserted, invariably transposed to further domains of Conrad's American mediation—fundamentally derives, not simply from Conrad's rich world latitude and uncanny U.S. historical resonances but also from heterotopic qualities in his writings that simultaneously negate and compel claims of boundary and order. Furthermore, as I explicitly demonstrated in the previous chapter and have been implicitly suggesting throughout this one, the complexity of Conrad's mediation of the international sphere carries equally complex and crucial obverse implications in the domestic sphere. The double mapping of the two spheres is the true full field of Conrad's cultural production as a "master" literary figure in the United States; and we turn now, subject to the reverse polarity of this chapter, to the two domains of domestic "Anglo-Saxon" contention not yet focally revisited earlier: immigration politics and black/white racial politics. As we shall see, not only the continuing gravity, multiplicity, and mutability of Conrad's meaning in the United States but also a complex recovery and estrangement of U.S. American voices and vantages, contact and colloquy, are at issue in these (manifestly related) lines of inquiry.

The first matter is the more straightforward. Simply put, whereas Mencken seizes on Conrad's "foreignness" to map resistance to British alliance and affinity in the international sphere onto resistance to "Anglo-Saxon" cultural and political hegemony in the domestic sphere, the Doubleday pole of Conrad's production does the reverse: it combines Conrad's Anglophile militarization in the international sphere with a domestic construction of Conrad, not simply as a perfect national patriot, but also as an immigrant perfectly committed to Anglo-Saxon cultural assimilation. A touchstone text in this regard is Alfred Knopf's *Joseph Conrad: The Romance of His Life and of His Books* (1913), the small book Knopf wrote to introduce Conrad to the American public and to commence Doubleday's marketing campaign. A genuinely remarkable text for its time—one reprinted and recycled by Doubleday countless times during the following decade; one regularly serving as a template for American biographical commentary on Conrad; one whose "sincere enthusiasm" and promise of "something unusual and individual in publishing" initially prompted no less than Willa Cather to turn to Knopf as a publisher in his own right[136]—Knopf's book initiates an assimilationist template of constructing Conrad by following the narrative example of Conrad's autobiographical *A Personal Record* (1912), which renders in parallel the "strange" yet "sympath[etic]" and "fascinating" peripatetic histories of both Conrad's own life and the material genesis of his first novel, *Almayer's Folly*.[137] Knopf's governing paradox is at work from the first page of his text, which presents a page-long excerpt of James Huneker's impressionistic account of a recent interview with Conrad, which Huneker wrote for the *New York Times* in November 1912. In the excerpt, Huneker begins by emphasizing Conrad's plurally "foreign" voice and appearance—"His shrug and play of hands are Gallic, or Polish, as you please, and his eyes, shining or clouded, are not of our race. . . . When Mr. Conrad speaks English, you can hear, rather overhear, the foreign cadence"—but he comes to emphasize Conrad's perfectly "sympathetic," transmutably "human," even American qualities: "His curiosity is prompted by his boundless sympathy for all things human. He is, as you may have surmised from his writings, the most human and lovable of all men. He takes an interest in everything except bad art, which moves him to vibrating indignation. . . . He is an admirer of Poe, Hawthorne, Walt Whitman, and Henry James among American writers."[138]

So, too, Knopf's narrative sets out to highlight the exotic range of "all the four corners of the earth—the Congo, the East Indies, Poland, England, Switzerland" through whose shifting contexts Conrad spent more than five years pursuing the writing of *Almayer*, and whose general "foreign" arc prompts Knopf's articulation of the diverse global contacts and composition of Conrad's life. But it is not the allure of otherness but rather two quite linear and domesticating metanarratives of Anglo-American normativity that provide Knopf's radiating narrative with its ultimate structure and romance. The first is a metanarrative of self-reliant hard work and its rewards: through many years and diverse conditions of deliberate and dedicated struggle, through his own individualist determination to work his way up "whenever and wherever the opportunity offered," through a tenacity that saw him rise first from the lowest proletarian rung to the highest rank of the British merchant marine, then "from conditions of obscurity to great fame" as an English writer, "Mr. Conrad," vindicating a kind of democratic "dream" and "romance" of upwardly mobile possibility, "has come slowly into his own . . . as a master of the art of fiction as great as . . . any living writer."[139] The fundamental "romance" at issue here is not really exotic so much as the American Dream: indeed, we understand little of the pervasive American fascination with Conrad's *biography* without understanding its ready "romantic" transposability to the terms of the Horatio Alger rags-to-riches American Dream story.[140]

The second metanarrative concerns the precise dream Conrad is chasing: Englishness. Though Knopf's narrative registers and even champions Conrad's alterity to a degree not true of the interpretive lineage he is opening up, the ultimate "romance of Conrad's life" lies, in Knopf's account, not in Conrad's "foreign" adventures or residual qualities but in their subjection to Conrad's romantic calling as an Englishman; it is not the autonomy or anarchy of cultural difference but rather the domestication and subjection of every conceivable world form of cultural otherness to and through the discipline and passion of Englishness, Anglo-Saxon normativity, that is the ultimate telos of the story. Hence, much as *Almayer's Folly*, notwithstanding its multiple foreign fields of concern and composition, is ultimately an *English* accomplishment, Conrad's life is also mapped from the beginning on a course toward and powerfully subsumed by Englishness. "From the age of five," Knopf observes, Conrad began "making his acquaintance" with, among other national authors and literatures, Shakespeare and other "English literature" translated into Polish by his father. When Conrad "from a very youthful age longed with unquenchable ardor to go to sea," such departure from Poland "meant an *absolute severing from his old, and the commencement of a totally new, life*. And young Conrad intended moreover, to be an *English* seaman." Though Conrad's prose, Knopf claims, "does not lend [itself] well to abstract quotation," this does not prevent Knopf's narrative from presenting at its center a long epiphanal quotation from *A Personal Record* in which the young adult Conrad, freshly emigrated to southern France and first encountering the English ship *James Westoll*, experiences rapturous self-discovery as an "English" man:

A few strokes brought us alongside, and it was then that, for the very first time in my life, I heard myself addressed in English—the speech of my secret choice, of my future, of long friendships, of the deepest affections, of hours of toil and hours of ease, and of solitary hours too, of books read, of thoughts pursued, of remembered emotions—of my very dreams! And if (after being thus fashioned by it in that part of me which cannot decay) I dare not claim it aloud as my own, then, at any rate the speech of my children. Thus small events grow memorable by the passage of time.[141]

Here, linguistic and cultural assimilation come together: though Knopf could have quoted many very different passages from *A Personal Record*—for example, any of several articulating Conrad's identification with what he would later call "the whole Polish mentality" (*PR* vii)—Knopf here picks the one emphasizing Conrad's zeal in being "fashioned" by the English language and its contexts of friendship, affection, labor, *culture*. To present Conrad testifying, with whatever provisional humility in 1912, to his almost reverential commitment of self and children to the "dream" of English; to present the once foreign, even *still* not completely deforeignized, Conrad proudly embracing the power of English language and culture permanently to "fashion" the most essential "part in me which cannot decay"—these are evidently to foreground the language of "Anglo-Saxon" cultural assimilation. Such Anglo-Saxon assimilation—or rather, Anglo-*Americanization*, for this specific U.S. context of immigration, of course, is what principally prompts Knopf's presentation of questions of assimilation here—is an ultimate ideological (and commercial) agenda complemented by at least two further strategies in Knopf's *Joseph Conrad*. First, Knopf counterbalances the centrifugal narration of Conrad's diverse "foreign" voyages with a steady refrain of "return," "rest," and eventuation in England: whence the "universal[ity]" of Conrad's "human interest" can be calibrated, articulated, ultimately enfolded. Second, Knopf's text is interspersed with a series of contemporary photos insisting on Conrad's commitment to and achievement of the life of a supremely domesticated English gentleman. Against one strangely blurred and one descriptively evasive picture of Conrad himself, Knopf presents two photos of Conrad's English wife; several involving their country estate at "Capel House, Orlestone, near Ashford, Kent, England"; three of their younger son John, with "family cat and dog," "his pet rabbits," and a toy wagon; and a final shot—patriotic, Anglified, gentrified—of "The Elder Son, Cadet Alfred Borys, in His Father's Cadillac, Known in His Family as the Puffer."[142] Knopf, though he does not completely erase the continuing possibility of Conrad's foreignness, expresses through these pictures what his narrative effects generally: a double narrativity whereby every expression of the "fascination" and residual possibility of "foreignness" becomes subordinated to and subsumed by the dedicated pursuit and "romance" of a very domestic and domesticating Anglo-Saxon normativity.

Knopf thus helps to generate a template for constructing Conrad which, to quite the reverse ends of his friend Mencken (Knopf could not see this at the time), and with the intelligent flexibility that typifies Doubleday's marketing efforts at their best, works to consolidate rather than subvert *domestic* Anglo-Saxon cultural hegemony and the various forms of American national order through which it was asserted. Unfolding through a familiar array of mainstream cultural institutions structurally associable with Doubleday, a dynamic culture of "our Conrad" mediating U.S. immigrant politics through evolving assertions of Anglo-American cultural order consequently emerges. This process happens in two overlapping historical stages, with significantly different vocabularies and ideological strategies of Conrad's Anglo-Saxon assertion at issue in each. First, prior to and with increasingly sharp emphasis during the war, the ideology of Americanization itself—the assimilation and/or subjugation of immigrant foreignness to Anglo-American language and culture norms, in line with the increasingly bellicose and Anglo-aligned politics of the State and country—serves as a primary frame of Conrad's advancement across Eastern mass media and major commercial magazines. Though it comes later, H. I. Brock's important assertion in the *New York Times* in May 1923, "Briefly, Conrad is a Briton by deliberate self-determination,"[143] effectively reiterates the domestic template of the pre-1919 years: for even as its internationalist rhetoric ("self-determination") begs contemporary questions of shared principle between the United States and Britain, its explicit meaning is to valorize Conrad's "deliberate" and determined assimilation as an (Anglo-Saxonized) immigrant in line with the construction of Conrad through Americanization discourse in the previous decade. Though there are occasional reservations of Conrad's "difference," usually toward authenticating the knowledge he provides of "other" places for the United States,[144] the general pattern in prewar and wartime U.S. mass commercial discourse is to marvel at the *feat* of Conrad's "literary naturalization";[145] to emphasize the accomplished extent of Conrad's gifts for self-translation and conversion;[146] to champion the dedication through which this "Man Who, Born Without a Country, *Made* Himself One of the Greatest Living Writers in English";[147] all in all, to dramatize the commitment through which Conrad, through his "twenty years [of] painstaking and admirable" service in the English merchant marine, "twenty years [of] unconscious amassing" and "slow absorption" and "assimilating" of English traditions, "twenty years [of] drilling himself in a language to which he was a total stranger up to his twentieth year," achieved a "thoroughness" of "Anglo" assimilation "that it is hard to duplicate."[148] "Duplication," of course, is precisely the point: it is as a model of Anglo-American cultural-national assimilation that Conrad is being advanced.

After the war, however, a change in emphasis arises. As I suggested earlier, Conrad's construction in mainstream U.S. discourse begins to shift at the end of the war, from model to object of Anglophilia, from admirer to essence and epitome of Englishness, to reflect new terms of international relation between the United States and Britain. A domestic agenda anchors this transition as well: at issue in Conrad's essentialization as an Englishman is not only the power internationally to pronounce on Britain in Conrad's image but also a domestic consolidation of Anglo-Saxon racial and cultural supremacy, *not* by offering Conrad as a blueprint of assimilation but rather by denying and delimiting this very possibility through Conrad's singular and newly essentialized example. As Walter Benn Michaels has explained, the earlier 1920s witness the rise of a new "nativist" (and isolationist) moment in U.S. history wherein dominant anxieties and energies are predicated less on assimilating immigrants than on designing racial and quasi-racial strategies of immigrant exclusion; the concern is less with acculturating foreignness than engineering a nation of boundaries, external and internal, whose essential referent is immutable racial difference, separation, monitoring—and cultural strategies designed to reinforce such absolutely exclusionary effects.[149] In this new context, "our Conrad," once so forcefully imaginable (and contestable) as an exemplary figure of American immigrant assimilation, now becomes an exceptionalized and essentialized means of foreclosing, or at least radically narrowing, American assimilationist possibility. Whereas before, mainstream media had followed Knopf in emphasizing Conrad's "English" epiphany alongside the *James Westoll* in *A Personal Record*, its "romance" lying in Conrad's "absolute severing of his old, and commencement of a totally new, life," postwar U.S. discourse turns heavily to Conrad's new language in the 1919 Author's Note to the autobiography, which is much more fundamentalizing of Conrad's relationship to English. Far from a rhetoric of transformative alien romance, article after article quotes Conrad insisting that "my faculty to write in English is as *natural* as any other aptitude with which I might have been *born*"; that "I have a strange and overpowering feeling that it has always been an *inherent* part of myself"; that "English was for me neither a matter of choice nor adoption. The matter of choice had never entered my head"; that "when I began to write it came as *natural* for me to write English as if it had been my own *native tongue*"; that "English seems to me *a part of my blood and culture.*"[150]

Here the overarching narrative is clearly not one of a twenty-year-old alien dramatically hailed by a "foreign" English tongue and culture, not one word of which he spoke, not one element of which he had directly experienced. Rather, the narrative is one of Conrad having actualized "English" aptitudes and qualities *that had essentially been part of him more or less from the beginning.* Either Conrad has always innately possessed special affinities with the English, or he acquired them through rich exposure to (translated) English language and culture so early on that it "seems to me a part of my blood and culture"— regardless, Conrad is not presented here as a broad license of Anglo-Saxon assimilation but as a restriction of who is capable of it. He reinforces the same Anglo-American cultural hegemony at issue before but through a very different essentialized vocabulary of order and strategy of construction. Similarly, whereas "Poland" once suggested the extreme "Slavic" difference Conrad had to overcome, it now suggests, in complementary relation to self-reflexive U.S. constructions of Poland against Russia in the international sphere, a narrow and essential "Western" *likeness* to "Anglo-Saxon" countries like Britain and the United States[151]—or in any event, a country where Conrad personally "from the stammering stage" was "so completely" exposed to English literature and culture in translation that "its very idioms I truly believe had a direct action on my temperament and fashioned my still plastic character."[152] Likewise, whereas Conrad's "mastery" once suggested a universal model of painstaking dedication to an Anglo-Saxon host culture, it now means a standard of English facility so high that only an exceptional immigrant—one of extremely rare gift, or one of unusually sympathetic essential racial/cultural background (e.g., being from Poland, also being immersed in contact with English from an early age)—could possibly achieve it. *Exclusion* and *exclusiveness*, the narrowing of immigration acculturation possibilities (of nationalized self-actualization as a "true" American) through Conrad's essentialized Englishness and personal singularity, is the new mechanism of Conrad's "Anglo-Saxon" assertion; and one finds such "nativist" premises at work not simply among Conrad's champions but also among his detractors, such as Columbia literature professor and writer Mark Van Doren. Van Doren, in a memorably pompous article in the *Nation* in January 1925, expresses his "conviction that Conrad, try as faithfully as he might, never learned how to write English"—but precisely because, extending the logic of nativism through the repudiation of Conrad, the "strange" and "strained" quality of Conrad's prose is marked by a "defective accent" which no amount of "labor" to learn an "adopted language" can overcome.[153] So, too, even liberal mainstream defenses of both Conrad and immigrants tend to effect profound nativist recoveries. In Lawrence Abbott's remarkable article in *Outlook* (NY) in May 1923, Conrad's recent visit to the United States prompts Abbott to reflect enthusiastically on how "in its literary life London is a greater melting-pot than the whole of the U.S."; indeed, as epitomized by Conrad, the cultural diversity of contemporary British authors suggests not only the true "variety" of a melting pot but "a literary league of nations which is greater, more inclusive, and more important than any political league of nations." However, the inclusive vision Conrad triggers is one of "Anglo-Scotch-Irish-American literature," perhaps with "a little Polish" sprinkled in; Conrad licenses, this is to say, if not strictly an "Anglo-Saxon" vision, nevertheless a profoundly Anglocentric and racially consolidating (as white) one, one aggressively marginalizing (and "melting" away) most of the ethnic minorities most acutely victimized in the United States at the time, and doing this all, of course, in explicit relation to a "British" model.[154] Similarly, the article "Joseph Conrad: The Gift of Tongues," printed as a lead editorial in the *Nation* the same month, directly challenges nativist dogma by offering in Conrad proof of "what many have long believed, that a language and with it an entire national culture can be absorbed after the years of infancy, and that thus the friendliness and flexibility of life can be indefinitely increased." But it is not, qua Mencken, as an attack on Anglo-American cultural dominance but rather in thorough deference to its "entirely native" standards of "correct[ness]," that the "friendliness" and "flexibility" of Conrad are contemplated as such.[155]

Willa Cather offers a final means of revisiting the entire historical field of Conrad's mediation of U.S. immigrant politics presented in this book: as complex, as we have just seen, in its facilitations of order as it was in its subversions of it. Much more engaged with Conrad than criticism acknowledges, Cather's literary career unfolds over a period that strikingly overlaps Conrad's (1895–1925). Conrad, of course, comes to maturity first, in part because he began writing much later in life, but in Cather's lifetime of literary engagements with him, not all of which can be discussed here and some of the most illuminating of which, as we shall see, predate the advent of "our Conrad," Cather remarkably anticipates the full latitude of vicissitudes and contradictions through which Conrad's cultural elaboration in matters of immigrant politics ultimately unfolds. I am less concerned, in other words, with questions of "influence" between the two authors than how Cather's writings, through their self-conscious sensitivity to and framing of Conrad, effectively *read* Conrad in comprehensive advance of (and eventual intersection with) an entire political subeconomy of Conrad's production.

Cather's clearest literary encounter with Conrad is the short story "Behind the Singer Tower" (1912): the last story but one Cather wrote before her breakthrough novel *O Pioneers!* (1913); perhaps the only story of direct political criticism, "muckraking" in certain elements, Cather ever wrote; and a transparent, self-conscious imitation in large part of *Heart of Darkness.* Set at twilight on a small boat on the North River just outside New York City, Cather's story presents six characters—an anonymous frame narrator; a philosophical engineer named Fred Hallett, who soon takes over the story with one of his long and inconclusive yarns; and four other professional men, including a journalist, a lawyer, a draftsman, and a Jewish doctor named Zablowski—who gather together on the water to reflect at some critical distance on a "horrifying" event that occurred the day before. This event is the burning of the Mont Blanc Hotel, the tallest and most extravagant hotel in New York: "Its prices, like its proportions . . . outscaled everything else in the known world."[156] When the Mont Blanc burns, the casualties include the hotel's many rich and powerful visitors, many of them foreigners killed in the fire or while attempting to jump from the building, as well as the very burgeoning "idea" of New York itself. Hallett's boat is in turn liminally positioned to produce both exotic reflection and domestic cross-implication: coming to rest at the river's edge of the home country, off the southeastern tip of Manhattan island, the boat allows the six characters simultaneously to gaze *out* along the outbound river—"that narrow, much-traveled highway, the road to the open sea," which more than anything else is dotted by *in*bound ships carrying immigrants to New York that "come steaming up the big sea road"—and also "behind us" at a haunted vision of the great city itself, a "brooding" "darkness" hovering over its "wide circle of lights that rim the horizon from east to west and west to east." Of course all of these details—the incipient nocturnal setting, the professional cast of characters, the convention of the anonymous frame narrator, the reference to the "idea," the motif of the delayed and liminalized boat and its bifocal significance, the somber mood, the oral tale to follow—take their cues from *Heart of Darkness,* as does the story's very framing narrative idiom. Here is the frame narrator's description of the six characters sitting in darkening, ruminative silence, meditating on obscure and ominous connections between their two zones of vision:

Boats of every shape and purpose went about their business and made noise enough as they did, doubtless. But to us, after what we had been hearing all day long, the place seemed unnaturally quiet and the night unnaturally black. There was a brooding mournfulness over the harbor, as if the ghost of helplessness and terror were abroad in the darkness. One felt a solemnity in the misty spring sky where only a few stars shone, pale and far apart, and in the sighs of the heavy black water that rolled up into the light. The city itself, as we looked back at it, seemed enveloped in a tragic self-consciousness.[157]

To read these words with any sensitivity to Conrad is to *hear* the intimacy of Cather's engagement with Conrad in this story; it is to recognize "behind" the singer Cather, and as part of the crisis of writerly identity that Sharon O'Brien demonstrates is crucially at issue in the story,[158] Cather turning to Conrad and engaging in not only a rewriting of Conrad but a reading and revealing of him. The political terms of this revelation become clear in the doubleness of the tale Hallett has to tell. Much as Marlow begins *Heart of Darkness* with a critique of colonial atrocity, the disclosure of a chaos of imperialist energy transacting a ruthlessness of African exploitation, Hallett's tale, triggered in his mind by an inbound immigrant ship that helps him to reframe the meaning of the Mont Blanc tragedy, concerns an "exotic" disclosure of imperialist victimization not abroad but at home. Hallett's tale recounts the American experience of a young Italian immigrant named Caesarino. Lured to the United States by the cheap labor needs and false promises of American capital, Caesarino—like so many "fur workers and garment workers" and high-rise window washers of foreign background, their "names unpronounceable to the American tongue"—once worked in oppressive and ungainful conditions on the "foundation" of the Mont Blanc with Hallett, where he was killed in a massive drilling accident caused by the extreme indifference of his rapacious and exploitative employer to safe working conditions. Just as Kurtz ends his life with the words, "The horror! The horror!" Caesarino ends his with the whispered and resonating summation, "ma, perché?" (but, why?). Following the immigrant Jewish Zablowski's formula, "You've used us for your ends—waste for your machine," Hallett and Cather thus set out through the story of Caesarino to reveal American capitalism as a species of indefensibly exploitative imperialism; Cather reads Conrad, this is to say, as a means of diagnosing *as imperialism* immigrant labor

exploitation in the United States, against the grain of American exceptionalist self-conception.[159]

However, the Jewish Zablowski is by no means a celebrated or authoritative figure in Cather's story; rather, he is on Hallett's boat as a kind of inter-
loper in the American scene, whose racialized terms Hallett's story moves on
to address. Just as *Heart of Darkness* begins (or so Conrad once suggested to
Cunninghame Graham) at the level of liberal political critique, but quickly
moves on to a larger racialized frame of "darkness" which, while obviously
not unrelated to imperialism, refuses to confine itself to reformist politics, so
too Hallett's story uses immigrant exploitation as an occasion to advance more
fundamental claims and anxieties about the racialized—or rather, increasingly deracialized—composition of the United States. The parallel is pointed
and unmistakable: just as in Conrad the true "horror" ultimately lies less in
Congolese oppression than in the disclosure of a "savage" racialized essential
commonality between oppressed and oppressor, in Cather's story the victimization of immigrant labor ultimately makes for an indictment less of unre-
strained American capitalism in itself than of its indexing of a foreign, vaguely
"Semitic" and "Oriental," racialized appropriation of the American national
soul and body politic, and the American capacity to maintain standards of
civilized human conduct. Such anxieties of a racial appropriation and degeneration, though plentifully available in 1912, strikingly anticipate the crest of
racialized nativism and anti-Semitism in the United States in the 1920s; and
they are expressed in a number of ways in "Behind the Singer Tower": for example, the suspect and insinuating presence of the Jewish Zablowski "on the
boat"; the "racial characteristics" of the Jewish employer Merryweather, who
is responsible for Caesarino's death and who has taken over the construction
industry; and overarching all, the eponymous "Singer Tower" itself, variously
described as a "Jewy-looking thing," "Persian," and reminiscent of "a Magi" or
"Buddha." The Singer Tower is an icon of American "foreign" racial appropriation—a "colossal figure . . . watching over the city and the harbor like a pre-
siding Genius" which "had come out of Asia quietly in the night, no one knew
just when or how," leaving "the Statue of Liberty, holding her feeble taper in
the gloom off to our left, . . . but an archaeological survival."[160] Racial infiltra-
tion thus underlies the economics of American imperialist depravity; and it
is, indeed, genuinely unclear whether in the story Cather's agenda is racially,
"orientally," to distinguish "bad" Jewish immigrants from "good" immigrants

like the Italian Caesarino; or whether the specter of racialized foreignness, of those who never properly belonged at the "foundation" of the American Mont Blanc ("*white* mountain") in the first place, applies to *all* the "new" immigrants.[161] What is clear, however, is that Cather's reading of *Heart of Darkness* is ultimately one of racialized license. One response, indeed, to those who have argued that Cather's story is actually meant to critique Hallett is that Cather had been telling the same racialized story, of the Jewish/Asian hijacking of American identity, without complication as far back as "The Affair at Grover Station" (1900)—a story that also articulates its racial agenda through a sense of self-conscious affiliation with *Heart of Darkness*.[162]

But *Heart of Darkness* was not the only, or even the primary, Conrad text of seminal interest to Cather. Rather, in "The Sculptor's Funeral" (1905)—an important early Cather text, first published in *McClure's Magazine* in January 1905 and later reprinted in both *The Troll Garden* (1905) and *Youth and the Bright Medusa* (1920)—a very different text and interpretive thread of engagement with Conrad emerges. Set in the stiflingly provincial town of Sand City, Kansas, "The Sculptor's Funeral" concerns the relationship between two characters: Harvey Merrick, an internationally famous sculptor, now dead, whose corpse is returned to his Kansas home at his request, and in implicit confirmation of the agonized indebtedness of his "beautiful" art to the home he always despised; and Jim Laird, a lawyer educated in the East who could have followed his friend Merrick's migratory example, but who at the crucial moment hesitated and remained behind in Kansas, where he has ever since served as an angry, tormented factotum of the crude ostentations and vindictive cupidity of the locals. Significantly, Jim Laird is named both in repetition and as a reversal of Conrad's "Lord" Jim. Like Conrad's Jim, Laird is a figure of perpetual isolation, anguished sensitivity, "fierce resentment" at missed opportunity; hiding his wounded pride behind an "astonishing cataract" of red beard, his "red face convulsed with anger," his shoulders "heavy and dogged" with the burden of memory, Laird carries in his body the shame of his failed courage to depart home, and its continuing lifetime of debasing implications of and for his character.[163] Yet "Lord" Jim's failing, of course, was that he *did* "jump" from familiar circumstances and his presumptive station, not that he stayed: as his name suggests, Jim Laird reverses the trajectory of "Lord" Jim's experience while sharing the essential terms of ambivalence that make up his condition. As such, Cather offers a most prescient and insightful reading of

Conrad's central character: whereas it would take twenty-five more years for Gustav Morf to offer the world its first standardized interpretation of "Lord" Jim and his "jump" as expressions of Conrad's personal emigration from Poland, and as expressions of the ambivalences (ethical, cultural, psychological) attending transcultural migration generally,[164] Cather understands this in 1905: this is what it means to name a character who stays, but who is tempted and haunted by the same migratory ambivalences as one who departs (Merrick), both after and as the reverse/obverse of "Lord" Jim.

But Cather does more than this. In "The Sculptor's Funeral," she does not simply map a single character from Lord Jim onto a single character in her story; she effects a web of cross-correlations between the two texts that effectively decodes Lord Jim, not only in terms of problematics of transcultural migratory experience but also as an exploration of the possibilities of imagined community, that may be generated from and in relation to it. Harvey Merrick, the actual migrant and exile in Cather's story, whose "romantic" figure and art both depend on and are haunted by the inescapable hail of "home," actually approximates certain aspects of "Lord" Jim more closely than Laird does. Laird, in turn, is an unsettled and unusual insider, sensitive to problems and analogies of transition that transcend literal travel, whose determination to narrate and intensely self-identify with the final "meaning" of Merrick's life is not unlike that of Lord Jim's Marlow. Steavens, one of Merrick's pupils and a bridging character, significantly exists in Cather's story to attest to its eminently Conradian search[165] for communal common ground between the displaced Merrick and any resident of Sand City: the search for "the feeling, the understanding, that must exist in someone, even here."[166] And all in all, Cather's story thus reads not simply one character from but the larger field and form of Lord Jim—that is, the obverse reciprocity between Jim and Marlow, the larger networks of social association generated around Jim, the novel's fundamental narrativity of empathy for a figure of departure—in terms of Cather's own explicit thematics of transcultural migration and the bonds of empathy, self-analogy, and self-identification that may be forged in relation to it. Though foreign immigrants (like Conrad himself) are not expressly at issue in "The Sculptor's Funeral," a template is clearly being developed for the kind of intercultural bonding between foreign émigrés and variously displaced U.S. natives, the kind of pluralist imagined community dynamically predicated on diverse cultural experiences of and analogies with what Joseph Urgo has described as "migratory consciousness,"[167] that Cather presents in her major fiction between characters like Alexandra Bergson and Carl Linstrum, and Ántonia Shimerda and Jim Burden. In "The Sculptor's Funeral," Cather hence mobilizes a reading of *Lord Jim* that is not only a sensitive and prescient interpretation of its (im)migratory premises, but also a powerful challenge to later developments of Anglo-assimilationist "Americanization" and "Anglo-Saxon" racialized exclusion—notwithstanding, of course, Cather's own licensing of the latter through the equal force of Conrad in "Behind the Singer Tower."

How, then, are we to talk about the place and terms of Conrad's construction at work in Cather's major fiction and later prose? To answer this question, it is important to understand that the literary engagements with Conrad we've been tracing, arising in the important period immediately before Cather's breakthrough as a novelist, emerge not only in a historical but in an institutional context: namely, the publishing world of S. S. McClure. For the seven years prior to January 1905, when Cather shrewdly sent "The Sculptor's Funeral" for publication in *McClure's Magazine*, McClure had been Conrad's principal promoter in the United States. As early as 1898, McClure had secured the advance American rights to the Conrad novel at the time entitled *The Rescuer*; and shortly thereafter, the McClure houses published the U.S. editions of *Lord Jim* (1900), *The Inheritors* (1901), *Youth: A Narrative and Other Stories* (1903); *Falk and Other Stories* (1903); and *Romance* (1904). These texts were heavily advertised in *McClure's Magazine*, and this culture of Conrad's strident promotion, though unsuccessful in the largesse of its ambitions, by no means ceased when Cather began working as an editor of the magazine in December 1905, shortly thereafter becoming its managing editor through 1912. As Edith Lewis recalls in a biographical treatment of Cather that takes its subtitle from Conrad's autobiography, Conrad was a "name" at *McClure's* throughout this time; more to the point, Elizabeth Sergeant remembers Cather's comment prior to introducing her to McClure: "'He reveres genius,' said Willa Cather in an intimate admiring tone. 'He's lost more money on Joseph Conrad than any editor alive!'"[168] Conrad's "The Brute" appeared in *McClure's* in November 1907: it had received truly remarkable promotional fanfare in six separate prior issues of the magazine, some of whose advertisements involve and cross-correlate themselves with Cather's work; and when "The Brute" appeared, it was lavishly printed with four full-page specially commissioned oil paintings by noted artist E. L. Blumenschein.[169] In 1908, the McClure houses also published in book form Conrad's *The Point of Honor* and steadily promoted it and Conrad generally in the magazine as well.[170] In 1909, Cather was sent personally to England on, among other things, an ultimately unsuccessful attempt to visit Conrad to secure an additional story for the magazine, which the magazine had already implicitly advertised. Also in 1909, Sarah Orne Jewett apparently expressed to Cather her "most rejoicing and reverent admiration" of Conrad; as Cather later recollects in her famous essay "Miss Jewett" (1936), Jewett "was one of the first Americans to see the importance of Conrad" and, indeed, "was reading a new volume of Conrad, late in the night, when the slight cerebral hemorrhage occurred from which she died some months later [in 1909]."[171]

These comments and the overarching institutional context of McClure are important because, without forcing a rubric of "influence" that I do not think is especially useful in the case of Conrad and Cather, they clarify the central seriousness, and also suggest some of the politics, of Cather's several later affirmations of Conrad as a *license* for her own self-assertion as a novelist—and for American writing more generally. Conrad was not a private whim but a central public condition of Cather's struggle to emerge as a novelist: that is what the institutional context of *McClure's* makes clear, even as the rise of "our Conrad" lay in the immediate future. However, unlike the familiar narrative of the earlier Cather's studied and ultimately stifling relationship to Henry James, Conrad's meaning to Cather is more that of the fraternally licensing empowerment of a parallel "pioneering" spirit (like many of Cather's primary character dyads). This is the essential symptomology of "Behind the Singer Tower" and "The Sculptor's Funeral" (and the several other earlier Cather stories that invoke Conrad): *not* ultimately one of mimicry or "tutelage," but rather of empowering *impact*: the authorizing precedent and enabling license to conduct the kind of experimentation—of theme, social domain, and form, of aesthetic as well as political expression—in some ways uncannily resonant of Conrad, but fundamentally answerable to Cather's own material and exigencies of expression in themselves. Cather often talks about herself through a rhetoric of larger arcs of American fiction; here, from the famous address "On the Novel" that Cather presented before the Pulitzer Prize Committee in 1933, is the most considered summation we still have by Cather of Conrad's liberating place in the development of the American novel—and in her own emergence as a novelist as well:

[The great Russian novelists of the nineteenth century] fixed the attention of every sensitive imagination the world over; the old icebergs began melting, the old forms began to break up. Joseph Conrad wrote *The Nigger of the "Narcissus"* without a woman in it, and no glory or promotions for anybody at the end of the voyage. Gradually our own writers began to look around and see a few things in God's world. So long as their eyes were fixed on youth, love, and success they could see nothing whatever; they were like men being carried to an operating table; they were in a nervous chill because they weren't always bubbling over with these three desirable things, and they wondered how long they could go on making the gesture. *Constantly putting the accent in the same place is a terribly degrading habit for a writer.*[172]

Though Cather presents the watershed significance of *The Nigger of the "Narcissus"* through its general negation of prior formal and thematic conventions, it is not difficult to see in Cather's special enthusiasm for the novel—a study of ethnic and social outsiders, hitherto "voiceless" and unrepresented in literature, struggling for survival and community beyond the "frontier" of established civilization, requiring "pioneering" forms and strategies of articulation to do "justice" to the "task," to "make you *see*" a domain until now rendered invisible in both its details and more general significance—Cather's expression of the novel's quite *specific* and *positive* license for *O Pioneers!* (1913).[173] Indeed, more so than I have space to trace here, many of the details of *O Pioneers!*, including an opening epigraph from the *Polish* Adam Mickiewicz and several analogies to conditions at sea, suggest the novel's inscribed proximity to Conrad; contemporary reviews of *O Pioneers!* and *The Nigger of the "Narcissus"* emphasize strikingly similar terms of unexplored location, unfamiliar people, and thoroughly disregarded conventions of plot, character, and narrative consistency; and Cather herself, unsure of her ability to find a U.S. publisher for a novel so unusual as hers, first sent the manuscript to Heinemann, the eventual English publisher of her novel, who had fifteen years earlier published *The Nigger of the "Narcissus."*[174] The matter here is as political as it is aesthetic: if Conrad's novel generally relieved the burden of "constantly putting the accent in the same place," the novel also, in a more literal sense of the word *accent*, authorizes and anticipates the diversity of foreign accents, voices, cultures, registers, and foreignized places foregrounded in Cather's novel. Similarly, though "On the Novel" mentions neither novel, it is difficult to read *My Ántonia* (1918) in the literary/political climate of its own moment without appreciating some heightened sense of proximity to *Lord Jim*. Cather's novel's practice of "elegiac romance,"[175] its nostalgic, retrospective, framed first-person narration concentrated on yet another "romantic" figure of departure and transcultural transition, its patchwork of internal tales, most especially the highly symbolic tale of Peter and Pavel's ethical betrayal of their passengers and consequent perpetual exile, the novel's emphases on empathy and forged community, its insistences of epic analogy, even the name "Jim," all suggest striking proximity to Conrad's novel; whatever "influence" there may be, it is Cather's text that effectively and objectively frames Conrad's in anticipatory relation to itself—and in precisely the same terms of pluralist, intercultural, dynamically (im)migrant-centric imagined communal possibility that Cather had been reading *Lord Jim* since "The Sculptor's Funeral." Finally, Cather's remarks before the Pulitzer Prize Committee foreground an important element of gender and erotics: the diversity of the world one is able to "look around and see," and the bodily directions in which one's "eyes" are "fixed" in seeing it, intersect Conrad as much at the level of gender and sexuality as they do race/ethnicity and aesthetics. Yet whereas we have seen several women writers variously affirm and politically extend Conrad's presentation of his women characters; and whereas Cather's friend Mary Austin wrote an essay critiquing the limitations of Conrad's women characters as an expression of their *essential* gender difference;[176] and whereas other writers, as we shall see, like Frances Newman sharply criticized Conrad for overly representing and overly authorizing male characters, Cather interestingly praises Conrad for writing *The Nigger of the "Narcissus"* "without a woman in it"—yet precisely for this reason liberating conventional constraints of gender and the strict routinization of all "love" and "desir[e]" through banal heteronormative formula. At issue here is not only a pluralization of Conrad's contexts of readership, social implication, and writerly precedent, all licensed by the "accent" of performed gender and erotic possibility being "placed" outside the norm; it's Cather's reading of texts like *Lord Jim* and *The Nigger of the "Narcissus"* as the eroticized, "queer," and gender-bending texts that they profoundly really are. Politically, then, and in resistance to the full field of "Anglo-Saxon" domestic order thus far traced in this section, it is toward the accentuation and intersection of "foreign" differences of all kinds that Cather's ultimate political construction of Conrad in her major fiction and prose tends.

. . .

The viciousness with which race is asserted in Conrad's image in "Behind the Singer Tower," combined with the more general pattern of Conrad's racially inflected "Anglo-Saxon" essentialization in the 1920s to authorize "foreign" immigrant exclusion, naturally raises the question of Conrad's parallel mediation of black/white U.S. race relations. The short initial answer to this question is as clear as it is unsettling. Just as Mencken, with serious limitations of his own, mobilizes Conrad to interfere with "Anglo-Saxon" assertions of white racial supremacy, the open secret of Conrad's more conventional production lies in his confirmation of black/white racial hierarchy and racialized assertions of black inferiority. This is an important subtext of Joyce Kilmer's review of a new book (on Jefferson Davis) by Thomas Dixon in the *New York Times* in July 1914, in which Kilmer conspicuously pairs up Conrad and Dixon, ostensibly to distinguish Conrad from the notorious author of *The Clansman* whose "utterances on the negro question had evoked much adverse comment," but actually to "contrast" only the discretion and "full possession of myself" with which Conrad articulates himself on such "adverse" subjects.[177] Such an open secret, however, when it did come into view, often baldly outed itself. Perhaps the most egregious, or at least bewilderingly outrageous, instance of Conrad's express articulation to racist construction comes in the work of Vachel Lindsay, an important poet of the 1910s, whose combinations of vatic pose and populist American material, whose pressing of evangelical and popular oratorical traditions into fresh idioms of poetic performance, led Harriet Monroe (founding editor of *Poetry* [Chicago]) among others to herald Lindsay as, in Rachel Blau DuPlessis's phrase, "the proof of an autonomous, burgeoning American modernism."[178] Among the many sources of Lindsay's most famous poem, "The Congo (A Study of the Negro Race)" (1914), a poem he performed on countless occasions in his sojourns across the country, Lindsay repeatedly drew particular attention to the inspiration of "Joseph Conrad's haunting sketches full of fever and voodoo and marsh."[179] In a letter that appeared in the *Boston Evening Transcript* on February 6, 1915, written to and forwarded by Doubleday employee Christopher Morley, and printed just above a Doubleday advertisement for Conrad extolling "his marvelous command and understanding of his material, human and otherwise, [to the] fullest measure," Lindsay explains the genesis of "The Congo" by writing: "I hoped to imply Joseph Conrad's fatalistic atmosphere, in his story 'Heart of Darkness.' I reached for the spiritual African fever he had in there that is the sure death to the soul. In my devices and settings for such phrases as 'Mumbo Jumbo will hoo-doo you,' I often had him consciously in mind."[180] Elsewhere, Lindsay explains even more directly of "The Congo": "Perhaps no one thing influenced me more than the story I have before mentioned, Joseph Conrad's 'Heart of Darkness.' I wanted to reiterate the word Congo and the several refrains in a way that would echo stories like that. I wanted to suggest the terror, the reeking swamp-fever, the forest splendor, the black-lacquered loveliness and above all the eternal fatality of Africa, that Conrad had written down with so sure a hand."[181]

"The Congo" thus offers an ideological "vision" of Conrad—that is, it self-reflexively interprets *Heart of Darkness* in the attempt to re-create it—precisely as, in each of the poem's three sections, the poem proffers a series of demotic, carnal, generally angry African-American bodies, only spiritually to "reveal" them through a "vision" of a fantastically atavized "Congo." Here, for instance, is how the first section of the poem, subtitled with faux-ethnographic numerical precision "I. Their Basic Savagery," begins; I reproduce it at some length because the aggregating, incantatory quality of the rhythms and pulsating rhymes are as important to the attempt to re-create "Conrad" as the thematic elements of Lindsay's (palpably disconcerting) "vision" experience:

Fat black bucks in a wine-barrel room,

Barrel-house kings, with feet unstable,

Sagged and reeled and pounded on the table,

Pounded on the table,

Beat an empty barrel with the handle of a broom,

Hard as they were able,

Boom, boom, BOOM,

With a silk umbrella and the handle of a broom,

Boomlay, boomlay, boomlay, BOOM.

THEN I had religion. THEN I had a vision.

I could not turn from their revel in derision.

THEN I SAW THE CONGO, CREEPING THROUGH THE BLACK,

CUTTING THROUGH THE FOREST WITH A GOLDEN TRACK.

Then along that riverbank

A thousand miles

Tattooed cannibals danced in files;

Then I heard the boom of the blood-lust song

And a thigh-bone beating on a tin-pan gong.

And "BLOOD" screamed the whistles and the fifes of the warriors,

"BLOOD" screamed the skull-faced, lean witch-doctors....

Listen to the yell of Leopold's ghost

Burning in hell for his hand-maimed host....

Listen to the creepy proclamation,

Blown through the lairs of the forest-nation. . . . —
"Be careful what you do,
Or Mumbo-Jumbo, God of the Congo,
And all of the other
Gods of the Congo,
Mumbo-Jumbo will hoo-doo you,
Mumbo-Jumbo will hoo-doo you,
Mumbo-Jumbo will hoo-doo you."[182]

"A steady, ponderous, fake-ritualistic" incantation of the "mindless frenzy of first beginnings"; "dehumanizing" expression which "while pretending to record scenes, incidents and their impact is in reality engaged in inducing a hypnotic stupor . . . through a bombardment of emotive words and other forms of trickery"—this is how Nigerian author Chinua Achebe describes *Heart of Darkness* in his famous essay of 1977 critiquing the novella as a "thoroughgoing racist" text;[183] and these are exactly the terms in which Lindsay, in a poem of enormous American distributive range and contemporary fascination, reads Conrad too. In the lines quoted above from "The Congo," a raucous, physical scene of pent-up African-*American* frustration becomes "spiritually" revealed through a "vision" of radical primitivism in the "Congo," itself presented through a mystically and lexically trivialized spirit of voodoo ("hoo-doo") bloodthirst whose perverse effect is to render the *Africans* ultimately culpable (the true and essential "horror" lies with them) for the imperialist victimization they seek to avenge. This is what *Heart of Darkness* means to Lindsay: a "spiritual African fever" that is "sure death to the soul" precisely as it is linked to "the eternal fatality of Africa," a "horror" that is in turn a baseline for all people of African descent. Ironically, Lindsay was by all accounts, as a historical matter, strongly and outspokenly committed to the cause of eliminating race prejudice and effecting "love and goodwill and witty conversation" between the races in the United States;[184] he sought through spiritual means to eliminate a mutual history of mistrust and hatred between the races, and in "The Congo," which ends with the light of Christian salvation overcoming racialized animosity, Lindsay thought he was doing just that. But as DuPlessis observes, "Lindsay's yearning to do something helpful to extirpate race prejudice . . . is totally swamped by the poem's raucous, sinister primitivisms": his "bombastic response" to race hatred only discloses and reinscribes his fascination with some of its most fundamental discursive and animating terms, beyond whatever good intentions he may have had.[185]

Not all racist channelings of Conrad, moreover, were so progressively well intentioned. Virginian John Powell's *Rhapsodie Négre* (1918), dedicated "To Joseph Conrad in appreciation of and gratitude for 'Heart of Darkness,'"[186] was originally imagined as an opera version of *Heart of Darkness*. When his friend Conrad could not be persuaded to authorize an opera-libretto version of the story, Powell, an "old-family" Virginian and an accomplished Vienna-trained pianist, also recently the founder of the Society for the Preservation of Racial Integrity at the University of Virginia, composed instead "a symphonic poem or, in the event, a piano-and-orchestra rhapsody loosely based on a program in which the novella's wild, cannibalistic tribesmen became transported Afro-American slaves."[187] Powell's "symphonic poem" endeavors to align itself with and render the essence of Conrad as much as Lindsay's "Congo" does, and the program notes for the 1922 Powell / Monteux / Boston Symphony performances of *Rhapsodie Négre* declare in luridly unabashed terms the racialized principles from which Powell's music proceeds: "the negro . . . is, *au fond*, in spite of the surface polish and restraints imposed by close contacts with white civilization, a genuine primitive"; "his musical utterance, when really direct, not imitative, brings with it always the breath of the jungle"; he "at . . . best glows with naïve simplicity and deep fervor, [which] at its worst descends to a nadir of frantic sensual fanaticism."[188] Equally revealing is how the three movements of *Rhapsodie Négre* effectively rewrite the three sections of Lindsay's "Congo": whereas the latter ends with racial animosity dissolved by Christian salvation, the former ends with "a frenzy of Voodoo orgy, which degenerates into a maniacal licentiousness," a "flood of madness" and closing "shriek" which the harmonies of "Sweet Chariot" are "incapable of maintaining."[189] Powell thus evokes Conrad as a means of confirming the very racial impasse—the ultimate fact of incompatible racial difference, and the ultimate urgent need for racial separation—that Lindsay recognizes in Conrad (in painfully self-undermining fashion) as a challenge to overcome. Powell is not alone in this ideological framing. South Carolinian Warrington Dawson's various outbursts of enthusiasm for Conrad—which came to annoy Conrad, at least once in the explicit context of race—must be understood in the context of the kind of violent racism Dawson advocates in *Le Nègre aux États-Unis* (1912); much of Conrad's efflorescence in the U.S. South in the 1920s, as we shall see, turns on strong affirmations and inhibitions not only of declaring but of *seeing* race; and even in the blandest mainstream national-commercial formulations of Conrad in the 1910s, one finds a striking propensity with which a basic social agreement *not* to talk about race almost casually breaks down, when the writer writes long enough, into solemnly grand appeals to Conrad's "presentment of the clashing of two continents," his "symbolic picture of the inborn antagonism of the two races, the white and the black"—before changing the subject back to Conrad's "exoticism."[190]

Such details lend support to Achebe's charge of "thoroughgoing racism" against Conrad and *Heart of Darkness*: not, in my view and as I will continue to show, because Conrad's extremely protean, multiply heterotopic in effect, and context-dependent text is reducible to any single, stable, abstract political formulation, but rather because both text and author here actively facilitate what can only be described as "thoroughgoing racism" in precisely the terms, plausibly derived from certain elements in Conrad's texts, that Achebe outlines. Indeed, it is worth considering that this *U.S. context* is actually a concrete and central, though by no means exclusive, target of Achebe's essay. Originally composed as the second Chancellor's Lecture at the University of Massachusetts in Amherst, where Achebe was a visiting professor in 1974–75, "An Image of Africa: Racism in Conrad's *Heart of Darkness*" begins with a discussion of two personal encounters with U.S. Americans invested in demeaning conceptions of "the customs and superstitions of an African tribe": it is these American encounters that prompt discussion of, and whose ideology Achebe argues finds exemplary expression in, *Heart of Darkness*.[191] Throughout the essay, moreover, Achebe hints at the true forces "guilty" of not only disseminating and promoting Conrad but doing so in a fashion that radically obfuscates the concerns of race and ideology to which Achebe's oppositional account draws attention; by the end of the essay, it is "English Departments in *American* universities" that are singled out for particular responsibility in this respect. Achebe's essay thus, among its many priorities, pointedly calls for American political attention to the ideological terms and concrete cultural history of its fascination with Conrad and *Heart of Darkness*; and yet, if I may be polemical for a moment, this is precisely the kind of inquiry, one of comparativist "capillary" endeavor, that the field imaginaries of both Americanist criticism and modernist/Conrad criticism have worked quite effectively to exclude. To this day outside the United States, the many global cultures of Conrad's engagement remain separated from consideration of the history of U.S. engagements; and within the United States, it is my experience that we teach and think about *Heart of Darkness* as a fundamentally "other" text:

one, to be sure, whose racial/ideological implications are *like* and compellingly *relevant* to the United States, but one that fundamentally takes place and comes from elsewhere: *one that has no concrete racial-political history of its own within the United States.* This is a mistake: *Heart of Darkness* should be taught in the United States with concrete sensitivity to its historical status as an internality (as well, obviously, as an externality) of U.S. culture; and the problems and possibilities become even more acute here when we consider that one of the most productive effects of Achebe's essay, even beyond its pedagogical indictments of Western culture, has been its performative and provocational effect of attention redirected to a wide diversity of "other" voices: i.e., voices from the colonized and postcolonial world, as well as other minoritized subject positions, whose remarkable latitude and subtleties of response to Conrad are now fundamental to our sense of him, such contrapuntal networks of global discourse and concern increasingly offering up the terms for justifying and critically coordinating Conrad's study. In the context of the above discussion of U.S. race relations, the question thus naturally arises concerning the history of modern African-American responses to Conrad. Here, I do not mean to suggest a centering of modern African-American writing around Conrad, to the contrary of the way this book does advance this kind of centering argument about other strands of American modernism and modern U.S. culture generally; nor do I mean to suggest a necessary symmetry between modern African-American engagements with Conrad and later global/postcolonial responses to Conrad—though the diversity and sensitivity of the former and latter do match up, intersect, and overlap in intriguing ways. But I do mean to argue modern African-American voices were profoundly aware of and are crucial to our understanding of the literary and cultural meaning of the contemporary rise of Conrad in the United States; that the larger "Anglo-Saxon" contestations and convulsions propelling the rise of "our Conrad" were acutely observed and actively negotiated by the African-American community; that in their strategic silences and complexities of express engagement with Conrad, African-American writers introduce particular subtleties of interpretation, revelation, and political agency; and overall, that modern African-American writers demonstrate the same expanse of diverse heterotopic response to Conrad—albeit in different terms, and through different exigencies and vocabularies of plural and polarizing elaboration—that one finds in other American economies of Conrad's contemplation.

At one extreme of modern African-American responses to Conrad is Langston Hughes, probably the most innovative poet of the Harlem Renaissance and a prolific writer in many other genres as well. We reinforce current efforts to estrange Hughes's location exclusively as a poet, and also to illuminate the broad world-cultural archive and field of redoubling complications that inform all his writings, including his poetry, by recovering his engagements with Conrad— by no means a "central" writer for Hughes, yet far more pointedly, powerfully, and even formatively negotiated than has been acknowledged.[192] Hughes's most direct public encounter with Conrad comes in his first autobiography, *The Big Sea* (1940), in the penultimate section of part 1 entitled "Haunted Ship." In this section, Hughes recounts that during the winter of 1922, at the age of twenty, he served as mess boy in a "ghost" shipyard for decommissioned merchant vessels in the Hudson River. Often left alone and effectively stranded aboard the most remote ship in that "dead fleet," the young Hughes "read all the ship's library"—including, among three conspicuously named works, "Conrad's *Heart of Darkness*."[193] As Arnold Rampersad observes biographically of this moment, Hughes "struggled with the Africa of Conrad's *Heart of Darkness*, consoling himself with Jessie Fauset's confirmation that Conrad was very difficult reading indeed."[194] This *resistance* to Conrad—a pointedly oppositional construction, as we shall see—*The Big Sea* underscores in two very important ways. First, in the central and eponymous episode of "Haunted Ship," the young Hughes accepts a dare by his white crewmates to spend a night alone on board a "haunted ship" in the shipyard; it is "haunted" not simply in the sense that it is a decommissioned "ghost" ship like all the others but also because it was the scene of a bloody "mutiny," "a pitched battle between the officers and the crew," during the war. Though Hughes ultimately has no trouble—indeed, finds himself serenely at home—sleeping soundly among the ghosts of mutinies past, this is notwithstanding his crewmates' best efforts to terrify him earlier in the day:

To frighten me, all day they kept on repeating the mutiny story with gruesome variations. They declared I had picked out the very cabin of the slain mate. They said I would turn white by morning from pure fear. They said I had better leave the door unlocked so I could run.

Though Hughes goes on here to explain his triumph in terms of deflating his white crewmates' "moving-picture" stereotypes of African-Americans as "superstitious and frightened," it is clear from the *literary* framing of the entire section—its equating of "ghost" ships with their "librar[ies]"; its pairing of a "dead fleet" of ships "going nowhere" with prior practices of *writing* that can only be a dead (and/or "haunting") end—that what is fundamentally being expressed, vindicated, contemplated through the vignette of the "haunted ship" is Hughes's refusal, as an emerging writer, to be haunted by the ghosts of the white, Western literary past—or rather, the young Hughes's great and quite seditious comfort in declaring a kind of *literary mutiny* on the authoritative voices, traditions, and present manifestations of that literary heritage. This is what it means for Hughes *not* to have fled, but rather quite comfortably inhabited, the "mutinous" space of the "haunted" ship; it is also what it means for Hughes not to have "turned white . . . from pure fear"—a simultaneously racial and literary disavowal—by morning. This sense of liberating and "mutinous" self-emergence as a writer, this oppositional and defiant literary and cultural declaration of independence that would seem pointedly to include Conrad among the dead racist hand of the past, is further confirmed by the signature gesture with which the circular part 1 of *The Big Sea*, entitled "Twenty-One" to suggest a coming of maturity, both opens and closes. This gesture happens when Hughes leaves the dead shipyard behind to "get on a boat actually going somewhere," whereupon, from the deck of his new ship, the SS *Malone*, Hughes "throws" overboard "all the books" he had recently been reading—"all the books I had had at Columbia, and all the books I had lately bought to read"—tossing them "as far as I could out into the sea." Conrad would seem to be included in this expulsion, whose significance is far more than simply "literary"; "It was like throwing a million bricks out of my heart—for it wasn't only the books I wanted to throw away, but everything unpleasant and miserable out of my past: . . . the stupidities of color prejudice, black in a white world, . . . the bewilderment of no one to talk to about the things that trouble you, the feeling of always being controlled by others . . . by some outer necessity not your own."[195]

Heart of Darkness, then, is a pointed instance that *The Big Sea* offers of the kind of "book" and racialized constraints of the world—the two categories, literary and cultural-political, being enmeshed—that the young Hughes of 1923 (the same year Conrad visits the United States, the apex of Conrad's dialogic championing in white U.S. discourse) determines absolutely to jettison and "mutinously" to overthrow and resist. Anticipating Chinua Achebe fifty years later, and engaging directly with the white culture of Conrad epitomized by Lindsay and Powell, this oppositional construction of Conrad becomes clarified in its terms, and elaborated in its complexity, in the first fiction the young Hughes writes thereafter: in what is effectively not only the mature beginnings of Hughes's prolific career as a prose writer but also the first world instance, to my knowledge, of a post-colonial "writing back" to Conrad's most famous novella. The "somewhere" to which Hughes was headed in 1923 on the SS *Malone*, a merchant ship, was Africa; and upon his return, Hughes began planning a cycle of six stories, four of which he completed, based on his experiences steaming up, down, and within the West African coast—both very like and very unlike, as Hughes well knew, the experience of Conrad. The four stories—the first Hughes ever wrote excepting high school juvenilia—appeared in *The Messenger* and *Harlem* in 1927 and 1928. They are written, as Rampersad observes, in the same racial and political "spirit of independence that dominates [Hughes's] landmark essay 'The Negro Artist and the Racial Mountain,'"[196] published in the *Nation* in June 1926; and though all of these stories, as I will show, presuppose a foundational frame of reference in Conrad, the fourth story, "Luani of the Jungles," rewrites *Heart of Darkness* clearly and directly in the "mutinous" spirit outlined in *The Big Sea*.

"Luani" begins with an anonymous first-person narrator, a seaman on a cargo freighter whose character is based loosely on Hughes himself, haggling with a Nigerian merchant over the price of a wild monkey, his boat having stopped at a wharf along the Niger River to unload goods. The seaman/narrator is persuaded to pay more than he should through the intervention of an "unknown voice," that of a "strange, weak-looking little white man" who speaks with a "queer accent" and "in a foreign sort of English," and who perhaps for these aestheticized reasons "*seemed* to know whereof he spoke"; the "stranger" is a self-styled expert connoisseur, and "poet" of all things authentically, remarkably, mysteriously "African." This strange faux-Africanist "poet"—whose "queer," "foreign," hyperaestheticized "accent" picks up on much of the current U.S. discourse on Conrad, as does Hughes's narrator's tweaking description of how the "strange" "poet" has a "vague far-off air about him as though he were not really interested in what he was saying"—joins the seaman's freight boat in its trip down the Niger. That Hughes has his sights on Conrad with this "poet" character and story is now directly suggested by the broodingly lush echoes and unmistakable parody of *Heart of Darkness* with which Hughes has the seaman/narrator describe the boat's resumed course downstream:

Soon we seemed to be floating through the heart of a dense, sullen jungle. A tangled mass of trees and vines walled in the sluggish stream and grew out of the very water itself. None of the soil of the riverbank could be seen—only an impenetrable thickness of trees and vines. Nor were there the brilliant jungle trees one likes to imagine in the tropics. They were rather a monotonous gray-green confusion of trunks and leaves with only . . . the flash of some bright-winged bird to vary their hopelessness . . . broken by a muddy brook or a little river joining the larger stream and giving, along the murky lengths, a glimpse into the further depths of this colorless and forbidding country.[197]

Such fantastically teeming, inscrutable, otherworldly cadences clearly echo and evoke Conrad's Marlow; and like Marlow, Hughes's "poet," finding himself on deck with the seaman/narrator, wrests narrative control from that anonymous frame narrator and proceeds to tell a long, dark, inconclusive, mostly uninterrupted tale about his "dark" experiences in "Africa." The tale is introduced by an interchange that is a brilliant comic send-up—worthy of quotation in full— of the high aesthetic, moral, and psychological seriousness with which *Heart of Darkness* takes itself; it is rendered against the topos of the setting sun, which "Luani" takes from and uses to "signify" on the opening of *Heart of Darkness*:

"Good evening," I said.

"*Bon soir,*" answered the little man [the "poet"].

"*Vous êtes français?*" I asked, hearing his greeting.

"*Non,*" he replied slowly. "I am not French, but I lived in Paris for a long while." Then he added for seemingly no reason at all, "I am a poet, but I destroy my poems."

The gold streak on the horizon turned to orange.

There was nothing I could logically say except, "Why?"

"I don't know," he said. "I don't know why I destroy my poems. But then there are many things I don't know. . . . I live back in that jungle." He pointed toward the coast. "I don't know why."

The orange in the sunset darkened to blue.

"But why?" I asked again stupidly.

"My wife is there," he said. "She is an African."

"Is she?" I could think of nothing other to say.

The blue on the horizon grayed to purple now.

"I'm trying to get away," he went on, paying no attention to my remark. "I'm going down to Lagos now. Maybe I'll forget to come back—back there." And he pointed to the jungles hidden in the distant darkness of the coast. "Maybe I'll forget to come back this time. But I never did before—not even when I was drunk. I never forgot. I always came back. Yet I hate that woman!"

"What woman?" I asked.

"My wife," he said. "I love her and yet I hate her."

The sea and the sky were uniting in darkness.[198]

Here, most of the mysteries of Conrad's "Africa"—its metaphysical incitement of "fascination" and "abomination," manifest in a perennial ambivalence of "going—back"; its aesthetic incitement of both poetic creativity and testimony and the defacement and concealment of such;[199] even its radical Difference by which even the most "atypical" narrator can become normalized, "one of us"—become laughably deflated as racialized nonsense: incapable, not because of profundity but rather inanity, of even the most basic accounting of itself. This racialized critique is advanced through the prism of gender, moreover: for while *Heart of Darkness* presents women, in Marlow's phrase, as significantly "out of it" (*YOS* 115), "Luani" confronts its "poet" with a central figure of resistance who is *both* African and a woman, *conjointly* misperceived: the poet's wife, Luani. In Hughes's story, the "poet's" tale essentially concerns an exoticized passion he conceives for the Nigerian Luani while both are students at the Sorbonne—"She seemed to me the most beautiful thing I had ever seen—dark and wild, exotic and strange"—which becomes the poet's eternal torment when the two marry and follow Luani's lead back to Nigeria, where Luani takes other lovers and more generally cannot be controlled by the poet. Whereas *Heart of Darkness* presents "Africa" in fundamentally primitivizing, bestializing, and metaphysical terms, "Luani" aggressively rewrites *Heart of Darkness* by materially decoding such appeals to "the jungle" as the stylized ignorance of a poet who simply understands none of the customs, "none of [the] ceremonies, none of [the] dances," "nor a word of [the] language" that constitute the local culture "in which I could take no part." Whereas *Heart of Darkness*, probably more than Hughes lets on, explores how a culture's "ideas" and knowledge are produced in the service of systems of power and domination, "Luani" takes the extra step of challenging a general mind-set that is incapable of conceiving any forms of knowledge or social relation that are *not* predicated on possession and dominance. (Luani's community welcomes the poet's cultural assimilation; Luani also quite sincerely, caringly appeals to him "with emotion" that a "woman can have two lovers and love them both"; but the poet cannot relinquish, except in the form of torment, his investments in racial and gendered mastery.) Finally, whereas *Heart of Darkness* struggles to register the agency, the culture, the human power and resistance and complexity of Congolese people, a primary purpose of "Luani" is to recover and vindicate the voices of racial and gendered difference whose genuine humanity—as opposed to "all the romance I'd ever found in books"[200]—its Conradian "poet" is incapable of entertaining. "Luani," hence, is the world's first postcolonial rewriting of *Heart of Darkness* in the sense that it is the first story to reinscribe Conrad's novella from outside and in resistance to the vantage of the colonizer; it is also a feminist rewriting for similarly resistant and critical reasons.

Yet this purely oppositional model of Conrad's construction, without at all taking away from the uncompromisingly principled politics we have been elaborating in Hughes to this point, does not entirely do justice to the full complexity of Hughes's relationship with Conrad. A brief return to *The Big Sea* helps us see why. Despite this autobiographical text's evident sympathy for a young protagonist with strong swelling sentiments of "mutiny" against and tossing "overboard" books like those by Conrad, *The Big Sea* does not really allow us for a moment (the following quote comes from the very first page) to take at face value the twenty-one-year-old Hughes's earnest, exhilarated sense of his own absolute transcendent liberation from the books he has attempted to throw away, "as far as I could out to sea":

The books went down into the moving water in the dark off Sandy Hook. Then I straightened up, turned my face to the wind, and took a deep breath. *I was a seaman going to sea for the first time—a seaman on a big merchant ship. And I felt that nothing would ever happen to me that I didn't want to happen. I felt grown, a man, inside and out. Twenty-one.*[201]

Parts 2 and 3 of *The Big Sea* thoroughly refute the young Hughes's convictions that "nothing would ever happen to me that I didn't want to happen," and that at twenty-one he is fully "grown, a man, inside and out"; and just so, *The Big Sea* insists in this passage—and as a subtext of the "Haunted Ship" section that comes later—that we question the degree of Hughes's simple transcendence of (Western) books. Indeed, for a text that has just explicitly tossed Conrad overboard, the italicized words above, in the full bloom of their naïveté, sound a note remarkably like that other tale of youthful exuberance in first setting off to sea on a big merchant ship so widely admired in the United States in 1923: Conrad's "Youth." So, too, we might speculate, may the "ghost" of Conrad be heard in the curiously technical sea language—referencing "booms" and "winches," the "afterdeck" and the "scupper," "four bells"—of the next substantial paragraph;

or at the close of that paragraph, which—expressly figuring the general (ironizing, antitranscendent literary) point I am making—references a "last book" that stubbornly *refuses* to be blown away: "I believe it was a book by H. L. Mencken."[202] Whatever the case may be for the specific place of Conrad in *The Big Sea*, what I do want to emphasize is the usefulness of *The Big Sea*'s complex engagement with "books" as a general model—one predicated on overdetermined assertions of liberation and disavowals of "haunting" that, in something of the manner of Freud's notion of "negation," thus allow for the fresh engagement and appropriation of presumptively oppositional material—for understanding the place of Conrad in the four Hughes stories of 1927 and 1928 where Conrad's imprint and engagement are unmistakable. For just as "Luani" both refutes *and* assumes (precisely to refute) the "Africanist" template of *Heart of Darkness*, so the nautical narrative framework of the three other Hughes stories—in their panoramic, impressionist descriptions of "sea and sky"; in their dignifying and mimetic emphasis on the dialogue and daily realities of a lower-class, multiethnic crew; in their loftier meditations on the "strange comradeship" and "brother[hood]" of the crew and the "wide-armed mother" of the "ship" and "sea"[203]—is simply unthinkable without the very precedent of Conrad's sea stories (especially "Youth" and *The Nigger of the "Narcissus"*) that those stories would also ultimately disavow; Conrad is a precondition, if an alienating one, of the very project of freedom (from, among other things, Conrad) that these stories narratively undertake. Natalie Melas, in *All the Difference in the World*, coins the term "dissimilation" to describe the process by which postcolonial authors—including Chinua Achebe, Wilson Harris, and V. S. Naipaul—are "hailed" (in an Althusserian sense) by Conrad but in a fashion that produces "dislocation" and "differentiation" rather than an absorption into Conrad's nonetheless enabling racial/imperial premises.[204] Though "dissimilation," I have suggested, is only one among many different heterotopic response patterns Conrad elicits, it is an excellent description of the mode of Hughes's response: both in *The Big Sea*'s theory of "books" one *needs* to jettison, and in Hughes's first fiction cycle which absolutely repudiates the Conrad that in important ways it presupposes as an archival resource and articulative condition. Thus Hughes's *oppositional* construction of Conrad is richly self-revelatory and of lasting significance to the interpretation of Conrad—even if Conrad himself, beyond the U.S. culture of "our Conrad" of which Hughes is both an antagonist and a part, is not ultimately a central figure of aesthetic interest and engagement for Hughes.

Hughes engages Conrad, of course, as a means of raising challenge both to colonial discourses of the international sphere and to specific U.S. discourses of race, the former providing the template through which to reimagine and deexceptionalize the latter. Such transnational reimaginings—re-placing the United States as part of the African diaspora; reconceiving U.S. templates of perception and ideology through other world colonialities of power—naturally raise the subject of W. E. B. Du Bois: the seminal twentieth-century U.S. theorist of transnational horizons of color, and the focal point of a significantly different conception of and strategy for engaging Conrad, nevertheless sharing Hughes's fundamental ideological distrust of his object and uncompromising commitment to the cause of racial justice. Du Bois, notwithstanding his own unparalleled gifts as a polemicist in contemporary texts like *Darkwater* (1920), in his two most direct engagements with Conrad does not follow Hughes, himself anticipating Achebe, in adopting an intertextual mode principally predicated on attack, opposition, and polemical reversal. Rather, Du Bois, who directly invokes Conrad very seldom, in these two moments invokes Conrad in anything but starkly confrontational or oppositional terms. While Hughes would declare "mutiny" on and violently cast Conrad overboard, Du Bois, when Conrad dies in September 1924, writes in "The Looking Glass" column of the *Crisis* simply, temperately: "Joseph Conrad, the great novelist, is dead. Young colored folk who want to write should read his life and novels."[205] Similarly, whereas Achebe, based in part on Conrad's repeated use of offensive racial epithets for black people, condemns Conrad as a "thoroughgoing racist," Du Bois, when Carl Van Vechten's controversial *Nigger Heaven* (1926) appears, writes a famous review attacking Van Vechten's book and title by *approving*, among other distinguished book titles, the example of Conrad's *The Nigger of the "Narcissus"*: "'Nigger' is an English word of wide use and definite connotation. As employed by Conrad, Sheldon, Allen, and even Firbanks its use was justifiable. But the phrase, 'Nigger Heaven,' as applied to Harlem is a misnomer."[206] The key to understanding these invocations and their constructions of Conrad, which are not at all simple endorsements of him, lies in appreciating how little they actually say and authorize about Conrad. The first statement, whose defining characteristic is its discreet reticence, beyond observing the simple empirical fact of Conrad's cultural status as a "great" novelist, affirms nothing about Conrad's life or works other than that young aspiring writers of color should be aware of them; nothing specific about Conrad is either endorsed as a model or authority or even elaborated in its terms. Likewise, Du Bois's Van Vechten review neither expresses nor legitimizes the content of the Conrad novel in question, nor even mentions it by name; rather, Du Bois simply (or rather, very carefully, narrowly) uses a penumbral invocation of Conrad's book to license Du Bois's own fundamentally class-based distinction between proper usages of the key term[207]—effectively immunizing the majority of literary and upwardly mobile Harlem from its ambit, and in the process *neutralizing* Conrad as a figure of potential resistance, counterauthority, difficulty, *discussion*. In a U.S. culture and moment when Conrad means a great deal, Du Bois both engages the necessity of Conrad's a priori cultural authority and strategically eliminates and minimizes his role in the conversation. This *silencing* of Conrad, this carefully managed narrowing, neutralization, and absorptive appropriation of his potential difficulty, becomes even clearer in the context of the other authors and texts invoked alongside Conrad in the Van Vechten review. During this time, Edward Sheldon's *The Nigger* (1910), a progressive three-act play concerning a racist Southern governor's discovery that he is the grandson of a slave, is repeatedly and quite freely extolled by Du Bois and other writers in the *Crisis* as "the finest play in favor of the Negro yet written," "the one notable early effort" in early twentieth-century U.S. drama in which "the Negro was sincerely treated by [a] white author."[208] So, too, Du Bois writes a very warm—almost puzzlingly so—review of British author Ronald Firbanks's "delicious book" *Prancing Nigger* (1926), a West Indian farce of social mobility in which the title, Du Bois argues, does not "translate" to U.S. circumstances of racial vitriol, and in which "the writer is unbound by convention, white or black."[209] Finally, the *Crisis* has many positive things to say about the "admirable" writings of the poet and novelist Clement Wood, whose *Nigger: A Novel* (1922) is a deeply sympathetic treatment of several generations of African-Americans abused by that name, and whose *Eagle Sonnets* lead Leslie Pinckney Hill to write in the *Crisis* in 1923: "The whole disadvantaged colored world is raised in hope when a seer of the white stock can wither up in song the blighting race prejudices and the terror of the war spirit of our times."[210] This stream of discussion is the context of the language above quoted from the Van Vechten review; in that language, Du Bois is not approving the use of the racial epithet in question but rather creating a strategic firewall to contain the extent of its abuse by invoking an array of sympathetic and/or culturally distinguishable white authors; and yet Conrad, aligned with but conspicuously unlike all the other authors here concerned, receives none of the praise nor even any of the *elaboration* of the others in the pages of the *Crisis*. Conrad instead seems to provoke a model of strategically enforced silence (on both sides); one finds this phenomenon instanced again by Alaine Locke in *The New Negro* (1925), which simply lists Conrad's *The Nigger of the "Narcissus"* without elaboration in its bibliographic section on "The Negro in Literature"—and, even more significantly and quite brilliantly, does not list *Heart of Darkness* at all.[211]

It is a mistake, however, to assume that this Du Boisian strategy of managing Conrad during the 1920s is fundamentally rooted in Hughes's sense of Conrad as a clear racial/colonial antagonist—or even someone whose larger Western and "high modernist" filiations are best simply jettisoned (though this is not really, as we have seen, at all Hughes' position). On the contrary, where clear colonial and racial antagonists are concerned, Du Bois characteristically lambasts the figures in question, ranging from Thomas Dixon to Rudyard Kipling, with precisely the transparency and expanse, the directness and the freedom of expression, lacking in the case of Conrad.[212] Likewise, just as the epigraphs of each of the chapters of *The Souls of Black Folk* (1903) meaningfully pair white/Western and black voices in a gesture toward unison, Du Bois's articles in the *Crisis* during the 1920s by no means forgo detailed invocations of sympathetic white "Western" literary and/ or political writers (H. G. Wells is a prominent example of both); while *Dark Princess* (1928) makes clear, if not overly synthesized with its "political" story, that Du Bois's many multicultural omnihistorical affirmations of "Beauty" are not exclusive of contemporary "high modernist" tastes in Picasso, Proust, Schönberg, and Kandinsky.[213] The "silenced" Conrad, the (mostly) *indiscutable* Conrad, is different from and somehow at cross-purposes with all these clearly delineated and expressively enabling categories: the paradox in turn being that Conrad is actually much closer—in the African, imperialist, racialized, internationalized, aestheticized coordinates of his fiction—to the central interweave of issues that define Du Bois's writings in the 1920s than most artists of this period. This paradox of disarticulate proximity—and the specific construction and "reading" of Conrad underlying it—is usefully clarified by Du Bois's important essay "Criteria of Negro Art" (1926), written two months before the Van Vechten review. Here Du Bois closes his impassioned defense of the function of "Art" in politically menacing times with his famous claim that "all art is propaganda": "I stand in utter shamelessness and say that whatever art I have for writing has been used always for propaganda for gaining the right of black folk to love and enjoy. I do not care a damn for any art that is not used for propaganda."[214] This *identification* of "art" and "propaganda" returns us, with African-Americanist and pro-propagandist complication, to the question of the relation between Conrad's fiction and propaganda discussed earlier in this chapter; and what I want to suggest here is that Du Bois understands, constructs, and approaches Conrad *neither* simply as racist propaganda *nor* as the kind of literary "Beauty" or "Truth" or "Goodness"[215] defined by its capacity to be mobilized as positive (progressive, antiracist) propaganda. Rather, Du Bois understands Conrad's fiction as a heterotopic practice, one whose erasure of articulative boundaries and categories and whose plural internal self-contradictions and indeterminacy defy propagandistic purposes altogether, leaving ultimately only difficulties of articulation, and dangers and liabilities that are best left un- or underspoken. That this is so is pointedly suggested by one of the central and most polemical essays in *Darkwater* (1920), "The Souls of White Folk."

"The Souls of White Folk" opens with something very rare in Du Bois: a direct allusion to *Heart of Darkness*. The allusion is to the same passage, indeed, that Achebe reprehends with much force fifty years later: the moment when Marlow, observing primitive "Africans" on shore and "truth stripped of its cloak of time," describes how "they howled and leaped and spun, and made horrid faces; but what thrilled you was just the thought of their humanity—like yours—the thought of your remote kinship with this wild and passionate uproar. Ugly" (*YOS* 96).[216] Du Bois, conducting his own savage racial odyssey into the heart of whiteness, at the close of the first substantive paragraph of his essay turns the tables on Marlow: such "white folks" may "deny my right to live and be and call me misbirth"—"Yet as they preach and strut and shout and threaten, crouching as they clutch at rags of facts and fantasies to hide their nakedness, they go twisting, flying by my tired eyes and I see them ever stripped,—ugly, human."[217] Marlow, however, in *Heart of Darkness* is just about to experience the very reversal Du Bois enacts: Conrad's text directly repays Marlow's aggressive racism with an attack on his ship in which Marlow is startled to discover his African crewmen behaving with much more dignity and composure, "honor" and "restraint," than the truly degenerate "pilgrims" (as the white company officials are satirized) on board with him (*YOS* 103–5). This raises the question of precisely what construction of *Conrad* underlies Du Bois's introductory allusion to him; and the answer with respect to the opening substantive paragraph itself is that the construction is remarkably unclear. On the one hand, Du Bois begins by positioning himself as something of a native informant when it comes to white culture: "Not as a foreigner do I come, for I am a native, not foreign, bone of their thought and flesh of their language. Mine is not the knowledge of the traveler or the colonial composite of . . . memories, words, and wonder." This sounds like someone elaborating an oppositional frame into which Conrad will fit: that is, *he* is an example of the quintessentially "foreign," "colonial," portentously empty and self-referential white "traveler" and writer whose racist presumption requires his explicit evocation and repudiation at the end of the paragraph. Yet on the other hand, two sentences after categorically distinguishing himself from such "colonial" praxis, Du Bois sharpens the authority of his "singularly clairvoyant" perspective, *not* by opening up further grounds of potential distance from the likes of Conrad, but rather by adopting and identifying himself in terms of the very signature trope of "entrails" by which *Heart of Darkness* asserts its own authority to pronounce on the "emptiness," "hollowness," and hypocrisy of European imperialism—and the *souls* of white folk (surely this is the point [Conrad's] of saying one has no entrails, that one is fundamentally a "hollow man," that one is a false "pilgrim") who carry its torch: "Rather, I see these souls undressed and from the back and side. I see the working of their entrails. I know their thoughts and they know that I know."[218] There, though it is matter of tone, Du Bois is quite clearly not "reversing" or parodying or "writing back to" Conrad. He is evoking, channeling, enlisting, even reveling in the empowering precedent and parallel proximity of Conrad's sympathetic figure; and read this way, the final sentence of the paragraph is also not a repudiation of Conrad—whatever it may be with respect to a specific moment in Marlow's political psychology—but rather an allied echo and elaboration of the very kind of reversal that, as we have seen, Conrad's text itself actually does significantly carry out.

This tension in Du Bois's first full paragraph, the fundamental *indeterminacy* of the construction of Conrad at work in it, *because of the directly contradictory logics mutually serviced in Conrad's image that make it impossible to place him*, is not resolved but intensified by the remainder of "The Souls of White Folk." Without ever strictly or unmistakably "alluding" to Conrad again, the essay elaborates itself in terms that make clear why Du Bois should have such grave difficulty—precisely because he is such a sensitive heterotopic reader of Conrad—locating *Heart of Darkness* as either friend or foe, routing and containing it as any particular form of "propaganda"—despite (or precisely because of) the constant and ever-expanding field of opportunities to do so. On the one hand, so much of Du Bois's critique of white Western imperialism—its fundamental bankruptcy and atrocity, its central intertwining with legitimating ideologies and culture, its emphatic and strategic racialization, its political centrality in historical modernity—finds close, even uncanny, anticipation in *Heart of Darkness*. Here are some examples:

- Du Bois's observation that "whiteness is the ownership of the earth" and that white Western imperialism, unmasked of its grandiose self-castings in the mold of the "modern Sir Galahad," essentially amounts to "rubber and murder, slavery in its worst form," powerfully coincides with Marlow's famous claim that "the conquest of the earth" means "the taking it away from those who have a different complexion or slightly flatter noses than ourselves," and that imperialism is ultimately only "robbery with violence, aggravated murder on a great scale," quite the reversal of any of Conrad's opening frame narrator's vision of "knights."[219]

- Du Bois's observation that a world presupposing that "the one virtue is to be white" will lead to the "inevitable conclusion" of "Kill the nigger!" is exactly Conrad's insight in having Kurtz scrawl as a postscript to his grandiloquent report to the International Society for the Suppression of Savage Customs, "Exterminate all the brutes!"[220]

- Du Bois's deflation of white claims to "super-humanity," his critical disclosure of white agency in imperialist contexts as essentially "weak and pitiable and cruel," and his fundamental concern that in comparison with earlier periods in interhuman domination, there is a fresh present "evil" and "horror" by which "ideas" about and the fundamental "lie" of race all powerfully legitimize unspeakable and unspoken atrocity, all have very familiar and pointed counterparts in *Heart of Darkness*.[221]

- There could be no more Conradian summation of the greater significance of Belgian atrocities in the Congo—which Du Bois, no less than Conrad, saw as a horrifying epitome of the modern world political system—than Du Bois's formulation, which so remarkably, if (perhaps) only incidentally, also articulates a central meaning of Kurtz: "This is not Europe gone mad; this is not aberration nor insanity; this *is* Europe; this seeming Terrible is the real soul of white culture—back of all culture,—stripped and visible today. This is where the world has arrived,—these dark and awful depths and not the shining and ineffable heights of which it boasted. Here is whither the might and energy of modern humanity has really gone."[222]

None of these quotations from "The Souls of White Folk" directly "allude" to Conrad, but they all explain why the essay's initial allusion to Conrad may very well be read in sympathetic and elaborative terms—as well as mark Conrad's remarkable proximity to the field of racial-political-world issues Du Bois cares about the most. But at the same time—and here we may expand beyond the specific essay "The Souls of White Folk," for my overarching point is the difficulty and liability of Conrad being made explicitly to signify in Du Bois's work of this decade generally—*Heart of Darkness* also is centrally predicated on the rescription and aesthetic reinforcement of some of the very narrative and ideological racializing strategies Du Bois's work of this period most forcefully resists. Du Bois's *The Negro* (1915), for instance, is a breathtaking scholarly endeavor to recover the *material* history and cultural achievements of African-descended peoples extending back to the most ancient of times: not only long before any claims to "Western" accomplishment can be made (*Heart of Darkness* has trouble imagining such things), but in direct repudiation and demystification of a metaphysics of prehistorical and eternally primitive "Time" whose stereotypical association with Africa *Heart of Darkness* not only assumes but to significant degrees depends on and actively reinforces. Similarly, a series of articles written in the *Crisis* in early 1919 when Africans were *not* being seated at the Paris Peace Conference find Du Bois (in Paris at the time) aggressively protesting a chronic Western mischaracterization of African cultural differences through primitivizing and essentializing narratives of racial atavism and "regression";[223] *Heart of Darkness,* even as it collapses the difference between white and nonwhite claims to "civilization," assumes African atavism as the ground of commonality and only faintly at best opens the question of African cultural difference. Finally, in "Criteria of Negro Art," Du Bois illustrates his claim that "all art is propaganda" with positive reference to "those who believe black blood human, lovable and inspired with new ideals for the world"; *Heart of Darkness* almost by titular definition—and whatever appeals might be made to Marlow's "helmsman" notwithstanding—profoundly presupposes the reverse of this fundamental appeal for a loving, inspired, dignified, and full conception of black ("dark") *humanity*. Conrad's novella powerfully negates the fundamental humanizing ambition of "Criteria of Negro Art," that "the point today is that until the art of black folk compels recognition they will not be rated as human."[224]

All of these values may be found deeply inscribed in "The Souls of White Folk," where Du Bois describes as a "descent to Hell" the gradient of much recent "pale, white" writing: "a writing of human hatred, a deep and passionate hatred, vast by the very vagueness of its expressions."[225] Yet for the very contradictory reasons we have been observing, notwithstanding the essay's clear opening invocation of Conrad and the starkly oppositional language of "hatred" used here, it is simply impossible to tell whether the essay considers *Heart of Darkness* an exemplar of precisely this form of hate literature or a harbinger of its own critical narrative of a descent into Hell in which that hate is unmasked. Conrad's text is both amenable to and emphatically *not* containable, controllable, reliable within either single stream of interpretive—"propagandistic"— processing; it is rather, Du Bois understands perfectly, precisely that kind of heterotopic space wherein the boundary between "racist" and "antiracist" textuality breaks down, wherein the two become significantly indistinguishable; it witnesses a Conrad who simply cannot be used, in a way that *either* Gandhi or Thomas Dixon can, for purposes of propaganda. As with Hughes, this reading is among the theoretical beginnings of a much larger postcolonial world discourse concerning Conrad; but unlike for Hughes, responding though they both were to a larger U.S. cultural machinery of "our Conrad," the answer for Du Bois, for whom art assumes primary significance insofar as it lends itself to propagandistic purposes, could only be a carefully guarded strategy of silencing and disarticulative management—not encouraging within the conversation that which cannot dependably ultimately work for the betterment of the conversation. The "Conrad" whose construction "The Souls of White Folk" cannot ultimately declare is the same Conrad who, despite remarkable proximity, cannot simply or easily surface, either to be championed or vilified, in Du Bois's discourse generally: he is both too complex to risk animating through critique and too much of a liability to invoke as an authority; he is neither simply a friend or enemy to be articulated but rather an occasion on which this kind of political articulation breaks down and hence must be contained in advance.

A third image and mode of constructing Conrad in the contemporary African-American community, different from that of both Hughes and Du Bois, appears in the work of Countee Cullen, for many commentators both then and now the exemplary poet of the Harlem Renaissance. Like Hughes and Du Bois, Cullen does not posit Conrad as a "central" writer but nonetheless, as a function of the larger dialogic U.S. culture of "our Conrad" in and adjacent to which they are all situated, engages Conrad in his own suggestive and sensitive fashion. Cullen's one direct public invocation of Conrad is quite conspicuous: it comes in Cullen's inaugural book of poetry, *Color* (1925), in the second "Epitaphs" section consisting of a sort of textual graveyard of some two dozen short epitaph poems. Though most of the poems are entitled with reference to general social or personal types (e.g., "For a Cynic," "For an Anarchist," "For One Who Gayly Sowed His Oats"), the sequence closes with epitaph poems for four named literary figures: for Keats (Cullen's most admired poetic inspiration), for white Oregon poet Hazel Hall, for Paul Laurence Dunbar, and—"buried" right next to the epitaph poem for Cullen himself—"For Joseph Conrad":

Not of the dust, but of the wave
His final couch should be;
They lie not easy in the grave
Who once have known the sea.
How shall earth's meager bed enthrall
The hardiest seaman of them all?[226]

The sequence of Keats, Hall, Dunbar, and Conrad once again raises the question of *archive* (of "library") we have already seen at work in Hughes and Du Bois: the key issues being not only the catholicity of reference and resonance at work in African-American writings but also their demonstration of the falseness, as Keith Leonard has demonstrated in the larger context of African-American formalist poetry generally, of most attempts categorically to distinguish between "white" and "black," Western/American and African-American, traditions of writing generally—as if somehow in a U.S. context the idioms of the colonizer and colonized were presumptively immune and distinct from one another.[227] Conrad is important today in large part because of his diverse postcolonial world legacies, and what Cullen likewise expresses here is Conrad's imbrication within (as well as beyond) specifically African-American practices of writing—though Cullen does so with such manifest sympathy for Conrad, so very different from the tense ambivalence and oppositional stances of Hughes and Du Bois, that one is forced to ask what the terms of this embrace, and what the construction of Conrad underwriting it and making it possible, can be. The first aspect to notice in the poem—so easy to underestimate in its whimsical formal brevity, just as Cullen's poetry generally closets (in every sense of the term) much of its danger and true emotional gravity through conventional poetic appearance—is that it is not simply a proposition about

Conrad; it is an engaged, dialectical and dialogic *argument*. Indeed, the structure of Cullen's argument suggestively presupposes and responds to both the
oppositional and indeterminate frames through which Hughes and Du Bois
respectively present their conceptions of Conrad. When Cullen, this is to say,
writes that Conrad's "*final* couch *should be*" not of the dust but wave, he is *arguing* that Conrad *ultimately* should be associated with the "sea"—*against* those
who would associate Conrad with the oppositional figure of "earth" ("dust"
is one of the poem's several related figures), or who understand Conrad as too
indeterminate to be firmly grouped in either category. When Cullen continues
by arguing that people like Conrad "*lie not easy*" in an earthen grave having
known the sea, and when he closes by rhetorically asking how the earth's meager bed can "*enthrall*" the hardiest seaman of them all, Cullen is both acknowledging and rejecting those other interpretive possibilities (the oppositional
category of the earth, the indeterminacy of being ultimately enthralled in any
conceptual space), in favor of the master figure and category of the "sea." The
stakes here become clearer when we contextualize and decode the key tropes
in question: more than once throughout *Color*, the "sea" is posited as a fluid,
otherworldly domain liberated from the violence, constraints, and boundaries
of lived historical racial experience; so, too, is the "sea" repeatedly opposed in
Color to "earth" and "dust," terrestrial, grounded figures of past and present
real-world racialized ensnarement, agony, and violence.[228] Conrad and Cullen
would seem to meet here (specifically in the Conrad poem) in an aestheticized
realm ("the sea") beyond capture or confinement by material experiences of
race; this idea is confirmed both by the remarkable picture (by the white artist
Charles Cullen, no relation to the poet) found in the second edition of *Color*
(1928) at the bottom of "For Joseph Conrad," which presents a white spiritual-
ized body surrounded by birds of one white and one black wing rising from a
tumultuous black sea, in a kind of resolved aesthetic harmony beyond differences and frictions of color, and by the earlier postracial interauthorial template of the poem "Tableau," in which Cullen presents two artist figures, "a
black boy and [a] white," "Locked arm and arm" "in unison" as they proceed
essentially to "walk" and "pass" out of the world—toward another and better
aestheticized world of their own.[229]

   This arm-in-arm vision is more or less the opposite of Hughes's conception of Conrad figured on board the *Malone*; and Hughes is not wrong, I am
suggesting through what I think is the very revealing mediating occasion of

Conrad, in "The Negro Artist and the Racial Mountain" to suggest an important impulse toward an aesthetics of racial transcendence circulating in and engaged by Cullen's poetry generally. But the matter does not stop there: for as the poem "For Joseph Conrad" quite self-consciously makes clear—indeed, as is surely the point of Cullen's dangerous and beautiful, ultimately saddening decision to bury himself right next to the hyperracialized Conrad, this hyperracialization organizing even as it is repudiated by the argumentative form and the master tropes of the poem itself—this kind of postracial aesthetic transcendence can only be genuinely imagined in the tenuously otherworldly space of death, through the textualized site of an epitaph. If much of the tension in "Color" (the first section of *Color*) turns on sincere visions, psychic yearnings, of interracial and postracial aspiration becoming deflated by stark "Incident[s]" and psycho-social-political entrenchments of an inescapable real-world color line; if "Yet I Do Marvel," a signature poem in the volume, offers the *discrepancy* between aesthetic beauty and a material history of lived racial violence as the ground for "marvel[ing]" that God would "make a poet black *and* bid him sing"; if "The Shroud of Color" by no means does away with this discrepancy, but rather tries to translate this dualized structure of feeling into a simultaneously race-specific and more broadly exemplary poetics of expulsion, death drive, and agonized mutability—then the poem about Conrad has its distinct poignancy and pathos too.[230] For the pathos of this African-American writer's burial next to Conrad—the poignancy of Cullen's imagining himself *ultimately* in full "aesthetic" sympathy with Conrad—lies in the entire living world that must be done away with for this imaginative conjunction to happen: the tenuous world-negation that must be presupposed (and eternally repeated) for this aesthetic construction to be maintained; the structure of feeling generated by such a world which refuses its gratified resolution. At issue here is not an oppositional construction of Conrad, because it is not Conrad's "racism" but his broad inextricability from living complications of race that is the rub; and whereas for Du Bois, Conrad's very endless indeterminacy with respect to precisely such questions requires his careful management and ultimate sequestration, for Cullen there could be no more perfect bedfellow to illustrate the tension and gap between the psychic reality of a strong cultural longing to inhabit a space uninhibited by the punitive effects and legacy of race, and the living material opportunities of doing so. There is, moreover, a profound heterotopic construction of Conrad at work in Cullen, one that does not turn, as with Du Bois, on the slippery boundary between racist and antiracist articulation but on the boundary, which Conrad's works seem both radically to license and to reject, between "art" and "race" in themselves. Cullen is able to make the case (however he goes on to complicate it) that Conrad is imaginable as a "final[ly]" postracial and universal-human transcendent artist precisely because a text like the famous "Preface" to *The Nigger of the "Narcissus,"* which (the Preface itself) has no immediately visible anchors in race, lavishly encourages this conception; yet at the same time, as the title of this very Conrad book highlights, race is indissociable from the novel proper, especially its most aestheticized elements. Cullen *reads* this signature kind of heterotopic tension throughout Conrad; it is the two-way premise of Cullen's complex evocation of Conrad in "For Joseph Conrad"; and it is further picked up on in the famous Cullen poem "Heritage," whose equivocal emphasis on the "book[s] one thumbs / Listlessly" to come up with images of "Africa," themselves both absolutely necessary to one's need for self-articulation and probably ultimately only a "lie,"[231] racially/materially grounds and complicates the more abstract literary heritage formation of Keats, Hall, Dunbar, and Conrad that Cullen iconizes in "Epitaphs." All in all, Cullen's is thus a sympathetic construction of Conrad—but one whose aestheticized sympathy is self-consciously predicated on a wide-ranging peril of material resurgence and deformation, a perpetual project of world- and self-cancellation that makes sympathy and distance curiously commensurate (and emptied out) items.

A final African-American mode of constructing Conrad, that of Richard Wright, completes a spectrum of alternatives being traced here. Though Wright's major work falls mostly outside the historical scope of this book, we may briefly advance three propositions of immediate relevance, to be elaborated elsewhere. First, the dynamic modern U.S. culture of "our Conrad"—particularly, the Southern regional economy of Conrad's production traced later in this book—*is* genuinely central to Wright's emergence as a writer. In *Black Boy* (1944), Wright famously recounts the story of his first encounter in 1927, through clever manipulation of a Memphis library and out of curiosity concerning H. L. Mencken's reprobate reputation in the South, with Mencken's *Book of Prefaces.* That book, Wright explains, its "clear, clean, sweeping sentences" written by "a raging demon, slashing with his pen, consumed with hate, denouncing everything American, extolling everything European or German, laughing at the weaknesses of people, mocking God, authority," first sparked Wright's "fighting" theory of writing—that "words" could be used as "weapons"; *A Book of Prefaces* further, in Margaret Walker's phrase, became an early "literary Bible" for Wright to read other writers in this spirit as well.[232] Conrad is among those first mentioned in *Black Boy*; and, as readers of the present book will appreciate, to read *A Book of Prefaces* was for Wright to become frontally exposed to not only a literary lionization but also a cultural/political U.S. dialogue and discourse of Conrad (in this case, national, regional, and interracial in dimension, as well as inherently transnational)—the effect on Wright being quick, significant, formative. Seven Conrad titles appear in Wright's library during this time (*The Arrow of Gold, Chance, Nostromo, Typhoon, The Shadow-Line, Victory, Youth*),[233] and it is very clear Wright read closely two other Conrad texts, *The Nigger of the "Narcissus"* and *Lord Jim*. Wright's first short story ("Superstition") to be placed in a major magazine, the black magazine *Abbott's Monthly* in April 1931, is a pointed and sensitive rewriting of *Heart of Darkness*—as we explore further later. The eminent Wright scholar Michael Fabre follows the logic of *A Book of Prefaces* in confirming of the early Wright that "Conrad and Dreiser undoubtedly dominated Wright's writing at this time"; and as Wright himself would later observe of his earliest period of self-discovery as a writer: "I only know that up until that moment [of reading Stein's "Melanctha" in 1935] I had been trying to write and I had been trying to write in the English of Joseph Conrad."[234]

The second point is that Wright's interest in Conrad continues after 1935. Even after Wright embraces writing in vernacular American idioms and emerges as a major writer in his own right, and thereafter throughout the various major phases and movements of his thinking, writing, travel—for example, across genres, toward and away from Marxist-Leninist analytic paradigms and praxes, interthreading different existential and ethnological interests with changing national, international, and transnational domains and stations—Wright's works return to and rework Conrad, perhaps not with the towering importance of Dostoevsky but in a quite similar vein and at a foundational level: as Wright's returns to Conrad in interviews and statements in each of the final three decades of his life (d. 1960) make clear.[235] Conrad's "Preface" to *The Nigger of the "Narcissus"* in particular bears a lasting trace: one hears its echoes in Wright's earlier grapplings with the art of fiction in the 1930s and in "How 'Bigger' Was Born" (1940), as well as in Wright's foreword to *Lest We Forget* (1955).[236] *Native Son* (1940), as we shall see, bears a pointedly self-referential reference to *Lord Jim*, just as *Black Power* (1954), Wright's copious nonfictional chronicle of his trip to revolutionary Ghana, both explicitly references Conrad and more generally articulates itself through a field of reference and phenomenological-ideological transaction that includes *Heart of Darkness*. Wright, a major *novelist* (i.e., different from most of the other voices discussed above), also introduced Conrad to other emerging African-American novelists including Ralph Ellison—whose *Invisible Man* (1952) closes with an explicit reference to "heart of darkness," as does James Baldwin's first novel, *Go Tell It on the Mountain* (1953).[237] Hearkening back to previous discussions of Jessie Fauset and Langston Hughes, the (African-American) poet/novelist Margaret Walker, a close colleague of Wright's, summarizes her own resistance to Conrad against the very different lifelong interest and inspiration Wright took across Conrad's works:

I have never felt as sympathetic toward Conrad as Wright did. I liked the element of adventure in his sea tales such as *Typhoon*, but I have never liked the short fiction, such as "Heart of Darkness." I realize now that I have deeply resented what I feel is ersatz in Conrad's treatment of Africa and the Negro. The two works by Conrad that Wright and I discussed most and like the most were *Lord Jim* and *The Nigger of the "Narcissus."*[238]

The third point, then, is that contrary to Walker's sense of the ersatz African in *Heart of Darkness*, and rather more in line with the important agency and resistance (the opposite of "ersatz") even Walker seems potentially to entertain of *The Nigger of the "Narcissus,"* Wright privileges an understanding of Conrad, not as an instrument of racialized oppression (Hughes) or dysfunctional ambivalence (Du Bois), and not as a complex register of an aesthetic will to transcend politics (Cullen), but rather as an active novelistic means of critically diagnosing and politically challenging world systems of race oppression—in the image of the same uneasy intertwining of existentialist and Marxist analytic techniques which, as many observers have noted, in important ways structure Wright's writing from beginning to end. The seed of this antiracist political and "existential" construction of Conrad may be found in Wright's early story "Superstition," a much more interesting and complex story than criticism acknowledges, and Wright's contribution to the early U.S./postcolonial tradition of rewriting *Heart of Darkness*. Interweaving Gothic elements of Poe and the Jamesian ghost story, "Superstition" identifies itself as a rewriting of *Heart of Darkness* through the usual signature conventions: an opening scene related by an anonymous frame narrator among potential storytellers;

the emergence of an especially compelling storyteller whose puzzling tale of self-reflexive mystery and "horror" will dominate the story; a tale itself of a "long and arduous" "journey" into a "dark" and "primitive" place that "Time had forgotten"; and more broadly, a pervasive Conradian rhetoric of "deep, penetrating silence," "overwhelming gloom," and unfathomable mystery that identifies *Heart of Darkness* as Wright's primary idiom of contemporary literary engagement.[239] The story itself is complex because, while it fundamentally concerns race politics and ideology, Wright is emphatically coy about declaring the racial contexts and identities of key scenes and characters; this is a story that significantly poses as race-neutral, race-indifferent, precisely to raise questions about the inescapability and invisible pervasiveness of racial ideology across various "American" domains. This complex inquiry happens primarily through the narrative means of Fently Burrow, Wright's Marlow figure, a Northern, white, but visually racially ambiguous real estate agent—the reader must work hard to infer all aspects of Burrow's racial profile, and even then is never absolutely certain—who is sent by his "company" to a small town in the heart of the remote South to review some property and leasing arrangements. Burrow, a credulous if introspective figure, easily puzzled and profoundly inattentive to racialized codes and concerns, arrives in the distant and disorienting Southern town only to be told by a hotel clerk that "alas, every one [of the hotel rooms in town] was filled"—whereupon, accepting this account at face value, Burrow is directed to the "suburbs" to stay with a bizarre mixed-race African-American family, the "Lancasters," their "estate . . . separated from the rest of the world" by a "white-washed picket fence." Burrow's "mysterious" tale concerns his stay with the Lancasters on two consecutive Christmases: on each occasion, the family, its elders shrouded in imagery of death and decay, becomes preoccupied with the idea that a "family re-union" will result in the death of one of its members; and on each occasion, this "superstition," galvanized by the unexpected holiday return of all the family members, seems literally to cause the death of the only two women in the family, the mother and one daughter, set off from the others by their light ("pale," "pallid," a "marked" resemblance thereof) skin color. The irrationally morbid and apprehensive superstition concerning the "re-union" of this mixed-race family in itself, one character notes, not anything the returning family members actually say or do, seems to cause the death of the "pale" women within it: "They act and think as if [their] death is a foregone conclusion."[240]

In ways Burrow can neither understand nor articulate, this "family" drama is essentially a political drama of the ideology of segregation in modern crisis. It witnesses separatist racial ideology meeting the combined social forces of economic modernization (which is what brings the "other" family members home) and a new conceptual horizon of desegregation; it dramatizes morbid and compulsive residual anxieties concerning the "reunification" of a Southern polity whose artificially polarized racialized parts were always historically constitutive of and "related" to one another in the first place. Against images of a "sagging and almost down" "white-washed picket fence" and an absurdly self-immolating "superstition" that would refortify its doomed purposes, Wright attacks on both sides of the Southern color line (in a white hotel in town, on the "estate" of the ironically named "Lancasters") the fierce persistence of white separatist and supremacist race ideology against inevitable forces of modernized outlook and socioeconomic circumstance. Wright tells this story through the template of *Heart of Darkness* precisely to cast white Southern race ideology, against its own "civilized" grain, as a kind of "primitive" "superstition"—and the segregated South itself as one of the true imperialist "horror"-spots and "dark places of the earth."[241] Conrad here is read not as exponent of race primitivism so much as a strategic and adaptable means of assaulting white racialized arrogance, European or U.S. Southern, through leveling, self-canceling primitivist technique.

But the even more important, and integrating, interface with *Heart of Darkness* concerns the "white" narrator Burrow: for it is Burrow's *misrecognition* of the "Lancaster" drama, his disorientation and confusion that can only speak themselves in "unfathomable" Gothic and Conradian idioms, the puzzle of Burrow's own racial identity, and the field of (white Northern) "superstition" and ideology Burrow projects onto a South he does not understand, its very disruption and *self*-implication leading Burrow to become haunted by the Southern drama, that is the ultimate frame and interest of the story . Wright critiques not only white Southern but also white Northern (Burrow lives in Chicago) race ideology, the two in important ways mirroring, "haunting," one another, even as the latter disavows its grounding implication in the South or by "race" altogether. Wright traces the hidden racial premises of white liberal Northern ideology, elaborately mapping its compulsive attraction to and pathological effacement of implication by disorienting Southern circumstance, and Wright does so by presenting Burrow through the narrative mode

of Marlow—and implicitly *reading* Marlow in his narrative rendering of Burrow. Wright thus rewrites and reads the narrative form of *Heart of Darkness*
not (qua Hughes) as a political instrumentation to be "written back" to but as
an enabling narrative-political mode of critically exploring (and forcing the
reader *actively* to explore) through a figure like Burrow/Marlow *how ideological
and epistemological systems elaborate and reproduce themselves when confronted
with disorientation and crisis—and what the invisible moorings and chronic pathologies of such systems are.* Put simply, Wright's rewriting of Conrad emphasizes in a way Hughes and Achebe do not the critical narrative and political
distance between Conrad and Marlow; Wright's reading of *Heart of Darkness*
foregrounds not its ersatz representation of Africa and Africans but the status
of those "representations" as ideology: the register of Marlow's culturally and
colonially derived investments in and narratives of "race" (entwined with other
"idea[s]" [*YOS* 51]), which *Heart of Darkness* sets out critically to chart as such
ideology becomes challenged, reproduced, and revealed in systemic operation
amid circumstances of radical disorientation and crisis.

   This conception of Conrad—on the one hand, as radically committed to
tracing the totalizing force and scope of ideological and socioeconomic systems
from a dislocated perspective, and, on the other hand, as radically in touch with
the profoundly immense but also dark and threatening existential "freedom"
that lies in being cast outside any ultimately arbitrary system—lies at the core
of Wright's fundamental (and self-reflexive) construction of Conrad ever after.
When Wright expresses particular interest in *The Nigger of the "Narcissus,"* he
is responding at least in part to the disruption the black character James Wait
poses to a field of perception which, even as it is exposed in its comprehensive
intricacy, never can finally place either the significance of race or the threat of
radical annihilation ("death") its totalizing force depends on disavowing.[242]
Similarly, Wright in *Native Son,* directly following an allusion to Poe's "Murders
in the Rue Morgue," references a newspaper article describing Bigger Thomas:
"His shoulders are huge, muscular, and he keeps them hunched, as if about to
spring upon you at any moment. He looks at the world with a strange, sullen,
fixed-from-under stare, as though defying all efforts of compassion."[243] Wright
is alluding to the opening paragraph of *Lord Jim*: "He was an inch, perhaps two,
under six feet, powerfully built, and he advanced straight at you with a slight
stoop of the shoulders, head forward, and a fixed from-under stare which made
you think of a charging bull" (*LJ* 7). Wright's point is the parallelism between

Bigger and Jim, between the totalizing systems that both produce and radically expel each as "criminals"; this existential yet ultimately unsustainable freedom of the "criminal" is also the fundamental "content" of the many echoes critics have observed between "The Man Who Lived Underground" (1942/1944) and *Heart of Darkness*.[244] Finally, though this is not the place to pursue a full reading of *Black Power* (1954), Cornel West's observation that Wright's "Virgil-like role of guiding frightened and bewildered Europeans through the Inferno of their colonial possessions and legacies *turns Joseph Conrad on his head*,"[245] which makes the important point that we do learn much more about Africa and African voices from Wright than we do *Heart of Darkness*, can be qualified by the following observations: (1) Wright's dialogic method in *Black Power*, akin to that he practices in *Pagan Spain* (1957), was one Wright himself understood in parallel relation to Conrad;[246] (2) Wright's one explicit reference to Conrad in *Black Power* is also one of parallelism, not reversal/opposition;[247] and (3) Wright's text, a controversial one for reasons not wholly distinct from the problems *Heart of Darkness* poses, does often turn self-reflexively on Wright's own ambivalent and double relation to "Western" tradition amid disorienting African circumstance, an epistemologically and ideologically dislocated framing of himself that had also been, from the beginning, Wright's framing of Conrad.

Wright's "Conrad" is fundamentally an epistemological and ideological expatriate and exile, sensitive to both the tenacious compulsion and absolute contingency of any given ideological system. Wright's Conrad is heterotopic in the sense, particularly vexed for U.S. individualist ideology but also extending to various African-American, European, Black Atlantic, and more general world domains, that what's free is revealed as most determined, and what's most determined is revealed as ultimately radically arbitrary. Engulfing frames of race, region, nation, imperialism, and transnationalism, Wright stands at the far modern frontier of Conrad's U.S. cultural interest, but he also points the way back to the second major historical economy of "our Conrad": among literary expatriates of the postwar period. This is the central subject of Part 2 of this book.

PART II

American Modernism Abroad

3

ALL A CONRAD GENERATION
F. Scott Fitzgerald and Other Expatriates

Has any man ever known, as this one knows, the soul of the human derelict?

—Review of *Victory*, *Dial* (May 13, 1915)

Did he live his life again in every detail of desire, temptation, and surrender during that supreme moment of complete knowledge? He cried in a whisper at some image, at some vision,—he cried out twice, a cry that was no more than a breath—"The horror! The horror!"   —Original epigraph of T. S. Eliot's *The Waste Land* (1922)

But from nothing else I have ever read have I gotten what every book of Conrad has given to me.   —Ernest Hemingway, *Transatlantic Review* (1924)

We hanker for loveliness on the horizon, we are inapprehensive of loveliness close to hand; desperately we struggle to discern indiscernibles, to be simultaneously obedient to all the voices of command. Playing feverishly with ideas that are both too heavy and too fragile for our powers of jugglery, it is comforting for those of a younger generation to look upon the novelist who, as much as any now living, has taught us that art may not be an answer but it is always a consolation.

—Christopher Morley, *Conrad and the Reporters* (1925)

You are all a lost generation.

—Gertrude Stein, epigraph to Ernest Hemingway's *The Sun Also Rises* (1926)

OUVERTURE TRANSATLANTIQUE

Zelda Sayre Fitzgerald sometimes told the story of F. Scott Fitzgerald sitting on a balcony in Hyères one morning in August 1924, his eyes gazing out at the sea, solemn, preoccupied, not unlike Jay Gatsby staring across the waters at the green light at the tip of East Egg. A friend approached and waited a good while before becoming noticed, at which point Fitzgerald, his eyes still on the sea, slowly said: "Conrad is dead."[1] This story is generally understood to express what will become the ultimate conceptual puzzle of this chapter: the exceptional bond of intimacy that led F. Scott Fitzgerald to become, in Zdzisław Najder's phrase, "perhaps the most effusive of all twentieth-century authors in his confessions of how much he owed to Conrad in the shaping of his work."[2] This puzzle, however, is best understood as a limit instance of a much larger U.S. expatriate cultural economy and field of significance already at issue in Zelda Fitzgerald's story. More than an accidental or purely personal site of Conradian reverie, Hyères is the general setting of Conrad's most recent (in 1924) and autobiographically evocative novel, *The Rover* (1923). So, too, Zelda Fitzgerald's evocation of France entwines Conrad with the modern U.S. expatriate literary imagination. Not only did her husband write nearly the entirety of *The Great Gatsby* in France during the summer of 1924 while deeply contemplating Conrad; in addition, in his very act of European expatriation, F. Scott Fitzgerald joined the ranks of many young U.S. writers (mostly male) who went abroad, not only in vague repetition of Conrad's various national displacements but also because, in Frances Newman's contemporary and disapproving phrase, "they purpose[d] *being* Joseph Conrads to France."[3] Zelda Fitzgerald's story raises the question of how, and toward what fresh insights and revaluations, we might reconsider the "lost generation" in terms of a "Conrad generation."

This is not to reduce the postwar U.S. "lost generation," many of whom did not care for Conrad (though often, as we shall see, for very "American" reasons), to Conrad's exotic, exilic models and scripts. But this is to say that through the galvanizing countercultural force of Mencken (a tremendous influence on F. Scott Fitzgerald); through the newly avant-garde pages of the *Dial*, which printed three new Conrad prefaces in December 1920; through the *living* image of "Ulysses" that Conrad offered a modernist generation preoccupied with that image; and through a prior U.S. wartime culture of "our Conrad" predicated on national confirmation and contestation, an *expatriate* economy of U.S. literary contemplation of Conrad, occupying a different position in the "field" of Conrad's production, evolves during the postwar period. Whereas the domestic field we have explored in the previous two chapters emphasizes how world vectors shape and sculpt "national" struggle, the expatriate field explored in this chapter emphasizes Conrad's contrapuntal production through recoveries of the question of "nation" from displaced, estranged, internationalized vantages. In critical conversation with Ernest Hemingway and T. S. Eliot, F. Scott Fitzgerald, I will be showing in this chapter, became one of the most steeped and sensitive Conradians of them all because of the keen "metanational" intelligence with which he understood and internalized Conradian forms—in the process writing one of the great "American" novels. But to appreciate this critical intelligence—a quality not always emphasized in discussions of Fitzgerald—we must pursue a bit further the expatriate cultural field in which it is situated, itself as plurally contested as the mainland wartime U.S. economy of Conrad from which it ultimately derives.

The list of expatriate and peripatetic modern U.S. writers whose life and literary movements find scripting in relation to Conrad is truly formidable. Eugene O'Neill, to take one prominent example, on several occasions attributes the sailoring period of his life to the inspiration of Conrad, a debt O'Neill acknowledges in the title of his early maritime play *The Children of the Sea* (1914), as well as in his many other plays—for example, *Bound East for Cardiff* (1914), *The Emperor Jones* (1920), *The Iceman Cometh* (1940)—that reflect expansive understanding of Conrad generally.[4] Similarly, John Dos Passos, shortly before relocating to France and Italy to join the ambulance service in 1917, wrote a precocious essay analyzing *Lord Jim* as "a sort of mental grindstone"; the essay's crux, however, is to emphasize the novel's "vast impression of romance made actual"—its "tropical jungles, sunbaked seaports, the glittering blue Indian Ocean"—in terms that would soon become commensurate with the wandering arc of Dos Passos's own life.[5] Moreover, William Faulkner writes a striking letter to his mother concerning his visit to Conrad's grave during his expatriate venture in 1925; Christopher Morley repeatedly associates his initial English expatriation in the 1910s with Conrad, and not only his own but the sea travels and writings of others with Conrad as well; John Gould Fletcher on his first arrival in England comments on the happy accompanying circumstance of Conrad's rising acclaim; James Thurber, at a London cocktail party in the early twenties, was once accused with very good reason, "You're all Joseph Conrads and William McFees at heart"; Jack London and Orson Welles, to pick an earlier and a later figure, carefully track important moments in their lives and artistic output with respect to Conrad; and even Ezra Pound, who despite his appreciation of Conrad is responsible for Eliot's excising the original Conradian epigraph of *The Waste Land* (1922), may be found in the famous picture of him at Sylvia Beach's bookshop standing underneath a portrait of Conrad.[6] Much archival work remains to be done in recovering the local terms of any of these individual constructions of Conrad. However, with respect to the questions of "national" and transnational assertion and estrangement fundamentally at issue in this book and its study of the various modern U.S. economies of Conrad's production, there are two expatriate voices of special framing and clarifying resonance: Ernest Hemingway and T. S. Eliot. By recovering the nationalized premises that underlie the direct conflict between their two accounts of Conrad, we can envision a wider field of debates and vocabularies through which the U.S. expatriate contrapuntal economy of Conrad unfolds—and the precision with which Fitzgerald offers a kind of "third space" (or means) of Conrad's conception.[7]

Hemingway, who in the aftermath of the Great War was taken to referring to Conrad as "the king," makes perhaps his most memorable comment concerning Conrad *and* Eliot in a brutal quip infamously included in the memorial piece he wrote for the "Conrad Supplement" of the Paris-based *Transatlantic Review* when Conrad died. Here, shortly before observing, "But from nothing else that I have ever read have I gotten what every book of Conrad has given me," Hemingway writes:

It is agreed by most people I know that Conrad is a bad writer, just as it is agreed that T. S. Eliot is a good writer. If I knew that by grinding Mr. Eliot into a fine dry powder and sprinkling that powder over Mr. Conrad's grave Mr. Conrad would shortly appear, looking very annoyed at the forced return, and commence writing I would leave for London early tomorrow with a sausage grinder.[8]

This grisly fantasy has been interpreted by critics in many suggestive ways: as a visceral assault on Eliot's overly technical aesthetics; a self-promoting instance of crude masculinist self-fashioning; an imagined revenge on Eliot for winning the *Dial* prize in 1922, which Hemingway thought promised to him; and a displaced expression of Hemingway's struggle for control of the *Transatlantic Review* with founder and chief editor Ford Madox Ford.[9] What all of these interpretations leave out, however, is the U.S. American specificity of Hemingway's engagement with both Eliot and Conrad, without which Hemingway's memorial piece—the object of egregious mistakes in transmission over the years[10]—cannot centrally be understood. As Bernard J. Poli describes, the *Transatlantic Review*, though founded with the broad goal of establishing in and through Paris an "international republic of letters," was in fact principally a binational vehicle of communication between artists in Britain and the United States. Hemingway was one of several midwestern "cowboy-ish" Americans who dominated the staff of the review,[11] his rugged "national" self-fashioning at work both in his sparring with the Tory Ford and in his maverick "letter to the U.S." that regularly appeared in the *Review*. The opening of Hemingway's Conrad memorial, in the string of American references that make up the third paragraph and the reference to "the country" in the fifth paragraph, makes very clear that Hemingway's fundamental question—"What is there you can write about [Conrad] now that he is dead?"—presupposes a central "American" frame of reference (and anxiety) as well. This is how the untitled memorial piece begins:

What is there you can write about him now that he is dead?

The critics will dive into their vocabularies and come up with articles on the death of Conrad. They are diving now, like prairie dogs.

It will not be hard for the editorial writers: Death of John L. Sullivan, Death of Roosevelt, Death of Major Whittlesey, Death of President Coolidge's Son, Death of Honored Citizen, Passing of Pioneer, Death of President Wilson, Great Novelist Passes, it is all the same.

CONRAD, OPTIMIST AND MORALIST

Admirers of Joseph Conrad, whose sudden death is an occasion of general regret, usually think of him as an artist of the first rank, as a remarkable storyteller and a stylist. But Mr. Conrad was also a deep thinker and serene philosopher. In his novels, as in his essays etc.

It will run like that. All over the country.

And what is there you can say about him now that he is dead?[12]

"You" and "the country" here are unmistakably U.S. American, as Hemingway parodies U.S. journalistic processing of Conrad's death to make the point that it is precisely the greater U.S. celebration of "our Conrad" that makes it difficult to "say [anything] about him" in expatriate and extra-American literary circles. The insipid ease with which *U.S.* newspapers will cast Conrad as "optimist and moralist"; the vapid forms that will enfold Conrad in an *American* lineage of sporting, presidential, and military heroes; the bland, blind, embarrassing profanity that "will run like that. *All over the country*"—these are the immediate circumstances of Hemingway's transnational anxiety of self-expression. Hemingway thus uses the occasion of Conrad to dissociate himself from normative "American" discourse and practice—including the practice of volubly celebrating Conrad. Concerned with his reputation in expatriate and non-American circles and anxious not to be condescended to in normative nationalized terms, Hemingway preoccupies himself with the fundamentally disciplinary question of "what . . . you can say . . . now." "It is fashionable among my friends to disparage [Conrad]," Hemingway observes. "It is even necessary"—because to reverence Conrad would be to risk identification with the very U.S. provincialism the "lost generation" made the transatlantic journey to Paris to lose. Similarly, T. S. Eliot, the perfect and permanently postnational U.S. expatriate, is the ideal "good writer" to pair with the "necessary" designation of Conrad as "bad"[13]—because both gestures in their disavowals of American anchorage, although articulated through a vocabulary of aesthetic preference and intergenerational hostility, mean fundamentally the same thing.

Yet having demonstrated his critical mastery of both the empty forms of American conventionalism and the arbitrary codes of "literary politics" in an expatriate milieu where "the wrong opinion often proves fatal," Hemingway pulls out the (very American) sausage grinder. He rips through *both* sides of the provincial/expatriate framework with a fresh recovery of national narrativity in Conrad's idealized image. For if the impulse to praise Conrad as a "Great Novelist" and to imagine him as fundamental to one's sense of genealogy is what marks one as an "American," this is exactly what Hemingway does in graphically rejecting the denationalized ideal of Eliot and foundationally affirming that "from nothing else that I have ever read have I gotten what every book of Conrad has given to me." Indeed, a series of pointedly "American" references follow. Though he is careful to distinguish himself from a "girl" in "Toronto" ("women" and "Canada" serving as diminutive, insulting metonymies for the United States[14]) who has "all of [Conrad's] books on her shelf" but has read only (the "popular") *Victory* and *The Arrow of Gold*, Hemingway is clearly more at home in *her* library than anywhere else: "One after another I borrowed [Conrad's books] from [her]. . . . Knowing I could not re-read them I saved up four that I would not read until I needed them badly, when the disgust with writing, writers, and everything written and to write would be too much. Two months in Toronto used up the four books." And again, in recounting the apparent ignominy of reading serial installments of *The Rover* in the women's magazine the *Pictorial Review* in a hotel in Sudbury, Ontario, Hemingway manages both to disdain continental North America and to naturalize his consumption and inheritance of Conrad there: "[I] read *The Rover,* sitting up in bed in the Nickle Range Hotel. When morning came I had used up all my Conrad like a drunkard, I had hoped it would last me the trip, and felt like a young man who has blown his patrimony. But, I thought, he will write more stories. He has lots of time."

Implicit in Hemingway's acid denigration of Eliot as a "great, acknowl-edged technician of a literary figure," the specific U.S. national narrative that Hemingway attempts to articulate through Conrad emerges in the sentence immediately following the "sausage grinder" reference: "One should not be funny over the death of a great man, but you cannot couple T. S. Eliot and Jo-seph Conrad in a sentence seriously any more than you could see, say, André Germain and Manuel Garcia (Maera) walking down the street together and not laugh."[15] The distinction Hemingway draws first between Eliot and Conrad, then between a minor French belletrist and one of Hemingway's most revered Spanish bullfighters, is one of strenuous *experience*. Hemingway draws the same distinction nine months later in "Banal Story" (1925), a short piece that ironically juxtaposes a reader of *Forum* magazine, convinced that through his reading he experiences the true "Romance" that is "everywhere" in the world, with the same heroic bullfighter Maera, a genuine romance figure who through his actual experiences in the ring lies wounded and moribund: "stretched flat on his bed . . . with a tube in each lung, dying of pneumonia." Like Conrad in 1924, Maera dies with "all the papers in Anadalucia devot[ing] special supple-ments to his death"; also like Conrad (or so one suspects from Hemingway's point of view) Maera leaves in his wake several fellow artists who are "very re-lieved that he was dead, because he always did in the bull-ring the things they could only do sometimes."[16] But most important, both Hemingway's story and the Conrad memorial piece—clearly written in palimpsestic relation to one another—work together to group Conrad, Maera, and Hemingway against Eliot, Germain, and the *Forum* reader to privilege an art based on concrete experience and the engagement of extreme circumstance: i.e., not "technique" alone, but technique in the context of Conrad's sea, Maera's bull ring, Heming-way's war experience, and so on. This valorization of the perilous actual; this determination that innovations in art derive from exceptional and unfamiliar circumstance; this insistence on extreme experience as the testing condition of aesthetic expression; this equation of the masterful artist and the master-ing person—collectively, this *ideology of strenuous and authentic experience*—is the linchpin of most twentieth-century critical attempts to conceptualize Conrad and Hemingway together: leading, indeed, to Leo Gurko's subtle, suggestive, and probably overstated contention that Hemingway is Conrad's "chief heir in our time."[17] But what we must emphasize, of course, is that this aesthetic and kinetic ideology is also a *nationalizing* ideology: Hemingway's construction of the "foreign" signifier "Conrad" is just as nationalized as the Rooseveltian ideal of the "strenuous life" that Hemingway both draws on and powerfully validates. Produced in estranged conditions and through a series of negative operations, it is a nationalized sense of (multi-)oppositionality that Hemingway ultimately recovers in the Conrad memorial piece. Like the shadow-boxing for which the ever-defensive Hemingway was famous in Paris, and also like the "civil war" by which Hemingway attempted to take over the *Transatlantic Review* in self-consciously "American" terms, Hemingway reads in Conrad a combative means and style of engaging both the world *and* various forms of U.S. domesticity that is simultaneously a *national* posture and *transnational* derivation.

T. S. Eliot's rejection of U.S. national identity, however, has equally strong and catholic claims on Conrad's interpretation. When Conrad died, Eliot, too, commemorated the occasion in the *Criterion* with an opening tribute saluting Conrad as "beyond question a great novelist," "one whose reputation is as secure as any writer of his time."[18] As with Hemingway, a certain stiffness and reticence in Eliot's manner only underscores the intensity of his appreciation of Conrad—and its "American" perils.[19] Ever spiritually inclined, Eliot would come to formulate his attraction to Conrad in terms of the latter's "essential moral preoccupation"—"Evil is rare, bad is common. Evil cannot even be perceived but by a very few," Eliot explains of Conrad's fundamental insight[20]— and indeed, at the heart of the intense and long-standing intimacy Eliot finds in Conrad lies a sense of "Original Sin" which, as Albert Gelpi, Kenneth Asher, and others have shown, constitutes a continuous foundation of Eliot's evolving views of aesthetics and politics throughout his life.[21] Though Conrad would not use a religious vocabulary, the "classicist point of view" that the earlier Eliot champions and "defines as essentially a belief in Original Sin—the necessity for austere discipline," and whose implications "may roughly be characterized as *form* and *restraint* in art, *discipline* and *authority* in religion, [and] *centralization* in government,"[22] is very much a point of view assumed by Conrad, who expresses his equally anti-Romantic, vehemently anti-Rousseauian first principles in a famous letter to his friend R. B. Cunninghame Graham:

Man is a vicious animal. His viciousness must be organised. Crime is a necessary condition of organised existence. Society is fundamentally criminal or it would not exist. . . . [Therefore] a definite first principle is needed. If the idea of nationhood brings suffering and its service brings death, that is worth more than the service to ghosts of a dead eloquence—precisely because the eloquence is disembodied. Believe me if I tell you that these questions are very real to me. . . . I look at the future from the depths of a very dark past, and I find I am allowed nothing but fidelity to an absolutely lost cause. (*CL* 2.159, 160)

Given the "dark past" of Poland, Conrad knows something about both the depths and fundamentality of human depravity as well as the remarkable power of concrete "national" traditions (as opposed to mere "disembodied" ideals and rhetoric) to sublimate, discipline, and "organise" human vulnerability. Such principles animate the tricky passage in *Heart of Darkness* in which Marlow speaks of human "darkness" being "redeem[ed]" by an "unselfish belief in the idea—something you can set up, and bow down before, and offer a sacrifice to" (*YOS* 51). Moreover, in the essay "Tradition" (1918)—which, as we have seen, applies *Heart of Darkness*'s valorization of "restraint" and "work" to the disciplines of the British merchant marine, as does most of Conrad's "sea" fiction—Conrad articulates a conception of "tradition" whose emphases on self-negation, constraint, and aestheticized central authority are fully commensurate with Eliot's "Tradition and the Individual Talent" (1920). Conrad's letter thus demonstrates the appropriateness of Eliot's original intention to use as the epigraph of *The Waste Land* (1922) Marlow's famous words concerning Mr. Kurtz at the end of *Heart of Darkness*: "Did he live his life again in every detail of desire, temptation, and surrender during that supreme moment of complete knowledge? He cried out at an image, at some vision,—he cried out twice, a cry that was no more than a breath—'The horror! the horror!'" Eliot was right to recognize these words as "somewhat elucidative" of his poem, and Pound, playing the perfect part of the insecure expatriate U.S. American, was wrong to advise change: because the shocking "horror" of human depravity and the consequential necessity of "surrender" to a higher "organising" structure speaks more fully to the peculiar vision and trajectory of the poem than the simple life-in-death sterility foregrounded in the eventual epigraph.[23] Indeed, when Eliot wants to make the latter point, he knows the right epigraph from Conrad to choose. As several critics have observed, "Mr. Kurtz—he dead" resonates as the epigraph of Eliot's "The Hollow Men" (1925) *not* because Kurtz is a "hollow man" but rather precisely because he isn't. It is not Kurtz, who dies, but the false "pilgrims" (with "crossed staves," as in Eliot's poem) in Conrad's novel who work for the Company, combining false and facile faith with the most petty hypocrisy and ambition, and whom Marlow repeatedly describes as "hollow" as they make their way up the river to *replace* Kurtz, who are the analogues for Eliot's "hollow" and "stuffed men" of the empty, sterile, banal modern world that ends "Not with a bang but a whimper."[24]

But the moral and political logic of Eliot's attraction to Conrad is also deeply entwined with an aesthetic negotiation of Conrad that itself has as its inevitable conclusion Eliot's renunciation of U.S. "national" narratives and categories of identification. We see this in an important essay Eliot wrote on Rudyard Kipling in 1919, which reverses Doubleday's formula by placing Conrad as "in many ways the antithesis of Mr. Kipling." Anticipating a central distinction drawn the following year in "Tradition and the Individual Talent," Eliot argues that whereas Kipling's poetry depends for its power on the expression and contingent presence of "personality," in Conrad "the emotion" is fully and objectively "there" by itself: "simply, coldly independent of the author . . . there and forever like Shakespeare's and Aeschylus's emotions."[25] Whereas Kipling's poems require the idea of an adjacent personality, Conrad's work *negates* his personality—Eliot writes in "Tradition and the Individual Talent" of "this process of depersonalization," of the artist's "continual self-sacrifice, a continual extinction of personality"[26]—and in a manner that extends to Conrad's negation of the significance of *matter* and *experience* as well. Pace Hemingway, Eliot makes clear that the "matter" and "the experience of the man himself" are fundamentally irrelevant to processes of art: "the more perfect the artist, the more completely separate in him will be the man who suffers and the mind who creates"; "the difference between art and the event is always absolute."[27] Conrad thus is an important figure in whose image this antimaterial, antiexperiential program of literary aesthetics is conceived; as John Gould Fletcher explains in a letter to John Cournos in 1921, in words that effectively reverse Hemingway's view of Conrad the anti-"technician": "The school [of Eliot and Pound] lays its stress on technique, exclusively. . . . This school is always talking about . . . the beauty of form. They incline to rate Conrad higher than Hardy, and probably James higher than Conrad. . . . They favor experiment in form but argue that subject-matter is unimportant."[28]

Even more important, moreover, is Eliot's construction of Conrad in terms of the negation of *ideas*, especially as ideas may relate to politics and ideological doctrine. Whereas writers like Kipling and Swinburne use the force of their "personalities" to advance "concepts or ideas" like "Empire" and "Liberty" (respectively), Eliot, in a crucial formulation, identifies Conrad as the repudiation of such things: "He is . . . the antithesis of Empire (as well as of democracy); his characters are the denial of Europe, of Nation, of Race almost, they are fearfully alone in the Wilderness."[29] Conrad, it would seem, is very much the exponentially negative and anarchic force—that singularity "revolutionary and abysmal"—one finds in Mencken: only whereas for Mencken Conrad's infinite negations *consolidate* a sense of "superior" personality and *license* a radically agnostic and iconoclastic relation to anyone else's declarations concerning the world, in Eliot Conrad's endless eviscerations of personality *and* substance *and* ideas (politically left or right) all make for a curiously immutable and ineffable world: "Mr. Conrad has no ideas, but he has a point of view, a 'world'; it can hardly be defined, but it pervades his work and is unmistakable. It could not be otherwise. Had Mr. Kipling taken Liberty and Swinburne the Empire, the alteration would be unimportant."[30] Eliot places "world" here very advisedly in quotation marks, because what he means by the term is not a material externality but rather "a point of view that holds" one's impressions of the world "together," a narrative mechanism of "cohesion."[31] Eliot means, in essence, a *tradition* of conceiving the world that has been so internalized and fundamentalized that one confuses it with the world itself. Conrad is "the denial of Empire, of Nation, of Race"—all of these being essentially synonyms for an imperial project of "restraint"—not in the Menckenian sense that he opens up questions of other worlds, and not in Hemingway's sense that he engages new extremes and elements of the uncharted world, but in the "classical" sense that every last sinful (or, in the Conrad lexicon, "anarchic") negation that he performs becomes the justification for the "austere discipline" of world structures of empire as they are. "I am all for empires, especially the Austro-Hungarian Empire,"[32] writes Eliot in a letter to the *Transatlantic Review* in January 1924 (*after* the fall, the negation, of the Austro-Hungarian Empire); and for Eliot what is so magnificent about Conrad is his ability to harness all the subversive energy in the world and yet ultimately plug it into—to sublimate it within, like Conrad's "vicious" but vanished personality itself—an unchanging, depoliticized conception of the world that must consequently continue to be administered by the oldest imperial traditions. To posit a Conrad who has "no ideas" but rather "a point of view, 'a world,'" is not only to present the ideas that underlie one's point of view as the world itself: it is to posit a world that exists in elementally unchanging relation to *any* ideas, and hence to insist that the world continue to be administered by traditions that are as fundamentally unchanging as it is.

In the same letter to the *Transatlantic Review*, Eliot, worried about the collapse of empires like Austria-Hungary in the aftermath of the Great War, bemoans "the present age" as "a singularly stupid one" of "mistaken nationalism": an era of an "outburst of artificial nationalities, constituted like artificial genealogies for millionaires"—among whose many culprits is the United States. For Eliot, "a *genuine* nationality depends upon the existence of a genuine literature, and you cannot have a nationality worth speaking of unless you have a national literature," and especially as these questions of "national" and "genuine litera-ture" ultimately turn on the "very small" "number of languages worth writing in," Eliot ultimately reaches the conclusion—which Ford Madox Ford at the time would have agreed with, but not most of the rest of the staff at the *Trans-atlantic Review*—"that there can only be one English literature: that there can-not be British literature, or American literature."[33] Eliot had earlier made this argument in "A Preface to Modern Literature" (1923), in which he laments the "disintegration" of "English literature" "into at least three varieties of provin-cialism" (British, Irish, U.S. American) and in particular the "excessively local" emphases of U.S. critics like Mencken who are "chiefly occupied in chastising the vices and stupidities of their own nation—a work useful at home . . . but of no interest abroad."[34] Eliot mentions Conrad in "A Preface to Modern Literature" as one of the few "solitary figures" in recent English letters to point the way to the present,[35] and it is not difficult to see how Eliot's greater understanding of Conrad implies the repudiation of independent U.S. nationality articulated in the "Preface." Not only does Conrad stand for the veneration of tradition and the rejection of "personality" that Eliot in "Tradition and the Individual Talent," which so squarely targets Emersonian doctrines of individualist self-reliance and "natural" originality, asserts *against* the U.S. American grain. Not only does Conrad stand for the irrelevance of "provincial" material or charismatic figures that might form the basis of a "usable" U.S. American tradition. As well, Conrad fundamentally appreciates that the antagonisms that underlie the world are so severe that the "austere discipline" of Empire is necessary: places like the United States that lack tradition, any American will-to-independence (and its support-ing ideologies) that belies tradition, and the very momentum of displacement from cultural, linguistic, and imperial systems like the "English," all are in op-position to the "essential morality" and conservative politics Eliot understands at the heart of Conrad. In "Tradition and the Individual Talent," Eliot repeat-edly returns to the idea of "nation," carefully balancing appeals to both "the mind of Europe" and "the mind of [one's] own country," meticulously insisting that the "traditional" writer internalizes both "the whole of the literature of Europe" *and* "the whole of the literature of his own country."[36] Eliot does this in significant part to subsume the United States within the greater "nation" of "the English": to reannex the United States for, and annihilate the meaningful possibility of its existence outside, the realm of "English." So, too, does Eliot's Conrad stand for "the denial of Empire, of Nation, of Race almost," precisely insofar as any of these three terms might become dissociated from one another.

. . .

The certainty with which Hemingway forges a resurgent image of the "American" through Conrad, and the equal certainty with which Eliot understands in Conrad the need to reject the United States as anything but the most factitious political category, may be compared with the political and conceptual *ambivalences* that inform the Conradian enthusiasms of F. Scott Fitzgerald. Indeed, though Fitzgerald's critical tenacity and range are generally taken less seriously than Eliot's or Hemingway's, the case of Conrad, whose heterotopic fiction probably really does turn more on generative uncertainties and metacritical inquiries than on tamable "positions" or "points of view," may reveal Fitzgerald to be the most sensitive intelligence of the three, at least in this instance. The very sophistication of Fitzgerald's understanding of Conrad, moreover, may help to explain the "effusive" nature of Fitzgerald's comments concerning Conrad—whose singularity Najder is quite right to point out, though it is the product of a larger cultural economy and counterpoint of "Conrad" in which Fitzgerald participates. Remarkably, Fitzgerald mentions Conrad in at least 124 letters and essays written over the course of his life. He was also unusually eager to parade the formal and thematic indebtednesses of each of his three mature novels to Conrad,[37] and in 1925 he actually protested when Mencken failed to include him in a public list of Conrad's "imitators."[38] Fitzgerald wrote numerous critical reviews supremely exalting several Conrad texts, among them *Nostromo* ("the greatest novel" ever written); "Youth" (contains "the most remarkable passages of English prose written these thirty years"); and the Preface to *The Nigger of the "Narcissus"* (in which Conrad "defined" "the serious business of writing . . . more clearly, more vividly, than any man of our time").[39] And if, in 1927, Fitzgerald was insisting to Hemingway that "my theory of fiction is derived from Conrad," as late as 1941, the month before his death, Fitzgerald was still writing his daughter and would-be writer Frances a letter advising her that "all writers line themselves up behind a solid gold bar like . . . Joseph Conrad's art."[40]

Such testimonials have produced something of an explosion of critical writings on the aesthetic relationship between Conrad and Fitzgerald, only one of which, however, explores this relationship in situated historical and political terms,[41] and all of which blink the central paradox of Fitzgerald's attraction to Conrad: that it is in some sense difficult to imagine two stranger aesthetic bedfellows than Conrad, the brooding, maritime, reclusive, Anglo-Polish champion of the work ethic, and Fitzgerald, the dapper, high society, hyper-American, eternally adolescent "Playboy of the Western World." The Fitzgerald, however, who wrote *The Great Gatsby* entirely from the distance of Europe has more "nationally" in common with the eternally displaced Conrad than might immediately meet the eye. For Fitzgerald, the fantasy of imagining oneself, as Nick Carraway puts it at the end of *The Great Gatsby* (1925), "unutterably aware of our identity with this country" exists in constant tension with the suspicion, as Fitzgerald confesses in *The Crack-Up* (1936), that beneath the "false face" of his national performances there lay a man who had more in common with the U.S.'s "Strangers, Virginians, Negroes (light or dark), Hunting People, retail clerks, and middlemen in general."[42] Such counter-impulses both to define "America" and to pull it apart at the seams lie somewhere near the heart of Fitzgerald's famous observation that "the test of a first-rate intelligence is the ability to hold two opposed ideas in the mind at the same time, and still retain the ability to function";[43] and it is not only this criterion but this context of "intelligence" that informs Fitzgerald's intimate appreciation and internalization of Conrad.

As Avrom Fleishman was the first to point out, Conrad's writings are virtually "unstinting" and "compulsive" in the interest they take, not in enumerating national "character" but in studying the processes and difficulties of national imaginings.[44] Stemming from the national difficulties of Conrad's Polish youth, "the idea of nationality" (*NLL* 96) surfaces as a focal and impassioned subject in Conrad's three essays on Poland, other political essays like "Autocracy and War" (1905), and many of Conrad's longer letters.[45] *L'idée nationale* is also a crucial (and often explicitly decoded) subtext of Conrad's greater metaphors of the collective ship; nervously repeated signature tropes like "our man" and "one of us"; and the key Conradian ideals of "solidarity," "fidelity," and "community."[46] And like Fitzgerald, what makes Conrad special is the double attitude he brings to this subject: exclaiming, in one breath, that "the national spirit . . . can alone give us the feeling of an enduring existence and of an invincible air of power against the fates," and in the next, that he found all "national egoism repulsive and destructive."[47] The result in Conrad's fiction is a dual propensity, in Hunt Hawkins's phrase, both to "make and un-make" nations;[48] the genuine vacillation, as Paul Armstrong argues, "between endorsing and demystifying the ideal of community";[49] and a "factor of ex-cess," as Geoffrey Harpham has most recently emphasized, by which Conrad both invests himself in national imaginings and then "erases" the legitimacy of those imaginings.[50]

   In what follows, I argue that much of Conrad's fiction can usefully be considered "metanational," and that Fitzgerald gravitates toward Conradian forms and aesthetic strategies precisely because he understands this and un-derstands in them a critical means of expressing and engaging with modern U.S. problematics of nationality and nationhood. By "metanational," I mean to suggest, in line with Benedict Anderson's seminal study of nationhood in 1983, that Conrad's fiction forgoes the ambition of representing distinctive national "qualities" for a culturally situated investigation of the techniques, strategies, and styles by which people attempt to "imagine" themselves as members of a national "community";[51] and if Fitzgerald initially approached "our Conrad," as we shall see, in the hopes of discovering a means to articulate an "utterly national" vision of "America,"[52] what Fitzgerald ultimately discovered was a means of "undiscovering" his country: of approaching nationhood as not an objective fact but an imaginative social construct, and anatomizing the vari-ous imaginative techniques and material interferences through which U.S. nationalist imaginings advanced and receded in the 1920s. I advance this ar-gument in two stages: first, by examining Fitzgerald's "national" construction of Conrad and Conrad's major fiction in his expository prose of the 1920s; and second, by exploring the formal and national intersections of two novels that have not received critical cross-consideration: Fitzgerald's *The Great Gatsby* and Conrad's *Nostromo*. Throughout, I am interested in teasing out the con-tours and contextual implications of a particular Conradian formal strategy that captivated Fitzgerald: that of constellating a novel of intense perception and socially conjunctive will around an *absent* character center—like Gatsby or Nostromo—whose status as a fundamentally vacant projective tableau, a vague surface and phantasmal mirror, allows Conrad and Fitzgerald to study both the procedures and cultural fractures that give rise to what Homi Bhabha calls "the impossible unity of 'nation' as a symbolic force."[53] Though Fitzgerald did in fact hold *Nostromo* in singular esteem at the time he wrote *Gatsby*—and very much because *Nostromo* alone among Conrad's novels literally tells the story of an imagined country and problems of collective imagining arising within it—I offer what follows as the beginning, not the end, of considerations of the cultural materialities that make it so Conradian tropes and aesthetics at large seem to saturate the very marrow of Fitzgerald's prose.

"MATERIAL" DIFFICULTIES

Alongside his novels, plays, and many short stories of the 1920s, F. Scott Fitzgerald also wrote a substantial stream of book reviews and essays on the state of U.S. fiction. These writings bear a family resemblance in their consistent return to two intertwined subjects: one, the failure of U.S. novelists to produce an authoritative national voice; and two, Joseph Conrad as the aesthetic benchmark of not only what is missing in U.S. fiction but also what it possibly could be. Fitzgerald's essay "How to Waste Material: A Note on My Generation" (1926) offers a representative account of the terms and assumptions that frame Fitzgerald's assessment of the nation's articulative difficulties. The essay begins by placing the entire U.S. literary tradition in an oft-voiced predicament of lacking worthwhile "material" substance:

Ever since [Washington] Irving's preoccupation with the necessity for an American background, for some miles of clear territory on which colorful variants might presently arise, the question of material has hampered the American writer. For one Dreiser who had made a single-minded and irreproachable choice there have been a dozen like Henry James who have stupid-got with worry over the matter, and yet another dozen who, blinded by the tail of Walt Whitman's comet, have botched their books by the insincere compulsion to write "significantly" about America.[54]

With an implicit temporal line drawn between James and Whitman, the orthodox tenor of Fitzgerald's argument quickly changes. The *modern* American problem, in Fitzgerald's view, is not that U.S. writers lack fertile domestic resources but that they are lacking in the imagination and style required to transform what is actually a U.S. cultural superabundance into a genuinely meaningful, "sincere" and "significant," vision of the nation. Fitzgerald goes on to describe how, "over the past seven years," there have been nearly "a dozen treatments of the American farmer, ranging from New England to Nebraska"; "at least a dozen books about [American] youth"; "more than a dozen novels respecting various aspects of New York, Chicago, Washington, Detroit, Wilmington, and Richmond"; and "innumerable" others "dealing with American politics, business, society, science, racial problems, art, literature, and moving pictures." Though Fitzgerald's tone is unmistakably caustic, his dissatisfaction does not attach to the unworthiness of the featured American "materials"—which were excavated in a "sort of literary gold rush" and should have provided the "literary beginnings . . . of a golden age"—but to the books and authors themselves, as they leave such rich pockets of national ore "as dead as if they never had been written." For lack of "effort," "intelligence," "imagination," and authentic "American instinct," the authors of all those books fail "to get hold of any material at all." Sounding not unlike Nick Carraway at the end of *The Great Gatsby*, Fitzgerald concludes the opening and major section of "How to Waste Material" with an elegiac anatomy of why U.S. novelists seize on domestic cultural resources only to waste them:

> But perhaps it was already too late. . . . Now the business is over. . . . The public, weary of being fooled has gone back to its Englishmen, its memoirs, and its prophets. [The Americans] were never sufficiently aware that material, however closely observed, is elusive at the moment in which it has existence unless it is imaginatively purified by an incorruptible style and by the catharsis of a passionate emotion.[55]

With the stage set for English "prophets," Conrad enters in the second section of "How To Waste Material," itself principally devoted to the one beacon of American hope Fitzgerald can see amid the national literary gloom: Ernest Hemingway's *In Our Time* (1925). Fitzgerald introduces *In Our Time* with the praise: "I read it with the most breathless unwilling interest I have experienced since Conrad first bent my reluctant eyes upon the sea."[56] The standard of Conrad doubles with the achievement of Hemingway in the discussion that follows; but the preliminary invocation of Conrad itself is noteworthy for at least two reasons. First, in the very gesture of introducing a "national" text— good or bad—through the superlative lens of Conrad, Fitzgerald is following in a customary ritual of his essays throughout the 1920s. In his review of Grace Flandrau's *Being Respectable* (1923), for example, Fitzgerald opens with the corrective standard of Conrad's *Nostromo*, which comes to represent the difference between the "utterly national . . . materials" Flandrau "clumsily" draws upon, and the "clear stream" of an "utterly national" style and vision that could have made her "our Conrad."[57] In his review of Thomas Boyd's *Through the Wheat* (1923), Fitzgerald similarly begins by quoting an extensive passage from Conrad's "Youth"—"one of the most remarkable passages of English prose these past thirty years"—and then, through a curious process of logic, makes the case that Boyd is faintly worthy of the "national" company of Stephen Crane and John Dos Passos in part because *Through the Wheat* contains "an echo of [Conrad's] lift and ring," in addition to upholding other Conradian aesthetic norms.[58] More idiosyncratically still, Fitzgerald introduces Sherwood Anderson's *Many Marriages* (1923) through an ostensibly irrelevant opening meditation on the "almost intolerable influence of Conrad" and three of his peers, which only becomes clarified near the end of the review when Fitzgerald discloses that Anderson's successful evacuation of national "illusions" reminds him of Conrad's *The Secret Agent*.[59] On the model of "one of those Conrad characters who so enthrall him," Fitzgerald further praises H. L. Mencken for his tragi-heroic efforts in the area of "shaping national letters"; and in his own preface to the 1934 reissue of *The Great Gatsby*, Fitzgerald defends the novel's "honesty of imagination" and "American" sincerity by reminding the reader that as he sat down to write *Gatsby* in 1924, "I had just re-read Conrad's preface to *The Nigger [of the "Narcissus"]*.[60]

Here and elsewhere, this habit of invoking Conrad as a yardstick of national achievement and as a talisman of national self-discovery comes coupled with yet another consistent practice: the rhetorical grouping of Conrad rigidly on the "imaginative" and "stylistic," as opposed to the mere "material," side of the literary dichotomy Fitzgerald presents in "How to Waste Material." This is a second point underwriting Fitzgerald's invocation of Conrad in praising *In Our Time*. When Fitzgerald champions Hemingway's short novel by comparing its appeal to a degree of readerly rapture he had not experienced "since Conrad first *bent my reluctant eyes* upon the sea," Fitzgerald is recalling his own initial resistance to reading Conrad as a writer whose "sea" material was so prohibitively distinct from his own. So little, in fact, did the younger Fitzgerald expect to have any use for Conrad that, as he put it in 1921, he had been "literally *forced*" to read Conrad's fiction.[61] This preliminary impression of Conrad as bearing no "material" relationship to himself, moreover, did not change but rather became strengthened as Fitzgerald became quickly infatuated with Conrad. In a letter to Mencken in 1925, Fitzgerald emphasizes that although he had "learned so much" from Conrad, it is Conrad's "approach and his prose [that] are naturally more imitated than his material."[62] Likewise, in another letter in which Fitzgerald meditates on both his own relationship to Conrad and Conrad's relationship to Henry James, Fitzgerald credits Conrad himself with the insight that "real authors must learn from other writers *whose material does not touch theirs at a single point.*"[63] One finds Fitzgerald, in fact, making much the same point up to the very month of his death;[64] and the significance, for our purposes, is not simply to accede to Fitzgerald's firm rhetorical grouping of Conrad on the side of "style" rather than "material," form rather than content, but rather to recognize that for Fitzgerald, the content of Conrad's appeal comes embedded within Conrad's formal practices. That this embedded content is in some sense a *national* content, moreover, seems rather strikingly telegraphed by the fact that in all those reviews in which Fitzgerald valorizes Conrad's "style," "utterly national" self-expression provides the focal content.

Two adjacent entries concerning Conrad in Fitzgerald's private *Notebooks* of the 1930s are of particular help in elucidating Fitzgerald's attempts to place Conrad as a formal model of national self-articulation. The first is a somewhat perfunctory entry reading: "Conrad influenced by *Man Without a Country*."[65] The reference is to Edward Everett Hale's short story of 1865; and the entry itself would be of marginal value—the "influence" claim is implausible, though the comparison is not wholly inapt[66]—were it not for the fact that it shows Fitzgerald meditating on Conrad in a context of national remove: not in a country but outside; not of a nation but rather metanationally and externally pondering national mechanisms of inclusion and exclusion (a central concern of both "The Man Without a Country" and *Lord Jim*). The second entry interjects into this metanational construction of Conrad a "secret theory" of social form Fitzgerald astutely discerns across much of Conrad's major fiction. The passage reads:

Conrad's secret theory examined: He knew that things do transpire about people. Therefore he wrote the truth and transposed it to parallel to give that quality, adding confusion however to his structure. Nevertheless, there is in his scheme a desire to imitate life which is in all the big shots. Have I such an idea in the composition of this book?[67]

Because of the long period over which the entries in Fitzgerald's *Notebooks* were compiled, the exact "book" Fitzgerald references at the close remains a secret.[68] Fitzgerald's use of the word *secret* at the outset, however, is not nearly so mysterious: the word is used analytically rather than dramatically to describe a theory *of* secrecy that, in Fitzgerald view, connects and socializes the form of most of the Conrad novels in which he took greatest interest. This "theory," Fitzgerald suggests, is one in which Conrad places dark and menacing "secrets"—which began as "truth" but become "transposed to parallel" beyond their recovery as "truth"—into removed, blocked, central, and strategically elusive character sites: "parallel" object sites whose names probably include James Wait, Mr. Kurtz, Karain, "Lord" Jim, and Nostromo. These characters are parallel both in the sense that they exist at a profound perceptual remove from interested narrative observers—who experience great barriers and delays in accessing what even *seems* to be their subjectivities—and in the sense that these characters seem to inhabit a parallel universe: one not of "imitated life" but rather fiction, such that their subjectivities, even when belatedly expressed, retain the mediated instability and implausibility of projected romantic artifice. "Nevertheless," Fitzgerald suggests, there seems in "Conrad's scheme" a genuine "desire to imitate life"—but precisely because perceptualized dynamics of fiction, projection, and mediation play a crucial role in social "life." Secrets "*do* transpire about people," drawing others collectively together in social relation around the central and "parallel" pockets of mystery and fascination. The mystery itself, however, remains fundamentally absented or "transposed": the connective webs of secrecy that envelop and circulate around such mystery-characters bear no necessary relation to their internal "truth," and may indeed be precisely a projected and protective shield designed to prevent the "truth" from arising. What is postulated here is not only a "lifelike" model of knowledge acquisition as a gradual and perhaps interminably thwarted process but also a metasocial understanding of collective formations arising through and around ambiguous central icons that serve as sites of projection and mediation for surrounding imaginations.

Such an understanding of the social production and accretion of meaning around the *outside* of secretly sequestered spaces is precisely what Conrad emphasizes about Marlow's unusual practice of storytelling in *Heart of Darkness*. Ordinary seamen may spin yarns of "direct simplicity, the whole meaning of which lies within the shell of a cracked nut" (*YOS* 48). Such "typical" yarn spinners, in fact, generally end up producing for the listener an ultimate "secret" that the listener "finds . . . not worth knowing": "But Marlow was not typical. . . . To him the meaning of an episode was not inside a kernel but outside, enveloping the tale which brought it about only as a glow brings out a haze, in the likeness of one of these misty halos that, sometimes, are made visible by the spectral illumination of moonshine" (*YOS* 48). The personal webs of intimacy and loyalty, of course, that can be spun through the hazy accretions around the outside of a central mystery provide the privileged concern of the next Conrad novel to feature Marlow: *Lord Jim*. But regarding the social and national implications of a magnetic and mediating social mystery, one may turn—as a matter of heightened attention rather than categorical difference—to the one Conrad novel Fitzgerald described, sometime on or around April 1923, as "the greatest novel of the past fifty years."[69] That novel is *Nostromo*, itself literally the story of an imagined country beset by "national" imaginative difficulties; and of interest is not only Fitzgerald's esteem for that novel at a time so close to his composition of *Gatsby*, but also the specific formal aspect of *Nostromo* which captivated Fitzgerald the most—in singular contradistinction, as we shall see, to every major critic of *Nostromo* in the first half of this century.

Fitzgerald's first extended reference to *Nostromo* comes in the aforementioned Flandrau review (March 1923). If *Nostromo* is the formal antidote to *Being Respectable*'s national underachievement, it quickly becomes clear that by *Nostromo* Fitzgerald principally means the *character* Nostromo. Though Flandrau is frequently "impressive" in her "documentation" of American culture, her novel itself is "inferior" primarily because "there is no one Nostromo in it to draw together the entire novel."[70] This comment, which initially seems to be one of Fitzgerald's somewhat bland appeals to Jamesian standards of "selective" concentration,[71] becomes more intriguing as Fitzgerald moves on to assault Sinclair Lewis's *Babbitt*, a book "in many ways inferior" to Flandrau's, even though it does fulfill Fitzgerald's borrowed requirements of a focal and centered character space. Fitzgerald asserts in the Flandrau review that there is an "imaginative"[72] national dynamic present in Nostromo that is lacking in both *Being Respectable* and *Babbitt*; but what this imaginative dynamic is, as it implicates Nostromo's place in *Nostromo*'s form, comes out most clearly in a revealing public statement Fitzgerald made two months later. The occasion was a question publicly posed to Fitzgerald—"what novel he would rather have written than any other"—and Fitzgerald's response is again important for both the novel he pinpoints and the "chief reason" why:

I would rather have written Conrad's *Nostromo* than any other novel. First, because I think it is the greatest novel since *Vanity Fair* . . . but chiefly because "Nostromo" the character intrigues me so much. Now the Nostromo who exists in life and always has existed, whether as a Roman centurion or a modern top sergeant, has often crept into fiction, but until Conrad there was no one to ponder over him. He was dismissed superficially and abruptly even by those who admired his efficient handling of the proletariat either in crowds or as individuals. Kipling realized that this figure . . . is one of the most powerful props of the capitalist system, and under various names he occurs in many of Kipling's stories of Indian life—but always as a sort of glorified servant.

Now Conrad didn't stop there. He took this man of the people and imagined him with such a completeness that there is no use of any one else pondering over him for some time. He's one of the most important types of our civilization. In particular he's one that always made a haunting and irresistible appeal to me. So I would rather have dragged his soul from behind his haunting and inarticulate presence than written any other novel in the world.[73]

Yet again, *Nostromo* has become Nostromo; and the key to appreciating the "national" import of Fitzgerald's words lies in a recognition of just how utterly marginal this view of *Nostromo* was among Fitzgerald's contemporaries. In the first half of the twentieth century, and from the very moment of *Nostromo*'s publication, the great debate framing the novel's reception history drew its lines over whether *Nostromo* was an "astonishing" success, an admirable "failure," or some hybrid of both. The one issue, however, that everyone agreed on— with voices ranging from essentially critical reviewers like Virginia Woolf to positive reviewers like John Buchanan, W. L. Alden, and Conrad's close friends Edward Garnett and R. B. Cunninghame Graham[74]—was that the character of Nostromo himself was an arbitrary inclusion and a fundamental mistake. The common charge, to combine Garnett, Buchan, and Woolf, was that Conrad had unwisely included within a properly panoramic political and historical novel—which "is" about and "ought to have been called 'Costaguana'"—a figure of inexcusably obvious fictionality: a species of "inanimate" and "hollow" "still-life," a "handy *deus ex machina* [who] misses being a masterpiece because of his habit of suddenly becoming a puppet."[75] These readers jointly indict Conrad for an artificiality in Nostromo that would seem precisely the reverse of Fitzgerald's admiration of the "completeness" with which Conrad "imagines" Nostromo.

The contradiction, however, is only a surface appearance, for as one reads Fitzgerald closely, one discovers that it is precisely the fictive barriers that surround Nostromo that "intrigue" Fitzgerald "so much." Fitzgerald never says that Conrad succeeds in "dragging" Nostromo's "soul from behind his astounding and inarticulate presence"; and he certainly never states exactly what it is that Conrad may have glimpsed at the essence of the "Nostromo who exists in life and has always existed." Rather, Fitzgerald's words are an extended meditation on the imposed fictionalities that make it so difficult to see *through* the Nostromo type: on the pat formulas of romance from Rome to Kipling that have enabled men like Nostromo to be "superficially dismissed"; on the social formulas of "prop" and "type" that betray a social and political investment in *not* seeing Nostromo, and hoping he does not "see" himself; and perhaps most importantly, on the patina of romance—"his haunting and irresistible appeal"—that, for observers like Conrad and Fitzgerald, creates a gap between the Nostromo type's "astounding and inarticulate *presence*" and the hidden "soul" that lies elusively behind, to be "dragged out" or not, as the case may be. The quality that Fitzgerald praises in Conrad, then, lies not in his realist exposition of the material fundaments of historical Nostromos, but rather in his commitment to pursuing in the extreme the social difficulties of "pondering" over and through such a type. Likewise, the "completeness" Fitzgerald esteems in Conrad does not lie in his understanding of people like Nostromo but in his pressing the limits by which cultures strive and have historically striven *not* to understand such people—precisely because the evacuated fiction of their presence serves crucial ideological purposes.

The model that Fitzgerald is positing is one in which a "man of the people," residing at the dead center of class and racial tensions, exists as a collective and fictionally constructed object site precisely to the extent his personal existence is evaporated—precisely what Conrad himself meant when he exasperatedly responded to Cunninghame Graham's indictment of Nostromo: "But truly N is nothing at all—a fiction—embodied vanity of the sailor kind—a romantic mouthpiece of 'the people'" (*CL* 3.142). No-stromo, then, is constructed along very much the same lines as James Wait in *The Nigger of the "Narcissus,"* whom Conrad similarly describes, in his American preface to that novel, as a "*nothing* . . . merely a centre of the ship's collective psychology and the pivot of the action."[76] If these comments suggest Fitzgerald as the first good reader of Nostromo, and one of the first good readers of *Nostromo* as well, they also suggest both the formal strategy and the metanational opportunity afforded by Conrad's novel and titular character. The formal strategy is one of positing a mediating site of fictional construction at the center of a novel of intensely perceptualized and otherwise "real" social relations. The metanational opportunity is one that arises from a means of expressing national formations as not facts of culture, nor even consciously held political ideologies, but rather a series of collectivizing imaginative techniques arising from and imposed upon local cultural fractures. It is to such ambivalent metanational questions, as they underwrite the formal cross-pollination of *Nostromo* and *The Great Gatsby*, to which we now turn.

NATION AND NEGATION:
ABSENT CENTERS, CENTRIPETAL GAZES

In their titles and at their centers, *Nostromo* and *The Great Gatsby* offer two "great" national figures: Nostromo, Conrad's "undoubted Great Man of the People" and the co-"creator of the New State" (*N* xl–xli); and Fitzgerald's "great" Jay Gatsby, similarly of "popular" origin and romantic national dimension. Few would object to my characterization of Gatsby as the formal center and symbolic pivot of Fitzgerald's novel, as the novel itself is controlled by a first-person narrator who gazes intently upon Gatsby throughout. As to Nostromo, however, there may be reservations: *Nostromo*'s immense and fluid interweave of shifting narrative perspectives—what Keith Carabine calls the novel's "massive tensile design"[77]—makes such centralizing claims inherently more problematic. Comparison of the unique place of the two characters in both novels reveals four important respects in which my claim may be considered useful. The claim itself, moreover, ultimately turns on the recognition of a particular formal practice of constellating observing perspectives around a mediating and opaque character center: one whose very centered opacity enables Conrad and Fitzgerald to use character as a means of analyzing how national collective imaginings take shape. It is precisely because, furthermore, neither Conrad's "Costaguana" nor Fitzgerald's (U.S.) "America" is ultimately amenable to satisfactory imagination or narration as a nation, despite the best efforts of authors and characters alike, that the two novels are able to pursue the distortionary extremes of nationalizing imaginative techniques to the extent they do.

As to centrality, it should first be noted that Nostromo and Gatsby share a similar and singular *social* location in their respective novels. In *Nostromo*, perhaps the primary significance of Nostromo's being "of the people" is that he provides the novel with its only major character who concretely interfaces *with* the people—in all their diversity and potential hostility: including the "outcast lot of very mixed blood, mainly negroes" who comprise his cargadores

(N 14); the town's ethnically mixed and riot-inclined "ladrones and matreros" whose unrest Nostromo dependably foils (13); the impoverished locals to whom Nostromo passes out his last quarters as he roams the streets; and the likes of Hernandez and his secret band of outlaws, to whom only Nostromo has access at the crucial moment of national need. *Nostromo*'s empowered classes depend upon these "people"—who provide them with labor, who offer them moral authority (the Ricos invariably justify their ambitions in terms of the best interests of "the people"), and who must be kept docile if "material interests" are to succeed. But it is only Nostromo who actually knows, "handles," and interacts with the populace; while at the same time, Nostromo is also the only member of the populace who knows, handles, concretely interfaces with, and is an "invaluable fellow" to all of the novel's major imperialist and aristocratic characters (25). Nostromo, then, occupies a unique social centrality in Conrad's novel because the novel positions him as a unique border figure; and as such, he inhabits much the same singular space of social in-between-ness—not "one of us," yet not quite "one of them"—that Fitzgerald accords Jay Gatsby. Gatsby's "overpopulated lawn"—as the many readings of Nick's famous "guest list" attest[78]—provides that anomalous site at which, literally and figuratively, most of the sealed off and significantly antimonious cultural components of the United States momentarily come together (*G* 83, 65–67). Just as, moreover, Gatsby personally serves as the missing center of his parties—no one ever seems quite sure where he is—Gatsby also narratively serves as an elided site through which the novel ponders the class, racial, and ethnic boundaries his presence seems to blur. Gatsby is of the humblest social origins yet the highest class approximation; he is a concrete intimate of Wolfsheim yet has had (and will have again) concrete intimacy with Daisy; he summons images of ethnic immigrants and internal racial minorities, yet he also captivates Nick Carraway's imagination as cricket-playing associate of the Earl of Doncaster at Oxford (71). Gatsby, then, like Nostromo occupies the social center of his novel not because he is of two social worlds but because he marks the border zone where worlds blur in their distinction and ultimately collide.

This social centrality provides the occasion for other characters in the two novels to imagine unusually wide social relationships *through* Gatsby and Nostromo, which results in a second and *magical* centrality that accrues to the two titular figures. Both *Nostromo* and *Gatsby*, of course, present broad fields of romantic illusions, inscrutable forces, and spellbinding charms; but these magical qualities seem to land with an almost definitional weight on Gatsby and Nostromo. The former, who "sprang from a Platonic conception of himself" and "was a son of God—a phrase which, if it means anything, means just that" (*G* 104)—is almost limitless in his capacity to generate "romantic speculation" in the world around him (48). Concerning Nick Carraway in particular, Gatsby's "enchanted life," "romantic readiness," and "compelling" presence routinely induce bouts of "absorption," "fascination," "wonder," and "aesthetic contemplation"—"charms" of a caliber that Nick has "never found in any other person and which it is not likely I shall ever find again" (6, 58, 60, 70, 71, 189). Similarly Nostromo—who seems literally to spring from a Platonic conception of the *Arabian Nights*, and whose real name, Gian' Battista, suggests proximity to the "son of God"—is the most universally recognized magic figure in Costaguana. Nostromo's "providential" powers, his "incorruptible genius," and his "peculiar talent" for "being on the spot whenever . . . something striking to the imagination needs to be done" are all part of a larger "spell" he casts: "the spell of that reputation the Capataz de Cargadores had made for himself by the waterside, along the railway line, with the English and with the populace of Sulaco" (*N* 211, 213, 19). Even Dr. Monygham, the incorrigible skeptic who believes in little but Mrs. Gould, is "under the spell of [Nostromo's] established reputation. . . . It seemed to be part of the man, like his whiskers or teeth. It was impossible to conceive him otherwise" (406–7).

It is a seductive mirrorlike function both Gatsby and Nostromo perform at the center of their cultures that combines their social and magical singularities. Nostromo, as Conrad summarizes his life near the end of the novel, has throughout led a "life whose very essence, value, and reality consisted in its *reflection* from the admiring eyes of men" (494, emphasis added). Until well into the novel, Nostromo cares for nothing more and nothing less than the preservation and reproduction of the perfect image others see in him; and even after embarking upon his "desperate affair" with the silver, Nostromo stands determined that everyone in Sulaco "shall learn that I am just the man they take me for" (251). Mirroring what "admiring eyes" would most like to see and confirming that he is just the hero they take him for provides the generating matrix of Nostromo's broad social "spell"; and as such, it is worth considering the reflective and heroic qualities of Jay Gatsby's "unusually prepossessing" smile:

It was one of those rare smiles with a quality of eternal reassurance in it, that you may come across four or five times in life. It faced—or seemed to face—the whole external world for an instant, and then concentrated on *you* with an irresistible prejudice in your favor. It understood you just so far as you wished to be understood, believed in you precisely as you would like to believe in yourself and assured you that it had precisely the impression of you that, at your best, you hoped to convey. Precisely at that point it vanished. (*G* 53)

Gatsby's smile is every bit the idealized mirror Nostromo's persona is: the latter is a "reflection" of the hero others would like to see; the former reflects the hero you would like to be and see in yourself. What unites these two magic-mirrors is the social opportunities for collective mediation and combination they afford. Located at the social center of his novel, Gatsby's image—not just in the previous passage but everywhere—is strategically open and utterly ambiguous. Outside of his "tanned" skin, itself a pointedly blurred and multivectored figure, Gatsby's *person*—the color of his hair or eyes, the shape of his face, the dimensions of his body—remains profoundly undescribed (54). Nick's description of Gatsby's smile itself is singularly devoid of any concrete and fixable details *about* Gatsby; and the magical effect is that *anyone* can look into the mirror of Gatsby's smile and see in it the idealized, privileged, and connected reflection of himself or herself—part of "the whole external world," yet a very special part at that. Similarly, Nostromo serves his novel as both its most ambiguous and opaque *and* its most stick-figurish and streamlined character—for precisely the same collective reasons. Nostromo caters to *all* of Sulaco's many intensely heterogeneous "admiring eyes"; and because he does, because he aims to exist at the idealized intersection of all those radically incommensurate parts, he can only be an intensely subtracted and narrowly delineated figure—surrounded by an overarching negative aura of ambiguity and opacity into which anyone can read himself or herself. The "quality of eternal reassurance" that emanates from both Gatsby and Nostromo—often magically, and sometimes quite precariously—takes place through the negativity that defines and distorts them as collective social mirrors: through the fantasies of dyadic collective oneness their ambiguity opens up, and through the axes of cultural difference their airbrushed images disavow. Both the narcissistic and the fetishistic aspects of this mediating social function will receive further examination. Here, however, we must be content to make this final magic observation: for both Gatsby and Nostromo, once their function as social mediators has been exhausted—once one crosses the line between what they ideally reflect of others and who they are beyond their social role—"precisely at that point" they seem to "vanish."

Vanishing, like a ghost, points the way to the third aspect of centrality shared by Gatsby and Nostromo in their respective novels: their *fictive* centrality in a greater web of writers and writing. One notes that the two novels abound in writer figures. As Edward Said has argued of *Nostromo*, "Nearly everyone [in the novel] seems extremely anxious about both keeping and leaving a personal 'record' of his thoughts and action"; and because these characters are so anxious about keeping written records, the novel seems to turn "auto-referentially" on itself—characters mirror the author's project of fictional composition, and "*Nostromo* reveals itself to be . . . a record of *novelistic* self-reflection."[79] *Gatsby* foregrounds the same writerly role in Nick Carraway: Nick not only literally pens Gatsby's story but also draws self-reflexive attention to his process of writing ("reading back over what I have written . . ."), as well as his ambitions to write (Nick was "rather literary in college" and arrives in West Egg intending "to bring back all such things in my life") (*G* 8–9, 60). Nick, moreover, is far from the only writer in Fitzgerald's novel: virtually everyone at one point or another has a fantastic story to weave about Gatsby, or the occasion to author himself or herself through texts like the *Saturday Evening Post, Simon Called Peter* (a book Fitzgerald despised), and "'The Rise of Coloured Empires' by this man Goddard" (referring to the historical Lothrop Stoddard's *The Rising Tide of Color*) (17).

At the centers of the two novels, however, there seem to be two characters who are both writers and *writing* itself—pure fiction. What Tracy Seeley so provocatively suggests of Jim in Conrad's *Lord Jim* is even more true of Nostromo: "he is a kind of romance character who has wandered into a modernist novel."[80] One recalls the fantastic and improbably fictive mode of Nostromo's appearances, especially in the first two-thirds of the novel: his is "the appearance of a phantom-like horseman mounted on a silver-gray mare" who solves labor problems with "the thundering clatter of his blows" (*N* 91); he is an abstract image of "black mustache and white teeth" who "shoots off his revolver" and "then, once he sees they're safe, cries '*Avanti!*' and rides off to the next danger zone" (22); he is the "dark figure of a man wrapped in a poncho to the neck" who emerges from campfire embers to see Sir John safely into the Sulacan night (41); and at one point, Nostromo literally emerges from Decoud's fallen pencil, "roll[ing] on the floor," as Decoud falls despairingly to sleep over his Declaration of Secession (235). Similarly, Gatsby also is consummately figurable through the tropes of romance: he is initially mentioned for his singular "romantic readiness"(*G* 6); the allure of his presence is anticipated in a "romantic" reverie in which Nick fancies himself a "pathfinder" (a clear allusion to Cooper's Leather Stocking) (8); Gatsby then first appears as a "shadow" in the moonlight "standing with his hands in his pockets and regarding the silver pepper of the stars" (25); and thereafter, his life seems all too easily and comprehensively circumscribed by a single quest narrative that locates Daisy as its "golden" object—"the following of a grail" (156). Just as Nostromo, moreover, seems often to appear purely through the writerly will and pens of others, so, too, is Gatsby pinpointed as a purely textual phenomenon: listening to him is "like skimming through a dozen magazines" (71); "the songs of Tin Pan Alley," as the original drafts of *Gatsby* make explicit, author the "Platonic conception of himself" from which Gatsby "springs;"[81] an odd hybrid of Benjamin Franklin's *Autobiography* and Clarence Mulford's *Hopalong Cassidy*, as the reader learns at the end, scripts Gatsby's younger efforts of self-definition; and, as Arnold Weinstein points out, the significance of the novel's "Blocks Biloxi" vignette consists in its mirror image of how Gatsby builds himself purely out of blocks of words.[82]

This *fictive* centrality of Gatsby and Nostromo ties to their social and magical centralities because it pinpoints at the level of novelistic *form* the very evacuation and negativity that defines them at the level of socioperceptual thematics. The form of both *Nostromo* and *Gatsby* depends upon their two titular characters remaining fundamentally absent: not subjectivities and textualized psychologies in and of themselves, but rather projective phantasms of what other characters and both novels desperately wish to see. One notes the striking structural correspondences between the two characters as they formally evolve throughout the two novels. Earlier on, the two characters are each presented as captivating names and obscurely "providential" images only: they both uncannily appear and reappear in most of the earlier chapters, but only briefly and at the charged margins, only to "vanish" or "ride off to the next danger-zone." Then, for over half of both novels, Nostromo and Gatsby are treated as purely external and intensely performative spectacles: the reader is given access to the inner psychologies and background histories of many other characters but never to these two, who instead seem mappable only in terms of the lavish parties or dramatic performances they stage and the material trappings that surround them (Nostromo's silver costume, Gatsby's "pink rag of a suit" and other surrounding gaucherie). It is, indeed, a puzzling secret why these two "props of the capitalist system" do what they do: why Nostromo is so eager to serve as a slavish "universal factotum" to the Blancos (*N* 43),[83] and what motivating force exists at the "womb" of Gatsby's "purposeless splendor" (*G* 83). Yet later on, when the two novels ultimately do divulge the secret operations of the two characters' minds, their private secrets turn out to be utterly public phenomena. Nostromo, Conrad's novel seems to insist, does not even have a secret life until his affair with the silver; but after he has hidden the silver, after he has tasted "the dust and ashes of the fruit of life" and "fallen" into a sense of split public and private identity, the one and only secret that defines Nostromo's private identity—that he is enslaved to the silver—is little more than an allegorical mirror image of the public secret that defines all of Sulaco (*N* 416). To the extent the silver is a personal burden on Nostromo, no one else in Sulaco knows, and no one else fundamentally cares to know; and to the extent that Nostromo's private self exists outside the dimensions of his internalization of an utterly public social phenomenon, the novel does not know or fundamentally care to know. Likewise Gatsby—a character who perfectly replicates Nostromo's "direct, uncomplicated, and naive" outlook on life as it is coupled with "a complete singleness of motive behind the varied manifestations of a consistent character" (*N* xl)—has a secret that is everyone's secret. Everyone is "compelled by" and "leans toward" Daisy's "thrilling voice" (*G* 25); and everyone seems vaguely amenable to the broad array of public American cultural markers—the originary "Dutch sailors"; Ben Franklin; Hawkeye; Emerson; Buffalo Bill Cody; the Rockefellers; the Roosevelts—that Nick Carraway flags in assembling his version of Gatsby's "personal" history. *Personal*, in fact, is the very word Gatsby uses to disdain any "love" Daisy may have felt for Tom; and the crucial significance of *im*personality, for both Gatsby and Nostromo, is that it marks the space where their socioperceptual importance and their fictiveness coincide. They are the fiction—the absent solution, the fantastic and phantasmal wish—by which other characters and authors alike attempt to write themselves into a continuity and direction that are insupportable by facts alone.

The final aspect of centrality, then, uniting the two absent centers that are Gatsby and Nostromo consists in what all the major "observing" characters who gather around them are trying to write: the narrative of a nation. In *Nostromo*, to be a resident of Costaguana seems to imply one's investment in an impossible project of national authorship. There are as many different national plans as there are national authors: Don Jose Avellanos envisions a loose neo-

Federalist Costaguana in his *Fifty Years of Misrule*; Decoud authors the birth
of a separate Occidental Republic in his Declaration of Secession; Gould "pins
[his] faith to material interests" in attempt to author, through his mine, the
social foundations of greater Costaguanan "justice," "stability," and "unity"
(*N* 80); Giorgio Viola, in his Inn of Unified Italy, authors a national space in
which Sulacan locals are not welcome at all; Pedro Montero composes lofty
speeches in which he claims to bring "Caesarism" to a unified Costaguana; and
Antonia Avellanos closes the novel with a democratic vision of "re-annexing"
Costaguana in the interests of assisting "our countrymen" who are "groaning
under oppression" (479). Though these plans range in motivation from the utterly private and self-interested to the genuinely public and disinterested, the
one characteristic they all share is an ultimate sense of futility—a sense that
whatever the plan, those who work to impose national terms on Costaguana
have merely "ploughed the sea" (175). The transience of national arrangements
in Costaguana, and the inevitability with which they are overhauled, seems to
derive from what Christopher GoGwilt calls the territory's "impossible political
identity of antagonistic interests"—racial, ethnic, and classed.[84] Dr. Monygham,
moreover, virtually paraphrases Conrad's "Autocracy and War" (1905) in his
closing indictment of how "material interests"—unchecked capitalist norms of
social organization—only replicate the collective problem rather than resolve
it. He declaims to Mrs. Gould,

No! There is no peace and rest in the development of material interests. They have their
own law and their justice. But it is founded on expediency, and is inhuman; *it is without
rectitude, without the continuity and force that can be found only in a moral principle.*
Mrs. Gould, the time approaches when all that the [San Tomé mine] stands for shall
weigh as heavily upon the people as the barbarism, cruelty, and misrule of a few years
back. (481, emphasis added)

In this attack upon "material interests," Monygham strangely raises, in the
ideal moral negative, the very "turn to the national spirit" that Conrad valorizes in a momentous passage at the close of *The Mirror of the Sea*. That passage—written at the same time Conrad was writing *Nostromo*—insists that in
times of great difficulty, "we must turn to the national spirit, which, *superior in
its force and continuity to good and evil fortune, can alone give us* the feeling of an
enduring existence and of an invincible air of power against the fates" (*MS* 194,
emphasis added). Reading through Conrad's code words, we can appreciate that

Monygham indicts "material interests" with an implicit "turn" to a national spirit that simply does not exist in Costaguana. This sense of nationhood as an ideal but impossible social limit—both the only effective mechanism of social cohesion imaginable, and a mechanism impossible to imagine in Costaguana—runs throughout the novel. In *Nostromo*'s many meditations on how "the old, stable political and national organizations" of Europe are not transferable to Costaguana (*N* 299); in its greater thought experiment of hopelessly planting English, French, and Italian norms of national organization in Costaguana; and in its repeated alternations between national aspirations and an ultimate resignation to the "political immaturity of the [Costaguanan] people, the indolence of the upper classes and the mental darkness of the lower" (364), *Nostromo*'s characters and narrator alike reveal themselves to be impossibly invested in fantasies of nationhood. National cohesion is what they would like to see in Costaguana but cannot. Local cultural conditions cannot ultimately support such national imaginings, yet they are incapable of conceiving social stability in any other terms. And at the center of this imaginative impossibility there lies the fantastic, fictive, and "providential" compensation of Nostromo: the "action" figure who seems uniquely indispensable ("absolutely the only one") to everyone's national plan; the iconic enforcer of social stability and reciprocity; the magical emblem of continuity between Sulaco's empowered and popular classes; and the mediating mirror image who makes a moral virtue of evacuated difference. "Ah, Nostromo!" as Dr. Monygham says, "that fellow has some continuity and force. Nothing will put an end to him" (481).

Much the same is true of Jay Gatsby and *The Great Gatsby*. Like *Nostromo*'s various author-characters, Nick Carraway, a "*bond* man" in more ways than one, sets out to write the United States "pedagogically" into a collective national existence: he aims to seize upon historical and contemporary cultural materials to articulate an elusive sense of "unutterabl[e] awareness of our identity with this country" (*G* 184). Like Dr. Monygham, Nick finds the expression of this national vision possible only in the negative: it is only "some deficiency in common" that he is ultimately able to locate among the novel's five major characters, and this common deficiency—as Nick explains with a most Conradian sensibility—is but a feeble guarantor of peaceful and orderly social "conduct" (6, 184). And if Mr. Gatz, Gatsby's father, says of his son at the novel's dark end, "He'd of helped build up the country" (176), Nick has clearly already entertained such impossible national fantasies in Gatsby from the moment Gatsby first spoke to him about the medal of valor he received from the people of Montenegro:

Little Montenegro! [Gatsby] lifted up the words and nodded at them—with his smile. The smile comprehended Montenegro's troubled history and sympathized with the brave struggles of the Montenegrin people. It appreciated fully the chain of national circumstances which had elicited this tribute from Montenegro's warm little heart. (71)

Like Nostromo, Gatsby offers up the heartwarming fantasy of combined and comprehensive national unity amid a space of "troubled history"; yet also like Nostromo, this fantasy takes place through an ambivalent relationship to cultural difference. "Montenegro" (read: rising blacks) is clearly the novel's anticipatory figure of U.S. norms of cultural difference and internal fracture that Nick imaginatively enlists Gatsby to solve. Here, however, Nick's momentary exhilaration betrays a curious double allegiance: on the one hand, it is precisely the possibility of a "sympathetic" and conjunctive bridge with difference that excites Nick about Gatsby; and on the other hand, Nick bookends his glee with diminutive nullifications of that difference: that is, through Gatsby, "Montenegro" must be rendered "little" and unthreatening, "warm" and familiar, before Nick can open himself up to the difference Montenegro marks. This double movement reflects a genuine ambivalence—a genuinely double attitude—toward national imaginings whose informing techniques, narcissism on the one hand and fetishism on the other, *The Great Gatsby* is using Nick to tease out. A similar ambivalence—though not identical—is also archaeologized in *Nostromo*, to which we now turn for one final look en route back to *Gatsby*. To combine each of the aspects of "centrality" enumerated above, however, we may say that such metanational investigations become possible because of a shared practice of novelistic form: one that magically posits, at the perceptual center of insurmountable social contradictions, a character of pure idealized fiction—one who exists only insofar as he mediates and facilitates imagined relationships between others.

WE THE "PEOPLE":
TECHNIQUES OF NATIONAL IMAGINING

In *Nostromo*, much is made of Sulaco's gradual captivation by the fetish of silver. Mrs. Gould watches the San Tomé silver "with misgivings turning into a fetish," one of "monstrous and crushing weight"; Charles Gould, who began his involvement in the mine with noblest intentions, comes to "dwell alone within a circumvallation of precious metal"; and Nostromo himself, that ostensibly "incorruptible" fellow, ultimately becomes enslaved by the silver he has stolen (*N* 209). No one ever knows, however, that Nostromo has either stolen or become enslaved to the silver. Indeed, just as Captain Mitchell's public narrative of Sulacan history will come to insist upon Nostromo's "perfectly fearless and incorruptible character," Nostromo's public image has always been one of *in*susceptibility to the influence of the silver—the reason he was entrusted with the lighter in the first place, and what he aims to broadcast when he cuts off all the silver buttons from his coat in his theatrical dalliance with Morenita (454). In the obsessive emphasis that Sulaco's Blancos place on Nostromo's "irreproachability" and "incorruptibility," there lies a phantasmatic disavowal of their own susceptibility to the "mine"—which marks both the "material interests" over which the Blancos think they have control, and the naked self-interest they continually repress through illusory narratives of "saving the country." The "gaping maw" of the mine, hence, is not unlike Freud's castrated mother in his fetish narrative: it threatens the Blancos with a specter of lack, and this threat is compensated for by fixation on the phallic, spellbinding, and otherwise self-reassuring image of Nostromo (267).

Already, this helps to explain Dr. Monygham's construction of Nostromo as a singular figure of "force and continuity": Costaguana may lack the force and continuity to fend off material interests, but Nostromo provides the fetishistic site of worship where such threats can be provisionally denied. The more important fetishistic function Nostromo serves, however, lies in his unusual relationship to "the people"—the radically heterogeneous popular classes of Costaguana, many of whom actively despise and resist the aristocratic and foreign presences in Sulaco. Nostromo is both *of* these people and the utter evacuation of and the overwhelming counterforce to any threat posed *by* them. When the locals revolt, Nostromo dependably crushes them. If there were any hint of personal revolt or threatening difference within Nostromo himself— whose real name is Gian Battista Fidanza, and whose original title, which the English corrupt, is *nuostromo*, Italian for "boatswain"—these become erased and recouped through an Anglicized fantasy of possession: "our man" (which the Blancos take "Nostromo" to mean). Nostromo has "the gift of evolving safety out of danger" (394); and in the Blancos' eyes, a crucial component of this gift lies in the ease with which the popular elements who oppose Nostromo can be either safely dismissed from the body or safely dismissed through familiar stereotypes. Given that Nostromo marks the true contours of "the people," those who oppose him are merely outside agents who have "infested, infested" the "body of the people"; given that Nostromo's own cargadores are a racially mixed lot, those who oppose them must be "the worst kind of nigger out here" (12–13). It is Nostromo's cargadores, however, who are actually the targets of the most violent action we see Nostromo take in the novel. When, on the days following fiestas, they do not answer to their names as Nostromo attempts to rouse them for work, "admiring eyes" require Nostromo to take brutal action: the "fellow in a thousand!" menaces them with a revolver, beats them in a "ferocious scuffle," and sends them "fly[ing] out head first and hands abroad, to sprawl under the forelegs of a silver-gray mare" (92). This is what it means in *Nostromo* to occupy a position of difference that has not been routed through familiar names and preconceived slots.

Nostromo, then, mediates the Blancos' relationship to the populace by serving as the site through which genuine, threatening popular difference becomes diffused, disavowed, and punishingly eliminated. If there are certain elements of "the people" who are not as subordinate as Nostromo, they are not really of "the people" at all. Nostromo, in fact, makes it so that the Blancos need not acknowledge popular difference at all: the thousands of dissidents are replaced by this one "fellow *in* a thousand"; "the people" are averted by a simple and magical gaze upon their one "Great Man"—the capital mirror image of the perfectly tamed populace all the Blancos wish to see, and the fetish through which all threatening differences are charmed away. The iconic ambiguity of Nostromo, hence, is significantly a function of differences that are erased through Nostromo's attempts to reflect "admiring eyes"; but the very stiffness and two-dimensionality that also define his social persona similarly derive from his fetishistic function. In the context of colonial discourse, Homi Bhabha has argued that figural strategies of stereotyping may be considered fetishistic because they turn on an impulse of *fixity*: one freezes an Other through a familiar narrative template, momentarily taming difference, but then is compelled to repeat the functionally overdetermined narrative to keep the differences tamed.[85] *Nostromo* is well aware of this insight: its presentation of "stereotyped relations"—say, in the moment when Emilia processes General Montero through the fixed image of a "cruel caricature," or when Sotillo erroneously convinces himself that Hirsch *must* be lying because he is Jewish— inscribes the momentum of compulsive repetition (445, 116, 310). Throughout

Nostromo, however, there is no more compulsively repeated practice than that of affirming the incorruptibility and dependability of Nostromo; and similarly, the very frozenness, two-dimensionality, vacuity, and fictive familiarity of his persona are precisely that of a stereotype—as he says: "It concerns me to keep on being what I am: everyday alike" (238). Nostromo, then, raises the interesting case of the stereotype that must be compulsively repeated as it signifies not "the other" but "our man." And as such, Nostromo mediates not only the Blancos' relationship to the populace but also the Blancos relationship to one another: perpetually disavowing difference through performative ritual, and perpetually reaffirming what it means to be "one of us."

Gatsby conducts a parallel investigation of fetishistic techniques of imagined collectivity—though it ultimately pushes this investigation in a different direction that will allow us to reconnect Fitzgerald with Conrad's fiction as a whole. In Fitzgerald's novel, Nick Carraway encourages a sharp distinction between two characters: Tom Buchanan, who is "a national figure in a way," and Jay Gatsby, who is a national figure in quite another (*G* 10). Tom's "way" is that of the historical Lothrop Stoddard: that of a racialized conception of U.S. identity emphatically closed to the idea that nationality might be acquired through civic and/or cultural performance. Gatsby, the consummate performer, suggests aracial national alternatives, and Nick's allegiances seem clearly with him—the romantic mediator of those alternatives. This sharp dichotomy, however, becomes problematized by the two moments in the novel when Nick finds himself so overwhelmed by a "renewal of faith" in Gatsby that he feels the urge to "get up and slap [Gatsby] on the back"—both moments precariously coupled with Gatsby's experiences at Oxford (71, 136). The first moment—in which Gatsby "proves" he went to Oxford by presenting a photograph of himself dressed for cricket alongside the Earl of Doncaster—is especially striking because it presents one of the few moments in the novel when the utterly ambiguous Gatsby becomes frozen into a brilliant, blazing, and yet somehow cardboard scene. This is how Nick describes the Oxford photograph and its imaginative effect upon him:

It was a photograph of a half a dozen young men in blazers loafing in an archway through which were visible a host of spires. There was Gatsby, looking a little, not much younger—with a cricket bat in hand.

Then it was all true. I saw the skins of tigers flaming in [Gatsby's] palace on the Grand Canal. I saw him opening a chest of rubies to ease, with their crimson-lighted depths, the gnawing of his broken heart. (71)

The significance of this vignette is that Gatsby suddenly becomes "true" to Nick when Gatsby can validate his aristocratic associations. In Nick's mind at the time, it is unclear exactly what Gatsby's background is: whether he is of fine "breeding" and a fine family like Nick's own, or something outside. Yet here and in the other "Oxford" moment, Gatsby becomes strikingly alive to Nick, becomes "truly" American to Nick, because he can flash experiential credentials that identify him with the former category. The opportunity to disavow social difference becomes the occasion to believe in Gatsby, to freeze Gatsby in a romantic scene (that must be repeated), and to embrace Gatsby as national mediator pursuant to terms that make genuine nationality a function of "breeding" and narratives of racial proportion and social hierarchy commensurate with it. As Walter Benn Michaels has argued, this actually places Nick in rather close company with Tom.[86] For Tom, the principal anxiety is U.S. national insularity; he wants to keep the American "family" closed and uses "race" as a rhetoric of doing so—a functional understanding of race that is underscored when Tom, at the Plaza Hotel, suddenly conceives Gatsby as black when he recognizes in Gatsby a threat to his own nuclear family (136–37). Nick, however, is compelled into rapture by a similarly closed model of national compass: it just so happens, due to the quirky aftermath of World War I, that Gatsby did go to Oxford for a few months; but what appeals to Nick is that Gatsby's attendance at Oxford and association with the Earl of Doncaster imply that Gatsby came from a fine family—a closed circle of "breeding" that, as Michaels suggests, "requires that the question of who we are continue to be understood as prior to questions about what we do."[87] The terms are not as crudely racialized and closed as Tom's, but the de facto closure, emphasis on family genealogy, and ultimate insularity are much the same. We may call Nick's gaze upon Gatsby fetishistic, moreover, because it is predicated not on embracing Gatsby's difference but rather on cultivating a static fixation ("Oggsford": Wolfsheim's corruption captures the tension nicely) to mask, displace, disavow it.

But this is only half the story at most. For Nick is nothing if not a distinctively ambivalent and divided character: both "within and without" (40); a "normal person" and utterly abnormal (6); conflicted in his relationships with both the Buchanans and Gatsby; at "home" neither in the East nor the West; and manifestly uncertain about the terms framing "the dark fields of the republic" (189). Consequently, there is little surprise that against Nick's fetishistic imaginative inclinations, which construct Gatsby as truly "American" to the extent he may be "placed" in relation to the social elite, one finds also certain narcissistic inclinations whose effect is precisely the reverse. Narcissism, of course, is generally understood as a project of ego-directed libidinal gratification predicated just as much as fetishism on a refused acknowledgment of difference; yet the term as inscribed by *Gatsby* also speaks more widely to the process by which alienated subjectivity projects and protects itself in self-supporting and identificatory relation to spaces of imagined self-similarity—as Nick does, for instance, in reflecting, "At metropolitan twilight I felt a haunting loneliness sometimes, and felt it in others—poor young clerks who loitered in front of windows waiting until it was time for a solitary restaurant dinner—young clerks in the dusk, wasting the most poignant moments of night and life" (62). As such, in a social context gridded by racial and crypto-racial insulations of the American "family," a narcissistic gaze upon an Other (or mediating site of potential otherness) can effectively subvert the terms through which the "family" logic is administered. Gatsby, one notes, when he is not being fixed in the image of "Oxford," generally harbors a strategically *open* and irreducible mirror-smile, and one whose effect is consistently coupled with two affects: the "familiar," which is to say *not* of the family but somehow like it, suggestive of alternative and displaced *affiliative* lines of kinship (51, 57); and the "absorbing,"[88] which is to say, like Gatsby's parties, open to and capable of integrating and bridging large companies of difference. Here, following the story of Montenegro and a description of Gatsby's "infinitely absorbing" smile, is Nick's description of their drive across the Queensboro Bridge:

The city seen from the Queensboro Bridge is always the city seen for the first time, in its first wild promise of all the mystery and beauty in the world.

A dead man passed us in a hearse heaped with blooms, followed by two carriages with drawn blinds and by more cheerful carriages for friends. The friends looked out at us with tragic eyes and short upper lips of south eastern Europe and I was glad that the sight of Gatsby's splendid car was included in their somber holiday. As we crossed Blackwell's Island a limousine passed us, driven by a white chauffeur, in which sat three modish Negroes, two bucks and a girl. I laughed aloud as the yolks of their eyeballs rolled toward us in haughty rivalry.

"Anything can happen now that we've slid over this bridge," I thought; "anything at all. . . ."

Even Gatsby could happen without any particular wonder. (73)

These words constitute an antithesis to the Earl of Doncaster vignette, and precisely because they are predicted on a different imaginative technique. This technique—which does not "fix" Gatsby in a particular image but rather apotheosizes Gatsby as an open interface between self and difference; which does not freeze otherness but encourages its mutable, multiple, metonymic, and "included" contemplation in relation to the self; and which is all fundamentally predicated on a narcissistic drive to escape culture, to recapture the "first time" and "first wild promise" of undifferentiated existence—presents the opportunity for Nick to self-identify *across* racial and crypto-racial lines of demarcated difference. The scene itself is an attempt to imagine "American" identity in terms of a very different kind of "race": one figured through cars rather than blood, determined by culture rather than heredity (racial or familial). And through the specific imaginative technique deployed, southeastern European immigrants and African-Americans become "included" in the race; "blinds," stereotypes, and taboos obscuring the dignity, the priority, the power, the fashionability, the sexuality, and the autonomous agency of racial others become lifted, penetrated, reversed; and all in all, the Queensboro Bridge becomes a suggestively *heterotopic* site at which all the different segregations structuring the United States as a residual and hierarchical imaginative field become negatively folded into one another—to the grammatical desiccation of that field, and Nick's ability to narrativize it.

The Great Gatsby, hence, recovers Conrad in ways that are larger than *Nostromo*. As we have just seen, Fitzgerald's novel turns fundamentally on an ambivalent alternation between *two* imaginative strategies and ideological projects: both perpetually in crisis due to a failure of the one to engage racial and ethnocultural difference, and the other to engage *dialectically* with the "race" (and "modern" cultural landscape) of modern commercial and industrial capitalism. *Gatsby*, this is to say, enlists the absent-centered and metanational form of *Nostromo* to express and analyze in U.S. circumstances one technique of national imagining (the fetishistic) that Conrad's novel directly theorizes, and another (the narcissistic) that lies latent within it. Another way to put this point, however, is to say that in conducting its metanational investigations in self-conscious relation to *Nostromo*, *The Great Gatsby* also recovers both of the imaginative technical movements of another absent-centered, metacommunal Conrad novel, *Lord Jim*. For what is the narrative movement of the first half of *Lord Jim* if not an ambivalent alternation and uncanny looping between

Marlow's festishistic affirmations that Jim, simply (essentially) because he has the "right looks" (*LJ* 27), *must* be "one of us," and Marlow's narcissistic, erotic solicitations of Jim's deviance to effect a "bond" with that which is *not* "one of us"? Surely *Gatsby*'s unmistakable echo of *Lord Jim* in introducing the flickeringly "normal" Nick as a lifelong magnet of abnormal "confidences" (*G* 5; *LJ* 21) is meant to suggest a narrative connection with Marlow; surely also Marlow's relation to Kurtz in *Heart of Darkness* (a text often compared with *Gatsby*) is governed by a similar ambivalence; and surely, as prior criticism extensively suggests, all three of Fitzgerald's mature novels evoke the forms and traces of several other Conrad texts as well. My point here is not to identify, alongside *Nostromo*, other individual Conrad texts that may have "influenced" Fitzgerald, but to suggest why all the many attempts to engage in precisely this kind of critical endeavor have inevitably failed: lost, as it were, in a sea of "possible" Conradian traces.[89] The reason is that the Fitzgerald/Conrad relation is not fundamentally driven by any individual text or even an ultimately individuated sense of Conrad's work. One may *see* the metanational stakes of Fitzgerald's investments in Conrad most clearly from the explicitly national and metanational text that is *Nostromo*, but Fitzgerald's underlying relation to Conrad, the textual ground through which he locates Conrad's political aesthetics, is much more a matter of underlying mode, even Conradian spirit. Fitzgerald's relation to Conrad is that of a superbly sensitive reader and organic expanse of understanding that runs across Conrad's works, and whose sympathetic extensions and reactualizations continually and *excessively* raise the signs of Conrad (or their uncanny likeness; it is often hard to tell the difference). Whereas for Hemingway, Conrad is fundamentally an object in whose image certain visions of the United States become globally defashioned and refashioned; and whereas for Eliot, Conrad serves as a prism for banishing the United States from vision altogether; for Fitzgerald, Conrad is not an instance but an agency of exilic national vision, not an exilic representation of the United States but a means of rendering the United States in terms of exile. Put another way, whereas for Hemingway, Conrad is "heterotopic" in the sense that his external virtual vantage both erases and reconstitutes the boundaries of the United States; and whereas for Eliot, Conrad's heterotopic qualities emerge to the degree Conrad's "American" advent interferes with Eliot's ability simply to declare Conrad as part of a project of U.S. erasure; for Fitzgerald, Conrad is not about either asserting or erasing an image of the United States. It is about both and neither:

Fitzgerald's Conrad is heterotopic in the sense that he assumes the exilic space of Conrad—the "man without a country" who nevertheless understands the compulsive appeal of "country"; the writer "at sea" whose thoughts/ships are nevertheless tangent to (Po/Eng)land; the writer in Hyères who authorizes the great American novel—and through his narrative mode, writes a novel that both expresses every technique of imagining "country" and materially archaeologizes why "country" must ultimately remain a figure of expulsion. To understand *The Great Gatsby* as a Conradian novel is to understand why, for all its striking command of U.S. cultural materiality, Fitzgerald's novel is a text that is fundamentally located *elsewhere*: in the "floating" rhetoric (to use a favorite *Gatsby* trope) and (as it were) offshore distance that both sutures and dissolves, consolidates and negates, discovers and *un*discovers, the boundaries of "country."

Fitzgerald, hence, is not only a key dialogic participant in a conflicted expatriate U.S. culture of Conrad, but also a key integration of "national" self-conception with the exilic structure of feeling/criticism dyad through which Mencken first offered "our Conrad" to the U.S. public. A brief quotation from a passage that both Fitzgerald and Mencken deeply admired from the end of "Youth" nicely rounds out this point. It is the moment just after Marlow mentions "the heat of life in the handful of dust" (*YOS* 37) that T. S. Eliot inverts to express the fearful stasis of modern existence ("fear in a handful of dust"); it is the moment when Marlow recounts how, after the sinking of the *Judea* and rowing for days in an open boat at sea, he first glimpsed the tropical shores of the East:

And this is how I see the East. I have seen its secret places and have looked into its very soul; *but now I see it always from a small boat*, a high outline of mountains, blue and afar in the morning; like faint mist at noon; a jagged wall of purple at sunset. I have the feel of the oar in my hand, the vision of a scorching blue sea in my eyes. And I see a bay, a wide bay, smooth as glass and polished like ice, shimmering in the dark. A red light burns far off upon the gloom of the land, and the night is soft and warm. We drag at the oars with aching arms, and suddenly a puff of wind, a puff faint and tepid and laden with strange odours of blossoms, of aromatic wood, comes out of the still night—the first sigh of the East on my face. That I can never forget. It was impalpable and enslaving, like a charm, like a whispered promise of mysterious delight. (*YOS*, 37, emphasis added)

The story shortly closes with a remembrance of such moments of "youthful" triumph—with a sadder, wiser Marlow and his close company of listeners reflecting on "our faces marked by toil, by deceptions, by success, by love; our weary eyes looking still, looking always, looking anxiously for something out of life, that while it is expected is already gone—has passed unseen, in a sigh, in a flash—together with the youth, with the strength, with the romance of illusions" (42). To read all of these lines is to *hear* the end of *The Great Gatsby*: the "transitory enchanted moment" in which "Dutch sailors' eyes" first glimpsed "the fresh, green breast of the new world"—a moment when "man must have held his breath in the presence of this continent, compelled into an aesthetic contemplation he neither understood nor desired, face to face for the last time in history with something commensurate to his capacity for wonder" (*G* 189). And as for Marlow and his friends, the problem for Nick and Gatsby is being both everlastingly compelled by and distanced from a "dream" space that, even as it was first being actualized, "was already behind him, somewhere back in that vast obscurity beyond the city, where the dark fields of the republic rolled on under the night. . . . It eluded us then, but that's no matter—tomorrow we will run faster, stretch our arms out farther. . . . And one fine morning—" (*G* 189). For Marlow, the specific issue is the "East": it is a fantastic dreamscape that he simultaneously needs as the only "home" in which his desires could be truly satisfied, and never had from the moment of his first contact with it (as Conrad brutally dramatizes with the profane arrival of a fellow "Western" ship [*YOS* 39]). With Fitzgerald, the issue is also the East (as opposed to the "Western" United States): it is also a fantastic dreamscape whose irreconcilable "quality of distortion" (*G* 185) derives from a tension between the need for it as the truly satisfying home "my middle west" (184) neither is or ever was, and the contact with it that makes it so being "unutterably aware of our identity with this country" (183) can never happen in its proximity. Conrad's global transmutations of exile (explored along one East/West axis) become Fitzgerald's domestic poetics of exile (articulated through another East/West axis), itself fundamentally predicated on expatriate distance (raising a third, transatlantic East/West axis, itself palimpsestically inscribed and opening like a door upon the others). And so we beat on, boats against the current—or rather in a "small boat" slightly offshore, from whose heterotopic vantage both "Youth" and *The Great Gatsby* produce their ultimate wisdom.

PART III

Regions of Conflict

4 UNDER SOUTHERN EYES
Visions of the South in the 1920s

When the last aqueduct shall have crumbled to pieces, the last airship fallen to the ground, the last blade of grass have died upon a dying earth, man, indomitable by his training in resistance to misery and pain, shall set this undiminished light of his eyes against the feeble glow of the sun. . . . Man is delightful in its pride, its assurance, and its indomitable tenacity. . . . [F]rom a short and cursory acquaintance with my kind, I am inclined to think that the last utterance will formulate, strange as it may appear, some hope now to us utterly inconceivable.

—Conrad, "Henry James: An Appreciation" (1905)

It is easy enough to say that man is immortal simply because he will endure: that when the last ding-dong of doom has clanged and faded from the last worthless rock hanging tideless in the last red and dying evening, that even then there will still be one more sound: that of his puny inexhaustible voice, still talking. I refuse to accept this. I believe that man will not merely endure: he will prevail.

—William Faulkner, Nobel Prize Speech (1950)

A beautiful picture, a fine sonata, a novel of Joseph Conrad seem to us more darkly significant to human life than the result of a gubernatorial primary.

—"The Politically Minded," *New Orleans Double Dealer* (April 1922)

OUR CONFEDERATE

Since its delivery in Stockholm on December 10, 1950, critics have observed that William Faulkner's Nobel Prize speech, as it builds toward its famous closing affirmation of humanity's ability not simply to "endure" but to "prevail," extensively echoes a long passage from Conrad's 1904 essay on Henry James.[1] Less well known is that Robert Penn Warren, the following summer in his landmark introduction to the Modern Library edition of *Nostromo* (1951), closes by quoting the very same passage. What remains unremarked altogether is how these two prominent U.S. Southern, highly literary, deeply political evocations of Conrad in the 1950s have their origins in the literary and political culture of

Conrad that emerged in the modern South during the 1920s. This was the cultural milieu in which *Notes on Life and Letters* (1921), the volume of Conrad's literary and political essays that contains the Henry James piece, first became available to Faulkner and Warren. The wide Southern interest in Conrad's volume and (oft-quoted) essay in the 1920s, moreover, derives from much the same questions of postwar devastation, sectional endurance, literary significance, and racial discord that prompt Faulkner's and Warren's invocations of the 1950s. Hence, when Faulkner and Warren present "their" Conrad through an opposition between mere "endurance" and "prevailing," they are not naïvely attempting to place Conrad's fiction simply on one side or the other. They are reiterating a *problem* of cultural extension—of boundary, self-constitution, longevity, relation, redemption—whose controversies and uncertainties Conrad had been mediating in the South, and under the master mystery sign of "the South," since the 1920s.

The rise of Conrad in the modern U.S. Southern imagination, fundamentally as a cultural-historical function of multifaceted, polyvocal competition over the terms and boundaries of "the South" as advanced in Conrad's image, is the subject of this chapter and the next. An offshoot of Conrad's "nationalized" production during the war and a complex counterpart of Conrad's contestation in U.S. expatriate circles, Conrad's advent in the modern South is traced in this chapter as a matter of contrapuntal, cultural-political friction within and among three broad ideological poles of "Southern" production: the first, a Menckenite pole grounded in three "modern" literary reviews emerging in Virginia, New Orleans, and Arkansas, and conceiving Conrad as a *critical externality* of the South; the second, a more conservative and aggressively sectionalist pole centered in the Vanderbilt Fugitive and Agrarian writers, and conceiving Conrad as a *sympathetic internality* of Southern culture and experience; and the third, a loose idiosyncratic nexus of writers including Thomas Wolfe, W. J. Cash (author of *The Mind of the South* [1941]), and Faulkner, all of whom understand Conrad as a *critical internality* from which to engage and articulate the operations of Southern ideology. In conducting its broad cultural history of Southern self-constitutions and disruptions through Conrad, this chapter also advances this book's strongest case for three of its principal macroarguments: first, that it is untenable to assume that even the most aggressively insular U.S. regions and nativist cultural-political battles are not deeply, intelligently saturated by "foreign" cultural-discursive weapons; second, that it is equally untenable to assume that careful contrapuntal attention to historical articulations of the "literary" (like "Conrad") will not result in remarkably estranging and enhancing constellations and archaeologies of U.S. culture; and third, that Conrad's fundamental place in the U.S. imaginary is a heterotopic one, of special interest to Southerners as a crisis space not only for *national* metanarratives of isolationism and exceptionalism but also for Southern *sectional* metanarratives of absolute boundary and self-exclusion. Indeed, the decoding of Conrad's modern Southern cultural fascination and proliferation as an expression of multifaceted interference and engagement with Southern sectional metanarratives (subject, of course, to a tangle of local and extraregional concerns) is the principal intellectual labor of what follows.

The subsequent chapter probes a deeper sense of structural and cultural-historical intimacy between Conrad and the modern South by turning to and attempting materially to account for uncanny aesthetic intimacies that run throughout the works of Conrad and William Faulkner. I argue that Faulkner's fiction, the place where Conrad's "Southern" affinities are expressed with most expansive and nuanced fecundity, writes and rewrites, and reads and rereads, Conrad's fiction in two mutually self-discovering ways: in a manner that uses Conrad's investigations of the centrality of "race" to Western imperialist systems gradually to overcome race blindness and to theorize the centrality and functionality of "race" in a Southern ideological context; and in a manner that silently capitalizes on profound historical continuities that run between Conrad's native Poland and Faulkner's U.S. South, allowing us to conceive through the confluences of the two authors' aesthetics possibilities of global literary history that are as plural and precise as the planetary reception history of each author is in itself. Curiously enough, Donald Davidson, the most conservative of the Vanderbilt Agrarians, anticipated something like this when he wrote in the *Nashville Tennessean* on August 17, 1924: "His place will be great. His work is lasting. And some day, perhaps, to later generations, Joseph Conrad will stand as a first great figure in a new literature that has become international rather than national in character. Not England, not Poland, but the whole world may justly claim Joseph Conrad."[2]

CONRAD IN THE SAHARA

It is pretty certain that the Southern variety of American writer must first see himself, if at all, through other eyes.

—Allen Tate, "Last Days of a Charming Lady" (1925)

I think that "Cinderella" is the best story ever written. If your letter, however, refers to a story written in English, I should say that perhaps the best story I know is the "Heart of Darkness" by Conrad.

—Thomas Nelson Page, *New York Times* (January 25, 1914)

"My greatest regret was not being able to visit the South," Conrad wrote Warrington Dawson after returning from the United States in July 1923.[3] Indeed, since at least 1897, when Conrad wrote to Stephen Crane's wife, Cora, that "I was so pleased to hear my tales are a success among the socialists of Tennessee" (*CL* 2.74), the South presented Conrad with a prospect of sympathy and familiarity he did not expect elsewhere in the United States. Despite a narrow circle of "private, precious friendships"—"you know there are not many," Conrad wrote John Powell on May 18, 1923—two of Conrad's three intimate friendships with younger American men (the third being Crane) were with Southerners: Powell, the Virginia-born, Vienna-trained pianist and composer who wrote *Rhapsodie Nègre* (1917) as a "symphonic poem" based on *Heart of Darkness*, and who understood the sailor Powell in Conrad's *Chance* to be named after him; and Dawson, the French-exiled South Carolinian who consulted with Conrad on several of his works and is an important source for the character of Captain J. K. Blunt in *The Arrow of Gold*.[4] Moreover, Conrad's correspondence demonstrates an insider's fondness for Southern social graces. At different moments in his life, Conrad commends the gentility of Walter Hines Page (of North Carolina) and Colonel Edward Markham House (of Texas); the "brave and tragic pages" of Sara Dawson's (Warrington's mother) *A Confederate Girl's Diary* (1913) and Grace King's tales of New Orleans; the long-standing literary traditions of Poe (of Virginia) and Twain (of Missouri); and "the insight, the mastery of craft, the interest and charm—all of the very first order" of Conrad's friend and "fellow-craftsman" Ellen Glasgow (of Richmond).[5]

All of this exists in sharp relief from the presumptive distaste and distance with which Conrad regarded U.S. Americans generally—and is the product, or so the letters strongly suggest, of a certain perceived "common ground" of social, moral, and stylistic code with the South, one whose true fit is an interesting subtext of *The Arrow of Gold* (1919). In *The Arrow*, Conrad's protagonist, the self-declaredly autobiographical Monsieur George,[6] is "brought into the world . . . out of the contact of two minds" (*AG* 6) who consist of the *English* Mills and the exiled *South Carolinian* Captain J. K. Blunt. As such, the novel meditates—at precisely the moment of Conrad's skyrocketing popularity in the United States, and through the novel that would shortly become the second best-selling novel in the United States in 1919—on the prospect of "Conrad" being brought into the world through the contact and mutual satisfaction of two very different "minds" and audiences: one European, localized as English, and the other American, epitomized by South Carolina. But if South Carolina is the ideal "American" choice precisely because its social, moral, and stylized conventions most closely resemble the "language" of Europe and Conrad's own fiction; if, indeed, this prospect of cross-identification is part of the point of Conrad's naming Blunt with his own initials (J. K.) and having Blunt introduce himself in terms of an old Polish formula Conrad himself once used;[7] then the point of *The Arrow of Gold* is that the project is not ultimately viable. For Blunt and George become enemies: the product of an "antagonism of feeling," as Conrad put it to Dawson, that "had of course to come out because it is the very foundation of the story's psychology" (*CL* 6.491). Though not as distant as the U.S. consulate is from all the European consulates gathered together with Blunt's abode "on the other side of town" (*AG* 20); though not as distant, this is to say, as Conrad thinks "Yankee" Americans are from understanding the complexities of Europe in the aftermath of the Great War, the U.S. South, figured through Blunt and the surreptitiously Polish, adoptively English M. George offer perspectives that both temptingly intersect and ultimately fail to coincide.

Neither *The Arrow of Gold* nor Conrad's feelings about the South, however, triggered the surge of modern Southern interest in Conrad that began in the early 1920s. Rather, the key animating and agitating agent—as in the north, further west, and to a significant extent abroad—was H. L. Mencken, the publication of whose infamous incendiary essay "The Sahara of the Bozart" in *Prejudices: Second Series* (1920) generated not only what Van Wyck Brooks would call "the birth of the new Southern literature,"[8] but also, in the process, the extension of Conrad as an object of urgent interest and debate below the Mason-Dixon Line. "Bozart" is an unflattering corruption of "beaux arts"; and although Mencken could be identified (and sometimes did strategically self-identify) as a Southerner, this was not because the urban, German-American, Baltimore Anti-Christ had any special sympathy for white Southern tradition or its "culture." Rather, Mencken's purpose was to spark the same sort of cultural revolution—or rather, civil war—in the South that he had waged against what he understood as the autocracy of Anglo-Saxon "Puritan" democracy in the North. This is the context of Mencken's opening salvo in "Sahara," placing the South as a cultural "desert":

It is, indeed, amazing to contemplate so vast a vacuity [as the South]. One thinks of the interstellar spaces, of the colossal reaches of the now mythical ether. Nearly the whole of Europe could be lost in that stupendous region of worn-out farms, shoddy cities and paralyzed cerebrums: one could throw in France, Germany, Italy, and still have room for the British Isles. And yet, for all its size and all its wealth and all the "progress" it babbles of, it is almost as sterile, artistically, intellectually, culturally, as the Sahara Desert. There are single acres in Europe that house more first-rate men than all the states south of the Potomac; there are probably single square miles in America. If the whole of the later Confederacy were to be engulfed by a tidal wave tomorrow, the effect upon the civilized minority of men in the world would be but little greater than that of a flood on the Yang-tse-kiang. It would be impossible in all history to match so complete a drying-up of civilization.[9]

Mencken continues in an oft-quoted passage reminiscent of Sydney Smith's famous attack on U.S. culture ("who reads an American book?") in the *Edinburgh Review* in 1820:

In all that gargantuan paradise of the fourth-rate there is not a single picture gallery worth going into, or a single orchestra capable of playing the nine symphonies of Beethoven, or a single opera-house, or a single theater devoted to decent plays, or a single public monument that is worth looking at, or a single workshop devoted to making beautiful things. Once you have counted James Branch Cabell . . . you will find not a single Southern prose writer who can actually write. And once you have—but when you come to critics, musical composers, painters, sculptors, architects and the like, you will have to give it up, for there is not even a bad one between the Potomac mud-flats and the Gulf. Nor a historian. Nor a philosopher. Nor a theologian. Nor a scientist. In all these fields the South is an awe-inspiring blank—a brother to Portugal, Serbia, and Albania.[10]

Such invective, as expansively cultural in its terms as it was sharply political in its implications, provoked in the South both widespread outrage and passionate conversions to Mencken's point of view. Above all, Mencken stimulated, and would continue to stimulate, Southern cultural-political controversy; yet regardless of the position one assumed in this maelstrom, it was impossible to conceive Mencken himself as anything but an *externality* of the South: an outside and purely negative agent whose affinities and concrete intimacy with the South were as empty as his assessment of it as desertlike. If, as Fred Hobson has meticulously demonstrated, Mencken's "war with the South" during the 1920s is essentially a repetition of his earlier "national" "war on Puritanism" and "similar crusades against England, the Anglo-Saxons in America, prohibition, religious fundamentalism, and moralism, cant, and sentimentality in American literature,"[11] this is to say that Mencken's new campaign is waged with no sense of Southern locality or particularity. In "The South Begins to Mutter" (1921), for instance, Mencken revives the trope of the "public enemy" he had earlier used to describe Conrad in *A Book of Prefaces* and advises young Southern writers on how to proceed in purely negative terms: "The artist is, in the highest sense, a public enemy. . . . His best work is always done in conscious revolt against the culture that surrounds him. . . . He is an anarchist or he is nothing."[12] Similarly, in "Confederate Strivings" (1921) and "Is the South a Desert?" (1923), Mencken insists that Southern writers engage "native" circumstances and materials but can only offer the analogy of Northern models: "It would not surprise me greatly if, on some not-distant tomorrow, a Confederate Amy Lowell arose suddenly and shrilly in New Orleans, or a Southern Edgar Lee Masters, or Dreiser, or Sherwood Anderson began horrifying the right-thinkers of Georgia."[13] All in all, even Mencken's many curiously romantic appeals to the "aristocratic" "Old South" of Washington and Jefferson—an odd but somehow perfectly commensurate pairing with Mencken's otherwise bludgeoning insistence on the trope of the "modern"—have a distinctly negative and empty ring.[14] Like Mencken's prospective appeals to "aristocracy" in the North, these romanticisms express less any genuine Southern history Mencken identifies with than his inability to identify with (and to a certain extent, even identify) anything genuinely Southern at all.

One result of Mencken's "Sahara" and its sequels was the appearance and efflorescence, within months of the essay's 1920 publication, of three Southern "little" magazines dispersed across the region which in different ways and to different degrees carried out Mencken's antitraditionalist, counter-hegemonic, "modernizing" literary and cultural-political project: the *Reviewer* (Richmond,

Virginia); the *Double Dealer* (New Orleans); and *All's Well, or the Mirror Re-polished* (Fayetteville, Arkansas), the latter published and largely written by the singular Charles J. Finger, a good friend of Conrad's close friend R. B. Cunninghame Graham. The first two of these magazines, especially the first, were strongly advised by Mencken; the third was a special Menckenian enthusiasm; and the central point to take with respect to all three—which together constitute the first of the three "poles" of Conrad's modern Southern production to be considered in this chapter—is that despite the vast diversity and conflict of sectionalist, imperialist, feminist, class- and race-based, erotic, and aesthetic agendas that inform and animate their constructions of Conrad, they all presuppose a "Conrad" foundationally framed not only by Mencken's hyperbolic enthusiasm for Conrad but by *the same sense of modernizing externality that comprises Mencken's own wholly external and aggressively critical relation to the South.* Whether coded as "modern" or "aristocratic," whether embraced or deprecated, and regardless of the cultural-political freight his image is made to carry, the Conrad of the Southern little magazines is always fundamentally an outsider and alienizing entity: *not* like and never quite "one of us"—no matter how compulsively, reverentially, plurally, and controversially his image is evoked to rethink what the South is and can be, and for whom. This filtering of Conrad through the vantage of Mencken is accompanied by a less predictable paradox of Conrad's construction and production in the Southern little magazines: the *more regional* the focus of the magazine, the more emphasis the "alien" Conrad receives in it. Conrad's heterotopic status in these magazines, indeed, exists in the ratio between the degree of their fascination with Conrad and the difficulty of demonstrating the regional spatial and ideological coordinations that always, empirically, underwrite their fascination with this "outside" space.

THUS QUOTH THE *REVIEWER*

A compelling blend of Southern cultural focus and cosmopolitan aesthetic sophistication and interpolation, the *Reviewer* was the most regionally conscious of the Southern little magazines, and for that reason, the most closely and consistently advised by Mencken and the most significant for Southern letters and culture generally. Begun in February 1921 and ending its Richmond run within weeks of Conrad's death in October 1924, the *Reviewer* has the ideal of Conrad built into its very foundations. Both of the principal editors, Emily Clark

and Hunter S. Stagg, have extensive pieces on Conrad whose tone is quite unlike nearly everything else the two write. Stagg's review of Conrad's *Notes on
Life and Letters* (1921), the volume of literary-critical and political essays that
includes the Henry James piece that Faulkner would later draw on in his Nobel
Prize speech, advances probably the boldest intelligent claim ever made for
that volume (in the process illustrating something of the milieu that would
lead writers like Faulkner and Robert Penn Warren toward it). Stagg begins by
observing the "astounding prophetic insight" of "Autocracy and War" (1905),
Conrad's early political essay on the Russo-Japanese War that clearly foresees
not only the rising internal instabilities within Russia that would result in the
Bolshevik Revolution but also the mounting European tensions with Germany
that would result in the Great War ("Le Prussianisme—voilà l'ennemi" [*NLL*
114], the essay concludes). Stagg, however, fundamentally champions *Notes on
Life and Letters* for its *literary* rather than political essays, and argues that they
demonstrate that Conrad "is pre-eminently *the* critic of letters." "Tired of its
poverty in the youngest of the arts, the English speaking world is eager to place
in its chair of Criticism someone it need not blush to show to France; and [given
Notes] it is ripe to recognize Conrad's fitness for this seat."[15] On a similarly adu-
latory note, Stagg's review of *The Rover* is really less a review than an expansive
meditation on a poetics of "mergence" across Conrad's fiction, one in which
Conrad's "gift of subjecting himself to the mood" of his scenes and characters
becomes "the secret"—and narrative methodology—"of his mastery over the
mood of the reader." This prescient insight[16] is complemented with the thesis
that although "[t]here are novelists of plot and novelists of character, novelists
of style, of place, of period, of manners, and . . . of course, plenty of novelists
of propaganda," "Joseph Conrad has been, and is, at will, *each of these*," demonstrating a curiously all-embracing power—despite his own irreducible singularity—somehow to comprehend and "merge" not only every category of place and
person but also nearly every form of fiction, such that ultimately "one cannot
say" of *The Rover* that "it is Conrad at his best" because that "statement really
means no more than it is a different Conrad," and one cannot say *The Rover*
is "Conrad at his worst, for so far as I can discover there is no 'worst' Conrad.
There is only Conrad, and that is enough."[17]

   This conception of Conrad—not at all particular to or materially evocative of the South, yet nevertheless highly suggestive of a transcultural model
of "mergence" wherein prior segregations of cultural territory and difference

become "subjected" to one another—may be compared with the equally monu-mentalizing and "personal" conception put forward by Clark. Clark's appre-ciation of Conrad is manifestly impacted by her close contact with Mencken and Joseph Hergesheimer (the latter, the single towering non-Southern writer most continually featured in the *Reviewer*; also a crucial adviser to it).[18] In her reminiscences, Clark recalls Mencken emphasizing, "There is no one like [Con-rad]. There is no one even remotely like him"; one of her articles on editorial procedure is playfully entitled "The End of the Tether" (after Conrad's novella, and apropos of a particular Hergesheimer enthusiasm); and many of Clark's expository pieces and fictional vignettes of Southern life demonstrate consid-eration of Conrad, albeit always with the sense of Conrad's corrective alterity that one would expect from a Menckenian frame.[19] Especially revealing in this respect is a series of essays resulting from Clark's early swaggering confession to lacking the "epic sense" to care about Dante on the six hundredth anniversary of his death in 1922. This mischievous trigger generates a sequence of medita-tions on how an "inadequacy" of "epic sense"—which for Clark means a heroic excess of form over native or grounding substance—can be remedied through a process of adaptation and acquisition: "Conrad is one of these acquired tastes. I regarded him once as I viewed oysters on the half-shell as a child, tremendous, yes, but difficult, damp, and gray. Now he is tremendous without those other shameful adjectives—shameful to me, I mean of course, not Mr. Conrad." For Clark, one of the "spoils of war" when it comes to cultural acquisition is an "epic"—what Edward Said, thinking of Dante and Conrad, would call "affili-ative"—extension of self, corroded of its former filiations and reconstituted at a superior level of dynamic aesthetic remove:

It is undeniable that acquired tastes are by far the most satisfactory.... Even after the triumphant thrill has departed there is a conscious and heart-warming knowledge that we are a degree above the herd in one respect at least.... For Conrad I am sure I have a special feeling which would not exist if he had been smooth going from the start.... [Those who] shrink from becoming vitally—and materially—interested in matters merely aesthetic, because that is not natural to them ... [forgo] results which are at once more thrilling and more soothing than the indefinite pursuance of what-ever one happens to be born liking.[20]

Both Clark's corrective, corrosive model of Conrad and Stagg's self-sub-jecting, "mergence" model of Conrad make up only a small part of the compulsive impulse to comment on Conrad that runs throughout the *Reviewer*, in its defining counterpoint of regional and metro/cosmopolitan concerns, its rich dialogue of analytic essays and literary experiments and artifacts (some of which, like Hergesheimer's sketch "Little Kanaka," import characters or landmarks from Conrad's fiction to make an explicit ideological point about issues like U.S. imperialism).[21] "Modern," moreover, is repeatedly the trope through which Conrad is presented: whether the writer's purpose is to trace the "modern" writings of America's "young intellectuals" or to place the paintings of Cézanne; to support the "basis for a modern musical criticism" or to support *and* reject the "ultramodern" musical practices of Schoenberg and Stravinsky; to personify "rebel[lion] against the existing literary order" or the "pursuit of pure literature" or, to the contrary, to represent an "older generation" that is *no longer* truly modern, or perhaps even the kind of once-modern artist who has sold out to a combination of "Victorian heritage" and "unspiritual materialism" to secure a "plush" place in "the mighty world of British letters."[22] Conrad, one may say, is less specifically "modern" than a space at which all the different permutations and even rejections of the "modern" experience contemplation, expression, and contact. This general principle of "modern" catholicity is evinced throughout the *Reviewer*'s many book reviews as well. The publication of any new novel by William McFee (generally concerning the sea) invariably provokes a meditation on how McFee "has evidently steeped himself in that very great man's [Conrad's] work" and how he has either admirably responded to his "great stimulus" or failed to demonstrate "the smallest notion of how to select and hold [a narrative] . . . à la Conrad."[23] Both Edwin Björkman's contemplation and Alfred Knopf's promotion of Knut Hamsun expansively reference the defining "stamp" of Conrad.[24] Frederick Eddy emphasizes the "thrill" of Walter de la Mare's prose at its best by comparing it to that "tense moment" in *The Secret Sharer*—which of all "moment[s] in literature linger[s] always in my memory"—when "the captain sees the steward making for his cabin where the fugitive lies hidden."[25] And so, too, the formal experimentations of British modernists May Sinclair and Dorothy Richardson, the "large personality" and "tempered melancholy" of Willa Cather, the sophomoric impatience of Frank Swinnerton, the banality of Clive Bell, the irony of John Partins, the collector's value of George Moore, the "subtle and colorful romance" of Morris Dallett, the "involved methods" of Wilbur Daniel Steele, and the "brooding" "Jungle" topos and Eastern exoticism of William

Beebe and Marjorie Greenbie, respectively, are all articulated in direct comparison with Conrad.[26]

Finally, it must be emphasized that even when the *Reviewer's* pages don't mention Conrad, he is in some sense implied by the virtual Who's Who gathering of Conradian appreciation that makes up a healthy plurality of its writers. It is difficult to find in one place a more dedicated group of Conrad's public admirers, friends, and instruments of advancement than the names that most frequently and/or prominently appear in the *Reviewer's* table of contents: most centrally (as linked to the *Reviewer*), Clark, Stagg, Mencken, Hergesheimer, and Cabell (not a great champion of Conrad but vitally linked to him as the single Southern writer Mencken championed with Conradian enthusiasm);[27] but also significantly, John Galsworthy, Hugh Walpole, Wilson Follett, H. M. Tomlinson, Ellen Glasgow, Vincent Starrett, Ernest Boyd, Burton Rascoe, Dawson, Powell, and Björkman. Small wonder that Carl Van Vechten, a tireless defender of Melville who never warmed to Conrad, would write in the *Reviewer* in January 1923 in an essay on "books that have that strange, indefinable quality known as glamour": "I am afraid I shall never be in fashion; I shall probably only begin to read Joseph Conrad and John Masefield when they are a little *démodés*."[28]

Most of the names and concerns just mentioned are not specifically, or even remotely, "Southern"—and it is precisely this sense of presumptive *externality*, the discrepancy between the breadth and intensity of interest in Conrad and the apparently "non-Southern" nature of that interest, that must first be emphasized of the Southern little magazines' constructions of Conrad. Indeed, it almost seems as if no local or sectional purposes at all account for the interest the *Reviewer* takes in Conrad—which is not to say, of course, that the magazine's traffic in Conrad is not heavily culturally and politically freighted. Rather, in the first full year of the *Reviewer* alone—the year after the Treaty of Versailles was signed—the magazine thoroughly flanks its references to Conrad with articles and creative works on various national and international topics that quite naturally suggest an interest in Conrad: anxieties of subservience to British interests and questions of "debt" between the United States and Britain; the allure of "Slavic" writers and writings about "revolutionary" Russia; intersecting concerns of immigrant writers, "national" literatures, and modes of "Americanizing America"; the future, present, and past of Africa, and problematics of race relations in the United States raised by the opening of Eugene O'Neill's *The Emperor Jones* (starring African American actor Charles Gilpin, inspired by *Heart of Darkness*).[29] Perhaps most important, moreover, is the general postwar climate of political skepticism and futility that Mencken had been cultivating through Conrad all along:

To-day American life—in common with the life of mankind everywhere—is more fluid than it has ever been. The war and its aftermath have awakened an intelligence and created such a general state of doubt, that there is left remaining little confidence in any institution, belief, doctrine, or idea. Everywhere there is profound skepticism. The older dogmas, creeds, shibboleths, which have crippled the free play of thought are bankrupt. . . . All the intellectual vitality of the planet was stirred by the war. It was focused by Wilson. It was betrayed at Versailles. The generous impulses, the latent idealism, of man were awakening only to be exploited and debauched. And now in America and the world the consequences are obvious.[30]

Just as in the rest of the country and against the grain of the confident political programs and didactic idealism of writers like Shaw and Wells that so appealed to younger U.S. intellectuals before the war, Conrad became a fascination through and after the war in Southern venues like the *Reviewer* significantly because of the radically skeptical relation his fiction assumes with respect to all political doctrines and much activism, his emphases on the corruptibility and vulnerability of human institutions and their agents, his sensitivity to the material complexities that delimit and the ideational certainties that invariably misconstrue human affairs, and an overall sense, as suggested earlier, that Mr. Wilson's fate was not all that different from Lord Jim's. This is the logic behind the extreme position of political disengagement adopted in Conrad's image by the lead editorial in the *Double Dealer* in April 1922:

We believe that there are more important and interesting things in the world than politics. A beautiful picture, a fine sonata, a novel of Joseph Conrad seem to us more darkly significant to human life than the result of a gubernatorial primary. We see a problem in our lives which is unaffected by the tariff revision, a hope and a despair which remain after the aspirations of all the liberals have been satisfied. And we would feel not a little stuffy in the new heaven and the new earth under the banner of any band of the politically minded.[31]

But the *Reviewer*, in fact, was a great deal more political than the *Double Dealer*—and in the process a great deal more "Southern" and more preoccupied with Conrad as well. Indeed, quite the opposite of the *Double Dealer* editorial, the previous quotation on post-Wilsonian disillusion comes from an essay written by the profoundly sectionally identified Marylander Jesse Lee Bennett, and far from dwelling on America's "lost idealism," Bennett's essay is a manifesto urging young Southerners to seize on the "rich soil," "deep roots," and "complex" raw "materials" of Southern tradition and history to forge—through "brooding, thinking, planning"—"an inchoate world yet in the making."[32] So, too, albeit generally far more critically, the *Reviewer* remained firmly committed to the twin sectional priorities of attempting "to develop young Southern writers" and to "build *The Reviewer* with Southern material insofar as this was possible," generating "a native product, rather than an exotic attempt to imitate magazines that have no essential connection with our own background."[33] Unlike the *Double Dealer*, whose increasingly aestheticist and cosmopolitan emphases would lead an exasperated Mencken to complain to Clark, "*The Double Dealer* is wholly un-Southern; *The Reviewer* is thoroughly of the South,"[34] the Richmond little magazine never let its extraregional awareness and contents confuse its central "determination to articulate the new Southern consciousness then becoming apparent." Such principles, of course, implied that the *Reviewer*'s concerns could not be "purely literary": and, indeed, in the scathing indictments of the Klan, Southern religion and politics, and New Southern commercialism written by Gerald W. Johnson and Paul Green; in the idiosyncratic investigative portraits of major Southern cities written by John Bennett, Glasgow, Clark, and others; and most especially, in the innovative fiction on frequently controversial subjects (for example, lynching, female sexuality, interracial contact) written by a number of extremely talented and sorely underdiscussed women writers— among them, Frances Newman, Julia Peterkin, Helen Dick, Amélie Rives, Mary Johnston, and Sara Haardt—the South received every bit the critical scrutiny Mencken had called for. The challenge, then, is to understand the *Reviewer*'s *non*-Southern contributors and contributions within the Southern grounding and signifying economy of the magazine: in relation to both the magazine's *literary* attempts, in Clark's phrase, "to show the young South what the young North and West are doing," and the magazine's *political* inclinations, whose most extreme formulation is Gerald Johnson's, to demand that "the Southerner must burst all bonds of conservative tradition, break with the past and defy the present with . . . bald, unequivocal and conclusive assertion."[35] By no means do all the authors in the (definitionally polyphonic, dialogic) *Reviewer* adopt Johnson's extreme Menckenian position; but this is the position that all the writers in the magazine are in some way engaging, precisely as they multiply engage the "modern" Conrad.

ENTER FRANCES NEWMAN

The crucial figure in this context, because of both the sparkling incisiveness of her engagements with Conrad and the complex field of Southern coordinates and codes at issue in them, is Frances Newman. A central essayist for the *Reviewer* and a key and controversial catalyst for its dialogic production of Conrad, Newman is also one of the most under-known and underrated U.S. prose writers of the earlier twentieth century.[36] Born in Atlanta in 1893, the last child of a family of elite social standing, Newman quickly found herself alienated from her presumptive social sphere by virtue of both her exceptional intelligence and unconventional appearance (which would come to include a penchant for dressing entirely in shades of purple). Prior to her untimely death in 1928, the well-traveled, highly literate, conspicuously caustic and flamboyant Newman achieved much that has become lost to contemporary criticism and scholarship. While working as a librarian at the Carnegie Library in Atlanta after the war, Newman became a literary critic of some celebrity status whose distinctive essays appeared regularly in the *Reviewer* and the *Constitution* (Atlanta) (the South's most influential paper at the time), and later by invitation in the New York *Herald-Tribune* and the *Saturday Review of Literature*. During the same period, Newman also became the first U.S. translator of Jules LaForgue's short fiction; the author of a book-length study, including translations from five languages, of the short-story form from Petronius to Paul Morand; a fellow at the Sorbonne and the MacDowell Colony for writers in Peterborough, New Hampshire; an award-winning short-story writer in her own right; and perhaps most notably, the controversial author of two published novels—*The Hard-Boiled Virgin* (1928) and *Dead Lovers Are Faithful Lovers* (1928)—that incited great scandal in the South (though they were in fact banned only in the North) for their erotic, gendered, socially satiric, and antiracist disclosures. These novels, as striking as their maverick feminist sensibility and stinging social critique of the urban upper-class South are, are equally striking for a distinctive prose *style* that runs across Newman's work: a "tight, glittering, extremely uncommon style,"[37] in Mencken's not entirely complimentary phrase, which combines the elaborate sentence structure of the later James, the comic rhetorical repetitions and whimsicality of Stein, a Swiftian sense of the satiric and grotesque, Wildean ostentation and mischief, Woolf's decorous interiority, and a penchant for allusivity whose density often out-Eliots T. S. Eliot. Given such literary coordinates—all explicitly mentioned by Newman herself in her letters and prose—one might expect Newman to have a strong point of view on Conrad, but what one might not expect is that this point of view should combine both a profound awareness of and a thoroughgoing aversion to Conrad's U.S. and Southern ascent. Theirs is an arch-antagonism under Newman's eyes, ultimately traceable, as careful examination of the rhetorical codes of Newman's first two major essays in the *Reviewer* and several essays in the *Constitution* (Atlanta) reveals, to the vision of the South that coordinates and grounds all of Newman's writings.

Newman's first major *Reviewer* essay, "The Allegory of the Young Intellectuals" (1921), constructs Conrad in line with the previous quotations from Bennett and the *Double Dealer* as a model and mythic archetype of the "lost generation"—albeit with precisely the reverse sympathies. In the essay, Newman assumes the role of critic of an imaginary "new great American allegory" that has so completely captured the spirit of the new younger generation of American writers, so compellingly won the "hearts and heads" of the "popular imagination" and the "most respectable critics" alike, that "there is now no reason why anyone should ever write a novel about contemporary life in a small town again."[38] Newman thus herself becomes the critical allegorist of this new generation of "unhappy young intellectuals": a "gloomy" group of "pessimistic" "young writers"—defined very broadly in terms of "point of view" rather than "age"—whose membership includes everyone from the *New Republic* intellectuals to "Mencken and his disciples," from T. S. Eliot and Ezra Pound ("excellent critics" if "unproven poets") to specific emblematic novelists like Theodore Dreiser, Sherwood Anderson, Sinclair Lewis, and the young F. Scott Fitzgerald. Pointedly responding to this overwhelmingly male roster of writers by making her exemplary figure a woman, Newman charts the symbolic course of these writers: they are born in what they discover to be "a small, ill-educated, rather avaricious village" in the United States; they evolve the conviction that their "true home" lies elsewhere in the "great cities" and "clouds of culture" of the "great" European "world"; and notwithstanding formidably "cerebral" and "universal" minds like Pound and Eliot, they physically and/or psychologically abandon their native land with little sense of style, "critical faculty," or literary and cultural range beyond their own temperamental "gloom."[39] Such limitations notwithstanding, these stern young writers—"who," Newman writes mischievously, "feel themselves forced to go to some alien country, where many of them will probably starve, but where at least they will be able, spiritually, to breathe"—set off for London because there lies the country where another fatally gloomy literary expatriate once found glory and a "true home": it is "the land that . . . long ago hailed Mr. Conrad her prince of prose." So, too, if their pilgrimage takes them to Paris, this is because "perhaps they purpose being new Joseph Conrads to France."[40] Such "hegiras" of the young intellectual are, of course, ultimately destined to fail, not because of any triumphal or insular nationalism on Newman's part, but rather because of the naïveté of the pilgrim and her failure, as Newman will put it in *The Hard-Boiled Virgin*, to confront the "horror" and "inevitability of her literary nationality."[41] But the immediate point is that Conrad here has become a figure and specular model of native dislocation and abandoned ground to which Newman, a deeply cosmopolitan figure with no "nationalist" sympathies whatever, is nevertheless intensely opposed.

The phrase "prince of prose," with its undertones of glamorous seduction and dark Satanic temptation, is important. In *The Hard-Boiled Virgin*, a semiautobiographical bildungsroman and "portrait of the artist" of sorts, the phrase is used twice near the end to describe two literary celebrities who nearly tempt Katharine Faraday from actualizing herself as a writer: to become seduced by them, to become "the mistress of a prince of prose," is to become seduced from herself and *of* her own voice as a "hard-boiled virgin."[42] Similarly, in her regular column in the *Constitution* (Atlanta) in July 1921, Newman describes Joseph Hergesheimer, a novelist widely identified with Conrad, as an "American prince of prose"—in her responding to a lecture Hergesheimer had recently delivered at Yale attributing the "disastrous" state of "American letters" and "all the arts" to their "hav[ing] been handed over to women."[43] The only other time Newman uses the phrase "prince of prose"—and this, along with the *Reviewer* essay, is clearly the context of its genesis[44]—is again to describe Conrad in one in a series of essays concerning "Joseph, the Polish Siren" in the *Constitution*, whose general burden is to argue that "Mr. Conrad is as contagious as the bubonic plague and nearly as dangerous," and that in these days when "so many people are getting laws passed to make other people do what they happen to fancy doing themselves," "there is no reason why an unusually severe bill, with some drastic penalty such as the loss of their license, should not be introduced to prevent young novelists from imitating the method of Joseph Conrad."[45] If part of the problem with Conrad, as we have just seen, is that his image, example, and aesthetic model encourage both the abandonment of one's native culture and the illusion that one will not ultimately be forced to confront the terms of her formative socialization, the case against Conrad—which obviously and complexly concerns patriarchal orchestrations of gender and seduction as well—is augmented in two further respects in Newman's second major *Reviewer* essay, "Herd Complex" (1922).

An essay of "tenacious" difficulty—to borrow Newman's favorite adjective for Conrad—"Herd Complex" manages to mention Owen Hatteras (one of Mencken's pseudonyms), Thomas Beer (who had just asked Conrad to write the introduction for his biographical study of Stephen Crane), *The Mauve Decade*, James K. Hackett, Rudolph Rassendyll, Macbeth, Silas Lapham, and Van Bibber all in the first two-thirds of its opening sentence. Another critique of the "young intellectual" writers—and evidently one with something to prove about the nature of intellectuality as such—this essay again advances its general claims and analysis through specific criticism of a new, exemplary work: this time an actual novel, Beer's *The Fair Rewards* (1922). Curiously for a text that flaunts its learning as aggressively as Newman's does, "Herd Complex" begins its attack by arguing that although there is by no means "an overeducated youth in America," Beer's book demonstrates certain overly "literary" qualities that speak to a disconcerting "herd" tendency in modern U.S. writing generally.[46] Though it is not ultimately objectionable that Beer's narrative, a tale of the recent stage, mixes within its fictional pages actual social personages like James Huneker and Charles Frohman, Beer crosses an alarming boundary of literary ontology when he imports into his own fictional world the characters of *other* novelists: for instance, Hergesheimer's Mariana Jannan, who is presented with two more children than she has in *The Three Black Pennys*; or those moments when Beer imagines "a liaison between Raskolnikov and Anna Karenina, or that the forgotten, unforgiven, and excessively romantic Lord Jim embarked on the *Patna* when the indiscreet Diana [of Meredith's *Diana of the Crossways*, one of Newman's favorite novels] was wedded to her Redworth."[47] These adulterations are troubling not because of their ludic excess or radical subversiveness with respect to established boundaries and categories, but rather because of the triviality of Beer's command of the texts he invokes—as if in "one of those parlor games which are the refuge of hostesses whose guests are too dull for conversation and too virtuous for bridge." Beer, indeed, reminds Newman of F. Scott Fitzgerald's recent practice of presenting characters reading his own work or named after himself—as if the world, as Newman puts it elsewhere, were "only the [duplication] of Mr. Fitzgerald's brain"—and of the wider prospect of writers turning to their valiant encounters with editors at the *Bookman* or the *Dial* or the *Smart Set* for the thematic matter of their fiction.[48] "Literature was never surely before literary in quite the informal fashion of our younger novelists," Newman argues, because "literary" knowledge has increasingly become a modish masquerade not of reading (of the world or other texts) but of superficial and self-referentiality. "Perhaps it is also becoming a trifle less difficult to write," Newman continues, because the obligations of fiction to reality—including the reality of other people's fiction—have also been relaxed. And if "things seem more real and vivid" in much modern fiction "when one can apply somebody else's ready-made phrase to them," the reason is that the "ready-made" word has in fact substantially eclipsed the "real": in the new fiction, the "real" derives from and has its referent entirely in the narcissistic author-subject and the "ready-made" clichés, expectations, and experiences of the commercial literary market.[49]

Such concerns are by no means lost on Conrad;[50] yet nevertheless, this usurpation and ungrounding of reality by fiction, this obfuscation and *not* penetration of material voices and otherness by a loose, smothering, seductive fog of words, once again produces Conrad as not an ally but rather an arch-antagonist. This happens at the end of "Herd Complex" when, as in "The Allegory of the Young Intellectuals," Newman places an anonymous Everyman figure of all the U.S. writers she has been critiquing—"our hero"—under the master narratively generative sign of Conrad: "The works of Mr. Joseph Conrad," she writes with stinging irony, "are usually found on those catalogues of books which have left our hero the brilliant maker of phrases that he is."[51] The Conrad who in the former essay was a Satanic menace for tempting U.S. Americans to leave and lose their native ground here is a menace for tempting them to make phrases that have no ground: that simply proceed, marrying whatever nominal concepts they like, of their own phallogocentric momentum. And that is not all. In the full paragraph with which "Herd Complex" closes, a passage so remarkably opaque and bizarre it merits quoting in its entirety, Newman ultimately makes the case that when Conrad *does* write of material things, he writes of them only *as* material things. The context here is the possibility of an "epic" "American" novel, given the tendency of modern U.S. novelists to model themselves on Conrad:

But if some American epic—the Domesday Book, perhaps, or Evangeline—should fire another Schliemann to dig another Troy, there is some reason to fear that our novel will look more like photographs of the original Floradora sextette than like the eternal

Hermes of Praxiteles. The works of Mr. Joseph Conrad are usually found on those cata-logues of the books which have left our hero the brilliant maker of phrases that he is—probably beginning with Henty and passing by Petronius to Carl Sandburg—and this, says his sometime collaborator, Mr. [Ford Madox] Hueffer, is one of the Polish siren's secrets of universality: "Never take for granted any special knowledge in your reader. For your reader may be Man, Woman, New Yorker, inhabitant of Tokio, or seller of grocer-ies behind a counter in Athens . . . or denizen of a century that shall come two thousand years after your own age. If, this rule implies, you have occasion to take your charac-ters somewhere in a four-wheeler—let the four-wheeler be projected as a dingy, rattling, glazed box on shaky wheels that the London four-wheeler used to be. If you just say: 'They went in a four-wheeler' the lady who will read you in Vienna in the year A.D. 4920, will fail to understand you and there will be a white spot on your page." Mr. Dreiser is evidently of the same opinion.[52]

The first point to take about this passage—whose difficulty is not an illusion of excerption but rather an expression of the difficulties Newman cathects in Conrad—is that the terms of its construction of Conrad seem initially unwor-thy of Newman. Whereas Newman's prior emphases on dislocations of cultural and textual ground are useful frames that lend themselves richly and complexly to the interpretation of Conrad's works, the emphasis here on an excess of situ-ating details is, like many cues provided by Ford, misleading: one recalls that *Heart of Darkness* refuses to specify even its location in the Congo, and also the famous letter Conrad wrote to Barrett Clark concerning *Victory* which empha-sizes the *avoidance* of details "tending to a definite conclusion" and how "the nearer [a novel] approaches art, the more it acquires a symbolic"—and hence, abstract—"character" (*CL* 6.210). Nor does there seem much promise in New-man's closing comparison with Dreiser, which is not premised on Mencken's sense of the "public enemy" or "cosmic skepticism" that unites Conrad and Dreiser but on the concept that invisibly organizes Newman's entire paragraph: the idea of the "journalistic." For Newman, as she makes the point repeatedly in her essays in the *Constitution* (Atlanta), Dreiser stands for "the worst style that has flourished since Laura Jean Libbey and a general literary incompetence."[53] Newman's objection to Dreiser's style may be paraphrased as an objection to the "documentary" or "journalistic." Given that philosophers have "categorically disposed of the pretensions of an art in which 'the *documentary* has dominated the aesthetic'"; and given that "the aesthetes, of course, long ago settled the lowly status of those to whom '*document*' in art is important," Newman argues that the Dreiserian style, premised on, at best, journalistic standards of "photographic accuracy" and "perfect truthfulness," will never suffice for anyone who has the taste to "prefer Venus to a red snapper" (referencing Botticelli).[54] This is the conceptual frame that produces Dreiser at the end of "Herd Complex." To imagine the next Heinrich Schliemann—the modern archaeologist who set out with the *Aeneid* to find Troy—setting out in search of modern U.S. America's epic roots with, as his guide, "our novel" that looks "more like *photographs* of the Floradora sextette" than the "eternal" Hermes of Praxiteles; and to identify (tongue firmly within cheek) Conrad "the Polish siren's secrets of universality" in terms of a similar standard of documentary detail and minimized abstraction, is "evidently" to bring up Dreiser and the journalistic style he epitomizes. Conrad's siren sway, this is to say, exists at the intersection of the journalistic priorities that he encourages in young "epic" U.S. writers and that he recalls and legitimizes in Dreiser: all in all, again, not a very promising reading of Conrad, whose fiction has in fact very little in common with journalism.[55]

But to say that Newman's objection is to "journalistic style" is to obscure the more fundamental point that for Newman this phrase is a contradiction in terms: the "documentary" is not the degradation of "style" but rather its absence and opposite; not the lowering of culture but rather, as Newman writes of Dreiser, "*nakedness of culture*—and of the simplest amenities of life and of literature."[56] Such a construction is not far from Mr. Kurtz, extraculturally "crawling on all fours" (*YOS* 142) and operating not with a bad method but with "no method at all" (*YOS* 138) at the heart of darkness; and it is, indeed, in the ultimate impossibility (for Newman) of ideas like "naked style" and "extracultural method" that the incisive intelligence of Newman's conception of Conrad emerges once again. *Style*, for Newman, consists quite precisely in that "special knowledge" "take[n] for granted in the reader" whose absence she deplores in Conrad at the end of "Herd Complex"—and whose presence defines the very essence of Newman's own highly allusive, richly exclusive prose voice. Newman defines herself as having style, this is to say, precisely to the extent that Conrad may be understood as not having it; and the kind of style Newman has, contrary to the democratic (because not insular) and discontinuous (because neither culturally nor textually grounded) example of Conrad, is the formal product of continuously acquired, layered, integrated, and sublimated knowledge and social experience. Not unlike Eliot's notion of "tradition"—though the politics, as we shall see, are trickier—Newmanian "style" is constituted through strategic, palimpsestic recuperations and filtrations of the past; selective extensions and critical elaborations of prior cultural reference points and systems; robust integrations of textual and experiential knowledge that are the very opposite of Beer's depthless and discontinuous literary borrowings; and a firm refusal to accommodate every "Man, Woman, New Yorker, inhabitant of Tokio, or [Greek] seller of groceries" in a manner that might compromise the rigor of this deeply sedimented and cumulative cultural project.

Clearly elitist and insular in several respects, yet advanced from the gendered margins, toward maverick social critique, with tremendous cosmopolitan sympathy and awareness, and in a spirit of Adornian critical "difficulty," Newmanian style turns on a direct but never exactly flush relationship between style and continuous cultural history—especially Anglo and English models of continuous cultural history—that Newman emphasizes throughout her *Constitution* essays. Picking up on a contemporary oil dispute between Britain and the United States, Newman remarks that "if patriotism required the abandonment of all traffic with British literature we would be in a very bad case indeed"; and elsewhere Newman—equally playfully but also not frivolously—compares Mencken's efforts to divorce the "American" from the "English" language to the extreme activities of "Messrs. Lenin and Trotzky [*sic*]."[57] Similarly, A. A. Milne's "irresistible" style and ability to "write with felicity on any [subject]" is traced to the continuous stream of "without-which-nothings" in his birth and upper-middle-class breeding that have centered him as the "Perfect Type of Briton"—universally curious yet fundamentally "as British as a tight little isle surrounded by gulf streams and untrustworthy channels"—just as Norman Douglas's "quite evident" background as a "public school and university-bred Englishman" has enabled the "wandering" Douglas to combine in his fiction and person "that mellow and charming type" of the "inglese italiano."[58] The problem with Ezra Pound, on the other hand, is precisely that this "*monstrous clever fellow*" has no grounding and integrating native tradition to wed his "formidable erudition" and omnivorous creative and critical appetites to. "The offspring of the unthinkable mating of Henry Mencken and Henry James," Pound's voice is the urbane yawp of world sophistication rendered in U.S. American anti-style: a freakishly dazzlingly but ultimately sterile combination and dissipation of energies lacking in a cumulative cultural framework—which is why (this being a moment prior to any substantial offering of *Cantos*—and surely as good a reading of Pound as any in this moment) Pound hops from one aesthetic and avant-garde enthusiasm to the next (imagism, vorticism, etc.) with no sense of aggregative continuity.[59]

Given this context, it's easy to see how Conrad—notwithstanding the irrelevance of the "documentary" to his aesthetics; and notwithstanding as well that most Conrad scholars would object to the overly categorical nature of this portrait—could emerge as the "siren" of anti-style, the aesthetic "prince" of darkness, and the aesthetic anti-image and enchanting center of the deluded American "herd" at the end of "Herd Complex." As a Polish native whose novels not only never mention Poland but also frequently seem enamored of radically "jumping" from—or "drifting" from or "kicking oneself free of" or "making a clean sweep of"[60]—continuous prior traditions; as a British emigrant who was *not* raised in England, was *not* the product of a cumulative or circumscribing English sensibility, but was the author of fiction that generally insists upon the *partiality* and synthetic *limitations* of British and Western imperial projects of knowledge; and as a "democratic" writer, both in the sense (epitomized by open-ended leitmotifs like "our man" and "one of us" and the exotic places Conrad frequently sets his fiction) that his alien relation to his presumed audiences precludes aggressively insular or sedimented assumptions of knowledge, and in the sense that as a former sailor, his proletarian maritime background and thematics and his sophisticated literary register make up every bit the "monstrosity" that distinguishes Pound from the congenitally "well-bred" Milne and Douglas, *Conrad is the supreme illusion of style without continuous cultural mechanism and inscription.* The seductive appearance of what simply cannot be—i.e., style without the continuous and cumulative cultural integrations that define it as such—Conrad is in fact the negation of style (and of Newman): the radical dissociation (or at least its appearance, temptation) of form from aesthetic and cultural history; the siren space wherein "nakedness of style" and "no method at all"—which is not far, we should remember, from how many readers first responded to *Lord Jim*—threaten to become indistinguishable from style.

National, textual, and now stylistic dislocation ("ungrounding"): having established these overarching codes and their seminal intertwining with Conrad, we are now in a position to understand and unpack the specific Southern coordinations and animations that frame Newman's constructions of Conrad as well as the entire dialogic system of Conrad's (multiple, contested) production in the *Reviewer*, in which Newman's voice plays a crucially illuminating, because aggressively dissonant, part. To proceed backward through the codes:

Style is a pointedly "Southern" issue for Newman because it is through the signature idea of style, even when its sectional bearings remain undeclared, that Newman theorizes and comes to principal terms with her sense of the South's interregional and intraregional distinctiveness. Responding to Mencken's "Sahara" essay in "The New Carthaginians" (1921), Newman argues that the South, whatever its literary shortcomings may be, is by national consensus the only U.S. region that has successfully preserved the traditions, "good manners," and "well-bred way" of England; hence, the "mysterious prestige" that "clings round us" ("from the vicinity of Greenwich") despite sectional economic and political deprivations. "If we have nothing else," Newman continues, "we have *traditions* at least," and as such "we"—a pronoun Newman invariably uses in describing Southerners—"are far from likely to write in that *distressingly crude fashion which, apparently, is an inevitable characteristic of the middle-western author and the most distressing effect of the rise of the urban proletariat.*"[61] Such a conceptual binary between the stylish South and its continuously "English" traditions, on the one hand, and the urban-industrial Northeast and "raw" Middle West where "crude[ness]" and a "poverty of experience and of traditions are their ultimate characteristics," on the other, runs throughout Newman's *Constitution* essays. It is the regional framework and structuring set of anxieties that stand behind Newman's more general meditations on continuous "traditions" and "modern" style; it is the ideological and social space whose boundaries are threatened both by Northern interference and by its surreptitious assertion through Conrad; and, hence, there is little coincidence that "The New Carthaginians," a thoroughly sectionalist essay, clinches its case by referencing "some poor young [Southern] journalist who carries about with him . . . the blue-bound copies of Mr. Conrad's tenacious prose, or perhaps some conscientious library assistant weary with searching the shelves for descendants of Mr. Conrad."[62] Both are supreme examples of Southern distinctiveness gone absurdly awry not only through the "modern" clarion call of Mencken but also through the specific kind of Trojan-horse anti-traditionality for which Conrad, in this reading, stands.

But if "style"—or at least, the material and cultural conditions requisite to it—is what distinguishes the South from the "crude" and traditionless North and Middle West, the specific context in which many of Newman's essays actually appeared—on the editorial page of the *Constitution* (Atlanta), with its emphases on statewide business and politics—emphasizes that "style" was a matter of *internal* Southern social contestation and control as well. And it is here that the politics and Southern specificity of Newman's relationship to Conrad begin to defy all simple categorizations altogether: "modern" as opposed "traditional"; "critical" or "radical" as opposed to "conservative"; "regionalist" or "nativist" as opposed to "cosmopolitan." To be sure, unlike the straightforward and concrete discussions of the editorial page—of cotton, railways, race relations and state suffrage—Newman's rarefied conception of style comes from and in many respects lends itself quite naturally to a wide variety of mystifying Southern elitisms: i.e., the idea of "aristocracy" and its preservation and insulation as a social category; the disdain and disavowal of the "New Southerner," whose thoroughly bourgeois and capitalist character was in fact the historical condition of all Southern wealth; and the exclusion, erasure, and imagined domestication of even more marginalized class and racial groups. The curiosity of Newman's deployments of style, however, is that they consistently work against their own grain. It is not social exclusivity, for instance, but rather rigorous, empowered social inclusivity that offers up the basis for the immense cultural capital presupposed by Newman's conception of style in her important exchange with Hergesheimer. Challenging Hergesheimer's dismissive characterization of American women as earnestly overeager readers, Newman responds that of course women, like "all subject races, all emerging proletarians, show a more avid desire for education than do the lords of creation"; what matters—in a conceptual frame that collapses gender, race, and class—is that such marginalized groups receive *full* access to culture so that they may move "in another generation or two" from "the branches of culture" to a position of power and control at "its roots."[63] At the level of style, the implicit objection here against more "democratic" forms of narrative like those practiced on the editorial page or licensed by Conrad (which require no "special knowledge" in the reader) is not that they let too many people in but that they do so with insufficient cultural and social rigor.[64] Lest one think, moreover, that this is neither a serious nor a "Southern" argument, one may compare the central emphasis *The Hard-Boiled Virgin* places on literary knowledge and cultural capital as a means of feminist resistance against the punishing, imprisoning ideal of the Southern lady—and also the moment in *Dead Lovers* when we learn of Isabel Ramsay:

She always remembered her father's sufferings on the day when he wanted his words to scream out his horror of a state in which hundreds of young gentlemen from America's oldest state university could stand still and hear another human being scream out of the agony of a body which was burning a slow exit from a world that dozens of virgins' sons had lived and died to save.[65]

Mr. Ramsay was a newspaper editorialist; and his inability (as a matter of newspaper policy) to print the "horror" of Southern lynching, so clearly replicated by his daughter's imprisonment within an opaque and censorious labyrinth of (Southern, ladylike, polite) words, is framed by an ultimate opposition between (1) the unheard "agony" of Southern women, African Americans, and non-"gentle" classes alike, and (2) the power of those who gain their cultural capital and social authority from the "oldest state university" in the South, neutralized of any progressive force by sanitized, monadic, "democratic" newspapers.

This link between cultural acquisition and social power is directly reinforced, in even more immediately "Southern" terms, by the *collective and critical social intelligence* that Newman understands as perhaps the most crucial potentiality made available by style. Newman's novels are revealing here. Read for their thematics, both *The Hard-Boiled Virgin* and *Dead Lovers* conduct unsparing and comprehensive critiques of a certain "mind-space of the South"—white, female, upper class, urban: in the full context of its psychosocial production—whose relentless assault on the patriarchal South may seem difficult to square with any notion of "tradition." Read for their aesthetics, however, the two novels also suggest the degree to which style in Newman constitutes both a critique and a recovery of tradition: the degree to which, as Anne Goodwyn Jones incisively explains, "Newman's style, simultaneously innovative and conservative," serves as not only a critical agency of "but also a metonymy for the novels' social preoccupations as well as the protagonists' subjectivity."[66] Style, this is to say, *through its own critical relationship to itself,* evolves a peculiar and cumulative form of progressive Southern social intelligence—and this not simply because style is the native idiom of the privileged classes featured in Newman's novels, and hence a natural place to concentrate critical observations of that class. In addition, as we have already begun to see, style becomes a means of reflecting upon the South as an imagined, historical, political totality: its (style's) elaborateness (allusions, exclusions, infinite pains of phrase) is an expression of contextual and historical sensitivity; its "experienced mirror"[67] is not only the record of one's social interpellation but the opportunity and means to exercise critical acumen and social agency; its abstract, ironic, and comic proclivities are the very opposite of the South's dangerous racial, religious, and other fundamentalisms; and its mechanism presupposes a living, continuous cultural mechanism against which objections can be advanced and within which they can be integrated and preserved. In *The Hard-Boiled Virgin*, "style"—which is "more important than any subject"[68]—fundamentally means a "hard-boiled" (seared but also stimulated), "virginal" (seduced but also separate), *dialectical* relationship to the very Southern culture one cannot subsist without; it is the very *integration* of the intellectual and literary resources denied to Southern women within a cultural framework that becomes mastered by those resources that makes for the "style" of the novel. Similarly, in *Dead Lovers* Isabel Ramsay's drama is never one of attempting to "transcend" or "escape" patriarchal Southern culture; rather, it is the struggle to preserve "the hard little core of consciousness she had instead of a soul" *with respect to that culture*; it is the continual fear that "her memory was bleeding" or that "her whole mind" and "her whole memory had been cut across by a hot, jagged knife" when Charlton Cunningham enters the room; it is the persistent concern that "she could not go on enduring the consciousness of her own consciousness . . . cutting her mind and body into such ugly, heavy minutes."[69] Charlton Cunningham is the personification of patriarchal Southern culture—but so thoroughly enmeshed in both his wife's and his mistress's sense of subjectivity (the book is constructed to emphasize their uncanny sociopsychic positions) that if either simply attempted to abandon Charlton, "her mind and her memory would tear as helplessly as wet squares of paper." "Mind" and "memory" are critical and cumulative resources in Newman through which one preserves a dialectical, intelligent, informed, empowered relationship to that which, often threateningly, will always be a part of you:

But she was disturbed when her mind astonished something which she did not think was her mind, and which she called herself. And she was disturbed because her mind was able to look past its image of Charlton Cunningham, and because it could realize suddenly that writers of old-fashioned love-stories seem to punish a villainess for wanting the very things with which the writers are preparing to reward a heroine for not wanting them.[70]

Hence the *social* power of having *literary* resources at one's disposal. Style is neither the full ambit of aesthetic, social, and historical forces that have their seductive culmination in nor the critical and creative ability to "look past" the image of Charlton Cunningham; it is the ability to express both at the same time.

Such is the spirit of Newman's relationship to "tradition": thoroughly, even dangerously skeptical, yet tactically, unreservedly, inescapably committed. If one irony of this formulation is that a more Conradian combination of energies is difficult to imagine[71]—clearly the proximity of Conrad has much to do with Newman's aggressive repudiations of him—another irony is that notwithstanding Conrad's own partiality to the South *precisely because of its style*, Newman constructs Conrad as the supreme lure away from the cumulative/dialectical social intelligence Southern "style" makes possible. For if, unlike H. L. Mencken, a Southern writer recognizes that a "remarkably acute critical mind" presupposes a "distinguished critical style"; if, this is to say, "truly aesthetic judgments" must reflect maximal engagements with history, context, aesthetics, critical thought, and the social tradition one is working within; and if, to the contrary, "a man who writes with the brain of a provincial journalist also thinks with the brain of a provincial journalist" (not unlike the many "young intellectual" writers who proceed "with an exaggerated idea of their own [semantic and analytic] powers"), Conrad the Polish Siren makes it seem as if "style", its "elaborate preparations," and its enabling "traditions" are unnecessary.[72] His sui generis fiction caters—less in itself than for the U.S. Americans who catch his "disease"—to painfully naïve models of "original" and "radical" insight;[73] in addition, the fatalistic pessimism that pervades his fiction—when received and emulated by "gloomy young American writers" like Eugene O'Neill, for whom "gloom is their one link with greatness"[74]— encourages that solemn, hopeless, humorless profundity and vast insuperable systemic doom be made out of what is actually only the author's staggering critical, cultural, and imaginative deficiency. We learn in *The Hard-Boiled Virgin* of "certain great celebrated novelists" who fascinate by not "condescending to allow" "character" and "chance" their "small share in the union which becomes fate";[75] and similarly, of "Mr. Conrad with his tenacious prose," Newman argues elsewhere, "one may at least question whether he would be called a prince of prose if he did not find man's conscious existence of this planet an irreparable calamity": indeed, the fact that "Mr. Conrad considers man's conscious existence on this earth as a fundamental and irreparable mistake" is fundamental to his "bubonic" outbreak.[76] "It takes a very much cleverer man to be merry in print rather than gloomy," Newman continues; and it is not only in her commitment to making "joy" or "beauty" or "grace" or satire or any other form of socially productive knowledge from the *cumulative* foundations of the South that Newman's objections to Conrad arise.[77] It is also in the *agency* his fiction denies while also erasing the very traditions that both provoke and preserve such agency. As such, to catch the "germ" or "disease" of Conrad's "icy prose" is to be overwhelmed by a "suicidal and homicidal feeling": the suicidal part, Newman teases, is "no doubt connected with sad memories of the ocean, seas, and lakes on which one has been very ill, and of crews lifting themselves shudderingly from a very uneven sea."[78]

The "homicidal" part is more directly concerned with gender. Indeed, both Newman's violent seducer/destroyer preoccupation with Conrad and the second major rhetorical code through which it is expressed—the usurpation of reality (plural, autonomous) by textuality (male, narcissistic)—extend directly out of the concerns of authentic Southern female expression and of resistance to punitive, silencing constructions of white Southern womanhood that centrally animate Newman's novels. In her bull's-eye review of *Dead Lovers* that appeared in the *New York Tribune* in 1928, Isabel Patterson writes: "It will give offense. It is meant to. The head of its offending is that it shows women as autonomous emotional beings. No man could have written it. Most men will be unable to read it. It says a good many of the things men have tried by every social and economic device to avoid hearing."[79] So, too, Newman wrote her publisher of *The Hard-Boiled Virgin*: "I do think that it is the first novel in which a woman ever told the truth about how women feel"—an undertaking whose erotic disclosures and "pervasive and corrosive feminism," in Anne Firor Scott's felicitous phrase, led Vanderbilt Fugitive/Agrarian Donald Davidson to protest its "ugly whisperings of a repressed and naughty child," and Elmer Davis (of Atlanta) to describe every line in the book as "grounds for lynching, unless Georgia and the South at large have lost all their pristine vigor."[80] One may compare, moreover, precisely what Newman *does* in her two novels—namely, use subtle, elaborate, free indirect discourse directly to articulate a fullness of female subjectivity in corrosive and incriminating opposition to prolix patriarchy and its conventions of the Southern lady—against its categorical antithesis, as described in the essay recommending a law against Conrad's influence, in the homosocial web of self-ratifying patriarchal discourse that Newman traces emerging between the "tenacious" Conrad and the "tedious" books of his disciples.[81] First, "there is Brett Young," whose *Tragic Bride* may be easily diagnosed as "pure Conrad" given the book's predication on the "technical stunt" of "tell[ing] the highly psychological story of a hapless Irish beauty" while "not know[ing] one thing about her except what a haunting old gentleman and the jealous mother of one of the tragic damsel's admirers have been kind enough to tell the penman." Then there is William McFee, whose "taste for capable ladies" once resulted in the "really good" novel *The Casuals of the Sea*, which features, among other things, a number of genuinely "interesting" female characters, including "Mrs. Gaynor, almost the only American in English fiction who is more than a caricature." In those "good old days," "McFee had not yet abandoned his novelist-given birthright of being able to see right through his characters' bodies, brains, and hearts"—as Newman does in her novels (apropos of their use of free indirect discourse), and as Conrad, of course, does not as a matter of aesthetic signature in his "Marlow" stories, especially *Chance*, which because of its deeply and multiply psychologized (almost always by male storytelling voices) and irretrievably distanced female protagonist, is clearly of principal interest here. With *Aliens*, however, McFee "caught the Conradian germ" and begins to demonstrate a "well-developed but not necessarily fatal case for thought": one in which "he could not know anything that his narrator did not know about his people" while this garrulous "narrator knew not only what he saw, but what the man next door told him and what a cousin in England wrote him about the wicked and dashing brother of the man next door and what the children of this man told him." With the most recent *Captain Macedoine's Daughter*, a clear kindred of *Chance*, McFee's "apparently incurable malady has progressed to its crisis"; for this novel "can only be distinguished from the master" by its idiom and lapses in execution; and, as with Brett Young's novel, McFee's book is at its most Conradian not only in combining male storytelling superabundance—"there must be a good deal of leisure in a sea-faring life"—with a "beautiful" and "very romantic" female object of speculation, but also in ultimately "killing Artemisia off" for "no reason at all" other than the doomed and inconsequential fatality it is her purpose in the novel to illustrate.[82]

Newman, hence, objects to Conrad as the hypercontagious masculinist effacement of the very authentic and autonomous terms of female experience ("the truth about how women feel") that her novels set out centrally to express and recover. Propelled by their aura of pseudoprofundity and a glamorizing romantic fatalism whose effect is to silence both alternatives and alternative voices, Conrad's novels both incarnate—through their multiple male narrators—and incite—through Conrad's multiple male imitators—a web of homosocial, patriarchal discourse that is not the recovery but rather the heightened obliteration "of the things men have tried by every social and economic device to avoid hearing" from and about women. From "The Allegory of the Young

Intellectuals," this gendered concern has always underwritten—and, one re-calls, offers up the terms for expressing—Newman's aesthetic objections to genealogies of Conrad in the United States. Similarly, in "Herd Complex" the master conceptual codes that first generate Conrad as an overarching aesthetic villain—spectacularly bad and insular acts of *not* reading, narcissistic and phallogocentric usurpations of reality that pretend to *be* readings—substan-tially derive from and inscribe such feminist concerns. Indeed, the very politi-cal aesthetics of Newman's novels—wherein free indirect discourse (i.e., the "novelist-given birthright to see right through [her] characters' bodies, brains, and hearts") is used directly and critically to express female experience—simply must be understood, as a function of the cultural work performed by "Conrad" in the United States at the time, as in some measure a corrosive repudiation of the political aesthetics of Conrad's "Marlow" texts, whose dense masculine narrativity, in this reading, inscribes and perpetuates the prolix patriarchy it pretends to call "radically" into question.

All of these concerns, moreover, though not lacking in implications outside the South, are pointedly "Southern" in the sense not only that they are animated by and grounded in the political and cultural struggles of a specific Southern location, but that their application to Conrad is sculpted by the entire sphere of social concerns (racial, classed, gendered, antinationalist, anti-imperialist, etc.) through which Conrad was produced as a *sectional* phenomenon. Neither the intensity nor the distinctiveness of Newman's feminist response to Conrad can be understood, in other words, without considering the specific disciplinary culture of the white Southern lady from which it is advanced, the context of the *Constitution*'s (Atlanta) editorial page on which it was printed, the championing of the *Reviewer* as a "truly southern" organ in which Newman's most complex articulations of Conrad were expressed, and the various intersectional and in-trasectional issues intersecting with gender that made Conrad a locus of interest and controversy in the South after Mencken's "Sahara." All of which, finally, is to decode the last major code through which Newman attacks Conrad in the *Reviewer*—*national* abdication—as the *sectional* metonymy it really is. There is nothing in Newman's writings that suggests a political, social, or aesthetic/ cultural investment in the category of "nation" per se—as anything other than a provincial barrier to planetary currents of knowledge or a vulgar imperial-ist corrosive of the South's horrifically imperfect but nevertheless extant and usable cultural "traditions." Read carefully, autobiographically, alongside *The*

Hard-Boiled Virgin, "The Allegory of the Young Intellectuals" discloses that its anonymous heroine is actually Newman herself; and what's wrong with the tempting allure of Conrad in this context is not the loss of and failure to confront "the inevitability of literary nationality,"[83] but rather the loss of and failure to engage the total sphere and space of Southern relations that, as *The Hard-Boiled Virgin* and *Dead Lovers Are Faithful Lovers* insist, will always and inevitably require a Southern subject's dialectical resistance.

AXES OF CONTROVERSY

There could be nothing further, hence, from the *Double Dealer*'s proffering Conrad to reject *any* relationship between aesthetics and politics, and yet also nothing further from the specific kind of "documentary" political aesthetics (i.e., naturalism) that Southerners might associate with Conrad through comparisons with Dreiser, than the politically engaged aesthetics of "style" Newman champions through the repudiation of Conrad. Moreover, within the "truly Southern" context of the *Reviewer* itself, many contrary images of and appeals to Conrad appear. Newman's Conrad, for instance, is *in himself* very much the opposite of editor Emily Clark's Conrad. Whereas for Clark, Conrad is fundamentally a negative agent of cultural demystification through whose corrosive nexus native Southern tastes and habits may "sink into the background" and become replaced by the "thorough and complete" acquisition of a new cultural foundation,[84] for Newman Conrad is the epidemic perpetuation of the worst aspects of the old patriarchal Southern cultural foundation, and also the pyrotechnic obfuscation of and seduction away from any Southern grounding or cultural tools through which social demystification might be effected. Whereas Clark (following Mencken) constructs Conrad as the emblem of a new (Southern) aristocracy of "taste"—one whose "acquisition," beyond the usual capacities of "the mass of people," produces the "conscious and heart-warming knowledge that we are above the herd in one respect at least"[85]—Newman locates Conrad (in the same issue of the *Reviewer*, the rhetorical overlap is not a coincidence, it is a response) as the center of a "herd complex": not only a parody of aristocracy but one that does not even effect the rigorous, trenchant, empowering social goals of genuine democracy. Whereas Clark's Conrad is "epic" in the sense that his elaborate forms and the "super-cultivated taste"[86] that his fiction requires send the South on an odyssey with respect to the rediscovery and reinvention of the totality of its own social relations, Newman's Conrad is "epic" because of precisely the totalizing degree to which his *un*cultivated register and seductive distractions from native history threaten to keep the South exactly where it is.

Hunter Stagg's Conrad is "epic," however, because of the comprehensive totality of *literary* relations offered up by Conrad's fiction; and in fact, Stagg's Conrad, no less positioned by Southern concerns than Newman's or Clark's, exists in dialogic tension with them both. Unlike Newman, Stagg understands Conrad not as an antagonist but as a catalyst of feminist attention. When Newman criticizes *Captain Macedoine's Daughter* as a Conradian doppelganger of the South's prolix patriarchy, she is responding to the kind of review Stagg and Mary D. Street wrote of that novel recognizing it as "evidently" the product of McFee's being "steeped" in the "great stimulus" and "great work" of "that very great man" Conrad, and applauding the novel for its sensitive and penetrating portrait of Artemisia Macedoine, who "becomes for us one of the faces, the questioning unanswered faces, of the world itself."[87] Similarly, in a series of short essays in the *Reviewer* that begins with Newman praising Paul Morand for a "formula" that is the gendered, antiromantic reverse of Conrad—i.e., to "choose as model a lady . . . devoted to the doomed idea," then "tell her story in the same words that annihilate the idea"—Stagg responds with an essay praising Conrad generally as "phenomenal" beyond compare—and Conrad's *The Rover* in particular for the assiduous and effective degree to which it "gives you the girl" [Arlette] at the center of the story.[88] Unlike Newman and also like Clark, moreover, Stagg champions Conrad on intellectually progressive and socially transformative (and also ultimately elitist, but not on a "traditional" basis) grounds. In Stagg's view, the peculiar quality of Conrad's fiction—with respect to his characters and readers—lies in "Conrad's mergence with their moods for their elevation above the commonplace majority one simply does not see." This kind of "elevation"—both one of insight and of *conversion* of the commonplace, whose prejudices are checked and put under erasure—is the reason why, again as opposed to Newman, Stagg believes Conrad should be considered the "master steersman" of the "English speaking world" rather than its rudderless undoing.[89]

But Stagg's framework for understanding Conrad is actually ultimately closer to that of Newman than of Clark. Clark's Conrad, transposed to Southern circumstances, is essentially Mencken's Conrad, urged upon Southern circumstances; and the Conrad of both, thoroughly negative and corrosive in its terms, has no clearer expression than Hergesheimer's major essay in the *Reviewer* on the late U.S. (Southern, on his mother's side) novelist John Partins. Partins, Hergesheimer argues, making the kind of argument Mencken had put to much *national* cultural-political work in the preceding decade, was fundamentally an "aristocratic" literary talent and genius: both in the sense that his social background was highly privileged and in the sense that Partins writes in an "ironic mode" that is "by essence" indigenous to the "aristocratic . . . spirit." Partins' "special" gift of presenting an illusion he "apparently agreed with" only to "fill his audience first with a doubt and then with an absolute distaste for what he was proclaiming"; and Partins' unfailing capacity to leave his readers "absorbed" in "the subversive conclusion[s]" "the vast majority of humanity spends its time resolutely avoiding"—these "ironic" qualities unavoidably lead to the "ideal" analogy of Conrad:

> Joseph Conrad is an example of this—he has ideally the aristocratic genius. Mr. Conrad, to the vulgar mind, must seem a compound of hopeless bitterness and arbitrary ill nature. No one, in all his books, ever conquers the circumstances of living. In the end the men and women he writes of are secure in neither mind or body; and the rewards toward which the majority of men and novels strive he shows to be empty and cold. What his men and women struggle to do is not be victorious over surroundings but to conquer themselves. The ships his captains drive through catastrophes of storm are no more than figures of the lonely valor of spirits brave for the sake of that quality only. There are no peaceful harbors for those men, only a moment, perhaps, of accomplishment, of invincible courage, and then death.[90]

This is the "gloomy" fatalism Newman distrusts as (or at least as an inducement to) bad faith; but for Hergesheimer, as for Mencken and Clark, Conrad is, in a word, productively, destructively *above*. Looking down with perfectly "aristocratic" security and analytic immunity on the "great moral and spiritual spectacle" transpiring farcically beneath him, Conrad deploys his "spirit of irony" in a manner that, like Partins, "deals with an unfailing zest in today."[91] Conrad by no means avoids or reinforces or temporizes with the reigning social illusions of the day, whether they concern African imperialism or political "terror" or the patriarchal, racist, fundamentalist, and even "democratic" South. Rather, as Clark puts it, Conrad is in effect a "tremendous" and "difficult" "special" mechanism of "war": an agency and emblem of acid critical assault on "the indefinite pursuance of whatever one happens to be born liking"; a mechanism for the breaking up and "sinking into the background" of the South's native and nativist paradigms of belief and conduct.[92]

Stagg's Conrad, however, is neither above nor the negation of the objects of his scrutiny. Quite the contrary, Stagg's Conrad achieves "mastery over the mood of his reader" through "the gift of *subjecting* himself to the mood of [the character], the theme, the scene and the moment" privileged in any given portion of a Conrad text. Whereas Hergesheimer's Conrad (and Mencken's) is a creature of categorical elevation and endlessly severe ironic distance and dominance, and whereas Clark implicitly glosses her "self-satisfaction" in learning to read Conrad with the analogy of befriending "a difficult person whom almost no one else likes and who likes almost no one else," Stagg's Conrad "certainly . . . never writes of friendless people because he is a friend of them all"—and he is a friend of them all precisely through his willingness to become "*the slave of their scene*." The difference between these two Conrads—one, the ironic, the other, consummately submissive—is the difference between a Conrad whose "modern" propensities lie purely in the negation of cultural landscape, and one whose "modern" gift is rather that of fusion and rediscovery, of forging and reconstitution of elements within a cultural landscape that have become arbitrarily separated, segregated—hitherto unseen in relation to one another or considered incompatible, irreconcilably antagonistic. "What happen[s] when Conrad create[s]," Stagg argues, is

precisely what happens when any of us creates, *out of some one who had been about for years*, a figure never seen by us before and never seen by others at all: in other words, when out of an acquaintance we make a friend. Such creations are made, like Conrad's characters, in mergences, sudden or gradual, of mood, after which neither party to the chance intangible contact can ever appear the same to the other. And that similar wonders are daily performed by others upon the most (to us) impossible material is one of the mysteries of life.[93]

Apropos of Stagg's interest in African-American folk culture and also apropos of Stagg's use of metaphors of the "slave" to gloss *Conrad*—the "master" who cross-identifies with the impossibly opposite space of the slave—throughout his essay, Stagg's premise is that in Conrad there is a model for reengaging the South itself: for remaking and reforging its culture from the contact of hitherto "unfriendly" and untouchable pieces, black and white among others, that actually make for remarkably fecund resources *within* the South. The same cultural logic underwrites Gerald Johnson's outspoken essay "The Congo, Mr. Mencken," which, even though it does not mention Conrad, in its thesis that "the South is not [a] sterile . . . Sahara" but rather "the Congo of the Bozart" helps to explain why Conradian metaphors and models are of such interest in the *Reviewer*; for the proper management of the South's (cultural) resources, black and white, and in relation to the South's wider sociopolitical administration (including "horrors" like lynching), is always an underlying animation of Conrad's invocations in the magazine.[94]

All of the above writers, despite intense disagreements about the terms and value of Conrad, place Conrad as "modern." Each writer, in other words, coordinates the larger "modern" framing of Conrad in the *Reviewer* with the specific Southern priorities of the magazine, Conrad's power in this respect ultimately deriving from the multiple and mutable heterotopic interferences his fiction poses to traditional articulations of Southern boundary and structure. Overall, even when Conrad is being used to articulate a model of "mergence" and sympathy, he is consistently presumed as an externality of the South: a foreign agent to be inserted within or imitated by the South, but not in itself fundamentally indigenous or materially akin to the cultural history of the region. There are, however, occasional hints that blur this final point, anticipating alternative and more intimate "Southern" vantages with respect to Conrad. Ellen Glasgow, for instance, self-consciously assumes the place of *Heart of Darkness*'s Marlow, and adopts his strategy of gazing upon a prominent river in the present to contemplate the "dark" mysteries suggested by its past, when she situates her ruminative essay on Southern history in the *Reviewer* with the remark: "This thought came to me again last April, when I stood at Jamestown, and looked over the beautiful grave river, and felt the mystery and darkness that surrounded those dauntless pioneers."[95] Though the ultimate point of Glasgow's essay, very much apropos of her status as a sea-change figure in modern Southern fiction, is that the South must *not* continue to "live and brood" in the "dark" image of the past, this very dissociation effected through and from Conrad's novella—which Glasgow expressed lifelong admiration of, as she also expressed familiarity "with every book, and almost every line" her friend Conrad wrote—*presupposes* a latent similarity.[96] The "burden" of Southern history could not be disavowed so evocatively through *Heart of Darkness* (itself rewritten and disavowed in the process) were there not vital tactile links between the racial, historical, and imperialist significance of the Jamestown River Glasgow gazes on and the Thames, with the Congo River conceptually attached, that Marlow gazes on. This same sense of latent intimacy—strikingly felt, if not clearly expressed or even understood—between Conrad and the cultural-material South appears at the end of John Bennett's impressionistic piece "Grotesque Old Charleston," whose climactic passage has the unmistakable ring of the "Eastern" epiphany at the end of Conrad's "Youth":

One suddenly gets the startling notion of a common summer's day that somehow, suddenly, time and place are nothing, geography of no account, that the whole earth is transformed. One hears, as in a fantastic dream, a strange, high-keyed fredonnement like the shrill hum of insects, the shuffling stamp of a girl's dancing feet, and the hollow reverberations of the sallow palms which base the passionate, lazy, ecstasy of the dance. And, turning in the alleyway, one finds himself face to face with the glamour and mystery of the East. . . . Everywhere the pathetic beauty and faded grace speak more of Malabar than on anything western. . . . The nightwind whispers, "Bombay!"[97]

This is Charleston, South Carolina, one recalls; and for Bennett to put the matter in this transparently Conradian way is, indeed, to make "time and place . . . nothing, geography of no account": to "transform" "the whole earth" by replacing, reimagining, one of the oldest citadels of the hyperboundaried South as an expression *of* the other, in its most globally reaching and racially and culturally alteritous aspects of continuity and relation. The vision, the "fantastic dream," here is advanced only and overwhelmingly at the level of "impressionist" aesthetics—yet the heterotopic prism of Conrad does its "modern" work through at least the intuition, the phantasm, of Southern intimacy.

We are approaching a second "Southern" pole of conceiving Conrad—but first let us quickly confirm that both the *Double Dealer* (New Orleans) and *All's Well* (Fayetteville, Arkansas) conform to the basic patterns of *plural externality* observable in the *Reviewer*. Originally Mencken's greatest enthusiasm among Southern little magazines, the *Double Dealer* assumes from its outset sufficient knowledge of Conrad to be able to say in a memorial piece on James Gibbons Huneker in March 1921 that "the fascinating playboy of the arts who kept nine muses guessing has checked out of this 'garish unrestful hotel'"[98]—without mentioning that the quotation comes from *Victory*. With the publication of the second volume of the *Double Dealer* in July 1921, moreover, the magazine briefly changed its subtitle to the regionally specific "A

National Magazine from the South"; provisionally focused its attention on engaging Southern culture and providing a "medium for Southern writers and readers";[99] and, in the process of being heavily advised by Mencken in each of these matters, came under the influential sign of Conrad as well. The manifesto editorial "A National Magazine from the South" is followed by a squarely Menckenite appeal to Conrad: "Joseph Conrad speaks in his last book of the illiterate (that is the ordinary man, you or me) '. . . who even from the dreadful wisdom of their evoked dead have so far culled nothing but inanities and platitudes.' . . . We need tearers-down, clearers-of-the-ground. We need liberation from the iron rule of the dead hand."[100] As did the Glasgow essay published in the *Reviewer* a few months earlier, this editorial uses *Heart of Darkness* to advocate a complete break with the Southern past, albeit through the very different (and fundamentally abstract) strategy of generating primitivizing tropes to malign Southern pretenses to "civilization": "Scratch a taxpayer and you have a Tahitian; a senator a Senegambian. . . . [Our] world of affairs is cluttered with dead men's ideals and dreams. We refuse to look into the heart of the problem at all."[101] These are the months leading to the claim in April 1922 that "a novel by Joseph Conrad seems to us more darkly significant to human life than the result of a gubernatorial primary"; these words are both a radical renunciation of politics and an affirmation to resist a cultural stranglehold that effectively neutralizes politics (this contradiction is fundamental to the *Double Dealer* in this moment); and throughout these months, one finds Conrad presented through the general template of the *Reviewer*: as a variously corrosive and corrective figure of U.S./Southern culture;[102] as a figure of "modern" contemplation and contention;[103] and as an overwhelmingly presumptive Southern externality—with the one possible exception of Charles J. Finger's short imitation of *Heart of Darkness* entitled "A Very Satisfactory God," in which a Marlovian narrator orally recounts his venture into the "heart" of South America, where a black U.S. Southerner has assumed dangerous godlike control over a native village.[104] *After* mid-1922, when the *Double Dealer*'s priorities shift to the avant-garde and cosmopolitan ambitions of metropolitan little magazines generally, and when Mencken's interest in the magazine wanes as a consequence, Conrad's presence in the *Reviewer* declines as well. Though not disappearing entirely, Conrad is increasingly proffered through reactionary constructions of the "modern," or in terms much more analogous to Mencken's twilight, "old-fashioned," superannuated Southern "aristocracy" than the "superior" Nietzschean image he cut in the *Double Dealer*'s pages in 1921 and 1922.[105] Overall, Conrad loses his sense of contemporary urgency, contextual vitality, disruptive edge. As much as the *Reviewer*, the *Double Dealer* perfectly instantiates the proposition that Conrad is fundamentally of interest in the Southern little magazines insofar as he is fundamentally a "Southern" interest *of* those magazines.

This point may be finally confirmed by brief mention of Charles Finger's magazine *All's Well, or the Mirror Repolished*—brief precisely because this remarkable magazine, though published in Arkansas and written by one of the more exceptional minor figures of this period, does not assume a regional focus and consequently only sporadically references Conrad, and never, in this magazine, as part of the Southern aesthetic and political counterpoint of Conrad we've been tracing to this point. Nevertheless, the rugged, world-traveled wanderer Finger, a friend of Conrad's friend Cunninghame Graham and the spouse of the editor of a 1925 edition of Conrad's and Ford's *The Inheritors*, was as deeply committed a Conradian as they come. In August 1924, on the occasion of Conrad's death, Finger organizes an entire issue of *All's Well* in terms of the significance and thematics of Conrad, beginning with an extensive, very personal article on the passing of a "giant," "one of the great figures of world literature" and someone who, in "slash[ing] his way out of the labyrinth of conventions" and helping "America" out of its "forest of ignorance," made "priceless contributions to the treasury of literature."[106] The cover of this issue presents the poem "Ulysses" as a tribute to and figural tombstone for the poet and sailor commemorated inside (Figure 9). It is not a lack of love that precludes more discussion of Conrad in *All's Well*; it is a lack of Southern discord, animation, heterotopic interference.

OUR AGRARIAN

At about the same time Conrad was reaching his peak interest in the Menckenite Southern literary magazines, John Crowe Ransom, the unofficial leader of the group of poets at Vanderbilt University who called themselves Fugitives, four of whom would soon compose the core of the conservative Vanderbilt Agrarians, began writing a poem that as a mature poet he would look back on as his "first poem," "the first made by my present Self."[107] Below is the original version of "Conrad at Twilight," which appeared in the *Fugitive* in July 1923. Ransom would revise this poem under several titles—"Conrad

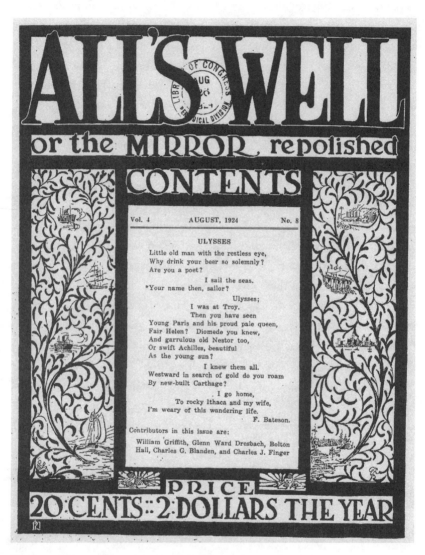

FIGURE 9. Joseph Conrad RIP, cover of *All's Well*, August 1924.

in Twilight" (1923), "Conrad Sits in Twilight" (1945), "Master's in the Garden Again" (1962)—throughout his life:

Conrad, Conrad, aren't you old
To sit so late in your mouldy garden?
And I think Conrad knows it well,
Nursing his knees, too rheumy and cold
To warm the wraith of a Forest of Arden.

Neuralgia in the back of his neck,
His lung filling with such miasma,
His feet dripping in leafage and muck:
Conrad! you've forgotten asthma!

Conrad's house has thick red walls
And chips on Conrad's hearth are blazing,
Slippers and pipe and tea are served,
Butter and toast, Conrad, are pleasing!
Still Conrad's back is not uncurved
And here's an autumn on him, teasing.

Autumn days in our section
Are the most used-up thing on earth
(Or in the water under the earth),
Having no more colour nor predilection
Than cornstalks too wet for the fire,
A ribbon rotting on the byre,
A man's face as weathered as straw
By the summer's flare and the winter's flaw.[108]

As Ransom later noted, he chose the name "Conrad" for this poem "in the earlier 1920's because it had been the pen-name of a brooding and intellectual Pole who wrote novels."[109] "Conrad in Twilight," moreover, is a quintessentially Ransomian poem of this period, its lightly teasing tone and jocular diction and sound play ("muck," "butter and toast," "miasma"/"asthma") offering the dispassionate ironic medium through which the very serious emotional concerns of impending death and an utterly indifferent universe—"twilight" in the Ransom lexicon is another permutation of the "shadow-line" for Conrad—are whipped into objectivized shape. The poem's invocation of Conrad, furthermore, is not without historical specificity and significance. First printed two months after Conrad's U.S. visit (during much of which Conrad was ill), the poem blends into its larger vision a sense of twilight and shadow-line by which many U.S. Americans were personally haunted by Conrad: the discrepancy between the almost miraculously romantic nature of his fiction, persona, and their implied sense of possibility, and the nagging sense, reinforced by Conrad's fading health, that his "Forest of Arden" charms were doomed to superannuation and extinction in the much more prosaic, faithless, industrialized wasteland of the contemporary world. But what we must emphasize here, of course, is that Ransom associates this "autumnal" sense of Conrad with not the world or country but rather "our section." Unlike the presumptively alien Conrad of the South's Menckenite literary magazines, Ransom's Conrad is not only *not*, as a matter of his aging person or his shadow-line preoccupied fiction, an externality to the concerns and terms of the agonized modern South; he is also quite familiarly and sympathetically—"Conrad, Conrad!"—"one of us."

Ransom's poem is thus an aperture to a second U.S. Southern pole of conceiving Conrad, one centered in Vanderbilt's more conservative circles and premised on engaging Conrad not as a critical externality but as a *sympathetic internality*: as a site of almost indigenous intimacy and profound interior kinship with, and harmonizing, healing, suturing relationship to, traditionalist cultures and conceptions of the South. Though Ransom was himself, despite acute insight into and much teaching of Conrad, only a secondary figure in the Vanderbilt machinery of Conrad, he did introduce Conrad to the two Fugitive/Agrarians who would become its principals: Donald Davidson and Robert Penn Warren. If both Davidson and Warren are remarkable for, like Ransom, understanding Conrad in conceptual and dialogic opposition to all the myriad "external" and "modern" oppositional constructions of Conrad advanced in the *Reviewer*, the two are also remarkable for *in themselves* composing a dyadic and dialogic opposition: each reading Conrad in light of the extreme antithetical poles he would come aesthetically and politically to occupy *within* the Vanderbilt group. This is, of course, to be expected: as we have already observed in different domains, Conrad's production as a figure of U.S. literary mastery—nationally, internationally, now regionally—assumes infinite subeconomies of ideological fracture whose collective remnants Conrad is curiously able to both mobilize and neutralize; the resulting dialogue itself is the engine of Conrad's "mastery."

Donald Davidson, though central to and often described as the "dean" of the Vanderbilt group in all its incarnations, was actually a ruggedly self-made, self-supporting, temperamentally alienated and brooding figure,[110] one who became attracted to Conrad for many reasons and with the extreme commitment and partisanship he would later bring to his unwavering reactionary defenses of Southern tradition, sectional distinction, racial segregation, and Confederate mythic ideology. Davidson first came to Conrad through an elaborate master's thesis—well over one hundred pages, addressing all of Conrad's works to that point—which he wrote under Ransom's direction at Vanderbilt from 1920 to 1922. Davidson published a condensed version of this thesis, the essay "Joseph Conrad's Directed Indirections," in the *Sewanee Review* in 1925; a surviving long typed lecture, heavily augmented with clippings and annotations made over time, makes clear that Davidson taught Conrad frequently, passionately, polemically at Vanderbilt during the next several decades; and various later Davidson works, academic/literary and political/polemical, contain sprinkled references to Conrad confirming his continued and commingled interest. Davidson was also the editor (from February 4, 1924, to November 30, 1930) of what has not implausibly been described as "the best literary page ever published in the South"[111]—the Book Review and Literary Page of the *Nashville Tennessean*—and among Conrad's many appearances on this page, not one of which is included in the volume that most substantially collects Davidson's writings from this page, is the inaugural installment, in which the Book Review and Literary Page introduces itself quite literally *under* the master sign of Conrad (Figure 10). At the top of the page dead center, under the heading "No Typewriter for Joseph!", is a reproduction of a manuscript page of Conrad's *The Rover*; and to the top left, Davidson's lead article celebrates *The Rover* and Conrad's "achievement" generally:

The achievement has continued through these 30 years without a break. In his list of 22 volumes, which does not include his collaborations with Ford Madox Ford, there is not a single weak book, not a single cheap book, not a single experiment that is not also achievement. It is an amazing record. One reflects that, whatever Conrad may or may not have imbibed of the "English Tradition," he has at least the English quality of productivity, the faculty of repeating again and again a masterly performance in a way that puts to shame our often skimpy American writers. He stands among the four or five great novelists of the day, meeting the test of both quality and quantity.[112]

The Tennessean's Book Review And Literary Page

Conducted By Donald Davidson

"The Rover," Conrad's Twenty-Third Volume, Ranks With Predecessors

All Regular Conrad Constituents Present in New Work of Great Stylist and Psychologist.

EGOISTIC CANON NEATLY SCALPED BY MAY SINCLAIR

"A Cure of Souls" Study of Comfortable Clergyman

No Typewriter for Joseph!

QUANTITY TEST ADDS TO WORTH OF MISS MILLAY

Still Foremost Among Lyric Poets Of Country

Rockefeller's Ideas for Solving Industrial Problems Advanced

New Spirit in Relationship Between Capital and Labor Urged in Book by John D., Jr.

JOHN D. ROCKEFELLER, JR.

"Great Open Space" Still Theme Of Zane Grey in Newest Novel

Romance of King Tut's Tomb Revealed in Discoverer's Book

South Carolina Poets

Latest Books

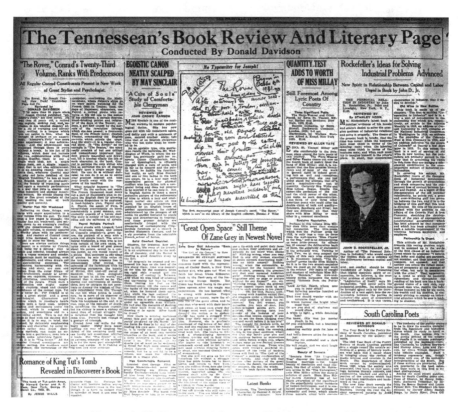

FIGURE 10. The *Nashville Tennessean*'s inaugural book review and literary page. At the bottom of this newspaper page (not shown here) is a small box entitled "By Way of Introduction."

FIGURE 11 (opposite). Text of Donald Davidson's review of Conrad's *The Rover* from the *Nashville Tennessean*.

"The Rover," Conrad's Twenty-Third Volume Ranks With Predecessors

All Regular Conrad Constituents Present in New Work of Great Stylist and Psychologist

T'IS more than 30 years since Joseph Conrad published "Almayer's Folly," his first novel. He was then 33 years old, a retired sea captain, seeking rest and seclusion in his adopted country after a life of voyaging and adventure; writing, in a tongue which was not native to him, what he thought of perhaps as an experiment. "Almayer's Folly" was more than experiment; it was achievement. And the achievement has continued through these 30 years without a break. In his list of 22 volumes, which does not include the two collaborations with Ford Madox Hueffer, there is not a single weak book, not a single cheap book, not a single experiment that is not also achievement. It is an amazing record. One reflects that, whatever Conrad may or may not have imbibed of the "English Tradition," he has at least the English quality of productivity, the faculty of repeating again and again a masterly performance in a way that puts to shame our often tentative and skimpy American writers. He stands among the four or five great novelists of the day, meeting the test of both quality and quantity.

Master Has Not Weakened

Reflecting on these things, one turns with eager expectation to a new volume from his pen. To read even a few pages is enough; the master has not weakened; one settles down to an evening's reading with the consciousness that this, the 23rd volume, is already assured a worthy place with its predecessors. And readers of Conrad (may their tribe increase) have a new delight in store for them.

There are always certain things to expect in a volume by Conrad. One looks for a setting that is exotic and colorful, touched always with a vague mystery and wonder. Happenings must be exciting, even melodramatic, and often drawn out to excruciating suspense. The characters, harmonizing with the setting and story, are men and women from the outer fringe of life--freebooters, moody or adventurous sea captains, outcasts, Malay chieftains, anarchists, daughters of the jungle. From such a combination one might expect sheer claptrap, blood and thunder melodrama of the rawest type. Yet it is never so. For Conrad is at once a great stylist and a great psychologist. Characters and events which in another's hands might take a lurid cast, acquire dignity and seriousness under his method, which is original and unique, and sometimes odd to a provoking extent. This is not the place to deal with his devices. Sufficient it is to say, in brief, that Conrad, by delicately emphasizing motive and character, by using indirect rather than direct slambang methods, can make an ex-pirate into a gentleman, even into a tragic, noble admirable figure.

So it is in "The Rover." All the regular Conrad constituents are there: setting, the southern coast of France, the farmhouse of Escampobar, overlooking the Mediterranean, where Nelson's ships go on wary patrol, watching for the French fleet in Toulon; time, the days of Napoleon; characters, one Peyrol, a retired pirate who returns in old age to the scenes of his childhood; a certain Scevola, blood-drinking patriot and informer of the days of the Terror; Arlette, a girl half crazed by the horrors of the revolution through which she has passed; a lieutenant Real, of the French navy; Captain Vincent, commanding the English corvette which patrols the coast. And the story--it is a regular Conrad story. In "The Rover," as for example in "The Rescue," the story really consists of but one critical and tremendously important incident, greatly magnified and drawn out, till it touches vitally the life of each character in the book. Conrad is perhaps the only writer who has so perfected the art of playing daringly upon a single major incident. He can do it without dullness; he can do it so as to excite your greatest interest and take your breath away with the suspense of his handling.

What actually happens in "The Rover"? On the surface, not much. The French lieutenant must carry out a part of Napoleon's plan to deceive the English fleet by allowing fictitious dispatches to be captured. A land-lubber's plan, Peyrol calls it. Peyrol, the agent of Fate, is nevertheless conveniently on hand, conveniently a great seaman, conveniently capable of a heroic deed. The story is mainly of his self-sacrifice and the salvation of Arlette.

Peyrol Notable Portrait

Peyrol stands with Lingard, Lord Jim, Nostromo, Heyst, and others of Conrad's creation--a great figure, the portrait of a man with a noble and simple heart. The whitehaired freebooter, a man who is not even certain of his own name, returns with a hoard of gold pieces about his person, sewed in a canvas jacket, as one would expect of a pirate. But, contrary to our ideas of pirates, he sets little value on the treasure. His treasure lies in contentment after roving, the calmness of the farmhouse with its mysterious occupants, the loyalty of Michel, that cast-off parcel of mankind, who, since somebody must be last in the world, was content that it should be he. The alarms and excitements of revolutions, love or intrigue do not penetrate or dismay the wisdom of Peyrol's detachment from life. Though he can act when action is necessary, he is more an observer of life than a participant in life. He finds his happiness at the end. It is true, even in the moment of death, in outwitting the English captain, but his victory is more a victory of mood than of actual struggle. He is delighted that his thought has come true. Peyrol's last voyage is a gesture of triumph.

Conrad does not write for the hasty reader. Many have found baffling his way of tangling the thread of his narrative until one can hardly tell sometimes whither it leads. But "The Rover" is not an extreme example of his method. It is for the most part straightforward and simple. It is Conrad at his best and most readable.

Such praise—the zeal of Mencken from the anti-Mencken—is complemented by even stronger language and an even more remarkable claim in the
Tennessean piece Davidson wrote when Conrad died:

There is [in Conrad] power of narration unsurpassed in English literature. There is in
his works a gallery of great human characters that no reader can ever forget. . . . His
work is highly individual, and his methods will hardly be copied by others. But his place
will be great. His work is lasting. And some day, perhaps, to later generations, Joseph
Conrad will stand as the first great figure in a new literature that has become international rather than national in character. Not England, not Poland, but the whole world
may justly claim Joseph Conrad.[113]

How is that the most reactionary figure of the Vanderbilt circle—a sectionalist, isolationist, and, in Theodore Hornberger's phrase of 1960, "the leading
proponent of literary regionalism in our time"[114]—would come to and persist
in such consummate admiration for the endlessly "roving," progenitively "international" Conrad? Davidson's master's thesis and *Sewanee Review* essay,
though these works appear to date from the period before Davidson's sectionalist convictions become solidified, hold much of the answer in incipient form.
Ostensibly, these two works turn on the purely technical claim that Conrad's
fiction practices an "inversive method": a "daring disregard of chronological
order in narrative" that, executed by Conrad in different ways, releases the
reader from "too great an absorption in moments" so that the reader may contemplate, against the racing flow of events, the "inner forces" that underlie and
the larger "significance of the human situation" one may locate in the course
of "history."[115] Conrad's various scramblings of chronology draw attention to
"the significance rather than the sequence of events"; they prepare the reader
"to intellectualize episodes more or less"; and all in all, they make for a "conflict between mood and chronology" that displaces the "history of fiction" as
mere forward movement—"the suspense of mere melodrama," the simple and
"animal" race of "rapid, thrilling narrative"—with an emphasis on the "unique"
"spirit" by which the artist and reader may find understanding and meaning in
life by writing and reading against the flow of time.[116] As I hope this description
suggests, Davidson's readings of how one Conrad text after another is amenable
to "inversive" technical description is far less tedious than it should be, in part
because Davidson writes in pellucid, alert prose that insists on evolving and
permuting its vocabulary,[117] but also because this very pungency of language

is evidently the product of a deeply searching, not-quite-conscious substantive political impulse. Far from an exercise in mere formalistic and technical acrobatics, Davidson's essay *thinks* it is praising Conrad for releasing the reader from the trivialities of "suspense" (plot, action) when what it is actually expressing is the joy of being caught up in a state of suspension with respect to the past, *against* the flow of modern events. Conrad's "directed indirections," this is to say, are not indirections at all: they are quite clearly directions and a directive to look backward, to resist the momentum of (U.S. Southern) modernity. Even more, they encourage this resistance project to recognize itself in intellectualizing, spiritualizing, and moralizing terms. Conrad's "inversions" make looking backward and looking for meaning into the same question.

Davidson's early "technical" writings on Conrad thus perfectly anticipate the many variations on the lecture "Joseph Conrad and the Vision of His Youth" that Davidson would give at Vanderbilt over the next several decades: the fundamental ideological project of which is to locate in and vindicate through Conrad a backward-looking, spiritually redeeming analogue of conservative Southern traditionalism. For Davidson, ironically like Mencken, "Youth" is a touchstone Conrad text. But whereas for Mencken the *Judea*'s impossible voyage—"You fight work, sweat, nearly kill yourself, sometimes do kill yourself, trying to accomplish something—and you can't" (*YOS* 4)—expresses the doomed exile that is and the false crusades that misconceive and misrepresent human experience, Davidson—sounding curiously like Edward Said, and not for the first time—understands "Youth" as the story of the *value* of stubborn and inexorable commitment to a Lost Cause.[118] Observing that "Youth" ends with the older Marlow affirming his "looking still, looking always, for something out of life" (*YOS* 44), Davidson—leaning implicitly on Conrad's own formulation in the "Familiar Preface" to *A Personal Record*,[119] recovering a wartime locution of Conrad but to different ends—argues that if "we seek to find that 'something out of life' which Conrad sought," "we shall find it, I believe, chiefly in the word *fidelity*."[120] With the determination with which he had once exhaustively anatomized Conrad's formal "inversions," Davidson now surveys the course of Conrad's fiction as a pragmatic series of lessons concerning the value of fidelity to past traditions: that "the 'something out of life' is always attained by looking backward"; that "ethical fibre" depends on "allegiance to solid abiding principles . . . that are a matter of loyalties and fatalism"; that fidelity itself constitutes "a faculty which brings

[one] to sorrow as often as not, but which leaves [one] with so magnificent an equipment of courage that he falls thundering when he does fall and gloriously shakes the globe, as with the fall of a Titan."[121] We can see here, though in blemished fashion, just how right Zdzisław Najder is to emphasize ethical codes of "honor" that unite the Polish Conrad's and much of modern Southern fiction.[122] Moreover, frequently referencing the struggles of postpartition Poland against "the harshness of Tzarist rule,"[123] Davidson reads all of Conrad's fiction and much of his life in terms of fidelity to infinitely embattled but ultimately humanizing and redemptive personal and cultural projects. *Almayer's Folly*—the title of which literally refers to an incomplete, always-already doomed house, much like Sutpen's in *Absalom, Absalom!*—becomes a tale of Almayer's heroic commitment to a dream which Davidson cannot see that the text itself considers a folly. Conrad's authorship of *Almayer's Folly*, moreover, which took many years and involved the text being transported through numerous hazards and world circumstances (including the Congo), similarly becomes an allegory of commitment to a cause opposed by the very materiality of the world itself. *Heart of Darkness* is a story of Kurtz's *loss* of fidelity to European traditions, the opposite of which include Nostromo, who remains faithful in social conduct despite his personal corruption by capitalism; Lena and Heyst in *Victory*, who vindicate fidelity to one another even in the hopeless circumstances that imply their death; and Conrad's father, the "active patriot" in Poland who cherished Polish traditions and "endured with no cowardly resignation the harshness of Tzarist rule."[124]

For Davidson, of course, this general championing of fidelity as a humanizing, purposive, heroic, and moral project, no matter how doomed the outcome, services a specific defense of Southern agrarian and mythic traditions as a means of fending off the debasing incursions of Northern-style materialism, capitalism, industrialization, urbanization.[125] And just as Davidson's Conrad falls very much in line with the antimodern, anti-Northern substantive priorities of Southern tradition and its (never sufficiently) Lost Cause, so, too, this Conrad also licenses the racial phobias inextricably enmeshed within this Southern tradition. Part of what Almayer, whose most "crushing blow" is his daughter's decision to marry a Malay chieftain, is demonstrating fidelity *to* is his "white pride": "His daughter goes because he is powerless to prevent it. But she does not go with his forgiveness. . . . [His] is the story of a lonely and tortured fidelity, a white man's battle fought and lost by a remote river in a savage land."[126] Similarly, Kurtz's "meetings and struggles with death or shame in the African jungle" that comprise the undoing of his "fidelity" certainly involve his infidelity (he has a fiancée) with an African mistress and his very negation of the idea of racialized segregation. Finally, in *The Nigger of the "Narcissus,"* the struggles of white fidelity against the rising tide of color are "ironically" dramatized in what is for Davidson clearly the upside-down story of "a worthless, dying negro [who] gets a complete hold on the ship's crew until he becomes the most important person on board."[127]

Such racism, and the deeply uncritical "moral" sense of tradition with which it is entwined, is precisely the reverse of the self-critical ethical Southern tradition championed by Frances Newman, who nevertheless hated Conrad and whom Davidson explicitly uses Conrad to attack.[128] Davidson's reading of Conrad by his own "traditional" lights, moreover, has one final twist, which emerges most powerfully in a moment when Davidson comes closest simply to declaring that Conrad is, mutatis mutandis, a veritable archetype of his conservative Southern program. Having already suggested historical parallels between the struggles of Poland and the South, both the proud objects of external invasion, defeat, and colonial subordination, Davidson summarizes his understanding of "fidelity" by quoting a sentence from "Prince Roman," Conrad's only tale that explicitly and focally concerns either Poland or its feats of patriotic subsistence and resistance:

It requires a certain greatness of soul to interpret patriotism worthily—or else a sincerity of feeling denied to the vulgar refinement of modern thought which cannot understand *the august simplicity of a sentiment proceeding from the very nature of things and men.*[129]

In part, the significance of this statement derives from Davidson's immediate gloss of it: "Patriotism is, of course, a kind of fidelity rather out of fashion in these days of internationalism."[130] The Davidson who champions Conrad in the *Tennessean* in 1924 as the progenitor of "a new literature that has become international rather than national in character" thus never really means to suggest Conrad as a figure of postnational cosmopolitanism: Davidson's Conrad rather confirms a kind of nationalism that is transnationally applicable.

But the greater significance of the above quotation concerns the specific *style* of national imagining that Davidson perceives in Conrad—and whose principles of "patriotism" he is ultimately applying, of course, not to a nation at all but rather to the South. Quite unlike most of his elitist friends in the Vanderbilt group, Davidson took the job as editor of the *Tennessean*'s Book Review page precisely because he relished the opportunity to participate in a broad Southern public forum: to speak in a language and to people not of cultivated exclusion but rather of "the very nature of things and men" generally. Likewise, unlike Tate's and Ransom's abstract and esoteric attractions to religion, a subject that bored and "repelled" Davidson generally;[131] and equally unlike the pre- and postconversion T. S. Eliot, whose notion of "tradition" centrally involves elaborate arrays of intellectualized constraint for shackling the sinful human soul, Davidson abjures all such "vulgar refinement of modern thought"—a phrase Davidson repeats three times, and for this reason—and embraces instead a "patriotic" conception of tradition that turns on the glorious expression of the "sincerity of feeling" and "august simplicity" of the "sentiments" of the general run of "things and men." Two points are important here. The first is that Davidson is in some sense a genuine democrat—a man whose sense of tradition prioritizes (at least within its own race-blind self-conception) application and availability to all—and so, too, is his Conrad. One may compare Davidson's commitment to *teaching* his popular Southern audience, to helping the South at large to "explore its own mind and rediscover itself," to his description of Conrad in the *Tennessean*: "Remember that Conrad never 'writes down' to the cheap and popular level. He demands intelligence of his readers. And if you will learn his ways; if you will read not one but several books; if you will bring to your reading an open and attentive mind—you will finally get the rare flavor of his style, and you will love him all the more because he is different."[132] (How very different from Newman's contention that precisely because there is no "specialised knowledge" required as a barrier to reading Conrad, nothing can be learned from him; how equally different from Emily Clark's and Mencken's presumptions that there must be a "herd" from whom readers of Conrad must be distinguished.) The second point is that Davidson's conception of tradition is not critical but *epic* and *heroic*—about learning the political and historical myths of the past so as to live and love living them, and in *living* as such provide the raw material for further myths contributing to the "traditional" continuum—and so too is Davidson's Conrad "epic." Painfully incapable of addressing the inequities of race, gender, class, and really any form of nonnormativity whose inequality "tradition" freezes and elides, Davidson nevertheless coherently—and in an important sense correctly—understands his Conrad as an "epic" Conrad who writes the myths of "august simplicity" that found and reproduce the social body:

Fidelity is the keystone of his art. Fidelity comes to his lips as naturally as to these elder men of action and contemplation—the bards who made our race epics. There is something in him of their epic insistence on human fundamentals. Like that olden seafarer, Beowulf, he is a servant of the mysterious Wyrd that rules men's lives. . . . He rejoices in the grandeur of men's deeds, even when men and deeds and motives are most obscure. . . . Fidelity becomes in Conrad's case a philosophy of life—the one absolute necessity in human affairs.[133]

There is no coincidence that Davidson ends his lecture with a long passage from *Lord Jim*: a novel whose very structure is that of converting the life quandaries of its first half (the *Patna* chapters) into the epic myth of the second (the Patusan chapters). Davidson is, indeed, something of the "Lord" Jim, or rather Captain MacWhirr, or U.S. Southern Conradians. Precisely because of the tenacious ("romantic") simplicity of Davidson's relation to authorizing scripts, or rather, the dogged lack of imagination through which Davidson refuses to see the complexities of both Conrad and the world around him, Davidson is ultimately able to thrive so successfully, so steadily, so fortuitously, and actually quite profitably, in waters significantly beyond his range and depth. Davidson's Conrad is heterotopic, to put this another way, because of the amazing difficulty and conceptual energy actually involved in placing the South through *Patusan* and *not* experiencing any shift or disruption of Southern boundary.

Robert Penn Warren is the Marlow to Davidson's MacWhirr.[134] Discovering Conrad through the prism of "illusions" and romance in his "youth," Warren evolves through Conrad a lifelong pattern of thinking that is the contemplative, gradualist undoing of both Davidson's traditionalism and Vanderbilt conservatism generally. In the process he becomes one of the very finest readers of Conrad—Southern, U.S. American, or otherwise—in the twentieth century. Though Warren may have written an essay on *Lord Jim* in high school,[135] the first evidence of his contact with Conrad that I have been able to verify is an undergraduate term paper Warren wrote for Ransom with the help of Davidson at Vanderbilt in August 1924.[136] The paper is entitled "Joseph Conrad: Master of Illusion," and in discussing Conrad's emphasis on the "necessity of illusion," Warren draws particular attention to the famous passage in *Heart of Darkness* we have seen before in which Marlow speaks of the "redeem[ing]" power of the "idea":

The conquest of the earth, which mostly means the taking it away from those who have a different skin complexion or slightly flatter noses than ourselves is not a pretty thing when you look into it much. What redeems it is the idea only. An idea at the back of it; not a sentimental pretence but an idea; and an unselfish belief in the idea—something you can set up, and bow down before, and offer a sacrifice to. . . . [137]

As several critics have noted, Warren's early attention to this passage is the seed of Warren's later and recurring mediations on the metathematics of the "true lie" and "the incorrigible and ironic necessity of the 'idea'" in Conrad: that is, the paradox of the fundamental human psychic and social need for idealization despite a skeptical recognition of the alienating quality and self-generated facticity of idealizations.[138] "We live, as we dream—alone," as Marlow puts it (*YOS* 82)—but not because we are simply born apart from one another, but rather because the artificial "dreams" (idealizations) which we need to survive inevitably cast us out, leaving us always already at tenuous odds with the very medium of self and social integration. Well beyond the 1920s (though curiously returning to them, repeatedly begging the question of their continued proximity), this conception of the "idea" recurs and develops in various permutations throughout Warren's lifetime of engagements with Conrad. At the dawn of the New Criticism, the relation between "structure" and "the 'idea' in a piece of fiction" informs the enthusiasm with which Warren and Cleanth Brooks add *Heart of Darkness* to the second edition of *Understanding Fiction* (1946).[139] In a series of more politically focused interviews in the early 1950s, Warren speaks of "still being under the spell of having re-read a lot of Conrad a year or so ago," and links Conrad's status as "one of the big seminal writers of the century" to the "special kind . . . of truth" that Conrad presents in his notion of the "idea": "It must be created by man. It is not inherited or given or revealed."[140] Finally, in prescient post-Americanist fashion, Warren uses Conrad's "doctrine of illusions" to place the fiction of Theodore Dreiser and F. Scott Fitzgerald in *Homage to Dreiser* (1971); and, in a similarly complicating Americanist gesture, Warren's *New and Selected Essays* (1989) reprints his landmark introduction to the Modern Library edition of *Nostromo* (1951) in the conspicuously U.S. company and genealogy of consecutive essays on Hawthorne, Twain, Hemingway, and Faulkner.[141] The new title given the

Modern Library piece is "The Great Mirage: Conrad and *Nostromo*," and here, too, the "idea" receives central consideration.

Like many of the most sensitive figures in the U.S. cultural history of "our Conrad," Warren is special in that he does not simply identify (or absolutely disidentify) with Conrad. He rather grows in his sense of identity and the mechanics of identification through his interactions with Conrad; and it is in light of the *Southern* specificity of Warren's identifications with Conrad, in tandem with the momentous transitional cultural-historical circumstances of the mid-century, that we must consider the seminal significance of Warren's meditations on the "idea" in the Modern Library introduction of 1951. Written on the eve of *Brown v. Board of Education* (1954) and the civil rights movement; written in a stream of writing that includes both *All the King's Men* (1946), Warren's Pulitzer Prize–winning novel based on the world of Louisiana politician Huey Long, and the remarkable nonfictional works *Segregation: The Inner Conflict* (1956) and *Who Speaks for the Negro?* (1965); and written in the very moment of William Faulkner's Nobel Prize speech (1950), which closes, as we have seen, by extensively invoking the very passage from Conrad's essay on Henry James that Warren's introduction quotes at its close, Warren's essay reveals an author positively steeped in Conrad as a means of thinking through and moving beyond the very tradition of racialized Southern conservatism epitomized by his own "Briar Patch" essay in *I'll Take My Stand* (1930). Dialogically positioned against both Menckenite anti-Southern nihilism and static Southern agrarian conservatism, Warren's *Nostromo* introduction articulates a fresh vision of moral redemption and pragmatic action whose terms of *deliberative and dynamically polyvocal relation to the "idea"* are fundamentally gridded by the specific "imagined community" and cultural-political circumstances of the South. As such, Warren's essay is not simply the landmark work of literary criticism that all Conrad scholars know but also, with the possible exception of Faulkner, the greatest vindication of Conrad's U.S. Southern internality and the political purposiveness of its contemplation. Indeed, the very moral intensity of Warren's introduction turns on a presumption of Conrad's Southern intimacy that formalist criticism has endlessly obscured: namely, the substantial interchangeability between Warren's American South and *Nostromo*'s "South America."

Much in Warren's framing of "Costaguana"—the imaginary South American country of *Nostromo*—recalls the terms, discourses, and historical and social problematics of the modern U.S. South. Like the South, Sulaco (the key province of Costaguana in question) is largely a preindustrial, isolated place experiencing the shock of modernization through the intervention of Yankee-financed imperial capitalism. Also like the South, Sulaco has had a history of "aristocratic" posture and brutality including slavery—though this is not to say that Conrad, any more than many U.S. Southerners, dispenses with the critical "analysis and unmasking of capitalism and imperialism" that present themselves in the name of pure "progress."[142] If in the South, as Warren describes in *Segregation*, many worry that Northern historical forces of "abstraction" threaten the terms of Southern "community," "concreteness of life," and "massiveness of experience,"[143] the same problem presents itself with the advent of "material interests" in Sulaco. There, Warren writes in the *Nostromo* essay, Gould, the emblematic figure who runs the silver mine, becomes "the slave of his silver" and loses his capacity for "love to the enormous *abstraction* of his historical role," while his wife, Emilia, the tenuous compensatory figure, struggles vainly "against the abstractions" to "set up the human community, the sense of human solidarity in understanding and warmth and kindness outside the historical process."[144] But Warren is writing these texts in a moment of not only general modern socioeconomic transition but also acute racialized conflict and apprehension. "Progress," Warren notes in *Segregation*, has become an especially charged word in the climate of *Brown*, as it implies a full range of socioeconomic as well as judicially racialized and sociological intervention on the part of the Northern "power-state," interpreted by many as an assault on an "entire way of life" and understood by all as part of an atmosphere of increasing tension, violence, and threateningly imminent "revolution."[145] So, too, in Sulaco, Warren notes in the *Nostromo* essay, is "progress" a profoundly contentious and political claim "hedged about with all sorts of ironies" and destabilizing antagonisms; so, too, is racial antagonism fundamental to Sulaco's instability; and so, too, is the "historical moment" of *Nostromo*—combining the densest and most explosive issues of "capitalism, imperialism, revolution, social justice"—one of impending and, indeed, actualized revolution. ("So foul a sky clears not without a storm," Warren quotes the epigraph of *Nostromo*: "Necessarily this involves the topic of revolution.")[146] We might add here that the very *form* through which the South is articulated in *Segregation* and *Who Speaks for the Negro?* owes much to the politico-narratological topography of *Nostromo*. In the Modern Library introduction, Warren emphasizes that Conrad's characters are not only "personal stories" but also "carriers of variation" on a common field of social "illusion" whose terms they constitute through their historical intersection as social types: "That is, each character is a carrier of attitude toward, a point of view about, society; and each is an actor in a crucial historical moment." In *Segregation* and *Who Speaks for the Negro?* (whose epigraph is taken from Conrad's *Under Western Eyes*), Warren's strategy of gathering together many voices—always fundamentally identified by social type ("Southern Negro professor," "rich businessman active in segregation," etc.) and shown collectively to constitute the contemporary field of race relations—unmistakably follows *Nostromo*'s example.[147] The form through which Conrad renders "South America" enables the articulation of the content Warren recovers in the U.S. South.

But for a text this self-conscious of its own social grounding, Warren's *Nostromo* essay curiously begins by emphasizing at length (three pages) the uncharacteristic *lack* of *Nostromo*'s grounding in any actual experience of Conrad or place in the world. Despite the personal experiences of people and places that generally underwrite Conrad's fiction, Conrad, Warren points out, had never been to the "West Coast of South America" and only fleetingly had contact with any part of Latin America. *Nostromo* thus must be understood as an act of pure "imagination and not recollection": "In the end, the land, its people, and its history all had to be dreamed up. . . . [Yet] it is one of the most solid and significant dreams we know, more solid and significant than most of our actualities."[148] Warren's point, of course, is that it is the "idea" of, not any integrated objective reality found in, a place or social polity that constitutes its "national" significance and solidity; and apropos of his own ultimate investments in engaging the "Southern" idea, Warren proceeds to read Conrad against the grain of two prior Southern deployments of Conrad, and toward a third. The first is the Davidsonian "fidelity" narrative, wherein simple allegiance to established cultural codes and normative values is what Conrad vindicates. Though acknowledging the seriousness with which "fidelity and the job sense"[149] make for the human community in Conrad, and the ultimate epic sincerity with which Conrad pursues "the solidarity of all mankind in simple ideas and sincere emotions," Warren notes that there is something a bit obvious about Conrad's insistences, generally in his prefaces and nonfiction, on "the idea of Fidelity," and something indeed quite "ambiguous, contradictory, false, or blandly misleading" about the relation such statements bear to the fiction itself.[150] This fiction, rather, is typified by a "dark inwardness" and radical "skepticism" that belie simple commitment to the social order or acquiescent piety of spirit.[151] This reading of Conrad has consequences for Warren well beyond the contours of his *Nostromo* essay. Whereas Davidson's Conrad, for instance, easily affirms the racism endemic to Davidson's larger "Southern" vision of "fidelity," Warren, emphasizing a Conrad text that had been historically used (as we have seen) to critique racialized arrogance in the international sphere, presents Conrad in *Who Speaks for the Negro?* as an *interference* with racist white paternalism: "The situation was, to the Negro at least, a paradigm of the behavior of the white liberal, who long ago, in *The Rescue*, was described by Conrad, in the person of Captain Lingard: 'He prided himself upon having no color prejudice and no racial antipathies. . . . Only he knew what was good for them.'"[152] Similarly, whereas Davidson is simply incapable of entertaining that "tradition" often exists to facilitate and justify inequalities and abuses of power, Warren raises in the *Nostromo* essay the example of *Lord Jim*'s Gentleman Brown, who, even in maliciously betraying Jim's trust and gratuitously leading the slaughter of Dain Waris's unsuspecting men, cannot see his action as "a vulgar and treacherous massacre" but idealizes it as "a lesson, a retribution" carried out with the "superiority as of a man who carries right—the abstract thing—in the envelope of his common desires." "Even bloodthirstiness or villainy must appeal beyond itself to the [justifying] 'idea,'"[153] comments Warren; and Warren, effectively using *Lord Jim* as a template to theorize the same project of idealized villainy in the modern South, makes the very same point in perhaps the most memorable scene of *Segregation*:[154] the scene in which he encounters the "quick, vituperous" boy from Alabama at the "replica" of the historical Fort Nashborough in Nashville. The boy's sudden outburst of racialized "automatic violence" when asked about African Americans—"Niggers—you mean niggers? . . . I hate them bastards"—cannot stand by itself but must find justification in the "idea" and idealizing codes of the South inscribed in the (simulated) historic site in which they stand:

This, too, is a cliché. The boy, standing on the ground of history and heroism, his imagination stirred by the fact, shudders with that other, automatic emotion which my question had evoked. The cliché had come true: the cliché of hate. And somehow the hallowedness of the ground he stood on had vindicated, as it were, that hate.[155]

Finally, more than anything else, Warren objects to the simple "fidelity" reading of Conrad because it mistakes "the static image of the condition" that

Conrad valorizes (community, solidarity) for the "earned" and "dynamic" terms, achieved only through difficulty and "by accepting the logic of experience," through which Conrad understands the individual's only meaningful, socially productive, and ultimately "significant" participation in structures of "fidelity." This MacWhirrian act of bad faith—this failure "to take the full risk of humanity" required to achieve "*earned* redemption"[156]—is Warren's fundamental objection to Davidsonian Southern traditionalists as well:

> In . . . taking refuge in the vision of a South redeemed in unity and antique virtue, they are fleeing from the burden of their own individuality—the intellectual rub, the moral rub. To state the argument another way, by using the argument of *mere* social continuity and the justification by mere *mores*, they think of a world in which circumstances and values are frozen; but the essence of individuality is the willingness to accept the rub which the flux of things provokes, to accept one's fate in time. What heroes would these idealists enshrine to take the place of Jefferson and Lee, those heroes who took the risk of their own fate?[157]

It is remarkable how this formulation repeats Warren's sense in the *Nostromo* essay of what he is doing as a reader of Conrad[158]—but here we must add that just as Warren rejects Conrad as an exemplar of static traditionalism, he also rejects the Southern Menckenite reading of Conrad as an agency of pure negative, skeptical, corrosive force. Though taking very seriously the letter to Galsworthy in which Conrad describes "Scepticism" as "the tonic of minds, the tonic of life, the agent of truth—the way of art and salvation," Warren points to *Nostromo*'s Decoud as the "key parable" of the human inability to exist by skepticism alone. Like Kurtz, who "kicks himself free" of any idealization only to be consumed by horror; like Captain Brierly, whose brittle arrogance results in suicide when Jim's "jump" collapses it as a self-idealizing mechanism; and like Heyst, who comes to learn only too late, "Ah, Davidson, woe to the man whose heart has not learned while young to hope, to love—and to put its trust in life!"—Decoud is a man who fancies himself beyond the need for "illusion," "outside of . . . human commitments, outside the influence of the 'idea,'" and when left with his skepticism alone on the Great Isabel, he takes his own life.[159] For "it is not some, but all, men who must serve the 'idea,'" Warren argues; and this very "incorrigible and ironical necessity of the 'idea'"—the human necessity to participate in structures of narrative and sanction, the human need to idealize oneself and one's actions into moral significance of some order, despite having the skeptical faculties to recognize such structures and idealizations as a species of falsity—is for Warren the key to the famous "in the destructive element immerse" passage in *Lord Jim*:

A man that is born falls into a dream like a man who falls into the sea. If he tries to climb out into the air as inexperienced people endeavor to do, he drowns—*nicht wahr?* . . . No! I tell you! The way is to the destructive element submit yourself, and with the exertions of your hands and feet in the water make the deep, deep sea keep you up.[160]

Here, the "sea"—a metaphor for "dreams," "the idea," idealizations that derive from and are connected to moral visions of social order—is a "destructive element" precisely because human beings both require and are *not* indigenous to it. As a creature of "black egotism and savage impulses" at elemental odds with the idealizations it requires; and/or as a species of trivial and utterly self-generated "meaning" in a vast and indifferent universe against which it must be protected; and/or as a type of social subject destined to experience dislocation from the "home" that was always only an "idea," the human will necessarily experience estrangement from idealizations that are nevertheless necessary for survival. The MacWhirrs of the world disavow in various ways that the dislocation ever fundamentally happened, and become "static" creatures of "fidelity" alone. Equally unsatisfactory, however, are the Kurtzes and Decouds, who use their skeptical awareness to deny and disavow the very self-division that constitutes the terms of their existence as "specifically human." *They* are the ones who have truly "feared to take the full risk of humanity."[161] In committing themselves to a purely Menckenite skepticism that is an assault on the "idea" alone, they reject the idealizing predicament that defines the human condition; they arrogantly and unwisely fancy themselves beyond investment in social structures; they consequently embrace "the denial of life and energy" that flows from their misunderstanding that "against all reason man insists, *as man*, in creating and trying to live by certain values"; and perhaps most importantly, they refuse to confront the terms of their alienation so as to be able to reenter and participate in the human community: to "swim" in the ideational "destructive element" out of which one cannot "climb" or swim.[162] A third position, hence, emerges, which is that of "Lord" Jim (in this reading), Dr. Monygham, Heyst in the end, Flora de Barral, Captain Anthony, and Marlow himself. Theirs is the "type of story that engages Conrad most fully," the story of "*earned* redemption," and it is a story of "the effort of the alienated [individual], whatever the cause of his alienation, crime or weakness or accident or 'mystic wound,' to enter again the human communion. And the crisis of this story comes when the hero recognizes the terms on which he may be saved, the moment, to take Morton Zabel's phrase, of the 'terror' of the awakening."[163]

Warren's Conrad's central parable, hence, is one of engaging the fact of alienated self-division so as to reenter the human community. Through confronting the terms of one's alienation, through experiencing "the cost of awareness and the difficulty of virtue,"[164] one is able to rise to the terrifying self-confrontation whose rejections and renunciations allow for productive reentry into the sphere of social relations. Though these terms may sound suspiciously abstract, it would be difficult to find a more precise formulation for the specific diagnosis of and the recommended terms of engagement for Southern race conflict that Warren offers in *Segregation*. Though acknowledging the great significance of "division between man and man in society"—the tremendous social conflict, for instance, incited by the murders of Emmett Till and Clinton Melton, and the outrageous acquittals of their murderers—Warren argues that the most fundamental impediment to Southern movement beyond race conflict is "the division within the individual man."[165] For Warren, the fundamental problem is not the white Southern extremist who clings to a reactionary Southern "idea" as a license for violence, hate, simple and amoral self-aggrandizement. The problem is the many Southerners—Warren emphasizes white Southerners here, though he suggests parallels for black Southerners as well—who are so compromised by divided allegiance and alienated anger that they fail to commit themselves to the very "idea" of desegregation (and of a racially open and equal South generally) that they *know* to be both just and inevitable. What makes it so difficult for so many white Southerners to "submit" to the "idea" of a racially just South? Why is it so difficult to immerse in the destructive element of this ideal?

It is the fact of self-division. . . . Within the individual there are, or may be, many lines of fracture. It may be between his own social idealism and his anger at Yankee Phariseeism. (Oh, yes, he remembers that in the days when Federal bayonets supported the black Reconstruction state governments in the South, not a single Negro held elective office in any Northern state.) It may be between his social views and fear of the power state. It may be between his social views and his clan sense. It may be between his allegiance to organized labor and his racism—for status or blood purity. It may be between his Christianity and his social prejudice. It may be between his sense of democracy and his ingrained attitudes toward the Negro. It may be between his own local views and his concern for the figure America cuts in the international picture. It may be between his practical concern at the money loss to society caused by the Negro's depressed condition and his own personal gain or prejudice. It may be, and disastrously, between his sense of the inevitable and his emotional need to act against the inevitable.

There are almost an infinite number of permutations and combinations, but they all amount to the same thing, a deep intellectual rub, a moral rub, anger at the irremediable self-division, a deep exacerbation at some failure to find identity. That is the reality.[166]

Northern hypocrisy, federal will-to-power, family history, historical racism, social appearance, personal financial circumstance: there are so many reasons here *not*, in the words of the *Nostromo* introduction, to "purge the self and enter the human community"; *not* to confront "the terror of the awakening" and rise to "the terms on which [one] may be saved"; *not* to "submit" to the very "idea" of the South that, though the terms themselves, of course, are quite new, are part of the stream of idealizations that have always informed articulations of the South. And not only white Southerners are caught in this trap of self-division: "Negroes, they must be split up, too. . . . I can imagine the grinding anger, the sense of outrage of a Negro crying out within himself: *After all the patience, after all the humility, after learning and living those virtues, do I have to learn magnanimity too?*"[167]

In the *Nostromo* essay, Warren conceptualizes through Conrad a twofold strategy of "awakening and redemption" that, beyond the analysis just given, becomes central to his political vision for the South—in which the "idea" of the South (as an "imagined community") is not rejected so much as adapted to ever-evolving progressive terms. The first element is that one can never abandon one's commitment to—as Kurtz and Decoud do, as Mencken does, and as Emily Clark's and Frances Newman's "gloomy" Menckenite understandings of Conrad imply—an ultimate vision of the "triumph of concord and justice" (in Conrad's phrase from "Autocracy and War"). The following quotation from *Under Western Eyes* appears both in the closing movement of Warren's *Nostromo* essay and as the opening epigraph of *Who Speaks for the Negro?* "I believe that the future will be merciful to us all. Revolutionist and reactionary, victim and executioner, betrayer and betrayed, they shall all be pitied together when the light breaks." The point of this quotation in both circumstances—which are,

I have argued, *the same circumstances*, Conradian and Southern—is that even in the moments of greatest turbulence and conflict, it is necessary to preserve an ultimate "vision of concord": to continue to "submit" to an "idea" of ultimate disinterested and ethical purposiveness in one's actions; to continue to believe, as Conrad insists in "Books," "not necessarily that the world is good" but "that there is no impossibility of it being made so."[168] This is also Warren's point in echoing Faulkner when quoting from Conrad's "Henry James" essay, though whereas Faulkner's invocation is immediately prompted significantly by the threat of the atomic bomb, Warren's purpose is squarely to affirm the "redeemed" *meaning*, "moral identity," and social value that can emerge from the South's present struggles with respect to race:

> When the last aqueduct shall have crumbled to pieces, the last airship fallen to the ground, the last blade of grass have died up a dying earth, man, indomitable by his training . . . shall set this undiminished light of his eyes against the feeble glow of the sun. . . . For my own part I am inclined to think that the last utterance will formulate, strange as it may appear, some hope now utterly inconceivable.[169]

Such idealism, however, is only a condition of meaningful political action, not a program. And just as Warren in the *Nostromo* essay quotes Emilia Gould's famous reflection, "There was something inherent in the necessities of successful action which carried with it the moral degradation of the idea," Warren also notes in *Segregation* the inevitability with which "the bright world of Idea" loses shape "once it descends" to the world of "some quite concrete persons and specific actions." For this very reason, Warren is not an advocate of revolution, as he makes clear with reference to *Under Western Eyes* in the *Nostromo* introduction.[170] Rather his political program is fundamentally one of "moral regeneration" through complex awareness, participatory interchange, and historical specificity. Regarding the first of these, Warren references in *Who Speaks for the Negro?* a moment in *Under Western Eyes* in which a character mentions that revolutionists and reformers "hate irony" because "it seems to strike at the taproot of total commitment." Warren, however, picking up on the argument he had made through Conrad five years before, is forced to protest: "But must it? When the act of commitment is seen as fully as possible in its context, does not the pinch of glory, the flicker of tragic dignity, which is implicit in any human commitment—any real commitment—show more suddenly, like 'bright metal on a sullen ground'?" Warren emphasizes here the complex awareness of one's own subjectivity that is fundamental, far beyond political sloganeering, to his sense of the moral regeneration of a people. Moreover, this self-awareness is complemented—apropos of Warren's echo of the Preface to the *Nigger of the "Narcissus"* in his foreword to *Who Speaks*, where Warren announces as his purpose "to make my reader see, hear, and feel, as immediately as possible what I saw, heard, felt"—by a complex awareness of context and the voices of others as well.[171] Furthermore, one of the most Conradian aspects of both *Segregation* and *Who Speaks* lies in their emphasis on *performed* and participatory dialogue: as in *Lord Jim* it is precisely through the interchange and contact of voices that boundaries of subjectivity become loosened, that complex awareness of self and others and new bonds of identity become discovered and *enacted*. Finally, Warren is insistent that the task at hand is not to "legislate for posterity," not to develop a program of abstract and absolute right, but to confront the specific dilemmas of the present among the specific people and in the specific circumstances in which they have arisen, with an eye to working through the prejudices and conflicts that, in different terms, every generation must confront anew.[172] There is no more eloquent statement of this position, whose fundamental point is that the ethical health of a people is fundamentally a participatory and situated matter, not dictated by superimposed policy so much as a culture capable of integrating and sustaining it, than the following passage found near the end of the *Nostromo* essay:

Man must make his life somehow in the dialectical process of [its] terms, and in so far as he is to achieve redemption he must do so through an awareness of his condition that identifies him with the general human communion, not in abstraction, nor in mere doctrine, but immediately. The victory is never won, the redemption must be continually re-earned. And as for history, there is no Fiddler's Green, at least not near and soon. History is a process fraught with risks, and the moral regeneration of a society depends not on shifts in mechanism but upon the moral regeneration of men. But nothing is to be hoped for, even in the most modest way, if men lose the vision of the time of concord, when "the light breaks on our black sky at last."[173]

TOWARD FAULKNER

The example of Robert Penn Warren, whose preservation of the South would seem to someone like Davidson an evisceration of it, points naturally to a third pole of Conrad's reception in the modern South: one predicated on conceiving Conrad not as a critical externality (as with the Southern Menckenite maga-

zines), and not as a sympathetic internality (the baseline of the Vanderbilt circle, which Warren only gradually, and as a gradualist, evolves into a dynamic
position), but rather as a *critical internality*—an indigenous idiom of Southern
resistance, criticism, alienation, negation, escape. Whereas the Southern little
magazines generally present Conrad as an alien means of corroding or contesting hegemonic Southern cultural-political norms, the loose aggregation of authors gathered at this third pole understand Conrad as speaking a language of
resistance and critical diagnosis endemic to the domain of the South. Though
his robust contemplation is beyond the scope of this book, one such figure is
North Carolina native Thomas Wolfe, who in his diaries in the 1920s uses scathing tropes from *Heart of Darkness* to express what he considers the "horrors"
of the South, and even more importantly uses Conrad's experiences as an exile
to elaborate his own national and international experiences as a Southerner
in exile.[174] A more revealing example is fellow Tar Heel W. J. Cash, the author
of *The Mind of the South* (1941) and yet another Conrad enthusiast par excellence, whose story is in many respects one of recognizing a "Southern" voice in
Conrad which Cash attempted to but could not as a literary matter reproduce
himself. An ardent Menckenite—politically, as a matter of literary taste, and
ultimately stylistically—Cash discovered Conrad as an undergraduate in 1919
at Wake Forest, where incipient iconoclastic urges to articulate and critique the
South were accompanied by Cash's passionate attempts to fashion himself as a
writer in the manner of Conrad. As Bruce Clayton notes, a number of "Cash's
stories in the student literary magazine show the unmistakable influence of Conrad"; when Cash entered Wake Forest Law School at age twenty-three in 1922,
as he later wrote on a Guggenheim Fellowship application, he was attempting
"a novel in the manner of Joseph Conrad's *Lord Jim*, but concluded dismally
at the halfway mark that Conrad somehow knew more of life and the English
language than I knew, and burned it"; and all the way up through his suicide
in 1941, Cash wrote many journalistic pieces expressing the highest praise for
Conrad, particularly for *Lord Jim*, *Heart of Darkness*, and *Victory*.[175] Especially
revealing is the Book Page article Cash wrote in the Charlotte *News* on October 18, 1936, entitled "Realism and Romance: Southern View," which poses the
question of how to write "the great southern novel" "now that literature has
finally come upon Dixie" squarely in terms of Conrad. Cash argues that faced
with a sense of division about whether "to make their masterpieces realistic or
. . . to make them romantic," Southern writers pathologically fall prey *either*

to a "sentimental" romanticism that contains nothing of true "perception and the rendering of man's life as a whole," or to a merely "photographic" realism that captures nothing of the Southerner's "inexplicable images of Beauty and Glory," visions of "shining sword and a flame" against "stumbling and frequent apostasy," heroism against "condemn[ation] to death and inevitable defeat in the flesh." But this is a false exclusivity; for those who have trouble imagining a voice "all integrally and equally real" with respect to both the true "realistic" and "romantic" aspects of Southern experience, one need only consult Conrad:

Still, granting that there is, after all, perfectly good room for both a sound romanticism and a sound realism—that these [sons and daughters of the Confederacy] who are coming along can go either way in safety—you doubt that they can well go both ways, that the two can be combined in a single author and a single book? I point you to Joseph Conrad's magnificent "Lord Jim," and his scarcely less magnificent "Victory." Here are two of the finest romantic novels ever written in the world. And here also, and precisely, are two of the most perfect and sure-footed examples of realism which have appeared on this marvelous wheeling ball.[176]

Cash's comments suggest that in advance of modern Southern writers themselves, Conrad somehow speaks the language and constitutes an aesthetic register of the eponymous subject of The Mind of the South itself: i.e., "a fairly definite mental pattern, associated with a fairly definite social pattern—a complex of established relationships and habits of thought, sentiments, prejudices, standards and values, and associations of ideas, which, if it is not common strictly to every group of white people in the South, is still more common in one appreciable measure or another, and in some part or another, to all but relatively negligible ones."[177] Anne Goodwyn Jones, in an inspired response to the tendency to dismiss Cash on empirical historical grounds, has recently argued that in this formulation of Southern "mind" Cash presents a sophisticated analogue, put to much productive cultural work, of Antonio Gramsci's influential notion of "hegemony."[178] Frequently inaccurate as a matter of historical detail and causal explanation, The Mind of the South is nevertheless keenly attuned to documenting in the South the interlocking intermixture of assumptions ("fairly definite mental pattern") and practices ("fairly definite social practices") by which Gramscian hegemony expresses the production and perpetuation of large systems of socialized behavior over time through the "saturation of the whole process of living": not simply through formal ideas, beliefs, and values, but through their very integration with the activities, in-stitutions, practices, rituals, and even smallest daily habits and unconscious assumptions of a culture that work together to form the fabric of what seems like their indispensable and immutable "reality" (what Althusser calls their "lived relation to the real").[179] For Jones, Cash captures this full and intricately self-perpetuating network of "fixing" social forces that places social subjectivity and generates and regenerates a distinctive species of "mind" in the South. Cash becomes here a sort of "organic intellectual" who through recognizing, declar-ing, and theorizing "from within" the terms of Southern hegemony, is able to combat the mechanism and to initiate and facilitate alternative terms of social relation.[180] But for us the key point to take is that the very terms of Southern hegemony that Cash articulates in *The Mind of the South* and could *not* articu-late as a matter of his own literary expression are precisely the terms through which Cash understands the compulsive intimacy of the aesthetic forms and idioms of Conrad. The same is true, moreover, of William Faulkner, with the exception that Faulkner *does* actualize the aesthetic commerce and symbiosis with Conrad of which Cash's peculiar genius was not capable.

The following chapter traces symbioses between Conrad's and Faulkner's aesthetics in terms of two historical and ideological phenomena: first, continu-ities in Polish and Southern political history that make for similar investigations and elaborations of "hegemony"; and second, the ideological centrality of race within the Southern systemic of hegemony that Conrad's "imperial" fiction helps Faulkner critically over time to read and to write. My claim is both that it is possible and useful to think of Faulkner evolving his aesthetic experimen-talism from engagements with Conrad, and also that there are larger cultural and historical concerns animating both writers that almost autonomously leads them in the direction of one another. One way into these investigations is simply to consider the element of overripe, brooding, and even ponderous *prolixity* that, if it does not uniquely distinguish Faulkner and Conrad even among the most distinguished caliber of writers, establishes an uncanny nexus between the two that may, indeed, be of use in decoding the ideological and cultural content of the vast array of global writers who self-consciously write a lot like them. Adjectives heaped on adjectives, obscurities compounded by further obscurities, digressions and even sentences that take absurd control of entire chapters, a distinct flair for the florid and baroque—these are some of the qualities of *word* that put the "-ese" in "Conradese" and "Faulknerese," critical epithets whose joint suffix is meant to suggest that even though the two authors are never at a loss for words, they also tend to get lost in them. Indeed, it is sometimes unclear whether Conrad and Faulkner are truly masters of words or radically mastered by them:[181] victims of an anonymous power in language that never allows them to say exactly what they would like to. Some such logic, in any event, leads J. Hillis Miller to consider in Conrad's case the remarkable letter Conrad wrote to R. B. Cunninghame Graham in December 1897, the ultimate referent of which in Miller's reading is *language*:

There is a—let us say—a machine. It evolved itself . . . out of a chaos of scraps of iron and behold!—it knits. I am horrified at the horrible work and stand appalled. I feel it ought to embroider—but it goes on knitting. . . . And the most withering thought is that the infamous thing has made itself; made itself without thought, without conscience, without foresight, without eyes, without heart. It is a tragic accident—and it has happened. . . . It knits us in and it knits us out. It has knitted time, space, pain, death, corruption, despair, and all the illusions—and nothing matters. I'll admit however that to look at the remorseless process is sometimes amusing. (*CL* 1.425)

As Miller notes, Conrad's machine is a strangely autonomous force that "has no beginning, no foundation outside itself, and exists only as a self-generated web." One does not knit this web but is knitted by it: a commentary, in Miller's view, on the agonizing process of fictional composition, which Conrad experiences as ruthlessly determined by the self-governing machinery of language.[182] The immediate context and subtext of Conrad's letter, however, is not fiction or language but political ideology. Conrad is writing in direct and critical response to the utopic socialist politics of his friend and political activist Cunninghame Graham, and he uses the figure of the indomitable knitting machine to assert the futility of idealist attempts to "embroider" the world in the image of international socialism. In part Conrad's objection may be understood in terms of the "material interests" privileged in *Nostromo*: imperial capitalism has its own logic, and, moral or not, it will knit the terms of humanity and its history through it. But as we have also seen, nationalism is as well a singularly powerful constituent force in Conrad: it is *against* Cunninghame Graham's international socialism that Conrad posits "the idea of nationhood" as a compulsive and saving social force in the "Man is a vicious animal" letter (*CL* 2.160–61); and it is only "the national spirit" that provides "the feeling of enduring existence" against "the ceaseless rush of shadows and shades" in the final paragraph of

The Mirror of the Sea (194). One way—the Davidsonian way—to read the tortuous quality of Conrad's prose is thus in terms of the mighty struggle between the ordering power of the national "idea" and the dark chaotic and anarchic forces that seek to unravel it. But what the context of the "knitting machine" letter suggests is that it is "nationality" that is the inescapable and indomitable knitting force itself: that the hegemony of the national culture into which one is born is a "destructive element" and ideological sculpting mechanism that one never escapes. Here Conrad's thick fecundity of language is the product of an originary script that can be questioned, complemented, violently critiqued, and endlessly qualified, but never finally eclipsed.

Much in Conrad's fiction aligns with the proposition that one can never escape the ideological determination and grasp of the native culture into which one is born. In the Author's Note to *Under Western Eyes*, for instance, Conrad insists upon the collective and immutable pathology of *all* Russians which defines them *as* Russians: "The ferocity and imbecility of an autocratic rule rejecting all legality and in fact basing itself upon complete moral anachronism provokes the no less imbecile and atrocious answer of a purely Utopian revolutionism. . . . The oppressors and oppressed are all Russians together" (*UWE* x). Similarly, in *Nostromo*, Costaguana's political difficulties in establishing itself as an actual or imaginable stable "nation" notwithstanding, a number of different characters—Gould and Decoud among them—find themselves accounting for their behavior in terms of the mystic proposition that they were, after all, "born in Costaguana" (*N* 56, 122). Indeed, in *Lord Jim*, Conrad makes permanent enslavement to the hegemonic terms of one's native jump-off point into the very definition of what it means to be "one of us." Marlow, of course, frets a great deal over the "doubt" Jim's jump introduces into the idea of the "sovereign power enthroned in a fixed standard of conduct" (*LJ* 32), but Jim's haunted life is a testament to the very sovereign reverse. Even when the old codes are shown to be "mere rules of the game, nothing more," belied by history and personal experience alike, Jim continues to experience them as "all the same so terribly effective in [their] assumption of unlimited power over natural instincts, by the awful penalties of [their] failure" (50). For Jim, the problem is not the failure of the old ideology but rather his own failure to live up to it as it exists as an indelible part of him. So completely has he internalized the ideology of his father and the British merchant marine (the book continually equates the two), so utterly has he been interpellated by the hegemonic machinery of his native culture whose terms have processed him as the inexpiable warp and woof of his existence, that Jim seems at times less a "character" than a textual trace of the "uncanny vitality" by which a certain ideology insists on knitting itself (92).

All of these novels bear specially on Conrad personally insofar as they speak to a proposition Conrad made in the earliest letter we have from him, to Stefan Buszczysnski on August 14, 1883: "'Remember'—you said—'wherever you may sail you are sailing towards Poland!' That I have never forgotten and never will!" (CL 1.8). Though none of Conrad's novels explicitly mention Poland, with the same consistency and intensity with which all of Faulkner's novels hyper-emphasize the American South, each of the above mentioned books bears the mark of Polish "knitting": the revolution in *Nostromo* begins on May 3, the date of the signing of the Polish Constitution in 1791, and an event that immediately resulted in the final partitioning and sovereign erasure of Poland for over a century; *Lord Jim* is a text wherein Jim's "jump" from the *Patna* has long been recognized in relation to Conrad's own historical "jump" from the sinking ship of his Polish *patria*; and Keith Carabine has powerfully suggested in *Under Western Eyes* that the "figure[s] behind the veil" in Conrad's overt interrogations of the Russian character and Russian revolutionism are, to profound degrees, Conrad's own Polish character and his father's Polish revolutionism.[183] Indeed, Geoffrey Harpham has recently argued that what he calls the "concept" of Poland constitutes the invisible but supremely situating Lacanian "real" of all Conrad's fiction—"that which guarantees the consistency of [its] symbolic order, but which cannot appear within that order except as a disfigurement or 'stain'"[184]—a proposition that I would connect to the argument that Conrad's fiction expresses a "mind" of Poland: a sense of inescapable knittedness to and by the terms and obligations of Polish culture, of which diagnosis may be had but never escape. Throughout his political essays, Conrad refers to Poland as a "ghost" and "corpse" that "refused to grow insensible and cold"; as a literally groundless "*pays du rêve*" that "never ceas[ed] to inspire a sense of awe, and a strange uneasiness"; as an "absent" and "erased" country that nevertheless insisted on knitting itself and "intruding its irresistible claim into every problem of European politics, into the theory of European equilibrium, into the question of the Near East, the Italian Question, the question of Schleswig-Holstein, and into the doctrine of nationalities itself" (*NLL* 113, 118–19, 142). So, too, at a more personal level does Conrad write in the Author's Note to *A Personal Record* of the "haunting reality" of the "Shades" of his Polish past, in which he also describes his place within "the whole Polish mentality" in remarkably Gramscian terms that include not only ideas like a "chivalrous view of moral restraints and an exaggerated respect for individual rights," but also institutional matters like Poland's "traditions of self-government," social practices like "simple fellowship and the honorable reciprocity of services," and all the little rituals, habits, and unconscious assumptions that made up "the mental and moral atmosphere of the houses which sheltered my hazardous youth" (*PR* x, vi, vii). Finally, in "Poland Revisited" (1915), in which Conrad describes returning to Poland after many years, he poignantly expresses the fear of discovering that everything in his present is but the inescapable scripting of his Polish past:

Cracow is the town where I spent with my father the last eighteen months of his life. It was in that old royal and academical city that I ceased to be a child, became a boy, had known friendships, the admirations, the thoughts and indignations of that age. It was within those walls that I began to understand things, form affections, lay up a store of memories and a fund of sensations with which I was to break violently by throwing myself into an unrelated existence. It was like the experience of another world. The wings of time made a great dusk over all this, and I feared . . . that if I ventured bodily in there I would discover that I who have had to do with a great many imaginary lives have been embracing mere shadows of my youth. I feared. . . . My present, all that gave solidity and value to it, would stand by me in this test of the reality of my past. (*NLL* 145–46)

The relevance to Faulkner of a past system of ideology, a past domain of hegemony, a residual matrix of "mind" exerting powerful social force, hardly needs to be overemphasized. In *Intruder in the Dust*, Chick Mallison is presented as the product of a long-standing Southern hegemonic process, one that "had bred his bones and those of his fathers for six generations before him and was still shaping him into not just a man but a specific man, and not with just a man's passions and aspirations and beliefs but the specific passions and hopes and convictions and ways of thinking and acting of a specific kind of race."[185] The autogenerative quality of Faulkner's prose reinforcing the self-replicating social process he describes, Mallison's predicament is that of capture within a recursive social project that looks back on an old idealized enemy: "the North: not north but North, outland and circumscribing and not even a geographical place but an emotional idea, a condition of which he had fed from his mother's milk to be ever and constant on the alert and not at all to fear and not actually any more to hate but just . . . to defy."[186] Many Faulkner characters fit the pattern of inescapable capture within Southern ideology—the younger Bayard Sartoris, Benjy Compson, the Reverend Hightower, Ike McCaslin, Gavin Stevens—but the Quentin Compson of *Absalom, Absalom!* is perhaps Faulkner's supreme example of a character for whom, as Gavin Stevens says, "The past is never dead. It's not even past":[187]

Quentin had grown up with that; the mere names were interchangeable and almost myriad. His childhood was full of them; his very body was an empty hall echoing with sonorous defeated names; he was not a being, an entity, he was a commonwealth. He was a barracks filled with stubborn back-looking ghosts still recovering, even forty-three years afterward, from the fever which cured the disease, waking from the fever without even knowing it had been the fever itself which they had fought against and not the sickness, looking with stubborn recalcitrance backward beyond the fever into the disease with actual regret, weak from fever yet free of the disease and not even aware that the freedom was that of impotence.[188]

Faulkner's "fever" here is analogous to Conrad's "knitting machine": both expressions of native ideological systems (in Faulkner's case positioned against the actual "sickness" and "disease" of the Civil War and the concrete concerns that produced it) that persist in processing one into and as a species of "commonwealth," forever generating from the past the essentially backward-looking "freedom . . . of impotence" that is the present. Here, too, we arrive at a deep sense of imprisoned sedimentation informing the crowded fecundity of Faulkner's language. What we turn to now is a more precise anatomy of how Faulkner's engagements with Southern ideology turn and return to Conrad, and what the specific historical terms are of their repeated aesthetic convergences.

FAULKNER'S CONRAD

One does become attached to things one has long known.

    —Januarius Jones in Faulkner, *Soldiers' Pay*

A PERSONAL RECORD

William Faulkner began reading Conrad at age twelve, when his mother rec-ommended Conrad's fiction as the kind of "manly fiction" her son should be reading.[1] Faulkner never stopped reading Conrad after this point. Over the course of his life the South's most prolific and intellectually omnivorous novelist would become keenly interested in many writers—Swinburne, Sher-wood Anderson, T. S. Eliot, Joyce, Mann, Cather, Melville, Dostoevsky, Twain, Sienkiewicz—but very few, if any at all, with the lifelong consistency of his interest in Conrad.[2]

  Faulkner's literary lifetime of winking, allusive testimonial references to Conrad is worth briefly sketching as a prelude to the puzzle of inescapable intimacy that runs throughout their major fiction—because this intimacy, even more so than we saw earlier with F. Scott Fitzgerald, is both more rooted in careful and sensitive study of Conrad than criticism acknowledges, and less ultimately attributable to that study than a kind of independent agency in Faulkner himself. Faulkner's first printed mention of Conrad comes in an important early essay Faulkner wrote on Eugene O'Neill for the *Mississippian* in February 1922, in which the future bard of "my own little postage stamp of native soil" marvels at Conrad, the progenitor of O'Neill, as "this man [who] has overturned all literary tradition" by *not* writing from a specific sense of "place."[3] One of the more place-specific and place-sustained (though not, of course, exclusive) giant imaginations in world literary history, hence, comes into being as a fiction writer through meditation on his ostensibly "place-less" or "displaced" reverse. During the next two years, one finds Faulkner praising Joseph Hergesheimer for "tricks of the trade [that] were never em-ployed to better effect unless by Conrad," and describing *Heart of Darkness* and Sherwood Anderson's "I'm a Fool" as "the two finest stories I ever read."[4] Many of Faulkner's early short stories of this period demonstrate careful attention to Conrad: "Chance" (1925) and "Victory" (1925) adopt Conradian titles;[5] "Country Mice" (1925) and "The Big Shot" (1926) adopt the anonymous frame-narrator and storytelling conventions of Conrad's "Marlow" stories; "Home" (1924), the tale of an immigrant and "alien" at a crisis moment who comes to realize that "he had pursued a phantom into a far land,"[6] pointedly recalls *Lord Jim*; and "Yo Ho and Two Bottles of Rum" (1925), a bizarre tale of English commerce and Asian superstition on the stormy high seas, is difficult to account for as anything other than a comic "tribute" to or ironic imitation of Conrad's *Typhoon*. Also from these years, the manuscript notes of Faulkner's first novel, entitled *Mayday* at the time (1925), explicitly name Conrad at what would become a significant autoreferential moment in the text;[7] Faulkner's second novel, *Mosquitoes* (1927), opens by parodically framing its river journey in relation to *Heart of Darkness*;[8] and the original manuscript of Faulkner's third novel, *Sartoris* (1929), names the founding member of the Sartoris clan "Aylmayer," perhaps in partial allusion to the title character of Conrad's *Almayer's Folly*, a text of significant resonance throughout Faulkner.

This stream of allusions to Conrad does not cease but rather becomes enhanced as a matter of suggestiveness and variety as Faulkner embarks on his major fiction. Of *The Sound and the Fury* (1929), the novel usually understood as Faulkner's first "masterpiece," one version of Faulkner's 1933 introduction describes Conrad as one of the authors by whom Faulkner "learned to judge the standards of [his] art," just as *The Sound and the Fury* itself (in an important phrase) "taught me both how to write and *how to read, and even more: It taught me what I had already read*"; while the other version describes how the "Flauberts and Dostoievskis and Conrads" he had "digested" came upon him "in a series of delayed repercussions like summer thunder"—which is to say, curiously *after* Faulkner had seen the light (so to speak) of his own prose.[9] Similarly, *Light in August* (1932) Faulkner would later describe as written "deliberately . . . measuring each choice by the scale of the Jameses and Conrads and Balzacs"; in a series of important interviews from 1933 to 1935 Faulkner names *The Nigger of the "Narcissus"* and *Moby-Dick* as "the two books I like best" and would "just like to have written more than any others I can think of"; and of *Absalom, Absalom!* (1936) Faulkner would confirm Albert Guerard Jr.'s sense of the significant relation between it and *Nostromo* with the coy reply:

"I can see why you would think so."[10] Nor does Conrad fade with the advent of "late" Faulkner. In *Knight's Gambit* (1939), Gavin Stevens tells his nephew Charles that lost places like Paris can be conceptually recovered by "simply opening up the right page in Conrad"; in 1942, Faulkner bought a small white boat and christened it *The Ring Dove* after Captain Whalley's ship in *The End of the Tether*; and in 1949—the year before the Nobel Prize speech in which he effectively impersonates Conrad, and in years following which he would continue to insist in lectures at the University of Virginia that "he got a lot from Conrad" and "read him every year"—Faulkner made a comment whose coda brings us back to the crucial paradox of "delayed repercussion": Conrad's curious capacity to be both a provoking catalyst and an evoked consequence of Faulkner simply being himself. When asked (as he often was) about his "greatest influences" by a member of a freshman English class at the University of Mississippi, Faulkner replied, as Blotner reports, that "the four greatest influences on his work were the Old Testament, Melville, Dostoevsky, and Conrad—the last perhaps more than he had ever realized."[11]

These testimonials suggest Conrad as something of a *cantus firmus*—to take Said's metaphor for his own relationship to Conrad—in Faulkner's imagination, a steady ground bass of creative contiguity and stimulus over a remarkable period of time, persisting through an endless series of contrapuntal combinations and expressive modes of intimacy.[12] Yet this pervasiveness of Conrad is combined with a signature evasiveness—the "delayed repercussion" of Conrad's recognition, the unexpected realization of Conrad's proximity, the uncanny recurrence of Conrad's name in otherwise general lists—that suggests *two* dynamics of convergence unfolding in inverse relation over time: the first, a fundamentally mimetic relation in which the younger Faulkner is learning through Conrad how to actualize himself as a writer; and the second, an independent conjunctive process guaranteeing their return and the inevitability of their sympathy even when mimesis in no longer at issue: such that the more Faulkner comes into his "voice," discovers and penetrates his "subject," becomes singularly, unmistakably, autonomously "Faulkner," the more his fiction also, of an invisible momentum and purposiveness of its own, seems to recover, rewrite, and reread a belatedly recognized Conrad. Concretely, we may identify the first dynamic with the young Faulkner's entry into the Southern Menckenite machinery of Conrad. Faulkner's early essays make frequent recourse to Menckenian commonplaces concerning Conrad, language, literature, and the United States;[13] and just as Faulkner's fiction is reticent to engage Southern cultural matter (on the model of the later *Double Dealer*) until *Sartoris* (1929), the early Faulkner experiments with Conrad as primarily a Southern externality. Yet the South was always, even if only in incipient and obliquely visible ways, a crucial animating and organizing coordinate of Faulkner's poetry and prose; and if the young Faulkner, like so many younger Southern and U.S. writers generally, was initially hailed into formative relation with Conrad on the assumption of the latter's "placeless" and/or displacing alien difference, even the earliest terms of Faulkner's engagements with Conrad betray the silent sympathetic routing of Southern history. This "Southern" historical proximity of Conrad, I argue, long after the "tutelary" dimensions of the Conrad/Faulkner relationship cease to be of interest, constitutes the second dynamic that steers the two authors together, as if their aesthetics do come from the same "place" after all. In his landmark study of Faulkner in 1975, John Irwin demonstrates just how structurally determined the "cosmos" of Faulkner's fiction is by the project of rewriting, rereading, revisiting itself: such that *Absalom, Absalom!*, for instance, rewrites *The Sound and the Fury* in a manner that illuminates the latter's psychic topography, or such that Eric Sundquist, building on Irwin's model with historicist and racial focus, argues that the second half of the "house divided" of Faulkner's major fiction politically rereads, revises, and relocates the first half.[14] Via Conrad, we will have occasion both to appreciate and to question Sundquist's "house divided" construction in particular; but here, the crucial question for us is how Faulkner's fiction, as it rewrites, rereads, and critically reveals itself, *also does the same for Conrad*—not ultimately because of the aesthetic tutelage with which the Faulkner/Conrad relationship begins, but rather because of objective historical confluences between (1) the powerfully coterminous residual force of Polish and Southern ideology in moments when the two "national" cultures were threatened with disappearance, and (2) the centrality of race to both the world imperial structures that Conrad's fiction studies and the Southern social structures that Faulkner's fiction studies. In this way, simply by following the logic of its own historical necessity, the ever-expanding site and the ever-experimentalist aesthetics that constitute Yoknapatawpha County continually find themselves—albeit almost unwittingly, inadvertently—both writing their way toward and clarifying the way from Costaguana, Patusan, and the decks of the *Narcissus*.

WAITING FOR CONRAD

The key entry text is Faulkner's impressive inaugural novel *Soldiers' Pay* (1926), a tale of postwar disillusion and grueling social transition set in Charleston, Georgia, in the year 1919. The novel is constellated around a single event: the return home of a young fighter-pilot named Donald Mahon, who has been shot down and gravely wounded in the closing days of the war. Mahon is a "sick man" (*SP* 167) who enters the novel dying, an invalid with a "horrible scar" (27) on his "poor terrible face" (28). The book itself is principally concerned with the other characters' reactions to and interactions through and around Mahon as they "*wait*"—a word the text uses forty-seven times, also a key word throughout Faulkner—for him "to die" (24) and wonder if he is "going to die" (35). Mahon's appeal has very little to do with his personality. In fact, he has none and, despite his centrality and ubiquity, is scarcely a "character" in the novel at all: he remembers nothing from and no one in his past; he rarely speaks, grows blind, and is largely incapable of social interaction; and throughout the novel, which, as a formal matter, rigorously blocks off (except for one brief moment at the end) Mahon's subjectivity from both the reader and other characters, it is generally unclear not only what Mahon is thinking but when and whether he is even conscious. Mahon is an empty character slot whose importance in *Soldiers' Pay* is *for others*—and what draws the other characters (and allows them to be drawn) to the cipher of Mahon is the simple fact of his face: the fact that "there is death in his face" (63), that "if I ever seen death in a man's face, it's in his" (35). It is said of Mahon that his "face" is impossible to "conform to a type" (68). What this means, however, is not that Mahon's face does not conform to the consistent type of death, but rather—as Noel Polk observes, and as the novel's many references to mirrors, reflections, Narcissus, and Mahon's own strategically open, "vividly undescribed scar" underscore[15]—that all the characters who gravitate around Mahon, regardless of their social type, can see in the "round mirror" (54) of his face some dying aspect of themselves: some element of the past they are attempting to preserve, however ambivalently; some element of their own sociomoral condition that is in mortal peril.

Defined only by an external scar and the unnerving, conflicting, doubt-engendering prospect of his death, Mahon is both a general symbolic emblem of the social condition and world of the novel and a centralized social site, which, as he is collectively tended, expresses the underlying entanglement, integration, intersection of all the various "traditional" values and illusions whose slow death anyone in or connected with the community of Charleston may envision (and disavow) in him: for Julian Lowe, the prospect of heroic glory; for Joe Gilligan, the project of human camaraderie; for Margaret Powers, the sanctity of marriage; for the Reverend Mahon, the continuity of various genealogical traditions (e.g., familial, doctrinal); for Cecily Saunders, any uncomplicated idea of social success; for Emmy, the vindication of a "natural" ethos. Even more, beyond the symbolic and ideational level of intertwined and mutually reinforcing projections, Mahon also serves as a concrete instrument and "apparatus" through which the traditionalist elements in the community practically attempt to reassert their embattled and compromised power. Mr. Saunders, for instance, attempts to resolve the threat of his daughter's liberated sexuality by seizing on the constraining occasion of her prewar promise to marry Mahon; Mrs. Powers and the Reverend Mahon, for their own reasons, are aggressively complicit in this tangled and unambiguous assertion of patriarchy; lower-class Mrs. Burney finds her fallen son—one of the novel's many doppelgangers for Mahon: "his absence accomplishing that which his presence had never done, could never do" (176)—reinforcing hierarchical Charleston's class structure, but with herself now at the top; and Miss Callie (Donald's mammy) uses the gravity of Mahon's condition, to the delight and relief of many white characters in the vicinity, to shame her son (another returned soldier) into a subservient racialized mode of behavior: "Don't you stand dar wavin' yo' arm at yo' Mist' Donald, nigger boy. Come up here and speak er him like you been raised to" (167).

Young Robert Saunders, of grade-school age, is something of an exemplary figure of all these characters in their relations to Mahon. Interested in Mahon only as a gruesome spectacle to impress his friends and to pry his way into the secrets of others, Bob proceeds in his enterprise with a childish tenacity— fierce, unyielding, essentially puerile and helpless—that is emblematic of the arrested development of the entire community in its compulsively retrograde coordinations of and by Mahon. What ultimately unites all the characters in *Soldiers' Pay*—all children, one might say, of a certain Southern seam of modernity—is a sense of desperation with respect to what the book calls a "certain conventional state of behavior" and "mental state" (194), what W. J. Cash would call a "state of mind," and what we might, following Gramsci, call a form of "hegemony"—i.e., an integrating and dominating formation of beliefs, values, assumptions, and practices—that has experienced a crisis of history:

displaced from its naturalizing and legitimizing foundations, and afflicted by that element of self-consciousness whose face is death and whose advent portends a transition from "dominant" to "residual" ideology.[16] *Soldiers' Pay* is a study of the autonomous afterlife of a once-dominant ideological system, the resurgence and persistence of its hegemony, in these conditions; and it uses an absent-centered form *not*, as in *The Great Gatsby* or (one reading of) *Lord Jim*, to emphasize the tenuously mediated nature of collective imaginings (how hard it is to imagine being "one of us"), but rather to underscore the tenacity, even in moments of mortal challenge and foundational decay, of the collective, impersonal forces that give rise to and enmesh subjectivity from the outset (how hard it is to *stop* being "one of us"). Through its spectacle of projections and intersections, ambivalences and reversals, delayed resolutions and recuperative pathologies that unfold around the central "departed" space of Mahon, the novel studies the power and persistence of a certain mode of socialized behavior to continue "knitting" the terms of social subjectivity even when history—here presented in terms of the shock of the Great War—has advanced itself in a different direction. This is a phenomenon for which the book has a superabundance of metaphors: plucked magnolia blooms that fade but never cease to captivate the imagination (74); the symphony that, though finished, lives on in "the studied completion of a rhythm carried to its *nth*" (220); "forces of gravity" that pull one back from "thundering at the very gates of infinity" (59); "the cracked scab on an ancient festering sore . . . on a corpse that would not be left to die" (289); the very idea of Mahon himself. And as these figures of suspension are invariably underwritten by characters' expressions of ambivalence,[17] so they also give rise to fantasies (pointedly avian and Christological in shape) of ascension, transcendence, resurrection, escape, and release from the burden of ideology.[18] Cleanth Brooks may be correct in arguing that *Soldiers' Pay*, despite its Southern setting, evinces "no special significance" as a register of Southern cultural matter.[19] Very clearly, however, the novel provides a crucial template—formally and rhetorically—for Faulkner's future engagements, beyond Mahon, with problematics of Southern "mind," culture, and history.

Faulkner intends the name "Mahon," of course, as an aural pun on "man" generally: a pun whose likely source is Conrad's short story "Youth," wherein it is said of the unfortunate chief mate of the *Judea* that "his name was Mahon, but he insisted it should be pronounced Mann" (*YOS* 5). Though this allusion to "Youth" is appropriate in a novel which itself emphasizes the lingering "thought of young days behind . . . the illusions of youth" (*SP* 121); and though Faulkner's character "Mr. Jones," especially in light of the author's contemporary fascination with the idea of "Victory,"[20] does bear a certain family resemblance to his equally fantastic, woman-obsessed, and wicked namesake in Conrad's *Victory*, another Conrad text provides the principal aesthetic model for the novel *Soldiers' Pay* and its absent character center Donald Mahon. This text is *The Nigger of the "Narcissus."* Like Faulkner's novel, *The Nigger of the "Narcissus"* is set at a moment of disturbing social transition: one Jacques Berthoud has described in terms of the (enormously consequential) transition from sail to steam in the British merchant marine in the later nineteenth century; one Ian Watt discusses in terms of a shift in social organization from *Gemeinschaft* ("community": a preindustrial mode predicated on traditional hierarchies and organic customs) to *Gesellschaft* ("society": an urbanized, atomized, liberalized, and class-conscious mode); one Cesare Casarino, as we have seen, locates in a shift in Western mode of production from mercantile capitalism to industrial capitalism; and one that may also be linked to the rise of the "New Imperialism" in Africa in the 1880s and 1890s.[21] Amid this palimpsest of interlocking historical sea changes, and without taking away from Berthoud's claim that there are uniquely valuable ways in which Conrad's text registers the historicity of the sea in his moment, I think we may also follow Fredric Jameson's line of argument that the *Narcissus* itself, like Faulkner's Charleston, is something of a stay against time: a vehicle of delaying, "derealizing" and "displac[ing] unwanted realities" associable with modernity.[22] Though it exists in a world whose "land" has already been thoroughly transformed to "modern" urban-industrial terms, and though it has already been irremediably infiltrated by contagious related conceptions of individual rights, class consciousness, and organized resistance that the novel tendentiously vocalizes and vilifies in the figure of Donkin, the *Narcissus* sails at a scrupulously maintained distance from "land" and is manifestly a figurative attempt at what Conrad knows is the "lost cause" of forestalling, containing, and sealing off the momentum of modernity. The text almost lovingly itemizes and valorizes all the various aspects of "old custom" (*NN* 28), "resumed routine" (29), "etiquette of the forecastle" (45), "discipline" (46), "force of habit" (84), "pace" (46), "place" (30), and "the half-hourly voice of the bells [that] ruled our lives" (30), which constitute the preindustrial (organic, hierarchical) traditions and social order of sail—and which the book attests, against the overdetermined adversary of the sea, are necessary for the ship's smooth operations and survival. Similarly, the "modern" Donkin has a curious way of speaking both to and for certain elements of discontent within the ship's crew, and then being ultimately produced—by text and crew alike—as an absolute other. Furthermore, the very intensity of the novel's "impressionist" aesthetics—its vivid attention to the cascading surfaces of sky and sea, which form the boundaries of the "great circular solitude" (29) that the novel incessantly draws around itself and the *Narcissus*, and that Conrad "makes us *see*" precisely as a function of making it very difficult to see *beyond* them—manifestly inscribes a will to distance and obscure "land" and its "modern" coordinations.

Jameson comments, in the context of *Lord Jim* but in a charge that also reverberates for the problems of social value at issue in *The Nigger of the "Narcissus"*: "Why should we be expected to assume, in the midst of capitalism, that the aesthetic rehearsal of the problematics of a social value from a quite different mode of production—the feudal ideology of honor—should need no justification and should be of interest to us? Such a theme must *mean something else*: and this even if we choose to interpret its survival as an 'uneven development,' a nonsynchronous overlap in Conrad's own values and experience (feudal Poland, capitalist England)."[23] One answer to this question is that it depends on who "we" are. Writing from the perspective of the contemporary metropolitan West, tellingly elided in "interest" with late nineteenth-century imperial "capitalist England," Jameson minimizes as personal ("Conrad's own values and experiences") the very kind of "nonsychronous overlap" that in postpartition Poland and the postbellum South—and, as Said extends the analogy in the important essay "On Lost Causes," the more recent experiences of many Palestinians, Vietnamese, Cubans, South Africans, Angolans, Armenians, American Indians, Tasmanians, Gypsies, and Jews[24]—was a primary cultural mode: an ideological resistance-formation whose principal "interest" and "justification" lay precisely in its "uneven" relation to adjacent modes of ostensibly insuperable domination; a resistant and "residual" matrix of ideology that must primarily "mean something else" only to a perspective unwilling to consider the marvel, priority, and perils of its resurgent autonomy in its own terms.

Such residual tenacity and struggle under the shadow of Death, in any event, comprise not only the project of *The Nigger of the "Narcissus"*—which is related by an obviously invested (and notoriously unstable) "narrator" long after the *Narcissus* and its brood are gone—but the essence of its plot as well.

Old Singleton, the ideal sailor of the old order, incarnates something of both the book's and the ship's embattled struggle to keep what can only be called the hegemony of the *Narcissus*—for as we shall see, what is fundamentally at issue is the instrumentations of its power relations—alive:

"Old Singleton" . . . through half a century had measured his strength against the favours and the rages of the sea. He had never given a thought to his mortal self. He lived unscathed, as though he had been indestructible, surrendering to all the temptations, weathering many gales. He had panted in sunshine, shivered in the cold; suffered hunger, thirst, debauch; passed through many trials—known all the furies. Old! It seemed to him he was broken at last. And like a man bound treacherously while he sleeps, he woke up fettered by the long chain of disregarded years. He had to take up at once the burden of all his existence, and found it almost too heavy for his strength. Old! He moved his arms, shook his head, felt his limbs. Getting old . . . and then? He looked upon the immortal sea with the awakened and groping perception of its heartless might; he saw it unchanged, black and foaming under the eternal scrutiny of the stars; he heard its impatient voice calling for him out of a pitiless vastness full of unrest, of turmoil, and of terror. He looked afar upon it, and he saw an immensity tormented and blind, moaning and furious, that claimed all the days of his tenacious life, and, when life was over, would claim the worn-out body of its slave . . . . (*NN* 99)

Among the infinite riches of this passage (to which we will return shortly) is its presentation of Singleton's embattled incarnation of the "old" order through images of him "fettered" by a "long chain," tormented in the "worn-out body" of a "slave," and gazing into the "black" mirror of the sea. These tropes pointedly connect Singleton and the backward-looking ideological project he epitomizes in and for the novel to the single black character who gives Conrad's novel its name: James Wait, the eponymous "nigger" of the *Narcissus*. And it is here that *Soldiers' Pay*, which already assumes a sociotemporal predicament commensurate with *The Nigger of the "Narcissus,"* becomes unmistakable and profound in its debt to (and insight into) Conrad's novel—and in a fashion that will reverberate with aesthetic and political significance throughout most of Faulkner's fictional career. For like Faulkner's novel, Conrad's prototype stages its essentially "realist" presentation of a social world in "a passing phase of life" (*NN* xlii) in relation to a central, spectral, dying character who coordinates the novel as a matter of collective psychology and social mechanism. Like Faulkner's Mahon, Conrad's Wait—his name implies the same residual hailing ("Wait!" [17]) and psychosocial burden ("weight") that the term does in Faulkner's novel[25]—enters Conrad's novel with the manifest symptoms of a shockingly "sick man" (39) (his thunderous tubercular cough has much the same effect as Mahon's scar)—and the "idea of stalking death" (31) ever around him. Though there is an important question of whether Wait is "shamming" sick that is not at issue in *Soldiers' Pay*, the crucial issue of *doubt* as to whether the central character is actually dying, and all the various *ambivalences* of anger and pity, attraction and repulsion, renunciation and resuscitation, that surround the spectacle of his dying, remain distinctively similar. Moreover, though Wait and Conrad's novel are less amenable to immediate reductions than Mahon and Faulkner's novel, *The Nigger of the "Narcissus"* nonetheless rigorously blocks off (with one exception even more brief and cryptic than with Mahon) Wait's subjectivity from other characters and the reader in the manner of *Soldiers' Pay;* and like Faulkner's "absent" Mahon, Wait is repeatedly presented as a species of the fundamental evasiveness that he constitutes for the novel as a matter of form: a "hollow" man (41); an "empty man—empty—empty" (113); "nobody" (150); "no one at all" (151); a "black phantom" (150); an "empty cask" (111); "all his inside . . . gone" (113); "distrustful of his own solidity" (140); someone who "did not like to be alone in his cabin, because, when he was alone, it seemed as if he hadn't been there at all" (148). Wait, one might say, like Mahon is less a "character" than the amorphous mirror and tangled intersection of a social condition—and this Conrad *does* say (though trust the tale, not the teller, Faulkner's rereadings over his first reading) in his American preface to the novel: "He is nothing . . . merely the centre of the ship's collective psychology and the pivot of the action."[26] "Immaterial like an apparition" (138), Wait slides through many different and radically inconsistent postures, each varying with the specific audience he is reflecting—the evangelist cook, for instance, believes Wait is a "black devil" (119) and genuinely dying as a function of the cook's own missionary zeal; Donkin believes Wait is shamming because of the cynical self-interest that underlies his (Donkin's) every action—while everyone on board, including the captain (127), the officers (44), and Donkin (153), are generally compelled by the anxieties of death he elicits from, intermingles for, and reflects and deflects in them. The mortal vulnerability of the ship's traditional structures of cohesion exist under the "fit emblem" of Wait's "moribund carcass" (122) and the collective psychology of the ship that he not only emblematizes but centralizes and organizes. And as in

Soldiers' Pay, the very contours of Conrad's novel are determined by a "return" voyage "home" in which the social community waits for and wonders if this centralized character is going to die.

The parallels here are so close and extensive that it becomes possible to speak of *Soldiers' Pay* not simply as a rewriting but as a disciplined reading of *The Nigger of the "Narcissus"*: "reading" being what we generally mean by close, extensive conceptual superimpositions of one narrative-hermeneutic framework on another. But as a reading of *The Nigger of the "Narcissus"*—Faulkner's first of many rereadings of this text which, along with *Moby-Dick*, he would "just like to have written more than any others"—*Soldiers' Pay* is especially interesting in what it appears to *mis*read or *not* read in Conrad's novel: most notably, the interrelated elements of (1) *subversiveness* and (2) *race* that are clearly integral to the meaning of Wait and all but completely evacuated from the thematic and formal construction of Mahon. To take the first element first (for as we shall see, not thinking carefully about subversiveness generally in Conrad's novel has resulted in notable historical and critical tendency not to think at all about race in the novel): though both novels are clearly invested in an absent-centered form and a collectivizing narrative impulse so as to express the collective social psychology and centralized hegemonic formations that are of thematic priority, Mahon is a genuinely absent character slot whose meaning exists *only* "for others" and *only* as a function of the past's allure. This is not a simple allure, but its complexities are a full degree less than those of Wait, a much more substantial though fundamentally mysterious character, who alongside the substantial homologies and metaphors that he offers up for the novel's retrograde "waiting" project as a whole also paradoxically acts as an emblem and agency of what is *causing* the past to die. Mahon is a dying hero; Wait is an undying nuisance. The people of Faulkner's Charleston tend to Mahon in a desperate attempt to preserve the old order; the crew of the *Narcissus*, Singleton *not* among them, tend to Wait in a fashion that actively disrupts and subverts the ship's order and functional cohesion. Indeed, most readings of *The Nigger of the "Narcissus"* place Wait in *opposition* to Singleton and as a "psychological" analogue and equivalent of the "political" Donkin; in this view, the individual attention Wait draws to himself, the weakening sentimentality and pity he encourages in the crew, and the divisive egoism he inculcates within the ship's social order all parallel—and re-express in a different narrative "key" and code—Donkin's self-interested and disruptive "modern" political agitation.[27] Faulkner, of course, is free to write whatever he wants; but to the extent *Soldiers' Pay* is the beginning of a project of—in the words of the first 1933 introduction to *The Sound and the Fury*—"learn[ing] to read" Conrad, has Faulkner, in making over the subversive character and form of Wait into the thoroughly "residual" Mahon, started out on the wrong note?

That Faulkner's reading is, in fact, a quite insightful and healthy corrective to much subsequent criticism is initially suggested by three basic asymmetries that careful reading of *The Nigger of the "Narcissus"* will detect between Wait and Donkin: (1) the two characters are only infrequently and tenuously allies, much more often enemies, in the novel; (2) the power they exercise over the crew is neither equivalent nor commensurate, as Wait is the far more compelling, appealing, and masterful figure; and (3) the two are profoundly divided as a matter of the novel's rhetorical taxonomy between domains of "land" and "sea," Wait living only in the latter and necessarily dying (as ship superstition has it) before the *Narcissus* can reach the former, Donkin being the only character on board truly at home in the former rather than the latter. So, too, as Chris Bongie observes, is the apparent opposition between Wait and "Old" Singleton "hardly, as it were, one of black and white."[28] Not only in the long, Faulknerian, color-coded passage on Singleton quoted above, but also in, for instance, the obsessive chiaroscuro through which Singleton is introduced— his "enormous and blackened hands" descending from "the muscles of his big white arms" (*NN*7); his "white mustache" above the "tobacco-juice that trickled down his long beard" (7); his "black-rimmed glasses" leaning over the white pages of *Pelham* (6–7)—it is clear that the two characters are significantly, reflexively cross-implicated. Bongie argues that this curious "proximity of [Wait and Singleton], who should be opposed as black to white, as present to past, signals the existence of a blind spot in Conrad's historicist strategy, one that produces many of the often-remarked and now glaring 'polyphonies' in the novel."[29] But that Bongie's eloquent and not insensitive account fundamentally misconstrues a problem *Soldiers' Pay* understands all too well is suggested by Irwin's study of Faulkner, a text of rich use in glossing the fundamental psychoanalytic codes of *The Nigger of the "Narcissus"* without which, I have come to believe, there can be no convincing discussion of the politics of Conrad's novel.

Following Freud and Otto Rank, Irwin uses a vocabulary of narcissism, doubling, and death obsession to explain the projective relation between the Quentin of *The Sound and the Fury*, who drowns himself in dark water after a day's preoccupation with race and his shadow, and Henry Sutpen and Charles Bon of *Absalom, Absalom!* For the Quentin of *Absalom*, Irwin argues, Henry and Bon comprise a means of psychic splitting whereby Quentin's own narcissistic ego (projected onto the white Henry) can be severed from the dark double of his unconscious, imagined in the black, seductively aristocratic, powerfully and irreducibly mysterious figure of Bon. At a level rarely considered by recent critics but so clearly emphasized in the title of Conrad's novel, this is very much the psychosymbolic template of *The Nigger of the "Narcissus"*: its presentation of James Wait as the "dark" shadow of a crew of white narcissists, its fascination with dark doubles and dark reflective water and erotically vexed death drives, its very anticipation in Wait of so many of Bon's defining social characteristics, all attesting less to any "influence" between Conrad and Faulkner than to the plausibility of their mutual claims never to have read Freud, which apparently neither author needed to do.

But Irwin is even more suggestive in his discussion of the specific myth of Narcissus he sees applying throughout Faulkner. Though he writes without Conrad in mind, his opening sentence directly glosses the troubling place of James Wait, a figure of doubling and death, on board the aptly named *Narcissus*; from there the analysis resonates even more intimately with Conrad's "sea" novel:

The difference that the ego senses in the double is the implicit presence of the unconscious and particularly that form of unconsciousness which the narcissistic ego finds so offensive to its self-esteem—death. In the myth, Narcissus sees his image reflected in the water; he recognizes the image as himself, yet sees that it is shadowed on a medium whose fluidity, whose lack of differentiation, whose anarchy continually threaten to dissolve the unity of that image at the very moment that the medium itself seems to supply the force to sustain the image. What Narcissus sees is that unified image of his conscious life buoyed up from moment to moment by a medium whose very constitution, in relation to the ego, seems, paradoxically, to be dissolution and death.[30]

This analysis, precisely as it emphasizes the subversive ("anarchic") threat posed by death/the unconscious, also highlights the *economy* of ego and unconsciousness systemically presupposed by and functionally necessary for the "force," "medium," and "very constitution" of the "unified image" of Narcissus. So, too, on board Conrad's *Narcissus*—to stay purely at this level of psychoanalysis and social psychology for the moment—the subversive threat of death posed and expressed by James Wait, like the sea on which the ship floats, is *not* an externality to the system but rather a fundamental and presupposed condition of the economies of light and dark, egoism and death disavowal, *narcissism as a mode of social administration*, upon which the "unified image" and collective functioning of the ship depends. The ship is named *Narcissus*, this is to say, not because "repressing" an "egoistic" narcissism is its primary project but because the fundamentally narcissistic project of disavowing and containing death is the essence of the ship's most basic social processes: i.e., mind-numbing, physically fatiguing, heavily routinized work that prevents the crew from "feeling themselves" (*NN* 91), especially their doubts and fears; and ubiquitous rituals of imagined mastery, wherein officers inspirationally abuse the sailors, the sailors ("romancing on principle" [6]) strategically "abuse the ship" (6) and one another, and wild stories are told about dumping tarpots on officers' heads (9) or knowing all about the "characteristics of gentlemen" and "Admirals" (32–33)—all as a means of "forgetting" the toil, marginality, and utter helplessness that defines these "lifelong prisoners of the sea" (25), and facilitating the "concloosion," as one sailor puts it, that things "ain't that bad now, if you had the taming of them, sonny" (9). James Wait, hence, is right to introduce himself by saying, "I *belong* to the ship" (18, emphasis added), for the threats of death, fear, uncertainty, and powerlessness he incarnates not only are shared by every member of the ship,[31] but also constitute the fundamental psychological rest position that the disciplinary culture of the *Narcissus* both assumes of its subjects and has been designed to manage and administer ("You . . . hold!" says Singleton [26]). Likewise, the crew is also right to experience Wait's eventual death—like that of the *Narcissus* which soon follows—not as the triumphal repulsion of a new and alien system of beliefs, like those associable with the "modern" Donkin, but rather as "the death of an *old* belief, [one that] shook the foundations of our society" (155, emphasis added). For all along, Conrad's crew has tended ambivalently to their beloved Jimmy—"we lovingly called him Jimmy to conceal our hatred of his accomplice [Death]" (36)—not as a form of incipient revolution or mutinous social resistance, but rather as a way to contain and disavow the threats of death that they see in Wait; that they do not wish to see as the permanent condition of themselves (as "lifelong prisoners of the sea" and descendants of the victims of "press gangs" [172] and other "fighting prototypes" [172] of abuse); and that *they desperately wish to isolate from the hegemonic system of the* Narcissus *that they are trying to preserve*. How the crew treats Wait, in other words—and this regardless of any subversive intentions Wait might have or incidental disruptive effects of their own actions—is not the rejection of but their desperate phantasmic attempt to recover the *Narcissus* as a functioning paternalistic system: one that answers all their questions and will without doubt take care of them (as they attempt to do for Wait). The crew tends to Wait as a function of their continuing capture by the hegemony of the *Narcissus*—and this is why they do not for a moment follow Donkin's plans of violent mutiny, whereas, in the famous storm chapter, the very moment they recover the ship is also the moment they set out to rescue and recover Wait. The two "recovery" projects are coterminous.

Soldiers' Pay is right, then, in a way no critical reading of *The Nigger of the "Narcissus"* since it has been, implicitly to decode the social project unfolding around Wait—by explicitly reading and transcribing so much of Wait's character-function and the absent-centered form associable with him—not in insurrectionary but rather in reactionary, residual terms. *Soldiers' Pay*'s acuity in this respect, however, makes all the more striking the novel's *failure* to transcribe and incorporate race as part of the residual ideological machinery and field of investigation it perceives. For if the point of the above paragraph is that the "psychological" unconscious that Conrad's book manifestly posits in Wait doubles as a *political* unconscious, then the project of political management and preservation that Conrad depicts gathered around James Wait equally manifestly concerns race. Both layers of this observation are readily revealed by returning to the long passage quoted earlier on Old Singleton, Conrad's figure of ideological stasis par excellence in the book. In sedimented relation to its overarching concern with social transition from "old" to "new", the immediate point of the passage is that the physical and psychological crisis Singleton is experiencing—as, for the first time, he experiences his body as *not* "indestructible"; as, for the first time, a lifetime of "never [having] given a thought to his *mortal* self" is opened to a new "modern" psychology—is coterminous with the political crisis of confronting the thought that the "burden," the "terror," and the "turmoil" of his life are not that different from the experiences of a black slave. This is what it means for an "ever unthinking" (*NN* 24) person suddenly to wake up "*fettered by the long chain* of disregarded years"; and this moment of Singleton's incipient awakening to "sinister truth" (100) is not unlike Nostromo's moment of awakening both to his own mortality and to class consciousness in *Nostromo*—only whereas Nostromo, a kind of "organic intellectual," succeeds at least to some degree in assuming a critical relationship to the "chains" he recognizes, Singleton is almost allegorically defined (as befits the struggles of everyone else on board the *Narcissus*) by his resistance to this process. But race here is not simply an analogy for class consciousness or even a more general figure for a "political unconscious" lodged against a dominant hegemonic formation. Rather, race is *part* of the hegemonic formation in question—an active, reciprocal, interconnected, indissociable element of the system and culture of the *Narcissus* that everyone on board (except Donkin and Wait) is trying to preserve. Indeed, we get nowhere with the politics of race in *The Nigger of the "Narcissus"* until we realize that just as Singleton, in repeated acts of false consciousness, defines himself in categorical opposition to the black Wait, so too do both the crew's amorous eagerness to help the dying, sickly, helpless, childlike, fundamentally immature Wait—to whom they are "as sentimentally careful . . . as a model slave owner" (140)—and the crew's paroxysms of rage and hysteria when they suspect that "our nigger" (64) may be actually "shamming," manipulating a conventional facade, derive from the crew's own fantasies of racial difference, superiority, and control. These racialized fantasies are part of what they are trying to take care of as they take care of Wait, and they take care of both as a function of the larger paternalistic imperialist system of which the *Narcissus* (a mercantile ship) is an instrument *and race itself a baseline organizing discourse.*

Race, then, according to Conrad's text, is a fundamental, inextricable part of the backward-looking, contra-modern ideological system that the novel scrutinizes. Indeed, one of the great paradoxes of *The Nigger of the "Narcissus"* is that for a text that lends itself with such disturbing ease to racist affirmation and appropriation, it is also, I believe, one of the most searching archaeologies of racial prejudice and its systemic persistence in the English language, especially by a white writer of the late nineteenth and early twentieth centuries.[32] Yet *Soldiers' Pay*, which so keenly understands and transposes to Faulkner's incipient scrutiny of the modern South the general ideological structure, form, and concerns of Conrad's novel, fails conspicuously to extend Conrad's concomitant attention to and engagements with race—the very sort of engagement that, for many critics from Sundquist to Walter Benn Michaels, constitutes the animating "problem" of Faulkner's best fiction.[33] That is, notwithstanding the good number and generally sympathetic (if representationally limited) nature of the black characters in *Soldiers' Pay*; notwithstanding the community's several references to Mrs. Powers, hovering around Mahon, as "that black woman" (*SP* 138), hence insinuating the theme of miscegenation that will become a fixation in Faulkner's later fiction; notwithstanding even the much more precise and prescient (with respect to the Yoknapatawpha novels) focus on Southern ideology than is usually acknowledged of *Soldiers' Pay*, the novel itself fundamentally, as Thadious Davis observes, keeps both African Americans and issues of race in a zone of "autonomous knowing"—sealed off from a genuinely reciprocal, mutually constitutive relation to the "frenetic pace and structures in the dominant world shaped by the text" that it is precisely the purpose of Conrad's novel to place aggressively in question.[34]

That this is a blind spot with respect to race *and* Conrad that we would not want simply to write off to Faulkner's "first" novel or freedom to "write what he likes" is suggested by two important facts about the reception history of *The Nigger of the "Narcissus."* First, the blind eye *Soldiers' Pay* turns to race in Conrad's novel is not at all idiosyncratic but rather typical of the reception of Conrad's novel from the beginning—especially, though not exclusively, in the United States. Originally published in the United States as *The Children of the Sea*—the title was altered "in deference to American prejudices"—on November 30, 1897, one year after *Plessy v. Ferguson* and four months before the formal commencement of the Spanish-American War on April 21, 1898,[35] *The Nigger of the "Narcissus"* during the first half of the twentieth century enjoyed a popularity in the United States that is probably inconceivable to most readers in the second half. The original American reviews, as Donald Rude and Kenneth Davies have carefully demonstrated and as an article in *Bookman* (NY) put it in October 1898, championed the novel with "unanimous praise" and "exceptional vigor" that was not the case in Britain.[36] When the title was changed back to *The Nigger of the "Narcissus"* (with similar general acclaim in the U.S. press) in 1914,[37] the book was supplemented with a special "American" preface and helped to spearhead F. N. Doubleday's momentous campaign to sell "uniform" editions of Conrad in the United States and to market Conrad as a "deep sea" writer during and after the war. And by the time of Conrad's American iconization in the early 1920s, the book had reached something of mythical status: reverentially invoked as the inaugural text of Conrad's "genius";[38] credibly referenced as "what most people consider his best work" (*LA Times*, August 5, 1924);[39] perpetually underwriting Conrad's claim as "the greatest sea storyteller the English language ever had" (*Chicago Daily Tribune*, September 6,

1942);[40] and regularly championed by a motley array of public voices well into the 1950s as simply one of the twentieth century's very greatest novels.[41] Though the novel's original title and the character James Wait did elicit objections and anxieties from the beginning;[42] and though race, of course, shaped earlier U.S. reactions to the novel no less gravely or complexly than it has since Achebe and Said focalized race issues for academic discussion of Conrad in the 1970s, what is most remarkable about the entire U.S. historical stream—especially early on, but also up through the present—of white, public, mainstream, journalistic, and academic discourse on *The Nigger of the "Narcissus"* is the overwhelming *elision* of race, the *difficulty* of its emergence, as a topic of conversation. This is not true, at least to the same degree, of the U.S. reception of either *Heart of Darkness* or Conrad's Malay novels, which, although they too have found their racialized content often sterilized, aestheticized, "philosophized" beyond rec-ognition, expressly were discussed (as we have seen) from the moment they appeared in terms of interracial contact and theories of racial "degeneration." For the eponymous James Wait, however, over half of the U.S. reviews of the novel do not mention him at all;[43] those reviews that do mention him and/or his color engage in a remarkable series of conceptual acrobatics to avoid their significance as markers *of* race;[44] and by the 1920s, when Faulkner was begin-ning his own immersion in Conrad, *The Nigger of the "Narcissus"* had found broad recognition and lionization for its great *sea* story, its famous Preface, its special American introduction emphasizing James Wait as *nothing*, its great *conclusion* (i.e., after Wait has died), its remarkably *British* and also perhaps *Russian* temperament[45]—everything, that is, except those elements of race rela-tion and significance that the novel's title foregrounds as clearly as its (equally underdiscussed—and not coincidentally) psychoanalytic rhetorical coordinates.

Race, one might say, is the "open secret" of this earlier mainstream, white American discourse on Conrad's novel—i.e., what everyone knows, what no one dares say—but this, less as a function of vicious conspiracy or craven im-percipience (though these too no doubt had their roles in the kind of "genteel silence" at issue here) than a profound cultural will, well in advance of the New Criticism, *not* to recognize race as part of the fundamental, timeless, "universal" terrain not only of *literature* but also of the U.S. *American* literary and cultural sensibility reading and rewriting it. This desire not to be fundamentally impli-cated at the levels of both sovereign subject and sovereign nation by questions and historical legacies of race; this fear which, as Richard Gray points out, self-conscious racism to the side leads an aggressively sectionalist text like *I'll Take My Stand* largely to erase race from consideration[46]—*these* are the kinds of knowledge that the non-acknowledgment of race in *The Nigger of the "Narcissus"* is designed to conceal. And hence *Soldiers' Pay* reads *The Nigger of the "Narcissus"* not only with the blindness of its national and regional place and time—which is also, as Jeremy Hawthorn has crucially expressed, a blindness that extends across international, temporal, and professional boundaries[47]—but also as a function of a systemic, extensively imbricated, and formidable cultural project of race disavowal. What we must emphasize and turn to here, moreover—and this is the second element of Conrad's novel's reception history—is that *after Soldiers' Pay*, Faulkner's fiction returns again and again to *The Nigger of the "Narcissus,"* precisely as a trace and means of engaging, exposing, and overcoming this systemic racial disarticulation. Faulkner's major fiction becomes some of the very best readings of *The Nigger of the "Narcissus"* that we have, precisely because it is through a process of compulsively—uncannily, in the most strictly Freudian sense of the term—revisiting, reconceptualizing, and reiterating Conrad's novel that Faulkner's fiction wages its own struggle to make itself *see* the centralized and indissociable place and operations of race throughout the ideological arena of the modern South.

The first two Faulkner novels after *Soldiers' Pay* that effectively reimagine *The Nigger of the "Narcissus"*—and this without at all making them subservient to Conrad's text—are the first two novels usually understood to inaugurate the major phase of Faulkner's fiction: *The Sound and the Fury* and *As I Lay Dying* (1930). Indeed, there is little coincidence that the breakthrough novel of Conrad's own career, which Conrad frequently referred to as his "Beloved" and describes in the 1914 American preface as "the book by which . . . as an artist striving for utmost sincerity of expression, I am willing to stand or fall,"[48] bears such intimate relation to the two most spectacularly progenitive novels of Yoknapatawpha: the first of which Faulkner described as *his* "most splendid failure" and "heart's darling," and the second of which, with the same aesthetic and technical emphasis that is Conrad's point, Faulkner originally imagined as the "book by which, at a pinch, I can stand or fall if I never touch ink again."[49] Nevertheless, it is *The Secret Agent* rather than *The Nigger of the "Narcissus"* whose Conradian sign looms most immediately and visibly over *The Sound and the Fury*: Faulkner's Benjy—whom even Faulkner's detractors, as Sundquist notes, tend to view as the novelist's "one great creation"; of whom Phillip Weinstein suggestively writes that "all Faulkner's art is in getting Benjy to matter narratively"[50]—constituting something of the subjective narrative apotheosis of *The Secret Agent*'s Stevie, the first modernist "idiot" brother whose hopeless dependency on a protective older sister doubles with his general and representative status within the novel as a figure of defenseless ensnarement within the lived social systems of his time. Like Benjy in his complete inability to appreciate metaphor, his wholly acritical relation to the signs that appear before him; and also like Benjy in the wild extremes of docility and rage, stammering and fury, that emerge as a consequence of his automation by ideologically charged sign systems (Benjy responds to Southern landscape like Stevie responds to modern newspapers;[51] much of Faulkner's art is getting Conrad to matter politically in such narratively analogous ways), Conrad's Stevie lives in the endless cycles of suffering, dependency, and futility that he draws: in "circles, circles, circles; innumerable circles, concentric, eccentric; a coruscating whirl of circles that by their tangled multitude of repeated curves, uniformity of form, and confusion of intersection lines suggested a rendering of cosmic chaos, the symbolism of a mad art attempting the inconceivable" (*SA* 45). This formulation is actually first picked up in *Soldiers' Pay* by Faulkner's description of Cecily "running her fingers lightly over her breast, across her belly, drawing concentric circles upon her body" (*SP* 139) to express the "inevitable time" (139) in which she fears being locked. But in *The Sound and the Fury*, Conrad's "symbolism"—astutely decoded by Faulkner in terms of the helpless ideological captivity that is both an aspect of Cecily's condition and a primary meaning of Benjy's "idiocy"—becomes an invitation for the "mad art attempting the inconceivable" that Faulkner actually practices. Without minimizing either the long-standing tradition of the "divine idiot" that stands behind both Conrad and Faulkner or the many literary frames on which *The Sound and the Fury* draws, one may thus say quite literally that Faulkner's first major voice and voicing of Yoknapatawpha come into being through a mediated revoicing of Conrad.

If this is a good example (obviously not limited to Conrad) of what Faulkner might have meant in describing *The Sound and the Fury* as the book that "taught me *both* how to write and how to read, and even more . . . what I had already read," it also encourages us to appreciate that the performative conception of "voice" that Warwick Wadlington traces as a vital element in Faulkner is not only a matter of what characters do in or how readers activate the ("silent") "score" of Faulkner's texts, but also how Faulkner's texts themselves (as a distinctive aspect of their experimental artifice) engage in "voicing" other and earlier literary "scripts" like those of Conrad.[52] But when it comes to the Conrad text most extensively summoned by *The Sound and the Fury*, the focus must return to *The Nigger of the "Narcissus."* For if *Soldiers' Pay* significantly models itself on aesthetic and metathematic elements in that Conrad novel, *The Sound and the Fury* demonstrates internalization of this modeling to the point that the novel seems autonomously, as a function of its own experimentalism, to rediscover Conrad and to do so in ways that are *more* Conradian (albeit as a matter of relation and kinship rather than replication) than the earlier imitation. On the one hand, *The Sound and the Fury* evinces recognizable recoveries—though they now appear endemic to Faulkner's "world" and "voice"—of key Conradian tropes and strategies already evident in *Soldiers' Pay*: for example, (1) an absent-centered form that turns on a character (Caddy) of obsessive multiperspectival interest and suppressed narrative access and voice; (2) the suffusion of this character space with the idea of death and the infinitely lingering prospect of loss; (3) the protracted project of death management and death deferral that consequently constructs this space and constitutes the text; and (4) the ideological content of this psychic project, its liminal suspension in a place between life and death, (Caddy's) presence and absence, expressing the "residual" psychoideological efforts of the three Compson brothers whose commensurate Southern "mind(s)" would restore Caddy to her "ordered place" (*SF* 321). Yet at the same time, *The Sound and the Fury* without any sense of derivation at all recovers and evokes the field of *The Nigger of the "Narcissus"* with a depth and intimacy that far eclipses *Soldiers' Pay*. In its seamlessly integrated (as we have seen from Irwin) discursive topography of narcissism, shadows, mirrors, water, eros, *liebestod*; in its radically unstable (and hopelessly externally dependent) character psychologies and use of wild fluctuations in narrative perspective and mode to express them; in its actualization of the metaphor of *children* to express this subjective condition;[53] in its graphic accentuation of images of disease and sickness to put in question the looming fatality of a social order;[54] in its ultimate skepticism, very much *not* the case in *Soldiers' Pay*, that the residual hegemonic "mindsets" in question can really be transcended or eclipsed; and in the elements of subversion and resistance that one finds in Caddy (like James Wait, but not like Donald Mahon) at the center of an ideological project of containment,

The Sound and the Fury recovers *The Nigger of the "Narcissus"* with greater intimacy precisely by turning away from it as an "intentional" (in both the customary and the rhetorical sense) object.

It is as if Faulkner's self-conscious turn to Southern cultural and historical matter—which literally begins, of course, with *Sartoris*, but first emerges as a matter of Faulkner's autonomous voice in *The Sound and the Fury*—implicitly steers Faulkner into much more profound sympathy with Conrad's novel than the earlier process of premeditated transposition. This serendipitous synchronicity, I am arguing, fundamentally derives from the rich parallelism of historical experience and residual ideological struggle that runs between (and renders aesthetically coterminous) the two cultures seminally animating the two authors' fictions, Conrad's native Poland and Faulkner's post–Civil War South;[55] and it is this sense of aesthetic and residual ideological reciprocity and transposability that *The Sound and the Fury* itself self-consciously registers in connectives like the overarching sign of Stevie, or, importantly, Quentin's dramatic memory shortly before he commits suicide: "Father . . . teaching us that all men are just accumulations *dolls stuffed with sawdust* swept up from trash heaps where all previous dolls had been thrown away *sawdust flowing from what wound in what side that died for me not*" (*SF* 175–76, emphases added). Expressly articulated as a metaphor of death-in-life, the residue of a dead past still constituting the living, leaking terms of unresurrected life, this image of dolls leaking sawdust is an unmistakable echo of what we have already seen is one of the most (ideological, racially) significant moments in the novel:[56] the crew's vision of James Wait as a "ridiculously lamentable . . . doll that had lost half its sawdust" (*NN* 72) as they go to great lengths to rescue him during the storm. Faulkner, moreover, repeats the figure and allusion in *As I Lay Dying*, when Darl comments: "How do our lives ravel out into the no-wind, no-sound, the weary gestures wearily recapitulant: echoes of old compulsions with no-hand on no-strings: in sunset we fall into furious attitudes, *dead gestures of dolls*. Cash broke his leg and now the *sawdust is running out*. He is bleeding to death is Cash."[57]

Here, extending the "reading" of Conrad conducted in *The Sound and the Fury*, Darl lyrically evokes in the figure of "sawdust" Faulkner's two favorite tropes for wearily recapitulant, compulsively echoing "residual" ideological assertion: "saw" (the present seen through the past; also Cash's preferred instrument of embalming the past), and "dust" (the residue and "patina" [*SF* 359] of the past in the present). Indeed, even more than in *The Sound and the Fury*,

As I Lay Dying highlights the paradox that the further Faulkner extends his autonomous commitments to his own voice and the specific project of recovering and critically articulating material Southern culture, the more substantially and sensitively he effectively recovers and elaborates Conrad—especially as concerns the wider ideological significance of "race." Conrad, in turn, may help us reassess our sense and significance of *As I Lay Dying*: for though Eric Sundquist powerfully argues, as the linchpin of a very important account of Faulkner generally, that *As I Lay Dying* "can, more than any of [Faulkner's] major novels, be read independently [of the other major works],"[58] I want to suggest that "capillary" sensitivity to the traces of Conrad in Faulkner shows the opposite, in Sundquist's own historicist and racialized terms, to be the case. Through the mediating template of *The Nigger of the "Narcissus,"* a text that *As I Lay Dying* evokes both more self-consciously and more serendipitously than does any other Faulkner text, *As I Lay Dying* may be read as occupying the absolute dead center of the Faulkner canon, as (1) a moment of true technical emergence; (2) the key bridge text in which Faulkner's major voice (the sonorously choric voice of *Absalom*) organically emerges from his earlier individuated character speakers; and (3) the continuation of a consistent ideological project (which the consistent presence of Conrad from *Soldiers' Pay* forward highlights) that resists any stark formulations of Faulkner's fiction as a "house divided."

The politics of *As I Lay Dying* are what immediately link it to *The Nigger of the "Narcissus."* Like Conrad's novel, *As I Lay Dying* offers a queer mix of conservative and populist sympathies in a project whose primary purpose is to give voice to a group of "voiceless men" (*NN* 6): to articulate, with sympathy and authenticity, the social and psychological experiences of a class of poor, uneducated, all but irretrievably marginalized and disempowered social outcasts, whose tale remains not only untold but presumptively untellable. The joint narrative consequences are striking. On the one hand, the combination of prioritizing what is essentially an ethnographic "rescue" project (*NN* xlii) while also attending to a largely *indiscutable* social group gives rise to an uneasy alternation between stringent realist and elevating nonrealist techniques: i.e., an intense, almost technically insistent mimetic fidelity to local circumstance and speech pattern (Conrad's nautical discourse and crew jargon, Faulkner's rural exactness and dialect) played off against a variety of heroic, comic, mythic, Gothic, impressionist, symbolic, and other experimentalist strategies and registers. Moreover, the novels' very presupposition of the need to voice the experiences of people who are *by definition* crucially voiceless—both novels emphasize their characters' linguistic limitations; both titles foreground impossibilities of vocalization (Conrad's refers to the most vocally marginalized character in the book; Faulkner's, referring to an identical character slot, posits a speech act made *after* death that begs the question of the conditions of its possibility)—gives rise to a mutual inconsistency and fundamental impossibility of narrative form. The two texts not only make recourse (albeit through very different techniques) to a variety of different narrative perspectives; they also proceed through a fundamental narrative slippage—seamlessly interwoven throughout both texts, and beyond the internal ability of either to account for it—between immanent and externalized expressive registers: Conrad's notorious vacillations between "we" and "they" perspectives ("impossible" in the sense that the same narrator cannot assume *both* relations to the crew, one from within, the other from above, at the same time, although the text encourages precisely this illusion), and Faulkner's equally notorious and fluid movements between registers of language both within and above (in the several senses of that word) his characters' "realistic" expressive range. At issue here amid very different technical strategies is a profound structural similarity—effecting what John T. Matthews describes as Faulkner's novel's "disembodiment effect,"[59] and implicating concerns of community, ideology, subjectivity, and impossible transition—that is unique, surely as a matter of degree if not kind, in Anglo-American modernist prose.

So, too, *As I Lay Dying* mirrors—with a rich awareness, of course, of a long tradition of tragic and epic literary antecedents implicated in the process—the basic premise and plot trajectory of *The Nigger of the "Narcissus"*: i.e., a central, titular character dying, and a burial journey coextensive with this moribund state (and its extenuations) and the imperative of cooperative action (against the "elements") which exposes tensions in the social unit. Here, moreover, we enter the more familiar terrain of long-standing recoveries of Conrad: formal absent centers (this time, Addie) engineered in terms of death and the prolonged, liminal experience of responding to it; pervasive tropes of "waiting," "dying," and "burden";[60] a metathematics of grief and its incompletion; extraordinary perils of social and psychosubjective dissolution; and an overarching interest in the persistence of residual ideological formations, explored through the instance of the family and an absent-centered form that provides both a metaphor for absented social foundations and a narrative means for

dramatizing the centripetally organized and socially enmeshed nature of subjectivity, its hegemonic captivity despite the death and lost cause of the foundational Mother herself. Indeed, just as *The Nigger of the "Narcissus"* emphasizes
the practical element of lived social relationships and ritualized conduct that
makes for hegemony on board the *Narcissus*, *As I Lay Dying* moves away from
the solipsistic and epistemological emphases through which questions of ideology are primarily posed in *The Sound and the Fury*. Instead, although *As I Lay
Dying* does place much emphasis on the Bundrens doing what they do because
their *minds* and Addie's "*mind* are set on it" (*AILD* 30, 53, 86, 89, 115, emphasis
added); and although Peabody, in one of the novel's most famous expressions
of ideological captivity, says:

I can remember how when I was young I believed death to be a phenomenon of the
body; now I know it to be merely a *function of the mind—and that of the minds of the
ones who suffer bereavement.* The nihilists say it is the end; the fundamentalists, the beginning; when in reality it is no more than a single tenant or family moving out of a
tenement or a town. (44, emphasis added)

—what "mind" means in *As I Lay Dying*, apropos of Peabody's closing domicilic
figures, is not an opposition to bodies and others but rather an inhabitation by
embodied realities and others. The Compson brothers *think* like one another;
the Bundrens, who are not alike, are obsessed with seeing and being inside one
another. The Compson brothers—including Benjy, in his own way—*think* a lot,
in significantly autonomous relation to anything practical they are trying to
accomplish; for the Bundrens, thoughts and practicalities of action, like Cora's
opening meditation on hens, are inextricably enmeshed. The Compson brothers
are both elaborately and distinctively (we do not confuse their voices) enslaved
to conventional thought patterns; the Bundrens, who rarely speak long enough
to elaborate and whose thoughts and language are frequently in question as
their own, are enslaved to the simultaneously representative (because they have
trouble thinking beyond them) and performative (because what they effect is
more important than what they "mean") conventions *through which they use
and are used by one another.* As Warwick Wadlington powerfully summarizes,
individuality in *As I Lay Dying* is the product not simply of a cluster of social-
izing ideas but also "a cluster of social relations": "Not only one's death but
one's life happens in and through others."[61] Painfully limited resources (material and conceptual); excruciating and inescapable proximity; and radical de-

pendency and intersubservience—all of which Anse pathologically disavows in his exemplary appeals to Addie's "private" nature and his own refusal to be "beholden" to any man—all give rise to a concrete infrastructure of collective habit and lived social practices that are as integral to the "mind" of the Bundrens as the (quite large number) of ideological/epistemological "ideas" also inscribed within it. This same robust presentation of "hegemony"—simultaneously ideational and concrete—repeats an emphasis we have already seen in the practical regimentation of the crew, itself an emphatically blurred conflation of individuality and collectivity, on board Conrad's *Narcissus*.

Even more so than with *The Sound and the Fury*, then, *As I Lay Dying* demonstrates an *enhancement* of common ground with *The Nigger of the "Narcissus"* since the seed of *Soldiers' Pay*—and this, in significant part because problematics of residual ideology are important to both authors throughout. But this linear and continuous course across Faulkner's fiction also allows Faulkner to revisit concerns of "race" as a coordinating concern of ideology to which his work had been blind before: indeed, through its self-conscious relation to *The Nigger of the "Narcissus," As I Lay Dying* is able to conduct a critical anatomy of the invisibility of race within white Southern residual hegemonic formations that Faulkner criticism itself, because it has not looked with historicist attention to the element of Conrad in Faulkner, has been unable to see. Against the once predominant view that race is simply an "absence" in *As I Lay Dying*; and against even the more sensitive recent criticism that treats the scene near the end where Jewel "go[es] blind" (*AILD* 229) with respect to three negroes, but treats it only as an isolated picaresque episode within the greater Bundren odyssey, we may juxtapose the following passage from Anse's first speaking section, itself arguably the most metathematically significant section in the novel. "It" in the opening sentence refers either to Darl's threatened institutionalization or Cash's carpentry and recent injury; from there the subject is the bedridden, dying Addie:

Making me pay for it. She was well and hale as ere a woman ever were, except for that road. Just laying down, resting herself in her own bed, asking naught of none. "Are you sick, Addie?" I said.

"I am not sick," she said.

"You lay you down and rest you," I said. "I know you are not sick. You're just tired. You lay you down and rest."

"I am not sick," she said. "I will get up."

"Lay still and rest," I said. "You are just tired. You can get up tomorrow." And she was laying there, well and hale as ere a woman ever were, except for that road. (*AILD* 37)

Anse's opening monologue is arguably the most metathematic section in the novel because in its opening (and killingly comic) meditation on the evils of "roads," in its introduction of Darl "with his eyes full of the land" (36), and in its situating the dying Addie in these contexts, the novel explicitly introduces and glosses its own central concerns with the advent of modernity, the effect on Southern modes of perception and action, and the tenacity of "undying" residual hegemonic formations, respectively. But in the passage quoted above, Anse's section also effectively glosses the novel in *metaliterary* terms: for in its comedic back and forth over the question of whether Addie is truly "sick," in its confusions about how a person who appears as "well and hale as ere a woman ever were" could actually be dying, and in the dynamics of disavowal (from both sides, just as in Conrad) and modernity that inform these movements, all in advance of a storm "a-coming up that road like a durn . . . bloody egg upon a crest of thunderheads" (37, 40), Faulkner's text manifestly re-creates the terms and conditions of Conrad's crew's response to James Wait on board the *Narcissus*; this is a moment in which Faulkner's text self-consciously signals and frames its much larger engagement with *The Nigger of the "Narcissus."* Like *Soldiers' Pay*, moreover, this moment of self-conscious contact with Conrad would seem to be one in which race is erased: for not only does the passage fail to mention race in any way, but also, as with Donald Mahon and the field of ideology examined through his Conradian image, *As I Lay Dying* presents a field of social relations affected by Addie's death which consists only of the white members of her family and their white neighboring acquaintances. But immediately before this passage race *is* evoked: when Anse bemoans how the "bad luck" of the road and Cash's injury left "me and Addie *slaving and a-slaving*" (*AILD* 36, emphasis added). And so too immediately after the passage Anse religiously and rhetorically invokes the racialized self-analogy of the slave once again: "But peace is in my heart: I know it is. I have done things but neither better nor worse than them that pretend otherlike, and I know that *Old Marster* will care for me as for ere a sparrow that falls" (38, emphasis added). Whereas in *Soldiers' Pay*, reading and rewriting Conrad meant *not* reading and transcribing race—leaving it, as Addie would say, "outside the circle" (*AILD* 172)—in *As I Lay Dying* reading and writing in self-conscious relation to Conrad means critically *displacing* race: so that what Anse cannot focally think about himself, and what both *Soldiers' Pay* and the "mind" of the poor white South under scrutiny in *As I Lay Dying* cannot conceive about themselves (namely, their fundamental penetration by questions of race; their disavowal of class interests through presumptions of race), becomes critically exposed and strategically traced in the penumbral racialized tropes Anse himself speaks only because he does not take them too materially or literally. *The Nigger of the "Narcissus,"* whose racial content for *Soldiers' Pay* is only a matter of metaphor, becomes for *As I Lay Dying* a text whose racial erasure must be materially accounted for. In *As I Lay Dying*, the very intimacy of *The Nigger of the "Narcissus"* as a literary frame makes it so the issues of race that Anse cannot see, and that Faulkner in *The Sound and the Fury* only really begins to see, the novel itself must account for and theorize as a matter of systemic cultural blindness. This is what it means for a novel as sensitive and committed to a critical archaeology of Southern culture as *As I Lay Dying* to script itself through *The Nigger of the "Narcissus"*: a novel whose very title, after all, was bound to provoke racialized reflection at some point—and whose title character is the black face upon whom Addie's character is very self-consciously inscribed.

This is a point we can develop with reference to that other "most important" speech in *As I Lay Dying*: Addie's monologue. Again, this is a section whose larger metathematic and metaliterary qualities it is important to emphasize. As to the former, the section resembles Molly Bloom's soliloquy at the end of *Ulysses* in dramatically reversing and recontextualizing paradigms and perspectives privileged earlier in the novel, offering a counter-hermeneutic aperture for the entire text. As to the latter—and this, without at all restricting the section's intertextual ambit to Conrad—we may note, in words Albert Guerard Jr. uses to describe James Wait's narrative treatment in the middle of Conrad's novel, that Addie's section commits a "serious violation" of narrative expectations in its unprecedented, even unaccountable turn to an "interior monologue" by a character concerning whom "it has been the very convention of the novel that [s/he] must remain shadowy":[62] a repetition (once, briefly, dramatically, in the middle of the text) "with a difference" of Conrad's violation which, especially because it is transacted in the name of an eponymous character already modeled in relation to James Wait, marks this section *narratively* in self-conscious relation to Conrad. This section does what it does with sensitivity to what Conrad did before, and readers sensitive to both texts cannot help also being sensitive to this. At stake in this process, moreover, is the recovery of crucial racialized dimensions of Addie's text which, without recourse to Conrad, precisely because

these dimensions are simultaneously literary and ideological, have remained critically invisible, but with the restoration of Conrad become almost self-evident.
Here is how Addie's section, which I am arguing should be understood as narratively framed by the racialized idea and ambit of James Wait, famously begins:

In the afternoon when school was out and the last one had left with his dirty snuffling
nose, instead of going home I would go down the hill to the spring where I could be
quiet and hate them. It would be quiet there then, with the water bubbling up and away
and the sun slanting quiet in the trees and the quiet smelling of damp and rotting leaves
and new earth; especially in the early spring, for it was worst then.

   I could just remember how my father used to say that the reason for living was to
get ready to stay dead a long time. And when I would have to look at them day after
day, each with his or her secret selfish thought, *and blood strange to each other blood
and strange to mine*, and think that this seemed to be the only way I could get ready to
stay dead, I would hate my father for ever having *planted* me. I would look forward
to the times when they faulted, *so I could whip them. When the switch fell I could feel
it upon my flesh; when it welted and ridged it was my blood that ran, and I would think
with each blow of the switch: Now you are aware of me! Now I am something in your
secret and selfish life, who have marked your blood with my own for ever and ever.* (AILD
170, emphases added)

   The children's "other blood" that is "strange" to Addie's "blood" is, of
course, not what *Light in August* will call "black blood": that is, Addie teaches
at a segregated school, and the children are, as Jordan Baker says in the Plaza
Hotel in *The Great Gatsby*, "all white here" (*G* 137). But this is not to say that
race is not a defining issue in or that miscegenation is not the master trope
and underlying anxiety of Addie's meditation. For alongside the distant sug-
gestions of plantation economy and race hierarchy—akin to Anse's references
to "me and Addie slaving and a-slaving" and "Ole Marster"—synecdochally
implicated in the idea of being "planted"; and alongside the graphic images of
whipping that directly recall slave narratives like those of Frederick Douglass
and that effectively, as Addie assumes the place of the Master to return the
violence and submission patriarchally visited on her, equate gender and racial
oppression; and alongside the fact that "blood" in Faulkner is not only always
a racially charged trope but also racially charged precisely because it is always
also an *erotic* trope (eros being the reason Addie goes down by the water; erotic
desire being the quantity she first sublimates by whipping the children, then

gratifies by "tak[ing] Anse" [*AILD* 170] and in the tryst with Whitfield)—alongside all these factors that point to race and miscegenation, *blood mixing* itself is *the* fundamental trope and ambivalence of Addie's section. On the one hand, profoundly alienated by and defiantly skeptical of the artificial tools of language and social convention through which human beings "use one another . . . like spiders dangling by their mouths from a beam, swinging and twisting and never touching" (172), Addie yearns for the primary, unmediated contact of her "blood" and "other blood": to mark "your blood with my own for ever and ever," to make "my blood and their blood flow as one stream" (172), to join "the terrible blood, the red bitter flood boiling through the land" (174), to recover "the wild blood boiling along the earth, of me and all that lived" (175)—all as a complex function of the primary acknowledgment, intimacy, power, and voice Addie's world radically denies to her. Yet on the other hand, Addie is equally obsessed with keeping her "blood strange" and distinct: "liquify and flow" (173) as her thoughts may sometimes be inclined, she generally experiences sex, pregnancy, and childbirth (all variations on the idea of blood mixing) as horrifying instances of "my aloneness [being] violated over and over each day" (172); she insists, not only in opposition to the "conventional" Anse, that "I would be I" (174), but in opposition to the "terrible blood" (175) commingled with Whitfield that "I was I" and "he was he" (174); and she not only sets the family standard for "secret and selfish thought[s]," but also pathologically comes to think both of the "wild blood" of the world and of the individual blood relations in her family in terms of who belongs to "me alone" (175) and who is absolutely, categorically "not mine" (176).

The allure and absolute taboo of blood mixture here is unmistakably structured in terms of racialized discourse and anxiety: so much so that one is tempted to conclude Addie self-consciously structures her entire project of resistance and revenge in strategic relation to the ultimate taboo of miscegenation. After all, she explicitly begins with simultaneously racialized and eroticized images of whipping children; she repeatedly (eight times in less than eight pages) expresses erotic desire through tropes of "wild darkness" (170), most notably in the key bridge passage where she lies by Anse and thinks erotically toward Whitfield:

I would lie by him in the *dark*, hearing the *dark* land talking of God's love and His beauty and His sin; hearing the *dark* voicelessness in which the words are the deeds, and the other words that are not deeds . . . coming down like the cries of the geese out of the wild *darkness*. (174, emphases added)

Indeed, Addie's erotic desire is precisely for that which is most sinful, unspeakable, convention breaking, and taboo, "the more utter and terrible" (174) the better; and if Addie does not come right out and say—as her near namesake in *Light in August*, Joanna *Burden*, will—that her ultimate fantasy is to sleep with (or do something like sleep with) a "Negro," this is exactly what we should expect in a chapter whose fundamental point is that "words are no good," that they "don't ever fit even what they are trying to say at" (171). But the point with respect to race in Addie's section is very much the opposite. Far from critically discerning and subtly inscribing cross-racial parallels and miscegenative tropes of contact and subversion, Addie is most remarkable in that she could so superabundantly raise the possibility of such relations and connections and then *not* make the connection. As with Anse, from whom "slaving" and "Old Marster" are only the most displaced and distant of tropes, Addie is someone for whom race, to the extent it could come up and would implicate her "circle" of existence, is simply beyond her field of vision. Much more enslaved to convention than she knows, Addie naively invests herself in Emersonian fantasies of simply "escaping" convention and language only to plunge herself in racialized conventions of which she is completely unaware. "Blind to sin" (176), as Cora suggests, and in much the same way that Jewel "go[es] blind" (229) with respect to three African Americans in the later town encounter, Addie cannot see that her very conception of "sin" is structured not only in terms of race but in terms of the racialized conventions that invisibly (to Addie) colonize her thinking. The character who is modeled in dialogic relation to the "Nigger" of the *Narcissus*, in the chapter that is both the centerpiece of her book and metanarratively directed squarely at *The Nigger of the "Narcissus*," simultaneously erases and *everywhere* leaves traces of the racialized frame through which she came into being. Or to put this another way: what is fundamentally, truly miscegenative about Addie's section is its *narrative* commingling of Addie and James Wait, and through this narrative miscegenation Faulkner's novel is prompted to elaborate and theorize the race blindness that circumscribes Addie herself.

Conrad alone, of course, does not force the critical anatomy of race invisibility conducted in Faulkner: but just as contiguous consideration of the two texts, *As I Lay Dying* under the star of *The Nigger of the "Narcissus*," in itself forces something of a sea change in the reading of Faulkner's novel (much as Faulkner's novels earlier compelled a sea change in readings of Conrad's novel), the point here is that Conrad is part of the world that *As I Lay Dying* is reading, voicing, and conversing with in its increasingly attentive engagements with race. Conrad offers the resistance, the interpretive challenge, *of* that world, and as *As I Lay Dying* comprehends and "signifies on" Conrad's novel with greater fullness than any Faulkner novel yet, so, too, as part of that critical sympathy is an increasing awareness of race disavowal as a powerful mechanism of white Southern self-construction. Moreover, what is true of the two focal (in the geometric, elliptical sense) monologues of *As I Lay Dying*, which are also the two moments that most precisely point to *The Nigger of the "Narcissus,"* is also true of Faulkner's novella as a whole: whose general symbiosis with Conrad is coterminous with a broad and aggressive anatomy of race erasure that spans and subtends its entirety. This critical anatomy proceeds through two basic strategies, both of which are linked to Conrad, and neither of which has been critically discussed before. First, Faulkner is very careful repeatedly to use tropes of darkness and blackness—frequently associated, as in *The Nigger of the "Narcissus,"* with water, both as a medium of sublime disintegration and as a mechanism of failed narcissistic self-reflection—not only as an abstract expression of his characters' imminent sense of complete psychic and social dissolution, but also as a pointed gesture encompassing the threat race poses to an integrated understanding of the (white) Southern "family." Of a kind with Addie's narrative, blind to the racial concerns that simultaneously structure and threaten to dissolve its integrity, one may consider articulations such as these:

It would be *black*, the shelf *black*, the still surface of the water a *round orifice into nothingness*, where before I stirred it awake with the dipper *I could see* maybe a star or two in the bucket. (Darl 11, all emphases here and below added)

Pa looks down *at the face*, at the *black* sprawl of Dewey Dell's hair, the outflung arms, the clutched fan now motionless on the fading quilt. (Darl 50)

It is *dark*. I can hear wood, silence: I know them. But not living sounds, not even him. It is as though the *dark* were resolving him out of his integrity. . . . I see him dissolve—legs, a rolling eye, a gaudy splotch like cold flames—and float upon the *dark* in fading solution. (Vardaman 56)

I saw the *dark* stand up and go whirling away and I said "Are you going to nail her up in it, Cash, Cash, Cash?" (Vardaman 65)

Once I waked with a *black void* rushing under me. I could not see. (Dewey Dell 121)

Before us the thick *dark* current runs. It talks up to us in a murmur become ceaseless and myriad . . . as though just beneath the surface something huge and alive waked for a moment of lazy alertness out of and into light slumber again. (Darl 141)

[Of the mules:] They see it too; for a moment they also *shine black* out of the water. The downstream one vanishes. . . . Cash is half turned, the reins running taut from his hand and disappearing into the water. . . . They roll up out of the water in succession, turning completely over, their legs stiffly extended as when they had lost contact with the earth. (Darl 148–49)

These articulations of darkness, penumbral and apocalyptic, inscribe race precisely as race *keeps* them penumbral in the terms of their apocalypticism. That is, they are both explicitly disarticulated (like Addie's section) from any sense of race as an organizing rubric—from any self-conscious sense of inter-penetration or equation between poor white and Southern black experience—while at the same time they are shadowed by a "dark" force (which must at least *include* race) that presents itself both as a violent *reactionary* volatility and a vast, dissolving, all-encompassing threat to an entire way of life. In other words, like the historical James K. Vardaman, Mississippi's populist, progressive, and outspokenly racist governor (1904–8) and U.S. senator (1912–18), Faulkner's Vardaman and his family both fundamentally disavow any self-implication by racial otherness and its categories, yet curiously depend (in the histori-cal Vardaman's case, especially around election time) on apocalyptic visions of "darkness" violently to affirm and hysterically to imagine threats to the "family" unit. To repeat Irwin's earlier psychoanalytic formulation, a certain Southern paradigm of self-actualization is here "buoyed up . . . by a medium whose very constitution . . . seems, paradoxically, to be dissolution and death."

The second strategy is blackface, and it is directly connected to the meta-narrative awareness with which *As I Lay Dying* tells its tale of the poor white South, knowing that it has implicitly adopted and adapted and superimposed itself on the racialized framework of James Wait and *The Nigger of the "Nar-cissus."* Important here is the famous scene reported by Darl in which Cash, searching in the pouring rain for his saw to finish Addie's coffin, looks over at Anse, who holds the saw and stands "gaunt and streaming" (78) in the rain: "'Why don't you go on to the house, out of the rain?' Cash says. Pa looks at him, his face streaming slowly. It is as though upon a face carved by a savage caricaturist a monstrous burlesque of all bereavement flowed. 'You go on in,'

Cash says. 'Me and Vernon can finish it'" (78). Anse's face is a "monstrous bur-lesque" because it turns emotion inside out: the "streams" of "all bereavement flow[ing]" are not tears but rain. The illusion of tears is, in fact, a "savage" and "monstrous" mask—an idea that Darl in this section has already linked to blackface: first, in general images of Anse's "shabby and aimless silhouette" against a background of "feeble light" (76), and also Cash's body, its interior-ity and exteriority confused, leaning over the lantern "as though he had been abruptly turned wrong-side out, shirt and all" (77); and second, in the almost theatrical image of paint, light, set, and reversed exteriority with which the section begins:

The lantern sits on a stump. Rusted, grease-fouled, its cracked chimney smeared on one side with a soaring smudge of soot, it sheds a feeble and sultry glare upon the trestles and the boards and the adjacent earth. Upon the dark ground the chips look like *ran-dom smears of soft pale paint on a black canvas*. The boards look like long smooth tatters torn from the *flat darkness and turned backside out*. (73, emphases added)

It would be hard to find a better metaphor for Addie's relation to James Wait, *As I Lay Dying*'s relationship to *The Nigger of the "Narcissus,"* than that of inscribing "soft pale paint" on a "black canvas," or tearing strands of "flat darkness" from a fabric and turning them "backside out"; and this very process of imposing white faces on black models, or rather black faces on white models who remain strenuously oblivious to the implications, is as fundamental to *As I Lay Dying* as anything else the novel does. Always "there" in the dark voids of "splotched" (52) dissolution and interchangeability that haunt the novel from the beginning (themselves an expression of the radical dependency of subjectivity on "dark" exteriorities); and also liminally present in the black buzzards that increasingly hover over and threaten to descend on the material surface of the novel, blackface is a concrete aesthetic strategy Faulkner applies throughout the novel—with increasing explicitness and graphic intensity the closer the Bundrens get to "town" and the class antagonisms presented by it. Just as early on Anse is presented in "savage" silhouette and Cash is described with his hair "smooth and black as if he had painted it onto his head" (90), so, too, as the Bundrens approach Jefferson, a crescendo of imaginative castings of them in blackface occur. First, Dewey Dell walks into Moseley's store with, in Moseley's view, "as black a pair of eyes as I ever saw" and looking like someone who wants to buy "a bottle of nigger toilet water" to apply to her "complexion"

(199; significantly, this is the first time in the novel that the offensive racial epithet is used, and the key word *complexion* is used twice). Then Vardaman mentions to Dewey Dell that when they sleep in the moonlight, they "will lie half in the white and half in the black": "'Look,' I say, 'My legs look black. Your legs look black too'" (215–16). Then Cash's rebroken and cement-cast leg turns "black" so that, as Vardaman says, "Your foot looks like a nigger's foot, Cash" (224). Then Jewel's back is burned when the barn burns down, requiring the application of grease such that his back turns "black" and "looks like a nigger's" (225). Finally, Darl is ultimately captured and committed in a scene whose vigilante-like public violence and sexual undertones unmistakably evoke a lynching.[63] Everyone in the Bundren family, hence, is in some sense placed in blackface by the end of the novel, just as Addie Bundren herself is the product of racialized literary and social conventions that have become curiously white-washed. In both cases the point is the same: a powerful and deeply systemic hegemonic blindspot when it comes to race; an utter inability to recognize commonalities of interest, experience, and collective possibility across racial lines; an inability even to recognize race as a constitutive tool of poor white class subservience. This is what it means for Jewel, near the end of the novel, to "go blind" with respect to three negroes, turning the shock one of them quite reasonably expresses at the stench of Addie's coffin into a conflict of class and "honor" purely between two white men; this is the same blindness that every member of the Bundren family, relentlessly placed in blackface only so as *not* to recognize black experience as akin to their own, demonstrates throughout; and it is a blindness in which Faulkner criticism has also been complicit, precisely because it has not looked in politically meaningful ways to the genetic connections between *As I Lay Dying* and *The Nigger of the "Narcissus."*

The culmination, hence, of Faulkner's reengagements with *The Nigger of the "Narcissus"* in the form of *Light in August* (1932) is thus not a sudden discovery of "race" as a central relay site of Southern ideology, not a sharp transition to the second half of a "house divided" of Faulkner's fiction, but rather a project Faulkner had been working his way critically and continuously toward through engagements with Conrad since *Soldiers' Pay. Light in August* again assumes the form of an absent-centered text wherein the very ambiguity of Joe Christmas's racial identity confirms the dependency of the community on categories of race in much the same way that the ambiguity of James Wait's identity—is he dying or merely shamming sick?—plunges the *Narcissus* into social crisis because race itself, the fundamental coordinate of all mysteries attaching to James Wait, is foundational to its sense of order. This Conradian pattern finds further elaboration in the several Faulkner texts involving the black character Lucas Beauchamp, especially *Intruder in the Dust* (1948), wherein again Faulkner's primary concern is not the elaboration of his subjectivity as an African-American man but rather the use of him as a psychologically foreclosed narrative space to tease out the racialized topography that surrounds and constructs him in the white South. *Intruder in the Dust* was written shortly before the Nobel Prize speech in which, as we have seen, Faulkner accords a crucial place to Conrad. What I have argued in this chapter is that it is as much culture and history as art that dictate[s] this commemoration of Conrad: that through both important moorings in and continuities of Polish and Southern history that make residual ideological persistence a central concern of both authors, and through equally coterminous investigations of race as a central constituent of Western imperialist and white Southern ideological formations, Faulkner and Conrad revisit one another in ways that are ultimately no more personal to them than they are to the diverse strands of twentieth-century global writers who have in turn experienced the "delayed repercussion" of their historical and aesthetic examples.

Reference Matter

NOTES

INTRODUCTION

1. Amy Kaplan, "'Left Alone with America': The Absence of Empire in the Study of American Culture," in Kaplan and Donald Pease, eds., *Cultures of United States Imperialism* (Durham, N.C.: Duke University Press, 1994), 3.

2. Perry Miller, *Errand into the Wilderness* (Cambridge, Mass.: Harvard University Press, 1956), vii, viii.

3. Kaplan, "Left Alone," 5–11.

4. Ibid., 4, 18.

5. F. Scott Fitzgerald, "Minnesota's Capital in the Rôle of Main Street," *Literary Digest International Review* 1 (1923): 35–36, 36.

6. For more on Perry Miller's personal background, see Robert Middlekauff, "Perry Miller," in Marcus Cunliffe and Robin W. Winks, eds., *Pastmasters* (New York: Harper & Row, 1969), 167–90.

7. *YOS* 48; Miller, *Errand into the Wilderness*, viii.

8. Miller, *Errand into the Wilderness*, vii–ix.

9. Conrad himself was especially fond of this metaphor. To Curle on March 12, 1923, Conrad describes his impending U.S. trip as "the voyage of the New Columbus"; to Doubleday on March 14, 1923, he references "my voyage of discovery" and compares himself to John Cabot, the Venetian navigator who "discovered" the continent of North America for England; on April 3, 1923, he writes to Gerard Jean-Aubry that "the moment of the discovery of America nears." One may compare the special attention Conrad devotes to the "pathetic figure" of Columbus—"the greatest of them all, who has presented modern geography with a new world to work on," even as "the discovery of America was the occasion of the greatest outburst of reckless cruelty and greed known to history" (*LE* 3)—in "Geography and Some Explorers," written shortly after and originally published in *National Geographic* within months of Conrad's U.S. visit. See Curle, *Conrad to a Friend: 150 Selected Letters from Joseph Conrad to Richard Curle* (London: Sampson Low, 1928), 110; G. Jean-Aubry, *Joseph Conrad: Life and Letters*, 2 vols. (Garden City, N.Y.: Doubleday, 1927), 2.296; G. Jean-Aubry, *Lettres française* (Paris: Gallimard, 1929), 183.

10. The useful bibliography edited by Robert Secor and Debra Moddelmog, *Joseph Conrad and American Writers: A Bibliographical Study of Affinities, Influences, and Relations* (Westport, Conn.: Greenwood Press, 1985), illustrates both the achievements and limitations of prior U.S. contextualizations of Conrad. Though meticulously cataloguing hundreds of individual references to Conrad made by U.S. literary authors and in criticism related to U.S. literature through the New Criticism, the bibliography, per the emphasis on "writers" in its title, leaves fundamentally unconsidered the

cultural and political U.S. contexts and writings essential to understanding Conrad's "relations" with the United States. For this very reason, Secor and Moddelmog cannot ultimately offer up a sustained and convincing narrative of Conrad's U.S. allure because they have written out of the story in advance that which *is* (or is at least absolutely foundational to) the story. I have found especially useful as a supplement to Secor and Moddelmog's bibliography Theodore Ehrsam's *A Bibliography of Joseph Conrad* (Metuchen, N.J.: Scarecrow Press, 1969). Historical materials (U.S., British, and other reviews, historical references, etc.) I have found through these sources and independently will soon be available through an online digital archive. For more on this book's relation to contemporary and more long-standing traditions of Conrad studies, compare notes 11 and 37 below.

11. Regarding Conrad studies, this book innovates not by conceiving Conrad in global terms or deploying Conrad as a means of imagining world-literary or world-political contact but by joining with and restoring to such a framework of globalizing aspirations—one of the primary energizing baselines of Conrad studies today—a U.S. vantage that has been largely written out of the equation. Among those transnational formulations of Conrad from whom this book has benefited and to whose dynamic discourse it seeks to contribute are Terry Collits, *Postcolonial Conrad: Paradoxes of Empire* (London: Routledge, 2005); Jennifer French, *Nature, Neo-colonialism, and the Spanish American Regional Writers* (Hanover, N.H.: University Press of New England, 2005); Byron Caminero-Santangelo, *African Fiction and Joseph Conrad: Reading Postcolonial Intertextuality* (New York: SUNY Press, 2005); Padmini Mongia, "Between Men: Conrad in the Fiction of Two Contemporary Indian Writers," and Christopher GoGwilt, "Opera and the Passage of Literature: Joseph Conrad, Pramoedya Ananta Toer, and the Cultural Dialectic of Abysmal Taste," in Carola Kaplan, Peter Mallios, and Andrea White, eds., *Conrad in the Twenty-first Century: Contemporary Approaches and Perspectives* (New York: Routledge, 2005), 85–100, 101–20; Asako Nakai, *The English Book and Its Marginalia: Colonial/Postcolonial Literatures After Heart of Darkness* (Amsterdam: Rodopi, 2000); Zdzisław Najder, *Joseph Conrad: A Life* (Rochester, N.Y.: Camden House, 2007), and *Conrad in Perspective* (Cambridge: Cambridge University Press, 2002); Andrzej Busza, "Conrad's Polish Literary Background," 10 *Antemurale* (Rome, 1966): 109–255; Claudine Lesage, *Joseph Conrad et le Continent* (Montreuil-sur-Mer, France: IEH, 2003); Yves Hervouet, *The French Face of Joseph Conrad* (Cambridge: Cambridge University Press, 1990); and Anthony Fothergill, *Secret Sharers: Joseph Conrad's Cultural Reception in Germany* (Oxford: Peter Lang, 2006).

12. See Michaels's "The Road to Vietnam," *Modern Language Notes* 94 (Summer 1979): 1173–75.

13. Wai Chee Dimock, *Through Other Continents: American Literature Across Deep Time* (Princeton: Princeton University Press, 2006), 5, 35.

14. Ibid., 4–5.

15. Ibid., 3; Benedict Anderson, *Imagined Communities* (London: Verso, 1983), 28–32 (qtg. W. Benjamin); on the "contemporary" in relation to the untamed present and immanent futurity, see "Introduction," in Kaplan, Mallios, and White, *Conrad in the Twenty-first Century*, xv–xix, and Donald Pease and Robyn Wiegman, "Futures," in *The Futures of American Studies* (Durham, N.C.: Duke University Press, 2002), 1–44, 11–18.

16. For Gregory Jay's suggestion for renaming the academic field of U.S. American literature, see Jay, "The End of 'American' Literature: Toward a Multicultural Practice," *College English* 53.3 (1991): 264–81.

17. See Natalie Melas, *All the Difference in the World: Postcoloniality and the Ends of Comparison* (Stanford: Stanford University Press, 2007): 1–44.

18. See John Carlos Rowe, ed., *Post-nationalist American Studies* (Berkeley: University of California Press, 2000), 2.

19. The earliest articulation of this term I am aware of is in Donald Pease, ed., *National Identities and Post-Americanist Narratives* (Durham, N.C.: Duke University Press, 1994), 1–13, 5. In the introduction, Pease emphasizes the term's embrace of the "multiple interpellations" through which not only the internal constitution of the field but also its possibilities of extension and expansion—as a matter of boundary, domain, priorities, and discipline—may be pursued, a set of priorities also fundamental to this book.

20. See Lauren Berlant, *The Anatomy of National Fantasy: Hawthorne, Utopia, and Everyday Life* (Chicago: University of Chicago Press, 1994), 20; for various examples of counter-hegemonic/postnational and transnational strategies generally, see Pease and Weigman, *Futures*, and notes 21–28 below.

21. See, e.g., Arjun Appadurai, *Modernity at Large: Cultural Dimensions of Globalization* (Minneapolis: University of Minnesota Press, 1996); Martha Nussbaum, "Patriotism and Cosmopolitanism," *Boston Review* 19.5 (1994); Michael Hardt and Antonio Negri, *Empire* (Cambridge, Mass.: Harvard University Press, 2001); Immanuel Wallerstein, "The National and the Universal: Can There Be Such a Thing as World Culture?" in Anthony D. King, ed., *Culture, Globalization, and the World-System* (Minneapolis: University of Minnesota Press, 1997), 93–105; Masao Miyoshi, "A Borderless World? From Colonialism to Transnationalism and the Decline of the Nation-State," *Critical Inquiry* 19.4 (Summer 1993): 726–51; Frederick Buell, *National Culture and the New Global System* (Baltimore: Johns Hopkins University Press, 1994).

22. Qtd. in Paul Giles, "Transnationalism and Classic American Literature," *PMLA* 118.1 (Jan. 2003): 62–77, 64.

23. Julia Kristeva, *Nations Without Nationalism*, Leon S. Roudiez, trans. (New York: Columbia University Press, 1993), 50.

24. See, e.g., Amy Kaplan, *The Anarchy of Empire in the Making of U.S. Culture* (Cambridge, Mass.: Harvard University Press, 2004); John Carlos Rowe, *Literary Culture and U.S. Imperialism: From Revolution to World War II* (New York: Oxford University Press, 2000).

25. Paul Gilroy, *Black Atlantic: Modernity and Double-Consciousness* (Cambridge, Mass.: Harvard University Press, 1995), 28–29, 87.

26. Laura Doyle, "Transnational History at Our Backs: A Long View of Larsen, Woolf and Queer Racial Subjectivity in Atlantic Modernism," *Modernism/modernity* 13.3 (2006): 531–59, 532–33.

27. See Lawrence Buell, "American Literary Emergence as a Postcolonial Phenomenon," *ALH* 4.3 (Fall 1992): 411–42; Laura Doyle, *Freedom's Empire: Race and the Rise of Empire in Atlantic Modernity, 1640–1940* (Durham, N.C.: Duke University Press, 2008); Amanda Claybaugh, *The Novel of Purpose: Literature and Social Reform in the Anglo-American World* (Ithaca, N.Y.: Cornell University Press, 2006).

28. *Transatlantic Insurrections: British Culture and the Formation of American Literature, 1730–1860* (Philadelphia: University of Pennsylvania Press, 2001); *Virtual Fictions: Transnational Fictions and the Transatlantic Imaginary* (Durham, N.C.: Duke University Press, 2002); *Atlantic Republic: The American Tradition in English Literature* (Oxford: Oxford University Press, 2006).

29. Giles, *Transatlantic Insurrections*, 3, 10–11 ("bi-focal" as key metaphor); Giles, *Virtual*, 1–5 ("virtuality" as key metaphor).

30. Giles, *Virtual*, 6.

31. "From the standpoint of the mirror I discover my absence from the place where I am since I see myself over there. Starting from this gaze that is, as it were, directed toward me, from the ground of virtual space that is on the other side of the glass, I come back toward myself; I begin again to direct my eyes toward myself and to reconstitute myself there where I am. The mirror functions as a heterotopia in this respect: it makes this place that I occupy at the moment when I look at myself in the glass at once absolutely real, connected with all the space that surrounds it, and absolutely unreal, since in order to be perceived it has to pass through this virtual point which is over there." Michel Foucault, "Of Other Spaces" (1967), rptd. in *Diacritics* 16.1 (Spring 1986): 22–27, 23.

32. See Paul Giles, "The Deterritorialization of American Literature," in Wai Chee Dimock and Lawrence Buell, eds., *Shades of the Planet: American Literature as World Literature* (Princeton: Princeton University Press, 2007), 39–61; Giles, "Classic American," 73–74.

33. Here, in identifying the war with this entire decade, I am following recent political historians who emphasize that even the narrowest understanding of the "resolution" of the war must extend well beyond the Treaty of Versailles in 1919 to include the vast international sphere of negotiations, always involving and/or implicating the United States, leading up to the London reparations settlement of 1924 and the Locarno security pact of 1925. Not coincidentally, this was the very decade of the American "invention" of Conrad. See Patrick Cohrs, *The Unfinished Peace After World War I: America, Britain, and the Stabilisation of Europe, 1919–1932* (Cambridge: Cambridge University Press, 2006).

34. Indeed, Giles's consideration of Alexander Pope in the eighteenth-century United States valuably anticipates certain aspects of my approach. See *Transatlantic Insurrections*, 17–39.

35. John Muthyala, "Reworlding America: The Globalization of American Studies," *Cultural Critique* 47 (2001): 91–119, 98.

36. On aesthetics, this book is crucially addressed to the issue of their political praxis, as raised for recent revisionist Americanist consideration in Christopher Castiglia and Russ Castronovo, "A 'Hive of Subtlety': Aesthetics and the End(s) of Cultural Studies," *American Literature* 76.3 (2004): 423–35, and the special issue that follows; regarding "the author"—or rather, "author function"—and the ideological *constellating* function that images of the author can perform, effecting through a single personal image a *bricolage* of ideas or forum of intersectional political dialogue, I have benefited much from Alan Sinfield's study of the complex idea of the "queer" consolidated in Oscar Wilde's image beginning in the late 1890s, in *The Wilde Century: Effeminacy, Oscar Wilde and the Queer Moment* (New York: Columbia University Press, 1994).

37. With respect to Conrad studies, I would add to notes 10 and 11 above that two important—and largely productive—internal developments have powerfully discouraged contact between the study of Conrad and U.S. cultural history. One is an emphasis, not started but formidably solidified by Ian Watt's *Conrad in the Nineteenth Century* (Berkeley: University of California Press, 1979), on Conrad as a "nineteenth-century" author, his "greatest" works and most substantial historical contexts and themes dating from on or around the end of that century, as opposed to the second and third decades of the twentieth century, when Conrad soared to popularity in the United States and wrote many more books, substantially critically underappreciated, very much aware of his U.S. audiences. The second is a fundamental shift from psychological and psychoanalytic academic criticism of Conrad, often by U.S. Americans, in the 1950s, to more "empirical" and historicist treatments of Conrad thereafter—which have tended to privilege the interpretation of Conrad's fiction through domains of Conrad's actual personal and historical contact (Poland, France, the Malay Archipelago, etc.) and/or places he concretely represents in his fiction, neither of which immediately lends itself to treatment of the United States. Regarding the complex and rapidly changing and diversifying field that is "modernist studies," the gaps between it and historical and historicist trajectories of U.S. American studies are beyond the scope of this book— though I would suggest that traditional articulations of the former have in many respects mirrored the exceptionalist premises of the latter.

38. I borrow the phrase "Conrad's heterotopic fictions" from, and reproduce it in appreciative conversation with, Robert Hampson's pioneering essay "Conrad's Heterotopic Fiction: Composite Maps, Superimposed Sites, and Impossible Spaces" (2005), in Kaplan, Mallios, and White, *Conrad and the Twenty-first Century*, 121–36. For more on this book's relation to Hampson's and other "heterotopic" conceptions of Conrad, see notes 50 and 55 below.

39. See Peter Mallios, "Here and 'There': Conrad's 'American' Vision," forthcoming in *Conradiana*.

40. Letters from Conrad to Eric Pinker, Dec. 17, 1922 (TS Berg), Jan. 30, 1924 (TS Berg).

41. For one account of the Yale English Department naming Conrad's fiction the subject of the competition for the John Hubbard Curtis Prize, see "In a Few Words," *New York Times* (Dec. 6, 1914): BR554; Mencken, "A Glance at the Novels," *Town Topics* 72 (Jan. 13, 1915): 14.

42. *New York Times* (Apr. 3, 1915): 9; "A Hamlet of the South Seas," *Current Opinion* 58.5 (May 1915): 8; "A Set of Six," *America: A Catholic Review of the Week* 12 (Feb. 6, 1915): 418.

43. For more on an "Evening with Conrad's People" and its sequel, see *CL* 6.71–72, 101–3, 114; on the American "Conrad Committee" (and written on the society's official letterhead), see Letter from E. F. Saxton to John Quinn, May 3, 1919 (Berg).

44. See *Publisher's Weekly* annual best-seller list, rptd. at *www.gnupooh.org/pwbs* *.html*; compare Doubleday, Page's not implausible and tirelessly repeated claim in the same year that Conrad was the "most read" novelist in the United States (*CL* 6.389).

45. See, among many instances, Fanny Butcher, "Tabloid Book Review," *Chicago Sunday Tribune* (May 30, 1920): 1.7 (lists *The Rescue*, just above F. Scott Fitzgerald's *This Side of Paradise*, as the number-one best seller in Chicago); *CL* 6.389 and "Best Sellers,"

Book Buyer 45 (July 8, 1921): 132 (also lists "best-selling" numbers for *The Rescue*); "The Sea Wizard Passes," *Los Angeles Times* (Aug. 15, 1924): A4 (upon publication *The Rover* [1923] "immediately jumped into the best-seller class"); "Best Sellers of the Week," *Chicago Daily Tribune* (Sept. 26, 1925): 19 (lists *Suspense* along with Willa Cather's *The Professor's House* and four others).

46. William Lyon Phelps, *As I Like It* (New York: Charles Scribner's Sons, 1924), 207; "Joseph Conrad's Heroic Pessimism," *Current Opinion* (Nov. 1924): 630–31, 630.

47. Christopher Morley, *Conrad and the Reporters* (New York: Doubleday, 1923), 54.

48. The critical commonplace that Conrad's stature as an author vanishes after his death in 1924, not to find recuperation until nearly two and a half decades later in F. R. Leavis's *The Great Tradition* (London: Chatto, 1948), has, like most narratives of this kind, some truth, but not much. One culprit here is an overemphasis on British and/or academic/literary genealogies of Conrad's reception, when the picture has always been much larger. In the United States, while Granville Hicks, in the *New Republic* in 1930, significantly observes a "depreciation" in Conrad's fiction because of its inability to speak to Depression-era "problems of industrial civilization," and while the *Saturday Review of Literature* in 1947 is able to reference a "complete" "eclipse" of Conrad's reputation, much contemporary commentary cuts the other way, attesting to Conrad's continuing U.S. interest. Always hostile to Conrad, the *Nation* in 1926 finds it difficult to imagine an "unhysterical reader of Conrad (we assume there are some despite the full-page advertisements)"; Richard Curle in 1928 describes Conrad as "to numbers of Americans . . . the author of authors, the one writer to whom they pay single-minded homage"; Wilbur Cross in 1929 in the *Yale Review* prophesies a "new Conrad" for a "new generation"; the *New Republic* in 1933 issues a call to "re-read Conrad"; Edith Mirrelees in the *Saturday Review of Literature* in 1938 describes Conrad as one of "four major epidemics of influence in undergraduate writing courses," where the "real" teaching of literature actually happens; the *Literary Digest* in 1938 features an article extolling to bibliophiles the extraordinary value of an original edition of *Chance*; much of this book excavates Conrad's American significance between 1924 and 1948—always there if not necessarily on the cover of *Time*. See Hicks, "Conrad After Five Years," *New Republic* 61.788 (Jan. 8, 1930): 192–94; "New Editions," *Saturday Review of Literature* 50 (Nov. 15, 1947): 50; "*Last Essays*," *Nation* 123 (Oct. 13, 1926): 381–82; Curle, *The Last Twelve Years of Joseph Conrad* (London: Sampson Low, 1928), 122; Cross, "Hardy and Conrad," *Yale Review* 18 (Spring 1929): 580–83, 580; "Book Notes," *New Republic* 76 (Oct. 25, 1933): 316; Mirrelees, "Those College Writing Courses," *Saturday Review of Literature* 14 (Jan. 15, 1938): 4; Bob Brown, "Conrad by *Chance*," *Literary Digest* (Feb. 1938): 45.

49. Foucault, "Of Other Spaces," 24.

50. Cesare Casarino, *Modernity at Sea: Melville, Marx, Conrad in Crisis* (Minneapolis: University of Minnesota Press, 2002), 12; Natalie Melas, *All the Difference*, 26, 27, 54–95, 92–93.

51. Foucault, "Of Other Spaces," 24–27.

52. See Michel Foucault, *The Order of Things* (New York: Random House, 1994), xv–xxiv.

53. Most theoretical accounts of heterotopia tend to emphasize purely disruptive, subversive, aphasiac properties, very much in line with what Foucault describes in *The*

Order of Things as well as much in "Of Other Spaces." However, the double conception of heterotopia also offered in "Of Other Spaces"—in terms of sites both of "crisis" and "consolation"—suggests a different model, one in which the very intolerable excesses of radical crisis/dissolution are always entwined with and generative of a countervailing will-to-order. This heterotopic doubleness one might in fact then turn back on the Foucault of *The Order of Things*—whose privileged heterotopic example of the Chinese encyclopedia does in fact contain an expression of a will to totalizing order within it [i.e., animals "(h) included in the present classification"], and whose self-declaredly "stupefied" and "shattered" reaction to the Chinese encyclopedia is at some odds with the truly lyric eloquence and consummately systematized and ordered explanation Foucault himself brings to it. In any event, the reader of Conrad may be struck in this light by the example of *Lord Jim*: whose bipartite form, one-half devoted to the "illusion"-shattering crisis of Jim's jump from the *Patna* ("the ship is a heterotopia *par excellence*," writes Foucault), the second the possible romance-colonial compensation and consolation of Patusan (Foucault also describes "the colony" as a prime instance of heterotopia), suggests that if the novel is "heterotopic" at all, it is so in a fashion that comprehends *both* radical breakdowns in order *and* an overdetermined will to assert or locate in such crises and their plural opportunities of recoverable vocabulary—*each* a part of the same "double" heterotopic skein. This double impulse I have just described seems to me manifestly and deeply to run across Conrad's fiction as a whole; and the *oppositional overdetermination* of responses to Conrad it implies (in the form of radical contrarity, hot debate, excessive and provocational overassertions that presuppose their own resistance—none of this simply muddled "ambiguity"), which is the mechanism of responding to Conrad I chart in the United States in this book, is also a heterotopic pattern (as I am theorizing it here) that is true of Conrad more generally. See Foucault, *Order of Things*, xv; "Of Other Spaces," 26–27.

54. See note 38.

55. Hampson, "Conrad's Heterotopic Fiction," 128.

56. Christopher GoGwilt, *The Invention of the West: Joseph Conrad and the Double-Mapping of Europe and Empire* (Stanford: Stanford University Press, 2005), 149–89.

57. For more on how Conrad uses the statue of Rousseau ironically to "situate the institutions of European democracy and the rhetoric of Russian revolutionary and autocratic thinking under the same mistaken political legacy," see GoGwilt, *Invention of the West*, 150–60, 150.

58. As Conrad writes in the Author's Note, and emphasizes throughout the novel: "If [Razumov] is slightly abnormal it is only in his sensitiveness to his position. Being nobody's child he feels rather more keenly than another would that he is Russian—or he is nothing" (*UWE* ix).

59. Foucault, "Of Other Spaces," 27; Casarino, *Modernity at Sea*, 1–28, 186–245.

60. For more on Casarino's remarkable account of the nineteenth-century merchant sea as a historically desynchronized "outside" space of presumptively transnationalized, prematurely multiethnicized, queerly capitalized relation to "landed" chronologies of modernity, from which heterotopic space, interfering with and providing an alternative laboratory for conventional patterns of modernity, emerges the modernist sea narrative, see Casarino, *Modernity at Sea*, 1–18, passim.

61. Compare note 53 above. With regard to *Lord Jim*, and a parallel there is not space here to elaborate other than simply to point out a mutual superabundance of "heteroclite" linguistic registers, the latter of which is surely a synecdoche for the form of *Lord Jim* as a whole, compare Foucault's discussion of the "Chinese encyclopedia" in *The Order of Things* with Marlow's engagement with the ship master who speaks as if his English were derived "from a dictionary compiled by a lunatic" (*LJ* 144).

62. Consider, beyond the distant and disparate global scenes of Conrad's fiction, the unusually and extensively irregular, disparate, heteroclite *conjunction* of its major component parts: its far-flung colonial subjects and tenors; its fine-grained maritime portraits; its existential and psychological proclivities; its political tales of Euro-Russian anarchism, espionage, revolution, and terror; its generally erased subtexts of immigration and Poland; its forays into British social satire and the novel of manners; its peculiar combinations of Gothic, melodrama, adventure romance, modernist aesthetics, and the epic; its French and Italian instances of historical romance; its Spanish instance of popular love-romance; even its (coauthored) practices of science fiction and murder mystery. What is the "*tabula*," what is the "site" and coordinating ground, outside the redundancy of the author's name that simply reiterates and reanimates the problem (and ever more complexly, expansively, insolubly so), that could conjoin this remarkable panorama of irregular parts? What is the site, indeed, that would further conjoin these heteroclite elements of Conrad's fiction with the equally heteroclite *non*fictional components of "Conrad": i.e., Conrad's two volumes of essays demonstrating multiple frictions and inconsistencies (especially with respect to the fiction) of political, historical, literary, and temperamental posture; and two autobiographies that notoriously compound the mysteries of the persona that is their subject rather than resolving them? To appreciate the difficulty of these questions is to begin to see how the textual "world of Conradia," quite unlike "Dickens's London" or "Joyce's Dublin" or Hardy's "Wessex" or Faulkner's "Yoknapatawpha," refers less to a stable coordinated or coordinating site than the very absence or at least extreme difficulty of identifying one—giving rise instead to a (heterotopic) problem and process by which "fragmented regions" and "unconnected islets" may be continually mobilized in glittering "agglutinations" of provisional order, only to collapse or be all the more anxiously reasserted amid the "wide field of identity" that remains, ever untotalizable, to be considered. Compare Foucault, *Order of Things*, xvii–xviii.

63. Geoffrey Galt Harpham, *One of Us: The Mastery of Joseph Conrad* (Chicago: University of Chicago Press, 1996), chap. 3 (playing on Conrad's famous appeal in the preface to *The Nigger of the "Narcissus"* to "make you *see*").

64. Ibid., chap. 1; Edward Said, *Joseph Conrad and the Fiction of Autobiography* (Cambridge, Mass.: Harvard University Press, 1966), *passim*, and *Reflections on Exile* (Cambridge, Mass: Harvard University Press, 2002), xiv, 70–82.

65. Edward Said, *Culture and Imperialism* (New York: Vintage Books, 1993), 19–31, and "Through Gringo Eyes: With Conrad in Latin America," in *Reflections on Exile*, 276–81; Melas, *All the Difference*, 44–112.

66. Edward Garnett, for instance, writes of Conrad's Malay fiction in 1898: "The artist has spoken; a new world finds voice; and we understand. The blank solid wall of the familiar, the strange world of new and old that fronts the puzzled sensations of

those far off, has melted away before this artist . . . [who] can connect this tangible world with that vast unseen ocean of life around him." John Galsworthy sounds a similar "virtual" (in Giles's sense) and heterotopic note in 1908: "Joseph Conrad's writings have the power of persuading man to peep out now and then and see the whole of which he is so small a part. Prisoners in the cell of our own nationality, we never see ourselves; it is reserved for one outside looking through the tell-tale peep-hole to get a proper view of us." Arthur Symons's formulation of May 1915 is, with Van Wyck Brooks's formulation of November 1914, the first great heterotopic articulation of Conrad: "Conrad's inexplicable mind has created for itself *a secret world* to live in, some corner stealthily hidden away from view, among impenetrable forests, on the banks of untraveled rivers. From that corner, like a spider in his web, he throws out tentacles into the darkness; he gathers in his spoils, he collects them like a miser, stripping from them their dreams and visions to decorate his web magnificently. He chooses among them, and *sends out into the world shadowy messengers for the troubling of the peace of man, self-satisfied in his ignorance of the invisible.*" See Garnett, "Mr. Joseph Conrad," *Academy* 55 (Oct. 15, 1898): 82–83; Galsworthy, "Joseph Conrad: A Disquisition," *Fortnightly Review* 89 (Apr. 1, 1908): 627–33, 629; Symons, "Conrad," *Forum* 53 (May 1915): 579–92 (emphases added).

67. Van Wyck Brooks, "A Study of Joseph Conrad," *New Republic* (Dec. 26, 1914): 26–27.

68. Wilson Follett, "Joseph Conrad: A Salvation," *New York Tribune Book News and Review* (Apr. 29, 1923): 19–20, 19.

69. Foucault, "Of Other Spaces," 27 (emphasis added).

70. "The End of American Isolation," *New Republic* 1.1 (Nov. 7, 1914): 8–9, 8.

71. See Secor and Moddelmog's *Joseph Conrad and American Writers*.

CHAPTER 1

1. "Joseph Conrad: *A Great Novelist to Visit the United States*," *Time* 1.6 (Apr. 7, 1923): 15.

2. Picking up on Conrad's essentially explicit self-identification as "Young Ulysses" in *The Arrow of Gold* (*AG* 12), articles in a number of U.S. periodicals extend the metaphor: e.g., "The Greatest of Sea Writers," *Current Opinion* (Sept. 1924): 304, 313 ("His tales are one long Odyssey told by an Odysseus who regretted nothing but the necessity for the past tense"); Wilbur Cross, "The Illusions of Joseph Conrad," *Yale Review* (Apr. 1928): 464–82, 466 ("another Ulysses"); Muirhead Bone, "Joseph Conrad—a Modern Ulysses," *Living Age* (Sept. 13, 1924): 551–54. Others extend Conrad's own fondness (see Introduction, note 9) for the Columbus metaphor: e.g., Percy Hutchison, "Joseph Conrad, Master in Sail for All Oceans," *New York Times* (Apr. 29, 1923): BR6 ("Like Columbus, he failed to reach the mainland" of the United States in his first journey); "In Conrad's 'Last Essays' Is the Key to His Character," *New York Times Book Review* (Mar. 28, 1926): 3 (places Conrad in genealogy of "Great Navigators" headed by Columbus).

3. A phrase I borrow from the historian Barbara Tuchman, who coins it, in her imaginative study of Anglo-Norman medieval history, *A Distant Mirror: The Calamitous 14th Century* (New York: Knopf, 1978), to express a sense of transhistorical parallelism between the twentieth-century present and the politically proximate fourteenth-century past. My application of the phrase is less transtemporal than transnational.

4. William Lyon Phelps, *The Advance of the English Novel* (New York: Dodd, Mead,

1916), 198, 215; Phelps's essay on Conrad also appears in *Bookman* (NY) 43 (May 1916): 297–304. Phelps is quite explicit about the "mirror" metaphor: what's special about Conrad's fiction is that "Conrad does not have us look directly at the object, but rather at a mirror in which the object is reflected. The mirror may be simply the effect produced on some other person or persons by the leading character, or it may be simply the clear surface of Marlow's mind. At all events we regard the character in its reflected image, rather than in the direct gaze" (215).

5. Christopher Morley, "A Word About Joseph Conrad," *Mentor* (Mar. 1925): 24–26, 26.

6. Helen and Wilson Follett, "Contemporary Novelists: Joseph Conrad," *Atlantic Monthly* 119 (Feb. 1917): 233–43, 234, 236 (emphasis added).

7. Ibid.

8. Foucault, "Of Other Spaces," 24.

9. Richard Curle, *Last Twelve Years of Joseph Conrad*, 122 (emphases added).

10. Morley, "A Cross Section," *Saturday Review of Literature* 1 (Dec. 27, 1924): 415.

11. Consider the following, in descending order and as a single cultural formation, all governed by the central idea of debate/dissensus and its disavowal in relation to Conrad: Alaric Watson, "But We Know What We Like," *McBride's Magazine* 97.580 (Apr. 1916): 155 (social allegory whose point is that everyone—young and old, modern and conventional, intellectual, professional, and worker, cosmopolitan and religious, male and female—can agree to embrace Conrad, perhaps singularly among authors); Edwin Francis Edgett, "Joseph Conrad Visits the South Seas," *Boston Evening Transcript* (May 26, 1920): 3.4 (few authors have received such "universal and favorable appreciation," are "so widely read by so many different classes of readers"—though there is something suspiciously "hypnotized" about this collective exuberance); "Conrad and His Fame," *Nation* (NY) 119 (Aug. 13, 1924): 157 (everyone loves Conrad, but not because of his universality but rather the "multiplicity of his qualities" and, in reading Conrad, different classes of readers "all unite to admire him" but "not because they see the same thing but because they see . . . different things"); Thomas Moult, "A Romantic Portrait of Conrad," *Yale Review* 15 (Oct. 1925): 165–67 (there has "always been" a "difference of opinion" about Conrad's quality as a writer; in addition, the curiosity is that Conrad's detractors tend to "assign different reasons" for their views and even to "disagree" over which of Conrad's works show "genius" and which are "intolerable"); William McFee, "Praise for Film of Conrad's 'Rescue,'" *New York Times* (Jan. 27, 1929): X8 (there is a "sharp and irreconcilable division of readers for and against" Conrad; the "cleavage is fundamental," and there is "no neutral ground whereon we may discuss our differences"; "You either admire Conrad as one of the world's great writers, or you cannot endure him at all").

12. "Unhomely" is Homi Bhabha's term for "the symbiotic encounter with difference that enables 'home' to become a strange place." See Bhabha, ed., "Introduction," in *Nation and Narration* (London: Routledge, 1990), 1–15, 7–8.

13. Walter Lippmann, "H. L. Mencken," in *Men of Destiny* (New York: Macmillan, 1927), 61–70, 61; qtd. in William Nolte, ed., "Introduction," in *H. L. Mencken's Smart Set Criticism* (Ithaca, N.Y.: Cornell University Press, 1968), xii; H. L. Mencken, *The American Scene: A Reader*, Huntington Cairns, ed. (New York: Random House, 1982), 51; Vincent O'Sullivan, "The American Critic" (1919), rptd. in the United States in Burton Rascoe,

Vincent O'Sullivan, and F. C. Henderson, *H. L. Mencken* (New York: Knopf, 1920), 16–20, 17, 16 ("Among all this criticism there is one critic. His name is H. L. Mencken").

14. Marion Rodgers, *Mencken: The American Iconoclast* (New York: Oxford University Press, 2005), 3 ("No one had done more to change the attitude toward conventions and affect the literary tastes of an entire generation").

15. See Hobson, *Serpent in Eden: H. L. Mencken and the South* (Baton Rouge: Louisiana State University Press, 1974); for an explicit expression of Mencken's contemporaneity, compare Hobson, *The Menckenites and the South, 1920–1930: A Study in Criticism, Reaction, and Response*, Thesis (A.M.), Duke University, 1967.

16. Mencken, *Notes on Democracy* (New York: Knopf, 1926), 122.

17. For a truly chilling indictment of the institutional rage to "correctness" (Mencken's word) in academia, see Mencken's "The National Letters" (1920), in *Prejudices: Second Series* (New York: Knopf, 1920), 9–101, 78–88.

18. Terry Teachout, *The Skeptic: A Life of H. L. Mencken* (New York: HarperCollins, 2002), 126, 256, 342, passim. For helpful discussions of recent critical responses to Mencken's *Diary*, see the two other recent biographies: Rodgers, *Mencken*, and Fred Hobson, *Mencken: A Life* (New York: Random House, 1994), 405–14, 453–57, 535–48.

19. Hobson, *Mencken: A Life*, 412.

20. Two examples are Peter Carafiol, *The American Ideal: Literary History as a Worldly Activity* (New York: Oxford University Press, 1991), and John Carlos Rowe, *At Emerson's Tomb: The Politics of Classic American Literature* (New York: Columbia University Press, 1996)—both thoughtful studies though more invested in traditionalist Americanist narratives through the reinscription of the central figure of Emerson than they acknowledge.

21. Ralph Waldo Emerson, *Nature*, in Mary Oliver, ed., *The Essential Writings of Ralph Waldo Emerson* (New York: Modern Library, 2000), 3; H. L. Mencken, *A Book of Prefaces*, 1st ed. (New York: Knopf, 1917), 61. All references to Mencken's *Book of Prefaces* will be to this edition unless otherwise specified.

22. Mencken, *Book of Prefaces*, 61–62, 283.

23. Rodgers, *Mencken*, 181; Mencken, "Seven Pages About Books," *Smart Set* 54.1 (Jan. 1918): 137–43, 143.

24. H. L. Mencken, *My Life as an Author and Editor* (New York: Knopf, 1993), 127. What becomes clear in a text like *A Book of Prefaces* is that Mencken champions Dreiser significantly as a function of Mencken's own views; this is also to a certain extent true of Conrad, but there is a vast difference in deference Mencken accords the two authors, such that in reference to Conrad there is less self-conscious manipulation or an impulse to issue qualifying corrections. Mencken genuinely believes that in Conrad he has found a confirmation, and actually superior exponent, of his own worldview. Mencken does not accord such deference to Dreiser, whose comparisons with Conrad begin as early as a letter Mencken wrote to Dreiser concerning *A Traveler at Forty* (1913) on November 16, 1913: "But don't assume from the foregoing that the book has disappointed me. Far from it. You have got into it, not only a definite revelation of your personality, but also a clear statement of your philosophy. Do you know that this last is substantially identical with Joseph Conrad's? You will find his confession of faith in 'A Personal Record.' He stands in wonder before the meaninglessness of

life. He is an agnostic in exactly the same way you are—that is to say, he gives it up."
A Book of Prefaces repeats much of this language (94–96) and makes clear the con-
ceptual articulation and authorization of Dreiser through Conrad, the rich concep-
tual, cultural, and political terms of which are elaborated throughout this chapter.
See Guy Forgue, ed., *The Letters of H. L. Mencken* (Boston: Northeastern University
Press, 1981), 35–36.

25. "Oyez! Oyez! All Ye Who Read Books": Apropos of this title and on the occasion of the publication of *The Point of Honor* (1908), the article conducts a brief survey
of Conrad's works and hails him, in excited tones of prophetic discovery, as a "genius."
Smart Set 26.4 (Dec. 1908): 153–59, 153–55.

26. Teachout, *The Skeptic*, 326.

27. Mencken, "Conrad Revisited," *Smart Set* 70.4 (Dec. 1922): 141–44, 141, rptd. in
Nolte, *Mencken's Smart Set Criticism*, 239–43, 239–40. The Nolte text will be cited in future
references to "Conrad Revisited." The essay itself is printed in revised form in *Prejudices:
Fifth Series* (New York: Alfred A. Knopf, 1926) and *A Mencken Chrestomathy* (New York:
Alfred A. Knopf, 1949).

28. Mencken, "Conrad Revisited," 241.

29. Mencken, *The Days of H. L. Mencken* (New York: Knopf, 1947), 196.

30. Mencken, "Conrad Revisited," 241.

31. Ibid., 242.

32. Stephen Greenblatt, *Shakespearean Negotiations: The Circulation of Social Energy
in Renaissance England* (Berkeley: University of California Press, 1988).

33. See Edward Said, "Traveling with Conrad," in Kaplan, Mallios, and White,
Conrad in the Twenty-first Century, 283–303; for more on Said's intimate lifelong relation to Conrad, see the introduction to *Conrad in the Twenty-first Century*, xvii–xix, and
my "Contrapunctus: Edward Said and Joseph Conrad," in Andrzej Busza and Marcin
Piechota, eds., *Conrad's Europe* (Opole, Poland: University of Opole, 2005), 177–94.

34. See the letters to Harry Leon Wilson on October 25, 1911 (begins with the remark
that "Conrad is one of my superstitions, and so I can't argue about him intelligently,"
and tells stories of both distributing "Youth" to various friends with equally recipro-
cated enthusiasm and discovering "Youth" in 1904 aboard a boat in the West Indies and
responding particularly to "my pet scene" at the end of the story) and September 4,
1911 (describes "Youth" as "the best short story in English, and 'Heart of Darkness' the
next best, and 'Falk' the next best," and "Conrad the greatest of them all"), in Forgue,
Letters, 16–18, 18–20. See also Mencken, "The Publishers Begin Their Drive," *Smart Set*
48.4 (Apr. 1916): 151–56, 156.

35. Mencken, "Publishers Begin," 156.

36. Mencken, "Criticism of Criticism of Criticism," *Smart Set* 52.4 (Aug. 1917):
138–44, 144.

37. Mencken, *Book of Prefaces*, 12–13.

38. And again. In yet another essay describing "Youth" as "perhaps the best short
story ever written in English," "a tale inimitably succinct, sympathetic, archetypal,
and penetrating," Mencken draws attention to the older narrator compelled by the
possibility of returning to the space of "youth" that in the end can only be a fleeting, if
ever-enticing, feat of the imagination: "Conrad wrote ['Youth'] when he was already

a man of middle age—a man looking back, with . . . a clear understanding, upon the memorable moods and gropings of those far-off but unforgotten days. The result is that his story is not merely a chronicle of youth but also an interpretation of youth. It illuminates a universal experience, here lifted to pulsing drama, by the light of profound philosophy. To read it is, in some sense, to live again. And that, I think, is the highest praise that can be laid upon a work of the imagination." See Mencken, "Novels to Reread" (July 1913), in Nolte, *Mencken's* Smart Set *Criticism*, 294–98, 296.

39. See Hobson, *Life*, 81–82; Rodgers, *Mencken*, 80–92; Mencken, *Newspaper Days, 1899–1906* (New York: Knopf, 1947), 276–300, 277–78 (emphasis added; the interpolated quotation is from "Youth").

40. For tropes of the "alien," see especially *A Book of Prefaces* and section 6 of "The National Letters"; the quotes on "foreignness" are in Rodgers, *Mencken*, 116, 118; Mencken, *The Diary of H. L. Mencken*, Charles A. Fecher, ed. (New York: Knopf, 1989), 215 (emphasis added).

41. T. S. Eliot, *The Waste Land* (1922), line 30; F. Scott Fitzgerald, "Under Fire," *New York Evening Post Literary Review* (May 26, 1923): 715. For more on Eliot and Fitzgerald, see Chapter 3, infra.

42. Mencken, "Conrad Revisited," 240.

43. Ibid.

44. Mencken, *Book of Prefaces*, 17.

45. Ibid., 16.

46. Ibid., 11, 15, 16, 5. Compare the discussion of Lippmann later in this chapter.

47. Ibid., 39; Mencken, "The Grandstand Flirts with the Bleachers," *Smart Set* 45.4 (Apr. 1915): 430–36, 434; Mencken, *Book of Prefaces*, 15 (qtg. Arthur Symons).

48. Hence also Mencken's emphasis on Conrad as a figure of the autonomous and comprehensively neutralizing "outside": someone of "quite extraordinary detachment," "unresolved dissonance," "a world apart," "an implacable comprehension as of one outside nature," "plainly a stranger, and all himself"—and who is capable of an infinitely irresolved "whole point of view" precisely because "his attitude toward all moral systems and axioms is that of a skeptic who rejects them unanimously." Mencken, *Book of Prefaces*, 18, 36, 50, 19, 29, 20, 31. "What were to me all the countries of the globe?"

49. Harpham, *One of Us*, 10, 8, chap. 1; Mencken, *Book of Prefaces*, 19, 40, 43, 29, 16, 18. For an "abysmal" reading of Conrad—that is, placing Conrad's uses of *mise en abyme* in relation to infinitely regressive questions of cultural perspective—of direct relevance here, see Christopher GoGwilt, "Opera and the Passage of Literature: Joseph Conrad, Pramoedya Ananta Toer, and the Cultural Dialectic of Abysmal Taste," in Kaplan, Mallios, and White, *Conrad in the Twenty-first Century*, 101–20.

50. Mencken, "Conrad's Self-Portrait" (Oct. 1912), in Nolte, *Mencken's* Smart Set *Criticism*, 230–232, 232.

51. Mencken, *Book of Prefaces*, 33, 29, 49.

52. *Abrams v. United States* 250 U.S. 616, 613 (1919) (Holmes, J., dissenting) ("the best test of truth is the power of the thought to get itself accepted in the market"). For Mencken's strong endorsement of this implicitly agnostic view of "truth" and its production, and Mencken's equally strong rebuke of Holmes for not arriving at and

protecting speakers pursuant to this principle earlier, see "Mr. Justice Holmes" (1930), in *Mencken Chrestomathy*, 258–65. For the relation between Holmes and Conrad under Mencken's eyes, see later in this chapter.

53. Mencken, *Book of Prefaces*, 12, 16, 38.

54. Ibid., 19, 190; Mencken, "The Prometheus of the Western World," *Smart Set* 46.3 (July 1915): 444–50, 452.

55. Qtd. in Hobson, *Mencken: A Life*, 135, 134, 137; qtd. in Rodgers, *Mencken*, 142.

56. Qtd. in Rodgers, *Mencken*, 132.

57. Mencken, "The Ulster Polonius," *Smart Set* 49.4 (Aug. 1916): 138–44, 143; compare the Preface to the second edition of *A Book of Prefaces* (New York: Knopf, 1918), 5–6, 6, in which Mencken references "greater concerns overshadow[ing] all artistic questions" that, or so the implication runs, are not at issue in the book.

58. Mencken, *Book of Prefaces*, 164.

59. Ibid., 28.

60. Ibid., 28–29, 88; Mencken, "Novels, Chiefly Bad," *Smart Set* 59.4 (Aug. 1919): 138–44, 144; Mencken, *Book of Prefaces*, 19, 29.

61. Mencken, "Criticism of Criticism of Criticism," *Prejudices: First Series* (New York: Knopf, 1919), 9–21, 18.

62. From Conrad's Preface to *The Nigger of the "Narcissus"* but quoted emphatically and repeatedly by Mencken; see *Book of Prefaces*, 29. There are few more crucial points for Mencken than that moralizing artists, and U.S. novelists generally, simply do not "see" and express the complexities of the world because the world they express in their pages is, as a matter of first degree, derived from moral conventions.

63. Mencken, *Book of Prefaces*, 29, 19.

64. First report on the work of Wellington House, qtd. in M. L. Sanders and Philip M. Taylor, *British Propaganda During the First World War, 1914–1918* (London: Macmillan, 1982), 168. For a useful account of British (Great) War propaganda in the United States, see Sanders and Taylor, 167–207; for an overly polemical but nevertheless suggestive account of the same subject, see Stewart Ross, *Propaganda for War: How the United States Was Conditioned to Fight the Great War of 1914–1918* (Jefferson, N.C.: McFarland, 1996). For more on British war propaganda of this period, compare Sanders and Taylor with George G. Bruntz, *Allied Propaganda and the Collapse of the German Empire in 1918* (Stanford: Stanford University Press, 1938). For more on the Masterman project and the queer results that ensued when the attempt was made to recruit Conrad, see Mark Wollaeger, "Conrad's Darkness Revisited: Mediated Warfare and Modern(ist) Propaganda in *Heart of Darkness* and 'The Unlighted Coast,'" in Kaplan, Mallios, and White, *Conrad in the Twenty-first Century*, 67–84.

65. Mencken, "Arnold Bennett," in *Prejudices: First Series*, 47–48.

66. H. G. Wells, *The War That Will End War* (New York: Duffield, 1914), 88; Mencken, "The Late Mr. Wells," in *Prejudices: First Series*, 22–35, 24 (emphasis added).

67. Mencken, *Book of Prefaces*, 26. For an inspired account of the role of Kipling as a bard and catalyst of empire in the United States, see Christopher Hitchens, *Blood, Class, and Empire: The Enduring Anglo-American Relationship* (New York: Nation Books, 2004), 63–97. Hitchens makes a point that speaks to the larger Americanist argument of this book (i.e., beyond Conrad): "Almost all studies of the man [Kipling]

and his life and work discount the influence he exerted on American expansionism, or else seem unaware of it" (374).

68. Mencken, "Partly About Books," *Smart Set* 48.1 (Jan. 1916): 304–10, 308 (emphasis added).

69. Mencken, "The Mailed Fist and Its Prophet," *Atlantic Monthly* (Nov. 1914): 598–613, 599.

70. Mencken, *Book of Prefaces*, 35.

71. "Bibliography of the European War," *New York Times Book Review* (Nov. 29, 1914), qtd. in Ross, *Propaganda for War*, 34; George Bernard Shaw, *What I Really Wrote About the War* (London: Constable, 1930), 117.

72. Conrad's friend John Powell. Consider Emily Clark's letter to Joseph Hergesheimer of June 1923: "This is John's article, reprinted in the *Leader*—I told Mencken what he said about Roger Casement being Kurtz, and he didn't see how it was possible. But John told me that years ago. He is always saying that Conrad is misunderstood, and thinks he is the only person who understands him!" Casement and Conrad were acquaintances who first met in the Congo in 1890. See Gerald Langford, ed., *Ingénue Among the Lions: The Letters of Emily Clark to Joseph Hergesheimer* (Austin: University of Texas Press, 1965), 147.

73. Mencken, "Roosevelt and Others," *Smart Set* 61.3 (Mar. 1920): 138–44, 139.

74. Mencken, *Book of Prefaces*, 17 (emphasis in original).

75. Mencken, "The Grandstand Flirts with the Bleachers," 433. Compare Mencken's discussion of "A Point of Honor" (the text's original title when printed separately in the United States in 1908) as "coloured by senseless, insatiable ferocity"—surely with an eye on the war—in *A Book of Prefaces*, 42.

76. Mencken, *Book of Prefaces*, 42.

77. See my "Reading *The Secret Agent* Now: The Press, the Police, the Premonition of Simulation," in Kaplan, Mallios, and White, *Conrad in the Twenty-first Century*, 155–74, and my "Afterword: The Deserts of Conrad," in Joseph Conrad, *The Secret Agent*, Peter Mallios, ed. (New York: Modern Library, 2005), 261–90.

78. See Sanders and Taylor, *British Propaganda*, 168–71, 179–84; Wollaeger, "Conrad's Darkness Revisited," 70–71.

79. Mencken, *Book of Prefaces*, 13, 42 (emphasis added).

80. That Conrad has Wilson not exclusively but nevertheless squarely in mind referring to the "idealistic" subset of the "great and very blind forces" set free upon the world is clear from a number of contemporary letters. Referring to Wilson and his freshly embraced (by the Germans) Fourteen Points, Conrad wrote Christopher Sandeman on October 17, 1918: "Somehow an air of mystery hangs upon the clearest utterances, like a cloud over an open landscape. The force behind these plain words is immense. Immense in every sense. The fact is that the mind uttering these momentous declarations is a non-European mind; and we, old Europeans, with a long bitter experience behind us of realities and illusions, can't help wondering as to the exact value of words expressing these great intentions" (*CL* 6.289). Indeed, as early as March 18, 1916, just as Wilson was beginning to run for reelection on the slogans "Too proud to fight," "Neutrality in thought and deed," and "He kept us out of the war," Conrad wrote to Eugene Saxton, an American editor at Doubleday that Conrad respected very much, that "as a true friend of the U.S." he hoped "with all of my heart that you will

keep out of the war"—precisely because the conclusion of the war would bring "problems of peace, extremely complicated, purely European, involving deep-seated feelings, aspirations and convictions absolutely foreign to American mentality and even
to American emotions" (*CL* 5.568). In a revealing letter written to his agent J. B. Pinker
on May 2, 1917, Conrad references Warrington Dawson, the expatriate U.S. Southern
writer, as representative of the "sort of mysterious exalted fashion" that informs grandiose American thinking: "O! these Americans! They seem to have something just a
little wrong with their brains and it shows in a variety of ways—which are *not* amusing" (*CL* 6.83). The "true friend of the U.S." continues on the subject of what's wrong
with American "brains" in a letter of May 16, 1917, to New York lawyer John Quinn, in
which Conrad undermines a formulaic reference to the "luck" of U.S. entry into the
war with a stream of prickly remarks on "a certain *unreality* in the motives set forth in
[American] speeches" and sharp differences between American and Allied European
"watchwords," "formulas," and "ideals" (*CL* 6.86, emphasis added). Conrad brings this
point squarely back to the representative figure of Wilson in a letter to Quinn in February 1918: "I don't remember what Mr. Wilson said in his latest utterance. There is such
an awful air of unreality in the words that are being flung in the face of such appalling
realities. For the closer they are looked into the more appalling they are" (*CL* 6.181).
Finally, when the Fourteen Points appeared and the armistice approached, Conrad worried about the mirage of U.S.-inspired "democratic bawlings" of "felicity" and "peace"
and "self-determination" and "democracy" (*CL* 6.337), about less the malicious than
the awfully unreal "babble of League of Nations and Reconstruction and production
of Commodities and Industrial arrangements . . . and Conciliation Boards . . . set up
to bring about a union of hearts while the bare conciliation of interests is obviously
impossible" (*CL* 6.351). Mencken, without the help of Conrad's correspondence, is reading Conrad quite accurately, though Mencken also ultimately attributes the critiques
(moralizing, idealizing, transcendentalizing, exceptionalist) that both Mencken and
Conrad advance against Wilson and U.S. Americans generally to a mimetic reproduction of *British* cultural and ideological habits. As we shall see, it is Conrad's very ambivalence and ambiguity on this latter point that make him attractive to both Mencken
and Mencken's Anglophilic American antagonists.

81. Hitchens, *Blood, Class*, xv.

82. Mencken, "On Being an American," in *Prejudices: Third Series* (New York: A. A.
Knopf, 1922), rptd. in Mencken, *American Scene*, 6–38, 20 (emphasis added).

83. Ibid., 20, 26.

84. See Carroll Quigley, *The Anglo-American Establishment* (New York: Books in
Focus, 1981); Hitchens, *Blood, Class*, 63–75 (on the Kipling poem and Roosevelt; compare Mencken's comments with respect to each); Mencken, "The National Letters,"
92; Mencken, "On Being an American," 18, 24; Mencken, "The Armenian Buncombe,"
Baltimore Evening Sun (May 28, 1920) (discussed in Rodgers, *Mencken*, 218). The phrase
"special relationship" is not Mencken's, though the point, which is very similar to
Hitchens's point in using both those phrases, is.

85. Mencken, "On Being an American," 14.

86. Ibid., 24, 21, 22, 20; Mencken, "The Cult of Dunsany," *Smart Set* 52.3 (July
1917): 138–44, 142–44 (on the *Encyclopaedia Britannica*; compare Mencken's praise of

the American *New International* encyclopedia in "Seven Pages About Books," 137–43); Mencken, "On Being an American," 15, 24.

87. Mencken, "The National Letters," 104.

88. Hence Mencken's notorious rewriting of "The Declaration of Independence" in "American" (language).

89. Mencken, "The Books of the Irish," *Smart Set* 51.4 (Mar. 1917): 134–44, 138.

90. Ibid., 142–43.

91. Mencken, "Conrad Revisited," 242.

92. It was a commonplace of Conrad's early reception history in Britain that he would imaginatively "annex" for Britain the new exotic places he wrote about.

93. Mencken, "The National Letters," 94.

94. Ibid., 94–95.

95. Ibid., 96. Mencken refers to the moment in *A Personal Record* when Conrad describes the genesis of his first novel, *Almayer's Folly*, in terms of a "hidden, obscure necessity" (*PR* 68). Mencken's misquotation—or is it mistranslation?—has significant afterlife: see, for instance, (American) James Branch Cabell's *The Line of Love* (New York: Robert M. McBride, 1921), specifically the second paragraph of the introduction. The book remains to be written on misquotations, misspellings ("Marlowe": or is that how he "spelt" his name? [*YOS* 3]), mislabelings ("The Heart of Darkness," not really referring to the original short story), and the general issue of translation in and of Conrad.

96. Jean-Aubry, *Joseph Conrad*, 2.289 (emphasis added). Compare the Author's Note to *A Personal Record*, where Conrad argues that "nothing is more foreign than what in the literary world is called Slavonism" to his "individual" sensibility and "the whole Polish mentality" (*PR* vii). The truth, of course, lies in between—or rather with both—Mencken and Conrad, as the example of *Under Western Eyes*, in which Conrad both autobiographically inscribes and critically presents "Russia," signally demonstrates. The young Conrad, one notes, was quite capable of imagining the idea of "Panslavism" (see Zdzisław Najder, ed., *Conrad's Polish Background: Letters to and from Polish Friends* [Cambridge: Cambridge University Press, 1982], 79–80); the older Conrad, even when for eminently sound political and cultural reasons repudiating "superficial or ill-informed theorists [who] are trying to force [Poles] into the social and psychological formula of Slavonism," is still quite capable of imagining the Polish "Russophile" (albeit of necessity), the "Slavonic" Pole (albeit "in truth" a misnomer), and a Russian protectorate subsuming Poland (see *NLL* 134–40, 134, 135). See chapter 1 of Harpham's *One of Us* for more in this respect; for a different and equally suggestive account of how in *Under Western Eyes* "Conrad's determination to capture 'the very soul of things Russian' actually involved, as he slowly realized, an exploration and reassessment of his troubled, divided feelings with regard to his Polish past and heritage," see Keith Carabine, "'The Figure Behind the Veil': Conrad and Razumov," in *The Life and the Art: A Study of Conrad's "Under Western Eyes"* (Amsterdam: Rodopi, 1997), 97–127.

97. Mencken, *Book of Prefaces*, 13–14.

98. Ibid., 51, 253; Mencken, "Probing the Russian Psyche" (1912) in Nolte, 230, 226.

99. Mencken, *Book of Prefaces*, 88–89, 76, 79, 106. In referencing the hysterical American "organized movement" to "depict Dreiser as a *secret agent* of the Wilhelmstrasse, told off to inject subtle doses of *Kultur* into a naïf and pious people" (78), and in later

referencing attempts in American newspapers to "sound an alarm against both Huneker and me as German spies" (165), Mencken picks up on the reading and contemporary U.S. application of *The Secret Agent* discussed earlier. Mencken's idea of the childish, easily alarmed, fundamentally afraid, categorically uncritical newspaper-reading public is never very far from the Stevie of *The Secret Agent*.

100. Ibid., 190, 164, 184, 187–88, 166. Beyond specific mentions of Conrad, the key Conradian elements gridding the portrait of Huneker are (1) the cosmopolitan account of Huneker's style that, in insisting on how it draws cumulatively from the number of different places in the world, duplicates the story Conrad tells (and that Mencken and numerous Americans are fascinated with retelling) concerning the composition of *Almayer's Folly*, and (2) the returns to *Polishness* and Poles (like Chopin and Conrad) at the heart of Huneker's sensibility.

101. See John Higham, *Strangers in the Land: Patterns of Nativism 1860–1925* (West-port, Conn.: Greenwood Press, 1981), 213.

102. See ibid., 194–263; David Traxel, *Crusader Nation: The United States in Peace and the Great War, 1898–1920* (New York: Knopf, 2006), 211–39; David M. Kennedy, *Over Here: The First World War and American Society* (New York: Oxford University Press, 1980), 45–92, 60–75. As these commentators note, the "Americanization" movement originally sprang from two dissimilar sources: one deriving from settlement house and social re-form activists like Lillian Wald, Jane Addams, and Josephine Roche, whose principal purpose was to provide functional assistance to immigrants; the other deriving from older generations of Anglo-identified (for the most part) Americans concerned about the loss of their class power, social normativity, cultural values, and overall dominance in a United States increasingly filled with hundreds of thousands of "new" (principally southern and Eastern European) immigrants. During the buildup to U.S. entry into the war, and under the terrorizing guise of "preparedness" against enemies both within and without, the second movement overwhelmingly absorbed and supplanted the first.

103. Mencken, *Book of Prefaces*, 30, 88.

104. Ibid., 163, 159.

105. For a good example of Mencken's express denunciations of U.S. anti-Germanism in a moment of freer expression, see "The Genealogy of Etiquette," 47.1 *Smart Set* (Sept. 1915): 304–10, 307: "Nor is it astonishing to find quite intelligent Americans believing that the Kaiser started the war for his private pleasure . . . [or] the English philologist, Prof. Dr. Archibald Sayce, staking his professional honor on the doctrine that no German has ever contributed anything of worth to philology. These things are not aston-ishing; they are merely human. Even the unparalleled allegation of Prof. Dr. Sayce does not prove that he is a lunatic, but merely that he is an Englishman." Compare Mencken, "Savonarolas A-Sweat," *Smart Set* 49.3 (July 1916): 292–98, 294–95. On the War Issues Courses, see Kennedy, *Over Here*, 57–59; Carol S. Gruber, *Mars and Minerva: World War I and the Uses of Higher Education* (Baton Rouge: Louisiana State University Press, 1975).

106. Mencken, *Book of Prefaces*, 201–2.

107. See Kennedy, *Over Here*, 45–92. Education being a generally nonfederal matter, local districts and many states banned the teaching of German; the language quoted is from the Board of Education of California. The notorious language from Wilson— who at one point also recommended the "hazing" of disloyal foreigners—comes from

his December 1915 address before Congress; earlier in the fall he had supported (military) "preparedness" in an address warning those within with "alien sympathies," and as late as 1919 and 1920 Wilson was still using antialien and antiradical sentiment to shore up support for the Versailles Treaty and the League of Nations. Opponents of the League, he argued, are "the same sources . . . which threatened this country . . . with disloyalty. . . . Any man who carries a hyphen around with him carries a dagger that he is ready to plunge into the vitals of the Republic." See Higham, *Strangers*, 200; Kennedy, *Over Here*, 87. As Kennedy notes, Wilson's tactics, though repugnant, were not irrational or without foundation: "More than the other belligerent governments, the Wilson administration was compelled to cultivate—even to manufacture—public opinion very favorable to the war. Lacking the disciplinary force of quick-coming crisis or the imminent peril of physical harm, Wilson"—especially given grave political fault lines within the United States—"had to look to other means to rally his people: to the deliberate mobilization of emotions and ideas. Here, the Great War was peculiarly an affair of the mind" (46).

108. Mencken, *Book of Prefaces*, 19.

109. Mencken, "Roosevelt and Others," 144.

110. Qtd. in Rodgers, *Mencken*, 179.

111. See Werner Sollors, *Beyond Ethnicity* (New York: Oxford University Press, 1986), 1–39, 66–99, for more on the wide complexity of "consent" and "descent" relations that historically figured into diverse conceptions of "Americanization" and the "melting pot."

112. For Mencken's ridicule of Americans who restrict themselves and would restrict others to the English language, see *A Book of Prefaces*, 155–57.

113. Mencken, "The Anglo-Saxon," *Baltimore Evening Sun* (July 16, 1923), rptd. in *Chrestomathy*, 169–77, 171–72.

114. Ibid., 177 (emphasis added). Mencken fights here for the very same "free[dom] from that slavery to embalmed ideas," and "new concept of relations between fact and fact, idea and idea," generated through "constant transfusions" of the "strange and bizarre," that he fears will "die" in "Conrad Revisited." As the front page of the *New York Times* put it on May 4, 1921, in the article "Immigration Bill Passed by Senate: Reed Alone Votes Against the Measure Limiting Admission of Aliens," Senator Reed of Missouri responded to the Dillingham Bill with a long speech "ridicul[ing] the statement that the country was endangered by a threatened influx of undesirable immigrants."

115. Mencken, "A Gamey Old Gaul," *Smart Set* 45.1 (Jan. 1915): 458–64, 461; Mencken, "The Sub-Potomac Phenomenon," *Smart Set* 55.4 (Aug. 1918): 138–44, 144; Mencken, "The Stream of Fiction," *Smart Set* 55.1 (June 1918): 138–44, 138, 139; Mencken, "Consolation," *Smart Set* 64.1 (Jan. 1921): 138–44, 141, 142; Mencken, "Hark, Hark, the Lark," *Smart Set* 55.2 (June 1918): 138–44, 140; qtd. in Rodgers, *Mencken*, 227.

116. Mencken, "The National Letters," 49, 50, 42, 44, 50. In this "foreignized" spirit— one in which all that is good in the United States is "based upon a genuine alienness" and "radiate[s] an alien smell"—*Heart of Darkness* is strategically named as an absolute opposite of the normative American short story (45, 46, 43).

117. Mencken, "The Anglo-Saxon," 170–72, 177.

118. Matthew Frye Jacobson, *Whiteness of a Different Color: European Immigrants and the Alchemy of Race* (Cambridge, Mass.: Harvard University Press, 1998), 42. For

different views of the history of the category of the "Anglo-Saxon," its racialization, and its changing terms of racial and cultural otherness, see Gary Gerstle, *American Crucible: Race and Nation in the Twentieth Century* (Princeton: Princeton University Press, 2001); Eric P. Kaufmann, *The Rise and Fall of Anglo-America* (Cambridge, Mass.: Harvard University Press, 2004).

119. Originally delivered as a lecture at the University of Massachusetts in 1975, and revised and reprinted several times since then, Achebe's "An Image of Africa: Racism in Conrad's *Heart of Darkness*" situates and explains its impulse to diagnose the "thoroughgoing racis[m]" of Conrad's works in two experiences, described at the opening of the essay, that happened while Achebe was a visiting professor in the United States. For why Achebe is historically right to worry about racist applications of Conrad in the United States, and more on the complex place of Conrad as a historical mediator of black-white racial relations in the United States and the world, see Chapters 2 and 5 in this volume.

120. Mencken, "The Murray Case" (1935) (regarding an African-American refused admittance to the University of Maryland Law School on racial grounds), rptd. in Marion Rodgers, ed., *The Impossible H. L. Mencken: A Selection of His Best Newspaper Stories* (New York: Doubleday, 1991), 191–95.

121. Theodore Allen, *The Invention of the White Race*, vol. 1, *Racial Oppression and Social Control* (London: Verso, 1994), 23, passim; Higham, *Strangers*, passim.

122. Mencken, "The Anglo-Saxon," 176, 170, 173.

123. See Mencken, "Negro Spokesman Arises to Voice His Race's Wrong," *New York Evening Mail* (Sept. 19, 1917) (regarding Kelly Miller and equal political rights for African-Americans); Mencken, "Two Wasted Lives," *Chicago Sunday Tribune* (Apr. 26, 1925) (defending Berkman and Goldman, Russian Jewish and Lithuanian Jewish [respectively] radicals, from deportation; Mencken would later call on the Bureau of Immigration to return Goldman); "The Land of the Free," *Baltimore Evening Sun* (Jan. 12, 1925) (defending Italian-American and antifascist newspaper proprietor Carlo Tresca from government persecution enabled by Italian-American identity; also references "the great agencies of Americanism," a thoroughly racialized reference, that are letting Sacco and Vanzetti "rot in prison")—all in Rodgers, *Impossible Mencken*, 186–90, 160–64, 77–81, 80.

124. In matters of race, like most others, Mencken's preferred pathway to truth lay in provoking confrontation and letting the "marketplace" of contradictory assertions and conflict play themselves out—even when the contradictions came from Mencken himself—rather than attempting to offer a conciliating and harmonizing viewpoint whose *consistency* would foreclose the terms and speakers of dissent in advance. In a fascinating passage in his autobiography, James Weldon Johnson explains Mencken's offering him similar advice for African-American authors:

The first contact I made was with H. L. Mencken, then [in 1916] one of the editors of *Smart Set*. Mencken had made a sharper impression on my mind than any other American then writing, and I wanted to know him. . . . I had never been so fascinated at hearing anyone talk. He talked about literature, about Negro literature, the Negro problem, and Negro music. He declared that Negro writers in writing about their own race made a mistake when they indulged in pleas for justice and mercy, when they prayed indulgence for shortcomings, when they based their protests against unjust treatment on the Christian or moral or ethical code, when they argued to prove that they were as good as anybody else. "What they should do," he said, "is to single out the strong points of the race and emphasize them over and over and over; asserting, at least on these points, that they are *better* than anybody else." I called to his attention that I had attempted something of that sort in *The Autobiography of an Ex-Colored Man*. (James Weldon Johnson, *Along This Way: The Autobiography of James Weldon Johnson* [New York: Viking Press, 1933], 305)

125. See Michaels, *Our America*, 1–30.

126. To say that Mencken's invocations of race are often not reducible to a logic of identity, even though "race" is a powerful social fiction whose (modern) terms are precisely those of essentialized identity, is not a contradiction: both because (1) the aesthetics of Mencken's appeals to "race" tend, both pedagogically and performatively, to cancel one another out and to provoke and presuppose resistance, and contestation of "race" at the level of discourse, as their fundamental logic; and because (2) Mencken frequently foregrounds racially *hybrid* figures and individuals, as a means of confusing and ambiguating the significance and parameters of overarching "racial" categories.

127. For example, prior to and concurrent with Mencken, the idea of "aristocracy" had currency both in racist writings like those of Madison Grant and the reactionary white South and in antiracist writings like those of George Santayana and Van Wyck Brooks; as we shall see, Mencken, though inclining to Santayanan tropes, "does the aristocracy" in a voice quite his own.

128. Mencken, *Book of Prefaces*, 18, 20, 92; Mencken, "Conrad's Self-Portrait," 230; Mencken, "Conrad Revisited," 243; Joseph Hergesheimer, "A Note on John Partins," *Reviewer* 2.4 (Jan. 1922): 175–87, 177; Mencken, *Book of Prefaces*, 92.

129. "The National Letters," 65; Mencken, *Book of Prefaces*, 64, 89, 35.

130. Mencken, *Book of Prefaces*, 22.

131. In *The Novel of Purpose*, 1–51, Claybaugh compellingly demonstrates the transatlantic premises and economies underpinning and entwining British and American projects of social reform and literary realism in the nineteenth century. Here in the earlier twentieth century, Mencken is attacking, through the contrary image of Conrad and in this *Book of Prefaces* essay on Conrad, precisely this transatlantic Anglo-Saxon nexus of overly moralized and didacticized, simultaneously insufficiently nationalized (in Mencken's view, because conducted in purely "colonial" terms) and too narrowly and provincially transnationalized (unlike the "global" Conrad) political and literary predilection.

132. See Mencken, *Book of Prefaces*, 198–210.

133. Ibid., 240.

134. See ibid., 225–74; Mencken and George Jean Nathan, *The American Credo* (New York: Knopf, 1920), 14–27; Mencken, *Notes on Democracy*, 170, passim; and the first number of *American Mercury* (Jan. 1924), a vast blast against U.S. political heroes (the opening essay assaults Lincoln) and constrictive American laws generally.

135. Mencken, "The National Letters," 96.

136. Mencken, *Book of Prefaces*, 220, 222.

137. Ibid., 202, 251. Throughout "Puritanism as a Literary Force," Mencken relentlessly decries a baseline lack of judicially guaranteed civic protections—what we

would now consider fundamental civil rights—at this moment in modern U.S. society. Against a punitive culture and "body of law that is unmatched in any other country of Christendom" in the "fanatical harshness and vigilance" of its exercise, making "escape from [its] operations well-nigh impossible," Mencken emphasizes that there is no check against the assumption that "the sinner [has] *no rights* that anyone is bound to respect"; no meaningful protections afforded by the "judiciary" against the excesses of the "legislative arm"; and no ultimate legal or social reality for the alleged perpetrator of various forms of arbitrarily decreed social "immorality"—embracing issues such as free speech, collective organization, reproductive rights and sexual freedom, and racialized restriction —but that "its practitioner has no rights," its "defendant must do his fighting without weapons." Ibid., 226, 248, 263, 268 (emphasis added); for Mencken's most complete system articulation for how the judiciary, in its utter accommodationism, becomes captured by the larger economic-plutocratic and majoritarian-Puritan forces gridding contemporary U.S. democracy, see 251, 263–68.

138. Mencken, *Notes on Democracy*, 168.

139. Mencken, *Book of Prefaces*, 210–11; Mencken, "The National Letters," 65.

140. Mencken, *Book of Prefaces*, 20.

141. Ibid., 50.

142. Ibid., 20–21.

143. Ibid., 279, 251.

144. Walter Lippmann, "H. L. Mencken" (1926), in Walter Lippmann, *Men of Destiny* (New Brunswick, N.J.: Transaction Publishers, 2003): 61–70, 63 (emphasis added).

145. Ibid., 62.

146. Ibid., 62–63 (emphasis added).

147. Mencken, *Book of Prefaces*, 50–51.

148. Conrad's fiction does this, Brooks argues, not only through the diverse world spaces it conflates but also through the arrays of oppositional conceptual categories whose terms his work insistently enfolds: Conrad is "'thrillingly' romantic" in "an almost bitterly anti-romantic epoch"; he combines Henry James's "utmost subtlety of style with an exclusive interest in large [geopolitical] issues"; he "preserve[s] that elemental integrity which as a rule springs from being rooted in one spot . . . through an experience of the earth's surface greater than that of Stevenson, or even Pierre Loti"; "he acclimatize[s] in our own [Western] language the very mood for which we have gone to Russian literature"; and Conrad effects such a heteroclite array of enfoldings—such that it is "impossible" for the "English tongue" to put them together—without ever offering the consolation of a new "master" narrative: "His greatest good luck lies in the fact that he satisfies the revolutionary appetite of his epoch while remaining perfectly free of each and every type of revolutionary theory." Brooks, "A Study of Joseph Conrad," 26.

149. Ibid.

150. Van Wyck Brooks, *The Wine of the Puritans* (1908), in Claire Sprague, *Van Wyck Brooks: The Early Years* (Boston: Northeastern University Press, 1993), 59; Brooks, *America's Coming-of-Age* (1915), in Sprague, *Van Wyck Brooks*, 99.

151. Brooks, "Enterprise" (1916), in Sprague, *Van Wyck Brooks*, 160–62; Brooks, *Wine of the Puritans*, 56; Brooks, *America's Coming-of-Age*, 120, 127, 128, 155; "Toward a National Culture" (1917), in Sprague, *Van Wyck Brooks*, 180–91, 187.

152. Van Wyck Brooks, *The World of H. G. Wells* (New York: M. Kennerley, 1915), 49, 47, 166, 178, 179, 171–72 (emphases added).

153. Ibid., 153, 155 (emphases added).

154. *Ibid.*, 154, 156–57.

155. See, e.g., Brooks, *Wine of the Puritans*, 11 (emphasis added) ("There is in European societies an accretion of twenty centuries of *experience*, bound up with prejudice and instinct incalculably complex, which expresses itself in a silent sense of fatality. . . . But we Americans have no bonds with remote antiquity, nor traditions old enough yet to have become instincts"); Brooks, *America's Coming-of-Age*, 176 (emphases added) ("our literature . . . springs from a national mind that has been standardized in another sphere than that of *experience*"; the American presumption "is that the function of art is to turn aside the problems of life from the unrest of emotional *experience*").

156. Brooks, *America's Coming-of-Age*, 181, 158.

157. See Brooks, "Toward a National Culture," 188; Brooks, "Our Awakeners" (1917), in Sprague, *Van Wyck Brooks*, 202–14, 209; Brooks, "An American Oblomov" (1917), in Sprague, *Van Wyck Brooks*, 216–19.

158. Brooks, *America's Coming-of-Age*, 157.

159. Brooks was fond of George Russell's maxim "Democratic in economics, aristocratic in thought"; in *Wells*, he draws particular attention to Wells's notion of "samurai," "that self-conscious, highly selective open-minded, devoted, aristocratic culture, which seems to me to be the necessary next phase in the development of human affairs." Qtd. in Raymond Nelson, *Van Wyck Brooks: A Writer's Life* (New York: E. P. Dutton, 1981), 216; Brooks, *World of H. G. Wells*, 78–79.

160. Indeed, the "Russian" Conrad's ability to enter the English language and English-speaking world, regrouping its "ideas" through his own foundational point of view in "experience," makes him in the Brooksian narrative the exact reverse of Wells. Brooks also sometimes fundamentally identifies Conrad as a "Pole": and even more than the "Russian," what greater expression could there be for a national culture so established through traditions and "experience" that even the cruelest developments in modern "ideas" and politics could not erase it? See Brooks, "A Study of Conrad," 26.

161. Nelson, *Van Wyck Brooks*, 279.

162. Brooks, *World of H. G. Wells*, 184.

163. And this, even though in essays like "Our Awakeners" (1917), Brooks, while acknowledging his "cordial agreement" with "the real background of pragmatism" as articulated by its most prominent philosophers (e.g., James, Dewey), critiques pragmatist philosophy for being insufficiently "vital"—for accepting the material sphere as it is rather than offering it the transformative qualities he believes necessary. Sprague, *Van Wyck Brooks*, 209. Brooks is complicit in his own critique because he assumes as primary the need for a "national" point of view that, in ways his work systematically avoids confronting, *precludes* the transformation of the material sphere, reinscribing many of its most strongly fortifying techniques and elements, as much as it potentially might stand to liberate it. The analogy is with the exigency of war: to embrace the necessity of entering the Great War, on the pragmatist assumption that control will then be able to be effected over its terms, is to cede one's values to what is inexorable about war in the first place. This is not to underplay the value of

Brooks's critical insights into the culturally corrosive effects of competitive capital-ism as practiced in the United States (see Casey Nelson Blake, *Beloved Community: The Cultural Criticism of Randolph Bourne, Van Wyck Brooks, Waldo Frank, and Lewis Mumford* [Chapel Hill: University of North Carolina Press, 1990]); it is to identify the lacuna in his ability to envision how to overcome them.

164. Sprague notes, in her introductory comments on *America's Coming-of-Age* in *Van Wyck Brooks*, that "years later Brooks felt that the American past needed reclaim-ing, not only from academic critics who ignored or disparaged it, but from younger critics like H. L. Mencken, 'with a German-American mind,' and the younger genera-tion who were largely immigrant and 'detached from an American past or any sense whatever of an American tradition'" (80). The writings of the earlier Brooks, however, in themselves bespeak an ambivalence between Anglophilia and a lament for the pass-ing of Anglo-American and Anglo-Saxon traditions of culture that are no longer viable, perhaps someday to be recovered in a new vision of the "flowering of New England," and an aggressive Whitman-style commitment to embracing the full, living, diverse terrain of the United States, in opposition to its capitalist debasement of them. One does not find nativist politics in the earlier Brooks so much as an evasion of them.

165. Qtd. in Nelson, *Van Wyck Brooks*, 125.

166. Letter from Sedgwick to Bourne, Dec. 7, 1911, qtd. in Bruce Clayton, *Forgotten Prophet: The Life of Randolph Bourne* (Baton Rouge: Louisiana State University Press, 1984), 59. The advice was especially timely in light of a front-page feature essay the *At-lantic Monthly* was about to run by H. G. Wells, whose first paragraph proclaims: "One of my chief claims to distinction in the world is that I wrote the first long appreciative review of Joseph Conrad's work." See H. G. Wells, "The Contemporary Novel," *Atlan-tic Monthly* 109.1 (Jan. 1912): 1–11, 1. The U.S. appearances of the unexpectedly popular *Twixt Land and Sea* (1912), which includes "The Secret Sharer," and *Chance*, serialized with massive publicity in the *New York Herald* from January 21–June 30, 1912, were soon to follow.

167. Randolph Bourne, "H. L. Mencken," *New Republic* 13.160 (Nov. 24, 1917): 102–3, in Carl Resek, ed., *War and the Intellectuals: Essays by Randolph S. Bourne, 1915–1919* (New York: Harper & Row, 1964), 162–64. Compare Bourne, "Traps for the Wary" (Mar. 1918), in Resek, 179–83.

168. Bourne, "Mencken," 163.

169. "Inexorable" is something of the master term, regularly repeated, of Bourne's political essays in the *Seven Arts* and the *New Republic* during this period. It is also, I would suggest, a silent governing master term of his conception of Conrad in the "Mencken" essay.

170. Mencken, *Book of Prefaces*, 17.

171. Bourne, "A War Diary" (Sept. 1917), in Resek, *War and the Intellectuals*, 36–47, 41 (emphasis added).

172. Ibid. Compare Bourne, "The War and the Intellectuals" (June 1917) and "Twi-light of Idols" (Oct. 1917), in Resek, *War and the Intellectuals*, 3–14, 53–64.

173. See H. L. Mencken, "The Grandstand Flirts with the Bleachers," 430–36.

174. Bourne, "Twilight," 54, 59.

175. Bourne explicitly discusses Conrad in "H. L. Mencken" and "The Art of

Theodore Dreiser" (June 1917); there seems a glancing allusion to *Lord Jim* in "A War Diary" in the description of the United States having "jumped" into the war ("we are like brave passengers who have set out for the Isle of the Blest only to find that the first mate has gone insane and jumped overboard, the rudder has come loose and dropped to the bottom of the sea" [Resek, *War and the Intellectuals*, 40]) and other references to "jumping" in the wartime essays; there is also a steady stream of essays on manifold subjects—hybrid/pluralist immigrant models; Slavic/Russian authors; anti-Puritanism; cosmopolitan tastes in literature and internationalist perspectives—that would naturally seem, especially in Bourne's circles, to raise the subject of Conrad in this moment. Given this context, what is striking is the difficulty and/or underelaborated strictures with which Conrad does appear.

    176. Bourne, "Mencken," 164.

    177. Bourne, "War Diary," 43; "Twilight," 59.

    178. Bourne, "Trans-national America" (July 1916), in Resek, *War and the Intellectuals*, 107–23, 116.

CHAPTER 2

    1. "Mr. Conrad Is Not a Jew," *New Republic* 16 (Aug. 24, 1918): 109.

    2. See, for instance, C. F. Howard, "The Jewish Worker," *Pearson's Magazine* (NY) 39.1 (May 1918): 9–11; Frank Harris, "The Fall of Leon Trotsky," *Pearson's Magazine* (NY) 38.10 (Apr. 1918): 1–2, 1 ("The moment has not yet come to weigh Trotsky or determine the influence and effects of the Bolshevik Revolution. . . . Still, I may be allowed even now to state my conviction that the four months' rule of the Bolshevik constitutes the greatest event in world politics since the French Revolution").

    3. Frank Harris, "Books to Read and Skip," *Pearson's Magazine* 38.8 (Feb. 1918): 370–71.

    4. See Letter from Lewis Browne to Conrad, mid-Nov. 1918, in *The Conradian* 19.1/2 (1995): 132–33.

    5. See Letter from Conrad to Browne, May 15, 1918 (*CL* 6.215–18).

    6. Among contemporary essays explicitly and implicitly challenging anti-American and other demonizing constructions of Jews, see Florence Kiper Frank, "An Acquaintance," *New Republic* 17.219 (Jan. 11, 1919): 307–8 (stereotypes prevent Jewish friend from being understood in terms of a "spiritual" will to be American); "The Forty-four Hour Work Week," *New Republic* 18.222 (Feb. 1 1919): 7–8 (labor victory for Amalgamated Clothing Workers demonstrates, contra the "rather common prejudice against . . . Jewish workmen," Jews as true American patriots); editorial regarding Benjamin Glassberg, *New Republic* 18.222 (Feb. 1, 1919): 2–3 (high school history teacher presumptively and wrongly suspect in his teaching because Jewish); Horace Kallen, "Zionism: Democracy or Prussianism," *New Republic* 18.231 (Apr. 5, 1919): 311–13 (Jewishness/Zionism allied with progressive, nonassimilationist visions of U.S. democracy); Morris Cohen, "Zionism: Tribal or Liberalism," *New Republic* 18.227 (Mar. 8, 1919) (Zionism/Judaism allied with cosmopolitan, enlightened vision of United States).

    7. See Keith Carabine, "'Irreconcilable Antagonisms': Reflections on Conrad, Poland, and the English Political Novel," in Alex Kurczaba, ed., *Conrad and Poland* (Lublin, Poland: Maria Curie–Sklodowska University Press, 1996), 89–112.

    8. "Amy Foster," sometimes considered Conrad's spiritual autobiography, recounts

the story of Yanko Goorall, "a poor emigrant from Central Europe bound to America and washed ashore here [England] in a storm" (*TOT* 111).

9. On translation and strategic erasure as narrative modality in Antin, see Mihaela Moscaliuc's superb "Translating Eastern European Identities into the American National Narrative," Ph.D. diss., University of Maryland, 2006.

10. Since World War II, the potential Jewish implications and resonances of Conrad's fiction have expanded even further—in works as diverse as the fiction of Polish-born Israeli writer John Auerbach, the prose of Saul Bellow, the journalism of Morris Dickstein, and the academic criticism of Daphna Erdinast-Vulcan. See Auerbach's *Tales of Grabowski* and *The Owl and Other Stories* (New Milford, Conn.: Toby Press, 2003; stories of Jewish odyssey during or haunted by the Holocaust, profoundly mediated by Conrad); Bellow's 2002 introduction to the 2003 Toby Press editions of Auerbach's fiction (articulating triangular relation between Bellow, Auerbach, and Conrad); Dickstein, "From Ethnic Ripples, a Tidal Wave," *Forward* (May 7, 2004) (glossing and explaining the Holocaust through the frame of *Heart of Darkness*); and Erdinast-Vulcan's remarkable essays on problems of witnessing atrocity and desire at all costs for law: "*Heart of Darkness* and the Ends of Man," *The Conradian* 28.1 (Spring 2003): 17–33, and "Some Millennial Footnotes in *Heart of Darkness*," in Kaplan, Mallios, and White, *Conrad in the Twenty-first Century*, 55–66.

11. See my "Untimely *Nostromo*," *Conradiana* 40.3 (Fall 2008): 213–33.

12. See Ford Madox Hueffer, "Joseph Conrad," *English Review* 10 (Dec. 1911): 68–83, 68–69.

13. "Literature and Art," *Current Opinion* 5.58 (May 1915): 8.

14. "Is American Life Divorced from American Literature?" *Current Opinion* 64.3 (Mar. 1918): 206.

15. See Edward Sapir, "Realism in Prose Fiction," *Dial* (Nov. 22, 1917): 1; Constant Reader (Dorothy Parker), "Looking Backward: Joseph Conrad," *New York Evening Post Literary Review* (Apr. 28, 1923): 647. Yezierska visited Conrad in 1922.

16. Eleanor Palffy, "Drunk on Conrad," *Fortnightly Review* 132 (Oct. 1929): 534–38, 537; Perriton Maxwell, "A First Meeting with Joseph Conrad," *New York Herald and Tribune Magazine* (Aug. 24, 1924): 10.1; "A Rush of Anniversaries in Paris," *New York Times* (Mar. 4, 1928): 74.

17. R. L. Mégroz, "Joseph Conrad: Man and Artist," *Bookman* (London) 70 (Aug. 1926): 238–41, 240.

18. H. L. Mencken, "Various Books," *Smart Set* 270 (July 1921): 141.

19. Edward Preston Dargan, "The Voyages of Conrad," *Dial* 66 (June 28, 1919): 638–41, 639.

20. George Palmer Putnam, "Conrad in Cracow," *Outlook* 124 (Mar. 3, 1920): 382–83, 382. It is important to note that the final sentence quoted is not that of Buszczynski (according to Preston) but the direct words of Putnam and the (Protestant, mainstream) *Outlook*. Putnam and his magazine are using Conrad both to trivialize the reality of pogroms in Poland and to discredit the veracity of Jews in the United States—the *opposite* of Mencken's point in his nevertheless commensurately de-Semitized presentation of Conrad in the review of *Notes*.

21. A complex and important question, especially in Polish, Irish, and hemispheric

American contexts, whose modern U.S. historicization, beyond my intentions here, might begin with the consistently ambivalent and often quite sensitive grapplings one finds with the issue of "faith" in Conrad in the many reviews of Conrad and of commentators on Conrad in the Catholic magazine *America*. See also, for a truly remarkable claiming of Conrad in "eminently Catholic" terms, "Joseph Conrad: An Appreciation," *Dublin Review* 189 (Oct. 1931): 318–25, 318.

22. "Mr. Conrad Is Not a Jew," 109.

23. Though the *New Republic* never endorses Bolshevism, within or outside the United States, in the years following November 1917, it is extremely critical of anti-Bolshevist hysteria and rampant false information with respect to Russia promulgated by the mainstream press and government. One particular aspect of anti-Bolshevist hysteria the *New Republic* repeatedly attacks is an automatic anti-Semitic association between Bolsheviks and Jews. In taking on the "absurdity" with which Conrad could be labeled a Jew, the *New Republic*, in this context, is also unmistakably implicitly taking on arbitrary attributions of "Bolshevism" as well; the two kinds of attribution are not separable in punitive discourse of this period. Hence, too, the added significance of Conrad's cutting reference to the "Russian."

24. For a trenchant discussion of narrative strategies of this kind in the late 1910s and 1920s, see Michaels, *Our America*, passim.

25. Alfred Knopf, "A Footnote to Publishing History" (1958), in Alfred Knopf, *Portrait of a Publisher 1915–1965*, 2 vols. (New York: Typophiles, 1965), 1.127–40, 148.

26. Geoffrey Hellman, "A Very Dignified Pavane" (1948), in Knopf, *Portrait*, 2.53–112, 83.

27. Knopf, "Footnote," 136; Knopf, "For Henry with Love" (1959), in Knopf, *Portrait*, 1.145–60, 150.

28. See Letter from Knopf to Conrad, Oct. 30, 1913 (TS Berg) (regarding commissioned articles by Macy and Ireland); Letter from Knopf to Conrad, Jan. 22, 1914 (TS Berg) ("I am trying especially now to arouse the interest of our numerous English professors at our colleges in your work. *Lord Jim* is prescribed reading in one large course at Purdue University"); Adolph Kroch, "To Alfred Knopf from a Bookseller," in Knopf, *Portrait*, 2.39–44, 40; Knopf, "Some Random Recollections," in Knopf, *Portrait*, 1.3–25, 10.

29. Knopf, "Some Random Recollections," 10; *Chance* advertisement, *Country Life in America* 25.6 (Apr. 1914): 160.

30. Knopf, "Footnote," 139; Letter from Knopf to Conrad, Jan. 22, 1914 (TS Berg).

31. Qtd. in Hellman, "A Very Dignified Pavane," 84.

32. See Carl van Doren, "Presentation" (1940), in Knopf, *Portrait*, 2.13–17, 14; Knopf, "Some Random Recollections," 58.

33. The quoted phrase appears opposite the title page of Knopf's edition of Przybyszewski's *Homo Sapiens* (1915). Productively, and apropos of my larger point concerning the internationalist political context and overarching precedent of Conrad at issue here, Hellman speculates that Knopf's decision to publish Przybyszeweski, whose novel's erotic content actually got Knopf in trouble with censors, was "possibly an effort on [Knopf's] part to explain Poland, which at the time did not exist as a nation." See Hellman, "A Very Dignified Pavane," 87.

34. Knopf, qtd. in Hellman, "A Very Dignified Pavane," 87. Of the ten books Knopf published in 1915, seven were by or about Russians; in 1916, twelve of Knopf's twenty-nine

titles were by or about Russians. For more on how "Knopf's dedication made American readers aware of the reaches of Russian literature"—and also on how "Russia serves [only] as an example" of Knopf's plunging America "so much farther into alien climes" (fifty-three of the seventy-seven books Knopf issued by the end of 1917 were by European or Asian writers)—see B. W. Huebsch, "The Publisher" (1952) and Adolph Kroch, "To Alfred Knopf" (1940), in Knopf, *Portrait*, 2.125–31, 127, 39–44.

35. See, for example, "Knut Hamsun Hailed as One of the Greatest Living Writers," *Current Opinion* 70.1 (Jan. 1921): 106; compare ad for Walter de la Mare's *Memoir of a Midget*, *New York Times* (Feb. 5, 1922): 46 (only "peer in the language" is *Nostromo*).

36. The quoted phrase is Pierre Bourdieu's, which I use to emphasize the structural relation and interdependence between all the literary elements (e.g., genres) and institutions that together constitute a "field," and whose prohibitive parceling is precisely what Doubleday, if immediately and ultimately after the pursuit of profit, strove "spiritually" to resist, omnicapitalize. See Bourdieu, *The Field of Cultural Production: Essays on Art and Literature* (New York: Columbia University Press, 1993), 29–73.

37. The five collected editions are the Deep Sea (1915; in affordable blue limp leather), Sun-Dial (1921; its plates are the origins of the Uniform edition Conrad scholars will recognize; it was an autograph limited edition of 735 sets that sold for a total of over $129,000), Concord (1923), Memorial (1925; limited to 499 plus 10 presentation sets), and Kent (1926). The four selected volumes of Conrad's tales are *Joseph Conrad: Shorter Tales* (1924), *Sea Tales by Joseph Conrad* (1930), *The Famous Stories of Joseph Conrad* (1938), and *A Conrad Argosy* (1942). The volume of prefaces is *Notes on My Books* (1921); the five anthologies are Mary Reginald, *Wisdom and Beauty from Conrad* (1922), George Iles, ed., *Little Masterpieces of Autobiography* (1926), W. Somerset Maugham, ed., *Traveller's Library* (1933), *A Book of Great Autobiography* (1934), Edward Weeks, ed., *Great Short Novels: An Anthology* (1941); the testimonial volumes beyond Keating's *A Conrad Memorial Library* (1929) are Christopher Morley, *Conrad and the Reporters* (1923), Jessie Conrad, *Joseph Conrad As I Knew Him* (1926), and Richard Curle, *The Last Twelve Years of Joseph Conrad* (1928); the second volume of letters is Curle's *Conrad to a Friend* (1928). I also mention Jessie Conrad's *A Handbook of Cookery for a Small House* (1923), also put out by Doubleday, not infrequently referenced in the press, and with a preface by Joseph Conrad.

38. One important example, to which we will return because of its political significance, is *The Nigger of the "Narcissus"* (1914), restored to its original title, and also including both the suppressed original "Preface" to the novel and a preliminary note "To My Readers in America."

39. Among other examples to be elaborated in this chapter: *The Arrow of Gold* (1919) was advertised as an unprecedented "Great Love Story by Joseph Conrad" (see Advertisement, *Chicago Daily Tribune* [Apr. 19, 1919]: 12); *The Rescue* (1920), completed over a more than twenty-year period, was widely marketed as an exciting opportunity to compare Conrad's "early" and "late" manner, and to speculate on where the fault line lay between past and present in the text; *Notes on Life and Letters* (1921) was presented as Conrad's first and definitive critical statement with respect to letters (with important political concerns, too); *The Rover* (1923) was first Conrad's unexpected "latest" and then his "last complete" novel; *Suspense* (1925) was his mysterious "unfinished" novel

(and, as we shall see, one Americans were invited to complete); and *Last Essays* (1926) was Conrad's final unpublished articulation.

40. Of many examples to point to here, the first British edition of *Suspense* has an image of Napoleon on the cover, whereas Doubleday's first edition has a picture of Conrad.

41. See, for example, "Books and Authors," *New York Times* (May 30, 1915): BR208 (Conrad set the prize for high school essay competition); on the *Suspense* competition, see the discussion of *Suspense* later in this chapter.

42. "Joseph Conrad Tells Why He Chose English," *New York Tribune* (May 23, 1920): 7.9.

43. The 1917 Author's Notes to *Lord Jim* and *Youth* appear, respectively, in *Bookman* (NY) 46 (Jan. 1918): 539–40, and 47 (Mar. 1918): 31–32; the Author's Notes to *Lord Jim*, *Nostromo*, and *Outcast* appear in "Three Conrad Novels," *Dial* 6.96 (Dec. 1920): 619–30.

44. See "Notes on Conrad," *Bookman* (NY) 38 (Dec. 1913): 352–54 (excerpts and photos from Knopf's *Joseph Conrad: The Romance of His Life and of His Books*); Richard Curle, "Joseph Conrad: A Study," pts. 1–3 (Aug.–Oct. 1914): 39.662–68, 40.99–104, 40.187–201 (preview of Curle's *Joseph Conrad: A Study*); Helen Thomas Follett and Wilson Follett, "Contemporary Novelists: Joseph Conrad," *Atlantic Monthly* 119 (Feb. 1917): 233–43 (following up on W. Follett's Doubleday book, *Joseph Conrad: A Short Study*).

45. The special relationship between Conrad and Yale—which includes many Conradian articles (by Ford Madox Ford, Richard Curle, Wilbur Cross, and Thomas Moult, among others) in the *Yale Review* during the 1920s; Conrad's visit to Yale and Professor William Lyon Phelps during his May 1923 U.S. visit; an earlier wartime attempt to arrange dinner with Professor Henry Seidel Canby (*CL* 6.223–24), who would come to correspond with Conrad and serve as editor-in-chief of the *Saturday Review of Literature*; and George T. Keating's enormous donation of primary Conrad materials (including the letters to Marie Poradowska) in 1938—begins, as described in the Introduction, with Conrad serving as the subject of the Yale English department's annual essay competition in 1915; it is not a coincidence that this happens at the very moment Doubleday is making Conrad's texts readily purchasable and available. The same is true of the book clubs: the quotations come from "A Kansas Critic of Conrad," *New York Times* (Feb. 2, 1916): 10 (arrogant article attempting to belittle Sabetha book club for studying Conrad), and "The Appreciation of Conrad," *Manchester Guardian* (Aug. 5, 1924): 6 (equally arrogant article belittling U.S. midwestern Conradophile book clubs generally).

46. "The Arrow of Gold," *Bookman* (NY) 49 (July 1919): 640 (emphasis added).

47. For citation and further context, see note 39 above.

48. This is a general subject—Conrad and earlier cinema—upon which much of value has been written. For Gene Moore's analysis of the "popular" production of Conrad in film through strategies of excision, and also his thoughts on the benefits of cinematic infidelity and a marvelous short history of Conrad's (characteristically complex, ambivalent) interactions with film and the film industry, see his essays in Moore, ed., *Conrad on Film* (Cambridge: Cambridge University Press, 1997), 1–7, 31–47. For a transcription and excellent discussion of Conrad's "Author and Cinematograph," which Conrad probably delivered at the outset of his Doubleday-sponsored public reading of *Victory* on May 10, 1923, as well as at Doubleday's facility five days before, see Arnold T. Schwab, "Conrad's American Speeches and His Reading from *Victory*,"

Modern Philology 62.4 (May 1965): 342–47. For more on Conrad and film and popular culture generally, see Stephen Donovan, *Joseph Conrad and Popular Culture* (New York: Palgrave, 2005). I will not elaborate further the subject of Conrad and U.S. film (in part precisely because of the excellence of what's already been said, in part because there also remains too much to be said)—other than simply to note the following: (1) U.S. film versions of five Conrad books (*Lord Jim, Nostromo, Victory, Romance,* and *The Rescue*) were made by 1929; (2) these films' "popular" (in every sense of the word) nature contributed to the greater U.S. counterpoint of dialogue and debate concerning the essential nature of "our Conrad," in terms commensurate with the *Bookman* quotation prompting this footnote; and (3) it is clear from contemporary newspaper articles attesting to the number of Doubleday authors, among them Louis Vance, Booth Tarkington, and Stewart Edward White, whom Fiction Pictures, the first film company to approach Conrad, also approached in 1915, that Doubleday's role in making Conrad available and conceivable as a popular and profitable author was not unrelated to the interest the new film companies took in Conrad. See "Notes Written on the Screen," *New York Times* (Apr. 18, 1915): X8.

49. Reproduced from Gary A. Borkan, *World War I Posters* (Atglen, Penn.: Schiffer Publishing, 2002), 136. Compare Edward Eyre Hunt, "Winged Victory," *New Republic* 21.263 (Dec. 17, 1919): 858–59 (review of French politician Edward Herriot's *Créer,* using Winged Victory as counterpoint to the "wingless" Nike Apteros to figure surmounting of war-related disillusion); Hervey Allen, "The Wingless Victory," *New Republic* 23.298 (Aug. 18, 1920): 336 (poem using Winged Victory as figural converse of present war victory); Frank Lloyd Wright's reproductions of the statue in a number of his buildings; Doubleday's many advertisements of Conrad through the Winged Victory image; and a general militarized culture in the United States in which the term "Victory" was a prevalent rhetorical factor—e.g., in the American Women's Victory Conference in Washington, D.C., in February 1919 (supporting representation of women at Paris Peace Conference); the Victory Campaign of the National Committee of Baptist Laymen beginning in March 1919 (to "enthrone the Christian ideal" throughout the world); the commencement of a new federal Victory Liberty Loan in April 1919; appeals to repair the crumbling Victory Arch in New York in September 1919.

50. "In A Few Words," *New York Times* (Oct. 4, 1914): 50.

51. "Joseph Conrad Is War Bound," *New York Times* (Oct. 22, 1914): 5.

52. "In a Few Words," *New York Times* (Nov. 8, 1914): BR490.

53. Ibid. (Dec. 20, 1914): BR578.

54. "Conrad in Poland," *Bookman* (NY) 46 (Feb. 1918): 659.

55. Conrad himself, as discussed later, commemorates this "rescue" (his metaphor) both in "Poland Revisited" (*NLL* 172) and eventually in the dedication of *The Rescue* to Penfield.

56. *CL* 6.71–72, 103, 114. Howe's militarized conception and construction of Conrad seem also evidenced by his writing to Conrad about plans to reorganize U.S. Army Regulars, the National Guard, and reserves into a single force. Conrad's self-reflexive response of December 15, 1920, apparently written to be publicly reproduced, is "The impending amalgamation is most gratifying to my feelings of affectionate regard for each individual of that great mass of men, great in numbers, great in endurance and

fidelity, great in achievement—and now knotted together into one great Brotherhood-in-Arms" (*CL* 7.219).

57. For more on the critical reception of the novel, see my introduction to *Victory* (New York: Modern Library), xi–xliv.

58. Ibid.

59. Elia W. Peattie, "Conrad's Fascinating but Brutal Realism," *Chicago Daily Tribune* (May 1, 1915): 10.

60. This reading recognizes Lena's act of self-sacrifice as a spiritual affirmation and tends to emphasize as an interpretive priority Heyst's late revelation: "Ah, Davidson, woe to the man whose heart has not learned while young to hope, to love—and to put its trust in life!" (*V* 410).

61. Said, "Traveling with Conrad," in Kaplan, Mallios, and White, *Conrad in the Twenty-first Century*, 285–87.

62. Peattie, "Brutal Realism," 10 (emphasis added).

63. Ibid.; for more on Peattie, about whom much work remains to be done, see Susanne George Bloomfield, ed., *Impertinences: Selected Writings of Elia Peattie: Journalist of the Gilded Age* (Lincoln: University of Nebraska Press, 2005), 1–20.

64. Peattie, "Brutal Realism," 10.

65. Edith Borie, "Joseph Conrad," *New Republic* 2.24 (Apr. 17, 1915): 6–7; Doubleday's large advertisement centering on *Victory* and the Nike image at the front of this issue also includes surrounding advertisements for Victorien Sardou's *Patrie!* ("A stirring dramatic presentation of the Spanish occupation of Belgium. With a change of names, the play might well have been written of the Belgium of 1915") and Hendrik William Van Loon's *The Rise of the Dutch Kingdom* ("Substitute Germany for France and you have a close parallel between the position of Holland in 1795 and to-day. It is history told with all the interest of a novel").

66. Lead editorial, *New Republic* 2.24 (Apr. 17, 1915): 1.

67. Borie, "Joseph Conrad," 6–7.

68. Three other academic literary critics of note, not discussed further in this book, are William Lyon Phelps, Stuart P. Sherman, and Charles Townsend Copeland. Phelps, Lampson Professor of English at Yale and an ordained minister, a prolific literary-critical and religious writer, was important both to the culture of Conrad that early emerged at Yale and the use of Conrad (among other "modern" writers) to champion the place of "modern" literature within the academic humanities curriculum, as well as the professional study of literature in generalist-humanist rather than research-philological terms. Although capable of subtlety, Phelps's interpretations of Conrad are generally overinvested in conventional academic categories ("romance" vs. "realism"), "Slavic" stereotypes, and most significantly, moralistic affirmations and conventions ("Although no novelist preaches less, Conrad's books are based on the axiom of the moral law. Ethically, his novels are sound"), which Mencken, of course, directly attacks, often explicitly naming Phelps. See Phelps, *The Advance of the English Novel* (New York: Dodd, Mead, 1916), 192–217, 215–16; Gerald Graff, *Professing Literature: An Institutional History* (Chicago: University of Chicago Press, 1987), 124–28. Sherman, an English professor at the University of Illinois and outspoken disciple of Irving Babbitt and Paul Elmer More, blends the ethically driven conservative humanism of his teachers with an aggressive

contemporary affirmation of "essential Americanism" (Anglo derived and allied); Sherman's proudly patriotic and self-declaredly "Puritan" vision of moral conduct and letters, broadly disseminated in the public sphere from the First World War forward, is the reverse of both Mencken's and Bourne's conceptions. Sherman became an arch enemy of Mencken after a snide review Sherman wrote of *A Book of Prefaces* in the *Nation* in November 1917, repeatedly insinuating, which was easy to do but toxic in the current war-hysterical climate, Mencken's true "German" sympathies. The article itself avoids discussion of Conrad, but shortly thereafter Sherman, in his own Americo-Arnoldian terms, embraces the cult of Conrad as well: a letter in 1923 expresses that "last summer" he "immersed [him]self in C's books and tried to fill myself with his spirit," discovering "something great in the man—high and heroic in the face of the fathomless beauty and horror of the universe"; in *Men of Letters of the British Isles* (1924), a collection of portrait medallions by Theodore Spicer-Simson (including one of Conrad) with accompanying critical essays by Sherman, Sherman extols how in his tales "Conrad has made his voyages *religious* symbols and his heroes incarnations of a faith, simple, traditional, tenacious"; Conrad's final affirmations are those "of the honor and faithfulness and fortitude of a white man, an officer, and an English gentleman." Mencken, hence, is generally quite correct, as the different extremes of both Phelps and Sherman suggest, to attack the academic institution as a whole as a moralizing apparatus of the state and its dominant cultures. See Sherman, *Americans* (Port Washington, N.Y.: Kennikat Press, 1922), vii–xiii, ix; *The Genius of America* (New York: Charles Scribner's Sons, 1925), 33–70; "Beautifying American Literature," *Nation* (NY) 105.2735 (Nov. 29, 1917): 593–94; *Life and Letters of Stuart P. Sherman* (New York: Farrar & Rinehart, 1929), 1.577; *Men of Letters of the British Isles* (New York: William Edwin Rudge, 1924), 39–40 (emphasis added). Copeland, as early as 1907, was responsible for introducing Follett, Walter Lippmann, and Conrad Aiken, among many other Harvard undergraduates, to Conrad. Follett, "Joseph Conrad, 1907–: A Humble Apology," *Bookman* (NY) 67 (Aug. 1928): 640–47, 641.

69. The other two books are Wilson Follett, *The Modern Novel: A Study of the Purpose and the Meaning of Fiction* (New York: Alfred A. Knopf, 1918), and Helen Thomas Follett and Wilson Follett, *Some Modern Novelists: Appreciations and Estimates* (New York: Henry Holt , 1918), an important collection of essays from the *Atlantic Monthly* and *Yale Review*, climaxing with an essay on Conrad that originally appeared in the *Atlantic Monthly* in February 1917.

70. Follett and Follett, "Contemporary Novelists," 233–43, 234; Follett, *Joseph Conrad: A Short Study*, 20.

71. Follett, *Joseph Conrad: A Short Study*, 22; Follett and Follett, "Contemporary Novelists," 235, 233.

72. Follett, *Joseph Conrad: A Short Study*, 108, 49, 70; Follett and Follett, *Some Modern Novelists*, vi, 236.

73. Follett and Follett, "Contemporary Novelists," 236–38 (emphasis added).

74. Follett and Follett, *Some Modern Novelists*, 15, 9, 17, 324–25 (all emphasis but first added).

75. Follett's uncompromising attention to irreducible *particularity* of otherness, the universal status of *all* human beings and cultures *as* "others," and the kinds of progressive material changes necessary to effect a "just" "human community," all articulated

through Conrad with Conrad's very sense of the impossibility of absolute solution but the necessity of trying (of "immersing in the destructive element" [*LJ* 144]), is what distinguishes Follett and his Conrad from the conventionally patriotic Sherman and his (eventual) Conrad.

76. See Follett, "A Humble Apology."

77. "A Kansas Critic of Conrad," *New York Times* (Feb. 2, 1916): 10.

78. "The Kansas Spirit," *New York Times* (Jan. 20, 1916): 8; "Topics of the Times," *New York Times* (Jan. 12, 1916): 12 (linking Kansas and Nebraska, making fun of "Bleeding Kansas," "Env[ious]" Nebraska, Bryan); "The Murderer of Its Citizens," *New York Times* (Jan. 13, 1916): 10 (attacking Bryan, equating antipreparedness with mass murder); "Topics of the Times," *New York Times* (Mar. 21, 1916): 10 ("Pacifism May Be a Neurosis"; "all" "pacifists" are "of course . . . either consciously or unconsciously pro-German").

79. "Current Fiction," *Nation* (NY) 102 (Feb. 10, 1916): 164.

80. "Conrad in Poland," *Bookman* (NY) 46 (Feb. 1918): 659; Ernest Rhys, "An Interview with Joseph Conrad," *Bookman* (NY) 56 (Dec. 1922): 402–8.

81. "'In the Zone': A War Play by Our New Dramatist of the Sea," *Current Opinion* 65.3 (Sept. 1918): 159.

82. Letter from John Quinn to Jessie Conrad, Jan. 6, 1918: 6 (Berg Collection) (first quote is Quinn's; second quote is direct quotation of a letter from Edith Roosevelt to Quinn).

83. "A Conrad Hero's Quest for Truth," *New York Times* (Apr. 22, 1917): 7.157–58, 157.

84. Ibid.

85. Mark Wollaeger, *Modernism, Media, and Propaganda: British Narrative from 1900 to 1945* (Princeton: Princeton University Press, 2006), 26–35.

86. Ibid., 28 (qtg. *YOS* 51).

87. Ibid., 9.

88. The terms of Fredric Jameson's famous reading of Conrad: his historicist account of the "semi-autonomous" fate of the senses under late capitalism, simultaneously disrupted by and compensating for the materially dislocating effects of modernity, I am attempting to transpose to disciplinary and militarized terms here: these latter terms composing a compulsive aspect of modernity as well. See Jameson, *The Political Unconscious: Narrative as a Socially Symbolic Act* (Ithaca, N.Y.: Cornell University Press, 1982), 206–80.

89. Because the indulgence remains, after all, *only* at the level of impression—tied, as it were, to that restraining mast.

90. In "Tradition," Conrad argues that the "call to . . . service" and "perfect faithfulness to tradition" prioritized in the British navy is "fashioned" from the British merchant marine (*NLL* 196–97); all the essays in this section of *Notes* emphasize the coordinated efforts of the two during the war.

91. For a superb treatment of the complexities of "Englishness" in Conrad's earlier fiction, see Allan H. Simmons, "Art of Englishness: Identity and Representation in Conrad's Early Career," *The Conradian* 29.1 (Spring 2004): 1–26.

92. "Topics of the Times," *New York Times* (Mar. 21, 1916): 10 (emphasis added).

93. See, e.g., *Country Life* (Feb. 1915): 86 (pictorialized ad featuring limp leather editions of Conrad and Kipling); *Country Life* (Dec. 1915): 83 (exotic *Victory* ad juxtaposed

with ad for Kipling's *France at War: On the Frontier of Civilization*); *Country Life* (Apr. 1916): 16-I (juxtaposed "sea" ads for Kipling's *Fringes of the Fleet* and Conrad's *Within the Tides*); *Country Life* (May 1917): 150 (pictorialized ad connecting by a line Kipling and Conrad); *Country Life* (June 1919): 106 (Kipling's *Years Between* and Conrad's *Arrow of Gold* advertised together as "New Books of Lasting Importance"); *Country Life* (July 1919): 2 (pictorial ad for "The Two Most Distinguished Living Writers in English"); *Country Life* (Oct. 1919): 90 (juxtaposed ads of Kipling, "a man's man," and Conrad, whose *Arrow* is a "masterpiece" because of the "woman" at its center).

94. See Conrad, "Henry James: An Appreciation," *North American Review* 203.725 (Apr. 1916): 585–90; Elbridge Adams, "Joseph Conrad—the Man," *Outlook* (NY) 133 (Apr. 1923): 708–12, 708; "Another Conrad Preface: *Youth*," *Bookman* (NY) 27.1 (Mar. 1918): 31–32; J. M. Robertson, "The Novels of Joseph Conrad," *North American Review* 208.754 (Sept. 1918): 439–49; Katharine Fullerton Gerould, *Modes and Morals* (New York: Charles Scribner's Sons, 1920): 278, and "Eidolons of Ulysses," *Bookman* (NY) 49.3 (May 1919): 368–70, 368.

95. G. H. C., "*Notes on Life and Letters*," *Sewanee Review* 30 (Jan. 1922): 108; "An Interview with Joseph Conrad," *Bookman* (NY) 56 (Dec. 1922): 402–8 (qtg. Ernest Rhys, British writer and founding editor of Everyman Library); H. I. Brock, "Gentlest of Deep Sea Skippers," *New York Times Magazine* (May 13, 1923): SM6 (qtg. Muirhead Bone; a widely reproduced quotation); "The Genius of Joseph Conrad," *Christian Science Monitor* (Aug. 1924): 16; Review of *Last Essays*, *Christian Science Monitor* (Apr. 3, 1926): 4.24; "Joseph Conrad in the Role of Essayist," *Boston Evening Transcript* (Apr. 10, 1926): BS1; Brock, "Gentlest," *New York Times* (May 1926): SM6.

96. "The Meaning of Conrad," *New Republic* 39.507 (Aug. 24, 1924): 341–42, 342.

97. Ibid. (emphasis added).

98. "How We Make Enemies," *New Republic* 27.345 (July 13, 1921): 184; "Imperialism in Haiti," *New Republic* 27.343 (June 29, 1921): 128–29.

99. Indeed, pursuant to this slippage, Conrad can just as easily be mobilized elsewhere in the United States as an aggressive *license* of U.S. imperialism, or as a means of displacing the idea of self-determination from liberal internationalist goals and effective enforcement mechanisms (like the League of Nations). Consider Frank Pease, "Joseph Conrad," *Nation* (NY) 107 (Nov. 2, 1918): 510–13 (challenging *Nation*'s progressive liberal internationalism by championing Conrad as a prophet of the "sustained and secret sympathy between the outer aspect and the inner reality," the need for strong U.S. assertion in the international sphere so as to retain its powers of "inner" self-determination); Lawrence Abbott, "Joseph Conrad," *Outlook* (NY) 134 (May 23, 1923): 14–15 (Conrad's work, in the international translation of sympathies and standards of "civilization" it facilitates, is emblematic of "a literary league of nations which is greater, more inclusive, and more important than any political league of nations"); Henry J. Smith, Review of *The Rescue*, *Chicago Daily News* (May 26, 1920): 12 (*The Rescue* illustrates the imperialist folly of "a group of artificial Europeans dashed against the realities of a primitive east" as the same time it "dramatize[s] the idea of the solidarity of the white race" for U.S. Americans back home).

100. Compare, alongside the sales statistics and newspaper headlines presented in the Introduction, reactions to the novel from critics and in venues as diverse as Gilbert

Seldes, "A Novelist of Courage," *Dial* (Aug. 1920): 15 (*The Rescue* prompts reflection that rather than fail to appreciate its importance, "it would be more decent to surrender criticism entirely and only breathe a quiet word of gratitude that [Conrad's] miracle should happen in our time"); Elia Peattie, "Joseph Conrad's New Book," *Chicago Daily Tribune* (June 12, 1920): 13 (*The Rescue* prompts this meditation: "There are many fine vocations in this world, many services which the devoted may perform for mankind. But were I to choose, knowing that my wish would be granted by the assembled gods, I would be a teller of tales—tales that like Conrad's would transport the reader from the hard ways of daily toil into the spacious times of romance, and send the mind and spirit back to its duty refreshed"); Philip Littell, "Books and Things," *New Republic* 23.290 (June 23, 1920): 128 (Review of *The Rescue*) (see discussion of *The Rescue* later in this chapter).

101. Consider articulations by two noteworthy U.S. figures: Herbert Croly, "Disordered Christianity," *New Republic* 21.265 (Dec. 31, 1919): 136–39, 136 (United States responsible for "the rescue of the world from the desolation of the war and the redemption of the promise of appeasement"); John Dewey, "The International War in China," *New Republic* 20.251 (Aug. 27, 1919): 110–12, 122 (referencing the world "situation which has given Japan the role of despoiler and assigned to America the role of rescuer").

102. My point here, of course, is not at all that this is Conrad's "intended" reading—certainly the Conrad we know from the letters would never posit the United States as a heroic interventionist agency—but rather the American readerly obverse of Daniel Schwarz's sensitive writerly observation that Conrad had trouble completing this novel back in the 1890s, when he wrote more than half of it, because Tom Lingard's "ethics and personality are irrelevant to the world in which he writes." Daniel Schwarz, *Conrad: The Later Fiction* (London: Macmillan, 1982), 111. Apropos of Conrad's own statement in the Author's Note to *The Rescue* that at "about the end of the summer of 1918" he was seized by a "firm determination" and "sudden feeling" to complete the manuscript, that at last the story carried "an air of expectant life" (*Re* vii, x), the world circumstances of the Great War (and even more importantly, its imminent, looming aftermath) make this novel of Tom Lingard freshly relevant, writable, capable of completion; and its robust *openness* to U.S. projection and self-reflexive construction in this same historical context is, among other things, what fundamentally propels the novel's popularity in the United States at this time.

103. For a good discussion of other alternatives, many of which *The Rescue* itself explicitly gestures to, see Gary Geddes, *Conrad's Later Novels* (Montreal: McGill-Queen's University Press, 1980), 162–71.

104. See, e.g., Peattie, "Joseph Conrad's New Book" (presented from a U.S. American vantage, the otherworldliness of Conrad underwrites all Peattie's many celebrations of Conrad).

105. Littell, Review of *The Rescue*, 128.

106. For other complexities of convention and aesthetics in *Suspense*, see Susan Jones, *Conrad and Women* (Oxford: Oxford University Press, 1999), 192–220; Yael Levin, *Tracing the Aesthetic Principle in Conrad's Novels* (New York: Palgrave, 2008), 139–68. Compare also on the actual primary textual source of the novel, Léonie Villard, "A Conrad Heroine in Real Life," *Living Age* 328 (Mar. 20, 1926): 637–39.

107. William W. Bonney, "Suspended," in Kaplan, Mallios, and White, *Conrad in the Twenty-first Century*, 188–89, 191.

108. "The Significance of Napoleon," *New Republic* 26.336 (May 11, 1921): 311–12.

109. A historical ally and liberator of Poland—and enemy of the Prussian, Russian, and Austrian alliance of imperial powers at Vienna who had tripartitioned and erased Poland from the map in the late eighteenth century.

110. "Conrad's 'Suspense,'" *Saturday Review of Literature* 1 (June 20, 1925): 833.

111. David Lambuth, "Essays on Suspense," *Saturday Review of Literature* 2.16 (Nov. 14, 1925): 289–91, 289.

112. Ibid. (emphasis added).

113. These are the memorably acerbic words of historian Hebert Butterfield, *Napoleon* (New York: Collier Books, 1962), 117 (qtg. Napoleon on "United States of Europe").

114. Lambuth, "Essays on Suspense," 290–91.

115. Sylvère Monod, "Conrad and European Politics," qtg. *CL* 5.568–69, in Andrezj Ciuk and Marcin Piechota, eds., *Conrad's Europe* (Opole, Poland: Opole University Press, 2005), 93–104, 100.

116. "Conrad's Last Work," *Times* (London) (Sept. 16, 1925): 10 (emphasis added).

117. Sinclair Lewis, "Swan-Song of Joseph Conrad," *Literary Review* (Sept. 19, 1925): 1–2; Albert Guerard Sr., "Conrad's Unfinished Novel," *New York Herald-Tribune Books* (Nov. 29, 1925): 4.

118. "*Nostromo*," *New York Times* (Dec. 31, 1904): 944 (emphasis added). Nearly all the U.S. reviews of the novel during this time adopt similar essentializing rhetoric—accompanied by breathless attestations to the hyperreality of Conrad's portrait of Latin America, somehow more true than Latin America itself, thus reinforcing (against all material challenge) the essentialization. For an example of how *Nostromo* becomes extended into U.S.–Latin American politics of the 1910s, see Helen Bullis, "Perch of the Devil," *New York Times* (Aug. 30, 1914): BR1–2 (imagining Conrad "reproduc[ing] for us the pageant of modern Mexico").

119. H. L. Mencken, "The Conrad Wake," *American Mercury* 4 (Apr. 1925): 505–7; Follett and Follett, "Contemporary Novelists," 242.

120. Follett and Follett, "Contemporary Novelists," 242–3 (emphasis added). This is by no means a bad reading of *Nostromo*. "Nation" is a very plausible way of reading the "moral principle" that Monygham has negatively, counterfactually, impossibly ideally in the context of Costaguana, in mind (compare F. Scott Fitzgerald's understanding of *Nostromo* as discussed in Chapter 3); and Follett, as we have seen, compellingly locates affirmations in Conrad's works through what is persistently denied actualization in them.

121. In "a timely article in *Asia* (New York)," reproduced in significant part for popular consumption in *Current Opinion* (NY), Lovett articulates a "South Sea School" of art and literature which, although international in ultimate composition (including Stevenson, Gauguin), fundamentally consists in a genealogy of American encounter and expression—by writers and painters including Melville, Charles Warren Stoddard, Jack London, Frederick O'Brien, and George Biddle. "From Melville on," Lovett argues, "we can distinguish a genuine South Sea School"; its "characteristic phenomena are unmistakable": "No one picking up a tale of Joseph Conrad's, unfamiliar as the geography might be, could attribute it to the South Seas. His field is the Malayan archipelago,

which is as different from the South Seas as South from North America." It is the "natural" qualities of the South Sea Islands, their "pristine" native peoples, and U.S. American attractions to them that make for such contrast with the self-evident frictions and compulsions of race, power, and imperialism that animate Conrad's Malayan world. This is a characteristic U.S. disavowal of an internationalist imperialist agenda whose grave domestic (and equally imperialist) implications become clear when, unmistakably limning a narrative model of the "vanishing Indian" by which Native American genocide in the United States has been historically erased of its true villains and justified in its effects, Lovett describes the "tragic background" and "profound" "theme" of "death" among South Sea natives—"not by cannibalism, nor leprosy nor the elements, but by sheer failure of the will to live, resulting in the annihilation of the race." Conrad's fiction, which Lovett so anxiously distinguishes, would suggest other causal narratives of race annihilation, among natives of both Polynesia and North America. See "The South Sea Islands as Literary Inspiration," *Current Opinion* 70.5 (May 1921): 679.

122. Zdzisław Najder, *Joseph Conrad: A Life* (New York: Camden House, 2007), 507. Conrad later wrote a close Polish friend: "There is one thing I like the Americans for: they are friendly towards Poland." By 1914, some 4 million native Poles lived in the United States—the single largest group of U.S. immigrants from Central and Eastern Europe. Conrad conducted an interview on Polish subjects with Antoni Czarnecki, a Polish-American correspondent for the Chicago *Daily News*, in January 1919; it was not printed until August 19, 1924. See Donald Rude, "Anthony Czarnecki's 'An Evening with Joseph Conrad': An Interview on Politics and Poland Recovered," in Wiesław Krajka, ed., *Conrad: Western and Eastern Perspectives* (New York: Columbia University Press, 2004).

123. John Quinn, "Joseph Conrad on Poland," *New York Tribune* (Apr. 5, 1920): 10.

124. Ibid.

125. "Conrad's Poland," *New York Tribune* (Apr. 5, 1920): 10.

126. "The Resettlement of Europe," *New Republic* 24.302 (Sept. 15, 1920): 55–58, 56.

127. See Najder, *Conrad: A Life*, 494, 507. Piłsudski was the Polish military hero of the 1920 Polish-Soviet War and actually much more consistently and fiercely opposed to Russia, whom he attacked with his Rifle Troops during the war, ultimately under Austrian auspices, than Dmowski (who had favored Polish reunification within the Russian sphere of influence); but this does not take away from the significantly more moderate, federationist, tolerant, left-wing, and anti-imperialist vision of Poland, its sovereignty, and its dimensions that separated Piłsudski, very much a Romantic radical *szlachta* figure in the vein of Conrad's father, Apollo Korzeniowski, from his lifelong adversary Dmowski. For more on these two, see Norman Davies, *God's Playground: A History of Poland*, vol. 2, *1795 to the Present* (New York: Columbia University Press, 1982), 52–60, passim.

128. An early review of *Under Western Eyes* in the *New York Times*, for instance, opines: "Its attempt to translate the Russian into terms a little more intelligible to the Western understanding ought to make it very interesting to those readers who wish to follow the course of Russian events with comprehension." Interestingly, so far as concerns the complex pliability of Conrad's construction with respect to Russia over time, this review begins by observing, quite correctly in a strict historical sense, that "Joseph Conrad was born in Russia" and that his novel evinces to "good effect" his "knowledge

and *sympathetic* understanding of Russian character and conditions." "Conrad's Latest Novel," *New York Times* (Dec. 10, 1911): 818 (emphasis added).

129. H. L. Mencken, "Conrad, Bennett, James et al.," *Smart Set* 36.1 (Jan. 1912): 153–58, 155.

130. Though *The Secret Agent: A Drama* (original version completed in March 1920) was eventually performed at the Ambassador's Theatre, London, for ten performances beginning November 3, 1922, much energy was invested in "hav[ing] the play first performed in America—as there are people with open mouths over there," as Conrad put it to Eric Pinker in April 1920, based on a scouting report from Pinker's father from the United States (*CL* 7.81). Harold Meltzer, comanager of the Greenwich Village Theatre, U.S. theater mogul David Belasco, and a U.S. theater agent named Kommer all contacted Conrad quite seriously about an American production of the play—and one finds Conrad contemplating a (moneymaking) "attempt in the U.S." as late as June 1922 (*CL* 7.151, 152, 188, 388, 486). When the play appeared at the Ambassador's Theatre, it was principally produced by Joseph Henry Bonrimo, born in San Francisco and with directorial and production experience mainly in the United States—perhaps not inconsequential to Conrad's choice of him.

131. *Ro* 26, 2, 25, 81. The very name of "Citizen *Scevola* Bron" (28), the "blood-drinking" Jacobite antagonist of the novel, also suggests a contemporary "Sclavonic" (a Conrad word) context.

132. Adams, "Joseph Conrad: The Man," 710 (emphasis added).

133. C. E. A., "Nostr' Omo," *New Republic* 40.508 (Aug. 27, 1924): 391 (emphasis added).

134. "The Rover," *New Republic* 37.124 (Dec. 26, 1923): 124.

135. GoGwilt, *Invention of the West*, 150. See also Jacques Berthoud, *Joseph Conrad: The Major Phase* (Cambridge: Cambridge University Press, 1978), 169–75.

136. Willa Cather, "Portrait of the Publisher as a Young Man" (1940), in Knopf, *Portrait*, 2.108–12, 109–10.

137. Alfred Knopf, *Joseph Conrad: The Romance of His Life and of His Books* (Garden City, N.Y.: Doubleday, Page, 1913), 5, 1, 6.

138. Ibid., 1.

139. Ibid., 5, 9, 10, 15.

140. See, e.g., H. I. Brock, "Gentlest of Deep-Sea Skippers," *New York Times* (May 13, 1923): SM6 (explicitly invoking the American Dream as a metanarrative for Conrad's arrival in the United States: F. N. Doubleday's big "American" house [where Conrad stayed] and big "American" dog ["protector of the shy houseguest"] signal Conrad's "birthright to bigness" American-style as appropriately confirmed by his fanfare in the United States); Fredric Taber Cooper, "Representative English Storytellers: Joseph Conrad," *Bookman* (NY) 35 (Mar. 1912): 61–71 (rhetoric of Conrad's "working his way upward" "with painstaking and admirable effort" through "twenty years" of disciplined "amassing" and "assimilating [of] his material," clearly drawing on immigration tropes and American Dream ideology).

141. Knopf, *Joseph Conrad*, 6–7, 17, 10.

142. Ibid., 10–12, 1, 2, 7, 8, 23.

143. Brock, "Gentlest of Deep-Sea Skippers," SM6.

144. See, e.g., "Mr. Conrad in Literature and on the Sea," *New York Tribune* (Jan. 27,

1912): 8 (diagnostic power of *The Secret Agent* and *Under Western Eyes* derives from the fact that Conrad "the Pole, as well as the Russian, is an Oriental of the Occidental world").

145. "Novels, Foreign and American," *American Review of Reviews* 59 (June 1919): 670.

146. Two historically bookending examples of this very familiar articulative pattern: "Joseph Conrad's Profession of Artistic Faith," *Current Opinion* 52 (Apr. 1912): 471–72 (marveling at the *double* assimilation of "this anglicized Pole—this extraordinary seaman turned artist"—"with 'fidelity' as his watchword"); "Some British Novelists," *America* 32.1 (Oct. 18, 1924): 20 (Armenian-born English novelist Dikran Kuyukjian, "like Conrad," "has achieved an English style that is more refined than that of his native-born countrymen").

147. "Mr. Conrad's Own Story," *New York Times* (Feb. 18, 1912): 8 (emphasis added).

148. Cooper, "Representative English Storytellers," 62, 63.

149. Michaels, *Our America*, passim.

150. "Joseph Conrad Tells Why He Chose English," 7.9 (enormous full-page pictorial article, qtg. *PR* v–vi [emphases added]). See also Adams, "Joseph Conrad—the Man," 708–12 (full text reprinted separately as a book); "Conrad Did Not Consider Himself a Writer," *New York Times* (Aug. 9, 1925): BR13.

151. See "Joseph Conrad," *Contemporary Review* 127 (Jan. 1925): 128–29 (rewrites the Polish history of Conrad's family through a variety of English equivalents).

152. "Joseph Conrad Tells Why He Chose English," 9, qtg. *PR* v.

153. Mark Van Doren, "First Glance," *Nation* 120 (Jan. 14, 1925): 45 (review of *The Shorter Tales of Joseph Conrad*).

154. Lawrence F. Abbott, "Joseph Conrad," *Outlook* 134 (May 1923): 14–15.

155. "Joseph Conrad: The Gift of Tongues," *Nation* 116 (May 16, 1923): 561.

156. Willa Cather, "Behind the Singer Tower," in Virginia Faulkner, ed., *Willa Cather's Short Fiction, 1892–1912* (Lincoln: University of Nebraska Press, 1970), 43–54, 44, 45.

157. Ibid., 43–44, 45.

158. See Sharon O'Brien, *Willa Cather: The Emerging Voice* (New York: Fawcett Columbine, 1987), 212–25. O'Brien reads the image of the opera singer Graziani's hand, severed when he jumps to escape the burning hotel, as an expression of Cather's writerly sense of self-sacrifice while writing in a milieu of rising East Coast literary ambition.

159. Cather, "Behind the Singer Tower," 45, 46, 52.

160. Ibid., 46, 47.

161. "I know, I know. . . . *We* don't want 'em," Hallett says indiscriminately with respect to all recent immigrant labor at one moment. Hallett's story, even as it expresses sympathy for Caesarino and outrage at his victimization, is equivocal about whether the Italian, whom he repeatedly and jarringly refers to as a "dago," should have been at the "foundation" of the Mont Blanc in the first place. Ibid., 49.

162. "The Affair at Grover Station," a curious adaptation of the Helen of Troy story to American circumstances, begins with clear adoption of the framed-narrative story-telling form of *Heart of Darkness*, and also, on its way to telling a story of penetration to "horrors" committed at an inner "station," with an initial adaptation of Conradian idiom: "When the train pulled out of Grover Station, we were sitting smoking on the rear platform, watching the pale yellow disk of the moon that was just rising and that drenched the naked, gray plains in a soft lemon-colored light. The telegraph poles scored

the sky like a musical staff as they flashed by, and the stars, seen between the wires, looked like notes of some erratic symphony. The stillness of the night and the loneliness and barrenness of the plains were conducive to an uncanny train of thought." See Faulkner, *Willa Cather's Short Fiction*, 339.

163. Willa Cather, "The Sculptor's Funeral," in Faulkner, *Willa Cather's Short Fiction*, 173, 178, 183.

164. See Gustav Morf, *The Polish Heritage of Joseph Conrad* (London: Sampson, Low, 1930).

165. The story seems aware of this parallel: Banker Phelps's throwaway (and otherwise hard-to-account-for) remark on Merrick and his brothers, "They never hung together," ironically recalls and reverses Marlow's "We exist only insofar as we hang together" (*LJ* 223), as well as the fraternal project of community enactment "The Sculptor's Funeral" cross-correlates with and cross-identifies in *Lord Jim*. See Cather, "The Sculptor's Funeral," 181.

166. Ibid., 178.

167. See Joseph Urgo, *Willa Cather and the Myth of American Migration* (Princeton: Princeton University Press, 1994), 28–35.

168. Edith Lewis, *Willa Cather Living: A Personal Record by Edith Lewis* (New York: Alfred A. Knopf, 1953), 63; Elizabeth Sergeant, *Willa Cather: A Memoir* (Lincoln: University of Nebraska Press, 1953), 39–40.

169. On two occasions in the magazine's "*McClure's* for 1907" pages, Conrad and Cather are advertised on the same page; on a further occasion, two pages apart, a large pictorialized advertisement for Conrad, "foremost of the younger romantic writers," anticipating the appearance of "The Brute" as "admirably illustrated by Ernest L. Blumenschein," is presented in suggestive correlation with an advertisement for Cather's "The Namesake"—as it includes a small facsimile of a "drawing by E. L. Blumenschein." Blumenschein, a noted artist of the Southwest and cofounder of the Taos Society of Artists, illustrated only Conrad's and Cather's stories in *McClure's* in 1907. See "*McClure's* for 1907," in *McClure's* 28.2 (Dec. 1906): 11; 28.4 (Feb. 1907): 12; 28.1 (Nov. 1906): 10, 12.

170. A delightful, and essentially fraudulent, advertisement for "Stories of Adventure" to appear in *McClure's* in 1908 gratuitously places a picture of Conrad at its bottom—though *McClure's* had secured, and would secure, no further story to print in its pages after "The Brute." See "*McClure's* for 1908," 31.1 (Nov. 1907): 12.

171. Willa Cather, "Miss Jewett," in Sharon O'Brien, ed., *Willa Cather: Stories, Poems and Other Writings* (New York: Library of America, 1982), 855. The suggestion and symbolism of Jewett's fatality in response to Conrad are as important as the corollaries of her appreciation of him: at issue is the innovative departure of Cather's own fiction, beyond the limitations of Jewett's nevertheless sympathetic and enabling precedent.

172. Willa Cather, "On the Novel," in L. Brent Bohlke, ed., *Willa Cather: Interviews, Speeches, and Letters* (Lincoln: University of Nebraska Press, 1986), 170 (emphasis added).

173. All quotations in this sentence except "pioneering" are from the Preface and text of *The Nigger of the "Narcissus"* (viii, ix, 7).

174. See Willa Cather, *Willa Cather on Writing* (New York: Alfred Knopf, 1949), 95.

175. See Bruffee, *Elegiac Romance*, passim (positions Conrad at the seminal center of the modern narrative development, which includes Cather).

176. See Mary Austin, "Joseph Conrad Tells What Women Don't Known About

Men," *Pictorial Review* 24.12 (Sept. 1923): 17, 28, 30–31. This essay engages Conrad, simultaneously with sympathy and at arm's length from understanding women's experiences, as a means of affirming essential gender difference; compare the complementary essay "Making the Most of Your Genius" (Nov. 1923), where Austin again engages Conrad (through the narrowing, exceptionalizing strategy described earlier) in articulating a *racially* essentialized conception of artistic "genius." In Esther F. Lanigan, ed., *A Mary Austin Reader* (Tucson: University of Arizona Press, 1996), 158–63, 162.

177. Joyce Kilmer, "A Southern Hero," *New York Times* (July 5, 1914): 297.

178. Rachel Blau DuPlessis, "'HOO, HOO, HOO': Some Episodes in the Construction of Modern Whiteness," *American Literature* 67.4 (Dec. 1995): 667–700, 668. My description here and analysis of Lindsay in what follows owe much to DuPlessis's most insightful essay.

179. Vachel Lindsay, *Letters of Vachel Lindsay*, Marc Chénetier, ed. (New York: Burt Franklin, 1979), 89.

180. Vachel Lindsay, "The Inspiration of a Poet: The Author of 'The Congo' Discloses Its Origin," *Boston Evening Transcript* (Feb. 6, 1915): 3.8. The Doubleday advertisement immediately beneath is for its reissue of Conrad's *A Set of Six*.

181. Qtd. in part in Bliss Perry, *Study of Poetry* (Boston: Houghton Mifflin, 1920), 262–63.

182. Vachel Lindsay, *Selected Poems of Vachel Lindsay*, Mark Harris, ed. (New York: Macmillan, 1963), 47–48.

183. I quote from the amended version (1987) of Achebe's essay, "An Image of Africa: Racism in Conrad's *Heart of Darkness*," in Joseph Conrad, *Heart of Darkness*, 3rd ed., Robert Kimbrough, ed. (New York: Norton, 1988), 251–62, 252, 253, 257.

184. Qtd. in DuPlessis, "'HOO, HOO, HOO,'" 671.

185. Ibid.

186. Qtd. in R. D. Darrell, "The Music of Henry F. Gilbert, John Alden Carpenter, John Powell, Adolph Weiss," in booklet accompanying Los Angeles Philharmonic Orchestra Performance of John Alden Carpenter, *Krazy Kat*; Henry F. Gilbert, *The Dance in Place Congo*; John Powell, *Rhapsodie Nègre*; Adolph Weiss, *American Life* (New York: New World Records, 1977), 6–14, 10.

187. Ibid.

188. Qtd. in ibid.

189. Performance notes from 1922 Powell / Monteux / Boston Symphony performances of *Rhapsodie Nègre*, qtd. in ibid., 11.

190. Cooper, "Some Representative English Storytellers," 65.

191. Achebe, "Image of Africa," 251, 252.

192. For more on Hughes in the kind of "estranging" contexts that inform my thinking here, see Arnold Rampersad, "Introduction," in Akiba Sullivan Harper, ed., *Langston Hughes: Short Stories* (New York: Hill & Wang, 1996), xiii–xix, xiii (foregrounding questions of Hughes's "literary virtuosity"); Madhuri Deshmukh, "Langston Hughes as Black Pierrot: A Transatlantic Game of Masks," *Langston Hughes Review* 18 (Fall 2004): 4–15 (Hughes's engagement with Italian commedia dell'arte); Meta DuEwa Jones, "Listening to What the Ear Demands: Langston Hughes and His Critics," *Callaloo* 25.4 (2002): 1145–75 (challenging monodimensional accounts of Hughes as folk or race poet); Anita

Patterson, "Jazz, Realism, and the Modernist Lyric: The Poetry of Langston Hughes," *Modern Language Quarterly* 61.4 (Dec. 2000): 651–82 (jazz instancing profound doubleness and multiple hybridities of Hughes).

193. Langston Hughes, *The Big Sea* (New York: Hill & Wang, 1993), 95.

194. Arnold Rampersad, *The Life of Langston Hughes*, vol. 1, *1902–1941, I, Too, Sing America* (Oxford: Oxford University Press, 2002), 71. Fauset, the prominent African-American fiction writer, was managing editor of the *Crisis* at the time.

195. Hughes, *The Big Sea*, 95–96, 92–93, 3.

196. Rampersad, "Introduction," in Harper, *Langston Hughes: Short Stories*, xv.

197. Langston Hughes, "Luani of the Jungles," in Harper, *Langston Hughes: Short Stories*, 24–31, 24, 25.

198. Ibid., 26.

199. Conrad's text turns on an ambivalence between "Africa" as a site that stimulates poetic creativity (Marlow's poetics, Kurtz's "poetry" [*YOS* 140]) and testimony (Marlow's to those gathered on board the *Nellie*, arguably Kurtz's and/or the Harlequin's to Marlow), and "Africa" as a site that requires poetic defacement (Kurtz's "Exterminate all the brutes!" scrawled at the foot of his report on "Savage Customs") and suppression (Marlow's "lie" to the Intended). Hughes is making fun of this with his own (Conradian) "poet" whose mode of creativity is to make poems and "destroy" them—without even knowing why; much as everything about the poet's relationship to Africa—including his relationship to his wife ("I love her and yet I hate her")—is predicated on a farcical (Conradian) dialectic of "fascination" and "abomination."

200. Hughes, "Luani," 27, 29, 30.

201. Hughes, *The Big Sea*, 3 (emphasis added).

202. Ibid., 3–4.

203. See Hughes, "Bodies in the Moonlight," "The Young Glory of Him," and "The Little Virgin," in *Langston Hughes: Selected Stories*, 3–23, 3, 17. One may compare Hughes's first prose description of his encounter with Africa, which appeared in the *Crisis* in December 1923 and is revealingly subtitled "Random Impressions"; its highly impressionistic, ellipsis-filled, *anti*narrative form suggests an awareness of narrative templates for "Africa" (including *Heart of Darkness*) whose terms Hughes urgently, highly self-consciously resists, both producing a certain form of aesthetics and preventing a (narrative) other. See Langston Hughes, "Ships, Sea, and Africa: Random Impressions of a Sailor on His First Trip down the West Coast of the Motherland," *Crisis* 27.2 (Dec. 1923): 69–71.

204. Melas, *All the Difference*, 85–103.

205. W. E. B. Du Bois, "The Looking Glass," *Crisis* 28.6 (Oct. 1924): 275.

206. Achebe, "Image of Africa," 258; Du Bois, "Van Vechten's 'Nigger Heaven,'" in Nathan Huggins, ed., *W. E. B. Du Bois: Writings* (New York: Library of America, 1986), 1216–18, 1216.

207. Though Du Bois is actually careful to frame his objection in terms of "the overwhelming majority of black folk" and the "average colored man" in Harlem, it is clear that Du Bois's well-known notion of a Talented Tenth, of a natural aristocracy of talent discoverable through democratized opportunities of education in broad democratic spaces, lies at the heart of Du Bois's objection to Van Vechten's title, and the

distinction Du Bois is drawing with respect to Conrad, Sheldon, Firbanks. Du Bois knows very well that Van Vechten's book itself attempts to gloss its title in terms of a contemporary expression for segregated upper-level theater galleries for blacks; but Du Bois also knows that Van Vechten's is a sensationalist and opportunist title that will be taken "in common parlance" to refer to "a nasty, sordid corner," into which "black folk" who are sufficiently "fools" in their "crass ignorance" to enjoy it, will be "herded." Harlem and its people, Du Bois is saying, are not to be classed in such a fashion. Du Bois, "Van Vechten's 'Nigger Heaven,'" 1216.

208. W. E. B. Du Bois, "An Array of Books," *Crisis* 28.5 (Sept. 1924): 218–20, 219; William Stanley Braithwaite, "The Negro in Literature," *Crisis* 28.5 (Sept. 1924): 204–10, 205.

209. W. E. B. Du Bois, "An Array of Books," 219.

210. Leslie Pinckney Hill, "A Review of Four Books," *Crisis* 26.5 (Sept. 1923): 211–12, 212; compare "The Looking Glass," *Crisis* 26.2 (June 1923): 80–82, 81 (reproduction of Wood verses in pointedly progressive racial-communalizing context).

211. Alaine Locke, ed., *The New Negro* (New York: Albert & Charles Boni, 1925), 429. Whereas Hughes suggests Conrad gets Africa and Africans wrong, Locke, by not listing *Heart of Darkness* in its bibliography of "The Negro in Literature," suggests that Conrad's text has nothing fundamentally to say about people of African descent at all. These are two very different cultural strategies of making a similar point—and, as we are about to see, amenable to at least two very different larger constructions of Conrad and *Heart of Darkness*, their racial politics.

212. For a representative example of how the *Crisis* engages Dixon, see "The Looking Glass," *Crisis* 17.3 (Jan. 1919): 127; for Du Bois on Kipling, see "The Freeing of India" (1947), in Bill V. Mullen and Cathryn Watson, eds., *W. E. B. Du Bois on Asia: Crossing the World Color Line* (Jackson: University Press of Mississippi, 2005), 145–53, 156; compare Du Bois's perennial attacks on the idea of "the white man's burden" (in, for instance, "The Riddle of the Sphinx" in *Darkwater*).

213. For Du Bois invoking Wells, see W. E. B. Du Bois, "The Hands of Ethiopia," in *Darkwater* (New York: Washington Square Press, 2004), 43–56, 45; W. E. B. Du Bois, "Opinion," *Crisis* 17.2 (Dec. 1918): 63. For a suggestive reading of ultimate disjunction between the aesthetic and political priorities of *Dark Princess*, see Homi K. Bhabha, "Global Minoritarian Culture," in Wai Chee Dimock and Lawrence Buell, eds., *Shades of the Planet: American Literature as World Literature* (Princeton: Princeton University Press, 2007), 184–95.

214. W. E. B. Du Bois, "Criteria of Negro Art," in Huggins, *Du Bois: Writings*, 993–1002, 1000.

215. Ibid.

216. Compare Achebe, "Image of Africa," 253–54.

217. W. E. B. Du Bois, "The Souls of White Folk," in *Darkwater*, 21–37, 21.

218. Ibid.; the terms I have quoted from *Heart of Darkness*—"entrails," "emptiness," "hollow," "pilgrim"—are used throughout that text.

219. Du Bois, "Souls of White Folk," 22, 27; *YOS* 50, 47.

220. Du Bois, "Souls of White Folk," 25; *YOS* 119.

221. Du Bois, "Souls of White Folk," 26, 25, 23, 31.

222. Ibid., 31.

223. See, for instance, W. E. B. Du Bois, "Reconstruction and Africa," *Crisis* 17.4 (Feb. 1919): 165 ("The suggestion has been made that these colonies which Germany has lost should not be handed over to any other nation of Europe but should, under the guidance of organized civilization, be brought to a point of development which shall finally result in an autonomous state. This plan has met with much criticism and ridicule. Let the natives develop along their own line and they will 'go back,' has been the cry. Back to what, in Heaven's name? Is a civilization naturally backward because it is different?")

224. Du Bois, "Criteria of Negro Art," 1001, 1002.

225. Du Bois, "Souls of White Folk," 23.

226. Countee Cullen, *Color* (New York: Harper & Bros., 1928), 71. I cite from the 1928 edition because of its inclusion of the illustrations by Charles Cullen referenced in note 229 below.

227. See Keith D. Leonard, *Fettered Genius: The African American Bardic Poet from Slavery to Civil Rights* (Charlottesville: University of Virginia Press, 2006), 1–18.

228. Though there are many examples, both in the text of *Color* and its illustrations, the major poem "The Shroud of Color" is exemplary. Here, above and against "the touch of earth," never to be truly eclipsed in its grounding dialectic of temptation and agony, lies the transcendent domain of the poet's imagination: "For whom the sea has strained her honeyed throat / Till all the world was sea, and I a boat / Unmoored, on what strange quest I will to float; / Who wore a many-colored coat of dreams." The sea is repeatedly associated with transcendent freedom—"And I was wind and sky again, and sea, / And all sweet things that flourish being free"—and also with death, the ultimate (as we shall see) condition of this self-conscious fantasy. Cullen, *Color*, 29, 33, xiv.

229. Ibid., 12. Charles Cullen began working with Countee Cullen as an illustrator in 1927; the former's illustrations of *Color* first appear in the second American edition of 1928.

230. Ibid., 15–17, 3, 33–35 (emphasis added).

231. Ibid., 36–41, 37.

232. Richard Wright, *Black Boy* (New York: HarperPerennial, 1994), 293; Margaret Walker, *Richard Wright: Daemonic Genius* (New York: Warner Books, 1988), 75.

233. See Michael Fabre, *Richard Wright: Books & Writers* (Jackson: University Press of Mississippi, 1990), 29–30.

234. Michael Fabre, *The Unfinished Quest of Richard Wright* (New York: William Morrow, 1973), 82–85; Wright, "Memories of My Grandmother," qtd. in Fabre, *Richard Wright*, 30.

235. See, for instance, Marcia Minor, "An Author Discusses His Craft," *Daily Worker* (Dec. 13, 1938): 7 (interview in which Wright describes his method of studying other writers, including Dostoevsky, Chekov, Conrad); Joseph Gollomb, "Profile," *Book of the Month Club News* (Feb. 1945): 8–9 (Wright speaking with "awe" of Dostoevsky and Conrad); Peter Lennon, "One of Uncle Tom's Children," *Guardian* (Dec. 8, 1958): 8 (Wright describing his self-education, including reading Conrad).

236. When Wright writes in "How 'Bigger' Was Born," "my task, as I felt it, was to free myself of this burden of impressions and feelings, recast them into the image of Bigger and make them *true*" (emphasis in original), he is echoing Conrad's famous

language in the Preface to *The Nigger of the "Narcissus"* explaining that his "task" is to "make you *see*" (ix, emphasis in original); Wright is also echoing, in the name of sensory, empirical, secular truth, Conrad's call for liberation from artistic and ideological dogma. Wright's foreword to *Lest We Forget* similarly articulates its vision of "art" in terms of, "as Joseph Conrad put it, 'that modicum of truth for which you have forgotten to ask.'" Such echoes may be found throughout Wright's expository statements on the art of fiction; he knows Conrad's Preface foundationally, as it were, "by heart." See Wright, *Native Son* (New York: HarperPerennial, 1994), 525; Wright, "Foreword" to *Lest We Forget*, qtd. in Fabre, *Richard Wright*, 30.

237. See Ralph Ellison, "Hidden Name and Complex Fate: A Writer's Experience in the U. S.," *Shadow and Act* (1964), in John F. Callahan, ed., *The Collected Essays of Ralph Ellison* (New York: Modern Library, 1995), 189–209, 204; Ralph Ellison, *Invisible Man* (New York: Vintage International, 1995), 579 (explicitly figuring the U.S. South as "heart of darkness"); James Baldwin, *Go Tell It on the Mountain* (New York: Bantam, 1985), 195.

238. Walker, *Daemonic Genius*, 75.

239. Richard Wright, "Superstition," *Abbott's Monthly* 2.4 (Apr. 1931): 45–47, 64–66, 72–73, 45, 46, 64.

240. Ibid., 46, 64, 65.

241. Ibid., 66, 73 ("In that silence, there was revealed, hideously and repellently, the stark nakedness of the fearful hearts of primitive folk—fearful hearts bowing abjectly to the terror of an unknown created by their own imaginations": here the South has become Conrad's Congo, the South's race prejudices the very mirror of the "African" primitivism the white South would define itself against—and which, Wright suggests, Conrad critically captures Europe producing to define itself against); *YOS* 48, 156.

242. For contemporary elaborations of this reading of James Wait and Conrad's novel, see the Haitian Canadian novelist and scholar Max Dorsinville's *Erzulie Loves Shango* (Montréal: Editions du CIDIHCA,1998) and Kurt Vonnegut's *Galápagos* (New York: Delacorte Press,1985).

243. Wright, *Native Son*, 323.

244. See, for instance, Carla Cappetti, "Black Orpheus: Richard Wright's 'The Man Who Lived Underground,'" *Melus* 26.4 (Winter 2001): 41–68.

245. Cornel West, "Introduction," in Richard Wright, *Black Power: Three Books from Exile* (New York: HarperPerennial, 2008), ix (emphasis added).

246. "By going from spot to spot talking to this person and that one, I had to gather this reality as it seeped into me from the personalities of others. There might be some merit in that kind of getting and giving a reality. . . . Conrad wrote all his novels in that roundabout way." Letter from Wright to Paul Reynolds (referencing experiences in Spain), Mar. 19, 1954, qtd. in Fabre, *Unfinished Quest*, 403.

247. See Wright, *Black Power*, 106.

CHAPTER 3

1. Here I follow the story as eloquently retold by Robert Secor in the introduction to Secor and Moddelmog, *Joseph Conrad and American Writers*, xx.

2. Zdzisław Najder, "Conrad in His Historical Perspective," *English Literature in Transition* 14 (1971): 162–63.

3. Frances Newman, "The Allegory of the Young Intellectuals," *Reviewer* (Richmond, Va.) 1.12 (Aug. 1, 1921): 359–65, 365 (emphasis added).

4. For O'Neill commenting on Conrad as "a lasting and deep-rooted influence upon his life and work," and *The Nigger of the "Narcissus"* as having "given the immediate bent to the prevailing note in his creative outlet," see Pierre Loving, "Eugene O'Neill," *Bookman* 53 (Aug. 1921): 515, 517–19. The subject of Conrad and O'Neill is largely unexamined, but for those few who have written well on the subject, see Secor and Moddelmog, *Joseph Conrad and American Writers*, 178–82.

5. John Dos Passos, "Conrad's *Lord Jim*" (July 1915), rptd. in Donald Pizer, ed., *John Dos Passos: The Major Nonfictional Prose* (Detroit, Mich.: Wayne State University Press, 1988), 22–24, 23–24. Dos Passos later expresses distaste for Conrad, in part for political reasons (Dos Passos's radical activism of the 1920s resists reasonable construction of Conrad). Dos Passos writes to Edmund Wilson in 1934: "Read with pleasure your Anatole France remarks (I doubt if he's worth that amount of space). At least nobody will ever have to bring him up again in our lifetime—and I hope that goes for Joseph Conrad too." T. Ludington, ed., *The Fourteenth Chronicle: Letters and Diaries of John Dos Passos* (Boston: Gambit, 1973), 449–50. However, the panoramic perspectival and geographical shiftings, as well as the general postnational sensibility (i.e., telling the story of a nation without ever being able to stay within the boundaries of that nation), of Dos Passos's *USA* trilogy, may bear greater kinship to *Nostromo* than Dos Passos acknowledges. Indeed, if one follows Jean-Paul Sartre's famous reading of *1919*, what is special about its form is very close to the effect Dos Passos describes of *Lord Jim*: "Indeed, Conrad's books are staggering achievements. You start with prejudices, with dislikes, you complain of his style; by the time you have finished you are cowed, wonderstruck. . . . It is as though you were looking at life through some wonderful instrument, a microscope that, instead of magnifying, merely refines the outlines. . . . The great joy of reading Conrad, apart from the romance of it, from the liveness of it, lies in the fact that his books act as a sort of mental grindstone. When you have finished such a novel as 'Lord Jim' or 'Chance' your mind feels clearer, more efficient and capable than when you took it up. Your intellectual cobwebs have been blown away. You feel as if a little of Conrad's magic elixir had penetrated your own brain" (Dos Passos, "Conrad's *Lord Jim*," 23–24). Surely the corrosive and expulsive experience of reading *1919*!

6. See Joseph Blotner, ed., *Selected Letters of William Faulkner* (New York: Random House, 1977); Christopher Morley, "A Note on Conrad," *Saturday Review of Literature* 4.25 (Jan. 14, 1920): 519; Lucas Carpenter, ed., *The Autobiography of John Gould Fletcher* (Fayetteville: University of Arkansas Press, 1988), 39; James Thurber, "The Lady from the Land," *Punch* 240 (Apr. 19, 1961): 63, and *My Life and Hard Times* (New York: Harper & Row, 1933), 113–15 (ends on the thought of spending the rest of his days "wandering aimlessly around the South Seas, like a character out of Conrad, silent and inscrutable"; Thurber loved Conrad, and as Ian Watt points out, "Lord" Jim's ethos is parodied in *The Secret Life of Walter Mitty*). Jack London prided himself on being one of Conrad's "first discoverers and boomers in the United States" (see King Hendricks and Irving Shepherd, eds., *Letters of Jack London* [New York: Odyssey Press, 1965], 151), and in his semiautobiographical *Martin Eden* (1909) compares his opus to the singular standard of Conrad; Orson Welles did both a radio version and an ill-fated, very expensive cin-

ematic adaptation, whose collapse was the imminent precursor to *Citizen Kane*, of *Heart of Darkness* in the later 1930s.

7. "Third space" is the phrase Homi Bhabha uses to describe "the place of hybridity . . . where the construction of a political object that is new, neither the one nor the other, properly alienates our political expectations." See Bhabha, *The Location of Culture* (New York: Routledge, 1994), 25. The second half of this chapter explains in detail how Fitzgerald, and Conrad, can be elaborated in such metacritical and "hybrid" terms— "simultaneously within and without," as Fitzgerald's novel would have it, both alienated from and "unutterably aware of our identity with the country."

8. Letter from Theodore Brumback to Hemingway (1920) in Michael Reynolds, *Hemingway's Reading 1910–1940* (Princeton: Princeton University Press, 1981), 112; Ernest Hemingway, untitled Conrad essay, *Transatlantic Review* 2.3, Conrad supplement (Fall 1924): 341–42.

9. See Bernard J. Poli, *Ford Madox Ford and the Transatlantic Review* (Syracuse: Syracuse University Press, 1967), 112–14; Nicholas Joost, *Ernest Hemingway and the Little Magazines: "The Paris Years"* (Barre, Mass.: Barre Publishers, 1968), 113–17; Michael Reynolds, *Hemingway: The Paris Years* (London: Basil Blackwell, 1989), 225–26. There was also a talk given at the annual meeting of the Joseph Conrad Society, U.K., in the late 1990s, whose author eloquently touched on most if not all of these arguments.

10. The only widely available reproduction of Hemingway's essay for years, for instance, cuts and distorts the author's language beyond recovery. Among other infidelities, Hemingway's clearly ironic headline "CONRAD, OPTIMIST AND MORALIST" is inexplicably excised from the *body* of the article and relocated as its title, hence reversing the meaning of the original, in William White, ed., *By-Line: Ernest Hemingway* (New York: Bantam Books, 1968), 114–15.

11. See Poli, *Ford Madox Ford*, 39, 57 ("They were all would-be contributors, all American, nearly all Middle Westerners," wrote Ford), 59 ("They had all been cow-boys so that the office took on an aspect and still more the sound of a Chicago speakeasy, invaded by young men from a Wild West show," Ford continued).

12. Hemingway, untitled Conrad essay, 341.

13. Ibid.

14. This automatic metonymic association is an offensive formulation of Canada too, of course.

15. Ibid., 341–42.

16. Ernest Hemingway, *The Short Stories of Ernest Hemingway* (New York: Macmillan, 1986), 360, 361.

17. Leo Gurko, *Joseph Conrad: Giant in Exile* (New York: Macmillan, 1962), 222. Compare Albert Guerard Jr., *Conrad the Novelist* (Cambridge, Mass.: Harvard University Press, 1966), 157, 187 (emphasizing shared emphases on wounds and experiential difficulty); Jeffrey Berman, *Joseph Conrad: Writing as Rescue* (New York: Astra Books, 1977), 23–24, 92, and Frederick Karl, *Joseph Conrad: The Three Lives* (New York: Farrar, Straus & Giroux, 1979), 508, 895–96 (emphasizing moments of great duress and challenge threatening the destruction of character); Ivo Vidan, "Conrad's Legacy: The Concern with Authenticity in Modern Fiction," in W. T. Zylia and Wendell M. Aycock, eds., *Joseph Conrad: Theory and World Fiction* (Lubbock: Texas Tech University Press, 1974),

176–78, and Edward Said, "How Not to Get Gored: On Ernest Hemingway," in *Reflections on Exile* (Cambridge, Mass.: Harvard University Press, 2002), 230–38 (emphasizing technical knowledge and work in dangerous contexts); and Zdzisław Najder, "Conrad in Historical Perspective," 163 (emphasizing the ethical problematics and persistence in turbulent circumstances of "an autonomously defined code of behavior"). Somewhere Ian Watt also draws attention to Conrad's and Hemingway's mutual and unusual reliance on personal experience for material as integral to their aesthetics.

18. T. S. Eliot ["Crites"], "A Commentary," *Criterion* 3.9 (Oct. 1924): 1.

19. Eliot's editorial is followed by a full essay on Conrad by John Shand, whose peacock prolixity and sophomoric comfort in pronouncing definitively, discursively, and with painfully fashionable conventionality on Conrad's "many faults" as well as "virtues," reveals Eliot ironically to be in much the same position as Hemingway in the *Transatlantic Review*. "What is there you can write about him now that he is dead?" See John Shand, "Some Notes on Conrad," *Transatlantic Review* 3.9 (Oct. 1924): 6–14, 6.

20. T. S. Eliot, Lecture at Harvard University (Spring 1933), qtd. in F. O. Matthiessen, *The Achievement of T. S. Eliot* (New York: Oxford University Press, 1958), 24. Eliot's remarks are not unrelated to his observation in his introduction to *Huckleberry Finn*: "As with Conrad, we are continually reminded of the power and terror of Nature, and the isolation and feebleness of Man," which may itself be compared with Eliot's remark that as opposed to Rudyard Kipling—who writes, "Be well assured that on our side / The abiding oceans fight"—"Mr. Conrad would hardly issue this opinion about the oceans." For both Eliot and Conrad—and this is the exact point of both the quotations above from the Harvard lecture—"Nature," both human and physical, is a force of "sinister violence of intention," "purpose of malice," and "unbridled cruelty," "which means to smash, to destroy, to annihilate all he has seen, known, loved, enjoyed, or hated," and which only rarely declares on its surfaces "the true horror that lies behind the appalling face of things" (*LJ* 7, 19). Mencken would have agreed, both with the Twain connection and the underlying sense of cosmology attributed to Conrad here—but to very different ends. See Eliot, Introduction," *Huckleberry Finn* (London: Cresset Press, 1950), vii–xvi; Eliot, "Kipling Redivivus," *Athenaeum* 4645 (May 9, 1919): 297–98, 298.

21. Albert Gelpi, *A Coherent Splendor: The American Poetic Renaissance, 1910–1950* (Cambridge: Cambridge University Press, 1987), 91–168; Kenneth Asher, *T. S. Eliot and Ideology* (Cambridge: Cambridge University Press, 1995), 35–40.

22. Syllabus of Eliot's second Oxford University extension lecture on modern French literature, rptd. in A. D. Moody, *Thomas Stearns Eliot: Poet* (Cambridge: Cambridge University Press, 1979), 44.

23. T. S. Eliot, *The Waste Land: A Facsimile and Transcript of the Original Drafts*, Valerie Eliot, ed. (San Diego: Harcourt, Brace, 1971), 2; V. Eliot, ed., *The Letters of T. S. Eliot*, vol. 1 (San Diego: Harcourt Brace Jovanovich, 1988), 497, 504, 505, 506 (contains the Pound-Eliot interchange concerning the epigraph; begins with Pound's claim—not fully reducible to but indissociable from U.S. expatriate anxieties of association with a U.S. culture of "our Conrad"—that "I doubt if Conrad is weighty enough to stand the citation," and includes Pound's later remark: "Ditto re the Conrad; who am I to grudge him his laurel crown"). For a different view sharing my ultimate conclusion, see Bernard Bergonzi, *T. S. Eliot*, 2nd ed. (New York: Macmillan, 1978), 194–95.

24. See, e.g., Donald R. Benson, "Eliot's and Conrad's Hollow Men," *CEA Critic* 29 (Jan. 1967): 10; compare "A Hypertext Version of T. S. Eliot's 'The Hollow Men,'" at http://www.aduni.org/~heather/occs/honors/Poem.htm. T. S. Eliot, "The Hollow Men" (1925): lines 1, 2, 33, 95–98.

25. Eliot, "Kipling Redivivus," 298.

26. T. S. Eliot, "Tradition and the Individual Talent," in T. S. Eliot, *Selected Essays* (New York: Harcourt, Brace, 1950), 7.

27. Ibid., 7, 9.

28. Leighton Rudolph, ed., *The Selected Letters of John Gould Fletcher* (Fayetteville: University of Arkansas Press, 1996), 88.

29. Eliot, "Kipling Redivivus," 298.

30. Ibid.

31. Ibid.

32. T. S. Eliot, "Public Letter to Ford Madox Ford," *Transatlantic Review* 1.1 (Jan. 1924): 95–96, 95.

33. Ibid., 95, 96 (emphasis added).

34. T. S. Eliot, "A Preface to Modern Literature," *Vanity Fair* 21 (Nov. 1923): 44, 118, a revised version of "Lettre d'Angleterre," which originally appeared in *La Nouvelle Revue Française* 9 (May 1, 1922): 617–24.

35. Eliot, "Preface to Modern Literature," 44.

36. Eliot, "Tradition and the Individual Talent," 1, 4, 5.

37. Comments concerning *Gatsby* and *Tender Is the Night* will be discussed later in this chapter. Fitzgerald wrote the following to sell his publishers on *The Last Tycoon*: "I am going to treat it, remember, as it comes through to Cecilia. That is to say by making Cecilia, at the moment of her telling the story, an intelligent and observant woman, I shall grant myself the privilege, as Conrad did, of letting her imagine the actions of the characters. Thus, I hope to get the verisimilitude of a first person narrative, combined with a Godlike knowledge of all events that happen to my characters." Fitzgerald is thinking of the formal strategies of Conrad's Marlow stories. See Fitzgerald's letter to Kenneth Littauer (Sept. 29, 1939), in Fitzgerald, *The Last Tycoon* (New York: Macmillan, 1985), 139–40.

38. Letter from Fitzgerald to Mencken, May/June 1925, in Andrew Turnbull, ed., *The Letters of F. Scott Fitzgerald* (New York: Charles Scribner's Sons, 1963), 482 (henceforth, *Letters*).

39. See, respectively, Fitzgerald, "Confessions," *Chicago Daily Tribune* (May 19, 1923): 9; "Under Fire," *New York Evening Post Literary Review* (May 26, 1923), in Matthew J. Bruccoli and Jackson R. Bryer, eds., *F. Scott Fitzgerald in His Own Time* (Kent, Ohio: Kent State University Press, 1971), 143; "One Hundred False Starts," *Saturday Evening Post* 205 (Mar. 4, 1933): 66.

40. Letter from Fitzgerald to Hemingway, Apr. 1927, in Turnbull, *Letters*, 309; letter to Frances Scott Fitzgerald, Nov. 1940, in Andrew Turnbull, ed., *F. Scott Fitzgerald: Letters to His Daughter* (New York: Charles Scribner's Sons, 1963), 158.

41. Kenneth Bruffee, *Elegiac Romance: Cultural Change and Loss of the Hero in Modern Fiction* (Ithaca, N.Y.: Cornell University Press, 1983). Bruffee situates Conrad and Fitzgerald amid a modern "elegiac" development in the genre of romance, resulting, in

his account, from loss of confidence in traditional norms of heroism that accompany the advent and social dislocations of modernity. The consequence is a form of romance that prioritizes "a quest for self-consciousness" rather than a search for stable truth or moral absolutes. Though I have learned much from Bruffee's study, my account is quite different; as I explain in what follows, I see "romance" in Conrad and Fitzgerald as more a signifier than a genre, one marking social strategies of contact and mystification for critical contemplation rather than prompting a quest for their transcendent resolution. See Bruffee, 1–15, passim.

42. F. Scott Fitzgerald, *The Great Gatsby*, Matthew Bruccoli, ed. (New York: Simon & Schuster, 1991), 184; Fitzgerald, "The Crack-Up" (1936) and "Handle with Care" (1936), in Edmund Wilson, ed., *The Crack Up* (New York: New Directions, 1956), 69–74, 85–90, 73, 79. *The Great Gatsby* will hereafter be cited as *G*.

43. Fitzgerald, "The Crack-Up," 69.

44. Avrom Fleishman, *Conrad's Politics: Community and Anarchy in the Fiction of Joseph Conrad* (Baltimore: Johns Hopkins University Press, 1967), 28–46, 46.

45. See, for instance, the letter quoted earlier to Cunninghame Graham positing *l'idée nationale* as the one *principle defini* capable of containing and rendering socially useful humanity's naturally "anarchic" and "fratricidal" impulses. For a thoughtful reading of this letter in the context of the fetishizing of England in *Heart of Darkness*, see Pericles Lewis, "His Sympathies Were in the Right Place: *Heart of Darkness* and the Discourse of National Character," *Nineteenth-Century Literature* 53.2 (Sept. 1988): 211–44, 222–24.

46. I reference, respectively (beginning with the quotation), Conrad's Letter to Cunninghame Graham, Feb. 8, 1899 (*CL* 2.160); *The Nigger of the "Narcissus," "Youth"* (1897), and *The Mirror of the Sea* (1906); *Nostromo* and *Lord Jim*; and Conrad's various prefaces and autobiographical texts.

47. *MS* 106; comment to Maria Dabrowska, qtd. in Fleishman, *Conrad's Politics*, 19.

48. Qtd in Lewis, "His Sympathies," 223.

49. Paul Armstrong, "Conrad's Contradictory Politics: The Ontology of Society in *Nostromo*," *Twentieth Century Literature* 31.1 (1985): 1–21, 13, 19. A good deal of what I say about mediation, festishism, narcissism, and stereotyping in *Nostromo* in what follows owes its foundations to this most insightful essay.

50. Harpham, *One of Us*, 12, 15.

51. Benedict Anderson, *Imagined Communities: Reflections on the Origin and Spread of Nationalism* (Norfolk, U.K.: Thetford Press, 1983), 13–15, passim.

52. Fitzgerald, "Minnesota's Capital in the Rôle of Main Street," *Literary Digest International Book Review* 1 (Mar. 1923): 35–36, 36.

53. Homi Bhabha, "Introduction: Narrating the Nation," in Bhabha, *Nation and Narration*, 1.

54. Fitzgerald, "How to Waste Material: A Note on My Generation," *Bookman* (NY) 62 (May 1926): 262–65, 262, rptd. in Bruccoli and Bryer, *Fitzgerald in His Own Time*, 145–49, 145.

55. Ibid., 145–47.

56. Ibid., 148.

57. Fitzgerald, "Minnesota's Capital," 36.

58. Fitzgerald, "Under Fire: A Review of Thomas Boyd's *Through the Wheat*," *New York Evening Post* (May 26, 1923): 715, rptd. in Bruccoli and Bryer, *Fitzgerald in His Own Time*, 143–44.

59. Fitzgerald, "Sherwood Anderson on the Marriage Question," *New York Herald* (Mar. 4, 1923): 9.5, rptd. in Bruccoli and Bryer, *Fitzgerald in His Own Time*, 138–40, 138, 140.

60. Fitzgerald, "The Baltimore Anti-Christ," *Bookman* (NY) 52 (Mar. 1921): 79–81, rptd. in Bruccoli and Bryer, *Fitzgerald in His Own Time*, 119–21, 121; preface to *The Great Gatsby* (New York: Modern Library, 1934), vii–xi.

61. Letter to Maxwell Perkins, Dec. 1921, in Turnbull, *Letters*, 149–51, 151 (emphasis in original).

62. Letter to Mencken, May/June 1925, in Turnbull, *Letters*, 482.

63. Letter to Maxwell Perkins, June 1, 1925, in Turnbull, *Letters*, 183–88, 187 (most emphasis added).

64. See, for instance, the letter from Fitzgerald to Frances Scott Fitzgerald, Dec. 1940, in Turnbull, *Letters*, 100–102, 102.

65. Matthew Bruccoli, ed., *The Notebooks of F. Scott Fitzgerald* (New York: Harcourt Brace Jovanovich, 1978), 161.

66. Hale himself became a devotee of Conrad: see, for instance, his "Recent Fiction," *Dial* 60.713 (Mar. 2, 1916): 214–16, 216 (praising Conrad's stories for "a vital intensity, an absolute originality, which one recognizes at once as life"—and for "giv[ing] us . . . life"). Despite the implausibility of the influence claim, the basic connection Fitzgerald is making—that Hale's hero, who cannot return home to the United States because of a disgrace he has incurred, is akin to Conrad's Jim, who lives in exile because of his disgraceful "jump"—is insightful in more ways than one.

67. Fitzgerald, *Notebooks*, 161.

68. The possibilities are *Tender Is the Night* (1933) and *The Last Tycoon* (unfinished at Fitzgerald's death); the former, in my view, is the likely referent given its emphasis on "secrets" and Fitzgerald's very different Conradian modeling of *Tycoon*. If so, then *every mature novel that Fitzgerald wrote* was, in Fitzgerald's own mind, explicitly modeled on Conrad's fiction.

69. Fitzgerald, "The 10 Best Books I Have Read" (1923), qtd. in Matthew Bruccoli, *Some Sort of Epic Grandeur* (New York: Harcourt Brace Jovanovich, 1981), 178.

70. Fitzgerald, "Minnesota's Capital," 36, 37.

71. Fitzgerald's appeals to James are not always bland, though they are sometimes. For an excellent study of Fitzgerald and the Jamesian dichotomy of the novel of "saturation" versus the novel of "selection," see James E. Miller, *F. Scott Fitzgerald: His Art and His Technique* (New York: New York University Press, 1964), 80–95.

72. Fitzgerald, "Minnesota's Capital," 37.

73. Fitzgerald, "Public Letter to Fannie Butcher," *Chicago Daily Tribune* (May 19, 1923): 9, rptd. in Bruccoli and Bryer, *Fitzgerald in His Own Time*, 168–69.

74. See John Buchan, Unsigned Review of *Nostromo*, *Spectator* (Nov. 19, 1904); W. L. Alden, "Mr. Alden's Views," *New York Times* (Oct. 29, 1904); Virginia Woolf, "Joseph Conrad," *Times Literary Supplement* (Aug. 14, 1924), all rptd. in Keith Carabine, ed., *Joseph Conrad: Critical Assessments* (Mountfield, East Sussex: Helm Info., 1992), 1.310–12, 314; 2.420–22. For an account of Garnett's and Cunninghame Graham's praise

of *Nostromo* but not Nostromo, see Cedric Watts, ed., *Joseph Conrad's Letters to R. B. Cunninghame Graham* (Cambridge: Cambridge University Press, 1969), 156–60. As Watts describes, Garnett made his view publicly known in his September 1904 review of *Nostromo* in the *Speaker.*

75. The quotations are, respectively, from Garnett, Review of *Nostromo*; Woolf, "Joseph Conrad"; and Alden, "Mr. Alden's Views."

76. Joseph Conrad, "To My Readers in America," *The Nigger of the "Narcissus"* (New York: Doubleday, Page, 1914), v.

77. Keith Carabine, Introduction, *Nostromo* (Oxford: Oxford University Press, 1984), vii.

78. See Victor A. Doyno, "Patterns in *The Great Gatsby*," *Modern Fiction Studies* 12 (Winter 1966): 415–26; Ronald Berman, *The Great Gatsby and Modern Times* (Chicago: University of Illinois Press, 1994), 3–4.

79. Edward Said, *Beginnings: Intention and Method* (New York: Columbia University Press, 1975), 100, 137.

80. Tracy Seeley, "Conrad's Modernist Romance: *Lord Jim*," *ELH* 59.4 (Winter 1992): 360–82, 383.

81. Matthew Bruccoli, ed., *The Great Gatsby: The Revised and Rewritten Galleys* (New York: Garland, 1990), 162. In the original galley, the "springing" is described as follows: "The part of his life he told me about began when he was fifteen, when the popular songs of those days began to assume for him a melancholy and romantic beauty. He attached them to reveries as transitory as themselves, and attributed deep significance to melodies and phrases set down cynically in Tin Pan Alley." The adolescent spirit of this passage is not lost on the final version of *Gatsby*—which locates Gatsby's "Platonic conception of himself" in "just the sort of Jay Gatsby a seventeen year old boy would be likely to invent" (*G* 104).

82. Arnold Weinstein, "Fiction as Greatness: The Case of *Gatsby*," *Novel* 19 (Fall 1985): 22–38.

83. Dr. Monygham expresses his bepuzzlement over Nostromo—to whose mysterious motives everyone seems to bring a different point of view—this way: "Really it is most unreasonable to demand that a man should think of other people so much better than he is able to think of himself" (*N* 43).

84. GoGwilt, *Invention of the West*, 206.

85. Bhabha, *Location of Culture*, 66, 74.

86. Michaels, *Our America*, 41.

87. Ibid., 15.

88. For example: "he *absorbed* me" (*G* 60); he "absorbed me infinitely" (61); "I was too absorbed by him to be responsive" (88); and "this absorbing information about my neighbor" (59). Here Nick is not freezing difference pursuant to his own established scripts but being pulled into an arena of difference he does not understand but with which he feels a "bond."

89. For a summary of those who have written on points of thematic and formal contact between Conrad and Fitzgerald, see Secor and Moddelmog, *Joseph Conrad and American Writers*, 142–49. The apotheosis of the problem I am raising—copious receptivity to any possible Conradian resonance in Fitzgerald, yet without any model

of how to discern or articulate such resonances—is Robert Emmet Long, *The Achieving of* The Great Gatsby (Lewisburg, Penn: Bucknell University Press, 1964), 79–118. At the risk of replicating Long's ebullient model, I would add to the list of "possible" points of contact between Fitzgerald and Conrad the very title (with which Fitzgerald was never quite satisfied) and name of the eponymous hero of *The Great Gatsby* itself: which, or so it's fun to think, may derive from the moment in *Lord Jim* when a denizen of Schomberg's bar says of the "romantic" Jim: "for one so young he was 'of great gabasidy'" (*LJ* 120).

CHAPTER 4

1. The earliest critics to make the connection formally are Richard Adams, "The Apprenticeship of William Faulkner," *Tulane Studies in English* 12 (1962): 113–56; and Ian Watt, "Joseph Conrad: Alienation and Commitment" (1963), rptd. in Watt, *Essays on Conrad* (Cambridge: Cambridge University Press, 2000), 1–19. For an excellent summary of the critical history on this point since then, see Grażyna Branny, *A Conflict of Values: Alienation and Commitment in the Novels of Joseph Conrad and William Faulkner* (Kraków: Wydawnictwo SPONSOR, 1997), 25–28.

2. Donald Davidson, "The Spyglass," Book Review and Literary Page, *Nashville Tennessean* (Aug. 17, 1924): 12. Davidson, as we shall see, is unthinkable as a literary matter without reference to Conrad; yet in a manner revealing of the larger critique this book advances of American studies, past and present, even the most compendious and excellent collection of Davidson's essays does not contain even one of Davidson's many articles referencing Conrad. See John Tyree Fain, ed., *The Spyglass: Views and Reviews, 1924–1930* (Nashville, Tenn.: Vanderbilt University Press, 1963).

3. Letter from Conrad to Dawson, July 29, 1923 (TS Duke).

4. Conrad wrote to Dawson on September 22, 1919: "Nothing has given me greater satisfaction than your good words about the Arrow. You were often in my thoughts while I wrote. It was unavoidable. . . . I need not protest to you that I tried to be scrupulously fair in my treatment of the Blunts" (*CL* 6.491). Laurence Davies notes: "Like Dawson, Blunt is a South Carolinian devoted to his mother and voluble on matters of race" (*CL* 6.491n1). To this one may add (1) the change in the identity of Blunt (based on the historical soldier of fortune John Young Mason Key Blunt) from North Carolinian in *The Mirror of the Sea* to South Carolinian (like Dawson) in *The Arrow*; and especially (2) the trying interchanges Conrad had with Dawson immediately prior to beginning *The Arrow* in July 1917 concerning idealism generally and the U.S. entry into the Great War (in April 1917) and its resolution—very much an anxiety that underwrites *The Arrow of Gold*. See *CL* 6.75, 83.

5. See, respectively, *CL* 5.382 ("I like all the Page lot immensely. Can't say much of the others—tho' they are much more showy") and Letter to Jessie Conrad, May 4, 1923 (MS Yale, re House); *CL* 5.243, 261; *CL* 1.191, 5.239, 1.365, 3.499; *CL* 5.574.

6. Conrad emphasizes in the preface that the book is not the product of "the exercise of my inventive faculty" and that the story, relayed by M. George, consists in "an inherent part of myself" (*AG* ix, viii).

7. As Najder notes, Blunt's introduction of himself as "Américan, catholique et gentilhomme" (*AG* 18) is a "curious replica of a dedication ('Pole, Catholic, nobleman')

which the five-year-old Conrad wrote on his own photograph, given to his grand-mother" (*MS* 149).

8. Van Wyck Brooks, "Mencken in Baltimore," *American Scholar* 20 (Autumn 1951): 415 ("It was more than a coincidence that the birth of the new Southern literature followed the publication of Mencken's essay").

9. Mencken, "Sahara of the Bozart" (1920), in Mencken, *Chrestomathy*, 184–85.

10. Ibid., 186–87.

11. Hobson, *Serpent in Eden*, 6.

12. Mencken, *Smart Set* 65 (Aug. 1921): 138–44, 143.

13. Mencken, "Is the South a Desert?" *Southern Literary Magazine* 1 (Oct. 1923): 2; Mencken, "Confederate Strivings," *Evening Sun* (Baltimore) (May 16, 1921). See also Mencken, "Letters and the Map," *Smart Set* 63 (Nov. 1920): 139–40.

14. See, for example, Mencken, "Morning Song in C Major," *Reviewer* 2.1 (Oct. 1921): 1–5, 3 (appealing to "the enlightened minority whose forefathers founded what we remembered as Southern civilization"); and "A Class of Blunder" (1926) (fantastically immunizing account of the Southern upper classes with respect to the region's race problems), "The Calamity at Appomattox" (1930) (arguing that Northern victory in the Civil War was unfortunate), and "The Sahara of the Bozart," all in *Chrestomathy*, 184–200.

15. Hunter S. Stagg, "A New Critic of Life and Letters," *Reviewer* 1.9 (June 15, 1921): 285, 284 (emphasis added).

16. Compare the equally thoughtful and not dissimilar thoughts on mastery, identification, and fictively inscribed mappings of the reader's relationship to Conrad in Geoffrey Harpham, "Beyond Mastery: The Future of Conrad's Beginnings," in Kaplan, Mallios, and White, *Conrad in the Twenty-first Century*, 17–20.

17. Hunter S. Stagg, "A Novelist of Mood," *Reviewer* 4.2 (Jan. 1924): 152–55 (emphasis added).

18. On Hergesheimer's central advising role at the *Reviewer*, see Emily Clark, *Innocence Abroad* (New York: Knopf, 1931), 87–109.

19. See ibid., 122; Clark, "The End of the Tether," *Reviewer* 3.3 (June 1922): 530; Clark, "The Facts of the Case Are These," *Reviewer* 2.6 (Mar. 1922): 335–37; and other essays by Clark noted in this chapter.

20. See, respectively, Emily Clark, "Reflection Andante," *Reviewer* 2.2 (Nov. 1921): 95–97, 95; "Concerning Investigations," *Reviewer* 2.4 (Jan. 1922): 211–13, 211; "The Advantages of Acquisitiveness," *Reviewer* 3.2 (May 1922): 461–62. On "affiliation," see Edward Said, *The World, the Text, and the Critic* (Cambridge, Mass.: Harvard University Press, 1983), 1–31; compare Said, "Reflections on Exile," in *Reflections on Exile*, 173–86. Said, of course, would be troubled by the insularity and class politics—the Menckenite denigration of the "herd" and fetishization of a hierarchical "aristocracy"—that ultimately underwrite Clark's view, as we shall explore further. Clark's initial and casual—though by no means unimportant—use of "epic" to signify an excess of form over thematic or experiential grounding is a Southern reiteration of the form/experience binary mediated by and contested through Conrad in U.S. expatriate circles, as discussed in Part 2 of this book.

21. *Reviewer* 1.6 (May 1, 1921): 169–71. In Hergesheimer's sketch, the American captain-narrator recalls "how, in his memoir, Captain Whalley spoke of making—

after the frozen unendurable waste of Cape Horn—the harbor of Papeete; where . . . the Kanaka girls swam out to the ship with hibiscus flowers in their hair. . . . That phase of romance, reward was over" (169). Hergesheimer's point is to connect the imperialist context of Captain Whalley's missions in Conrad's *The End of the Tether* (the novella that follows *Heart of Darkness* in the *Youth* volume) to U.S. activity in Hawaii during the Spanish-American War, when this sketch is set; for such a point to be made in a *Southern* magazine is to raise the question of U.S. imperialism along a domestic North-South axis as well.

22. See, respectively, Frances Newman, "The Allegory of the Young Intellectuals," *Reviewer* 1.12 (Aug. 1, 1921): 359–65; Burton Rascoe, "Art and Clive Bell," *Reviewer* 3.3 (June 1922): 489–95, 493 (Bell's misunderstanding of Cézanne's innovative "form" likened to his misunderstanding of Conrad); John Powell, "A Basis for Modern Musical Criticism," *Reviewer* 1.9 (June 15, 1921): 263–68 (Powell's aggressively racialized "modern" exposition of "African" as opposed to "European" modalities of music presupposes knowledge of his recent "symphonic" version of *Heart of Darkness*); Harold Randolph (head of Peabody Conservatory of Music in Baltimore), "Notes on Ultra-Modern Music," *Reviewer* 3.5/6 (Oct. 1922): 646–50, 649 (suggestive essay in which objections to "ultramodern" music practices that—on the model of "Bolshevism"—"deliberately discard everything with which we are familiar and undertak[e] to speak to us at once in an entirely different tongue" are parried by analogy to "a story or novel [that presents] the dénouement first and the character drawing and descriptions last"; the fact that "Conrad, for instance" has "done very nearly this" is evoked by different voices both in justification and repudiation of the new music); Frances Newman, "With One Year's Subscription," *Reviewer* 3.1 (Apr. 1922): 374; Joseph Hergesheimer, "A Note on John Partins," *Reviewer* 2.4 (Jan. 1922): 179; Emily Clark, "Coquette," *Reviewer* 1.2 (Aug. 1, 1921): 373 (cites Frank Swinnerton for the "older generation" comment; it is clear that Clark does not agree with, is in fact challenging, the antimodern categorization: the debate from both sides being the point); and Douglas Goldring, "Plush," *Reviewer* 2.6 (Mar. 1922): 297–306, 306 (see note 28 below).

23. See, respectively, Mary D. Street (and Hunter Stagg), "*Captain Macedoine's Daughter*," *Reviewer* 1.8 (June 1, 1921): 247–48; Hunter Stagg, "Reflections," *Reviewer* 3.8 (Jan. 1923): 794–95. Compare Street, "*An Ocean Tramp*," *Reviewer* 1.11 (June 15, 1921): 343–44; Stagg, "Casuals of McFee and Others," *Reviewer* 2.3 (Dec. 1921): 165–66 (review of *Harbors of Memory*). Compare also Charles J. Finger, "*Captain Macedoine's Daughter*," *All's Well* 1.2 (Jan. 1921): 18 ("Thinking of McFee one thinks of and brackets him just under Conrad. . . . There is in McFee the same keenness of sympathetic observation that is found in Conrad, and the same refined and delicate art. . . . Few can approach McFee in the power to conceive and depict a character compounded of subtle and profound elements and show it wavering in a storm of emotion").

24. Edwin Björkman, "On Reading Hamsun," *Reviewer* 2.1 (Oct. 1921): 42–43 (implicitly enlists moonlight image at outset of *Heart of Darkness* to articulate effect of reading Hamsun); Stagg, "Decay and Dissolution," *Reviewer* 4.3 (Apr. 1924): 240–41 (notes how Knopf advertises Hamsun's *Children of the Age* by emphasizing that "Lieutenant Willatz Holmsen is a figure such as Conrad would delight in drawing and analyzing: one might even go further and say that he is, as he stands, as good as a figure out of

Conrad. Hamsun's methods of portrayal bear no resemblance to Conrad's, of course, but one recognizes the stamp").

25. "The Prose and Poetry of Walter de la Mare," *Reviewer* 3.5/6 (Oct. 1922): 655–60, 658.

26. See, respectively, Stagg, "The Delicate Question of Donkeys," *Reviewer* 2.2 (Nov. 1921): 111–12 (In *Mr. Waddington of Wyck* Sinclair "has employed an old trick of Joseph Conrad's. That is, she has produced an effect of difference with materials which no one knows better than she to be utterly usual, by throwing into exaggerated relief traits common in some degree to all men and in themselves commonplace. Yet while Conrad uses this trick, generally, on the outward appearance of his characters, she applies it to the soul"), and Wilson Follett, Review of Dorothy Richardson, qtd. in "Books of the Month," *Reviewer* 2.4 (Jan. 1922): 228–29; Follett and Mencken qtd. in Stagg, "About Books," *Reviewer* 3.5/6 (Oct. 1922): 711 (review of Cather's *One of Ours*); Emily Clark, "*Coquette*," 373 ("Mr. Swinnerton protests enviously that Mr. Conrad, Mr. Kipling . . . and others of the older generation, were never subjected in their infancy to such barbarous fondling"); Burton Rascoe, "Art and Clive Bell," 493 ("If he doesn't know what he is talking about when he is on the subject of literature [and it is apparent that he doesn't] he should refrain from committing such anti-climaxes as that of declaring that the greatest living novelists are Hardy, Conrad, and Virginia Woolfe [*sic*]"); Joseph Hergesheimer, "A Note on John Partins," 175–87, 177 ("essence of creative genius," as apotheosized by Conrad, is "aristocratic" and "ironic"), and 175 ("Only the early Conrads, the tall paper Masefields, and one of George Moore's privately printed volumes, exceed in value *The Alabaster Saint*"); Stagg, "Some Books and Some Readers," *Reviewer* 3.9/10 (Apr. 1923): 869 (review of Dallett's *Star of Earth*); Stagg, "A Cleared Shelf," *Reviewer* 3.11/12 (July 1923): 958 (review of Steele's *The Shame Dance*; "Too many writers, with the eye of admiration upon *Lord Jim*, neglect to consider that they cannot afford so well as Joseph Conrad to risk the dwarfing of matter by manner," and though Steele's "tendency is to fall into this error," "on the whole the book may be recommended as a safe investment"); and Stagg, "A Student of the Jungle and an Observer of the East," *Reviewer* 2.6 (Mar. 1922): 346–48.

27. Meaningful consideration of Cabell, who simply has very little to say about Conrad, is beyond the scope of this book. In *Straws and Prayer-Books* (1924), he makes reference to those "who have just seen or heard Mr. Joseph Conrad described as 'a master of English prose,'" and—on a similar note of mock amusement—to Conrad's status as an "impeccant prosateur" (with Proust, Melville, O. Henry, and Tagore) and "recent hierarch" (with Hardy) of the moment. Nevertheless, he does Conrad the complicated indignity of leaving him off his once "regretfully" compiled list of "the world's ten worst writers"; and in a letter of June 1918, perhaps captures his lack of interest best in referring to "the shadow of a name like Conrad." Though Cabell is not a U.S. author meaningfully recoverable or reunderstandable through Conrad, he is an example of this book's larger point concerning important, talented, politically and aesthetically significant writers—*Jürgen* was not only widely revered in its time but banned for its subversive content; it's also a very unusual aesthetic artifact that has become significantly lost to U.S. literary studies because of the internationalist aesthetic vocabulary required to engage his Southern locality. See *Straws and Prayer-Books* (New York: Robert McBride, 1924), 246, 249, 252. 271; Edward Wagenknecht, ed., *The Letters of James Branch Cabell* (Norman: University of Oklahoma Press, 1975), 23.

28. Carl Van Vechten, "On Visiting Fashionable Places out of Season," *Reviewer* 3.7/8 (Jan. 1923): 758–77, 776, 777. Compare Douglas Goldring's biting essay "Plush" in March 1922, which without naming names—"I know them all by name. So, if you think for a moment do you"—takes aim at some of the more recently successful giants emerging from "the mighty world of British letters" and accuses them of a "plush" capitulation in their latest fiction to standards of popularity, commerciality, and strategic self-promotion. Goldring, "Plush," 297–30. In context, this line of calumny almost certainly extends to Conrad—about whom Goldring had a number of unflattering anecdotes and impressions to share, frequently in defense of Ford Madox Ford. See Douglas Goldring, *South Lodge: Reminiscences of Violet Hunt, Ford Madox Ford, and the English Review Circle* (London: Constable, 1943), chap. 12.

29. See, respectively, Hunter Stagg, "The Abuses of Diversity," *Reviewer* 1.3 (Mar. 15, 1921): 83–87 (this article, suspicious of the suave but shallow (and immensely profitable) triumphs of G. K. Chesterton on the U.S. lecture circuit, must be understood in the context of widespread American suspicion of British (and French) motives in the aftermath of the Paris Peace Conference; for a good illustration of how British requests for U.S. debt forgiveness become comingled with questions of U.S. *cultural* indebtedness to Britain, compare two adjacent articles—Frances Newman's "Literary Introductions: F. Scott Fitzgerald," arguing that *This Side of Paradise* owes an extensive debt to Compton MacKenzie's *Sinister Street*, and M. Ashby Jones's "Lest We Forget," arguing that British war debts should be canceled "on the ground of pure and simple sympathy"—in *Constitution* (Atlanta), Feb. 13, 1921, 2G); Hunter Stagg, "The Friend of the Family and Another Story by Fyodor Dostoevsky" and "People Coming and Going," *Reviewer* 1.10 (July 1, 1921): 211–15, 224–28 (review of Louis Couperus's *Majesty*), and Joseph Hergesheimer, "Charlotte Russe," *Reviewer* 1.12 (Aug. 1, 1921); Edward Hale Bierstadt, "Americanizing America," *Reviewer* 1.11 (July 15, 1921): 327–32, and Hansell Baugh, "Urbana, Ill.," *Reviewer* 1.122 (Dec. 1921): 122–25; the writings concerning Africa (by Achmed Abdullah, about the historical experiences of Sir Harry Johnston and Wilfred Scawen Blunt, and commenting and fictional representations thereof) and the opening of O'Neill's play are ubiquitous.

30. Jesse Lee Bennett, "The Nation Wants—," *Reviewer* 2.1 (Oct. 1921), 12–18, 14.

31. "The Politically Minded," *Double Dealer* 3.16 (Apr. 1922): 170–71, 171. Compare Gordon King's assessment of Wells and Shaw in the *Reviewer* in April 1922: "Both of these authors were in a sense the intellectual leaders of English literature before the World War. Both were hopeful, pleasantly optimistic, and encouraging to their readers who were, for the most part, people of patient faith in the general progress of mankind. But the war had a crushing effect upon the faithful. The depression that has settled down upon the minds of men and women since the peace conference seems almost insurmountable. Both Wells and Shaw appeal to us to overcome this appalling disillusion of mind and spirit, and both appeals are addressed to the same quality of imagination." Gordon King, "Back to Methuselah with the Theater Guild," *Reviewer* 3.1 (Apr. 1922): 370.

32. Bennett, "The Nation Wants—," 17, 18.

33. Emily Clark, "At Random: Beginning the Second Volume," *Reviewer* 2.1 (Oct. 1921): 38, 41.

34. Qtd. in Clark, *Innocence Abroad*, 111–12.

35. Emily Clark, "Beginning the Second Volume," 41; Gerald W. Johnson, "Fourteen Equestrian Statues of Colonel Simmons," *Reviewer* 3.4 (Oct. 1923): 22, 24 (emphasis added).

36. As such, Newman is one of this book's foremost examples of its larger argument concerning the need for U.S. literary and cultural studies to develop greater sensitivity to the "capillary" traces and networks of "foreign" literary authorship circulating within and as a material and constitutive part of various domains of U.S. culture: for at issue in such "foreign" recoveries as "our Conrad" is also the recovery and conceptual reintegration of marginalized U.S. writers like Newman. For Newman, whose cosmopolitan aesthetic and critical sophistication are as striking (at least for those who have obtained access to her voluminous critical works, none of which have been reprinted) as the sociohistorical value and political fire of her writings are unmistakable, has curiously found the masculinist, nationalist, and ahistorical emphases responsible for her erasure from U.S. literary history in the first half of the twentieth century reproduced by more recent historicist Americanist, Southern studies, and feminist interventions, which, as Anne Goodwyn Jones has pointed out, have not been successful in restoring Newman to visibility—in part because of a conceptual separation of Newman's international-aestheticist/modernist and Southern-political/historical qualities and domains of consideration. But these qualities cannot be separated; the failure to integrate the two vocabularies has occasioned the loss of Newman; and if there is some irony, as we shall see, in a vigorous case for Newman's resurrection being occasioned by Conrad, there is no irony at all in Newman's restoration to visibility emerging from the kind of post-Americanist inquiry that would concentrate on the significance of an international figure like Conrad as a simultaneously aesthetic and political U.S. signifier. See Anne Goodwyn Jones, "Foreword," in Frances Newman, *Dead Lovers Are Faithful Lovers* (Athens: University of Georgia Press, 1994), xxxiii–xxxiv.

37. Qtd. in ibid., xxv.

38. Newman, "Allegory of the Young Intellectuals," 359.

39. Ibid., 360–64.

40. Ibid., 364–65.

41. Frances Newman, *The Hard-Boiled-Virgin* (1926), Anne Firor Scott, ed. (Athens: University of Georgia Press, 1980), 11, 12.

42. Ibid., 246, 252. Though he is not a writer, one may compare the "two forked veins" whose "green lines" wave their way up Charlton Cunningham's forehead in *Dead Lovers*: a devilish indication of the same kind of seductive power that wrests agency, expression, memory, and critical self-reflection away from Evelyn Cunningham and Isabel Ramsay. See Newman, *Dead Lovers*, 255.

43. "Mr. Hergesheimer on the Feminine Nuisance," *Constitution* (Atlanta) (July 10, 1921): 2G.

44. Newman originally derives the phrase "prince of prose" in association with Conrad from a review of *Notes on Life and Letters* that appeared in the *Times Literary Supplement* in March 1921, which, after wrestling with the question of whether Conrad "is a great man, a master of prose, a prophet, a man of genius," settles for the labels of "very sensible man" and "prince of prose." See "A Prince of Prose," *Times Literary Supplement* (Mar. 3, 1921): 141. This review emphasizes Conrad's Henry James essay and questions of humanity's ability to "endure" after the Great War—begging later

Southern formulations of Conrad, and also offering an austere "sacrificial" narrative of "endur[ance]" that Newman equates with "gloom."

45. "Living by Gloom Alone," *Constitution* (Atlanta) (July 3, 1921): 2G; "Literary Introductions IX: William McFee," *Constitution* (Atlanta) (Jan. 3, 1921): 2G. See also "The New Carthaginians," *Constitution* (Atlanta) (July 31, 1921): 2G (laments the fate of Southern librarians "weary with searching shelves for the literary descendants of Mr. Conrad"); "Vacation for the Brain," *Constitution* (Atlanta) (July 24, 1921): 2G ("it is a sad thing to find oneself on a lonely heath or a lonely strand, among a hundred strange people, from among whom the almost inevitable congenial spirit has not yet emerged, and there to discover one has brought *Lord Jim*"); "Literary Introductions XLV: Francis Scott Fitzgerald," *Constitution* (Atlanta) (Feb. 13, 1921): 2G (disturbed by Fitzgerald's self-comparison with Conrad in *This Side of Paradise*); and other essays noted in this chapter.

46. Frances Newman, "Herd Complex," *Reviewer* 3.2 (May 1922): 428–33, 428–29.

47. Ibid., 430.

48. Ibid., 430–31; Newman, "Francis Scott Fitzgerald," 2G.

49. Newman, "Herd Complex," 428–30.

50. Especially *The Secret Agent*. See my "Reading *The Secret Agent* Now," in Kaplan, Mallios, and White, *Conrad in the Twenty-first Century*, 165–71, and "Afterword: The Deserts of Conrad," in *The Secret Agent* (New York: Modern Library, 2004), 277–82.

51. Newman, "Herd Complex," 433.

52. Ibid., 432–33.

53. Newman, "Living by Gloom Alone," G2.

54. Frances Newman, "Literary Introductions XI: Henry Mencken," *Constitution* (Atlanta) (Jan. 16, 1921): 2G; Frances Newman, "The Novels of 1920—American," *Constitution* (Atlanta) (Feb. 27, 1921): 2G.

55. Conrad's own sense of the opposition between "journalistic" and "artistic" modes of discourse receives its most careful and considered expression in the opening of "Autocracy and War"; the opening of "Karain: A Memory" provides a powerful evocation; *The Secret Agent*, a relentless elaboration.

56. Newman, "Living by Gloom Alone," G2.

57. Frances Newman, "Literary Introductions XII: A. A. Milne," *Constitution* (Atlanta) (Jan. 23, 1921): 2G; Newman, "Henry Mencken," 2G.

58. Newman, "A. A. Milne," 2G; Frances Newman, "Literary Introductions XV: Norman Douglas," *Constitution* (Atlanta) (Feb. 20, 1921): 2G. Compare, pursuant to the same logic, Newman's praise for the *French* Paul Morand for having "become entirely cosmopolitan without ceasing to be entirely Parisian" (clearly a model, as will be demonstrated shortly, for the entirely cosmopolitan and entirely "Southern" Newman), in Frances Newman, "Open All Night," *Reviewer* 4.2 (Jan. 1924): 143.

59. Frances Newman, "Literary Introductions X: Ezra Pound," *Constitution* (Atlanta) (Jan. 9, 1921): 2G.

60. Key motifs, of course, in *Lord Jim, Victory, Heart of Darkness*, and *The Secret Agent*. One may also compare the important moment in the Preface to *The Nigger of the "Narcissus"* when Conrad writes of how the "gods" of the past "must, after a short period of fellowship, abandon him—even on the very threshold of the temple—to the

stammerings of his own conscience" (xi)—though Conrad's complicated tone of reverence for past inheritances (aesthetic, in this case) at the very moment he is confronting the need for radical departures introduces the element of *ambivalence* in Conrad that makes so many different readings of him plausible.

61. Newman, "The New Carthaginians," 2G. Compare (with respect to "we" Southerners) Newman's "Mencken" and "The Novels of 1920—American" essays, and also the subtle attention Newman draws to Burton Rascoe's Southern origins (and kindredly "British" spirit) in "A. A. Milne." See also Newman's defense of the *Reviewer* as opposed to the *Double Dealer* as "very properly" and "very truly Southern" (in "The New Carthaginians," 2G), and Newman's numerous letters assuming a regional subject position, as when she writes to Clark of Mencken, "I do not think he quite understands us" (qtd. in Clark, *Innocents*, 188–89).

62. Newman, "The New Carthaginians," 2G.

63. Newman, "Mr. Hergesheimer on the Feminine Nuisance," 2G (emphasis added).

64. Exactly the opposite of both Mencken's "aristocratic" conception of Conrad presented in Chapter 1 and the "poetics of democracy" arguably *vindicated* by readers of Conrad texts like *Victory* as described in Chapter 2.

65. Newman, *Dead Lovers*, 219. The university referenced: University of Georgia.

66. Jones, "Foreword," in *Dead Lovers*, xxxiv.

67. Newman, *Dead Lovers*, 68.

68. Newman, *Hard-Boiled Virgin*, 235.

69. Newman, *Dead Lovers*, 273, 205, 190, 211.

70. Ibid., 250, 215.

71. This "irreconcilable antagonism" and signature irresolvable combination is the point of Ian Watt's famous essay "Joseph Conrad: Alienation and Commitment."

72. Newman, "Henry Mencken," 2G; Newman, "Allegory of the Young Intellectuals," 362, 363, 364.

73. Compare, on the note of narcissistic faux "discovery" masquerading as "originality," Newman's remark in "Advice to Living Authors": "although Miss Willa Cather has stated, without any of Mr. James' self-distrust, that originality is never a very important thing, there is persistent charm in being the Columbus of something more than one's own soul." In *Reviewer* 2.1 (Oct. 1921): 71.

74. Newman, "Living by Gloom Alone," 2G.

75. Newman, *Hard-Boiled Virgin*, 20.

76. Newman, "Living by Gloom Alone," 2G; Newman, "William McFee," 2G.

77. Newman, "Henry Mencken," 2G; compare Newman, "Freud and the Flapper," *Constitution* (Atlanta) (June 26, 1921): 2G.

78. Newman, "William McFee," 2G.

79. Isabel Patterson, "Phantom Lovers," *New York Herald-Tribune Books*, (May 6, 1928): 3.

80. See Scott, "Foreword," in *Hard-Boiled Virgin*, xiii, xvi, xvii; Jones, "Foreword," in *Dead Lovers*, viii, ix.

81. Newman, "William McFee," 2G.

82. Ibid.

83. Newman, *Hard-Boiled Virgin*, 12.

84. Clark, "Advantages of Acquisitiveness," 460.

85. Ibid., 460, 462; compare Newman, "Herd Complex."

86. Clark, "Advantages of Acquisitiveness," 461.

87. Street and Stagg, "*Captain Macedoine's Daughter*," 247, 248.

88. Newman, "Open All Night," 145; Stagg, "A Novelist of Mood," 152, 154.

89. Stagg, "A Novelist of Mood," 153; Stagg, "A New Critic of Life and Letters," 285, 284.

90. Hergesheimer, "John Partins," 177.

91. Ibid., 178–79.

92. Emily Clark, "Advantages of Acquisitiveness," 460–62.

93. Stagg, "A Novelist of Mood," 153 (emphasis added).

94. Gerald W. Johnson, "The Congo, Mr. Mencken," *Reviewer* 3.11/12 (July 1923): 887–93, 891. For more on the South as the "American Congo," and "the Congo" as a trope for white Southern brutality and mismanagement of human and cultural resources, see Barbara Foley, *Spectres of 1919: Class & Nation in the Making of the New Negro* (Urbana: University of Illinois Press, 2003), 20–21.

95. Ellen Glasgow, "The Dynamic Past," *Reviewer* 1.3 (Mar. 15, 1921): 73–80, 74. The essay's penultimate paragraph also suggestively opens itself up to the problem and (Southern) parallel of *Heart of Darkness*: "We can be as great as we were in the past only when we open the floodgates of thought, and the river of the past flows through us and from us onward into the future. For the past and the present and the future are the same endless stream, and with all our efforts we can merely change the course a little—we can never break the eternal continuity of the race" (80).

96. Ibid., 75, 76; Ellen Glasgow, *The Woman Within* (New York: Harcourt Brace, 1954), 201.

97. John Bennett, "Grotesque Old Charleston," *Reviewer* 3.4 (July 1922): 551–58, 555–56.

98. "James Gibbons Huneker," *Double Dealer* 1.3 (Mar. 1921): 84.

99. "A National Magazine from the South," *Double Dealer* 2.7 (July 1921): 2.

100. "The Dead Hand," *Double Dealer* 2.7 (July 1921): 3–4. The essay quoted is "Books," the first essay (followed by "Henry James: An Appreciation") in *Notes on Life and Letters*.

101. Ibid., 3, 4.

102. See "The Sentimental Mr. Mencken," *Double Dealer* 2.8/9 (Aug./Sept. 1921): 49–50 (presenting Conrad as worthy favorite of disruptive Mencken); "The Great American Novel," *Double Dealer* 2.8/9 (Aug./Sept. 1921): 51–52 (Conrad as antithesis to the degraded and underachieving novels of the United States); H. C. Auer, "Frank Harris," *Double Dealer* 2.7 (July 1921): 29–31 (Conrad as superior to nonetheless worthy Harris).

103. See, for instance, "Defending Artificiality," *Double Dealer* 4.20 (Aug. 1920): 58–59 (opposes "modern" "realism" of a tradition of writers including Tolstoy, Zola, and Joyce to an equally "modern" tradition of "consummate artist(ry)" including Conrad); A. Donald Douglas, "The Modern Novel," *Double Dealer* 4.23 (Nov. 1922): 235–38, 236 (Conrad praised as a quintessential figure of the "modern novel" for his realistic courage in engaging in "the disinterested and dispassionate endeavor to interpret that strange and terrible thing, the soul of man, against the burning hues of the universe," one of "vast terrible indifference"). Compare Banbury Cross, "The Novel and the Drama: A Note," *Double Dealer* 5.27–28 (Mar./Apr. 1923): 116–17 (Conrad is one of the few "Anglo-Saxon" novelists who still can write—as opposed to the "cult[s]" of Joyce,

Proust, and Eliot—with both "sure craftsmanship" and "verve and sincerity"); Lawrence Morris, "Ohio and the Seine," *Double Dealer* 6.32 (Jan. 1924): 3–5 (Conrad, despite his "continental bonds," is essentially an "English genius"; he is the "essentially anarchistic" "modern" *opposite* of the sort of "over-aestheticism" and heightened attention to technique associated with France, and also the "conception of international literature," "a sort of spiritual Esperanto!" that has poisoned the "national" "note" whence all worthy literary expression derives); Basil Thompson (coeditor of *Double Dealer*), "Stephen Crane Finds His Biographer," *Double Dealer* 6.32 (Mar. 1924): 74–76 (clearly impatient with the "studied manner" of Conrad, "the solemn Pole who is England's master stylist"); Julius Weis Friend (coeditor of *Double Dealer*), "Joseph Conrad: An Appreciation," *Double Dealer* 7.39 (Oct.1924): 3–5 (defending Conrad's "nobility," "aristocracy," and permanent literary value, in the present moment as much as any other, against those who object to him as insufficiently "modern" on superficial grounds).

104. See Charles J. Finger, "A Very Satisfactory God," *Double Dealer* 2.8/9 (Aug./Sept. 1921): 70–77. As in the Glasgow essay previously described, Finger's story suggests more than a purely externalized "Southern" relation to Conrad in that it enlists the tropes, techniques, and terrain of *Heart of Darkness* to tell a story of a South American village that is itself a blurred figural middle ground between Conrad's "Africa" and the U.S. South (i.e., the obvious immediate subtext of Finger's story). Like O'Neill's *The Emperor Jones*, another Conrad-inspired text featuring a black character who experiences "imperial" power followed by madness and decay in the manner of Conrad's Kurtz, Finger's story is not simply a rewriting but also an intelligent reading of *Heart of Darkness*: the thematic commonality among all three being a collapse of the ideology of white/black racial distinctions and distinctiveness. This happens in O'Neill and Finger by virtue of a black character *repeating* what a white character (Kurtz) has already done, hence reenacting the collapse of racial categories precisely at the moment, in O'Neill's case, when having a black performer onstage (originally Charles Gilpin) was already O'Neill's primary assault on ideologies of segregation. *The Emperor Jones* is discussed throughout the Southern literary magazines at this time; the issue of racial separation and its incoherence, discontents, subversive appropriations are what Finger and Southern readers of O'Neill flirt with recognizing as a Southern commonality, *internality*, of Conrad.

105. The quotations are from Friend, "Joseph Conrad," 4–5; see note 103 for context.

106. Charles J. Finger, "A Giant Passes," *All's Well* 4.6 (Aug. 1924): 4–7, 5, 7.

107. See John Crowe Ransom, "Now the Grateful Author: On 'The Master's in the Garden Again,'" in Anthony Ostroff, ed., *The Contemporary Poet as Critic and Artist* (Boston: Little, Brown, 1964), 134–40, 134.

108. John Crowe Ransom, "Conrad in Twilight," *Fugitive* 2.3 (July 1923): 7.

109. Ostroff, *Contemporary Poet*, 136.

110. As Michael O'Brien observes, whereas the urbane "Ransom had drawn upon the largesse of the Rhodes trustees, [Donald] Wade had been pampered by his uncle's fortune, [Andrew] Lytle had a rich family past, [and the New York-accultured Allen] Tate and Warren had been prodigies," Davidson's life "had been a slow laborious grind in small Tennessee towns, where he had taught in schools to pay for his education." Davidson would continue to shoulder an enormous teaching load to support himself

while at Vanderbilt. See O'Brien, *The Idea of the American South, 1920–1941* (Baltimore: Johns Hopkins University Press, 1979), 185–90.

111. Qtd. in Virginia Rock, "The Twelve Southerners: Biographical Essays," in Twelve Southerners, *I'll Take My Stand: The South and the Agrarian Tradition* (Baton Rouge: Louisiana State University Press, 1977), 371.

112. Donald Davidson, "'The Rover,' Conrad's Twenty-third Volume Ranks with Predecessors," Book Review and Literary Page, *Nashville Tennessean* (Feb. 4, 1924).

113. Donald Davidson, "The Spyglass," Book Review and Literary Page, *Nashville Tennessean* (Aug. 17, 1924).

114. Qtd. in Fain, *The Spyglass*, xvii.

115. Donald Davidson, "Joseph Conrad's Directed Indirections," *Sewanee Review* 33 (1925): 163–77, 163, 177.

116. Ibid., 174, 175, 177.

117. O'Brien is wrong to dismiss this quality in Davidson—for the reason elaborated in the final clause of the referenced sentence, and later in this chapter—which a number of the Vanderbilt group insisted on as a distinguishing quality of Davidson's work as well. See O'Brien, *Idea of the American South*, 185.

118. Consider Edward Said, "On Lost Causes," in *Reflections on Exile*, 527–53.

119. "Those who read me know my conviction that the world, the temporal world, rests on a very few simple ideas; so simple that they must be as old as the hills. It rests notably, among others, on the idea of Fidelity" (*PR* xix).

120. Donald Davidson, "Joseph Conrad and the Vision of His Youth," Vanderbilt University Special Collections, 9 (emphasis in original). The date of the original typed manuscript is unclear, though context suggests the later 1920s. Many handwritten insertions and extra materials were added to the original typed manuscript over time.

121. Ibid., 4, 15.

122. "Blemished fashion" because, as Najder explains, honor is a Janus-faced concept in which fidelity to public code and need for public esteem are always counterbalanced by, and indeed must always be supplanted in relation to, concerns of conscience and self-approbation preceding right conduct. This critical element is lost on, effaced by, Davidson and his "Conrad." See Zdzisław Najder, "Conrad and the Idea of Honor," in *Conrad in Perspective* (Cambridge: Cambridge University Press, 1997), 188–98, 195–96; Najder, "Joseph Conrad and His Historical Perspective," in *Conrad in Perspective*, 153–64, 161–63; Najder, "Sienkiewicz—Conrad—Faulkner: A Prolegomenon," in Ilona Dobosiewicz, ed., *Crossing the Border: English Studies at the Turn of the Century* (Opole, Poland: Opole University Press, 1998): 57–62.

123. Davidson, "Conrad and the Vision of His Youth," 5.

124. Ibid.

125. For some of his more famous statements on such matters, see Davidson, "A Mirror for Artists," in *I'll Take My Stand*, 28–60; Davidson, *The Attack on Leviathan: Regionalism and Nationalism in the United States* (Chapel Hill: University of North Carolina Press, 1938).

126. Davidson, "Conrad and the Vision of His Youth," 12–13.

127. Ibid., 14, 20.

128. Distinguishing Conrad from a number of U.S. writers, Davidson writes: "Nor

is he like certain other young moderns, venomously impressed with his self-importance, and eager to exhibit the wounds which his self-importance has suffered at the hands of an unfeeling world." Above this sentence at the top of the page is penciled in "Frances Newman." The irony here, of course, is that Newman understands Conrad as largely the very annihilation of tradition Davidson attacks *in* Newman. Also on the subject of combative and dialogic constructions of Conrad, early in the lecture after first referring to Marlow's searching for "something out of life," Davidson pencils in: "for *something, something*, not like so many modern authors, for a *nothing*, a negation, a rejection, an escape, a drug of forgetfulness." Davidson likely would have included the Eliot of *The Waste Land* in this category—another advocate of "tradition," but not of Davidson's stripe, or construction of Conrad. See "Conrad and the Vision of His Youth," 10–11, 4 (emphases in original).

129. Ibid., 16 (emphasis added).

130. Ibid.

131. Qtd. in O'Brien, *Idea of the American South*, 186. For a helpful discussion of Davidson's commitment to public education and the popularization of literary discussions and access, see O'Brien, 186–89.

132. Davidson, "The Spyglass," Book Review and Literary Page.

133. Ibid., 15–16.

134. Or is it Davidson's Davidson, the ever sympathetic, never quite comprehending Captain of *Victory*?

135. See Floyd Watkins, *Then & Now: The Personal Past in the Poetry of Robert Penn Warren* (Lexington: University Press of Kentucky, 1982), 40.

136. See Letter from Warren to Davidson, Aug. 30, 1924, in William Bedford Clark, ed., *Selected Letters of Robert Penn Warren*, vol. 1 (Baton Rouge: Louisiana State University Press, 2000), 58–59 ("Might I see the Conrad paper"—surely the "Directed Indirections" essay—"you were working on while Allen [Tate] and I were there? I am trying to do Mr. Ransom a term paper on Conrad and I am in sad need of reference books for facts and criticism"). Note also that in the October 1924 issue of the *Double Dealer*, the second piece is Jules Weis Friend's memorial essay on Conrad. The first consists of two poems by Warren, "Autumn Twilight Piece" ("Now has the brittle incandescent day / Been shattered") and "Admonition to the Dead" ("Such be the end of all the red and gold; / . . . Such be the end. / Nor weep; but in the land where you are gone / Take rest until all, slow friend by friend, / Come to you there"). Apropos of Ransom's "Conrad at Twilight," it is difficult to read these poems, themselves pointedly Southern in evocation, in the printed context and not read them as—regardless of whose juxtaposition this is, and/or whether Warren had any role in it—anticipating what follows on Conrad, effectively connecting, as a matter of sympathetic internality, the South and Conrad. See *Double Dealer* 7.39 (Oct. 1924): 2.

137. *YOS* 50–51, qtd. in Robert Penn Warren, "Joseph Conrad: Master of Illusion" (1924), Beinecke Rare Book and Manuscript Library, Item 4426: 3–4. The date (1921) the library identifies with this manuscript is incorrect.

138. See, for instance, Marshall Walker, *Robert Penn Warren: A Vision Earned* (New York: Barnes & Noble, 1979), 87–89, 236. The (very famous) quotations are Warren's, and will be discussed in more detail.

139. See Cleanth Brooks and Robert Penn Warren, *Understanding Fiction* (New York: Appleton-Century-Crofts, 1946), xv; Letters between Warren and Brooks on May 26, 1946, and June 5, 1946, in James A. Grimshaw, ed., *Cleanth Brooks and Robert Penn Warren: A Literary Correspondence* (Columbia: University of Missouri Press, 1998), 108, 110.

140. See Gouverneur Paulding and Lyman Bryson, "Joseph Conrad: *Nostromo*," *Invitation to Learning* 2 (1953): 247–52, 247, 251 (transcription of a CBS Public Affairs radio broadcast, produced by George D. Crothers).

141. See Robert Penn Warren, *Homage to Dreiser* (New York: Random House, 1971), 166–68; Warren, *New and Selected Essays* (New York: Random House, 1989).

142. Robert Penn Warren, "Introduction," in Joseph Conrad, *Nostromo* (New York: Modern Library, 1951), vii–xxxix, xxix, xxxii.

143. Robert Penn Warren, *Segregation: The Inner Conflict in the South* (New York: Vintage Books, 1956), 26.

144. Warren, "Introduction," xii.

145. Warren, *Segregation*, 54, 82, 76.

146. Warren, "Introduction," xxix, xxvii, xxxi–xxxii.

147. Ibid., xxvii; Warren, *Segregation*, 98, 104.

148. Warren, "Introduction," vii, ix.

149. Ibid., xvi. As Warren points out, "fidelity" in Conrad is often a matter not only of adherence and allegiance to glorious traditions (of nation, merchant service, etc.) but simply of doing one's job. This is what keeps Marlow from going ashore "for a howl and a dance" in *Heart of Darkness* and is a basic disciplinary principle in Conrad generally.

150. Ibid., xvi–xviii; in the second quotation, Warren is quoting the opening chapter of *Chance*; in the third, he is quoting and exposing Davidson's oversimplified investment in the summary formula offered by the "Familiar Preface" to *A Personal Record* (as described earlier in this chapter).

151. Ibid., xviii–xix.

152. Robert Penn Warren, *Who Speaks for the Negro?* (New York: Random House, 1965), 118. Warren is directly commenting (with obvious sympathy) on the responses of Stokely Carmichael and others to the Freedom Democratic Party's attempts to avoid seating African Americans at its Atlantic City convention in the summer of 1964. However, on a more global scale, he is also effectively challenging the "liberal imperialism" that some Wilsonian liberals once justified and harmonized with the idea of "self-determination" through appeals to Lingard—and doing so by critically rereading as a simple imperialist the very same Conrad figure. Compare the discussion of *The Rescue* in Chapter 2.

153. Warren, "Introduction," xxi.

154. And not for the last time. The Gentleman Brown episode in *Lord Jim*—itself of pointedly racialized dimension and mediated through Brown's "aristocratic" class frame—was one that greatly interested Warren, especially in its Southern evocations and applications. For a convincing explanation of how Warren's interpretation of "Brown" (as it were) in a 1954 address at Columbia University closely anticipates the scene with the Alabama boy in *Segregation*, see Leonard Casper, *Robert Penn Warren: The Dark and Bloody Ground* (Seattle: University of Washington Press, 1960), 9.

155. Warren, *Segregation*, 18–19.

156. Warren, "Introduction," xvii, xix, xxii (emphasis added).

157. Warren, *Segregation*, 97.

158. Warren's introduction closes in a fashion that suggestively equates his understanding of himself as a member of the Southern community (as evinced by the preceding paragraph) and his understanding of himself as a member of the community of readers of Conrad (there being significant overlap): "I have tried to define my reading of Conrad's work in general and of *Nostromo* in particular. In these matters there is not, and should not be, an ultimate 'reading,' a final word and orthodoxy of interpretation. In so far as a work is vital, there will continually be a development, an extrapolation of significance. But at any one moment each of us must take the risk of his sensibility and his logic in making a reading. I have taken this risk, and part of the risk is repudiation, or at least criticism, of competing interpretations." Warren, "Introduction," xxxvi.

159. Ibid., xix, xx, xxiv.

160. Ibid., xxiii, xxi–xxii.

161. Ibid., xxii.

162. Ibid., xxiii.

163. Ibid., xix, xviii.

164. Ibid., xxvi.

165. Warren, *Segregation*, 91, 93.

166. Ibid., 94–95.

167. Warren, "Introduction," xxvii; Warren, *Segregation*, 106–7 (emphasis in original).

168. Warren, "Introduction," xix, xxxvii, xxxi; Warren, *Who Speaks?* viii; *NLL* 7.

169. Warren, *Segregation*, 155 ("If the South is really able to face up to itself and its situation, it may achieve identity, moral identity. Then in a country where moral identity is hard to come by, the South, because it has had to deal concretely with a moral problem, may offer some leadership"); Warren, "Introduction," xxxvi.

170. Warren, "Introduction," xxxiii; Warren, *Segregation*, 97; Warren, "Introduction," xxxii.

171. Warren, *Who Speaks?* 276–77, ix.

172. Warren, *Segregation*, 113–14 ("No moral problem gets solved abstractly. It has to be solved in a possible context for solution. . . . We have to deal with the problem our historical moment proposes, the burden of our time").

173. Warren, "Introduction," xxxiii.

174. With respect to exile, Wolfe wrote upon leaving the United States for the first time: "Upon a ship attention is focused on two targets—on people and on the sea. If I could represent the effect the sea had on these people—that interpenetration of its influence which Joseph Conrad noticed in its action on the lives of Englishmen—I might have represented something of its importance and beauty. . . . And it did this: it severed them from the earth, from town, from walls; it broke the mould of a hundred little patterns of existence; it removed one hundred people suddenly and violently from the contrived web of habit and custom and association their lives had fashioned. The sea had found men in chains and its had set them free. Was the result then social revolution?" Such references to "Youth," and also to "Karain: A Memory" (another story readily amenable to interpretation in terms of exilic displacement), and also *Heart of Darkness*, recur in the *Diaries*. Consider also in this respect an entry from January 25,

1927: "I am weary of the old forms—the old language—It has come to me quite simply these last three days that we must mine deeper—find language again in its primitive sinews—like the young man, Conrad." See R. S. Kennedy and P. Reeves, eds., *The Notebooks of Thomas Wolfe*, vol. 1 (Chapel Hill: University of North Carolina Press, 1970), xxvi, xxvii, 36, 49, 98.

175. Bruce Clayton, "W. J. Cash: A Mind of the South," in Paul Escott, ed., *W. J. Cash and the Minds of the South* (Baton Rouge: Louisiana State University Press, 1992), 15; qtd. in Joseph Morrison, *W. J. Cash: A Southern Prophet* (New York: Alfred A. Knopf, 1967), 35–36. For more on Cash and Conrad, see Bruce Clayton, *W. J. Cash: A Life* (Baton Rouge: Louisiana State University Press, 1991), 123–25.

176. W. J. Cash, "Realism and Romanticism: Southern View," Charlotte *News*, Oct. 18, 1936, 224–27.

177. W. J. Cash, *The Mind of the South* (New York: Alfred A. Knopf, 1941), vii, viii.

178. Anne Goodwyn Jones, "The Cash Nexus," in Charles W. Eagles, ed., *The Mind of the South Fifty Years Later* (Jackson: University Press of Mississippi, 1992), 23–59.

179. See Jones, "Cash Nexus," 30–34; Raymond Williams, *Marxism and Literature* (Oxford: Oxford University Press, 1977), 108–14, 110; Louis Althusser, *For Marx*, qtd. in James Kavanaugh, "Ideology," in Frank Lentricchia, ed., *Critical Terms for Literary Study* (Chicago: University of Chicago Press, 1990), 313.

180. On the "organic intellectual" as opposed to "traditional" professional intellectuals who, wittingly or not, are situated within and ultimately serve to preserve the dominant forces of the present regime of hegemony, see Gramsci, "The Intellectuals," in *The Prison Notebooks* (New York: International Publishers, 1971), 3–23.

181. Revealingly, one of Conrad's and one of Faulkner's most sensitive readers independently begin their studies with this very puzzle. See Harpham, *One of Us*, ix, and Philip Weinstein, *Faulkner's Subject: A Cosmos No One Owns* (Cambridge: Cambridge University Press, 1992), ix.

182. J. Hillis Miller, *Fiction and Repetition: Seven English Novels* (Cambridge, Mass.: Harvard University Press, 1982), 56–57, 25–28, 27.

183. See Gustav Morf, *The Polish Heritage of Joseph Conrad* (London: Sampson Low, Marston, 1928); Keith Carabine, *The Life and the Art: A Study of Conrad's "Under Western Eyes"* (Amsterdam: Rodopi, 1996), 64–127. I am indebted to Grażyna Branny for the (crucial) connection between *Nostromo* and the May constitution.

184. Harpham, *One of Us*, 10, 12.

185. William Faulkner, *Intruder in the Dust* (New York: Random House, 1948), 98.

186. Ibid., 99.

187. William Faulkner, *Requiem for a Nun* (New York: Vintage Books, 1978), 88.

188. William Faulkner, *Absalom, Absalom!* (New York: Random House, 1964), 12.

CHAPTER 5

1. Qtd. in Joseph Blotner, *Faulkner: A Biography*, vol. 1 (New York: Random House, 1974), 110.

2. Compare on this point the following two superb essays, which generally concern Faulkner's literary contexts and influences: Mick Gidley, "Faulkner and the British," in Doreen Fowler and Anne Abadie, eds., *Faulkner: International Perspectives* (University

Press of Mississippi, 1984), 74–96; and Michael Millgate, "Faulkner's Masters," in Millgate, *Faulkner's Place* (Athens: University of Georgia Press, 1992), 82–95.

3. William Faulkner, "Interview with Jean Stein Vanden Heuvel," in James D.
Meriwether and Michael Millgate, eds., *Lion in the Garden: Interviews with William
Faulkner, 1926–1962* (New York: Random House, 1968), 155; Faulkner, "American Drama:
Eugene O'Neill," in Carvel Collins, ed., *William Faulkner: Early Prose and Poetry* (Bos-
ton: Little, Brown, 1962), 86–89, 86.

4. Faulkner, "Books and Things: Review of *Linda Condon, Cytherea*, and *The Bright
Shawl*," in Collins, *Early Prose*, 101–3, 102; Faulkner qtd. in Carvel Collins, ed., *New
Orleans Sketches* (New York: Random House, 1958), vii.

5. "Victory," though first published in the short-story collection *These Thirteen*
(1931), was written shortly after Faulkner's return from his European trip in the fall
of 1925. It is typical of the "war" fiction, heavily imprinted by Conrad, of this period;
and, as Frederick Karl has observed, the story, apropos of its Conradian title, places
its protagonist Alec Gray "in the shadowy presence of a typical Conradian conflict."
See Karl, *William Faulkner: American Writer* (New York: Ballantine Books, 1989), 410.
Interestingly, the title of the cluster of war stories in *These Thirteen*—which would
become "The Wasteland" in *The Collected Stories*—is also "Victory"; and the original
title of another story in the cluster, "Crevasse," is also "Victory." For a suggestive account of why the title of *Sanctuary* (1931) and the name of its heroine, Temple, may derive from Conrad's *Chance*, see Cleanth Brooks, *William Faulkner: The Yoknapatawpha
Country* (New Haven, Conn.: Yale University Press, 1963), 136–37.

6. Faulkner, "Home," in Collins, *New Orleans Sketches*, 79.

7. A facsimile of this page of "Notes" appears in Blotner, *Biography*, 407, and reads in
relevant part: "Jones—There is a kinship between Napoleon, J. Conrad and John Brown:
Napoleon feels his actions are important, Conrad feels his emotions are important, John
Brown feels his beliefs are important." This passage, spoken by Mr. Jones, is repeated in
Soldiers' Pay, with "Conrad" changed to "Swift" (in part to effect a pun on "swift" that
becomes the ultimate comic note of the passage) and "Brown" changed to "Savonarola."
The passage is of autoreferential textual significance because it allows Mr. Jones—who
is something of a central character in the novel, a shadow of and even gloss on the novel
itself, and also, incidentally, the namesake of the antagonist of the equally fanciful villain
of Conrad's *Victory*—to identify with the Swift/Conrad slot: "'Say,' Gilligan repeated,
'who's swift anyway? . . . ' 'Mr. Jones is, according to his own statement.'" William
Faulkner, *Soldiers' Pay* (New York: Horace Liveright, 1926), 284 (hereafter cited as *SP*).

8. Though the "Nausikaan" reference is to Joyce, the opening of the river trip in
Mosquitoes unmistakably echoes the opening of *Heart of Darkness*: "The *Nausikaa* lay
in the basin—a nice thing, with her white matronly hull and mahogany-and-brass su-
perstructure and the yacht club flag at its peak. A firm steady wind blew in from the
lake. . . ." William Faulkner, *Mosquitoes* (New York: Liveright, 1997), 54.

9. Faulkner, "Introduction," *Southern Review* (1929): 708–9; Faulkner, "Introduction," qtd. in André Bleikasten, *The Most Splendid Failure: Faulkner's "The Sound and
the Fury"* (Bloomington: Indiana University Press, 1976), 44.

10. Qtd. in Stephen B. Oates, *William Faulkner: The Man and the Artist* (New
York: Harper & Row, 1987), 108; Meriwether and Millgate, *Lion in the Garden*, 21, 49, 52

(Faulkner adds: "One can learn something from *Lord Jim* and *Nostromo* too"); Albert Guerard Jr., *Conrad the Novelist* (Cambridge, Mass.: Harvard University Press, 1958), ix.

11. William Faulkner, *Knight's Gambit* (New York: Vintage Books, 1978), 244; Frederick L. Gwynn and Joseph Blotner, eds., *Faulkner in the University: Class Conferences at the University of Virginia, 1957–58* (New York: Vintage Books, 1965), 20, 50; Blotner, *Biography*, 2.1213.

12. See Edward Said, "Traveling with Conrad," in Kaplan, Mallios, and White, *Conrad in the Twenty-first Century*, 283.

13. In the early O'Neill essay, for instance, Faulkner's references to Conrad as a "Slav" and a "supreme contradiction," and the grounding of his discussion in a nationalist idea of "our language" as the "greatest source" of American "national" identity, are signature Menckenian gestures. See Collins, *Early Prose*, 87–89.

14. See John T. Irwin, *Doubling & Incest / Repetition & Revenge: A Speculative Reading of Faulkner* (Baltimore: Johns Hopkins University Press, 1975); Eric Sundquist, *Faulkner: The House Divided* (Baltimore: Johns Hopkins University Press, 1983).

15. See Noel Polk's superb essay "Scar," in Noel Polk and Anne Abadie, eds., *Faulkner and War* (Jackson: University Press of Mississippi, 2004), 138–59, 144. On mirrors and reflections, see *SP* 82–83, 87–88, 129, 154, 161. On Narcissus, consider not only "the bulky tweeded Narcissus of himself in the polished wood" (88) that Jones contemplates and the narcissi Emmy frequently carries about (60, 105), but the fact that even the plants in this novel are narcissists: "The small stream murmured busily like faint incarnation and repeated alder-shots leaned over it Narcissus-like" (305).

16. As opposed to "dominant" and "emergent" ideological practices and forces, Raymond Williams describes the "residual" as those ideological elements that have "been effectively formed in the past" but that are "still active in the cultural process, not only and not often at all as an element of the past, but as an effective element of the present. Thus certain experiences, meanings, values which cannot be expressed in terms of the dominant culture, are nevertheless lived and practiced on the basis of the residue—cultural as well as social—of some previous social and cultural institution or formation." "Dominant" here is an epochal term that refers to large historical movements like industrial capitalism; it is hence possible for a culture like some of those in the modern South to be principally invested in "residual" ideological practices (agrarianism, religion, etc.) even as a new dominant phase of cultural existence has begun. See Williams, *Marxism and Literature*, 121–27, 122.

17. Margaret Powers's inner monologue on her late husband Dick (for whom Donald is a proxy in her mind; both are expressions of the compulsions of residual ideology) is exemplary of this ambivalence, which arises from "the terror of parting, of that passionate desire to cling to something in the dark world" (32): "Dick, my love, that I did not love, Dick, your ugly body breaking into mine like a burglar, my body flowing away. . . . Kiss and forget me: remember me only to wish me luck, dear, ugly, dead Dick" (180).

18. The book's obsession with the image of "wings"—from pilots' wings to birds' wings ("shimmering birds on motionless gold wings" [18]; "regard the buzzard . . . supported only by the air" [59])—to angels' wings—derives its force from the book's underlying fantasy (as is more famously the case in many later Faulkner texts) of escape

and ascension from the crucifix of ideology. Very much in anticipation of the final section of *The Sound and the Fury, Soldiers' Pay* closes with a trip to a Negro church, and this soothing hope: "I am the Resurrection and the Life, saith the Lord" (290).

19. Brooks, *Yoknapatawpha Country,* 98.

20. See note 5 supra.

21. Jacques Berthoud, "Introduction," in Joseph Conrad, *The Nigger of the "Narcissus"* (Oxford: Oxford University Press, 1984), xiv–xix; Ian Watt, *Conrad in the Nineteenth Century* (Berkeley: University of California Press, 1979), 112–15; Casarino, *Modernity at Sea,* 3–9.

22. Berthoud, "Introduction," vii–viii; Fredric Jameson, *The Political Unconscious: Narrative as a Socially Symbolic Act* (Ithaca, N.Y.: Cornell University Press, 1982), 214, 217.

23. Jameson, *Political Unconscious,* 217 (emphasis in original).

24. See Said, "On Lost Causes," in *Reflections on Exile,* 543.

25. Related to the "burden" in question, there is also an aural pun here on "white"— which is how Wait's name as he pronounces it probably would have sounded—whose significance is crucial to the racialized trajectory of Faulkner's rereadings of this novel, as we shall see.

26. Joseph Conrad, *The Nigger of the "Narcissus"* (New York: Doubleday, Page, 1914), v.

27. For one influential articulation of this view, see Jacques Berthoud, *Joseph Conrad: The Major Phase* (Cambridge: Cambridge University Press, 1978), 26–29.

28. Chris Bongie, *Exotic Memories: Literature, Colonialism, and the Fin de Siècle* (Stanford: Stanford University Press, 1991), 169.

29. Ibid.

30. Irwin, *Doubling & Incest,* 33.

31. Hence Conrad's obsessive, omnipresent figuring of the crew in Wait's image: one particularly suggestive instance of which is a moment at the beginning the storm chapter: "Their eyes blinked in the wind; their *dark faces* were wet with drops of water more salt and bitter than *human tears.* . . . They were *fantastically misshapen*; in high boots, in hats like helmets, and *swaying clumsily,* stiff and bulky in glistening oilskins, they resembled men strangely equipped for some fabulous adventure" (51–52, emphases added).

32. If there is a more vivid description of the absurd, conceptually and ethically bankrupt, psychosocially compulsive lengths to which various white peoples have historically gone to rescue, preserve, defend, transmit, and carry the "hateful burden" of racial prejudice than the scene in which Conrad's sailors risk all to recover and carry the "hateful burden" of James Wait, who is clearly presented there as the empty (to the white crew, for whom he is "invisible" in Ellison's sense) embodiment of their own long-standing racialized conceptions, then it must be a very vivid description indeed. He [Wait] emitted no sound; he looked as ridiculously lamentable as a doll that had lost half its sawdust, and we started on our perilous journey over the main deck, dragging along with care that pitiful, that limp, that hateful burden. He was not very heavy, but had he weighed a ton he could not have been more difficult to handle. We literally passed him from hand to hand. Now and then we had to hang him up on a handy belaying-pin, to draw a breath and reform the line. Had the pin broken he would have irretrievably gone into the Southern Ocean, but he had to take his chance of that; and after a little while, becoming apparently aware of it, he groaned slightly, and with a great effort whispered a few words. We listened eagerly. . . . We

had so far saved him; and it had become a personal matter between us and the sea. We meant to stick to him. Had we (by an incredible hypothesis) undergone similar toil and trouble for an empty cask, that cask would have become as precious to us as Jimmy was. More precious, in fact, because we would have had no reason to hate the cask. And we hated James Wait. We could not get rid of the monstrous suspicion that this astounding black-man was shamming sick, had been malingering heartlessly in the face of our toil, of our scorn, of our patience—and now was malingering in the face of our devotion—in the face of death. (*NN* 72–73)

33. See Sundquist, *House Divided*; Walter Benn Michaels, "*Absalom, Absalom!*: The Difference Between White Men and White Men," in Robert Hamblin and Ann Abadie, eds., *Faulkner in the Twenty-first Century* (Jackson: University Press of Mississippi, 2003), 137–53, 151.

34. Thadious Davis, "From Jazz Syncopation to Blues Elegy: Faulkner's Development of Black Characterization," in Doreen Fowler and Ann Abadie, eds., *Faulkner and Race* (Jackson: University Press of Mississippi, 1986), 70–92, 82.

35. The context of *Plessy* and the "nadir" of U.S. race relations during this period is a vital, complicated, and disturbing element of the U.S. reception history of Conrad's novel from the beginning—as is the Spanish-American War, given the novel's multiply resonant (from various U.S. vantages) use of an insurrectionary Caribbean figure *both* as an occasion to champion an almost militaristic sense of discipline and authority (the references to the U.S. Navy lurking repeatedly in the story's margins are by no means exclusively figures of opposition) *and* to raise questions concerning the sentimentality, self-interest, and imperialist bad faith that frequently lurk behind jingoistic rhetorical appeals to "liberating" oppressed peoples from "tyrants." Consider in this light E. C. Martin, "How the War Works Against Space Writers," *Los Angeles Times* (May 29, 1898): 13 (claim that "war news and war 'stories'" are squeezing out the printing of all other material, especially fiction, followed by a long description of the recent success and interest of Conrad's fiction); Letter to Editor, *New York Times* (July 20, 1898): BR136 (through Conrad's novel one appreciates that the "exigencies of sea life may be so much worse than those of a soldier, not even excepting the wounded and lost on the battlefield"); and perhaps most importantly, the many uses of the trope "children of the sea" in U.S. discourse of the time to evoke and contemplate intervention (or not) among native, primitivized, colonized peoples: i.e., "Spain and Cuba," *Washington Post* (May 18, 1896): 4 (Cuba); "A Modern Cortez," *Los Angeles Times* (Mar. 26, 1906): 16 (Jamaica); "Hawaii's July Fourth and Real Celebration," *Christian Science Monitor* (July 1, 1916): 15 (Hawaii); "A Town That Was," *Christian Science Monitor* (Nov. 27, 1919): 12 (preindustrial Flint Island); "Where Diamonds 'Grow' in Southwest African Desert," *Christian Science Monitor* (Feb. 10, 1922): 10 (southwest Africa).

36. "Chronicle and Comment," *Bookman* (NY) 8.91 (Oct. 1898): 91; Donald W. Rude and Kenneth Davies, "The Critical Reception of the First American Edition of *The Nigger of the 'Narcissus',*" rptd. in Carabine, *Critical Assessments*, 2.264–70, 265; compare the British reviews in Norman Sherry, ed., *Conrad: The Critical Heritage* (London: Routledge & Kegan Paul, 1973), 82–100.

37. See, for instance, George Middleton, "Joseph Conrad's 'The Nigger of the Narcissus," *Bookman* (NY) 39 (July 1914): 563–65, 563 (praises Doubleday's "commendable desire" to reissue Conrad's novel under its original name); compare Fredric Taber Cooper,

"The Sustained Effort," *Bookman* (NY) 18 (Nov. 1903): 310–11 (references "unfortunate sea change" in the original title of Conrad's novel "during [its] passage into an American edition"); W. L. Alden, "Mr. Alden's Views," *New York Times* (Dec. 1, 1900) (remarks on "the absurdity of changing the title of *The Nigger of the 'Narcissus,'* a title that fitted the book to perfection, into the schoolgirl sentimentality of *Children of the Sea*").

38. See, for instance, Belle Cooper, "Home Is the Sailor, Home from the Sea," *Los Angeles Times* (Sept. 21, 1924): 34–37 (long elegiac article presenting *The Nigger of the "Narcissus"* as Conrad's "first real success"); "Conrad's Last Essays," *Christian Science Monitor* (Apr. 3, 1926): 6 ("for all who had eyes to see and imaginations to be kindled, with the publishing of *The Nigger of the 'Narcissus,'* there stepped upon the stage of fiction one of the greatest of modern writers"). Virginia Woolf also emphasized this understanding of and period in Conrad, albeit in a quite different tone.

39. "Sea Wizard Passes," *Los Angeles Times* (Aug. 5, 1924): A4.

40. "Immortal Sea Stories," *Chicago Daily Tribune* (Sept. 6, 1942): 17. This kind of claim was a commonplace in the United States and among Americans from the beginning: see, for example, Stephen Crane, "Concerning the English 'Academy,'" rptd. in *Bookman* (NY) 7 (Mar. 1898): 22–24 (famous article praising Conrad's novel as "unquestionably the best story of the sea written by a man now alive"); "Chronicle and Comment," *Bookman* (NY) (Oct. 1898): 91 ("one of the finest storms in literature," only comparable to the "almost forgotten" Herman Melville); W. L. Alden, "Mr. Alden on What London Is Reading," *Chicago Daily Tribune* (June 14, 1902): 17 ("far and away the finest description of a storm at sea that has ever been written"); "A Line o' Type or Two," *Chicago Daily Tribune* (Mar. 20, 1920): 8 (opens contest for "ten best books of the sea" by "start[ing] the list with *The Nigger of the "Narcissus"*).

41. Consider Temple Bailey, Open Letter to Fanny Butcher, *Chicago Daily Tribune* (July 14, 1923): 7 (Bailey, an immensely popular romance novelist introduced as "the nicest sort of person, 'home folks,' as they used to say," names *The Nigger of the "Narcissus"* as one among five books [*Lord Jim* is another] that "would have fought for first place" on her list of books she "would rather have read" than any other); "Fifty Great Modern Novels," *Los Angeles Times* (June 7, 1931) (list of "fifty great modern novels" compiled by "Professor William H. F. Lamont of Rutgers University" places *The Nigger of the "Narcissus"* among texts written by English novelists at the top); Vincent Starrett, "The Best Loved Books," *Chicago Daily Tribune* (Dec. 12, 1954): L2, and "Books That Will Last—Perhaps," *Chicago Daily Tribune* (Nov. 30, 1958): B14 (*The Nigger of the "Narcissus"* placed among the "Best Loved Books" and the eleven finest novels in English of the twentieth century); John Randolph, "Among the Best of the Recent Paperbacks," *Chicago Daily Tribune* (Mar. 27, 1960): B8 (Albert Guerard Jr.'s Laurel reissue [with *The End of the Tether*] placed at top of "sample listing of some of the best of last year's general paperback titles").

42. A review in *Bookman* (NY), for instance, references the novel's "ungainly title" in England, whereas "we understand that Mr. Conrad is delighted with the title given to the American edition, namely *The Children of the Sea*, which fits the book to a nicety." See *Bookman* (NY) 7 (Mar. 1898): 3. Similarly, U.S. novelist and journalist Harold Frederic, in an otherwise positive review of the novel in the *Saturday Review* (London), laments, after qualifying his appreciation of Conrad's presentation of the "shadowy"

Donkin: "It cannot be said that the 'Nigger' himself attains even that limited success. He worries the reader from the outset, as one feels he bored and fatigued the writer." See Frederic, "Mr. Conrad's Latest Story," *Saturday Review* 85 (Feb. 12, 1898): 211. On the title, compare British critic W. L. Courtney's much more unconstrained and critical reference to the novel's "ugliest conceivable title" in the *Daily Telegraph* on Dec. 8, 1897 (rptd. in Sherry, *Critical Heritage*, 85); and on Wait, compare more elaborated British criticisms in the *Daily Mail* on Dec. 7, 1897, and the *Spectator* on Dec. 25, 1897 (see Sherry, *Critical Heritage*, 83–84, 92–93). On the title change in the United States, one should note this change was repeatedly referenced by U.S. reviewers; the subject of at least one letter to the *New York Times* (Mar. 4, 1899: BR136); and further broadcast through the selling of English editions of the novel in the United States (see, for instance, the "Books" advertisement for R. H. Macy & Co. in the *New York Times* [Aug. 5, 1899]: BR 523, listing "Nigger of the Narcissus" at thirty-six cents). The title change accentuated rather than diminished attention to and awareness of the disconcerting title, whose difficulties of articulation precisely in circumstances of heightened awareness of it is the "American" point I am making.

43. These include Annie Logan's otherwise exceptionally articulate review in the *Nation* (NY) on July 21, 1898; the reprint of Stephen Crane's open letter to the *Academy* (London) in *Bookman* (NY) in March 1898; the subsequent review in *Bookman* (NY) in October 1898; repeated pieces in the *New York Times* by W. L. Alden; and reviews in the *Washington Post* (Apr. 18, 1898), the Atlanta *Constitution* (Apr. 10, 1898), and throughout the *Christian Science Monitor* and *Chicago Daily Tribune*. Also telling is that stock advertisements and blurbs promoting the novel in the United States *never* mention or refer to Wait.

44. A fair-sized essay could be written on this subject. Frederic Taber Cooper's *Bookman* essay of November 1903, for instance, draws specific attention to "the inert figure of a sickly, malingering negro" who "stands out" as an "ominous" "embodiment of fate" in the novel. But as Cooper's discussion moves to the tellingly misnamed "Heart of Blackness" and other Conrad tales in which the fundamental theme is the "in-born antagonism of two races" (i.e., "native" and European), it becomes clear that the earlier parsing of Wait *only* as a spectral "embodiment of fate" is a means of deracializing his significance. See Cooper, "Sustained Effort," 310–11. So, too, Harold Frederic, in his *Saturday Review* piece, describes *The Nigger of the "Narcissus"* as a "volte-face" from Conrad's usual "tales of racial degeneration." See "Mr. Conrad's Latest Story," 211. Middleton's piece in *Bookman* (NY) in July 1914 champions and takes great interest in the restoration of the novel's old title, but quotes extensively Conrad's description of Wait as "nothing" and then dwells entirely on the deracialized 1897 preface, now published in the American edition for the first time. See Middleton, "The Nigger of the Narcissus," 563. The *Bookman* (NY) review in March 1898 also emphasizes, in a dubious display of innocence, that Conrad's original English title "means nothing to the average mind." See Review, *Bookman*, 3. An early review in the *New York Illustrated Supplement* in April 1898 gushes over the "great deal" the novel owes to the "thrilling effects" of Wait—"What would [the novel] be without the Nigger?"—but then emphasizes that what is special about Wait (what and how he *really* means) is that he provides a "starting point for the *psychological analysis* which goes side by side with the author's purely descriptive work"

(which apparently includes the "malingering Donkin" and political problems of "discipline"). Indeed, "Mr. Conrad is most to be praised for having kept the psychological interest in its proper place"—which is to say, keeping Wait's race and its politics out of Wait's place. See "A Strong Sea Story," *New York Tribune Illustrated Supplement* (Apr. 3, 1898): 7 (emphases added). An anonymous review in the *New York Times* on May 21, 1898, begins by describing that "in deference, possibly, to Mr. Lincoln's celebrated dictum on the subject of the 'double g,' this story, known in England as 'The Nigger of the Narcissus' has been rechristened for American readers"—implicitly making the point, to the detriment of an otherwise acute article, that the domain of race relations Mr. Lincoln mentioned is unproblematically severable from and not fundamentally related to the entirely race-neutral account of the story that the critic relates thereafter. "The Nigger of the Narcissus," *New York Times* (May 21, 1898): 344. Similarly, W. L. Alden, another generally perceptive and prescient champion of Conrad, gives himself away in a *New York Times* column on October 13, 1900, in lauding the novel's "realist" aesthetics with the comment, "The 'Nigger' is realistic in the best sense of the word"—here, Alden reduces an entire novel to a racial epithet while at the same time parsing that novel in terms of everything but the object of that racial epithet (for James Wait is not simply a "realistic" standard and is all but never mentioned in Alden's many articles on the novel; nor does the "sea" paradigm through which Alden articulates his "best sense" of the "realistic" ever extend to race). See Alden, "London Literary Letter," *New York Times* (Oct. 13, 1900): 582. Less impressive but equally revealing is the early review in the *Boston Daily Globe*, which starts out forthrightly with the declaration, "The story in brief is: James Wait, a colored sailor, shams sickness, and the crew is very kind to him," but then gets so many of the novel's character names and plot details wrong that it almost confesses to its own incompetence in declaring: "Of course one cannot get from this abstract any adequate notion of the admirable manner in which the tale is unfolded." The closing claim that the novel's "pictures of sea life are natural and its character drawings not at all artificial" epitomizes the emptiness into which U.S. engagements with Wait as a black man are pulled generally. See "New Literature," *Boston Daily Globe*, (July 6, 1898): 2. One of the rare exceptions to this rule in the mainstream U.S. press is a short entry that appeared in the *Chicago Daily Tribune* in March 1917, referring to journalist Floyd Gibbons's wildly popular *And They Thought We Wouldn't Fight* (1917), concerning his travels to wartime Europe and experiences at Belleau Wood: "We wish Col. Gibbons had written more about the Negro stoker who was so picturesque a feature of his story. He reminded us a bit of the 'Nigger of the Narcissus.'" See "A Line o' Type or Two," *Chicago Daily Tribune* (Mar. 1, 1917): 6.

45. These are largely commonplaces: on the 1897 preface, see Burton Rascoe, "Some Impressions of Hergesheimer and 'Java Head,'" *Chicago Daily Tribune* (Mar. 8, 1919): 9 (Conrad's preface described as the "epitome" of "the creed of a novelist who, by common critical consensus, has beyond all others of his time approached by way of the novel the plasticity of sculpture, the color of painting, and the suggestiveness of music to which he in common with all serious artists in fiction aspires"); on the novel's ending, consider Vincent Starrett, "Books Alive," *Chicago Daily Tribune* (Feb. 2, 1947): C6 ("Christopher Morley wishes he had written the closing pages of *The Nigger of the 'Narcissus.'* In his mature lifetime, Mr. Morley asserts, he has 'absorbed only one full scale

and utterly magical talent in fiction'; and he plumps for the work of Joseph Conrad").

46. See Richard Gray, *Writing the South: Ideas of an American Region* (Cambridge: Cambridge University Press, 1986), 142–64.

47. Hawthorn begins an important chapter published in 1990, "When I first read *The Nigger of the 'Narcissus'* as part of an undergraduate course in English literature, what I wanted most of all was a reaction to that word 'nigger' in the title and body of the work. . . . Yet nowhere could I find any answer to these questions. . . . It is only in comparatively recent years that the issue of James Wait's race, and the significance which this is made to carry in *The Nigger of the 'Narcissus,'* has been discussed by literary critics." See Jeremy Hawthorn, *Joseph Conrad: Narrative Technique and Ideological Commitment* (London: Edward Arnold, 1990), 101.

48. Joseph Conrad, "To My Readers in America," v.

49. Qtd. in Bleikasten, *Most Splendid Failure*, 15; qtd. in Warwick Wadlington, *Reading Faulknerian Tragedy* (Ithaca, N.Y.: Cornell University Press, 1987), 16.

50. Sundquist, *House Divided*, 9; Philip Weinstein, *Faulkner's Subject: A Cosmos No One Owns* (Cambridge: Cambridge University Press, 1992), 63.

51. For more on *The Secret Agent*'s interest in social reproduction and ideologically recursive sign systems, see my "Reading *The Secret Agent* Now: the Press, the Police, the Premonition of Simulation," in Kaplan, Mallios, and White, *Conrad in the Twenty-first Century*, 155–72, 162–65.

52. See Wadlington, *Reading Faulknerian Tragedy*, chap. 1.

53. That is, just as Conrad presents his manifestly confused, unstable, and manipulable crew through the primary figure of "everlasting children of the sea" (*NN* 25; hence the original U.S. title), so Faulkner presents his subjects of ideological, epistemological, and familial confusion as (everlasting) children.

54. Phrases like Caddy's (in Benjy's memory) "Is Mother sick" (*SF* 61); the interchange on the final page of Benjy's section, "'Is mother very sick.' Caddy said. 'No.' Father said" (*SF* 75); Quentin's "Caddy you've got fever *You're sick how are you sick*" (*SF* 111, emphasis in original); and Quentin's and Caddy's "*Sick how are you sick. . . . I'm just sick I can't ask anybody*" (*SF* 111, emphasis in original) express their crisis—and the will conceptually to disavow them—in much the same tropes of uncertain illness that frame Conrad's crew's relation to James Wait.

55. This historical argument and its multiple transnational implications are larger than there is space to properly articulate here: where our primary concern must remain with simply decoding a general politics of residual ideology that constitutes the "content" of Faulkner's aesthetic intersections with Conrad, as well as the increased Southern racial sensitivity whose expression evolves and extends through them. Nevertheless, we may briefly note that the residual "Polish" sensibility that underwrites and coordinates Conrad's fiction—invisibly but formatively rooted in the political struggles of postpartition Poland, and mapping itself onto Conrad's explicit engagements with the transitional British merchant marine, the changing colonized world, and various fading world aristocracies—must also be understood as a complex *product* of a much wider array of Polish historical factors and contexts that also suggest remarkable continuities with the U.S. South after the Civil War. These historical factors, which situate and animate the very Polish and Southern patriotisms they also complicate, include shared

experiences of military conquest, external occupation and reconstruction, anxieties of imperial erasure, agrarian/plantation history, racialized reliance on bonded labor, impracticably weak traditions of centralized government, sudden needs and calls for a new kind of collective "national" solidarity in fractured social, ethnic, and political circumstances, galvanizing social codes of honor and gentlemanly aristocracy, and literary emphases on romance and the romanticized past. Concern with the complications of residual ideology is thus a good historicist way to *begin* talking about the conspicuous aesthetic proximities of Conrad and Faulkner—but ultimately as a means of accessing and theorizing a much wider field of transnational historical contiguity. The stakes are much larger here than "the South" and Poland alone, for one of the more remarkable traits of Conrad and Faulkner is their both having been broadly rewritten across many global domains. How might the historical axis of racialized bonded labor, which unites not only Poland and the South but a much larger circum-Western imperial periphery, be used via Faulkner and Conrad to theorize a new array of transnational literary economy, one capable of answering just why it is that both authors have found themselves so incisively rewritten throughout the Americas? Compare Zdzisław Najder's eloquent appeal for this kind of transnational inquiry facilitated by Conrad and Faulkner in "Sienkiewicz—Conrad—Faulkner," Dobosiewicz, *Crossing the Border*, 57–62.

56. This is the moment when the novel makes it most clear that it is an archaeology of the "hateful burden" (*NN* 72) of racial prejudice: when Wait, always already identified in terms of his "intimate . . . companion" of and "monstrous friendship with" death (*NN* 36), is being rescued by the crew after the storm and, in an image the novel goes on to recycle, "looked as ridiculously lamentable as a doll that had lost half its sawdust (*NN* 72). See note 32, and compare the discussion of race in *As I Lay Dying* that follows in this chapter.

57. William Faulkner, *As I Lay Dying* (New York: Vintage International, 1988), 207 (emphases added; hereafter cited as *AILD*).

58. Sundquist, *House Divided*, 28.

59. John T. Matthews, "*As I Lay Dying* in the Machine Age," *Boundary 2* 19.1 (Spring 1992): 69–94, 87.

60. The word *wait* and its variants—whose ample appearance in *The Sound and the Fury* I will leave it to someone else to count—appears seventy-four times in the very short novel *As I Lay Dying*.

61. Warwick Wadlington, *As I Lay Dying: Stories out of Stories* (New York: Twayne Publishers, 1992), 44.

62. Guerard, *Conrad the Novelist*, 107.

63. Consider Peabody's report of how the Bundrens—with apparently no initial assistance from the police—"throw that poor devil down in the street and handcuff him like a murderer" (*AILD* 240), and also the interchange between Anse and Jewel: "'You want to fix him now?' 'Fix him?' pa said. 'Catch him and tie him up,' Jewel said. Goddamn it" (*AILD* 233).

INDEX